בכאדמין

Tabularum Magicarum

ὁ ἀπόρρητος

999

### Books on the Western Esoteric Tradition by Stephen Skinner

*Agrippa's Fourth Book of Occult Philosophy* (edited) – Askin, Ibis
*Aleister Crowley's Astrology* (edited) – Spearman, Ibis
*Complete Magician's Tables* – Golden Hoard, Llewellyn
*Dr John Dee's Spiritual Diaries: the fully revised edition of 'A True & Faithful Relation of what passed…between Dr John Dee…& some Spirits'* – Golden Hoard
*Geomancy in Theory & Practice* – Golden Hoard, Llewellyn
*Goetia of Dr Rudd: Liber Malorum Spirituum* (with David Rankine) – Golden Hoard
*Grimoire of Saint Cyprian: Clavis Inferni* (with David Rankine) – Golden Hoard
*Key to the Latin of Dr John Dee's Spiritual Diaries* - Golden Hoard, Llewellyn
*Keys to the Gateway of Magic* (with David Rankine) – Golden Hoard
*Magical Diaries of Aleister Crowley* (edited) – Spearman, RedWheel Weiser
*Michael Psellus 'On the Operation of Daimones'* - Golden Hoard
*Millennium Prophecies: Apocalypse 2000* - Carlton
*Nostradamus* (with Francis King) – Carlton
*Oracle of Geomancy* – Warner Destiny, Prism
*Practical Angel Magic of Dr. Dee* (with David Rankine) – Golden Hoard
*Sacred Geometry* – Gaia, Hamlyn
*Search for Abraxas* (with Nevill Drury) – Spearman, Salamander
*Sepher Raziel: Liber Salomonis* (with Don Karr) – Golden Hoard
*Techniques of Graeco-Egyptian Magic* – Golden Hoard, Llewellyn
*Techniques of Solomonic Magic* – Golden Hoard, Llewellyn
*Techniques of High Magic* (with Francis King) – Daniels, Inner Traditions, Askin
*Terrestrial Astrology: Divination by Geomancy* – Routledge
*Veritable Key of Solomon* (with David Rankine) – Golden Hoard, Llewellyn

### Books on Feng Shui by Stephen Skinner

*Advanced Flying Star Feng Shui* – Golden Hoard
*Feng Shui Before & After* - Haldane Mason, Tuttle
*Feng Shui for Everyday Living* aka *Feng Shui for Modern Living* - Cico
*Feng Shui History: the Story of Classical Feng Shui in China & the West* – Golden Hoard
*Feng Shui Style* - Periplus
*Feng Shui the Traditional Oriental Way* - Haldane Mason
*Feng Shui: the Living Earth Manual* - Tuttle
*Flying Star Feng Shui* - Tuttle
*Guide to the Feng Shui Compass* – Golden Hoard
*K.I.S.S. Guide to Feng Shui (Keep it Simple Series)* – Penguin, DK
*Key San He Feng Shui Formulae* – Golden Hoard
*Living Earth Manual of Feng Shui* – RKP, Penguin, Arkana
*Mountain Dragon* – Golden Hoard
*Original Eight Mansion Formula* – Golden Hoard
*Practical Makeovers Using Feng Shui* – Haldane Mason, Tuttle
*Tibetan Oracle Pack* - Carroll & Brown
*Water Dragon* – Golden Hoard

# The Complete
# Magician's Tables

*The most complete set of Magic, Kabbalistic, Alchemic, Angelic, Astrologic, Chivalric, Demonic, Elemental, Emblem, Enochian, Gematric, Geomantic, Grimoire, I Ching, Isosephic, Pagan Pantheon, Planetary, Perfume, Plant, Polytheistic, Religious, Tarot, Zodiacal and Character Correspondences in more than 840 Tables*

by

Stephen Skinner

GOLDEN HOARD
2017

Expanded Fifth Edition 2015, 2017

Published by:
Golden Hoard Press Pte Ltd
PO Box 1073
Robinson Road PO
Singapore 902123

www.goldenhoard.com

Distributed in the US by Llewellyn Worldwide,
2143 Wooddale Drive,
Woodbury, Minnesota 55125-2989,
U.S.A

www.llewellyn.com

ISBN 978-0-9547639-7-8 Cloth Edition

Printed in Malaysia by
BS Print (M) Sdn. Bhd.
10, Jalan Indrahana
off Jalan Kuchai Lama
Kuala Lumpur 58200

# Acknowledgements

I wish to acknowledge Adam McLean's edition of the *Magical Calendar* as my original inspiration for writing this volume, and David Rankine for re-awakening my old interest in the Kabbalah. I would also like to thank Suguna Rethinasamy and Er Choon Haw who both worked unflaggingly on the research, typing, design and formatting of countless tables, without whose work this book might never have seen the light of day.

Special thanks to Dianthus Kim for Figures 3 and 4, to Gan Kek Hann for Figures 7 and 14, and to Linda Peh for technical help with the illustrations. I would like to thank Helene Hodge for her helpful suggestions in the Natural Magic and Pagan Pantheon sections. My thanks to Rita Henderson for her support and understanding during the gestation period of the book.

I would also like to thank Darcy Kuntz for permission to use the cover illustration of the variant Tree of Life from his book *The Complete Golden Dawn Cipher Manuscript*. The angel from the De Lisle Psalter is reproduced with the kind permission of the Trustees of the British Library. Robert Fludd's Angelic and Planetary Spheres is drawn from his *Utriusque Cosmi*, II, a, p. 219. Athanasius Kircher's Tree of Life comes from his *Oedipus Ægyptiacus*.

The cover illustration is from Peter Apian's *Astronomicum Caesareum*, published in Ingolstadt in 1540, which contains a series of beautiful cardboard discs forming a sophisticated circular tabular device. This work is significant as it was the last standard astronomical work to be based entirely on the Ptolemaic geocentric and magical view of the universe. This circular disk with rotating pointer enables the user to determine the points of intersection of the moon's orbit and the ecliptic, or *Caput* and *Cauda Draconis*, the head and tail of the dragon, for any time of the year. It is thus an early example of a Magician's Table.

Dedicated to Fra Volo Inteligere
Gerald Yorke (1901 - 1983)
friend and mentor
who preserved and kept alive the work of Aleister Crowley

# CONTENTS

## THE COMMENTARY                                                                     347

## REFERENCE                                                                            482

# List of Figures

# Subject Order Listing of Tables

# Introduction

The basis of Occultism can be summed up in a word *correspondence*. The theory of correspondence recognizes an implicit interdependence of all things with all other things, the existence of multiple relationships between various aspects of Nature's kaleidoscopic richness.

- James Wasserman, *Art and Symbols of the Occult*

# INTRODUCTION

This book contains all of the standard correspondences of the Golden Dawn as recorded in Aleister Crowley's *Liber 777*. But it also includes a lot more, including the real roots of the Tarot, Geomancy, the Olympic Spirits, Mithraic grades, and the hierarchy of spiritual creatures (be they angels, demons, intelligences, spirits or elementals) from grimoires such as the *Liber Juratus*, the *Key of Solomon*, the *Lemegeton (Goetia, Theurgia Goetia, Ars Paulina, Ars Almadel)*, and the *Book of Abramelin*. In fact it is a complete set of magician's tables.

A few attributions will appear to clash with the accepted attributions. This will undoubtedly upset some people, but upon closer inspection they will see that I have in such cases gone back to basics and corrected errors of transcription or deliberate 'blinds'. It may also upset some New Age writers who feel that it is justifiable to mix up *any* material or systems, regardless of its age, provenance or reality, just because the mix appeals to their intuition. Such systems may be valid, but I have attempted only to tabulate material with deep roots, and have tried to undo a few of the spurious associations of the recent past. I do not claim that this book is definitive, just that it pushes the boundaries of magic and magical correspondence further than they have previously been pushed.

We communicate by explaining how some new thing is *like* an existing thing, or how one thing corresponds with another. Words correspond to our thoughts and ideas. Words correspond with ideas, and the ideas in turn correspond with external reality. In fact without such correspondences we are reduced to grunting in a cave. With these correspondences we can communicate. The letters of one language correspond with the letters of another. The words of one language correspond to the words of another, because all our human concepts have similar roots. Even the letters that make up a word correspond with numbers, and allow us to do the calculations of Isopsephy and the Gematria of the practical Kabbalah, to investigate things which we otherwise may not have been able to grasp.

Correspondences not only form the basis of communication, but they are also the basis of magic. There is a whole stratum of thought which relates to emblems, colours, images, herbs and perfumes which was much more accessible to ancient man, and was still a part of Renaissance thinking, but which no longer forms part of the way we think at a conscious level. These correspondences are only vaguely guessed at by modern psychologists like Jung, who see the tip of the iceberg, but cannot easily trace its roots. These roots are not always obvious, but they are there as part of the subconscious memories, or the *egregore* of our culture, indeed of the cultures of all mankind.

Magic is based on correspondences. Magic most powerfully uses them when they are put together in a well constructed ritual. The denizens of other worlds and other spaces do not always speak our language, but they do respond to correctly assembled rituals where the colours, perfumes, gestures and words of power are all attuned to the same 'wavelength'. The whole science of magic, before the advent of universal literacy, was based on correspondences. Correspondences were used to store vast quantities of information, enabling feats of memory which are just not possible for modern man, who uses the written and electronic word to store his knowledge. Knowledge of these correspondences can help us understand the structure of thought, and the nature of memory, as well as the techniques of magic. These correspondences can even be used to *alter* this reality, not to just describe it.

A book of correspondences, such as this, is therefore basic to communication, communication between human beings, communications with one's own subconscious, even communication with angels and other non-human entities.

In a perfect holistic universe everything (and every non-thing) is connected to everything else. But not everything *corresponds* to everything else. Things are divided into categories, in order that they may function, and that we may be able to think about them. Thus, in the beginning was the 'Word', or the differentiation into yin and yang, or the Light, or the 'first swirlings', or whatever you wish to call it. However you like to phrase it, the essential act of creation was division. This is also reflected in biological necessity where growth comes about by the *division* of cells.

Such division is also necessary to the structure of thought. Until we categorise and label it is not possible to compare and contrast, therefore logical thought is not possible. Maybe the removal of such categories of thought might enable us to return to original bliss, but that is not the purpose of this book.

The categories I have chosen to use in this book are those of the Sephiroth of the Tree of Life of the Kabbalah, the Zodiac, the Elements and the Planets. I list the last three categories separately, despite the fact they are also included in the Tree of Life, for reasons that will soon become apparent.

Correspondences are the different things (often physically remote) that can be conceptually tied together using the 'chains of correspondence'. For example one chain of correspondences ties together the colour red, the god Mars, his planet, the fifth Sephirah, the sword, the ruby, and so on. Another ties together Aphrodite, Venus, the colour green, emeralds, and passionate love. On the other hand neither Ceres, cats, copper sulphate, corn, rock crystal or the smell of storax are on this chain. Each chain can therefore be clearly tabulated as a particular row of correspondences running across many tables.

# *History*

The work of discovering and collecting correspondences has been at the root of magic from time immemorial. Before looking at the way correspondences are structured we should take some time to look at the history of such work. The greatest synthesisers of these chains of correspondences were Henry Cornelius Agrippa, and in more recent times S L MacGregor Mathers.

Here we will just touch briefly upon those magicians and writers who have ordered these correspondences into tabular form. This work was begun by Greek and Arabic writers on magic, in books like the *Picatrix*. It was later codified in Latin by magical scholars like Peter de Abano (1250-1317) and Johannes Trithemius, Abbot of Sponheim (1462-1516) who was one of the main focuses for the recording and transmission of the magical traditions of his age. His pupil Henry Cornelius Agrippa (1486-1535) arranged much of this information in tabular form in his *Three Books of Occult Philosophy*[1] in 1509 (although these volumes were not published till 1533). Many animal, mineral and planetary correspondences were published in 1525 by Francesco Giorgio (1466-1540) in his *De Harmonia Mundi*. John Dee (1527-1604) used and extended much of Agrippa's work, especially that concerned with the knowledge and conversation of angels. He even drew up his own set of Kabbalistic tables in 1562.

Shortly after, much of this material was compressed into just one amazing page, the *Magical Calendar*[2] published in 1620. The conception for this is attributed to the famous astronomer Tycho Brahe (1561-1623) as its 'inventor' and to Johann Baptista Großschedel Von Aicha (who flourished around the 1620s) as its author. Using much of Agrippa's work and with the amazing engraving skills of Theodore de Bry,[3] the author produced one huge page, which is an almost comprehensive table of magical correspondences and sigils. I say 'almost' because the author deliberately left out all demonic references from his compilation, which were readily available in sources like Agrippa, and introduced other material instead.[4] Published in 1620, the *Magical Calendar*[5] contains tables of correspondences arranged by number, from one to twelve. The material is based largely on the extensive tables in Agrippa, book II, but goes beyond this, especially in its inclusion of sigils.

---

[1] In Book II Chapters 4-14.

[2] Or to give it its full name, *Calendarium Naturale Magicum Perpetuum Profundissimam Rerum Secretis Simarum Contemplationem, Totiusque Philosophiae Cognitionem Complectens*.

[3] De Bry also illustrated other important occult works such as those of Robert Fludd.

[4] It is interesting that a manuscript copy of this Calendar has the bogus date of 1503, which is a direct reference back to the work and times of Agrippa and Trithemius. As Adam McLean has pointed out, the date is definitely bogus because one of the calendar tables included can only have come after the 1582 revision of the calendar by Pope Gregory XIII.

[5] Carlos Gilly has identified the original manuscript on which the printed *Magical Calendar* was based as British Library Harley MS 3420.

The *Sigilla Decem Nomina Dei Principalia Complectentia* also has more detail than has survived in the engraving of the *Magical Calendar*. This Harley manuscript adds some very interesting details missing from the engraving, such as the 8 tables (or seals) of the Patriarchs[6] with particular virtues ascribed to them. So for example, Solomon's seal, which also appears in the *Goetia*, is to be used to secure wisdom, Jeremiah's seal for visions, Ezekiel's seal for health, and so on. These sigils were then used in lots of other magical manuscripts of the period. The sigils and images of the planets are two separate sets. Both sets are used in the *Ars Paulina* (Part 3 of the *Lemegeton*) table of practise. In addition to the *Lemegeton*, at least two other grimoires, Rabbi Abognazar's *Key of Solomon* and *Janua Magicae Reserata*[7] depend partly on the *Magical Calendar*.

During the late 19th century renaissance of magic, S L MacGregor Mathers and Dr Wynn Westcott organised much of this information into the knowledge lectures of the Hermetic Order of the Golden Dawn, and in the course of doing this generated a Book of Correspondences. As Adam McLean points out in his edition of *The Magical Calendar*:

> "Mathers 'Book of Correspondences' circulated among the members of the R.R & A.C., the inner order of the Hermetic Order of the Golden Dawn, which was later published by Aleister Crowley as his own work 'Liber 777'."

Like 'his' edition of the *Goetia*, and his publication in the *Equinox* of Mather's Golden Dawn rituals, Crowley's work was basically a light edit of the original scholarly work actually done by Mathers. As Crowley well knew, the main lists were assembled by the Golden Dawn founders, and he published them in 1909 anonymously, with impunity and without so much as a backwards look. Mathers did attempt later to sue Crowley over his publication of Mather's work in the *Equinox*, but failed through lack of funds. Gerald Yorke, in his Editorial Preface to *Liber 777*, states that:

> "Ninety per cent of the Hebrew, the four colour scales, and the order and attribution of the Tarot trumps are as taught in the Hermetic Order of the Golden Dawn with[in] its inner circle."

Israel Regardie gave Crowley the credit for creating the concept of tabulating the various sets of data (thereby producing 'a new type of literature'), even if Crowley did not generate very much of the content. But even that was not a new idea, as Agrippa had used tables 400 years before for the same purpose.

*Liber 777* was first published by the Walter Scott Publishing Company as a slim volume of just 54 pages in 1909. Several times Crowley planned to re-issue it in an

---

[6] One of these is the famous seal of Solomon, used as the Table of Practice in the *Lemegeton* grimoire *Theurgia Goetia*.

[7] Skinner & Rankine, *Practical Angel Magic of Dr John Dee's Enochian Tables*, published as Volume 1 of the Sourceworks of Ceremonial Magic, Golden Hoard Press, 2005.

expanded form, first via the original Mandrake Press, and later in an illustrated colour edition through Oskar Hopfer. None of these plans came to fruition, and so it was not reprinted till after Crowley's death in 1947.

In 1955 my old friend Gerald Yorke expanded the tables, added a lot of new notes from his Crowley archives, and published *Liber 777 Revised* in a beautifully printed and limited edition volume through Neptune Press, the publishing arm of Atlantis, the famous London bookshop. This beautiful edition has since become a collector's item. Almost twenty years later Samuel Weiser, over their own copyright, republished *Liber 777 Revised* in 1973 along with an Essay on *Gematria*, and *Sepher Sephiroth8* (both taken from Crowley's *Equinox* Vol. 1, Nos. 5 and 8 respectively) as *The Qabalah of Aleister Crowley*.

The tables of *Liber 777* are however all over the place in terms of their ordering, having been assembled partly in the order in which they were taught in the Golden Dawn, with some modifications to the order made for the printer's convenience. Accordingly, using that book is quite difficult for the beginner.

The most fruitful sources used to create the present volume were the works of Henry Cornelius Agrippa (as edited by Donald Tyson), the *Lemegeton* (as edited by Joseph Peterson), Peter de Abano (as edited by the present author), MacGregor Mathers (both published and unpublished works), Aleister Crowley (as edited by Gerald Yorke), the four volumes of *The Golden Dawn* (as edited by Israel Regardie) and the inventor (supposedly Tycho Brahe) of the *Magical Calendar* (as edited by Adam McLean). David Godwin, Bill Whitcomb and Alan Hulse's volumes have also been useful and encyclopaedic references.

This material, and much more drawn from both book and unpublished manuscript sources, in the British Library and Bodleian Library, has gone into the present book. I have re-grouped the information according to subject, and incorporated much new material which has become available with the recent publication of old Kabbalistic and magical texts. I have also tried to present the material in a more consistent and logical way. Of course sadly such an undertaking can never be complete.

No work of this size and complexity will ever be error free or 'complete' in any sense of the word, and for this I accept full responsibility. However in building on the shoulders of the giants who have gone before, like Agrippa or Mathers, I hope to provide the magical student with a classic which will weather the next 100 years as well as Crowley's *Liber 777* has weathered the last 100 years.[9]

---

[8] *Sepher Sephiroth* was another example of Crowley borrowing somebody else's work, in that case Allan Bennett, editing it, and then publishing it over his own name.

[9] "When Onkelos the Chaldean said בכבאדרמין (=777), i.e. 'with or by the Eternals', he understood the Thirty-two Paths of Wisdom" – Pico de Mirandola *Conclusiones* XXVI.

# Aleister Crowley's Liber 777

Of all the sources, in some ways Crowley's *Liber 777* is the most difficult for a beginner to read. There are several reasons why it is initially difficult to read:

1.      The ordering of the columns. These are neither grouped by subject nor presented in order of complexity. In many cases these appear to be grouped at random, as the information came to hand. For example, of the first eight columns, only two are in English. Unaccountably, things that would normally be grouped together are printed many pages apart, such as the gods of different cultures, which are separated from each other by many columns.

2.      The quirkiness of some of his inclusions. For example Crowley amended the age old list of Archdemons to include some of his personal favourites, taken from Mathers' *Kabbalah Unveiled*, like Isheth Zenunim and Chioa[10] and placed these, without comment, into a standard and otherwise well established list. I have accordingly shown the traditional ascriptions but also provided a comment outlining the alternatives. Undoubtedly the content of some of the tables reflects the distribution of the present author's interests, but my overriding consideration was to present traditional pre-20th century attributions.

3.      The lack of both translation and transliteration of many of the Hebrew columns. This is Crowley showing off his virtuosity with Hebrew, Latin and other languages, but it makes it very difficult for someone without a Classical education, or for the English-only reader. I have therefore supplied both translations and transliterations where necessary. The point of supplying letter for letter transliterations is so that the student who is not familiar with the Hebrew alphabet can still apply the techniques of Gematria to the words under consideration. In important and significant Tables there is also a numeration column, where these values have been calculated for the reader.

If you compare Crowley's columns with those in the present book you will see that some of his columns do not have a corresponding column in the present volume, because Crowley's columns were short on real information (e.g. his columns 4, 9, 25-32, 37, 124) or trivial (e.g. columns 10, 77 and 92).[11] Many columns contain much more information (e.g. columns 43 and 91) or completely new contents (e.g. column 46), and some of his columns containing several sets of incompatible information (e.g. column 49) are here rationalised. Some columns (e.g. the single geomancy column 49) appear here in a much more complete form, in this case as 30 columns on the same subject. Others (e.g. column 47) contain much more up to date, or more correct information (e.g. Table Y the *I Ching*).

---

[10] The Beast was the child of Samael and Isheth Zenunim from *Revelations* 17.
[11] I have refrained from using Crowley's Roman numerals, and refer to his columns by their Arabic number equivalents, as Roman numerals are no longer universally understood.

# *The Paths on the Tree of Life*

The Tree of Life is one of the basic diagrams of the Kabbalah. If you look at any of the illustrations of the Tree (Figures 1, 2, 3 or 4), you will see that the Tree of Life is composed of 10 circles, spheres or Sephiroth, connected together by 22 lines or Paths (or *netivoth*), making a total of 32 categories. In his book *Liber 777*, Crowley used the Sephiroth and Paths of the Tree of Life as his core reference points, and arranged all rows according to their numbers.

*Hebrew Letters on the Paths*

As we will see further down, as well as different Path arrangements, there are also several different arrangements of the letters on to the Paths on the Tree. It is interesting that even the secret Golden Dawn Cipher manuscript, upon which the Order was based, shows a completely different Path layout, with no horizontal Paths and a different arrangement of the Hebrew Letters.[12] Not only do these attributions differ within the Golden Dawn, but they also differ between main Kabbalistic schools. This means that the use of the Paths on the Tree of Life is not a rock solid basis for a definitive Table of Correspondences.

The Tree of Life is considered by Golden Dawn tradition Kabbalists to be a universal filing system, and although it may sound like heresy to say so, this approach in fact does not work so well.

Indeed Crowley soon found that there were at least four major problems with using the Path numbers of the Tree of Life in this way:

1.    There are two double attributions in the system because:
     a)      a row/Path for the 5th Element Aethyr is missing, and
     b)      there is a double attribution of both Earth and Saturn to the same 32nd row/Path

Crowley had to introduce two more theoretical rows/Paths to cover these multiple attributions, and these lines show up at the bottom of some of his tables. This made for an uncomfortable additional of the two 'paths' of 31-*bis* and 32-*bis*, '*bis*' being French for 'encore' or 'again'. As Crowley puts it:

> "31 and 32 must be supplemented by 31-bis and 32-bis, as these two paths possess a definitely double attribution; viz. 31-bis to Spirit as against 31 to Fire; 32-bis to Earth as against 32 to Saturn".

In fact these two Paths do *not* possess a double attribution. Crowley simply created one for tabular convenience, on rather flimsy theoretical pretexts.

---

[12] *The Complete Golden Dawn Cipher Manuscript.* Edited by Darcy Kuntz, Holmes Publishing, Edmonds, 1996. See cover diagram, and in the Cipher manuscript itself folios 53 and 54. These show, for example, the Hebrew letters on the Middle Pillar, as ק. ר. ש. ת rather than the accepted Golden Dawn attribution of ג. ס. ת.

It is obvious that any system of classification is not working too well if you have to bolt on another two categories before you even get started.

2.     The next thing Crowley realised was that many tables were only related to small parts of the Tree, and so (to the confusion of many students) he published a number of tables which were just sub-sets of the full 32+2 Paths, without fully explaining that some correspondences only belong to one subset.

3.     To help clarify why certain correspondences grouped together and other lines showed gaps, he then printed the numbers 1 to 32-*bis* in the right hand Key column in a horizontally staggered format.

This has confused even more students, although his rationale was as follows. His bold middle column numbers for the numbers 0-10 were associated with the zero (Ain Soph) and the 10 Sephiroth. Further down, this middle column is used differently, where it is also associated with Path numbers 12, 13, 14, 21, 27, 30 and 32. These apparently unrelated numbers are the 7 Classical Planets. Then there is a column staggered to the right containing the unlikely set of numbers 11, 23, 31, 32-*bis* and 31-*bis*. These are the 4 Classical Elements plus the fifth Element Aethyr. The remaining numbers, which are staggered to the left, 15, 16, 17, 18, 19, 20, 22, 24, 25, 26, 28, 29, are the 12 Zodiacal signs.

4.     The numbers 11-32 *bis* have no particular symbolic meaning, they are simply convenient numbering for the Paths. Even Crowley has to say "observe that the numbers [of this column] subsequent to 10 are not to be considered as real numbers."

These are the four main problems encountered when using this method. Crowley's treatment of these problems was to simply force everything into the Sephiroth and Path mould. Then he made shorter Tables for categories which simply involved just the Sephiroth, just the Zodiac, just the Planets, or just the Elements, but Crowley was well aware of the forcedness of the classification.

In fact the 22 Paths do their job satisfactorily *only* in the context of the 22 letters of the Hebrew alphabet (and other cognate alphabets), and just maybe in the context of the 22 Tarot trumps. Considerations of other categories, especially the 5 Elements, 7 Planets and 12 Zodiacal signs, are poorly served by this arrangement. Each of these categories are split up by the 32 + 2 Path arrangement, and interleaved, so you cannot easily see the clear patterns, which become apparent when like is grouped with like.

Accordingly I will not be using the Path model, but looking back in time to the more traditional system of enumerating correspondences.

In this book, I have mostly ignored the *order* of the 32+2 Paths, and have instead gone back to the traditional building blocks of esoteric classification using the Zodiac, Elements, and Planets.

## *A New Row Order*

The solution is to only show those things that are genuinely equivalent together on the same table. That is to show the Zodiacal, Elemental, and Planetary correspondences simply as themselves, without forcing them to conform to the (fairly arbitrary) Golden Dawn Path numbering order of the Tree of Life. Or to put it another way, these tables preserve Hebrew Kabbalistic categories for the Hebrew Kabbalah and its cognates, but return to ancient magical and Classical categories for those things that can be better grouped by Zodiacal, Elemental, and Planetary attributions.

From a practical point of view this means that in this book the Path *order* of the 32 + 2 Path sequence will not be used, except for the Hebrew alphabet (and the other alphabets which relate directly to it) and the 22 major trumps of the Tarot, whist the rest of the tables will revert to the Classical groupings which have ruled since ancient times, arranged by the Zodiac, Elements and Planets (or 'ZEP' order). I have therefore uncoupled the grouping of the symbols and entities from the arbitrary restriction of the Path number order.

Don't worry though, as the Golden Dawn Path numbers are still shown down the second column of most Tables for cross reference purposes, if you need them. However it is now the Zodiacal, Elemental and Planetary attributions that form the prime ordering mechanism for most of the Table structures. Surprisingly little has changed, except for the better, as immediately the significance of some symbolical groupings becomes *much* more apparent, and new patterns show up which were previously lost to sight.

For those purists who feel this is desecration, pause a while, and look at the groupings in the Tables. Where there were previously gaps in the Path order arrangement, the logic of the tables now stands out, with Planetary attributions all together, Zodiacal attributions falling together, and likewise for the attributions of the 5 Elements. Note that the Planets are of course duplicated in the first 10 numbers (Sephiroth). Where they appear as Sephiroth they are considered to be more universal, but where they appear lower down on the tables, they are more exclusively of a planetary nature.

Finally, a further and conclusive confirmation that this is the most natural way to group the correspondences is to be found in *Liber 777 Revised* itself, in the section headed 'Explanation of the Attributions.' Here the explanatory text for a number of the columns, such as Crowley's columns 15, 18, 19, 34, 35, 38, 39 and many more, are each subdivided up into separate sections for 'The Elements', 'The Planets' and 'The Zodiac', confirming that Crowley also found that *in practice* the 'ZEP order' is the most natural way of dealing with, and explaining, the correspondences.

In the present volume, the two left hand columns are used as the Key columns to the tables. The numbers 1 to 10 refer to the ten Sephiroth, the rest of the rows are divided into Zodiac, Element and Planets ('ZEP') groupings.

Where any *other* order is used, such as with the 16 Geomantic figures, this differing row sort order will be indicated in the box at the top left of the relevant Table. Incidentally, Crowley barely touched upon the subject of geomancy in *Liber 777* (only devoting *part* of one Column 49 to it), probably because the 16 figures wouldn't fit conveniently into his rows.

In Crowley's *Liber 777* the key identifiers, the Zodiac, Element and Planetary sign of each Path form only *one* column of their own (his Column 177), but I think these are so important that in this volume they appear in almost *every* table down the left hand side, so that you can see at all times if you are dealing with a Zodiacal sign, an Element, or a Planet.

This way it becomes much more instructive to see attributions of the 7 Planets grouped *together* in a table, and attributions of the 12 Zodiacal signs grouped together, and the 5 Element also grouped together, rather than having then intercut like a shuffled deck of cards.

## *Tarot on the Tree*

Talking of cards, it was of course the Tarot pack which, first Mathers, and then Crowley, used to bridge the symbolic gap between the Kabbalah and the attributes of ancient, Classical and mediaeval magic. This use of the Tarot was however based upon something that has now been proved, beyond a shadow of a doubt, to be a fallacy. This fallacy, that the origin of the Tarot pack is to be found in the 'Book of Thoth' of ancient Egypt, was only *invented* relatively recently, in 1781, by Court de Gebelin in his book *Le Monde Primitif*, and elaborated upon by Etteilia later in the same century, finally to be embraced by Eliphas Levi and later the Victorian English occultists. More details will be found in the commentary on Table T.

It was Comte De Mellet who (in the same book) first suggested the infamous connection of the 22 Hebrew letters with the Tarot, not Eliphas Levi, although it was the latter who popularised it and became associated with it.

When you are freed of this erroneous misconception, then the Tarot reveals that it is in fact a splendidly constructed mediaeval emblem pack, a series of archetypal designs that were rich with symbolic meaning to the members of Renaissance society. When that is realised, then we can look truly at the very concrete meanings embedded in these cards, and forget much of the modern superstructure of symbolical speculation and accretion. We can again call a spade a spade, rather than 'an instrument of divine excavatory intent'.

## *How to Use these Tables*

Because such a wide range of topics has been covered, to better keep them together a form of Alphabetic grouping has been utilised. For example, every Column to do with the Tarot has the prefix 'T', correspondence Columns concerned with Angels are prefixed with 'A', and all Geomancy correspondence Columns are prefixed with a 'G', and so on.

The Tables are listed in three ways: first in the Contents page alphabetically, then in the Subject Order Listing of Tables which follows. This Subject Order Listing can be used as a quick lookup for broader subject groupings. Under Magic, for example, you will find Dr John Dee's Angels ('D'), Geomancy ('G'), Magic of the Grimoires ('M'), Natural Magic ('N'), Orders, Grades and Officers ('O') and so on. Finally at the back of the book is a complete list of all Columns in the order they are printed. The Tables and the Commentary are printed in strict alphabetic and numeric order in order to aid in rapid location.

Some grouping has had to be slightly arbitrary. For example, all Hebrew angels could equally been put amongst Angels, or put in the Kabbalah section. For convenience angels that relate directly to the Tree of Life are grouped under Kabbalah, but other Biblical, Apocryphal and Gnostic angels are grouped under Angels, as otherwise the Kabbalah section would have become too unwieldy. This means there is some slight duplication, with the main Archangels of necessity appearing in both places.

I have refrained from using the spelling 'magick' which Crowley reintroduced into the language, as I do not think there is any further need to distinguish the magic of sorcery and Harry Potter from the parlour magic of the Victorians.

Note that where a Column is listed as a *transliteration* of another Column you should expect to see the Hebrew or Greek letters replaced one for one with Latin capital letters (some characters like Ch, Sh and Th have a *lower case* character following them to distinguish them from characters with similar sound values). This is so non-Hebrew or non-Greek readers can easily see how many characters make up the word, easily add up the value of the Hebrew letters, perform Gematria or Isopsephy on the word, and appreciate what the word actually 'sounds' like. If the Column is listed as a *translation* then you will instead find the word as it is usually written in English, or if it is not a proper noun, then the English meaning.

For example:

|  אמת | Hebrew original |
| --- | --- |
| = AMTh | *three* letter transliteration |
| = Aemeth | usual translation into English |
| = Truth | English meaning |
| = 441 | Numeration. |

## *Numbering Conventions*

The 'zero row' representing the Unmanifest, and favoured by Crowley, has not been used. With the exception of the Ain Soph Aur of the Kabbalah and the Wu Chi of Taoist cosmology (not the Tao, which is more appropriate to Kether) there are very few attributions suitable for a zero row. In fact it is certain that anything that is able to be written down in this row cannot adequately represent the Unmanifest, so there is no zero row used in these tables. Where appropriate a note will be made of this in the Commentary.

For the convenience of readers and for purposes of comparison, Crowley's column numbers have been included in the second row of any column which relates in any way to a similar column in *Liber 777*. These numbers do not have an intrinsic or Kabbalistic numerical value. They have been transferred out of Roman numeral format into modern number format, as Roman numerals do not come as easily for today's readers as they did in Mathers' time when they were much more common, so for example a reference to Crowley's Column LXXXVIII is simply marked as '88'.

This book does not claim to be a complete exposition of any of the subjects tabulated. It is a tabular presentation of correspondences in both Western and Eastern systems of magic, religion and mysticism, and as such must devote most of its space to tabulation, not to explanation. Therefore comment is not evenly spread across all columns. Most of the comment occurs where some point needs explaining or updating, or is controversial, or where its source will not be found amongst the usual texts. Another exception is where completely new material has been introduced, such as the numerical correspondences of the Olympic Spirits or the numerical values of the Grades of Mithras, which have never before appeared in print in this form. Some Columns appear without any comment at all. I refer the reader to the Bibliography for further research.

## *The Nature of Correspondences*

To understand how the correspondences are built up, it becomes important to see, and to test, the links in the chain. The basic Kabbalistic texts underlying these correspondences are the *Sepher Yetzirah*, the book *Bahir*, and the *Zohar*. It is no coincidence that Wynn Westcott (co-founder of the Golden Dawn with Mathers and Woodman) published a translation (from the Latin rather than the Hebrew) of the *Sepher Yetzirah* in 1887, as this is one of the main links of the chain of correspondences that links Western Magic through astrology to the Hebrew Kabbalah.

There is no problem with the *Sepher Yetzirah* correspondences for the 10 Sephiroth which are clearly documented in many Hebraic and Latin sources, but the 22 Paths connecting the Sephiroth have had scant attention paid to them in much of the literature, and it is these Paths that are the crux of many Western correspondences.

At this point I recommend that anyone who is quite happy with the internally consistent Golden Dawn synthesis, or who is new to it, skips the rest of this section. If you proceed to read the rest of this section, prepare to have some of your basic preconceptions shaken a little, but at the end you will be standing on a firmer conceptual ground.

The main chain of correspondences has four links (marked ①-④):

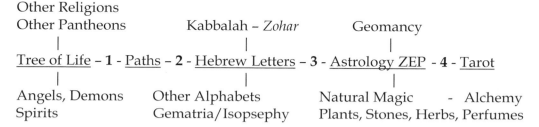

As you can see, the Hebrew letters are central to the chain, and to the Kabbalah. You can also see that the Tarot is actually a long conceptual distance from the Tree of Life[13], and we will later see why this has caused both Mathers and Crowley to make various tweaks to links 3 and 4 (like swapping the cards Strength and Justice, or the cards Emperor and Star), without perhaps addressing the root of the problem.

Taking each of the four links in turn:

*1. Tree of Life – Paths Link*

The Tree of Life diagram comes in three main 'flavours': the Gra, the Lurianic, and the Kircher/Golden Dawn Tree. The most familiar to modern readers is the Golden Dawn Tree shown in Figure 3 which shows three Paths radiating from Malkuth at the bottom but with only 4 paths crossing the so-called Abyss. The Lurianic Tree (named after its promoter Isaac Luria, called the 'Ari') in Figure 4 shows only one Path leading from Malkuth (it also occurs in older sources like the *Bahir*). All three Trees have 22 Paths, but obviously the numbering of the Paths differs, so this link yields variable results, and is not as firm as most commentators imply. I will be comparing the three Trees later in this introduction. Let us now look at how the chain of correspondence proceeds from there.

---

[13] It was not till the 19th century that the Tarot was first connected to the much more ancient symbolism of the Kabbalah, and this connection was made by French esotericists in the spirit of Romanticism rather than careful scholarship. Even A E Waite wrote "I am *not* to be included among those who are satisfied that there is a valid correspondence between Hebrew letters and Tarot Trump symbols."

2.      *Paths Numbers – Hebrew Letters Link*

All three types of Trees have 22 Paths, and as the *Sepher Yetzirah* states, one letter of the Hebrew alphabet is allocated to each Path. The problem is that the *Sepher Yetzirah* does not *diagrammatically* show what this allocation is. There are however definite allocations of the 3 *types* of Hebrew letters to the Paths:

a) The 3 Mother letters (א Aleph, מ Mem and ש Shin) are logically allocated to the 3 Elements (excluding Earth). On the Lurianic Tree, they are the three horizontal Paths on the Tree. The Golden Dawn Tree however applies Aleph to connect Sephiroth 1 and 2, Mem to connect 5 and 8, and Shin to connect 8 and 10: hardly a satisfactory distribution of these three most important letters.

b) The seven Double letters[14] (ב Beth, ג Gimel, ד Daleth, כ Kaph, פ Peh, ר Resh, ת Tau) are allocated to the 7 Planets. On the Lurianic Tree, these are the 7 vertical Paths on the Tree. On the Golden Dawn Tree they appear to be just randomly allocated.

c) The twelve Single letters (ה He, ו Vau, ז Zain, ח Cheth, ט Teth, י Yod, ל Lamed, נ Nun, ס Samekh, ע Ayin, צ Tzaddi, ק Qoph) are allocated to the 12 Zodiacal signs. On the Lurianic Tree these are systematically allocated only to the diagonal Paths on the Tree. On the Golden Dawn Tree they fill the remaining Paths, with no obvious pattern.

Obviously for this link to work we have to establish which allocation is correct. The clue to the positioning of the three different types of Hebrew letters on the Tree (and hence the Paths) occurs in the very clear differentiation of the three different types of letters. It also occurs in the last section of the *Sepher Yetzirah* (which is in fact dropped from some editions). This section lists out the qualities of each of the 32 'Intelligences.'[15] The symbolism of the first ten Intelligences show clearly that they are meant to be the 10 Sephiroth, and the texts show some interesting secret connections between the Sephiroth. The next 22 Intelligences are from the 22 Paths, and from the hints (particularly in the original Hebrew) you can see which two Sephiroth are connected by each Intelligence or Path. Crowley clearly did not understand the significance of this section when he wrote of it:

> "Column XII…These attributions arise from the description of the paths in the *Sepher Yetzirah*. This is one of the most ancient books of the Qabalah; but it is far from clear how the ideas correspond with the general scheme of symbolism. They seem of no use in practical magical work." [16]

---

[14] Those letters with two different pronunciations, the harder version indicated by a dot or *dagesh* in the centre of the letter.

[15] In fact Intelligence was an old name for an angel, and this perhaps suggests that you can pass from one Sephirah to another with the aid of an angel.

[16] Crowley, *Liber 777*, page 66.

On the contrary, they are the clearest *available* indicators of the correct order of the Paths. I will not pursue this here, except to say that these indications taken together with the real meaning of the Serpent and Lightning Flash give the correct order for the Path *numbers*. They also indicate the correct order of meditational practice. Note that I am only talking about the *numbering* here.

*3 - Hebrew Letters - Astrology (Zodiac /Element/Planet) Link*

This link is perhaps the most important for Western magic, as most of the other non-Kabbalistic correspondences depend upon it. Let us look at the parts:

a) The three Elements Aleph=Air, Mem=Water, Shin=Fire is clearly set out in Chapter 3 of the *Sepher Yetzirah.*

b) The Zodiac. This correlation of the 12 single letters to the 12 signs of the Zodiac is agreed upon by all commentators and is very clearly laid out in Chapter 5 of the *Sepher Yetzirah.*

c) The Planets however are a different matter, and occur in more than four variant arrangements in Chapter 4 of the various editions of the *Sepher Yetzirah.* The main variants are discussed below.

Westcott & Kaplan in their translations of the *Sepher Yetzirah* show:

| | | |
|------|---|--------|
| Beth | – | Moon |
| Gimel | – | Mars |
| Daleth | – | Sun |
| Kaph | – | Venus |
| Peh | – | Mercury |
| Resh | – | Saturn |
| Tau | – | Jupiter |

It is very curious that Mathers did *not* use this arrangement, especially as he probably had a hand in the translation of the Westcott version.[17]

For some reason, Mathers gave an order which is not included in any of these versions of the *Sepher Yetzirah.* This is the order that has influenced all of 20th century esoteric thought, but it is not an order with foundations in tradition:

---

[17] *Sheirat Yoseph* (quoted in Kaplan, *Sepher Yetzirah: The Book of Creation,* page 178-179) gives a completely different order, which I think is completely wrong, allocating Beth to Saturn, Gimel to Sun, Daleth to Moon, Kaph to Mars, Peh to Mercury, Resh to Jupiter, and Tau to Venus. Likewise, in associating the particular letters with each planet, the Jesuit Athanasius Kircher speculatively allots Beth to the Sun, Gimel to Venus, Daleth to Mercury, Kaph to Luna, Peh to Saturn, Resh to Jupiter, and Tau to Mars. I believe this attribution is also flawed.

| Beth | – | Mercury |
|------|---|---------|
| Gimel | – | Moon |
| Daleth | – | Venus |
| Kaph | – | Jupiter |
| Peh | – | Mars |
| Resh | – | Sun |
| Tau | – | Saturn |

By far the largest number of versions of the *Sepher Yetzirah* (including both the Long and Short Version of the text) give an order which follows exactly the order of the Planets on the Sephiroth, which is therefore the most Kabbalistically logical. This is also the arrangement favoured by the translation by Gershom Scholem, who could be said to have a broader perspective on the Kabbalah than any other 20th century scholar. More impressively, this order is reflected in the pediments of the Ziggurat of Ur, suggesting it also has the most ancient pedigree:

| Beth | – | Saturn |
|------|---|--------|
| Gimel | – | Jupiter |
| Daleth | – | Mars |
| Kaph | – | Sun |
| Peh | – | Venus |
| Resh | – | Mercury |
| Tau | – | Moon |

There are other hints of the rightness of this order, especially when using the Lurianic Tree which puts the Planets on the Paths connecting the Sephiroth vertically. The only conclusion open to us is that the planetary attributions in Mathers' working are in fact incorrect. I think it strange that Mathers preferred to preserve the fairly recent sequencing of the Tarot trumps in preference to retaining the considerably older and more valid instructions of the *Sepher Yetzirah*. I feel therefore that the time has come to turn back to this older attribution.

This arrangement has also been pointed out by Carlos Suares. I have not however made this change to the Tarot tables from Tables T1 to T28, which follow strict Golden Dawn attributions. Columns T38-T41 show how the Tarot would look if the ancient *Sepher Yetzirah* attributions had been adopted by Mathers. It is up to you, the reader, to decide for yourself if you wish to implement this material. The effect of correcting this, is to bring the 7 Planets on the Paths into line with the *Sepher Yetzirah* but to put their 7 corresponding Tarot Trumps on different Paths. If this ancient Planetary order is accepted, then the attribution of 7 of the Tarot Trumps to the Paths changes in a way which is infinitely more logical. The connection between each Tarot trump and its Planet is however not affected (as we will see below).

*4 – Astrology (Zodiac /Element/Planet) - Tarot Link*

Mathers' alignment of individual Tarot Trumps with the Zodiac, Element and Planets is very cogent. By retaining this, 7 of the Planetary Trumps now fall on different Paths, but remain linked to exactly the same Planets.

*Roman Numbering*

I also feel it is better to jettison the Roman numbering of the Tarot altogether, as it is a very recent addition, and intimately tied up with the basically wrong traditional French numerical attributions.

This is not as inflammatory a statement as it first seems. Remember that as Eliphas Levi put The Magician = Aleph, every one of his attributions is therefore wrong in Golden Dawn terms, or any other terms. Levi's excuse is that it was just a 'blind'. I don't believe in blinds. I think information should be given to the best of one's ability, or withheld, but not provided in an intentionally crippled form. Almost all writers of the French tradition followed this deliberately blinded attribution.

Accordingly the Roman numbering will *always* be out of step with both the Paths of the Tree and the Hebrew letters of *any* modern system anyway.

In addition, as the Tarot is itself a distillation of a series of broken emblem sets, something we will see in the commentary on the Tarot Table T, so the idea of assigning them a sequence of ordered numbers is intrinsically nonsense. In fact all the early packs were unnumbered. The current numbering of packs like the Visconti-Sforza was only applied in the last few decades of the 20th century). Finally, as Stuart Kaplan clearly shows, the order of the Tarot cards has changed many times in the 600 years of its existence, so the Roman numbering of the Trumps is at best a convenience, and at worst a very misleading distraction. These numbers have no intrinsic value, being useful only as identifiers, and the name of the Trump adequately fulfils that function.

So let me sum up. The links in the chain are as follows:

1. *Tree of Life - Path Link*. There are at least four Tree formats, the Cordovero/Kircher format used by the Golden Dawn, the Cipher manuscript, and the Lurianic versions, therefore this connection is not as fixed as one might think, and tables from *Liber 777* would have to be re-arranged accordingly for whichever Tree was used. The variant Tree arrangements have however no effect on the rearrangement of the present Tables, as these are dependent only on ZEP order rather than Path number order anyway.

2. *Path - Hebrew Letters Link*. These attributions are also *not* fixed. The Lurianic Tree's use of horizontal Paths for Elements, vertical Paths for Planets and diagonal Paths for Zodiacal signs has much to recommend it, is more ancient, and is more logical than the Golden Dawn arrangement.

3. *Hebrew Letters – Astrology. Link* As Mathers did not use any standard edition of the *Sepher Yetzirah* to associate the Planets with the Hebrew letters (not even Westcott's edition) his seven Planet to Hebrew Letter attributions are suspect. I recommend that you examine the realignment of the 7 Planets and their Tarot trumps with the Hebrew letters as shown in Columns T38-T41.

4. *Astrology – Tarot Link.* Mathers' clever attributions of the Tarot Trumps to the astrological Zodiac, Elements, and Planets (as shown in the Golden Dawn Cipher manuscript) still holds good.

With regard to the Tarot, I recommend that you also ignore or remove the Roman numbering of the Tarot to allow the Trumps to be assigned to the Paths correctly and smoothly without the usual sense of numerical dislocation.

## *Spelling and Transliteration*

The spelling of names, such as those of the Archangels, has been standardised to Golden Dawn style, except where a specific authority closer to the origin has been quoted, then that spelling has then been used. In the Kabbalistic section I have listed all entries in Hebrew, but have also provided columns with the English transliteration, and the English translation, making it more user friendly, rather than being only accessible to the Hebrew reading specialist.

Hebrew has been transliterated according to MacGregor Mather's table of equivalents in *The Kabbalah Unveiled*. Although that is not modern practice, and the mixed use of capitals and lower case looks very uncomfortable to the eye of modern Hebrew scholars, nevertheless this is the format most easily recognisable by those interested in Western occultism, and so has been the one used. For scholars who read the original Hebrew, the transliteration is redundant anyway, as they can go direct to the Hebrew letters and ignore the transliteration. At a late stage in production it was observed that, in the particular Hebrew font used here, there is very little difference between נ Nun and ג Gimel, and between ח Cheth and ה Heh, so be careful when reading these letters.

For Chinese columns, the Wade-Giles system of transliteration has been used as standard, rather than either modern *pinyin* or James Legge's antiquated Victorian system. *Pinyin*, although now almost universal as a system of Chinese transliteration is, surprisingly, based on Albanian sound values, which make it rather unnatural for English speakers. In addition the present author's books on Chinese metaphysics and feng shui are all presented in Wade-Giles format, so it is consistent for him to use the same system here.

## *Variant Attributions*

I will be predominantly observing Golden Dawn attributions throughout, especially where they are clearly and closely drawn from older sources like Agrippa. Where these have been corrected it will clearly be marked and explained. I will not be utilising the mid-20th century swap of Emperor and Star Tarot Trumps favoured by Crowley, and derived from a line in his *Book of the Law*.

The only notable exception to Golden Dawn practice is the reversal of the ascription of two magical weapons back to the traditional grimoire ascription of the Sword to Fire and the Wand to Air.[18] In addition, several well known and acknowledged 'blinds' have been silently removed, as we no longer live in the prudish atmosphere of Victorian England. One example of such a blind is Bishop Leadbeater's attribution of the Svadisthana chakra to the 'spleen', when he was certainly aware that this chakra maps directly onto the genitals.

## *Tree of Life Formats*

There are at least five different arrangements of the Paths on the Tree of Life:

1) The conventional geometrical arrangement of the Tree of Life of Moses Cordovero (1522-1570) as drawn by the Jesuit Athanasius Kircher (1601-1680) (see Figure 1). This was the basis for the Golden Dawn Tree (see Figure 3).

2) The Golden Dawn Cipher Manuscript showing a different arrangement of Paths, with Daath shown as a full blown Sephirah connected to the six other surrounding Sephiroth. The inclusion of this form of the Tree is not for use, but simply to demonstrate the fact that the 'standard' Golden Dawn Tree of Life was not the only one, even within the Golden Dawn itself (see Figure 2).

3) The Tree of Life as popularised by Mathers and the Golden Dawn, which became the standard version in the 20th century, especially in the context of magic (see Figure 3). This is very similar structurally to Figure 1.

4) The more logical and mystical arrangement of the Tree, favoured by Rabbi Isaac Luria (1533-1572) (see Figure 4).

5) The Gra version of the Tree of Life (which essentially shows the pre-Fall universe, and therefore theoretic rather than practical) is not shown here.

The Path numbers in the second column of most Columns refer to the Golden Dawn version of the Tree. However Tables in this book can be happily used on *any* of the Tree arrangements, simply by ignoring these Path numbers, and using the ZEP (Zodiac, Element, Planet) Column to place the correspondences.

---

[18] First outlined in modern times in Francis King and Stephen Skinner, *Techniques of High Magic*, C W Daniels, London, 1976.

## *Rebuilding the Tree of Life*

In conclusion I would like to just enumerate the steps involved in building your own Tree of Life, using the Luria format (Figure 4).

1.  Construct the Tree geometrically. Draw a vertical line. Use its lower end as the centre of a circle. Where this circle cuts the line, use this point as a centre to inscribe another circle of the same radius. Repeat this process to create five interlocking circles of the same radius, whose centres will now mark the positions of Kether, Daath, Tiphareth, Yesod and Malkuth.

The other intersection points of these circles mark the position of the other five Sephiroth. Using these points and a radius that is 20% of the radius of the original circles, draw in the 10 Sephiroth.

2.  Draw in the 22 connecting Paths between them (using Figure 4).

3.  Label and number the 10 Sephiroth (using Figure 4, or the first 10 rows of Column K3).

4. Label the 22 Paths with the Hebrew letters (using Figure 4).

5. Label the 22 Paths astrologically (using Figure 4 or Columns K8-K9) placing:

    a) Three Elements (Mother letters), Fire, Air and Water on the 3 horizontal Paths, and Earth upon Malkuth.

    b) Seven Planets (Double letters) on the 7 vertical Paths.

    c) Twelve Zodiacal Signs (Single letters) on the 12 diagonal Paths. Note these Paths form three groups, one at each level of the Tree, each of which contains all four Elements.

6.  Number the 22 Paths, using the Lightning Flash for the descending Path numbers and the Serpent for the ascending Path numbers (or using Column K12).

7.  If you wish, add the names of the 22 Tarot Trumps using Column T39 to match them with the astrological attributes already marked in. Do not use the Golden Dawn Path numbers for this operation.

From a practical point of view the seven vertical Paths, marked by the seven Double letters of the Hebrew alphabet, and attributed to the seven Planets are the key to Rising on the Planes. The numeration of the ascending Paths provides you with the key to Path Working. The astrological attributions to the diagonal Paths and 12 Simple letters provide the key for, amongst other things, the use of the Four Elements on the Tree. Other practical formulae arise from this Tree format that are totally lost on the Golden Dawn format of the Tree of Life.

## *Introduction to the Second Edition*

The Second Edition has incorporated a number of minor changes:
Columns A25, B9, C17, D17, D19, D22, F3, G27, H2, H37, J14-J17, K25-K28, K51, K99, M10, M19, M20-M23, M44, M65, N7, P29, S14, S15, T2, U1-U4, X1, Y1.

And some major amplifications:
Columns A10-11, A24, B8, C17, H13, H37-H38, K4, M15, M18, M26-M29, M69, O1, O25, P11, P13, T2, T38-T41, V18, W4, Y2.

Additional Columns have been included:
Columns B8a, B15, E4a, F56, H1a, H20a, H37a, K105a, K122, K123, L31a, L31b, L51, M10a, M20a, M27a, M70, N9a, O5a, O5b, R12, T3a, V21, Y3, Z12a.

This has been done without disturbing the existing Column numeration. The original Column numbers have therefore remained the same as in the First Edition for ease of reference. Some illustrations have been added, and a few replaced. Finally the full list of all 801 Columns (symbolically and isopsephically an A to Ω of correspondences) has been added at the very end of the volume, and the Bibliography has been expanded.

## *Introduction to the Third Edition*

The Third Edition has incorporated a number of changes:
Minor layout changes, amplifications and reorganisation to Columns H39-H45, K7, K9, K17, K26, K27, K40, K123, M18, M62, M63, P30, V3, Y1.

And some major amplifications:
Columns M26, M63, U3, U4

Additional Columns have been included:
Columns A45-A57, G6a, H23a, H23b, H39a, H40a, H77, H78, J14a, J18, M21a, M71, O27a, P13, P14a, P30, P14a.

It might be interesting for readers to know a little bit about the inception of this book. At one point when Gerald Yorke and I were chatting, before he died in 1983, he mentioned to me that *Liber 777* really needed to be extended, updated and re-issued. When my dear friend and co-author Francis King passed away in 1994, he left to me a very special copy of Crowley's *Liber 777*. It was the edition printed by the Neptune Press (which was and still is part of the famous Atlantis Bookshop in London) in 1955 which had been expanded and edited by Gerald. The copy, which had Francis' library plate pasted inside (itself derived from the cover symbol of Crowley's periodical *The Equinox*) was one of only 12 copies which had been printed on hand-made paper, royal octavo, and bound in full vellum, certainly a treasure in its own right.

While I still treasured it, the book sat on my shelves for twelve years, till one day I had the urge to take it down and peruse its beautiful pages. It was at that point that I conceived the project of fully researching the roots of the correspondences recorded there and of the many other correspondences of the Western Esoteric Tradition.

Although I was working on other projects and magical experiments at the time, this book would not let me rest. I woke up thinking about it, I went to bed thinking about how certain material could be better expressed or tabulated. Even after the first edition was published it would not let me rest, and it wasn't until I had completed the expanded second edition for Llewellyn that the book was content to rest. Only then I felt I could go back to working on the *Goetia of Dr Rudd,* or indeed anything else. Since then other information has come my way, and the updating of various Columns as listed above has lead to the issuance of this Third edition.

In the light of the new edition of *The Book of Abramelin,* the structure of Column M26 has been rationalised. A number of new tables have been introduced, including a complete Moon phase ephemeris. The section on the Mansions of the Moon in Table H has been expanded with reference to Christopher Warnock's excellent book on the subject, including the addition of the actual starting points of the Mansions for the year 2000 as well at the traditional points. This has resulted in a reordering of the Columns so that astrological extents are grouped together, and interpretations are grouped together, but the actual numbers of each Column have not changed and are therefore backwardly compatible with first two editions.

Finally an additional page has been added to the end of the main Introduction on the geometry of the Tree of Life.

## *Introduction to the Fourth & Fifth Editions*

The Fifth Edition has incorporated all of the changes above and a few more:

Minor layout changes and reorganisation to: Columns A44, E7, E10, E11, M30, O4, P17, S15, T35, U3, U4 and Y1.

Columns M71, M72, M73, M74, N21, N22, P12a, P12b and U9 have been added.

Note that in this edition Table M17 appears out of order before Table M15 so that the ranks of spirits in M15 are better able to be appreciated.

The Subject Order Listing of Tables has been expanded.

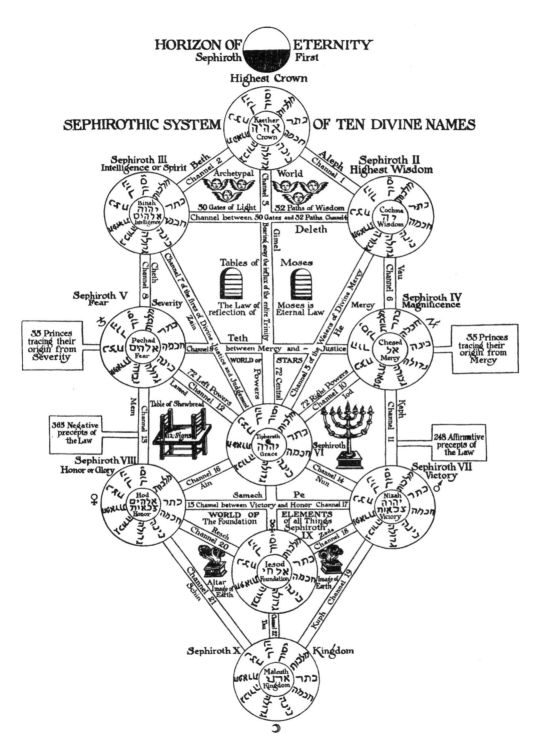

Figure 1: Athanasius Kircher's Tree of Life.

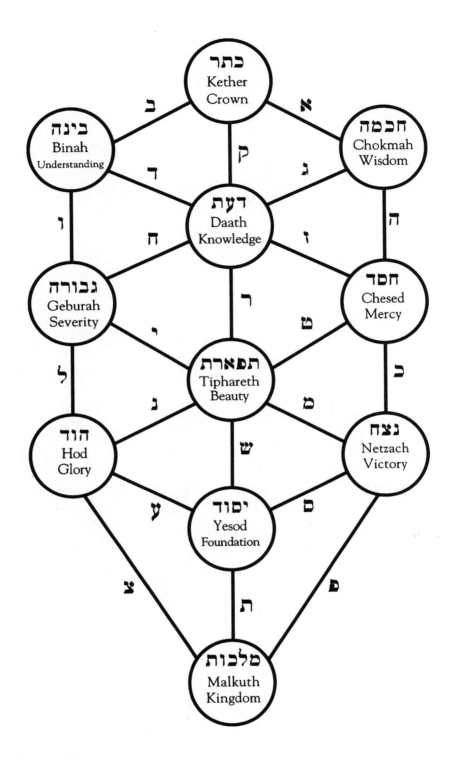

Figure 2: The original Golden Dawn Cipher Manuscript Tree of Life

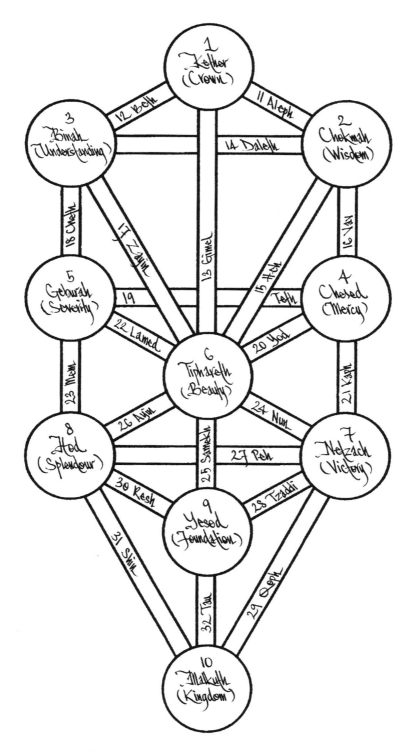

Figure 3: The Golden Dawn Tree of Life

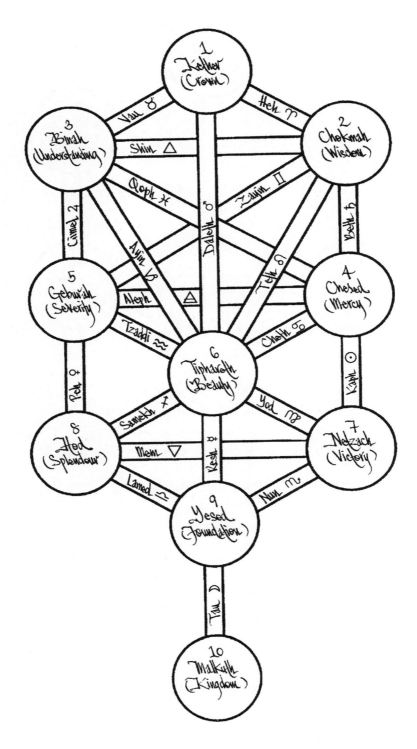

Figure 4: The Lurianic Tree of Life

# THE TABLES

# A. Angels – Biblical, Apocryphal and Gnostic

*Angels of Enoch*

| No. | A1. Watchers or Grigori from *Enoch* from Qumran – Aramaic names. | A2. Watchers or Grigori from *Enoch* I - Aramaic names. | A3. Watchers from *Enoch* I – variant Aramaic names. | A4. What the Watchers or Grigori taught Mankind. |
|---|---|---|---|---|
| 1 | Shemihazah – chief | Samiazaz[1] – leader | Samjaza | Enchantments, root-cuttings |
| 2 | Arataqoph | Arakiba | Artaqifa | |
| 3 | Ramatael | Rameel [maybe Arakiel] | Armen | The signs of the earth |
| 4 | Kokabel | Kokabiel = 'star of God' | Kokabel | Science of the constellations |
| 5 | [see number 18] | Tamiel = 'perfection of God' | Turael [also as 18] | |
| 6 | Ramael | Ramiel | Rumjal | |
| 7 | Daniel | Danel | Danjal | |
| 8 | Ziqiel | Ezeqeel | Neqael | Knowledge of the clouds |
| 9 | Baraqel | Baraqijal = 'lightning of God' | Baraqel | Astrology |
| 10 | Asael | Asael | Azazel | To make instruments of war, knives, swords, shields, ornaments, cosmetic colourings for beautifying women |
| 11 | Hermoni | Armaros [Arearos or Pharmaros] | Armaros | The resolving of enchantments |
| 12 | Matarel | Batarel | Batarjal | |
| 13 | Ananel | Ananel | Busasejal | |
| 14 | Stawel | Zaqiel | Hananel | |
| 15 | – | – | Turel | |
| 16 | Shamshiel | Samsapeel [or Shamshiel] | Simapesiel | The signs of the Sun |
| 17 | Shahriel | Satarel | Jetrel | |
| 18 | Tummiel | [see number 5] | Tumael | |
| 19 | Turiel | Turel = 'rock of God' | Turel [also as 15] | |
| 20 | Yomiel | Jomjael | Rumael | |
| 21 | Yehaddiel | Sariel [from 'Moon'] | Azazel | The course of the Moon |

---

[1] שמעזי שמחזא‎ or שמחזאי‎

# A. Angels – Biblical, Apocryphal and Gnostic

| No. | A5. Earliest names of the 7 Archangels from *Enoch* I. | A6. Earliest names of the 7 Archangels from *Enoch* I – function and rulership. | A7. The Four Presences on the four sides of the Lord of Spirits [God] from *Enoch* I. |
|---|---|---|---|
| | | | |
| 1 | | | |
| 2 | | | |
| 3 | Uriel | The world and Tartarus | |
| 4 | Raphael | Spirits of men | Raphael – set over all the diseases and wounds of man |
| 5 | Raguel | The world of the luminaries [Sun and Moon] | |
| 6 | Michael | The best part of mankind and chaos | Michael – merciful and long-suffering |
| 7 | Saraqael | Spirits | |
| 8 | Gabriel | Paradise, the serpent[s] and the Cherubim | Gabriel – set over all the powers |
| 9 | Remiel | 'Those who rise' | |
| 10 | | | Phanuel – set over repentance and the hope of eternal life |

| No. | A8. Chiefs of the Fallen Angels or 'Satans' from *Enoch* I - Aramaic names. | A9. The Chiefs of the Fallen Angels or 'Satans' from *Enoch* I – their actions. |
|---|---|---|
| 1 | | |
| 2 | | |
| 3 | | |
| 4 | | |
| 5 | Jeqon | The one who led astray the Beni Elohim (the Sons of God), and brought them down to Earth to couple with the daughters of men. |
| 6 | Asbeel | He imparted evil council to the Beni Elohim, and led them to defile their bodies with the daughters of men |
| 7 | Gadreel | Taught men how to kill, led Eve astray, showed men how to make weapons, swords, shields and coats of mail |
| 8 | Penemue | Taught the bitter and sweet, the secrets of wisdom, the use of ink and paper and writing |
| 9 | Kasdeja | Showed the wicked smitings of spirits and demons, even of the embryo in the womb, the smitings of the soul and of the son of the serpent named Taba'et/Taba'ta |
| 10 | Kasbeel | Was the chief of the oath (Akae/Biqa). He requested from Michael (and revealed) the hidden name, which enabled the creation of the mountains, seas |

# A. Angels – Biblical, Apocryphal and Gnostic

| | | A10. The Angel Prince Rulers of the Earth from *Enoch 3*.[2] | A11. The Angel Prince Rulers of the Earth from *Enoch 3* – Rulership. |
|---|---|---|---|
| | | | |
| | 1 | | |
| | 2 | | |
| | 3 | Rahatiel (3) | The constellations, with 72 great angels. He makes the stars run (*marhit*) in their orbits 339 thousand parasangs every night from East to West and West to East. |
| | 4 | Za'aphiel | Storm and wind |
| | 5 | Ra'amiel | Thunder |
| | 6 | Galgalliel (1) | The globe (*galgal*) of the sun, with 96 great angels |
| | 7 | Za'amiel | Vehemence[3] |
| | 8 | Kokbiel (4) | The planets (*kokab*), with 365,000 myriads of ministering angels who move the planets in the Heaven of Raqia. |
| | 9 | 'Ophanniel (2) | The globe (*'ophan*) of the moon, with 88 great angels who move the moon 354 thousand parasangs every night. |
| | 10 | Zi'iel | Commotion |
| ⊛ | 31b | Shimshiel | The day |
| | | Lailiel | The night |
| F | 31 | Gabriel | Fire[4] |
| | | Baraqiel / Barakiel | Lightning |
| A | 11 | Ruchiel | Wind |
| | | Shalgiel | Snow |
| W | 23 | Baradiel | Hail |
| | | Matariel | Rain |
| E | 32b | Ra'ashiel | Earthquake |
| | | Ziqiel | Sparks (*sic*) |

---

[2] This Column now also contains material that was originally in Column K77 in the First Edition.
[3] Za'amiel and Zi'iel are speculative attributions, as is the attribution of the Angel Princes of day and night to ⊛ Spirit.
[4] Fire is a rather surprising attribution of Gabriel by Enoch.

# A. Angels – Biblical, Apocryphal and Gnostic

| No. | A12. The Sarim or Angel-Princes. | A13. The Sarim or Angel-Princes – Attributes. |
|---|---|---|
| | **Name** | **Functions and Attributes** |
| 1 | Akatriel or Akrasiel | Revealer of the Divine Mysteries & Angel of Proclamation. |
| 2 | Anafiel | Chief of the Crown Judgement Angels of the Merkabah. |
| 3 | Azbuga or Azbugah | One of the 8 great Throne Angels of Judgement who clothes with the Garment of Righteousness those deemed worthy among the new arrivals in Heaven. |
| 4 | Barakiel or Barkiel or Barbiel | Ruler of the Order of the Seraphim; Governor of February and one of the 7 Archangels. |
| 5 | Camael or Kemuel | Chief of the order of Powers; one of the Holy Sephiroth; personification of Divine Justice; among the 7 that stand in the presence of God. |
| 6 | Chayyiel | Chief of the holy Hayyoth (Cherubim). |
| 7 | Gabriel | Angel of Annunciation, Resurrection, Mercy & Vengeance; ruling Prince of the 1st Heaven; Chief of the Angelic Guards over Paradise. |
| 8 | Galgaliel | Eponymous head of the order of Galgalim (chariots of the Merkabah); Chief Angel of the Wheel of the Sun. |
| 9 | Haniel or Anael | Chief of the orders of Principalities & Virtues; one of the 7 Archangels; Governor of December; reputed to have transported Enoch to Heaven. |
| 10 | Iofiel | Preceptor Angel of Shem; a prince of the Torah (like Yofiel, Zophiel, Yefefiah); one of the 7 Archangels; Chief of the Order of Thrones. |
| 11 | The Irin | Twin Angels who, together with the twin Qaddisin, constitute the Supreme Judgement Council of the Heavenly Court; among the 8 exalted hierarchs that enjoy a rank superior to that of Metatron. |
| 12 | Jehoel or Jaoel | Mediator of the Ineffable Name, Prince of the Presence |
| 13 | Metatron | Chancellor of Heaven, Prince of the Ministering Angels; Sustainer of Mankind. |
| 14 | Michael | Chief Angel of the Lord; Deliverer of the Faithful; Tutelary Prince of Israel; Angel of Repentance, etc. |
| 15 | Phanuel or Raguel | Archangel of Penance; Prince of the Presence; Identified with Uriel & Ramiel. |
| 16 | The Qaddisin | Twin Angels who, together with the twin Irin, constitute the Supreme Judgement Council of the Heavenly Court. |
| 17 | Radueriel or Vretil | The Recording Angel; Leader of the Celestial Choirs; Creator of the lesser Angels. |
| 18 | Raphael | Angel of Healing, Science & Knowledge; one of the Princes of the Presence; Regent of the Sun. |
| 19 | Raziel or Galizur | Chief of the Supreme Mysteries; One of the Archangelic governors of the Briatic World; Preceptor Angel of Adam, Herald of Deity and reputed author of *The Book Of The Angel Raziel*. |
| 20 | Rikbiel | Chief of the Divine Chariot; Prince of the Merkabah Angels. |
| 21 | Sopheriel Mehayye Sopheriel Memeth | Two of the Supreme Angels of the 8 Merkabah; Keepers of the Books of Life and Death. |
| 22 | Soqed Hozi | Keeper of the Divine Balances; One of the 8 Supreme Angels of the Merkabah; appointed by God to the Sword |
| 23 | Sandalphon | Angel of Power and Glory; Twin brother of Metatron. |
| 24 | Shemuil | The Great Archon, Mediator between the prayers of Israel and the Princes of the 7th heaven. |
| 25 | Suriel | Benevolent Angel of Death; Instructor of Moses; Also a Prince of the Presence. |
| 26 | Tzadkiel | Angel of Divine Justice. |
| 27 | Uriel | Archangel of Salvation; Regent of the Sun; Overseer of Tartarus. |
| 28 | Yefefiah or Dina | Angel of the Torah; Instructed Moses in the Mysteries of the Cabala. |
| 29 | Zagzagel | Angel of Wisdom; Chief Guard of the 4th Heaven; Angel of the Burning Bush. |

# A. Angels – Biblical, Apocryphal and Gnostic

| | Hall | Angels |
|---|---|---|
| | | A14. The 64 Angel Wardens of the 7 Celestial Halls (*Hekhaloth*). |
| 1 | | |
| 2 | | |
| 3 | 7th | 63-Zeburial 64-Tutrbebial |
| 4 | 6th | 55-Rumial 56-Katmial 57-Gehegial 58-Arsabrsbial 59-Egrumial 60-Parzial 61-Machkial (or Mrgial or Mrgiviel) 62-Tufrial |
| 5 | 5th | 46-Techial 47-Uzial 48-Gmial 49-Gamrial 50-Sefrial 51-Garfial 52-Grial 53-Drial 54-Paltrial |
| 6 | 4th | 38-Pachdial (Chief) 39-Gvurtial 40-Kzuial 41-Shchinial 42-Shtukial 42-Arvial (or Avial) 43-Kfial 44-Anfial |
| 7 | 3rd | 31-Sheburiel (Chief) 32-Retsutsiel 33-Shalmial 34-Savlial 35-Harhazial 36-Hadrial 37-Bezrial |
| 8 | 2nd | 23-Tagriel (Chief) 24-Maspiel 25-Sahriel 26-Arfiel 27-Shahariel 28-Sakriel 29-Ragiel 30-Sehibiel |
| 9 | 1st | 1-Suria 2-Tutrechial 3-Tutrusiai 4-Zortek 5-Mufgar 6-Ashrulya 7-Sabriel 8-Zahabrieli 9-Tandal 10-Shokad 11-Huzia 12-Deheboryn 13-Adririon 14-Khabiel (Head Supervisor) 15-Tashriel 16-Nahuriel 17-Jekusiel 18-Tufiel 19-Dahariel 20-Maskiel 21-Shoel 22-Sheviel |
| 10 | | |

| | | A15. Archangels of the Four Quarters. | A16. Archangels of the Four Quarters – Transliteration. | A17. Archangels of the Four Quarters – English. | A18. Archangels of the Four Quarters – Numeration. |
|---|---|---|---|---|---|
| | | | | | |
| F | 31 | מיכאל | MIKAL | Michael | 101 |
| A | 11 | רפאל | RPAL | Raphael | 311 |
| W | 23 | גבריאל | GBRIAL | Gabriel | 246 |
| E | 32b | אוריאל | AVRIAL | Auriel | 248 |

# A. Angels – Biblical, Apocryphal and Gnostic

*Gnostic Angels*

| | | Gener-ation [Tert-ullian] | Gener-ation [St. Irenaeus] | A19. Numeric Grouping. | A20. The 30 Gnostic Aeons. | A21. The 30 Gnostic Aeons – English. | A22. Angels of the 30 Gnostic Aeons. |
|---|---|---|---|---|---|---|---|
| | **1** | 5 | 6 | **Decad** | Bythios | Deep (adjective) | Udua |
| | **2** | 5 | 6 | " | Mixis | Mixing | Casten |
| | **3** | 5 | 6 | " | Ageratos | Unaging | Amphian |
| | **4** | 5 | 6 | " | Henosis | Union | Essumen |
| | **5** | 5 | 6 | " | Autophyes | Self-Existent | Vannanin |
| | **6** | 5 | 6 | " | Hedone | Pleasure | Lamer |
| | **7** | 5 | 6 | " | Akinetos | Immovable | Tarde |
| | **8** | 5 | 6 | " | Syncrasis | Blending | Athames |
| | **9** | 5 | 6 | " | Monogenes | Only-Begotten | Susua |
| | **10** | 5 | 6 | " | Makaria | Happiness | Allora |
| | | | | | | | |
| | | – | 2 | | Ennoae [*Irenaeus only*] | Thought | |
| | | – | 2 | | Thelesis [*Irenaeus only*] | Will | |
| ☽ | 13 | 4 | 4 | **Ogdoad** | Eccleasia | Church (as foundation) | Artababa |
| ☿ | 12 | 4 | 4 | " | Anthropos | Humanity | Metaxas |
| ♀ | 14 | 3 | 5 | " | Zoe/Vita | Life | Thardedia |
| ☼ | 30 | 3 | 5 | " | Logos/Sermo | Word | Ubucua |
| ♂ | 27 | 2 | 3 | " | Aletheia | Truth | Thartun |
| ♃ | 21 | 2 | 3 | " | Nous | Mind | Bucua |
| ♄ | 32 | 1 | 1 | " | Ennoia/Sige/Charis | Idea | Ouraan |
| | | 1 | 1 | " | Bythos | Deep (noun) | Ampsiu |
| | | | | | | | |
| ♈ | 15 | 5 | 6 | **Dodecad** | Parakletos | Advocate | Bucidia |
| ♉ | 16 | 5 | 6 | " | Pistis | Faith | Damadarah |
| ♊ | 17 | 5 | 6 | " | Patrikos | Fatherly | Alora |
| ♋ | 18 | 5 | 6 | " | Elpis | Hope | Dammo |
| ♌ | 19 | 5 | 6 | " | Metrikos | Motherly | Oren |
| ♍ | 20 | 5 | 6 | " | Agape | Love | Lamaspechs |
| ♎ | 22 | 5 | 6 | " | Aeinous | Ever-thinking | Amphiphuls |
| ♏ | 24 | 5 | 6 | " | Synesis | Understanding | Emphsboshbaud |
| ♐ | 25 | 5 | 6 | " | Ecclesiastikos | Church-like | Assiouache |
| ♑ | 26 | 5 | 6 | " | Makariotes | Felicity | Belin |
| ♒ | 28 | 5 | 6 | " | Theletos | Desired | Dexariche |
| ♓ | 29 | 5 | 6 | " | Sophia | Wisdom | Massemo |

# A. Angels – Biblical, Apocryphal and Gnostic

*Shem ha-Mephorash Angels*

| | Seraphim | Cherubim | Thrones | Dominations | Powers |
|---|---|---|---|---|---|
| | A23. Amberlain's table of the Shem ha-Mephorash Angels. | | | | |
| | *Metatron* | *Jophiel* | *Zaphkiel* | *Zadkiel* | *Kamael* |
| **1** | | | | | |
| **2** | 1 – Vehuiah | 9 – Haziel | 17 – Lauviah | 25 – Nilaihah | 33 – Iehuiah |
| **3** | 2 – Jelial | 10 – Aladiah | 18 – Caliel | 26 – Haaiah | 34 – Lehahiah |
| **4** | 3 – Sitael | 11 – Lauviah | 19 – Leuviah | 27 – Ierathel | 35 – Chavakiah |
| **5** | 4 – Elemiah | 12 – Hahaiah | 20 – Pahaliah | 28 – Seehiah | 36 – Menadel |
| **6** | 5 – Mahasiah | 13 – Iezalel | 21 – Nelchael | 29 – Reiiel | 37 – Aniel |
| **7** | 6 – Lehahel | 14 – Mehahel | 22 – Ieiaiel | 30 – Omael | 38 – Haamiah |
| **8** | 7 – Achaiah | 15 – Hariel | 23 – Melahel | 31 – Lecahel | 39 – Rehael |
| **9** | 8 – Cahetel | 16 – Hakamiah | 24 – Hahiniah | 32 – Yasariah | 40 – Ieiazel |
| **10** | | | | | |

| | Virtues | Principlalities | Archangels | Angels | |
|---|---|---|---|---|---|
| | A23. Amberlain's table of the Shem ha-Mephorash Angels (continued). | | | | |
| | *Raphael* | *Haniel* | *Michael* | *Gabriel* | |
| **1** | | | | | |
| **2** | 41 – Hahael | 49 – Vehuel | 57 – Nemamiah | 65 – Damabiah | |
| **3** | 42 – Mikael | 50 – Daniel | 58 – Ieialel | 66 – Manakel | |
| **4** | 43 – Veualiah | 51 – Hahasiah | 59 – Harael | 67 – Eidel | |
| **5** | 44 – Ielahiah | 52 – Imamiah | 60 – Mitzrael | 68 – Hahniah | |
| **6** | 45 – Sealiah | 53 – Nanael | 61 – Umahel | 69 – Rochel | |
| **7** | 46 – Ariel | 54 – Nilhael | 62 – Iahhel | 70 – Jabamiah | |
| **8** | 47 – Asaliah | 55 – Mehaiah | 63 – Ananel | 71 – Haiaiel | |
| **9** | 48 – Mihael | 56 – Poiel | 64 – Mehriel | 72 – Mumiah | |
| **10** | | | | | |

# A. Angels – Biblical, Apocryphal and Gnostic

| No | Hebrew Root | Name | Degrees Ruled | Characteristics |
|---|---|---|---|---|
| | | | | A24. The 72 Shem ha-Mephorash Angels, their Hebrew Root, Name, Degrees and Nature. |
| 1 | והו-יה | Vehuiah | 1-5° | Helps enlightenment & expands consciousness; dominates the sciences; influences the shrewd. |
| 2 | ילי-אל | Yeliel | 6-10° | Helps repress unjust revolts; aids conjugal peace; dominates kings & princes; influences all generations. |
| 3 | סיט-אל | Sitael | 11-15° | Protects against adversity and calamity; dominates magnanimity & nobility; influences lovers of truth. |
| 4 | עלמ-יה | Elemiah | 16-20° | Helps against spiritual torment; reveals traitors; dominates sea voyages; influences discoveries. |
| 5 | מהש-יה | Mahasiah | 21-25° | Helps all to live in peace; dominates occult magic & theology; influences learning. |
| 6 | ללה-אל | Lelahel | 26-30° | Serves to acquire "light"; cures contagious diseases; dominates love, fame & fortune; Influences the sciences. |
| 7 | אכא-יה | Achaiah | 31-35° | Helps discover natural secrets; dominates patience & temperance; influences the spread of light and industry. |
| 8 | כהת-אל | Kahetel | 36-40° | Serves to obtain blessing and protection against evil spirits. Dominates agricultural produce; influences the hunt. |
| 9 | הזי-אל | Aziel | 41-45° | Helps keep promises & obtain the friendship of the great; dominates good faith; influences sincerity and faith. |
| 10 | אלד-יה | Aladiah | 46-50° | Helps hide secrets; dominates plague and rabies; influences healing. |
| 11 | לאו-יה | Lauviah | 51-55° | Protects against lightning; serves to obtain victory; dominates fame; influences the famous learned. |
| 12 | ההע-יה | Hahaiah | 56-60° | Protects against adversity; helps those in need; dominates dreams; influences wise & spiritual people. |
| 13 | יזל-אל | Yezalel | 61-65° | Helps reconciliation & conjugal faithfulness; dominates friendship & affability; influences memory & shrewdness. |
| 14 | מבה-אל | Mebahel | 66-70° | Protects against those wishing to usurp the fortunes of others; dominates justice; influences & protects truth. |
| 15 | הרי-אל | Hariel | 71-75° | Serves against the ungodly & defeatists; dominates the sciences & arts; influences discoveries & new methods. |
| 16 | הקמ-יה | Hakamiah | 76-80° | Helps against traitors; serves for victory over enemies; dominates arsenals; influences frankness. |
| 17 | לאו-יה | Lauviah | 81-85° | Helps refresh at night time; helps against sadness; dominates the high sciences; influences musicians & poets. |
| 18 | כלי-אל | Kaliel | 86-90° | Serves to reveal the truth; aids the triumph of innocence; dominates trials; influences witnesses. |
| 19 | לוו-יה | Leuviah | 91-95° | Protects & helps in obtaining grace; dominates the memory; influences joviality & intelligence. |
| 20 | פהל-יה | Pahaliah | 96-100° | Helps conversions; dominates theology & religion; influences chastity & morals. |
| 21 | נלכ-אל | Nelekael | 101-105° | Protects against unfavourable spirits & slanderers; Dominates mathematics & geometry. |
| 22 | ייי-אל | Yeiael | 106-110° | Protects against storms & shipwrecks; dominates business fortunes; influences business trips. |
| 23 | מלה-אל | Melahel | 111-115° | Protects against weapons & perils of travel; dominates medicinal herbs & water. |
| 24 | חהו-יה | Chahuiah | 116-120° | Serves to obtain grace; dominates the exiled; protects against thieves & murderers. |
| 25 | נתה-יה | Nithahaiah | 121-125° | Serves to obtain wisdom & dream revelations; dominates the occult sciences & the wise. |

# A. Angels – Biblical, Apocryphal and Gnostic

| No | Hebrew Root | Name | Degrees Ruled | Characteristics |
|----|-------------|------|---------------|-----------------|
| | | | A24. The 72 Shem ha-Mephorash Angels, their Hebrew Root, Name, Degrees and Nature. | |
| 26 | האא-יה | Haaiah | 126-130° | Protects those seeking the true light; dominates peace treaties; influences ambassadors. |
| 27 | ירת-אל | Yerathel | 131-135° | Protects against unjust attacks; confounds one's enemies; dominates civilisation; influences peace. |
| 28 | שאה-יה | Sheahiah | 146-140° | Protects against fire, ruin & collapse; dominates health & longevity; influences prudence. |
| 29 | ריי-אל | Reiyel | 141-145° | Helps & protects against enemies both visible and invisible; dominates mystic feelings & sacred philosophy. |
| 30 | אומ-אל | Omael | 146-150° | Helps against desperation & trouble; strengthens patience; dominates the generation (birth) of men and animals. |
| 31 | לכב-אל | Lekabel | 151-155° | Casts light on one's profession; dominates vegetation; influences astrology. |
| 32 | ושר-יה | Vashariah | 156-160° | Helps against false & unjust accusations; dominates justice & judges; influences the word. |
| 33 | יחו-יה | Yechuiah | 161-165° | Uncovers plots & traitors; undoes their plans; dominates & influences just rulers. |
| 34 | להח-יה | Lehachiah | 166-170° | Maintains peace & harmony between countries; dominates faithfulness & respect & devotion. |
| 35 | כוק-יה | Kevaqiah | 171-175° | Recovers the friendship of those we have offended; dominates wills; influences friendly distribution. |
| 36 | מנד-אל | Menadel | 176-180° | Protects against slander; releases prisoners; dominates the return of exiles. |
| 37 | אני-אל | Aniel | 181-185° | Helps conquer & to obtain release from siege; dominates the sciences & arts; influences the meditation of the wise. |
| 38 | חעמ-יה | Chaamiah | 186-190° | Protects against lightning and infernal spirits; dominates creeds; influences & protects those who seek the truth. |
| 39 | רהע-אל | Rehael | 191-195° | Protects from & cures disease; dominates health & longevity; influences paternal love. |
| 40 | ייז-אל | Yeiazel | 196-200° | Helps release prisoners, releases from enemies; dominates the press & books; influences artists. |
| 41 | ההח-אל | Hahahel | 201-205° | Helps against the ungodly & slanderers; dominates missionaries; influences priests & prelates. |
| 42 | מיכ-אל | Mikael | 206-210° | Helps & protects the safety of journeys; dominates the powerful; influences curiosity & politics. |
| 43 | וול-יה | Vevaliah | 211-215° | Helps destroy enemies; frees from slavery; dominates peace; influences prosperity. |
| 44 | ילה-אל | Yelahiah | 216-220° | Helps win lawsuits; dominates victory; influences courage in battle. |
| 45 | סאל-יה | Saliah | 221-215° | Helps confound the evil & the proud; dominates vegetation; influences education. |
| 46 | ערי-אל | Ariel | 226-230° | Helps uncover hidden treasures; dominates night-time visions; influences difficult solutions. |
| 47 | עשל-יה | Aushaliah | 231-235° | Helps those who wish to raise themselves spiritually; dominates justice; influences contemplation. |
| 48 | מיה-אל | Mihael | 236-240° | Helps preserve harmony & union between spouses; dominates the generations; influences love. |
| 49 | והו-אל | Vehuel | 241-245° | Helps find peace against trouble; dominates great personalities; influences humility. |
| 50 | דני-אל | Daniel | 246-250° | Protects & consoles; inspires decisions; dominates justice; influences judges. |

# A. Angels – Biblical, Apocryphal and Gnostic

| No | Hebrew Root | Name | Degrees Ruled | Characteristics |
|---|---|---|---|---|
| | A24. The 72 Shem ha-Mephorash Angels, their Hebrew Root, Name, Degrees and Nature. | | | |
| 51 | חחש-יה | Hachashiah | 251-255° | Helps those who wish to know the occult mysteries; dominates chemistry; influences abstract sciences. |
| 52 | עממ-יה | Aumamiah | 256-260° | Destroys enemies; protects prisoners; dominates vigour; influences research. |
| 53 | ננא-אל | Nanael | 261-265° | Obtains enlightenment; dominates the higher sciences; influences teachers & men of law. |
| 54 | נית-אל | Nithael | 266-270° | Obtains mercy & longevity; dominates dynasties & stability. |
| 55 | מבה-יה | Mebahiah | 271-275° | Helps in consolation & those who wish to have children; dominates morals, religion & piety. |
| 56 | פוי-אל | Poiel | 276-280° | Obtains what is asked for; dominates fame, success & fortune; influences moderation. |
| 57 | נממ-יה | Nemmamiah | 281-285° | Helps prosper & release prisoners; dominates generals; influences combatants. |
| 58 | ייל-אל | Yeialel | 286-290° | Helps against trouble; heals eye diseases; dominates iron; influences locksmiths & knife-grinders. |
| 59 | הרח-אל | Harachel | 291-295° | Protects against female sterility & rebellious children; dominates treasures & archives; influences the press. |
| 60 | מצר-אל | Mitzrael | 296-300° | Heals the ills of the spirit; releases from persecutors; dominates men of virtue; influences faithfulness. |
| 61 | ומב-אל | Umabel | 301-305° | Obtains the friendship of a person; dominates astronomy & physics; influences the sensitivity of the heart. |
| 62 | יהה-אל | Yahehel | 206-310° | Obtains wisdom & knowledge; dominates philosophers & enlightened; influences virtue in solitude. |
| 63 | ענו-אל | Anuiel | 311-315° | Protects against accidents; maintains health & heals; dominates trade & businessmen; influences business. |
| 64 | מחי-אל | Mechiel | 316-320° | Protects against rabies & fierce animals; dominates the learned, orators & authors; influences the press & books. |
| 65 | דמב-יה | Damabiah | 321-325° | Aids against sorcery; obtains wisdom; dominates the waters; influences sailors & fishermen. |
| 66 | מנק-אל | Manaqel | 326-330° | Protects against & heals leprosy & anger; dominates vegetation; influences sleep & dreams. |
| 67 | איע-אל | Eiael | 331-335° | Helps and consoles in adversity; obtains wisdom; dominates change; influences the occult sciences. |
| 68 | חבו-יה | Chabuiah | 336-340° | Helps maintain health & cure disease; dominates fertility & agriculture & the earth. |
| 69 | ראה-אל | Rahel | 341-345° | Helps find lost or stolen objects; dominates laws & judges; influences fame. |
| 70 | יבמ-יה | Yabamiah | 346-350° | Protects & regenerates; leads to inner harmony; dominates philosophical knowledge; influences nature. |
| 71 | היי-אל | Hayiel | 351-355° | Confounds evil; grants release from enemies; gives victory; dominates weapons & soldiers, influences iron. |
| 72 | מומ-יה | Mumiah | 356-360° | Brings every experience to a happy conclusion; dominates medicine & influences longevity. |

# A. Angels – Biblical, Apocryphal and Gnostic

| No. | A25. The 72 Shem ha-Mephorash Angels with their corresponding Invocatory Psalm. | | |
|---|---|---|---|
| | **Angel** | **Psalm (KJV/ Vulgate)** | **Invocatory Psalm or *Tehilim*** |
| 1 | Vehuiah | 3:3 / 3:4 | *Et tu Domine susceptor meus es, gloria mea et exaltans caput meum.* (Deus Exaltator) <br> And thou, O Lord, art my guardian, and exaltest my head. |
| 2 | Yeliel | 22:19 / 21:20 | *Tu autem Domine ne elongaveris auxilium tuum a me, ad defensionem meam conspice.* (Deus Auxiliator) <br> Do not remove thy help from me, O Lord, and look to my defence. |
| 3 | Sitael | 91:2 / 90:2 | *Dicam Domino, susceptor meus es, et refugium meum, Deus meus, sperabo in eum.* (Deus Spes) I shall say to the Lord, Thou art my guardian, my God is my refuge, and shall hope in him. |
| 4 | Elemiah | 6:4 / 6:5 | *Convertere Domine, et eripe animam meam, salvum me fac propter misericordiam tuam.* (Deu Absconditus) <br> Turn, O Lord, and deliver my soul, and save me for Thy mercy's sake. |
| 5 | Mahasiah | 34:4 / 33:5 | *Exquisivi Dominum, et exaudivit me, et ex omnibus tribulationibus meis eripuit me.* (Deus Salvator) I called upon the Lord and he heard me and delivered me from all my tribulations. |
| 6 | Lelahel | 9:11 / 9:12 | *Psallite Domino qui habitat in Sion, annunciate inter gentes studia eius.* (Deus Laudabilis) Let him who lives in Zion sing unto the Lord, and proclaim his goodwill among the peoples. |
| 7 | Achaiah | 103:8 /102:8 | *Miserator et misericors Dominus, longanimus, et multum misericors.* (Deus Longanimis) The Lord is merciful and compassionate, long-suffering and of great goodness. |
| 8 | Kahetel | 95:6 / 94:6 | *Venite, adoremus, et procidamus ante facem Domini, qui fecit nos,* (Deus Adorandus) <br> O come let us adore and fall down before God who bore us. |
| 9 | Aziel | 25:6 / 24:6 | *Reminiscere miserationum tuarum Domine, et misericordiarum tuarum quae a saeculo sunt.* (Deus Misericors) <br> Remember Thy mercies, O Lord, and Thy mercies which have been for ever. |
| 10 | Aladiah | 33:22 / 32:22 | *Fiat misericordia tua Domine super nos, quemadmodum speravimus in te.* (Deus Propitiabilis) <br> Perform Thy mercies O Lord upon us, for we have hoped in Thee. |
| 11 | Lauviah | 18:46 / 17:47 | *Vivit Dominus, et benedictus Deus meus, et exaltatur Deus salutis meae.* (Deus Exaltandus) <br> The Lord liveth, blessed is my God, and let the God of my salvation be exalted. |
| 12 | Hahaiah | 10:1 / 10:1 | *Ut quid Domine recessisti longe, despicis in opportunitatibus in tribulatione?* (Deus Refugium) Why standest Thou afar off O Lord, why hidest thyself in the times of tribulation. |
| 13 | Yezalel | 98:4 / 97:4 | *Jubilate Domino omnis Terra, cantate, et exultate, et Psallite.* (Deus super omnia decantabilis) Rejoice in the Lord, all ye lands, sing exult, and play upon a stringed instrument. |
| 14 | Mebahel | 9:9 / 9:9 | *Et factus est Dominus refugium pauperi, adiniutor in opportunitatibus, in tribulatione.* (Deus Custos et Servator) <br> The Lord also will be a refuge for the oppressed, and in times of trouble. |
| 15 | Hariel | 94:22 / 93:22 | *Et factus est mihi Dominus in refugium, et Deus meus in adjutorium spei meae.* (Deus Sublenator) <br> The Lord is a refuge for me, and my God the help of my hope. |
| 16 | Hakamiah | 88:1 / 87:25 | *Domine Deus salutis meae, in die clamavi et nocte coram te.* (Deus Erector) O Lord, God of my salvation, by day have I called to thee, and sought Thy presence by night. |
| 17 | Lauviah | 8:9 / 8:2 | *Domine Dominus noster, quam admirabile est nomen tuum in universa terra!* (Deus Mirabilis) <br> O Lord our Lord, How wonderful is Thy name in all the world! |
| 18 | Kaliel | 35:24 / 34:24 | *Judica me secundum justitiam tuam, Domine Deus meus, et non supergaudeant mihi.* (Deus Invocandus) Judge me, O Lord, according to Thy loving kindness, and let not them be joyful over me, O Lord. |

# A. Angels – Biblical, Apocryphal and Gnostic

| No. | A25. The 72 Shem ha-Mephorash Angels with their corresponding Invocatory Psalm. | | |
|---|---|---|---|
| | **Angel** | **Psalm (KJV/ Vulgate)** | **Invocatory Psalm or *Tehilim*** |
| 19 | Leuviah | 40:1 / 39:2 | *Expectans expectavi Dominum et intendit mihi.* (Deus Festinus ad Audientum) I waited patiently for the Lord, and He inclined unto me, and heard my cry. |
| 20 | Pahaliah | 120:1-2 / 119:2 | *Et nomen Domini invocabo, O Domine, libera animam meam.* (Deus Redemptor) I shall call upon the name of the Lord, O Lord free my soul. |
| 21 | Nelekael | 31:14 / 30:15 | *Ego autem in te speravi Domine, dixi, Deus meus es tu.* (Deus Solus) In Thee also have I hoped, O Lord, and said, Thou art my God. |
| 22 | Yeiael | 121:5 / 120:5 | *Dominus custodit te, Dominus protectio tua super manum dexteram tuam.* (Deus Dextera) The Lord keep thee, the Lord be they protection on thy right hand. |
| 23 | Melahel | 121:8 / 120:8 | *Dominus custodiat introitum tuum, et exitum tuum, ex hoc, nunc et usque in saeculum.* (Deus Declinans Malum) The Lord keep thine incoming and thine outgoing from this time forth for evermore. |
| 24 | Chahuiah | 33:18 / 35:5 | *Beneplacitum est Domino super timentes eum, et in eos qui sperant super misericordiam eius.* (Deus Bonus ex seipso) The Lord is well pleased with those that fear Him and hope upon his mercy. |
| 25 | Nithahaiah | 9:1 / 9:2 | *Confitebor tibi Domine in tote corde meo, narrabo omnia mirabilia tua.* (Deus Largitor) I shall acknowledge Thee, O Lord, with all my heart and shall tell forth all Thy wonders. |
| 26 | Haaiah | 119:145 / 118:145 | *Clamavi in toto corde meo, exaudi me Domine, justificationes meas requiram.* (Deus Auditor in Abscondito) I have called unto thee with all my heart, hear me, O Lord, and I shall keep thy statutes. |
| 27 | Yerathel | 140:1 / 139:1 | *Eripe me Domine ab homine malo a viro iniquo eripe me.* (Deus Propulsator) Save me, O Lord, from the evil man and deliver me from the wicked doer. |
| 28 | Sheahiah | 71:12 / 70:12 | *Deus ne elongeris a me, Deus meus in auxilium meum respice.* (Deus Sublator Malorum) Let not God depart from me, look to my help, O God. |
| 29 | Reiyel | 54:4 / 53:7 | *Ecce Deus adjuvat me, et Dominus susceptor est animae meae.* (Deus Expectatio) Behold, God is my helper, and the Lord is the guardian of my soul. |
| 30 | Omael | 71:5 / 70:5 | *Quoniam tu es patentia mea Domine, Domine spes mea a juventute mea.* (Deus Patiens) For Thou are my strength, O Lord. O Lord, Thou are my hope from my youth. |
| 31 | Lekabel | 71:16 / 70:16 | *Introibo in potentiam Domini, Deus meus memorabor justitiae tuae solius.* (Deus Doctor) I shall enter into the power of the Lord, my God, I shall be mindful of Thy justice only. |
| 32 | Vashariah | 33:4 / 32:4 | *Quia rectum est verbum Domini, et omnia opera eius in fide.* (Deus Rectus) For the word of the Lord is upright, and all his works faithful. |
| 33 | Yechuiah | 94:11 / 93:11 | *Dominus scit cogitationes hominum quoniam vana sunt.* (Deus Omnium Cognitor) The Lord knows the thoughts of men, for they are in vain. |
| 34 | Lehachiah | 131:3 / 130:3 | *Speret Israel in Domino, ex hoc nunc et usque in saeculum.* (Deus Clemens) Let Israel hope in the Lord from this time forth and for evermore. |
| 35 | Kevaqiah | 116:1 / 114:1 | *Dilexi quoniam exaudi Dominus vocem orationis meae.* (Deus Gaudiosus) I am joyful, for the Lord hears the voice of my prayer. |
| 36 | Menadel | 26:8 / 25:8 | *Domini dilexi decorum domus tuae, et locum habitationis gloriae tuae.* (Deus Honorabilis) I have delighted in the beauty of They House, O Lord, and in the place of the habitation of Thy glory. |

# A. Angels – Biblical, Apocryphal and Gnostic

| No. | Angel | Psalm (KJV/ Vulgate) | Invocatory Psalm or *Tehilim* |
|-----|-------|----------------------|-------------------------------|
| | | A25. The 72 Shem ha-Mephorash Angels with their corresponding Invocatory Psalm. | |
| 37 | Aniel | 80:3 / 79:4 | *Domine Deus virtutum converte nos; et ostende faciem tuam, et salvi erimus.* (Deus Dominus Virtutum) O Lord God, turn Thy power towards us, and show us Thy face and we shall be saved. |
| 38 | Chaamiah | 91:9 / 90:9 | *Quoniam tu es, Domine, spes mea, altissimum posuisti refugium tuum.* (Deus Spes Omnium finium terrae) For Thou art my hope, O Lord, and Thou hast been my deepest refuge. |
| 39 | Rehael | 30:10 / 29:11 | *Audivit me Dominus et misertus est mei, Dominus factus est adjutor meus.* (Deus Velox ad Condonandum) The Lord has heard me and pitied me and the Lord is my helper. |
| 40 | Yeiazel | 88:14 / 87:15 | *Ut quid Domine repellis animam meam, avertis faciem tuam a me.* (Deus Vivum Laetificans) Why drivest Thou away my soul, O Lord, and turnest Thy face from me? |
| 41 | Hahahel | 120:2 / 119:2 | *Domine libera animam meam a labiis iniquis, et a lingua dolosa.* (Deus Triunas) O Lord, deliver my soul from wicked lips and a deceitful tongue. |
| 42 | Mikael | 121:7 / 120:7 | *Dominus custodiat te ab omni malo, et custodiat animam tuam.* (Deus Quis sicut ille) The Lord protects thee from all evil and will protect thy soul. |
| 43 | Vevaliah | 88:13 / 87:14 | *Et Ego ad te Domine clamavi, et mane oratio meae praeveniet te.* (Deus Rex Dominator) I have cried unto Thee, O Lord, and let my prayer come unto Thee. |
| 44 | Yelahiah | 119:108 / 118:108 | *Voluntaria oris mei beneplacita fac Domine et Judicia tua doce me.* (Deus Aeternum, Manens) Make my wishes pleasing unto Thee, O Lord, and teach me Thy judgments. |
| 45 | Saliah | 94:18 / 93:18 | *Si dicebam motus est pes meus, misericordia tua Domine adjuvabit me.* (Deus Motor Omnium) If I say that my foot is moved, Thou wilt help me of Thy mercy. |
| 46 | Ariel | 145:9 / 144:9 | *Suavis Dominus universes, et miserationes ejus super omnia opera ejus.* (Deus Revelator) The Lord is pleasant to all the world and his mercies are over all his works. |
| 47 | Aushaliah | 92:5 / 91:6 | *Quam magnificata sunt opera tua Domine, nimis profundae factae sunt cogitatones tuae.* (Deus Justus Judex) How wonderful are Thy works, O Lord, and how deep Thy thoughts. |
| 48 | Mihael | 98:2 / 97:2 | *Notum fecit Dominus salutare suum, in conspectu gentium, revelabit justitiam suam.* (Deus Pater Mittens) The Lord hath made thy salvation known in the sight of the peoples and will reveal his justice. |
| 49 | Vehuel | 145:3 / 144:3 | *Magnus Dominus et laudabilis nimis, et magnitudinis ejus non est finis.* (Deus Magnus et Excelsus) Great is the Lord and worthy to be praised, and there is no end to his greatness. |
| 50 | Daniel | 145:8 / 144:8 | *Miserator et misericors Dominus, patients, et multum misericors.* (Deus Judex Misericors) The Lord God is pitiful and merciful, long-suffering and of great mercy. |
| 51 | Hachashiah | 104:31 / 103:31 | *Sit gloria Domini in saeculam, laetabitur Dominus in operibus suis.* (Deus Secretus Impenetrabilis) Let the Lord be in glory for ever and the Lord will rejoice in His works. |
| 52 | Aumamiah | 7:17 / 7:18 | *Confitebor Domino secundum justitiam ejus, et psallam nomini Domini altissimi.* (Deus Caligine Rectus) I shall make known the Lord, according to his justice, and sing psalms to the name of the Lord, the greatest. |
| 53 | Nanael | 119:75 / 118:75 | *Cognovi Domine, quia aequitas judicia tua, et in veritate tua humiliasti me.* (Deus Superborum Depressor) I have known Thee, O Lord, for Thy judgements are just, and in Thy truth have I abased myself. |
| 54 | Nithael | 103:19 / 102:19 | *Dominus in Caelo paravit sedem suam, et regnum ipsius omnibus dominabitur.* (Deus Rex Coelestis) The Lord hath prepared His seat in heaven and His rule shall be over all. |

# A. Angels – Biblical, Apocryphal and Gnostic

| No. | Angel | Psalm (KJV/ Vulgate) | Invocatory Psalm or *Tehilim* |
|---|---|---|---|
| | | A25. The 72 Shem ha-Mephorash Angels with their corresponding Invocatory Psalm. | |
| 55 | Mebahiah | 102:12 / 103:13 | *Tu autem Domine in aeternum permanes, et memoriale tuum in generationem et generationem.* (Deus Sempiternus) Thou remainest for ever, O Lord, and Thy memorial is from generation in to generation. |
| 56 | Poiel | 145.14 / 144:14 | *Allevat Dominus omnes qui corruunt, et erigit omnes elisos.* (Deus Fulciens Omnia) The Lord raiseth up all who fall and setteth up the broken. |
| 57 | Nemmamiah | 115:11 / 113:19 | *Qui timent Dominum, speraverunt in Domino, adiutor eorum et protector eorem est.* (Deus Amabilis) They who fear the Lord have hoped in the Lord, He is their helper and their protector. |
| 58 | Yeialel | 6:3 / 6:4 | *Et anima mea turbata est valde, sed tu Domine usque quo.* (Deus Auditor Gemituum) My soul is greatly troubled, but Thou, O Lord art here also. |
| 59 | Harachel | 113:3 / 112:3 | *A Solis ortu usque ad occasum, laudabile nomen Domini.* (Deus Omnia Pentrans) From the rising of the Sun to the going down of the same, the word of the Lord is worthy to be praised. |
| 60 | Mitzrael | 145:17 / 144:17 | *Justus Dominus in omnibus viis suis, et sanctus in omnibus operibus suis.* (Deus Sublevans Opressos) The Lord is just in all his ways in blessed in all his works. |
| 61 | Umabel | 113:2 / 112:2 | *Sit nomen Domini benedictum ex hoc, nunc, et usque in saeculum.* (Deus Super Omne Nomen) Let the name of the Lord be blessed from this time forth for evermore. |
| 62 | Yahehel | 119:159 / 118:159 | *Vide quoniam mandata tua dilexi, Domine, in misericordia tua vivifica me.* (Deus Ens Supremum) See, O Lord, how I have delighted in Thy commandments according to Thy life-giving mercy. |
| 63 | Anuel | 100:2 / 99:2 | *Servite Domino in Laetitia, introite in conspectu ejus in exultatione.* (Deus Mansuetus) Serve ye the Lord with gladness and enter into his sight with exultation. |
| 64 | Mechiel | 33:18 / 32:18 | *Ecce oculi Domini super metuentes eum, et in eis, qui sperant super misericordia ejus.* (Deus Vivificans) Behold the eyes of the Lord are upon those that fear Him and hope in His loving kindness. |
| 65 | Damabiah | 90:13 / 89:13 | *Convertere Domine usque quo, et deprecabilis esto super servos tuos.* (Deus Fons Sapientiae) Turn, O Lord, even here also, and be pleased with Thy servants. |
| 66 | Manaqel | 38:21 / 37:22 | *Ne derelinquas me Domine Deus meus, ne discesseris a me.* (Deus Omnia Pascens et Lactens) Neither leave me, O Lord, nor depart from me. |
| 67 | Eiael | 37:4 / 36:4 | *Delectare in Domino, et dabit tibi petitiones cordis tui.* (Deus Deliciae Filiorum Hominum) Delight in the Lord and He will give thee the petitions of thy heart. |
| 68 | Chabuiah | 106:1 / 105:1 | *Confitemini Domino, quoniam bonus, quoniam in sæculum misericordia ejus.* (Deus Liberalissimus Dator) Confess to the Lord, for He is God, and His mercy is for ever. |
| 69 | Rahel | 16:5 / 15:5 | *Dominus pars haereditatis meae et calicis mei, tu es qui restitues haereditatem meam mihi.* (Deus Omnia Videns) The Lord is my inheritance and my cup, and it is Thou who restorest mine inheritance. |
| 70 | Yabamiah | Genesis 1:1 | *In principio creavit Deus Caelum et Terrum.* (Deus Verbo Omnia Producens) In the beginning God created the Heaven and the Earth. [The only scriptural passage not drawn from the Psalms from the 72 angels.] |
| 71 | Hayiel | 109:30 / 108:30 | *Confitebor Domino nimis in ore meo, et in medio multorum laudabo eum.* (Deus Dominus Universorum) I shall confess to the Lord with my mouth and praise Him in the midst of the multitude. |
| 72 | Mumiah | 116:7 /114:7 | *Convertere anima mea in requiem tuam quia Dominus benefeciet tibi.* (Deus Finis Universorum) Return to thy rest, my soul, for the Lord doeth thee good. |

# A. Angels – Biblical, Apocryphal and Gnostic

*Astrological Angels*

| | | A26. Angels Ruling the Astrological Houses. | A27. Angels Ruling the Astrological Houses – English. | A28. The Lesser Assistant Angels in the Zodiacal Signs. | A29. The Lesser Assistant Angels in the Zodiacal Signs – English. |
|---|---|---|---|---|---|
| | | **142** | | **143** | |
| ♈ | 15 | איאל | Ayel | שרחיאל | Sharahiel |
| ♉ | 16 | טואל | Tuel | ארזיאל | Araziel |
| ♊ | 17 | גיאל | Giel | סראיאל | Sarayel |
| ♋ | 18 | כעאל | Kael | פכיאל | Pakiel |
| ♌ | 19 | עואל | Ovel | שרטיאל | Sharatiel |
| ♍ | 20 | ויאל | Veyel | שלתיאל | Shelathiel |
| ♎ | 22 | יהאל | Yahel | חדקיאל | Chedeqiel |
| ♏ | 24 | סוסול | Susul | סאיציאל | Saitziel |
| ♐ | 25 | סויעסאל | Suyasel | סריטיאל | Saritiel |
| ♑ | 26 | כשני עיה [5] | Kashenyaiah | שמקיאל | Samaqiel |
| ♒ | 28 | אנסואל | Ansiel | צבמקיאל | Tzakmiqiel |
| ♓ | 29 | פשיאל | Pasiel | וכביאל | Vakabiel |

| | | A30. Angel Lords of the Elemental Triplicity in the Signs by Day. | A31. Angel Lords of the Elemental Triplicity in the Signs by Day – English. | A32. Angels Lords of the Elemental Triplicity in the Signs by Night. | A33. Angels Lords of the Elemental Triplicity in the Signs by Night – English. |
|---|---|---|---|---|---|
| | | **144** | | **145** | |
| ♈ | 15 | סטרעתן | Sateraton | ספעטאוי | Sapatavi |
| ♉ | 16 | ראידאל | Rayel | טוטת | Totath |
| ♊ | 17 | סערש | Sarash | עגנרמען | Ogameron |
| ♋ | 18 | רעדר | Raadar | עכאל | Akel |
| ♌ | 19 | סנחם | Sanahem | זלברהית | Zalberhith |
| ♍ | 20 | לסלרא | Laslara | ססיא | Sasia |
| ♎ | 22 | תרגבון | Thergebon | אחודראון | Achodraon |
| ♏ | 24 | בתחן | Bethehon | סהקנב | Sahaqanab |
| ♐ | 25 | אהוז | Ahoz | לברמים | Lebarmin |
| ♑ | 26 | סנדלעי | Sandali | אלויר | Aloyar |
| ♒ | 28 | עתור | Athor | פלאן | Polayan |
| ♓ | 29 | רמרא | Ramara | נתדורינאל | Nathdorinel |

---

[5] Or כשויעה

# A. Angels – Biblical, Apocryphal and Gnostic

| | | A34. Angels of the Ascendant Decans. | A35. Angels of the Ascendant Decans – English. | A36. Angels of the Succedent Decans. | A37. Angels of the Succedent Decans – English. |
|---|---|---|---|---|---|
| | | **146** | | **147** | |
| ♈ | 15 | זזר | Zazer | בההמי | Behahemi |
| ♉ | 16 | כדמרי | Kadamidi | מנחראי | Minacharai |
| ♊ | 17 | סגרש | Sagarash | שהדני | Shehadani |
| ♋ | 18 | מתראוש | Mathravash | רהדיץ | Rahadetz |
| ♌ | 19 | לוסנהר | Losanahar | זחעי | Zachi |
| ♍ | 20 | אננאורה | Ananaurah | ראידיה | Rayadyah |
| ♎ | 22 | טרסני | Tarasni | סהרניץ | Saharnatz |
| ♏ | 24 | כמוץ | Kamotz | כנדוהר | Nundohar |
| ♐ | 25 | משראת | Mishrath | והרין | Vehrin |
| ♑ | 26 | מסנון | Misnin | יסיסיה | Yasyasyah |
| ♒ | 28 | ססּפם | Saspam | אברון | Abdaron |
| ♓ | 29 | בהלמי | Bihelami | אורון | Avron |

| | | A38. Angels of the Cadent Decans. | A39. Angels of the Cadent Decans – English. | A40. Angels of the Zodiacal Signs from Francis Barrett's *The Magus.*[6] | |
|---|---|---|---|---|---|
| | | **148** | | | |
| ♈ | 15 | סטנדר | Satonder | מלכידאל | Malachidael |
| ♉ | 16 | יכסגנוץ | Yakasaganotz | אסמודאל | Asmodel |
| ♊ | 17 | ביתון | Bethon | אמבריאל | Ambriel |
| ♋ | 18 | אלינכיר | Alinkir | מוריאל | Muriel |
| ♌ | 19 | סחיבר | Sahiber | ורכיאל | Verkiel |
| ♍ | 20 | משפר | Mishpar | חמיאל | Hamiel |
| ♎ | 22 | שחדר | Shachdar | זוריאל | Zuriel |
| ♏ | 24 | ותרודיאל | Uthrodiel | ברכיאל | Barkiel |
| ♐ | 25 | אבוהא | Aboha | אדוכיאל | Advakiel |
| ♑ | 26 | יסגדיברודיאל | Yasgedibarodiel | חמיאל | Hamiel |
| ♒ | 28 | גרודיאל | Gerodiel | כאמבריאל | Kambriel |
| ♓ | 29 | סטריף | Satrip | וכביאל | Vakabiel[7] |

---

[6] See also Column G27.

[7] Corrected from First Edition.

# A. Angels – Biblical, Apocryphal and Gnostic

## Yezidi and Persian Angels

| | A41. Archangels of the Yezidi. | A42. The 7 Amesha Spentas. | A43. The 7 Amesha Spentas – qualities. |
|---|---|---|---|
| 1 | | | |
| 2 | Melek Taus | | |
| 3 | Kadir-Rahman | | |
| 4 | Sheikh Bakra | Asha-Vahishta (Arbidihist/Ardwahisht) | Spirit of righteousness, presides over Asha and fire |
| 5 | Sheikh Ism | Khshathra-Vairya (Shahriver/Shahrewar) | Desirable Dominion of the noble/warrior caste, original kingdom of god. Presides over metals |
| 6 | Sij-ed-din | Vohu-Mano (Bahman/Vohuman) | Spirit of good, grace, state of Earthly paradise, Good Mind |
| 7 | Nasr-ed-din | Haurvatat (Khordadh/Hordad) | Perfection (feminine) or Health. Presides over water |
| 8 | Fakr-ed-din | Ameretat (Amurdad/Mourdad) | Immortality (feminine), the Amahraspand presiding over the Earth |
| 9 | Shams-ed-din | Spenta Mainyu | Good Spirit |
| 10 | | Spenta Aramaiti (Sipendarmith/Spandarmad) | Piety or selfless love, daughter of Ahura Mazda. Presides over the earth |

## Solomonic Angels

| | | A44. Archangels & Angels of the Days from *Key of Solomon*. | | |
|---|---|---|---|---|
| | | **Day** | **Archangel** | **Angel** |
| ☽ | 13 | Monday | Gabriel | Gabriel |
| ☿ | 12 | Wednesday | Michael | Raphael |
| ♀ | 14 | Friday | Haniel | Anael |
| ☉ | 30 | Sunday | Raphael | Michael |
| ♂ | 27 | Tuesday | Khaniael | Zamael |
| ♃ | 21 | Thursday | Tzadqiel | Sachiel |
| ♄ | 32 | Saturday | Tzaphqiel | Cassiel |

# A. Angels – Biblical, Apocryphal and Gnostic

| | | | |
|---|---|---|---|
| | | **A45. The Angels of the 12 Hebrew Months in *Sepher Raziel*.** | |

| | | Hebrew Month | Angels |
|---|---|---|---|
| ♈ | 1 | Nisan | Oriel, Malaquiran, Acia, Yaziel, Paltifus, Yesmactria, Yariel, Araton, Robica, Sephatia, Anaya, Quesupale, Semquiel, Sereriel, Malgas, Ancason, Pacyta, Abedel, Ram, Asdon, Casiel, Nastiafori, Sugni, Aszre, Sornadaf, Adniel, Necamia, Caisaat, Benit, Quor, Adziriel. |
| ♉ | 2 | Iyar | Safuel, Saton, Cartemat, Aryel, Palthia, Bargar, Galms, Nocpis, Aaron, Manit, Aadon, Qwenael, Quemon, Abragin, Yehoc, Adnibia, Parciot, Marinoc, Galus, Gabmion, Resegar, Affry, Absamon, Sarsaf, Alxim, Carbiol, Regnia, Achlas, Nadib, Absafyabitan, Pliset. |
| ♊ | 3 | Sivan | Amariel, Tatgiel, Casmuch, Nuscifa, Almux, Naamab, Mamiazicaras, Samysarach, Naasien, Andas, Paltamus, Abris, Borhai, Salor, Hac, Yayac, Dalia, Azigor, Mabsuf, Abnisor, Zenam, Dersam, Cefania, Maccafor, Naboon, Adiel, Maasiel, Szarhyr, Cartalion, Adi, Ysar. |
| ♋ | 4 | Tammuz | Moriel, Safida, Asaf, Mazica, Sarsac, Adnyam, Nagrow, Galuf, Galgall, Danroc, Saracus, Remafidda, Luliaraf, Nediter / Delgna, Maadon, Saamyel, Amrael, Lezaidi, Elisafan, Paschania, Maday. |
| ♌ | 5 | Ab | Byny, Madrat, Amantuliel, Cassurafarttis, Nactif, Necif, Pdgnar, Tablic, Mamirot, Amacia, Qnatiel, Reycat, Qnynzi, Paliel, Gadaf, Nesquiraf, Abrac, Amyter, Camb, Nachal, Cabach, Loch, Macria, Safe, Essaf. |
| ♍ | 6 | Elul | Magnyny, Arabyel, Hanyel, Nacery, Yassar, Rassy, Boel, Mattriel, Naccamarif, Zacdon, Nafac, Rapion, Sapsi, Salttri, Raseroph, Malgel, Samtiel, Yoas, Qualabye, Danpi, Yamla, Golid, Rasziel, Satpach, Nassa, Myssa, Macracif, Dadiel, Carciel, Effignax. |
| ♎ | 7 | Tishri | Suriel, Sarican, Gnabriza, Szucariel, Sababiel, Ytrut, Cullia, Dadiel, Marhum, Abecaisdon, Sacdon, Pagulan, Arsabon, Aspiramo, Aquyel, Safcy, Racynas, Altim, Masulaef, Vtisaryaya, Abri. |
| ♏ | 8 | Marchesvan | Karbiel, Tiszodiel, Raamyel, Nebubael, Alisaf, Baliel, Arzaf, Rasliel, Alson, Naspiel, Becar, Paliel, Elisuaig, Nap, Naxas, Sansani, Aesal, Maarim, Sasci, Yalsenac, Iabynx, Magdiel, Sarmas, Maaliel, Arsaferal, Manistiorar, Veaboluf, Nadibael, Suciel, Nabuel, Sariel, Sodiel, Marcuel, Palitam. |
| ♐ | 9 | Kislev | Adoniel, Radiel, Naduch, Racyno, Hyzy, Mariel, Azday, Mandiel, Gamiel, Seriel, Kery, Sahaman, Osmyn, Sachiel, Pazehemy, Calchihay, Hehudael, Nerad, Minael, Arac, Arariqniel, Galnel, Gimon, Satuel, Elynzy, Baqwylaguel. |
| ♑ | 10 | Tebet | Anael, Aniyel, Aryor, Naflia, Rapinis, Raaciel, Pacuel, Hahon, Guanrinasuch, Aslaqwy, Naspaya, Negri, Somahi, Hasasisgafon, Gasca, Szif, Alzamy, Maint, Xatinas, Sargnamuf, Oliab, Sariel, Canyel, Rahyeziel, Pansa, Insquen, Sarman, Malisan, Asirac, Marmoc. |
| ♒ | 11 | Shebet | Gabriel, Israel, Natriel, Gazril, Nassam, Abrisaf, Zefael, Zamiel, Mamiel, Tabiel, Miriel, Sahumiel, Guriel, Samhiel, Dariel, Banorsasti, Satyn, Nasyel, Ranfiel, Talgnaf, Libral, Luel, Daliel, Guadriel, Sahuhaf, Myschiel. |
| ♓ | 12 | Adar | Romiel, Patiel, Guriel, Laabiel, Addriel, Cardiel, Aguel, Malquiel, Samiel, Sariel, Azriel, Paamiel, Carcyelel, Amaluch, Parhaya, Ytael, Beryel, Cael, Tenebiel, Pantan, Panteron, Fanyel, Falafon, Masiel, Pantaron, Labiel, Ragael, Cetabiel, Nyahpatuel. |
| | 13 | Adar *bis* / Bisertillis | Lantiel, Ardiel, Nasmyel, Celidoal, Amyel, Magel, Gabgel, Sasuagos, Barilagni, Yabtasyper, Magossangos, Dragos, Yayel, Yoel, Yasmyel, Stelmel, Garasyn, Ceyabos, Sacadiel, Guracap, Gabanael, Tamtiel. |

# A. Angels – Biblical, Apocryphal and Gnostic

| | | |
|---|---|---|
| | | A46. Angels of the 7 Days of the Week in *Sepher Raziel*. |

| | Day | Angels |
|---|---|---|
| ☾ | Monday | Semhahylyn, Stemehilyn, Jasyozyn, Agrasinden, Aymeylyn, Cathneylyn, Abrasachysyn, Abrasasyn, Layzaiosyn, Langhasin, Anayenyn, Nangareryn, Aczonyn, Montagin, Labelas, Mafatyn, Feylarachin, Candanagyn, Laccudonyn, Casfrubyn, Bacharachyn, Bathaylyn, Anmanineylyn, Hacoylyn, Balganarichyn, Aryelyn, Badeilyn, Abranocyn, Tarmanydyn, Amdalycyn, Sahgragynyn, Adiamenyn, Sacstoyeyn, Latebaifanysyn, Caybemynyn, Nabyalni, Cyzamanyn, Abramacyn, Lariagathyn, Bifealyqnyn, Baiedalin, Gasoryn, Asaphin, Dariculin, Marneyelin, Gemraorin, Madarilyn, Yebiryn, Arylin, Farielin, Nepenielin, Branielin, Asrieylin, Ceradadyn. |
| ☿ | Tuesday | Michael, Zamirel, Beerel, Dufuel, Aribiriel, Boel, Bariel, Meriol, Amiol, Aol, Semeol, Aaon, Berion, Farionon, Kemerion, Feyn, Ameinyn, Zemeinyn, Cananyn, Aal, Merigal, Pegal, Gabal, Leal, Amneal, Farnnial, Gebyn, Caribifin, Ancarilyn, Metorilin, Nabiafilyn, Fisfilin, Barsfilin, Camfilin, Aaniturla, Feniturla, Geniniturla, Elmia, Calnamia, Rabmia, Rasfia, Miaga, Tiogra, Bee, Ylaraorynil, Benenil. |
| ♀ | Friday | Hasneyeyl, Barnayeyl, Uardayheil, Alzeyeil, Szeyyeil, Uachayel, Zesfaieil, Morayeil, Borayeyl, Apheieyl, Arobolyn, Canesylyn, Anrylin, Zarialin, Marilin, Batoraielyn, Kelfeielyn, Azraieylin, Ambayerin, Ayayeylin, Cadneirin, Alserin, Afneirin, Abneyrin, Nonanrin, Eazerin, Orinyn, Gedulin, Hareryn, Nanylin, Halilin, Himeilin, Resfilin, Noraraabilin, Hayeylin, Laudulin, Et, Effilin, Thesfealin, Patnilin, Keialin, Lebraieil, Ablaieil, Talrailanrain, Barcalin, Bahoraelin. |
| ☉ | Sunday | Daniel, Elieyl, Saffeyeyl, Dargoyeyl, Yelbrayeyl, Comaguele, Gebarbayea, Faceyeyl, Caran, Neyeyl, Talgylnenyl, Bethaz, Rancyl, Falha, Hyeyl, Armaqnieyeyl, Roncayl, Gibryl, Zamayl, Mycahe, Zarfaieil, Ameyl, Torayeil, Ronmeyeyl, Remcatheyel, Barhil, Marhil, Barhil, Mehil, Zarafil, Azrageyl, Anebynnyl, Denmerzym, Yeocyn, Necyl, Hadzbeyeyl, Zarseyeyl, Zarael, Anqnihim, Ceytatynyn, Ezuiah, Vehichdunedzineylyn, Yedmeyeyl, Esmaadyn, Albedagryn, Yamaanyl, Yecaleme, Detriel, Arieil, Armayel, Veremedyn, Unaraxxydin. |
| ♂ | Wednesday | Samayelyn, Tartalyn, Dexxeyl, Racyeylyn, Farabyn, Cabyn, Asymeylyn, Mabareylyn, Tralyelyn, Rulbelyn, Marmanyn, Tarfanyelyn, Fuheylyn, Ruffaraneylyn, Rabfilyn, Eralyn, Enplyn, Pirtophin, Brofilyn, Cacitilyn, Naffrynyn, Impuryn, Raffeylyn, Nyrysin, Memolyn, Nybirin, Celabel, Tubeylyn, Haayn, Reyn, Paafiryn, Cethenoylyn, Letityelyn, Rorafeyl, Cannyel, Bastelyn, Costiryn, Monteylyn, Albeylyn, Parachbeylyn, Alyel, Uaceyl, Zalcycyl, Amadyeyl, Usaryeyel, Emcodeneyl, Dasfripyel, Unleylyn, Carszeneyl, Gromeyl, Gabrynyn, Narbell. |
| ♃ | Thursday | Sachquiel, Pachayel, Tutiel, Osfleel, Labiel, Raliel, Beniel, Tarael, Snynyel, Ahiel, Yebel, Ancuyel, Jauiel, Juniel, Amyel, Faniel, Ramnel, Sanfael, Sacciniel, Galbiet, Lafiel, Maziel, Gunfiel, Ymrael, Memieil, Pariel, Panhiniel, Toripiel, Abinel, Omiel, Orfiel, Ael, Bearel, Ymel, Syymelyel, Traacyel, [42ʳ] Mefeniel, Antquiel, Quisiel, Cunnyryel, Rofiniel, Rubycyel, Jebrayel, Peciel, Carbiel, Tymel, Affarfytyriel, Rartudel, Cabrifiel, Beel, Briel, Cherudiel. |
| ♄ | Saturday | Micraton, Pacryton, Pepilon, Capeiel, Themiton, Alsfiton, Chenyon, Sandalson, Panion, Almyon, Expion, Papon, Calipon, Horrion, Melifon, Aurion, Temelion, Refacbilion, Ononiteon, Boxoraylon, Paxilon, Lelalion, Onoxion, Quilon, Quiron, Vixalimon, Relion, Cassilon, Titomon, Murion, Dedion, Dapsion, Leuainon, Foylylon, Monichion, Gabion, Paxonion, Xysuylion, Lepiron, Belon, Memitilon, Saron, Salion, Pion, Macgron, Acciriron, Felyypon, Ymnybron, Raconeal, Zalibron. |

# A. Angels – Biblical, Apocryphal and Gnostic

| | | | |
|---|---|---|---|
| **A47. Names of the Planets by the Elements, with their Angels in *Sepher Raziel*.** | | | |

| | Planet | | Fire | Air | Water | Earth |
|---|---|---|---|---|---|---|
| ☾ | Levanah | | Claron | Becyla | Tasfit | Pantours |
| | | Angels: | Gabriel, Paticael, Daliel | Barasiel, Ztaziel | Caziel, Memyiel, Pazicaton | Simyllyel, Lafaqnael, Toniel |
| ☿ | Kokab | | Piztal | Cabran | Facayl | Tarzon |
| | | Angels: | Paradiel, Darifiel, Dameyel | Ramatiel, Loriqniel, Bengariel | Rinafonel, Mellifiel, Alatiel | Alapion, Beriel, Rabiel |
| ♀ | Nogah | | Dusuyon | Clarifon | Narubni | Cabras |
| | | Angels: | Capciel, Debitael, Deparael | Camirael, Cakaziel, Neraziel | Saloniel, Emyel, Expaoniel | Paziael, Amurael, Salainel |
| ☼ | Hamina | | Yeye, | Don | Agla | On |
| | | Angels: | Dandaniel, Saddaniel, Ellalyel | Karason, Berriel, Oliel | Muracafel, Pecyrael, Michael | Homycabel, Lucifel, Locariel |
| ♂ | Madim | | Roqnyel | Pyryel | Tasfien | Ignofon |
| | | Angels: | Kaliel, Cabryel, Raloyl | Pyroyinel, Flatoniel, Carbiel | Cazabriel, Pasaliel, Zebaliel | ??? |
| ♃ | Zedek | | Pheon | Fidon | Calidon | Mydon |
| | | Angels: | Tinsyel, Necanynael, Fonyel | ??? | Meon, Ykiel, Yryniel | Palriel, Tufiel, Quyel |
| ♄ | Sabaday | | Campton | Srynongoa | Synyn | Onion [*sic*] |
| | | Angels: | Libiel, Nybiel, Phynitiel | Arfigyel, Gael, Nephyel | Almemel, Hoquiel, Fulitiel | Lariel, Tepyel, Esyel |

| | | | |
|---|---|---|---|
| **A48. Names of the 4 Elements and the Lowlands [Underworld] in the 4 Seasons in *Sepher Raziel*.** | | | |

| | Spring | Summer | Autumn | Winter |
|---|---|---|---|---|
| **F** | Quoyzil | Enlubra | Mezayn | Aybedyn |
| **A** | Ystana | Furayl | Oadion | Gulynon |
| **W** | Angustiz | Theon | Maddrylk | Sebillgradon |
| **E** | Ingnedon | Yabassa | Coliel | Aradon |
| **UW** | Hahan<br>*Angel*: ? | Cipaon<br>*Angel*: Jacyel | Meresac<br>*Angel*: Ababaot | Aycyhambabo<br>*Angel*: Caaniel |

# A. Angels – Biblical, Apocryphal and Gnostic

A49. The 7 Heavens and the Angels ruling in each of their Directions in *Sepher Raziel*.

| Heaven | | North | East | West | South |
|---|---|---|---|---|---|
| Shamayim | 1 | Alael, Hiaeyel, Urallim, Veallum, Baliel, Basy, Unascaiel | Gabriel, Gabrael, Odrael, Modiel, Raamyel, Janael | Abson, Soquiel | Duraniel, Darbiel, Darquiel, Hanin, Anael, Nahymel, Alscini, Soquiel, Zamel, Hubayel, Bactanael, Carpariel |
| Raqia | 2 | Tyel, Jarael, Yanael, Nenael, Nenel, Quian, Uetamuel | Maachin or Carmiel, Carcoyel, Betabaat | Anulus, Yesararye [corrupt godname], in which is written the name Macareton | Mylba, Nelia, Balyer, Calloyel, Cyoly, Batriel |
| Shechaqim | 3 | Poniel, Penael, Penat, Raphael, Carmiel, Doranel | Satquiel, Quadissa, Taramel, Taryestorat, Amael, Hufrbria or Hifaliel | ??? | Parna, Sadiel, Lyenyel, Vastamel, Sanael, Samyel |
| Ma'on | 4 | Rahumiel, Haynynael, Bacyel, Serapiel, Matiel, Serael | Capiel, Braliel, Braaliel, Raguel, Gael, Daemael, Calcas, Atragon | Lacana, Astagna, Nobquin, Sonatas, Yael, Yas, Yael, Lael, Yyel | Saoriel, Mahamel, Gadiel, Hosael, Vanyel, Verascyer |
| Makon | 5 | Hayel, Hanyel, Veal, Quiel, Margabiel, Saeprel, Mamyel | Lanifiel or Barquiel, Zaquiel, Sanficiel, Zoaziel, Aciel, Farbiel, Uranacha | Anhael, Pabliel, Uslael, Bortaz, Suncacer, Zupa, Faly, Paly | ??? |
| Zebul | 6 | [no angels] | | | |
| Araboth | 7 | [no angels] | | | |

A50. Names of Heavens, and the names of the Directions, distributed over the 4 Seasons from *Sepher Raziel*.

| | Spring | Summer | Autumn | Winter |
|---|---|---|---|---|
| Names of the Heavens | Hacibor | Rumcaqnia | Mesfisnogna | Saaemaho |
| Names of the East | Acbedan | Cardrenac | Abrthel | Acritael |
| Names of the North | Henniyna | Abodich | Galdidur | Rabbifor |
| Names of the West | Mahanahym | Sugor | Zarzir | Rabiur |
| Names of the South | Naufor | Alparon | Machniel | Thaumy |

# A. Angels – Biblical, Apocryphal and Gnostic

| Heaven | Chapters [Capitulum] | Moses' Semiforas | Ordinary Semiforas |
|---|---|---|---|
| | | **A51. Angel Names for the Semiforas from *Sepher Raziel*.** | |
| Shamayim | 1 | Maya, Afi, Zye, Yaremye, Une, Bace, Sare, Binoe, Maa, Yasame, Roy, Lyly, Leoy, Yle, Yre, Cyloy, Zalye, Lee, Or, See, Loace, Cadeloy, Ule, Meha, Ramechi, Ry, Hy, Fossa, Tu, Mimi, Sehie, Nice, Yelo, Habe, Uele, Hele, Ede, Quego, Ramaye, Habe. | גגגג יהוה הוהי [no angel names] |
| Raqia | 2 | Abgincam, Loaraceram, Naodicras, Pecaccecas, Acaptena, Yeger, Podayg, Saccosicum. | אשר אהיה. [no angel names] |
| Shechaqim | 3 | Ena, Elaye, Sayec, Helame, Maace, Lehahu, Lehahu, Alielie, Qore, Azaye, Boene, Hyeha, Ysale, Mabeha, Arayha, Arameloena, Qleye, Lieneno, Feyane, Ye, Ye, Malece, Habona, Nechee, Hicers. | Adona[i], Sabaoth, Adonay, Cados [Kadosh], Addona, Annora. |
| Ma'on | 4 | Micraton, Piston, Yeymor, Higaron, Ygniron, Tenigaron, Mycon, Mycondasnos, Castas, Laceas, Astas, Yecon, Cuia, Tablinst, Tabla, Nac, Yacuf. | Lagume, Lamizirm, Lanagzlayn, Lagri, Lanagala, Lanatozin, Laifyalasyn. |
| Makon | 5 | Saday, Haleyos, Loez, Elacy, Citonij, Hazyhaya, Yeynimeysey, Accidasbaruc, Huadonenu, Eya, Hyebu, Ueu, Uaha, Oyaha, Eye, Ha, Hia, Zalia, Haliha, Eyey, Yaia, El, Ebehel, Ua, Ua. | Lihaham, Lialgana, Liafar, Vialurab, Lelara, Lebaron, Laasasilas. |
| Zebul | 6 | Yana, Yane, Sia, Abibhu, Uanoia, Accenol, Tiogas, Yena, Eloym, Ya, Uehu, Yane, Hayya, Uehu, Ahiacmed. | Letamynyn, Letaglogen, Letafiryn, Babaganaritin, Letarimitin, Letagelogin, Letafalazin. |
| Araboth | 7 | Saday, Samora, Ebon, Pheneton, Eloy, Eneiobceel, Messias, Jahe, Yana or Eolyen. | Eliaon, Yaena, Adonay, Cados, Ebreel, Eloy, Ela, Egiel, Ayom, Sath, Adon, Sulela, Eloym, Deliom, Yacy, Elim, Delis, Yacy, Zazael, Pabiel, Man, Myel, Enola, Dylatan, Saday, Alina, Papym, another [source gives] Saena, Alym, Catinal, Uza, Yarast, Calpi, Calsas, Safna, Nycam, Saday, Aglataon, Sya, Emanuel, Joth, Lalaph, Om, Via, Than, Domyfrael, Nimel, Lalialens, Alla, Phenox, Agsata, Tiel, Piel, Patriceion, Chepheron, Baryon, Yael. |

# A. Angels – Biblical, Apocryphal and Gnostic

## A52. Names of the Angels ruling over the 4 Elements in *Sepher Raziel*.

| | Angel |
|---|---|
| **F** | Michael, Rafael, Rasoiel, Acdiel, Roqniel, Myriel, Indam, Malqniel, Gazriel, Amynyel, Cariel, Yafrael. |
| **A** | Rafael, Quabriel, Michael, Cherubyn, Ceraphin, Orychyn, Pantaceren, Micraton, Sandalfon, Barachiel, Ragehyel, Tobiel. |
| **W** | Urpeniel, Armariel, Yyamnel, Abrastos, Sapiel, Uiotan, Oriel, Bachmyel, Porackmiel, Acceriel, Galliel, Zsmayel. |
| **E** | Samael, Yatayel, Baraniel, Oriel, Arfaniel, Latgriel, Daniel, Affariel, Partriel, Bael, Byeniel. |

## A53. Name of the Planets, and their Angels, in the 4 Seasons, in *Sepher Raziel*.

| | Angel | Spring | Summer | Autumn | Winter |
|---|---|---|---|---|---|
| ☾ | Anael | Salmi | Sarico | Naspilii | Afriqnym |
| ☿ | Satquiel | Armis | Angocus | Tholos | Ancholos |
| ♀ | Adzdiel | Aporodicy | Calizo | Niniptz | Pontos |
| ☼ | Dandaniel | Halyom | Adocham | Cantopos | Pantasus |
| ♂ | Balquiel | Aaryn | Daron | Bearon | Pantefos |
| ♃ | Satquiel | Amonor | Sahibor | Sayin | Eanynyel |
| ♄ | Capciel | Cuerues | Palicos | Quirtipos | Panpotes |

## A54. Angels ruling over 7 Heavens in *Sepher Raziel*.

| | Heaven | Angel |
|---|---|---|
| ☾ | Shamayim | Capciel |
| ☿ | Raqia | Saquiel |
| ♀ | Shechaqim | Samael |
| ☼ | Ma'on | Raphael |
| ♂ | Makon | Anael |
| ♃ | Zebul | Michael |
| ♄ | Araboth | Gabriel |

## A55. Names of Angels having power in each Direction in *Sepher Raziel*.

| Direction | Angels |
|---|---|
| Names of the East | Gabriel, Raphael, Uriel |
| Names of the North | Adriel, Yamiel, Zabdiel |
| Names of the West | Adtriel, Samael, Joel |
| Names of the South | Corabiel, Sariel, Michael |

# A. Angels – Biblical, Apocryphal and Gnostic

*Planetary Angels*

| | A56. Angels of the Planets | | | | | | |
|---|---|---|---|---|---|---|---|
| | Avenares 1145 | Peter de Abano | Trithemius | Agrippa Vol. III | Agrippa | Magia Naturalis | 'Schemham- phorasch' |
| ☽ | Gavriel | Gabriel | Gabriel | Gabriel | Gabriel | Gabriel | Gabriel |
| ☿ | Raphael | Raphael | Raphael | Raphael | Michael | Michael | Michael |
| ♀ | Anael | Anael | Anael | Anael | Haniel | Haniel | Haniel |
| ☼ | Michael | Michael | Michael | Michael | Raphael | Raphael | Raphael |
| ♂ | Samael | Samael | Samael | Samael | Camael | Camael | Camael |
| ♃ | Satkiel | Sachiel | Zachariel | Zachariel | Zadkiel | Zadkiel | Zadkiel |
| ♄ | Caffiel | Cassiel | Orifiel | Oriphiel | Zaphkiel Jophiel | Zaphkiel | Zaphkiel |

| | A57. Angel and Demons of the Days of the Week in the *Hygromanteia*. | | |
|---|---|---|---|
| | **Planet** | **Angel** | **Demon** |
| ☽ | Moon | Gabriēl | Mamonas |
| ☿ | Mercury | Ouriēl | Loutzipher |
| ♀ | Sun | Mikhaēl | Asmodai |
| ☼ | Mars | Samouēl | Kakistōn |
| ♂ | Jupiter | Rhaphaēl | Meltiphrōn |
| ♃ | Saturn | Sabapiēl | Klēndatōr |
| ♄ | Venus | Agathouēl | Gouliōn |

# B. Buddhism

| | B1. The Noble Eightfold Buddhist Path. | B2. The Noble Eightfold Buddhist Path – English. | B3. Buddhist Courts of Hell their direction in respect of Mount Meru. | B4. Buddhist Courts of Hell – President. |
|---|---|---|---|---|
| | **82** | | | |
| 1 | Samma Samadhi | Right Meditation or Rapture | 10th | Chuan-lun Wang |
| 2 | | | 9th – SW | Píng-teng Wang |
| 3 | | | 8th – W | Tu-ti Wang |
| 4 | Samma Sati | Right Mindfulness or Awareness | 7th – NW | Tai-shan Wang |
| 5 | Samma Vayama | Right Effort or Endeavour | 6th – N | Pien-cheng Wang |
| 6 | Samma Ajiva | Right Livelihood | 5th – NE | Yen-lo Wang |
| 7 | Samma Kammanta | Right Action or Conduct | 4th – E | Wu-kuan Wang |
| 8 | Samma Vaca | Right Speech | 3rd – SE | Sung-ti Wang |
| 9 | Samma Sankappa | Right Thought or Aspiration | 2nd – S | Chu-chiang Wang |
| 10 | Samma Ditthi | Right Understanding | 1st – W | Chin-kuang Wang |

| | | B5. The Ten Fetters of Buddhism. | B6. The Ten Fetters of Buddhism – English. | B7. The Four Noble Truths of Buddhism. |
|---|---|---|---|---|
| | | **119** | | **191** |
| | 1 | Arupa-raga | Desire for immaterial immortality | |
| | 2 | Vicikiccha | Sceptical doubt | |
| | 3 | Rupa-raga | Desire for bodily immortality | |
| | 4 | Silabbata-paramansa | Clinging to rules and rituals | |
| | 5 | Vyapada | Hatred | |
| | 6 | Udhacca | Restlessness | |
| | 7 | Mana | Pride or conceit | |
| | 8 | Sakkaya-ditthi | Belief in a personal 'soul' | |
| | 9 | Kama-raga | Bodily desire | |
| | 10 | Avijja | Ignorance | |
| ✳ | 31b | | | |
| F | 31 | | | Noble Eight-fold Path leads to the cessation of sorrow |
| A | 11 | | | The origin of sorrow is attachment |
| W | 23 | | | The cessation of sorrow is attainable |
| E | 32b | | | Life means sorrow |

# B. Buddhism

| | | B8. The Forty Buddhist Meditations. | B8a. The Forty Buddhist Meditations - Divisions. | B9. Twelve (Chinese) Buddhist Teachers (ta-t'ien shih). |
|---|---|---|---|---|
| | | **23** | | |
| | 1 | Reflection on Nirvana | Upekkha (Acceptance, Equanimity or Indifference) | |
| | 2 | Reflection on Generosity | Mudita (Joy) | |
| | 3 | Reflection on Ethics/Morals | Karuna (Compassion) | |
| | 4 | Reflection on Dharma | Metta (Friendliness) | |
| | 5 | Reflection on Death | | |
| | 6 | Reflection on Buddha | 1-10 = the 10 Recollections | |
| | 7 | Reflection on the Gods | | |
| | 8 | Reflection on the Sangha | 1 - 4 = the 4 Brahmaviharas or Sublime States also | |
| | 9 | Mindfulness of the Breathing | | |
| | 10 | Mindfulness of the Body | | |
| ⊛ | 31b | Akasha – the jewel - light | | |
| F | 31 | Fire – blood red triangle/cone | The 10 Kasinas: Meditation on the 5 Elements symbolized by the stupa, and the 5 colours (including Light) | |
| A | 11 | Wind – blue/green crescent | | |
| W | 23 | Water – white globe | | |
| E | 32b | Earth – yellow cube | | |
| ☾ | 13 | Odata – White | | |
| ☿ | 12 | Pita – Yellow | | |
| ♀ | 14 | Nila – Blue/green | | |
| ☼ | 30 | Aloka – Light | The 5 colour Kasinas plus Space | |
| ♂ | 27 | Lohita – Blood-red | | |
| ♃ | 21 | | | |
| ♄ | 32 | Akasa – Space | | |
| ♈ | 15 | Bloody Corpse | | Wen-shu yen-k'ung (Manjusri) |
| ♉ | 16 | Beaten and Scattered Corpse | | P'u-hsien hsin-li (Samantabhadra) |
| ♊ | 17 | Cut in Middle Corpse | | P'u-yen fa-chieh |
| ♋ | 18 | Worm-eaten Corpse | | Chin-kang-tsan ch'i-hsi |
| ♌ | 19 | Gnawed by Wild Beasts Corpse | The 10 Impurities (stages of decomposition of the corpse) as an Impermanence meditation. | Mi-lo shen-chih (Maitreya) |
| ♍ | 20 | Bloated Corpse | | Ch'ing-ching-hui shuo-fa |
| ♎ | 22 | Hacked in Pieces Corpse | | Wei-te san-kuan |
| ♏ | 24 | Skeleton Corpse | | Pien-yin wu-kuan |
| ♐ | 25 | Purple/Livid Corpse | | Ching-yeh ch'u-wo |
| ♑ | 26 | Putrid/Festering Corpse | | P'u-chio tse-fa |
| ♒ | 28 | Analysis of Physical Body into the 4 Elements | One Perception and one Analysis related to Impermanence | Yuan-chio k'o-ch'i |
| ♓ | 29 | Perception of the Loathsomeness of Food (as antidote to craving) | | Shan-shou chien-she |

# B. Buddhism

| | | B10. Buddhist Animal. | B11. Buddhist Symbol. | B12. Peaceful Buddhas (Dhyani). | B13. Terrifying Buddhas (Heruka). | B14. Dakini Consorts. | B15. Directions of the Buddhas. |
|---|---|---|---|---|---|---|---|
| | | | | | | | |
| ✸ | 31b | Lion | Wheel | Vairocana (White) | Buddha (Brown) | Akasa-Dhatesvari (Red) | Centre |
| F | 31 | Peacock | Open Lotus | Amitabha (Red) | Padma (Red-Black) | Pandarava-Sini (Red) | West |
| A | 11 | Bird-man | Double-headed sword | Amogha-siddhi (Green) | Karma (Dark Green) | Tara (Green) | North |
| W | 23 | Elephant | Lightning bolt (Vajra) | Akshobya (Blue) | Vajra (Black) | Locana (White) | East |
| E | 32b | Horse | Jewel | Ratna-Sambhava (Yellow) | Ratna (Tawny) | Mamaki (Yellow) | South |

# C. Christianity

*Virtues and Sins*

| | C1. Western Virtues. | C2. Western Mysticism – Visions. |
|---|---|---|
| | **50** | **45** |
| **1** | Accomplishment of the Great Work | Union with God |
| **2** | Devotion | The Vision of God face to face, Vision of Antinomies |
| **3** | Silence | The Vision of Sorrow |
| **4** | Obedience | The Vision of Love |
| **5** | Energy | The Vision of Power |
| **6** | Self-Sacrifice<br>Devotion to the Great Work | The Vision of the Harmony of Things<br>The Mysteries of the Crucifixion, The Beatific Vision |
| **7** | Unselfishness | The Vision of Beauty Triumphant |
| **8** | Truthfulness | The Vision of Splendour |
| **9** | Independence | The Vision of the Machinery of the Universe |
| **10** | Scepticism | The Vision of the Holy Guardian Angel or of Adonai. |

| | | C3. The 7 Deadly Sins, and their Order. | C4. The 7 Deadly Sins, their Opposing Virtues. |
|---|---|---|---|
| ☾ | 13 | Sloth/Idleness (4th) | Zeal |
| ☿ | 12 | Envy (2nd) | Love |
| ♀ | 14 | Lust (7th) | Self-control |
| ☉ | 30 | Pride (1st) | Humility |
| ♂ | 27 | Wrath (3rd) | Kindness |
| ♃ | 21 | Gluttony (6th) | Temperance |
| ♄ | 32 | Avarice/Greed (5th) | Generosity |

# C. Christianity

*Apostles*

| | | C5. Twelve Apostles. | C6. Apostle's Symbol. | C7. Greek Name. | C8. Greek Numeration. |
|---|---|---|---|---|---|
| ♈ | 15 | Simon Peter | Two crossed keys of Heaven | ΣΙΜΟΝΑ ΠΕΤΡΑΝ | 371 + 536 = 907 |
| ♉ | 16 | Andrew | Saltire cross | ΑΝΔΡΕΑΝ | 211 |
| ♊ | 17 | James the Elder | Three [pilgrim] scallop shells | ΙΑΚΩΒΟΝ | 953 |
| ♋ | 18 | John | Chalice containing a serpent | ΙΩΑΝΗΝ | 919 |
| ♌ | 19 | Thomas | Carpenter's square and upright spear | ΘΩΜΑΝ | 900 |
| ♍ | 20 | James of Alphaeus | Vertical saw | ΙΑΚΩΒΟΝ ΛΦΑΙΟΥ | 953 + 1012 = 1965 |
| ♎ | 22 | Philip | Cross and two loaves | ΦΙΛΙΠΠΙΟΝ | 840 |
| ♏ | 24 | Bartholomew | Three flaying knives | ΒΑΡΘΟΛΟΜΑΙΟΝ | 453 |
| ♐ | 25 | Matthew | Three money purses, two above one | ΜΑΘΘΑΙΟΝ | 190 |
| ♑ | 26 | Simon the Zealot | Fish on an open book | ΣΙΜΟΝ ΖΗΛΩΤΗΝ | 370 + 1203 = 1573 |
| ♒ | 28 | Jude or James | Ship with cross masts | ΙΟΥΔΑΝ ΙΑΚΩΒΟΥ | 535 + 1303 = 1838 |
| ♓ | 29 | Judas Iscariot | Moneybag with 30 silver coins | ΙΟΥΔΑΝ ΙΣΚΑΡΙΩΘ | 535 + 1150 = 1685 |

| | | The Twelve Apostles. | C9. Hebrew Name – Agrippa. | C10. Hebrew Name – Translation. | C11. Hebrew Name – Numeration.[1] |
|---|---|---|---|---|---|
| ♈ | 15 | Simon Peter | שמעון הכפי | Symehon Hacephi | 1234 |
| ♉ | 16 | Andrew | אלעוזי | Alouzi | 124 |
| ♊ | 17 | James the Elder | יעקבה | Jahacobah | 187 |
| ♋ | 18 | John | יוחנה | Johanah | 76 |
| ♌ | 19 | Thomas | תמני | Thamni | 500 |
| ♍ | 20 | James of Alphaeus | יעקב | Jahacob | 182 |
| ♎ | 22 | Philip | פוליפוש | Polipos | 512 |
| ♏ | 24 | Bartholomew | ברכיה | Barachiah | 237 |
| ♐ | 25 | Matthew | מדון | Medon | 750 |
| ♑ | 26 | Simon the Zealot | שמאם | Samam | 941 |
| ♒ | 28 | Jude or James/Thaddeus | כטיפא | Catopha | 120 |
| ♓ | 29 | Judas Iscariot/Matthias | מתתיה | Matattiah | 855 |

---

[1] Columns C12-C13 have now been embodied in the Commentary on Columns C9-C10, as their content was similar.

# C. Christianity

| Hell Level. | C14. Christian Hell – the levels of Dante's *Inferno*. | | |
|---|---|---|---|
| | **Location** | **Inhabitants** | **Punishment & Guard** |
| | Vestibule | The indecisive | |
| ≈ | River Acheron | | Boatman: Charon |
| 1 | Limbo | Good pagans, unbaptised souls, ancient philosophers and poets, Homer, Horace, Ovid, Lucan, Old Testament Patriarchs | Like the Elysian Fields – no punishments there |
| 2 | | The lustful | Tossed by storm winds *Guard*: Minos. |
| 3 | | The gluttonous | Live in the mud subjected to continuous heavy cold rain *Guard*: Cerberus |
| 4 | | The avaricious, misers and prodigals, spendthrifts | Continually roll stones up slopes *Guard*: Pluto/Plutus |
| 5 | | The wrathful and the sullen/surly | Wrathful fight in filthy water. Sullen are submerged in a filthy marsh |
| ≈ | River Styx | Boundary between Upper and Lower Hell | Boatman: Phlegyas |
| | Walls of the City of Dis | | The Furies and Medusa |
| 6 | | Heretics | Burn in fiery graves *Guard*: the Erinyes |
| ≈ | River Phlegethon | River of boiling blood | *Guard*: the Minotaur |
| 7 | | Violent Sinners – murderers, warmongers, tyrants, psychopaths (against their neighbours) | In boiling blood *Guard*: the Centaurs/Chiron |
| | | – suicides (violent against themselves) | Souls imprisoned in the trees of the Wood of suicides. *Guard*: Harpies |
| | | – squanderers (violent against their possessions) | |
| | | – blasphemers (violent against God) | Burning plain, a desert of flaming sand with fiery flakes raining from the sky |
| | | – sodomites (violent against fertility/Nature) | |
| | | – usurers (violent against money/fellow man) | |
| | | | *Guard*: the monster Geryon |
| 8 | Malebolge – the evil 'pouches' | Fraudulent Sinners – those guilty of deliberate and knowing evil | Giants, Malebranche (demons) |
| | | – panderers, pimps and seducers | Scourged by horned demons |
| | | – flatterers | Immersed in human excrement |
| | | – simoniacs (sellers of false religious pardons – priests mostly, e.g. Pope Nicholas III) | Upside down in holes with flames burning on their feet, baptized with fire |
| | | – sorcerers, false diviners, astrologers, magicians, false prophets | Heads twisted around backwards |
| | | – barrators (corrupt politicians) and swindlers | Plunged into a lake of boiling pitch |
| | | – hypocrites | Lead lined gilt cloaks |
| | | – thieves | Turned into reptiles. *Guard*: Cacus |
| | | – fraudulent advisors, lawyers, counselors | Burn in flames |
| | | – schismatics, scandal-mongers, sowers of discord, heretics | Continued disembowelment by devils with swords |
| | | – falsifiers (counterfeiters, perjurers, impersonators, coiners, alchemists) | Subject to diseases and deformities |

# C. Christianity

| Hell Level. | C14. Christian Hell – the levels of Dante's *Inferno*. | | |
|---|---|---|---|
| | **Location** | **Inhabitants** | **Punishment & Guard** |
| ♒ 9 | Cocytus – the frozen lake | Traitorous Sinners | *Guard*: the Giants – Antaeus |
| | | – Caina (traitors to kin and family) | Immersed in ice head down |
| | | – Antenora (political traitors, to homeland or party) | Heads bitten off |
| | | – Ptolomæa (traitors to guests) | Buried up to neck in ice |
| | | – Judecca (traitors to benefactors and masters) | Completely immersed in ice |
| | Satan | with three heads and six wings, waist deep in ice | |

| | | C15. Christian Theology. | C16. The 7 Early Churches of Asia Minor (Turkey). |
|---|---|---|---|
| | | **36** | |
| | 1 | God the Father | |
| | 2 | Logos, [Sophia] | |
| | 3 | Virgin Mary, Mary Magdalene | |
| | 4 | God as Storm God | |
| | 5 | Christ as Judge of the World | |
| | 6 | God the Son, Christ as Hanged Man | |
| | 7 | Messiah, Lord of Hosts | |
| | 8 | God the Sender/Healer of Plagues | |
| | 9 | God the Holy Ghost/Holy Spirit [Ruach ha-Qadesh] | |
| | 10 | The Church [Ecclesia Christi] | |
| ☾ | 13 | | Laodicea |
| ☿ | 12 | | Sardis |
| ♀ | 14 | | Thyatira |
| ☉ | 30 | | Smyrna |
| ♂ | 27 | | Pergamos/Pergamum |
| ♃ | 21 | | Philadelphia |
| ♄ | 32 | | Ephesus |

# C. Christianity

*Doctors of the Church*

<table>
<tr><td colspan="3">C17. Doctors of the Catholic Church.</td></tr>
<tr><td>Name</td><td>Lifespan</td><td></td></tr>
<tr><td>St. Athanasius</td><td>296 - 373</td><td>First Doctor of the Church and an arch enemy of Arianism. Bishop of Alexandria</td></tr>
<tr><td>St. Ephraem the Syrian</td><td>306 - 373</td><td>Author of On the Last Times, the Antichrist, and the End of the World</td></tr>
<tr><td>St. Hilary of Poitiers</td><td>315 - 367</td><td>Concerned with the arrival of the Antichrist</td></tr>
<tr><td>St. Cyril of Jerusalem</td><td>315 - 386</td><td>Against pagans, Jews and heretics</td></tr>
<tr><td>St. Gregory of Nazianzus</td><td>325 - 389</td><td>An enemy of Apollinarianism and Nestorianism</td></tr>
<tr><td>St. Basil the Great</td><td>329 - 379</td><td>Author of Hexaemeron, enemy of Arianism, Father of monasticism in the East</td></tr>
<tr><td>St. Ambrose</td><td>339 - 397</td><td>Part of a patrician Roman family. Well versed in Greek. Bishop of Milan</td></tr>
<tr><td>St. John Chrysostom</td><td>347 - 407</td><td>Bishop of Constantinople who wrote against the Jews</td></tr>
<tr><td>St. Jerome</td><td>347 - 419</td><td>Translator of the Bible into Latin, the Vulgate</td></tr>
<tr><td>St. Augustine of Hippo</td><td>354 - 430</td><td>Son of a pagan and follower of Manichaean religion before becoming a Christian. Author of City of God</td></tr>
<tr><td>St. Cyril of Alexandria</td><td>376 - 444</td><td>Patriarch of Alexandria at the time of the cruel murder by Christians of the Neoplatonist philosopher and pagan Hypatia. Responsible for the burning of the great Library of Alexandria.</td></tr>
<tr><td>St. Peter Chrysologus</td><td>406 - 450</td><td>Called 'the Golden worded'</td></tr>
<tr><td>St. Leo the Great</td><td>400 - 461</td><td>Against Nestorian, Monophysite, Manichean and Pelagian heresies</td></tr>
<tr><td>St. Gregory the Great</td><td>540 - 604</td><td>Pope. Fourth and last of the traditional Doctors of the Latin Church</td></tr>
<tr><td>St. Isidore of Seville</td><td>560 - 636</td><td>Introduced Aristotle to Spain and wrote a very important Summa of all learning, the Etymologiae. The most learned man of his time</td></tr>
<tr><td>St. John of Damascus</td><td>645 - 749</td><td>Well versed in music, astronomy and theology. Wrote against the interesting heresy of the Ishmaelites</td></tr>
<tr><td>St. Bede the Venerable</td><td>672 - 735</td><td>Wrote The Ecclesiastical History of the English People. Re-edited the Vulgate, the Latin Bible</td></tr>
<tr><td>St. Peter Damian</td><td>1007 - 1072</td><td>Ecclesiastical and clerical reformer. Benedictine</td></tr>
<tr><td>St. Anselm</td><td>1033 - 1109</td><td>Archbishop of Canterbury. Father of Scholasticism</td></tr>
<tr><td>St. Bernard of Clairvaux</td><td>1090 - 1153</td><td>Was involved in the founding of the Knights Templar and the rebuilding of Chartres Cathedral</td></tr>
<tr><td>St. Anthony of Padua</td><td>1195 - 1231</td><td>A worker of miracles who wrote about demons</td></tr>
<tr><td>St. Albert the Great</td><td>1206 - 1280</td><td>Albertus Magnus wrote books on Natural Magic. Patron of natural scientists; called Doctor Universalis, Doctor Expertus. Dominican</td></tr>
<tr><td>St. Bonaventure</td><td>1221 – 1274</td><td>Popular saint whose works were supported by Pope Sixtus V.</td></tr>
<tr><td>St. Thomas Aquinas</td><td>1226 – 1274</td><td>Author of Summa Theologiae, containing opinions about angels</td></tr>
<tr><td>St. Catherine of Siena</td><td>1347 – 1380</td><td>Visions of Heaven, Hell and Purgatory</td></tr>
<tr><td>St. Teresa of Avila</td><td>1515 – 1582</td><td>Intense visions of suffering and mortification</td></tr>
<tr><td>St. Peter Canisius</td><td>1521 – 1597</td><td>Leader in the Counter-Reformation. Jesuit</td></tr>
<tr><td>St. John of the Cross</td><td>1542 – 1591</td><td>Wrote Dark Night of the Soul. Reformed the Carmelites</td></tr>
<tr><td>St. Robert Bellarmine</td><td>1542 – 1621</td><td>Wrote two catechisms. Jesuit</td></tr>
<tr><td>St. Lawrence of Brindisi</td><td>1559 – 1619</td><td>Strong influence in the post-Reformation period</td></tr>
<tr><td>St. Francis de Sales</td><td>1567 – 1622</td><td>Patron of Catholic writers</td></tr>
<tr><td>St. Alphonsus Ligouri</td><td>1696 – 1787</td><td>Poet, painter, musician and author</td></tr>
<tr><td>St. Thérèse of Lisieux</td><td>1873 – 1897</td><td>Her autobiographical Story of a Soul has become a spiritual classic</td></tr>
</table>

# C. Christianity

*Saints*

<table>
<tr><td colspan="3" align="center">C18. Selection of Saints.</td></tr>
<tr><td align="center">Saint</td><td align="center">Patron of</td><td align="center">Country/City of Patronage</td></tr>
<tr><td>Adalbert of Prague</td><td>evangelizers</td><td>Hungary, Prague, Bohemia, Poland, Prussia</td></tr>
<tr><td>Albertus Magnus</td><td>natural scientists, chemists, magicians</td><td>Archdiocese – Ohio; Germany</td></tr>
<tr><td>Andrew the Apostle</td><td>fish dealers, fishermen, gout sufferers</td><td>Achaia, Amalfi (Italy), Patras (Greece), Russia, Scotland</td></tr>
<tr><td>Anthony of Padua</td><td>fishermen, swineherds</td><td>Brazil, indigenous peoples of the Americas, Portugal</td></tr>
<tr><td>Apollonia</td><td>dentists</td><td>Alexandria, Egypt</td></tr>
<tr><td>Augustine of Hippo</td><td>brewers, printers, and theologians</td><td>Cagayan de Oro, Augustine (Florida).</td></tr>
<tr><td>Barnabas</td><td>hailstorms, peacemaker</td><td>Antioch (Cyprus)</td></tr>
<tr><td>Bartholomew the Apostle</td><td>tanners, leatherworkers, curriers</td><td>Armenia</td></tr>
<tr><td>Benedict</td><td>agricultural workers; against nettle rash, poison, witchcraft</td><td></td></tr>
<tr><td>Bernadette of Lourdes</td><td>shepherds, shepherdesses</td><td>Lourdes (France)</td></tr>
<tr><td>Bernard of Clairvaux</td><td>bee keepers, wax refiners</td><td>Gibraltar</td></tr>
<tr><td>Brigid of Ireland</td><td>dairy farms and workers, healers</td><td>Ireland</td></tr>
<tr><td>Casimir of Poland</td><td>bachelors, kings, princes; against plague</td><td>Lithuania, Poland</td></tr>
<tr><td>Catherine of Siena</td><td>nursing services, nurses</td><td>Europe, Siena (Italy)</td></tr>
<tr><td>Cecilia</td><td>musicians</td><td>Albi (France)</td></tr>
<tr><td>Christopher</td><td>travellers</td><td>Rab (Croatia)</td></tr>
<tr><td>Clare of Assisi</td><td>gilders, embroiderers</td><td>Santa Clara Indian Pueblo (California, US)</td></tr>
<tr><td>Columba</td><td>bookbinders, poets; against floods</td><td>Ireland, Scotland</td></tr>
<tr><td>Crispin & Crispian</td><td>tanners, leatherworkers, curriers</td><td>Gaul</td></tr>
<tr><td>Cyprian of Carthage</td><td>ecumenicals</td><td>Algeria, North Africa</td></tr>
<tr><td>Cyril of Alexandria</td><td></td><td>Alexandria (Egypt)</td></tr>
<tr><td>David of Wales</td><td>doves</td><td>Wales</td></tr>
<tr><td>Dionysius the Areopagite</td><td></td><td>Zakynthos Island (Greece)</td></tr>
<tr><td>Edward the Confessor, King</td><td>kings, against bad marriages</td><td></td></tr>
<tr><td>Francis Borgia</td><td>against earthquakes</td><td>Portugal</td></tr>
<tr><td>Francis de Sales</td><td>writers, authors</td><td>Columbus (Ohio); Baker (Oregon), Diocese of Gilmington (Delaware)</td></tr>
<tr><td>Francis of Assisi</td><td>animal welfare organizations; environment</td><td>Assisi, Colorado (Italy); Santa Fe (New Mexico)</td></tr>
<tr><td>Francis Xavier Cabrini</td><td>immigrants, hospital administrators</td><td>Australia, Borneo, China, East Indies, India, Japan, New Zealand</td></tr>
<tr><td>George</td><td>soldiers, farms, farmers, farmhands, ranches, husbandry, equestrians, scouts</td><td>Aragon; Canada; Catalonia; England; Germany; Malta; Greece; Istanbul; Lithuania; Palestine; Portugal; Russia;</td></tr>
<tr><td>Gregory the Great</td><td>choirboys, gout-sufferers, stone masons, teachers</td><td>England, West Indies</td></tr>
<tr><td>Hedwig (Jadwiga)</td><td>brides, duchesses, victims of jealousy, widows; against bad marriages</td><td>Bavaria</td></tr>
</table>

# C. Christianity

C18. Selection of Saints.

| Saint | Patron of | Country/City of Patronage |
|---|---|---|
| James the Greater | veterinarians, equestrians, furriers, tanners, pharmacists, alchemists | Chile, Guatemala, Nicaragua, Spain |
| James the Lesser | pharmacists | Uruguay |
| Jerome | librarians, translators | Rome |
| Joan of Arc | soldiers | France; New Orleans (US) |
| John Bosco | apprentices, editors, printers, publishers | Turin (Italy) |
| John Chrysostom | lecturers, orators; against epilepsy | Istanbul (Turkey) |
| John the Almoner | Knights Hospitaller | Alexandria (Egypt) |
| John the Apostle | tanners | Asia Minor, Taos (New Mexico) |
| John the Baptist | farriers, bird dealers, Knights Hospitaller | Florence, Turin & Genoa (Italy), Quebec (Canada) |
| Julian the Hospitaller | shepherds | Western Europe |
| Luke the Apostle | doctors, surgeons, artists, bachelors | Hemersdorf (Germany) |
| Margaret of Scotland | death of children, learning, queens, widows, large families | Scotland |
| Mark the Evangelist | Attorneys, captives, barristers, prisoners; against impenitence, insect bites, lions | Venice (Italy), Egypt |
| Mary Magdalene | tanners, reformed prostitutes | Palestine |
| Matthew | bankers | Apostle |
| Methodius | ecumenicals | Bohemia, Bulgaria, Moravia, Czech Republic, Montenegro |
| Patrick | engineers | Ireland, Nigeria |
| Paul the Apostle | hospital workers, public relations | Malta, Poznan (Poland), Rome (Italy), Sao Paulo (Brazil) |
| Peter the Apostle | popes, fishermen, sailors, bakers, butchers, glass makers, carpenters, shoemakers, clockmakers, blacksmiths, potters, masons, cloth makers, penitents, virgins | Poznan (Poland), Rome (Italy) |
| Philip the Apostle | pastry chefs, hatters | Luxembourg, Uruguay |
| Simon the Apostle | tanners, curriers, sawyers | Egypt, Mesopotamia |
| Stephen of Hungary | bricklayers, kings, masons | Hungary |
| Teresa of Avila | against illness, loss of parents, headaches | Spain |
| Thomas a Beckett | | Portsmouth (England) |
| Thomas More | politicians, statesmen | Diocese of Arlington, Virginia; Pensacola, Florida (US) |
| Thomas the Apostle | architects, builders, blind people, stone masons | East Indies, India, Pakistan, Sri Lanka |
| Valentine | bee keepers, lovers, betrothed couples | |
| Vincent de Paul | hospitals and hospital workers | Madagascar |
| Walburga | Sailors; against cough, famine, plague, storms, dog bites | Antwerp (Belgium), Netherlands |
| Wenceslas, King | | Bohemia, Czech Republic, Moravia |

# D. Dr John Dee's Angels

*Liber Scientiae Auxilii et Victoriae Terrestris*

| D1. The 91 parts of the Earth. | D2. Planet – Agrippa. | D3. Zodiacal Sign – Agrippa. | D4. Names of the Parts of the Earth [with modern geographical location]. | D5. Names of the parts of the Earth drawn from Dee's reformed Angelic table. | D6. 30 Spheric Aethers of the good Princes of the Air. | D7. Tripartite number of good servants of each Order. | D8. Total Number of tripartite good servants in each Order. | D9. 12 Angel Kings ruling their 30 Orders, who rule also over 12 tribes. | D10. 12 Tribes of Israel at their dispersal. |
|---|---|---|---|---|---|---|---|---|---|
| I | | | II | III | V | VI | VII | VIII | IX |
| 1 | ☿ | ♊ | Aegyptus / Egypt | Occodon | 1 LIL | 7209 | 14931 | ZARZILG | Naphtali |
| 2 | ♂ | ♏ | Syria / South Syria | Pascomb | | 2360 | | ZINGGEN | Zebulun |
| 3 | ☿ | ♍ | Mesopotamia / North Iraq | Valgars | | 5362 | | ALPVDUS | Issachar |
| 4 | ♂ | ♏ | Cappadocia / Turkey | Doagnis | 2 ARN | 3636 | 15960 | ZARNAAH | Manasseh |
| 5 | ♃ | ♐ | Tuscia / Tuscany | Pacasna | | 2362 | | ZIRACAH | Reuben |
| 6 | ♀ | ♉ | Parva Asia / Asia Minor | Dialiva | | 8962 | | ZIRACAH | Reuben |
| 7 | ☿ | ♊ | Hyrcania / South East Iran | Samapha | 3 ZOM | 4400 | 17296 | ZARZILG | Naphtali |
| 8 | ♄ | ♑ | Thracia / Greece | Virooli | | 3660 | | ALPVDUS | Issachar |
| 9 | | | Gosmam / Artic Pole | Andispi | | 9236 | | LAVAVOTH | Gad |
| 10 | ♀ | ♎ | Thebaidi / Part of Egypt | Thotanp | 4 PAZ | 2360 | 11660 | LAVAVOTH | Gad |
| 11 | | | Parsadal / Persia | Axziarg | | 3000 | | LAVAVOTH | Gad |
| 12 | ♄ | ♑ | India / India | Pothnir | | 6300 | | ARFAOLG | Ephraim |
| 13 | ♀ | ♎ | Bactriane / Afghanistan | Lazdixi | 5 LIT | 8630 | 16738 | OLPAGED | Dan |
| 14 | ♂ | ♏ | Cilicia / Southern Turkey | Nocamal | | 2360 | | ALPVDUS | Issachar |
| 15 | ♄ | ♒ | Oxiana / N Afghanistan | Tiarpax | | 5802 | | ZINGGEN | Zebulun |
| 16 | ☾ | ♋ | Numidia / East Algeria | Saxtomp | 6 MAZ | 3620 | 20040 | GEBABAL | Asher |
| 17 | ♀ | ♉ | Cyprus / Cyprus | Vauaamp | | 9200 | | ARFAOLG | Ephraim |
| 18 | ♀ | ♉ | Parthia / Notrth East Iran | Zirzird | | 7220 | | GEBABAL | Asher |
| 19 | ♂ | ♏ | Getulia / West Sahara | Opmacas | 7 DEO | 6363 | 20389 | ZARNAAH | Manasseh |
| 20 | ♄ | ♒ | Arabia / Saudi Arabia | Genadol | | 7706 | | HONONOL | Judah |
| 21 | | | Phalagon / Greenland | Aspiaon | | 6320 | | ZINGGEN | Zebulun |
| 22 | ☿ | ♊ | Mantiana / North Iran | Zamfres | 8 ZID | 4362 | 13900 | GEBABAL | Asher |
| 23 | | | Soxia / Turkestan | Todnaon | | 7236 | | OLPAGED | Dan |
| 24 | ♂ | ♈ | Gallia / France | Pristac | | 2302 | | ZARZILG | Naphtali |

# D. Dr John Dee's Angels

| D1. The 91 parts of the Earth. | D2. Planet – Agrippa. | D3. Zodiacal Sign – Agrippa. | D4. Names of the Parts of the Earth [with modern geographical location]. | D5. Names of the parts of the Earth drawn from Dee's reformed Angelic table. | D6. 30 Spheric Aethers of the good Princes of the Air. | D7. Tripartite number of good servants of each Order. | D8. Total Number of tripartite good servants in each Order. | D9. 12 Angel Kings ruling their 30 Orders, who rule also over 12 tribes. | D10. 12 Tribes of Israel at their dispersal. |
|---|---|---|---|---|---|---|---|---|---|
| I | | | II | III | V | VI | VII | VIII | IX |
| 25 | ♄ | ♑ | Illyria<br>Balkans | Oddiorg | 9<br>ZIP | 9996 | 17846 | HONONOL | Judah |
| 26 | ♄ | ♒ | Sogdiana<br>Oxus River | Cralpir | | 3620 | | LAVAUOTH | Gad |
| 27 | ♃ | ♓ | Lydia<br>Coast of Turkey | Doanzin | | 4230 | | ZARZILG | Naphtali |
| 28 | ♀ | ♎ | Caspis<br>Caspian Sea | LEXARPH | 10<br>ZAX | 8880 | 11727 | ZINGGEN | Zebulun |
| 29 | ♂ | ♈ | Germania<br>Germany | COMANAN | | 1230 | | ALPVDUS | Issachar |
| 30 | | | Trenam<br>Ivory Coast | TABITOM | | 1617 | | ZARZILG | Naphtali |
| 31 | ☾ | ♋ | Bithynia<br>By Black Sea | Molpand | 11<br>ICH | 3472 | 15942 | LAVAUOTH | Gad |
| 32 | ☿ | ♍ | Graecia<br>Greece | Vsnarda | | 7236 | | ZVRCHOL | Simeon |
| 33 | ♃ | ♓ | Licia/Anatolia<br>South Turkey | Ponodol | | 5234 | | HONONOL | Judah |
| 34 | | | Onigap<br>China and Japan | Tapamal | 12<br>LOE | 2658 | 13821 | ZVRCHOL | Simeon |
| 35 | ♄ | ♑ | India Major<br>India | Gedoons | | 7772 | | CADAAMP | Benjamin |
| 36 | ☼ | ♌ | Orcheny<br>Tigris/Euphrates | Ambriol | | 3391 | | ZIRACAH | Reuben |
| 37 | ☿ | ♍ | Achaia<br>S. Greece | Gecaond | 13<br>ZIM | 8111 | 15684 | LAVAVOTH | Gad |
| 38 | ☿ | ♊ | Armenia<br>Armenia | Laparin | | 3360 | | OLPAGED | Dan |
| 39 | ♃ | ♓ | Cilicia (Nemrod)<br>Russia | Docepax | | 4213 | | ALPVDUS | Issachar |
| 40 | ♃ | ♓ | Paphlagonia<br>North of Turkey | Tedoond | 14<br>VTA | 2673 | 20139 | GEBABAL | Asher |
| 41 | | | Phasiana<br>East Turkey | Viuipos | | 9236 | | ALPVDUS | Issachar |
| 42 | ☼ | ♌ | Chaldei<br>Chaldea | Ooanamb | | 8230 | | ARFAOLG | Ephraim |
| 43 | | | Itergi<br>Mongolia | Tahando | 15<br>OXO | 1367 | 4620 | ZARZILG | Naphtali |
| 44 | ♄ | ♑ | Macedonia<br>North Greece | Nociabi | | 1367 | | LAVAVOTH | Gad |
| 45 | ♄ | ♒ | Garamantica<br>Phazania | Tastoxo | | 1886 | | ARFAOLG | Ephraim |
| 46 | ♄ | ♒ | Sauromatica<br>Poland/Russia | Cucarpt | 16<br>LEA | 9920 | 28390 | ZIRACAH | Reuben |
| 47 | ♄ | ♒ | Aethiopia<br>Ethiopia | Luacon | | 9230 | | HONONOL | Judah |
| 48 | | | Fiacim<br>North Pole | Sochial | | 9240 | | ARFAOLG | Ephraim |

# D. Dr John Dee's Angels

| D1. The 91 parts of the Earth. | D2. Planet – Agrippa. | D3. Zodiacal Sign – Agrippa. | D4. Names of the Parts of the Earth [with modern geographical location]. | D5. Names of the parts of the Earth drawn from Dee's reformed Angelic table. | D6. 30 Spheric Aethers of the good Princes of the Air. | D7. Tripartite number of good servants of each Order. | D8. Total Number of tripartite good servants in each Order. | D9. 12 Angel Kings ruling their 30 Orders, who rule also over 12 tribes. | D10. 12 Tribes of Israel at their dispersal. |
|---|---|---|---|---|---|---|---|---|---|
| **I** | | | **II** | **III** | **V** | **VI** | **VII** | **VIII** | **IX** |
| 49 | ☾ | ♋ | Colchica<br>Russian Georgia | Sigmorf | 17<br>TAN | 7623 | 27646 | ZIRACAH | Reuben |
| 50 | ☿ | ♊ | Cireniaca<br>East Libya | Aydropt | | 17389 | | OLPAGED | Dan |
| 51 | ♃ | ♓ | Nasamonia<br>N E Libyan coast | Tocarzi | | 2634 | | ZARZILG | Naphtali |
| 52 | ☾ | ♋ | Carthago<br>Tunisia | Nabaomi | 18<br>ZEN | 2346 | 19311 | GEBABAL | Asher |
| 53 | | | COXLANT<br>Eden | ZAFASAI | | 7689 | | ALPVDUS | Issachar |
| 54 | ♂ | ♏ | Idumea<br>Jordan | Yalpamb | | 9276 | | ARFAOLG | Ephraim |
| 55 | ♂ | ♈ | Parstavia/Bastarnia<br>E Romania | Torzoxi | 19<br>POP | 6236 | 15356 | ARFAOLG | Ephraim |
| 56 | ♃ | ♐ | Celtica<br>N W France | Abaiond | | 6732 | | CADAAMP | Benjamin |
| 57 | | | Vinsan<br>Kazakhstan | Omagrap | | 2388 | | ZINGGEN | Zebulun |
| 58 | | | Tolpam<br>Antarctica/Australia | Zildron | 20<br>CHR | 3626 | 14889 | GEBABAL | Asher |
| 59 | ☾ | ♋ | Carcedonia<br>Tunisia | Parziba | | 7629 | | HONONOL | Judah |
| 60 | ☼ | ♌ | Italia<br>Italy | Totocan | | 3634 | | ALPVDUS | Issachar |
| 61 | ♂ | ♈ | Brytania<br>British Isles | Chirspa | 21<br>ASP | 5536 | 16829 | ARFAOLG | Ephraim |
| 62 | ☼ | ♌ | Phenices<br>Phoenicia | Toantom | | 5635 | | CADAAMP | Benjamin |
| 63 | ♂ | ♏ | Comaginen<br>South Turkey | Vixpadg | | 5658 | | ZVRCHOL | Simeon |
| 64 | ☼ | ♌ | Apulia<br>South East Italy | Ozidaia | 22<br>LIN | 2232 | 6925 | ARFAOLG | Ephraim |
| 65 | ☿ | ♊ | Marmarica<br>North African coast | PARAOAN | | 2326 | | OLPAGED | Dan |
| 66 | ♂ | ♈ | Concava<br>North Syria | Calzidg | | 2367 | | ARFAOLG | Ephraim |
| 67 | | | Gebal/Byblos<br>Beirut | Ronoamb | 23<br>TOR | 7320 | 21915 | ZARNAAH | Manasseh |
| 68 | ☿ | ♍ | Elam<br>Iran | Onizimp | | 7262 | | LAVAVOTH | Gad |
| 69 | | | Idunia<br>Beyond Greenland | Zaxanin | | 7333 | | ZINGGEN | Zebulun |
| 70 | ♄/♀ | ♒/♉ | Media<br>North West Iran | Orcanir | 24<br>NIA | 8200 | 24796 | ZARNAAH | Manasseh |
| 71 | ♄ | ♑ | Ariana<br>Pakistan | Chialps | | 8360 | | LAVAVOTH | Gad |
| 72 | ☼ | ♌ | Chaldea<br>South Iraq | Soageel | | 8236 | | ZINGGEN | Zebulun |

# D. Dr John Dee's Angels

| D1. The 91 parts of the Earth. | D2. Planet – Agrippa. | D3. Zodiacal Sign – Agrippa. | D4. Names of the Parts of the Earth [with modern geographical location]. | D5. Names of the parts of the Earth drawn from Dee's reformed Angelic table. | D6. 30 Spheric Aethers of the good Princes of the Air. | D7. Tripartite number of good servants of each Order. | D8. Total Number of tripartite good servants in each Order. | D9. 12 Angel Kings ruling their 30 Orders, who rule also over 12 tribes. | D10. 12 Tribes of Israel at their dispersal. |
|---|---|---|---|---|---|---|---|---|---|
| I | | | II | III | V | VI | VII | VIII | IX |
| 73 | ♀ | ♎ | Serici populi Bosnia/Croatia | Mirzind | 25 VTI | 5632 | | ZARNAAH | Manasseh |
| 74 | ♀ | ♉ | Persia Iran | Obuaors | | 6333 | 18201 | ZIRACAH | Reuben |
| 75 | | | Gongatha Liberia | Ranglam | | 6236 | | ARFAOLG | Ephraim |
| 76 | | | Gorsim/Khorasim North Israel | Pophand | 26 DES | 9232 | | ARFAOLG | Ephraim |
| 77 | ♃ | ♐ | Hispania Spain & Portugal | Nigrana | | 3620 | 18489 | CADAAMP | Benjamin |
| 78 | ♃ | ♓ | Pamphilia South Turkey | Bazchim | | 5637 | | ARFAOLG | Ephraim |
| 79 | ♀ | ♎ | Oacidi Oasis West of Nile | Saziami | 27 ZAA | 7220 | | ZIRACAH | Reuben |
| 80 | ☿ | ♍ | Babylon Baghdad, Iraq | Mathula | | 7560 | 22043 | ZARNAAH | Manasseh |
| 81 | ♄/♀ | ♒/♉ | Median Sinai | Orpamb | | 7263 | | GEBABAL | Asher |
| 82 | ♂ | ♈ | Idumian Scythian Sea | Labnixp | 28 BAG | 2630 | | LAVAVOTH | Gad |
| 83 | ♃ | ♐ | Felix Arabia Yemen | Focisni | | 7236 | 18066 | ZARZILG | Naphtali |
| 84 | ♂ | ♏ | Metagonitidim Tangiers | Oxlopar | | 8200 | | ZVRCHOL | Simeon |
| 85 | ☿ | ♍ | Assyria Iraq | Vastrim | 29 RII | 9632 | | HONONOL | Judah |
| 86 | ☽ | ♋ | Affrica Africa | Odraxti | | 4236 | 21503 | ZARNAAH | Manasseh |
| 87 | ♀ | ♎ | Bactriani S of Oxus river | Gomziam | | 7635 | | ARFAOLG | Ephraim |
| 88 | | | Afran Africa North Zaire | Taoagla | 30 TEX | 4632 | | ARFAOLG | Ephraim |
| 89 | ☽ | ♋ | Phrygia Central Turkey | Gemnimb | | 9636 | | ZARNAAH | Manasseh |
| 90 | ☿ | ♍ | Creta Crete | Advorpt | | 7632 | 27532 | HONONOL | Judah |
| 91 | ♂ | ♏ | Mauritania Morocco | Dazinal | | 5632 | | ZVRCHOL | Simeon |

# D. Dr John Dee's Angels

| | | Teucer | Acts 2.7-11 | Paulus | Dorotheus | Manilius | Hephaistio Hipparchus & Egyptians (Odapsos) | Claudius Ptolemy |
|---|---|---|---|---|---|---|---|---|
| | | | | | | **D11. Zodiac Mapped on to the Geography of the Ancient World.** | | |
| ♈ | 15 | Persia | Parthians, Medes, Elamites | Persia | Babylon, Arabia | Hellespont, Propontis, Syria, Persia, Egypt | Babylonia, Thrace, Armenia, Persia, Cappadocia, Mesopotamia, Syria, Red Sea | Britian, Gaul, Germania, Bastarnia, Syria, Palestine, Idumaea, Judaea |
| ♉ | 16 | Babylonia | Mesopotamia | Babylonia | Media, Arabia, Egypt | Scythia, Asia, Arabia | Media, Scythia, Armenia, Cyprus | Parthia, Media, Persia, Cyclades, Cyprus, coast of Asia Minor |
| ♊ | 17 | Cappadocia | Judea, Cappadocia | Cappadocia | Cappadocia Perrhaebia, Phoenicia | Black Sea | Boeotia, Thrace, Galatia, Pontos, Cilicia, Phoenicia, India | Hyrcania, Armenia, Matiana, Cyrenaica, Marmarica, Lower Egypt |
| ♋ | 18 | Armenia | Pontus | Armenia | Thrace, Ethiopia | India, Ethiopia | Bactriana, Akarnania, Hellespont, Western Sea, Bretania, Thoule, Armenia, Cappodocia, Rhodes, Cos, Illium, Asia, Lydia | Numidia, Carthage, Africa, Bithynia, Phrygia, Colchica |
| ♌ | 19 | Asia | Asia | Asia Minor | Greece, Phrygia, Pontus | Phrygia, Bithynia, Cappadocia Armenia, Macedonia | Propontis, Hellas, Macedonia, Phrygia | Italy, Cisalpine Gaul, Sicily, Apulia, Phoenicia, Chaldea, Orchinia |
| ♍ | 20 | Greece, Ionia | Phrygia, Pamphylia, Egypt | Greece, Ionia | Rhodes, Cyclades, Peloponnese | Rhodes, Caria, Doris, Ionia, Arcadia | Ionia, Rhodes, Peloponnese, Arcadia, Cyrene, Doria, Sicily, Persia | Mesopotamia, Babylonia, Assyria, Hellas, Achaia, Crete |
| ♎ | 22 | Libya, Cyrene | part of Libya, Cyrene | Libya, Cyrene | Cyrene, Italy | Italy | Rome and surrounding, Arabia, Egypt, Ethiopia, Carthage, Libya, Cyrene, Sparta, Smyrna, Tyre, Thrace, Cilicia, Sinope | Bactriana, Casperia, Serica, Thebes, Oasis, Troglodytica |
| ♏ | 24 | Italy | Rome | Italy | Carthage, Libya, Sicily | Carthage, Libya, Cyrene, Sardinia, Mediterrean Isles | Italy, Iberia, Rome, Basternia | Metagonitis, Mauritania, Gaetulia, Syria, Commagene, Cappadocia |
| ♐ | 25 | Cilicia | Crete | Cilicia, Crete | Gaul, Crete | Crete, Sicily | Crete, Sicily, Cyprus, Red Sea, Tyrrhenia, Caspians, Euphrates, Mesopotamia, Carthage, Western Sea, Italy, Adria, Syria, Atlantic, Triballi, Bactriana, Sicily, Egypt | Tyrrhenia, Celtica, Spain, Arabia Felix |
| ♑ | 26 | Syria | Arabia | Syria | Cimmeria | Spain, Gaul, Germany | Aegean Sea, Corynth, Great Sea, Iberia, Cyllenia, Tyrrhenia, middle Egypt, Syria, Caria | India, Ariana, Gedrosia, Thrace, Macedonia, Illyria |
| ♒ | 28 | Egypt | – | Egypt | Egypt | Phoenicia, Cilicia, Lower Egypt | Syria, Euphrates, Tigris, Tanais | Sauromatica, Oxiana, Sogdiana, Arabia, Azania, Middle Ethiopia |
| ♓ | 29 | Red Sea, India | – | Red Sea, India | Red Sea | Chaldea, Mesopotamia, Parthia, Red Sea | Euphrates, Tigris, Syria, Red Sea, India, middle Persia, Arabian Sea, Borysthenes, Thrace, Asia, Sardo | Phazania, Nasamonitis, Garamantica, Lydia, Cilicia, Pamphylia |

# D. Dr John Dee's Angels

*De Heptarchia Mystica*

| | | King 1 | Prince 2 | 3 | 4 | Ministers 5 | 6 | 7 |
|---|---|---|---|---|---|---|---|---|
| | | | | | D12. John Dee's 49 *Bonorum Angelorum.* | | | |
| ☾ | 13 | 43–BLUMAZA | 44–BAGENOL[1] | Bablibo | Bulduma | Blingef | Barfort | Bamnode |
| ☿ | 12 | 29–BNASPOL | 30–BRORGES | Baspalo | Binodab | Bariges | Binofon | Baldago |
| ♀ | 14 | 1–BALIGON[2] | 2–BORNOGO | Bapnido | Besgeme | Blumapo | Bmamgal | Basledf |
| ☼ | 30 | 8–BOBOGEL | 9–BEFAFES | Basmelo | Bernole | Branglo | Brisfli | Bnagole |
| ♂ | 27 | 15–BABALEL | 16–BUTMONO[3] | Bazpama | Blintom | Bragiop | Bermale | Bonefon |
| ♃ | 21 | 17–BYNEPOR | 18–BLISDON | Balceor | Belmara | Benpagi | Barnafa | Bmilges |
| ♄ | 32 | 36–BNAPSEN | 37–BRALGES | Bormila | Buscnab | Bminpol | Bartiro | Bliigan |

| | | D13. Day of Week. | D14. The Heptarchical Kings (without their initial 'B'). | D15. The Heptarchical Princes (without their initial 'B'). |
|---|---|---|---|---|
| ☾ | 13 | Monday | 43 – Lumaza | 44 – Agenol |
| ☿ | 12 | Wednesday | 29 – Naspol | 30 – Rorges |
| ♀ | 14 | Friday | 1 – Aligon | 2 – Ornogo |
| ☼ | 30 | Sunday | 8 – Obogel | 9 – Efafes |
| ♂ | 27 | Tuesday | 15 – Abalel | 16 – Utmono |
| ♃ | 21 | Thursday | 17 – Ynepor | 18 – Lisdon |
| ♄ | 32 | Saturday | 36 – Napsen | 37 – Ralges |

[1] Or Hagonal.
[2] Aka Camara.
[3] Or Ulmono.

Figure 5: Dr John Dee's *Sigillum Dei Aemeth*

# D. Dr John Dee's Angels

*Sigillum Dei Aemeth*

| No. | D16. John Dee's *Sigillum Dei Aemeth*: Emeth *nuncupatem*.Dei.[1] | | | | | |
|---|---|---|---|---|---|---|
| | **Letters in Vertices of Pentagram** | **Names between Vertices of Pentagram** | **Letters inside Inner Heptagon** | **Letters in Inner [1st] Heptagon** | **Letters in Middle [2nd] Heptagon** | **In Vertices of Heptagram** |
| 1 | Z | EDEKI[EL$^2$] | Z | E[l] | S | El |
| 2 | M | ADIMI[EL] | A | An | Ab | Me |
| 3 | S | EMELI[EL] | B | Ave | Ath | Ese |
| 4 | N | OGAH[IEL] | A | Liba | Ized | Iana |
| 5 | C | ORABI[EL] | T | Rocle | Ekici | Akele |
| 6 | – | – | H | Hagonel$^3$ | Madimi | Azdobn |
| 7 | – | – | I$^{21}_8$ | Ilemese | Esemeli | Stimcul |

| No. | D16. John Dee's *Sigillum Dei Aemeth (continued)*[4] | | | | |
|---|---|---|---|---|---|
| | **In Main Heptagram** | **Seven Great Names of God inside the Heptagon** | **Letters in Outer [3rd] Heptagon** | **Letters inside Outer Circle** | **40 Letters in Outer Circle** |
| 1 | Heeoa | SAAI$^{21}_8$EME$^8$ | ZllRHia | + +OG + | $T^4G^9n^79'h^{22}n$ |
| 2 | Ih | BTZKASE$^{30}$ | aZCaacb | + H 14 + | $m^60^{22}a^{20}n^{14}a^6$ |
| 3 | Beigia | HEIDENE | paupnhr | + T 9 + | $ho^{18}p^{26}30'n8^p$ |
| 4 | Ilr | DEIMO$^{30}$A | hdmhiai | + XE 21 + | $G^7r^{13}12^Hog14^y11^t$ |
| 5 | Stimcul | I$_{26}$MEGCBE | kkaaeee | + +L 30 + | $8^O21^eb^{10}A^{11}I^{15}$ |
| 6 | Dmal | ILAOI$^{21}_8$VN | iieelll | + A 24 + | $a^816^rnA^610^OG^5$ |
| 7 | I | IHRLAA$^{21}_8$ | eellMG+ | + +G 5 + | $14^h17^Os\ 5^n24^A\omega^6$ |

---

[1] In a clockwise direction from the top in each case. The name around the central cross is Levanael.
[2] Probably should be *–el* but is actually *–ieil* in the manuscript.
[3] Here *-el* considered as one letter, hence the length of Hagonel is 6 letters.
[4] Superscript numbers below here are not footnotes, but occur in the original manuscript.

# D. Dr John Dee's Angels

*Clavicula Tabularum Enochi – Four Great Elemental Tables*

D17. *Clavicula Tabularum Enochi*[1].

| No[2] | | | | | | | | | | | | | | | | | | | | | | | | | No |
|---|---|---|---|---|---|---|---|---|---|---|---|---|---|---|---|---|---|---|---|---|---|---|---|---|---|
| 1 | r | Z | i | l | a | f | A | U | t | i | p | a | T | a | O | A | d | V | P | t | D | n | i | m | 24 |
| 25 | a | r | d | z | a | i | d | p | a | L | a | m | a | a | b | c | o | o | r | O | m | e | b | b | 48 |
| 49 | c | Z | o | n | s | a | r | O | Y | a | u | b | T | o | g | c | o | n | X | m | a | l | G | m | 72 |
| 73 | T | o | i | T | t | X | o | p | a | c | o | C | n | h | o | d | D | i | a | l | e | a | o | c | 96 |
| 97 | S | i | g | a | s | o | m | r | b | Z | n | h | P | a | c | A | x | i | o | V | S | P | S | yl[3] | 120 |
| 121 | f | m | o | n | d | a | T | d | i | a | r | i | S | a | a | i | x | a | a | r | v | r | o | i | 144 |
| 145 | o | r | o | i | b | A | h | a | o | z | p | i | m | p | h | a | r | s | l | g | a | I | O | l | 168 |
| 169 | C | n | a | b | r | V | i | x | g | a | z | d | m | a | m | g | l | o | i | n | L | i | r | x | 192 |
| 193 | O | i | i | i | t | T | p | a | l | O | a | i | o | l | a | a | D | a | g | a | T | a | P | a | 216 |
| 217 | A | b | a | m | o | o | o | a | c | v | c | a | p | a | L | c | o | i | d | X | P | a | c | n | 240 |
| 241 | N | a | o | c | o | T | t | n | p | r | a | T | n | d | a | z | n | X | i | V | a | a | s | a | 264 |
| 265 | O | c | a | n | m | a | g | o | t | r | o | i | l | i | d | p | o | n | s | d | a | S | P | i | 288 |
| 289 | S | h | i | a | l | r | a | P | m | z | o | X | X | r | i | i | h | t | a | r | n | d | I | L* | 312 |
| 313 | b | o | a | Z | a | R | o | P | h | a | R | a | d | o | n | p | a | T | d | a | n | V | a | a | 336 |
| 337 | V | N | n | a | x | o | P | S | o | n | d | n | O | l | o | a | G | e | o | o | b | a | v | i | 360 |
| 361 | a | i | g | r | a | n | o | o | m | a | g | g | o | p | a | m | n | o | O | G | m | d | n | m | 384 |
| 385 | o | r | P | m | n | i | n | g | b | e | a | l | a | p | l | s | T | e | d | e | c | a | o | p | 408 |
| 409 | r | s | O | n | i | Z | i | r | l | e | m | u | s | c | m | i | o | o | n | A | m | l | o | X | 432 |
| 433 | i | Z | i | n | r | c | Z | i | a | M | h | l | v | a | r | s | G | d | L | b | r | i | a | P | 456 |
| 457 | m | o | r | d | i | a | l | h | C | t | G | a | o | i | p | t | e | a | a | P | d | o | C | e | 480 |
| 481 | Æ | o | c | a | n | c | h | i | a | s | o | m | P | s | v | a | c | n | r | Z | i | r | Z | a | 504 |
| 505 | A | r | b | i | Z | m | i | i | l | p | i | Z | S | i | o | d | a | o | i | n | r | z | f | m | 528 |
| 529 | O | p | a | n | a | l | a | m | s | m | a | L | d | a | l | t | T | d | n | a | d | i | r | e | 552 |
| 553 | d | O | l | o | P | i | n | i | a | n | b | a | d | i | x | o | m | o | n | s | i | o | S | P | 576 |
| 577 | r | x | p | a | O | c | s | i | Z | i | X | P | O | o | D | P | Z | i | a | P | a | n | l | i | 600 |
| 601 | a | x | t | i | r | V | a | s | t | r | i | m | r | g | o | a | n | n | Q[4] | A* | C | r | a | r | 624 |

---

[1] As reformed by the Angel Raphael, the final version delivered April 20, 1587. * = letter reversed left right.
[2] Sequence number of the 624 letters in the Table.
[3] Or 'N' reversed left right.
[4] Or a reversed letter 'P'.

# D. Dr John Dee's Angels

| | | D18. The Tablet of Union. | | | | | | |
|---|---|---|---|---|---|---|---|---|
| | | **Quadrangle bound** | | | | | | |
| ⊛ | 31b | | | | | | | |
| F | 31 | South | b | i | t | o | m | |
| A | 11 | East | e | x | a | r | p | |
| W | 23 | West | h | c | o | m | a | |
| E | 32b | North | n | a | n | t | a | |

| | | D19. Watchtowers – Direction and Quadrant. | | | | D20. Watchtower Colour (Dee). | D21. Watchtower Colour (Golden Dawn). |
|---|---|---|---|---|---|---|---|
| | | **Direction** | **Angel** | **Original** | **Reformed**[1] | | |
| ⊛ | 31b | | | | | | |
| F | 31 | South | Michael | Lower Left | Lower Right | White | Red |
| A | 11 | East | Raphael | Upper Left | Upper Left | Red | Yellow |
| W | 23 | West | Gabriel | Lower Right | Upper Right | Green | Green/Blue |
| E | 32b | North | Auriel | Upper Right | Lower Left | Black | Black |

| | | D22. The Kings and Seniors of the *Tabularum Enochi*. | | | |
|---|---|---|---|---|---|
| | | **Table Quarter** | **Great Names of God**[2] | **King/Name of God** | **24 Angelic Seniors** |
| ⊛ | 31b | | | | |
| F | 31 | South | Oip Teaa Pdoce (Oip Teaa Pedoce) | Edlprnaa | Aetpio, Adoeoet, Alendood, Aapedoce, Arinnaq, Anodoin |
| A | 11 | East | Oro Ibah Aozpi (Oro Ibah Aozodpi) | Bataivah | Habioro, Aaoxaif, Hetermorda, Ahaozpi, Hipotga, Autotar |
| W | 23 | West | Mph Arsl Gaiol (Empeh Arsel Gaiol) | Raagiosl | Lefarahpem, Saiinou, Laoaxarp, Selgaiol, Ligdisa, Soaixente |
| E | 32b | North | Mor Dial Hctga (Emor Dial Hectega) | Iczhhcal | Laidrom, Aczinor, Elzinopo, Alhectega, Elhiansa, Acemliceve |

[1] As reformed by the Angel Raphael, the final version delivered to Dee April 20, 1587. Directions as used by the GD.
[2] Or three Ensign Bearers. Spelled out in full in brackets.

# D. Dr John Dee's Angels

| | | Lesser Angle | Name of God[1] | Invocatory Divine Names[2] | Anagram Angels of Lesser Angle[3] | 4 Angels of the Lesser Angle[4] |
|---|---|---|---|---|---|---|
| | | | | D23. Angels of the *Tabularum Enochi*. | | |
| ✳ | 31b | *East – AIR:* | | | | |
| F | 31 | E4 | Xgzd | Aovararzod, Moar, Alai | Exgezod, Gezodex, Zodexge, Dexgezod | Acca, Enpeat, Otoi, Pemox |
| A | 11 | E1 | Rzla | Idoigo, Ardza | Vrzla, Zlar (or Zodelar), Larzod, Arzel | Cezodenes, Totet, Sias, Efermende |
| W | 23 | E2 | Utpa | Ilacza (or Haeza), Palam | Vtepa, Tepau, Paute, Autep | Oyube, Paoc, Vrbeneh, Diri |
| E | 32b | E3 | Cnbr | Aiaoai, Oiit | Cenbar, Enbarc, Barcen, Vrcenbre | Abemo, Naco, Ocenem, Shael |
| ✳ | 31b | *West – WATER:* | | | | |
| F | 31 | W4 | Nlrx | Jaaasde, Atapa | Enlarex, Larexen, Rexenel, Xenelar | Expeceh, Vasa, Dapi, Reniel |
| A | 11 | W1 | Taad | Obegoca, Aabeco | Taad, Aadet, Adeta, Detaa | Paax, Toco, Enheded, Saix |
| W | 23 | W2 | Tdim | Nelapar, Omebeb | Tedim, Dimet, Imted, Emtedi | Magem, Leoc, Vsyl, Vrvoi |
| E | 32b | W3 | Magl | Maladi, Olaad | Magel, Agelem, Gelema, Lemage | Paco, Endezen, Fipo, Exarih |
| ✳ | 31b | *North – EARTH:* | | | | |
| F | 31 | N4 | Iaom | Espemenir, Hpizol | Iaom, Aomi, Omia, Miao | Mesael, Jaba, Jezexpe, Estim |
| A | 11 | N1 | Boza | Angepoi, Vnenax | Boza, Ozab, Zabo, Aboz | Aira, Ormen, Reseni, Jzodenar |
| W | 23 | N2 | Phra | Anacem, Sonden | Phra, Harap, Rapeh, Aphar | Omgege, Gebal, Relemu, Jahel |
| E | 32b | N3 | Æoan | Cebalpet, Arbizod | Æoan, Oanæ, Anæo, Næoa | Opena, Dopa, Rexao, Axir |
| ✳ | 31b | *South – FIRE:* | | | | |
| F | 31 | S4 | Ziza | Arzodionar, Narzefem | Ziza, Jzazod, Zazi, Azizod | Adre, Sispe, Pali, Acar |
| A | 11 | S1 | Dopa | Noalmar, Oloag | Dopa, Opad, Pado, Adop | Opemen, Apeste, Scio, Vasge |
| W | 23 | S2 | Anaa | Vadali, Obavi | Anaa, Naaa, Aaan, Aana | Gemenem, Ecope, Amox, Berape |
| E | 32b | S3 | Psac | Volexdo, Sioda | Pesac, Sacepe, Acepes, Cepesa | Datete, Diom, Oopezod, Vrgan |

---

[1] Or Kerubic God Names direct from the Tabularum Enochi without spelling expansion.
[2] Servient God Names spelled out in full.
[3] Or Kerubic Angels, spelled out in full.
[4] Servient Angels spelled out in full.

# E. Emblems and Alchemy

## Golden Dawn and Chemistry

| | E1. Alchemical Elements on the Tree of Life – 1. | E2. Alchemical Elements on the Tree of Life – 2. | E3. Chemical Elements (Golden Dawn). | E4. Chemical Symbol and Latin Names of Planetary Metals. | E4a. Periodic Table for Planetary Metals: Number, Row & Column. | | |
|---|---|---|---|---|---|---|---|
| | **112** | **113** | | | **Num** | **row** | **col** |
| **1** | ☿ – Mercury | Metallic Radix | Hydrogen | | | | |
| **2** | ♃ – Salt | ♄ – Lead | Oxygen | | | | |
| **3** | ⊖ – Sulphur | ♂ – Iron | Nitrogen | ♄ Pb – Plumbum | 82 | 6 | 14 |
| **4** | ☽ – Silver | ☽ – Silver | Fluorine | ♃ Sn – Stannum | 50 | 5 | 14 |
| **5** | ☉ – Gold | ☉ – Gold | Chlorine | ♂ Fe – Ferrum | 26 | 4 | 8 |
| **6** | ♂ – Iron | ♂ – Iron | Carbon | ☉ Au – Aurum | 79 | 6 | 11 |
| **7** | ♃ – Tin | ♅ – Brass | Bromine | ♀ Cu – Cuprum | 29 | 4 | 11 |
| **8** | ♀ – Copper | ♅ – Brass (hermaphroditic) | Iodine | ☿ Hg – Hydrargyrum Argentum Vivum | 80 | 6 | 12 |
| **9** | ♄ – Lead | ☿ – Mercury | Phosphorus | ☽ Ag – Argentum | 47 | 5 | 11 |
| **10** | ☿ – Mercurius Philosophorum | Medicina Metallorum | Sulphur | Sb – Stibium (Antimony) | 51 | 5 | 15 |

## Ripley and Lapidus

| | | E5. Alchemical Processes – Lapidus. | E6. Ripley - *Twelve Gates.* | |
|---|---|---|---|---|
| | | | **Process** | **Description** |
| ♈ | 15 | Calcination | Calcination | The conversion of a raw substance, through the use of intense heat. When a substance is heated to just below its melting point, all moisture is lost, its carbonates decompose, leaving behind a calx or ash. |
| ♉ | 16 | Congelation | Dissolution | The process of melting or dissolving with chemical solvents, making the operation of their future separation possible. |
| ♊ | 17 | Fixation | Separation | Separation of substances which are re-crystallized independently, separating the pure essence of the elements from their impure matter. |
| ♋ | 18 | Dissolution | Conjunction | Reuniting of fundamental substances, which may previously have been separated. |
| ♌ | 19 | Digestion | Putrefaction | The purification of substances through a moist disintegration. Organic matter is used to artificially induce oxidization, creating a spontaneous decomposition and corruption. |
| ♍ | 20 | Distillation | Congealation/ Coagulation | The process of binding or crystallizing substances from a fluid to a solid. Whether the substance is heated to evaporate excess moisture, or cooled after been dissolved by heat, it is reduced again into a homogeneous body. |
| ♎ | 22 | Sublimation | Cibation | The material within a sealed crucible is strengthened by saturating it with fresh nourishment. This is provided by the transformative tincture of the substance itself, condensed from the vapour circulating within the vessel. |
| ♏ | 24 | Separation | Sublimation | The process of vaporization by the gradual application of extreme heat, followed by dry precipitation. Transformation from a solid to gaseous state is made more precious by avoiding any loss of potency by earthly contact. |
| ♐ | 25 | Incineration/ Ceration | Fermentation | Organic substances converted into new compounds by the presence of a ferment. |
| ♑ | 26 | Fermentation | Exaltation | The process of heating a substance to concentrate its strength. This transmutation of the substance creates maturity. |
| ♒ | 28 | Multiplication | Multiplication/ Augmentation | The amplification of a substance through internal multiplication. This white or red tincture is also known as the Philosophers Stone. |
| ♓ | 29 | Projection | Projection | The tincture is introduced into molten base metals, causing the transmutation of their elements into gold or silver. |

# E. Emblems and Alchemy

*Emblems*

| Emb-lem | E7. *Splendor Solis* Emblems. | E8. *Splendor Solis* – Images in the Surrounding Frame. |
|---|---|---|
| | | |
| 1 | The Arms of the Art. A coat of arms being a Sun and blue ornate heraldic foliage, surmounted by a crowned helmet with three crescent moons. Above the shield another Sun shines down from a red hanging. Scroll: *Arma Artis.* | Two monkeys, herons, owl, plants |
| 2 | The Philosopher. A bearded philosopher stands wearing red and purple, pointing to a flask half full of golden liquid which he holds in his right hand – probably the finished elixir. Scroll: *Eamus Quesitum Quosuor Elementorum Naturas* | Deer, peacock, owl, birds, fly |
| 3 | Knight of the Double Fountain. A crowned knight in full gold-trimmed armour brandishing a sword in his right hand and holding a golden shield in his left, on which is inscribed *Ex duabus aquis una[m] facite. Qui quaeritis Solis…nafacem…date bibere inimico… Et videbitis cum mortuum. Dein[um?] de aquater era[t] facte Et lapide muleiblicositis.* He stands one foot upon each side of an ornate double fountain, which overflows. His buckler is coloured in sequence black, white, yellow, red, black. 7 stars encircle his head. | Peacock, birds, flowers |
| 4 | Lunar Queen and Solar King. The Queen (with scroll inscribed *Lac viramium*) in white standing on a ball with a face. Above her is a Moon. She faces a King with scroll (*Minsimetium? Coagula*), sceptre and wearing red and ermine robes. He stands under a Sun, and in a fire. A scroll above is inscribed: *Particularia*, and below *Via Universalis particularibus. Inclusis.* | Plants and birds. Below a frieze showing scenes of armies, a king visiting a philosopher in a barrel (Diogenes?). |
| 5 | Digging the Ore. Two miners dig into a small hill with pick-axes. In a lake nearby floats a crescent Moon. | A different framing like a gilt mirror. Below a king and queen in a court scene. |
| 6 | The Tree. Two philosophers talk under a tree which has a number of black and white birds flying from it. The largest pecks at the crown of the tree. A man is climbing a ladder propped against the tree which grows from a golden crown around its trunk. The philosophers are dressed in red & white. | Four naked woman bathe at a golden fountain attended by two attendants |
| 7 | The Dying (drowning) King. A Queen in yellow robes and ermine, with sceptre and orb, stands beside a lake. A white bird perches on the orb. Behind him is the sun, and above her is a golden star. In a lake a king in yellow is seen to be drowning or possibly wading. | Below are two mythological scenes, with man with club (Hercules?) |
| 8 | The Angel and the dark Man. A crowned and white winged angel with a six-pointed star shining above her head. She holds out a red cloak to a dark naked man who is emerging from a swamp. One arm is red, the other white. His head is like a black crystal ball. | Two deer, two monkeys, plants, flowers |
| 9 | The Hermaphrodite. A winged hermaphrodite in a black formal jacket holding an egg is its left hand, and a mirror in its right. Its right wing is red, its left is white. | Birds and plants |
| 10 | Dismembering the Body. A bearded man in armour with a sword has dismembered another man's naked body on the ground before him. The head is nowhere to be seen, instead he holds a solar mask in his left hand. In the background is an open sided Renaissance building. Probably set in Venice. | Two Classical vignettes |
| 11 | 'Cooked Philosopher.' A naked bearded man with a white bird perched on his head, is being cooked in water heated by a fire which is tended by an assistant with bellows, in an ornate Renaissance courtyard. A small flask is nearby. | Plants, birds and a bee |

| Emb-lem | | E7. *Splendor Solis* Emblems. | E8. *Splendor Solis* – Images in the Surrounding Frame. |
|---|---|---|---|
| ♄ | 12 | **Saturn**. A crowned flask with open top is heated upon flames, containing a naked child who pours liquid down the throat, and uses a pair of bellows on a winged dragon. | Chariot of Saturn drawn by two winged griffons/dragons. Wheels = Capricorn & Aquarius. Saturnian occupations: beggar, merchant, man drawing water, parchment preparation, pig castration, ploughing and a hanging. |
| ♃ | 13 | **Jupiter**. A crowned flask with sealed top supported upon a green wreath. Within this three birds (red, white and black) who are fighting or are following each other in cyclic succession. | Chariot of Jupiter (with thunderbolts) drawn by 2 peacocks. Wheels = Sagittarius & Pisces. Jupiterian occupations: king being crowned by the Pope, banker's treasure chests. |
| ♂ | 14 | **Mars**. A crowned flask with sealed top supported upon a red wreath. Within it is a crowned three headed bird, with wings outspread. | Chariot of Mars (with armour) drawn by two foxes/wolves. Wheels = Aries & Scorpio (hidden). Martial occupations: soldiers, burning house, battle, the slain. |
| ☼ | 15 | **Sol**. Within a crowned flask now sealed and not heated is a three headed green winged dragon. Its heads are white, red and black. | Chariot of the Sun (with crown) drawn by two horses. Wheels = Leo. Solar occupations: dueling, disputing, wrestling |
| ♀ | 16 | **Venus**. Within a crowned flask now sealed and not heated, a peacock displays its tail. | Chariot of Venus (with Eros and a golden arrow transfixed heart) drawn by two doves/birds. Wheels = Taurus & Libra. Venusian occupations: lovers, drinking and eating, playing music, reading, dancing |
| ☿ | 17 | **Mercury**. Within a crowned flask now with open top, a white crowned bare-breasted Queen stands holding an orb and sceptre within a golden egg shaped glow. | Chariot of Mercury (with caduceus wand and sickle!) drawn by two cocks. Wheels = Virgo & Gemini. Mercurial occupations: masons, geographers, scholars, musicians |
| ☾ | 18 | **Luna**. Within a crowned flask now again with sealed top, a King stands on an upturned lunar crescent, with an orb and sceptre in hand, bathed in a golden glow. | Chariot of the Moon (holding a Luna crescent) drawn by two girls. Wheels = Cancer. Lunar occupations: traveling, hawking, shooting, fishing |
| | 19 | In a bleak wintry landscape with dead trees, a dark Sun sets half behind a hill. See Emblem 22. | Butterflies, caterpillars, snails, birds, frog, dragonfly |
| | 20 | An indoor scene with 7 naked and 3 dressed children at play with a hobby horse and cushion, watched by two adults. Large middle European ceramic stove at the back. | Birds, plants, butterflies, dragonfly, strawberries, snail |
| | 21 | A village scene with a number of women doing the clothes washing by a stream, sheets hung up, and laid out to dry on the grass. Maybe the sheets are designed to absorb the dew. | Birds, flowers |
| | 22 | A tired but radiant Sun setting above the horizon in the countryside. It is winter. City in background. See Emblem 19. | Birds and flowers |

# E. Emblems and Alchemy

| Emb-lem | E9. *Book of Lambspring* Emblems. |
|---|---|
| 0 | *Title Page*. A coat of arms displaying a lamb surmounted by a helmet, surrounded by plumes and surmounted by a second lamb. The reference is to the author's name, Lambsprinck.<br>*Frontispiece*. A wand carrying Philosopher stands beside a flag surmounted furnace. He wears the image of a black double headed eagle (of Austria or of Mercurial volatility) with a cock at its centre. He has an eagle handled sword and stands beside a triple alchemic furnace. |
| 1 | The arduous voyage of alchemy. Two fishes lie dead on the surface of a lake facing in opposite directions. A boat draws near. |
| 2 | The slaying of the dragon or the dissolution of the *prima material*. An armed man with raised sword and shield faces a two legged winged dragon, with a river in the background. |
| 3 | A unicorn (Sulphur) meets with a stag (Mercury) in a forest with a lake in the background. |
| 4 | A lion (Philosophic Sulphur) and a lioness (Philosophic Mercury) in a forest clearing. Their union produces the Philosopher's Stone. |
| 5 | A wolf and a dog fighting on a river bank, with bridge and city in the background. |
| 6 | A winged ouroboros biting its own tail in a forest glade. |
| 7 | The Fixation of the Volatile. A bird (the Volatile) sits upon a nest high in a tree, while another bird flys by. At the foot of the tree is a snail (the Fixed). |
| 8 | The Whiteness (*Albedo*) is overcome by the Redness (Spirit). Two large birds fighting, one upside down, in a forest with a river in the background. |
| 9 | A crowned king with an orb and sceptre is seated upon a dolphin-armed throne mounted on a stone canopied pediment, reached by 7 steps (the seven operations of alchemy). His feet rest upon the dragon from Emblem 2. In the background is a river and town. |
| 10 | A bare-chested man with a loincloth uses a trident to control a Salamander in a blazing open fire fed from between two rocks, in a country landscape. The salamander has a line of stars along its spine. |
| 11 | In front of a castle beside a river, stands a crowned Prince in armour bearing a sword, a venerable bearded King with sceptre, and a winged bearded Angel or adept wearing the Phrygian cap of Mithra. All three hold hands. Mountains behind. |
| 12 | The Angel wearing the Phrygian cap (left) and the young Prince in armour (right) stand upon an unnaturally high mountain, with a radiant Sun on the left and the Moon and stars on the right. They overlook the landscape. |
| 13 | In the arcade of a palace the venerable bearded King sits upon a canopied throne. He holds the young prince affectionately but with wide open mouth as if to absorb him. The winged, bearded and crowned Angel gestures towards the other two. |
| 14 | The venerable bearded King lies ill, feverish and sweating in his bed in a bare and empty chamber. Outside a heavy rain falls. |
| 15 | The three principles, the Prince, the King and the Angel are united. In front of a cloth backdrop the winged, bearded and crowned Angel sits. On his right is the young Prince in armour holding a sceptre. On his left, the venerable bearded King holds an orb in his right and a sceptre in his left hand. |

# E. Emblems and Alchemy

| Key | E10. *The Twelve Keys* of Basil Valentinus Emblems. |
|---|---|
| 1 | A robed King with sceptre talks with a Queen holding a rose with 3 flowers and a peacock feather. In front of the King a fox jumps over a crucible placed on a fire. In front of the Queen, the figure of Death, an old man with a scythe and crippled leg, straddles a fire with a crucible. |
| 2 | A winged Mercury with winged feet stands holding a caduceus in each hand is attacked by two men. To his right is a man with a sword wrapped in a serpent, and to his left a man with a sword, with a bird perched upon its point. Either side of Mercury is a Sun and a Moon at the level of his thighs. In front of Mercury is a large pair of detached wings. |
| 3 | A winged dragon with curled tail and pointed tongue faces left, with rugged mountains and a castle in the background. Behind a fox runs off with a hen in its mouth. A cockerel attacks it. |
| 4 | Death. A skeleton stands on a draped coffin with pall-bearers' staves in a churchyard. On the left a candle burns, while on the right is a dying tree. |
| 5 | A crowned woman with a heart and seven-blossomed rose stands by a furnace. She is connected with flask on the furnace. Beside the woman stands an alchemist with flaming head and mouth, and bellows. A blindfold cupid fires an arrow at the woman. On the left is a regal lion with a crown above his head, and a S-shaped tail. A radiant Sun shines above the lion. |
| 6 | Chemical Wedding. A bishop performs the wedding service of a King and Queen under a dark rain cloud, above which a rainbow forms. On the left is the Sun, on the right the Moon. In front of the King a fire heats a distillation flask, behind which is a goose. In front of the Queen, an alchemist holding a trident tends a furnace, pouring water into a water bath holding an alembic which distils into a flask below. |
| 7 | Justice, a woman holding scales and a sword, stands behind a large circle above which is written '*Sigilum Hermalis*'. In front is a circular talisman with '*Chaos*' around it. Inside the circle is a square with the four seasons written one on each side, and '*Sal Philosophorum*' at the bottom. Inside that is a triangle labeled 'AQUA'. |
| 8 | Resurrection. In a circular graveyard with 12 arches, two men with crossbows fire at a target with a key above it. Seven arrows are imbedded in the target. Between the men is an open grave out of which a corpse is rising. Corn is sprouting from the grave, also symbolic of resurrection. Another corpse lies on the ploughed field which is being sown with grain, some is being eaten by four birds. The Angel of Resurrection holding a sceptre of dominion sounds her trumpet. |
| 9 | At bottom in a circle are three hearts with three serpents emerging in a clockwise direction. At the top are a man and woman with their bodies forming a cross joining 4 birds. To the South is a Peacock, to the West is a Swan, to the North is a crow, and to the East is a black Eagle. |
| 10 | A downward pointing triangle surrounded by the words "I am born out of Hermogenes. Hyperion elected me. Without Iamsuph I perish" in Latin. Inside the vertices is the Sun on the left with BLKShGO, the Moon on the right with DDHD or DDChD, and Mercury at the bottom with KRRK or KDDK, all in Hebrew. Within the triangle is a double circle with TOBCh in Hebrew. |
| 11 | Two lions attack each other. On the back of each rides a woman holding a heart from which springs a Sun and a Moon. Behind the left woman stands a knight with sword raised to strike her. Behind the right lion are four cubs. |
| 12 | Inside a laboratory an alchemist stands in front of a barrel furnace. Outside the window are the Sun and the Moon. The alchemist points to a triangular crucible on a bench with two roses growing out of it, and the symbol of Mercury above. On the right a lion devours a snake. |

# E. Emblems and Alchemy

| Emb-lem | E11. *Atlanta Fugiens* Emblems. |
|---|---|
| 1 | The famous sentence from the Emerald Tablet of Hermes: 'The Wind has carried him in its belly'. A man pregnant with child stands on a rock, his hands and head emitting wind. |
| 2 | The Earth is his Nurse. A woman with the globe of the Earth as her body, nourishing a child at her breast. She points to the earth, where a goat suckles a child, and a wolf suckles two children. |
| 3 | Do as the Woman Washing Clothes. A woman prepares to wash clothes, and pours water into a large wooden copper full of boiling water. From a tap at the bottom hot water is drawn off into a small bucket. |
| 4 | Join the Brother & the Sister in Love. A man with a cloak embraces a woman. Another man offers them a chalice or vase. A countryside scene. |
| 5 | In a town square, man approaches a woman to suckle a toad at her breast. |
| 6 | A man in the countryside is sowing seed into newly opened furrows. |
| 7 | On the summit of a strange mountain above a town one bird sits upon a nest as another leaves. |
| 8 | In a tessellated courtyard in front of a fire, a man in armour holds a sword with which he is about to cleave an egg balanced upon a low table. |
| 9 | In a round blue pavilion in a garden, a bearded old man sits eating fruit from a tree which grows within this pavilion. |
| 10 | An man in a tunic tends a fire, holding a burning log in his left hand. Two figures with winged helmets and sandals (Mercury) sit and stand nearby. Both hold a caduceus. |
| 11 | A woman sits beside a lake while two children play around her lap, one has a sun head, the other a moon crescent head. One man stands either side, sprinkling water upon her, and tearing pages from a book. |
| 12 | Saturn flies over a mountain holding a scythe in his right hand. He drops a large rock onto the mountain. In the foreground is a small chapel. |
| 13 | A naked man sits on the bank of a river, with a city in the background. |
| 14 | Among the ruins of a building a winged serpent dragon seizes its own tail to form the ouroborus. |
| 15 | A potter in his workshop is making a pot on his wheel. |
| 16 | Among the ruins of a building a winged lion (or perhaps lioness) is attacked by a lion without wings, which springs upon and claws at the first lion. |
| 17 | Four spheres filled with fire rise in a chain above a lake or river, upon which are small boats. |
| 18 | An artisan works at a furnace, a large bellows in the background. The artisan places a rod into the flames. On a block in front of him is a bowl with coins. Through an open doorway a Church is seen. |
| 19 | A man with a rough club stands on the right facing the onslaught of four naked men each attacking him with one of the four elements – fire, air water and earth – which emerge from their hands. |
| 20 | A knight in armour with shield and sword is urged to enter a flaming fire by a naked woman. |
| 21 | A philosopher or geometrician stands in front of a wall upon which he is drawing a circle with a large pair of compasses. He is constructing a square within a triangle. Within this central circle are a naked couple. On the ground in front of him are a protractor, a set square and a tablet with geometrical diagrams. |
| 22 | A woman stand in a kitchen in front of a large open fire on which pots are set. On the ground in front of her are three triangular rods and two rectangular blocks. On the right behind her is a wooden basin in which two fish swim in opposite directions (Pisces?). |
| 23 | An artisan stands at a furnace, with an anvil, tongs and hammers, holding an axe with which he has just struck open the head of an old bearded man (Zeus figure) who has fire in his hands, and an eagle at his back. Out of the cut in the skull a small naked woman emerges (Athena). Behind her a statue of a man with bow and arrows, while under a canopy a man with a Sun head embraces a woman while Cupid stands by. |
| 24 | A king with a crown lies on his back on the ground and is attacked by a wolf. In the background a king stands beside a fire within which a wolf is burning. |
| 25 | On the left a man with a Sun head, and on the right a woman with a Moon head, raise clubs and attack a winged serpent dragon. On the seashore, the man with the solar head shoots a winged dragon with bow and arrow, while the woman with the Moon head shoots at a man swimming in the sea. |
| 26 | A crowned queen stands in a landscape beside a tree and holds out two banners for us to see. That on the left has "*Longitudo dierum et sanitas*", and that on the right has "*Gloria ac divitiae infinitae*" |
| 27 | A man without feet stands outside the door of a walled formal garden. The door has three locks. On a small mound we see nine figures possibly Apollo, Pan and the seven planetary gods. |

# E. Emblems and Alchemy

| Emb-lem | E11. *Atlanta Fugiens* Emblems. |
|---|---|
| | |
| 28 | A crowned king lies in a wooden box with an oil lamp set over a steaming vessel of water. |
| 29 | A salamander with a line of stars along its back lies in a flaming fire. |
| 30 | A Sun headed man on the left and a Moon headed woman on the right, stand on the shore of a sea or lake. The woman gestures to a cock and a hen which are at their feet. |
| 31 | A crowned King swims far out from the land, on a wide lake or sea. |
| 32 | On the bank of a river crossed by a small bridge, a man stands with a pole and fishes out a piece of coral. Above in the sky on the left a wind blows. |
| 33 | At night under a crescent moon, a naked hermaphrodite, male on the right side and female on the left, lies in a ravine beneath crags and rocks, on a plate being heated over a fierce fire. |
| 34 | In a cave in the bank of a river, a naked man with a Sun head and a naked woman with a Moon head, stand up to their hips in water and embrace each other. On the left a naked woman crawls out of the river onto the bank. In the clouds above the man with the Sun head is raised to the heavens. |
| 35 | On the left a woman sits beside a corn field nursing her child. On the right a woman drags a naked man to a fire beneath a large rock or cliff, his armour and weapons lies at her feet. An old man stands on the right side of the rock, looking on the fire. To the left of the rock the woman turns and runs to the left. |
| 36 | A road winds through a valley along the bank of a river. Cubic stones lie in the mud of the road below, on the summit of a hill, in the water of the river, and in the air of the heavens above. Various people walking along the road or in boats on the river fail to see the stones, which might symbolize the *prima materia*. |
| 37 | A lion with a laurel wreath stands on the ground. Behind him on the right is a steaming swamp, while behind him on the left is a volcano with flames of fire and smoke. |
| 38 | A hermaphrodite, male on the right side, female on the left, stands with one foot on each side of a steep valley. Beneath this, Mercury or Hermes with winged helmet and sandals, lies embracing Venus or Aphrodite. At his feet is his caduceus, while to the right of Venus, a cherub plays. |
| 39 | In the foreground the three stages of life: child (with a square), a mature man (with a semicircle), and an old man with a stick (with a triangle). Behind them the myth of Oedipus and the sphinx is enacted out. Oedipus meets the sphinx. He meets his mother the Queen and kills his Father the King. |
| 40 | From the mouth of a male statue on the left built into a niche in a rocky hillside, a stream of water falls into a rectangular stone basin. On the right, a stream of water falls from the mouth of a similar female statue into another basin. Various figures with crutches are drinking from the fountains. |
| 41 | A hunter lies fallen on his back while his dog pursues the wild boar. A woman emerges from the forest her hands held up. In the middle distance a warrior with sword and shield watches the scene. |
| 42 | At night under a crescent moon a woman walks along a path which passes over a bridge across a river. She holds a bunch of flowers in her right hand and a bundle of fruits in her left. She is followed by an old man wearing spectacles, with a lamp in his left and a walking stick in his right hand, walking precisely in her footprints. |
| 43 | On the summit of a high rock an eagle perches holding a banner which proclaims "I am black, white, yellow and red." Lower down a black crow flies. |
| 44 | In the foreground three men open a coffin to reveal a king coming back to life. In the background his body is being cut into pieces by a man with a sword, witnessed by a woman. On the right the woman seated at a table discourses with the man in oriental dress. |
| 45 | The globe of the Earth is seen around which the Sun moves through the zodiac of the fixed stars. The shadow of the Earth is shown into which the Moon is about to enter in eclipse. |
| 46 | A Jupiter figure stands on a small island in the sea. He releases an eagle from each hand. |
| 47 | A dog and a wolf fight. |
| 48 | In the foreground a sick King, supported by a councilor and two soldiers, receives a cup of medicine from a man, at whose feet is a vessel. In the background the king lies in bed, with two physicians. |
| 49 | Three gods, Mars, Mercury and Neptune, Vulcan(?) hold the skin of an animal, as if attempting to divide it. Two servants, one on the left looks on while the other on the right gestures towards the group. |
| 50 | In a landscape of ruined buildings a woman lies in a fresh cut grave, a winged snake or serpent dragon coiling around her body, its mouth against hers. |

## Taoism and Trigrams

| | | F1. Taoism and Trigrams of the Former Heaven Sequence. | F2. Taoism and Trigrams of the Former Heaven Sequence – English. | F3. The *kua*. | F4. The Five Chinese Planets – Chinese. | F5. The Five Chinese Planets – English. |
|---|---|---|---|---|---|---|
| | | | **46** | | | |
| | 1 | 道, 太极, 乾 | Tao, T'ai Chi, T'ien, Ch'ien | | 乾 – 天 | Ch'ien – Heaven |
| | 2 | 陽, 乾 | Yang, Ch'ien | | 陽 | Yang |
| | 3 | 陰, 坤 | Yin, K'un | | 陰 | Yin |
| | 4 | 巽 | Hsun | | 木星 | Wood Star – Jupiter |
| | 5 | 离 | Li | | 火星 | Fire Star – Mars |
| | 6 | 艮 | Ken | | 太陽 | Tai Yang – Sun |
| | 7 | 震 | Chen | | 金星 | Metal Star – Venus |
| | 8 | 坎 | K'an | | 水星 | Water Star – Mercury |
| | 9 | 兑 | Tui | | 太陰 月亮 | Tai Yin – Moon |
| | 10 | 坤 | K'un [as Earth opposite Ch'ien at 1] | | 土星 | Earth Star – Saturn |
| ⊛ | 31b | | | | | |
| F | 31 | 离 | Li as Fire | | | |
| A | 11 | 巽 | Hsun as Air | | | |
| W | 23 | 坎 | K'an as Water | | | |
| E | 32b | 坤 | K'un as Earth | | | |
| ☾ | 13 | 兑 | Tui | | 太陰 | Tai Yin – Moon |
| ☿ | 12 | 坎 | K'an | | 水星 | Water Star – Mercury |
| ♀ | 14 | 震 | Chen | | 金星 | Metal Star – Venus |
| ☼ | 30 | 艮 | Ken | | 太陽 | Tai Yang – Sun |
| ♂ | 27 | 离 | Li | | 火星 | Fire Star – Mars |
| ♃ | 21 | 巽 | Hsun | | 木星 | Wood Star – Jupiter |
| ♄ | 32 | 坤 | K'un | | 土星 | Earth Star – Saturn |

## Five Chinese Elements

| F6. Five Chinese Elements. | F7. Five Colours. | F8. Seasons. | F9. Five Directions. | F10. Five Traditional Emperors. |
|---|---|---|---|---|
| Wood | Green | Spring | East | T'ai-hao (2953 BC) |
| Fire | Red | Summer | South | Yen-ti (2838 BC) |
| Earth | Yellow | – | Centre | Huang-ti (2698 BC) |
| Metal | White | Autumn | West | Shao hao (2598 BC) |
| Water | Black | Winter | North | Chuan hsu (2541 BC) |

# F. Feng Shui, Chinese Taoism, Taoist Magic

| Five Chinese Elements. | F11. Five Sacrifices and Five Key Feng Shui points. | F12. Five Spirits or *shen*. | F13. Later Heaven Sequence Numbers. | F14. Former Heaven Sequence Numbers. |
|---|---|---|---|---|
| | | | | |
| Wood | Door | Koumang | 3, 4 | 3, 8 |
| Fire | Stove/Hearth | Chujung | 9 | 2, 7 |
| Earth | Courtyard | Hou Tú | 2, 5, 8 | 5, 10 |
| Metal | Gate | Jushou | 6, 7 | 4, 9 |
| Water | Pond/Path | Hsuan ming | 1 | 1, 6 |

| Five Chinese Elements. | F15. Five Tastes. | F16. Five Odours. | F17. Five Organs. | F18. Five Musical Notes. | F19. Five types of Creature. |
|---|---|---|---|---|---|
| | | | | | |
| Wood | Sour | Rancid | Spleen | Chueh | Finned |
| Fire | Bitter | Scorched | Lungs | Chih | Feathered |
| Earth | Sweet | Fragrant | Heart | Kung | Naked |
| Metal | Sharp | Putrid | Liver | Shang | Furry |
| Water | Salty | Musty | Kidneys | Yu | Scaled |

*Heavenly Stems*

| Stem | F20. Heavenly Stems – Chinese. | F21. Heavenly Stems – English. | F22. Heavenly Stems – Yin or Yang. | F23. Heavenly Stems – Element. | F24. Heavenly Stems – Associated Spirit – Chinese. | F25. Heavenly Stems – Associated Spirit – English. |
|---|---|---|---|---|---|---|
| | | | | | | |
| 1 | 甲 | Chia | Yang | Wood | 閼逢 | O-Feng |
| 2 | 乙 | I | Yin | Wood | 旃蒙 | Chen-Meng |
| 3 | 丙 | Ping | Yang | Fire | 柔兆 | Jou-Chao |
| 4 | 丁 | Ting | Yin | Fire | 疆圉 | Chiang-Yu |
| 5 | 戊 | Wu | Yang | Earth | 著雍 | Chu-Yung |
| 6 | 己 | Ch'i | Yin | Earth | 屠維 | T'u-Wei |
| 7 | 庚 | Keng | Yang | Metal | 上章 | Shang-Chang |
| 8 | 辛 | Hsin | Yin | Metal | 重光 | Chung-Kuang |
| 9 | 壬 | Jen | Yang | Water | 玄默 | Hsuan-Yi |
| 10 | 癸 | Kuei | Yin | Water | 昭陽 | Chao-Yang |

# F. Feng Shui, Chinese Taoism, Taoist Magic

*Earthly Branches*

| | | F26. Chinese Astrology – 12 'Zodiacal' Animals. | F27. Chinese Astrology – 12 'Zodiacal' Animals. | F28. The Twelve Branches – Chinese. | F29. The Twelve Branches – English. | F30. The Twelve Branches – Yin and Yang. | F31. The Twelve Branches – Elements. |
|---|---|---|---|---|---|---|---|
| ♈ | 15 | 鼠 | Rat | 子 | Tzu | Yang | Water |
| ♉ | 16 | 牛 | Ox | 丑 | Chou | Yin | Metal |
| ♊ | 17 | 虎 | Tiger | 寅 | Yin | Yang | Fire |
| ♋ | 18 | 兔 | Rabbit | 卯 | Mao | Yin | Wood |
| ♌ | 19 | 龍 | Dragon | 辰 | Chen | Yang | Water |
| ♍ | 20 | 蛇 | Snake | 巳 | Ssu | Yin | Metal |
| ♎ | 22 | 马 | Horse | 午 | Wu | Yang | Fire |
| ♏ | 24 | 羊 | Goat/sheep | 未 | Wei | Yin | Wood |
| ♐ | 25 | 猴 | Monkey | 申 | Shen | Yang | Water |
| ♑ | 26 | 鸡 | Rooster | 酉 | Yu | Yin | Metal |
| ♒ | 28 | 狗 | Dog | 戌 | Hsu | Yang | Fire |
| ♓ | 29 | 猪 | Pig | 亥 | Hai | Yin | Wood |

| *Five Chinese Elements.* | F32. Triplicity of Harmonious Branches. | F33. Triplicity of Punishment Branches. | F34. Post Horse Branches. |
|---|---|---|---|
| Wood | Hai, Mao, Wei | Yin, Mao, Chen | Ssu |
| Fire | Yin, Wu, Hsu | Ssu, Wu, Wei | Shen |
| Earth | | | |
| Metal | Ssu, Yu, Chou | Shen. Yu. Hsu | Hai |
| Water | Shen, Tzu, Chen | Hai, Tzu, Chou | Yin |

# F. Feng Shui, Chinese Taoism, Taoist Magic

*Flying Stars*

| | F35. Nine Flying Stars – Chinese. | F36. Nine Flying Stars – Transliterated. | F37. Nine Flying Stars – English | F38. Nine Flying Stars – usual Chinese order. |
|---|---|---|---|---|
| | | | | |
| 1 | | | | |
| 2 | 貪狼 | T'an Lang | Greedy Wolf | T'an Lang – Greedy Wolf |
| 3 | 巨門 | Chu Men | Great Door | Chu Men – Great Door |
| 4 | 文曲 | Wen Ch'u | Civil Career | Lu Ts'un – Rank Preserved |
| 5 | 武曲 | Wu Ch'u | Military Career | Wen Ch'u – Civil Career |
| 6 | 廉贞 | Lien Chen | Honesty & Purity | Lien Chen – Honesty & Purity |
| 7 | 禄存 | Lu Ts'un | Rank Preserved | Wu Ch'u – Military Career |
| 8 | 破軍 | P'o Chun | Broken Army | P'o Chun – Broken Army |
| 9 | 左辅 | Tso Fu | Left Assistant | Tso Fu – Left Assistant |
| 10 | 右弼 | Yu Pi | Right Assistant | Yu Pi – Right Assistant |

| | F39. Talismans of the Nine Stars. | F40. The Nine Stars – Chinese. | F41. The Nine Stars – Secret Star Name. | F42. The Nine Stars – Compass Direction. | F43. The Nine Stars – Trigram. | F44. The Nine Stars – Position on the *lo shu*. | F45. The Nine Stars – Element. |
|---|---|---|---|---|---|---|---|
| | | | | | | | |
| 1 | T'ien-Feng | 天逢 | Tzu-Ch'in | N | K'an | 1 | Water |
| 2 | T'ien-Ping | 天芮 | Tzu-Hsu | SW | K'un | 2 | Earth |
| 3 | T'ien-Chung | 天衝 | Tzu-Ch'iao | E | Chen | 3 | Wood |
| 4 | T'ien-Fu | 天輔 | Tzu-Hsiang | SE | Hsun | 4 | Wood |
| 5 | T'ien-Ch'in | 天禽 | Tzu-Chin | Centre | – | 5 | Earth |
| 6 | T'ien-Hsin | 天心 | Tzu-Hsiang | NW | Ch'ien | 6 | Metal |
| 7 | T'ien-Chu | 天柱 | Tzu-Chung | W | Tui | 7 | Metal |
| 8 | T'ien-Jen | 天任 | Tzu-Ch'ang | NE | Ken | 8 | Earth |
| 9 | T'ien-Ying | 天英 | Tzu-Ch'eng | S | Li | 9 | Fire |
| 10 | | | | | | | |

# F. Feng Shui, Chinese Taoism, Taoist Magic

*Immortals and Spirits*

| | F46. Eight Taoist Immortals *pa hsien* – Chinese. | F47. Eight Taoist Immortals *pa hsien* – English. | F48. Eight Taoist Immortals – Qualities and Symbols. |
|---|---|---|---|
| 1 | | | |
| 2 | | | |
| 3 | | | |
| 4 | 韩湘子 | 7. Han Hsiang-Tzu | Poet and statesman |
| 5 | 吕洞宾 | 6. Lu Tung-Pin | Holds magic sword and fly whisk |
| 6 | 曹国舅 | 8. Ts'ao Kuo-Chiu | Resembles a genie |
| 7 | 锺离权 | 2. Chung-Li Ch'uan, | Able to transmute copper and pewter into silver. Holds a feather fan and the peach of immortality |
| 8 | 李铁拐 蓝采和 | 1. Li T'ieh-Kuai 3. Lan Ts'ai-Ho | With crutch and bag full of magic medicines Trickster and hermaphrodite with flute or cymbals |
| 9 | 何仙姑 | 5. Ho Hsien-Ku | Maiden holding a lotus blossom or peach, playing a reed-organ or drinking wine |
| 10 | 张果老 | 4. Chang-Kuo Lao | Hermit and necromancer, rides a white magic mule, carries a phoenix feather or peach of immortality |

| | | F49. 12 of the *shen* of the 60 *Chia-Tzu* Cyclical characters – Chinese. | F50. 12 of the *shen* of the 60 *Chia-Tzu* Cyclical characters – transliterated. | F51. The 12 *Ting-Chia* Spirits – Chinese. | F52. The 12 *Ting-Chia* Spirits – transliterated. |
|---|---|---|---|---|---|
| ♈ | 15 | 丁卯神 | Ting-Mao Shen | 司馬卿 | Ssu-Ma Ch'ing |
| ♉ | 16 | 丁丑神 | Ting-Chou Shen | 趙子壬 | Chao Tzu-Jen |
| ♊ | 17 | 丁亥神 | Ting-Hai Shen | 張文通 | Chang Wen-Túng |
| ♋ | 18 | 丁酉神 | Ting-Yu Shen | 臧文公 | Tsang Wen-Kung |
| ♌ | 19 | 丁未神 | Ting-Wei Shen | 石叔通 | Shih Shu-T'ung |
| ♍ | 20 | 丁巳神 | Ting-Ssu Shen | 崔石卿 | Ts'ui Shih-Ch'ing |
| ♎ | 22 | 甲子神 | Chia-Tzu Shen | 王文卿 | Wang Wen-Ch'ing |
| ♏ | 24 | 甲戌神 | Chia-Hsu Shen | 展子江 | Chan Tzu-Chiang |
| ♐ | 25 | 甲申神 | Chia-Shen Shen | 扈文長 | Hu Wen-Ch'ang |
| ♑ | 26 | 甲午神 | Chia-Wu Shen | 衛上卿 | Wai Shang-Ch'ing |
| ♒ | 28 | 甲辰神 | Chia-Ch'en Shen | 孟非卿 | Meng Fei-Ch'ing |
| ♓ | 29 | 甲寅神 | Chia-Yin Shen | 明文章 | Ming Wen-Chang |

# F. Feng Shui, Chinese Taoism, Taoist Magic

*60 Year Cycle*

| | | Animal \ Element > | Wood | Fire | Earth | Metal | Water |
|---|---|---|---|---|---|---|---|
| ♈ | 15 | Rat | 1924, 1984 | 1936, 1996 | 1948, 2008 | 1960, 2020 | 1972, 2032 |
| ♉ | 16 | Ox | 1925, 1985 | 1937, 1997 | 1949, 2009 | 1961, 2021 | 1973, 2033 |
| ♊ | 17 | Tiger | 1974, 2034 | 1926, 1986 | 1938, 1998 | 1950, 2010 | 1962, 2022 |
| ♋ | 18 | Rabbit | 1975, 2035 | 1927, 1987 | 1939, 1999 | 1951, 2011 | 1963, 2023 |
| ♌ | 19 | Dragon | 1964, 2024 | 1976, 2036 | 1928, 1988 | 1940, 2000 | 1952, 2012 |
| ♍ | 20 | Snake | 1965, 2025 | 1977, 2037 | 1929, 1989 | 1941, 2001 | 1953, 2013 |
| ♎ | 22 | Horse | 1954, 2014 | 1966, 2026 | 1978, 2038 | 1930, 1990 | 1942, 2002 |
| ♏ | 24 | Goat/Sheep | 1955, 2015 | 1967, 2027 | 1979, 2039 | 1931, 1991 | 1943, 2003 |
| ♐ | 25 | Monkey | 1944, 2004 | 1956, 2016 | 1968, 2028 | 1980, 2040 | 1932, 1992 |
| ♑ | 26 | Rooster | 1945, 2005 | 1957, 2017 | 1969, 2029 | 1981, 2041 | 1933, 1993 |
| ♒ | 28 | Dog | 1934, 1994 | 1946, 2006 | 1958, 2018 | 1970, 2030 | 1982, 2042 |
| ♓ | 29 | Pig | 1935, 1995 | 1947, 2007 | 1959, 2019 | 1971, 2031 | 1983, 2043 |

F53. Chinese Animal and Element Year 60-Year Cycle.

| Chinese Year | Animal Year | Start Date |
|---|---|---|
| 4704 | Dog | January 29, 2006 |
| 4705 | Pig | February 18, 2007 |
| 4706 | Rat | February 7, 2008 |
| 4707 | Ox | January 26, 2009 |
| 4708 | Tiger | February 10, 2010 |
| 4709 | Rabbit | February 3, 2011 |
| 4710 | Dragon | January 23, 2012 |
| 4711 | Snake | February 10, 2013 |
| 4712 | Horse | January 31, 2014 |
| 4713 | Goat/Sheep | February 19, 2015 |
| 4714 | Monkey | February 9, 2016 |
| 4715 | Rooster | January 28, 2017 |
| 4716 | Dog | February 16, 2018 |
| 4717 | Boar/Pig | February 5, 2019 |
| 4718 | Rat | January 25, 2020 |

F54. Start of the Chinese Lunar New Year.

# F. Feng Shui, Chinese Taoism, Taoist Magic

| No. | Combination | Combination Name | Vitality Element | Destiny Element | Luck Element |
|-----|-------------|------------------|------------------|-----------------|--------------|
| | | F55. Chinese Animal and Element Year – Luck, Vitality and Destiny Cycles.[1] | | | |
| 1 | Wood-Rat | Rat on the Roof | Water | Wood | Wood |
| 2 | Wood-Ox | Sea Ox | Earth | Wood | Water |
| 3 | Fire-Tiger | Tiger in the Forest | Wood | Fire | Metal |
| 4 | Fire-Rabbit | Rabbit dreaming of the Moon | Wood | Fire | Fire |
| 5 | Earth-Dragon | Dragon of Pure Virtue | Earth | Earth | Wood |
| 6 | Earth-Snake | Snake of Happiness | Fire | Earth | Water |
| 7 | Metal-Horse | Palace Horse | Fire | Metal | Metal |
| 8 | Metal-Goat | Lucky Goat | Earth | Metal | Fire |
| 9 | Water-Monkey | Elegant Monkey | Metal | Water | Wood |
| 10 | Water-Rooster | Barnyard Rooster | Metal | Water | Water |
| 11 | Wood-Dog | Guarding Dog | Earth | Wood | Metal |
| 12 | Wood-Pig | Traveling Pig | Water | Wood | Fire |
| 13 | Fire-Rat | Field Rat | Water | Fire | Wood |
| 14 | Fire-Ox | Lake Ox | Earth | Fire | Water |
| 15 | Earth-Tiger | Tiger Climbs the Mountain | Wood | Earth | Metal |
| 16 | Earth-Rabbit | Rabbit of the Woods and Mountains | Wood | Earth | Fire |
| 17 | Metal-Dragon | Dragon of Patience | Earth | Metal | Wood |
| 18 | Metal-Snake | Hibernating Snake | Fire | Metal | Water |
| 19 | Water-Horse | War Horse | Fire | Water | Metal |
| 20 | Water-Goat | Goat in a flock | Earth | Water | Fire |
| 21 | Wood-Monkey | Tree Monkey | Metal | Wood | Wood |
| 22 | Wood-Rooster | Rooster Crowing at Noon | Metal | Wood | Water |
| 23 | Fire-Dog | Sleeping Dog | Earth | Fire | Metal |
| 24 | Fire-Pig | Pig traversing a Mountain | Water | Fire | Fire |
| 25 | Earth-Rat | Granary Rat | Water | Earth | Wood |
| 26 | Earth-Ox | Ox in the Byre | Earth | Earth | Water |
| 27 | Metal-Tiger | Tiger leaves the Mountain | Wood | Metal | Metal |
| 28 | Metal-Rabbit | Rabbit in the Burrow | Wood | Metal | Fire |
| 29 | Water-Dragon | Rain Dragon | Earth | Water | Wood |
| 30 | Water-Snake | Snake in the Grass | Fire | Water | Water |

[1] For more information on how to use these see Stephen Skinner, *The Tibetan Oracle*, Carroll & Brown, London, 2005.

# F. Feng Shui, Chinese Taoism, Taoist Magic

| No. | F55. Chinese Animal and Element Year – Luck, Vitality and Destiny Cycles.[1] | | | | |
|---|---|---|---|---|---|
| | **Combination** | **Combination Name** | **Vitality Element** | **Destiny Element** | **Luck Element** |
| 31 | Wood-Horse | Horse in the Clouds | Fire | Wood | Metal |
| 32 | Wood-Goat | Serious Goat | Earth | Wood | Fire |
| 33 | Fire-Monkey | Mountain Monkey | Metal | Fire | Wood |
| 34 | Fire-Rooster | Solitary Rooster | Metal | Fire | Water |
| 35 | Earth-Dog | Mountain Dog | Earth | Earth | Metal |
| 36 | Earth-Pig | Monastic Pig | Water | Earth | Fire |
| 37 | Metal-Rat | Rat on the Crossbeam | Water | Metal | Wood |
| 38 | Metal-Ox | Ox on the Road | Earth | Metal | Water |
| 39 | Water-Tiger | Tiger Crossing the Forest | Wood | Water | Metal |
| 40 | Water-Rabbit | Rabbit Leaving the Forest | Wood | Water | Fire |
| 41 | Wood-Dragon | Dragon in the Whirlpool | Earth | Wood | Wood |
| 42 | Wood-Snake | Snake Leaving its Hole | Fire | Wood | Water |
| 43 | Fire-Horse | Traveling Horse | Fire | Fire | Metal |
| 44 | Fire-Goat | Lost Goat | Earth | Fire | Fire |
| 45 | Earth-Monkey | Independent Monkey | Metal | Earth | Wood |
| 46 | Earth-Rooster | Rooster Pecking for Food | Metal | Earth | Water |
| 47 | Metal-Dog | Temple Dog | Earth | Metal | Metal |
| 48 | Metal-Pig | Farmer's Pig | Water | Medal | Fire |
| 49 | Water-Rat | Rat on the Mountain | Water | Water | Wood |
| 50 | Water-Ox | Ox by the Gate | Earth | Water | Water |
| 51 | Wood-Tiger | Tiger Standing Firm | Wood | Wood | Metal |
| 52 | Wood-Rabbit | Enlightened Rabbit | Wood | Wood | Fire |
| 53 | Fire-Dragon | Dragon in the Sky | Earth | Fire | Wood |
| 54 | Fire-Snake | Snake in the Pool | Fire | Fire | Water |
| 55 | Earth-Horse | Horse in the Stable | Fire | Earth | Metal |
| 56 | Earth-Goat | Goat in the Pasture | Earth | Earth | Fire |
| 57 | Metal-Monkey | Monkey Eating Fruit | Metal | Metal | Wood |
| 58 | Metal-Rooster | Caged Rooster | Metal | Metal | Water |
| 59 | Water-Dog | Watch Dog | Earth | Water | Metal |
| 60 | Water-Pig | Pig in the Forest | Water | Water | Fire |

*Lo P'an*

| | | Direction | Compass Degrees | Mountain – Chinese | Mountain | Branch/Stem/Trigram |
|---|---|---|---|---|---|---|
| | | | F56. The 24 Mountains of the *lo p'an* or Chinese compass. | | | |
| | 1 | NW2 | 307.5-322.5 | 乾 | ch'ien | Heaven Trigram |
| | 2 | | | | | |
| | 3 | | | | | |
| | 4 | SE2 | 127.5-142.5 | 巽 | hsun | Wind Trigram |
| | 5 | | | | | |
| | 6 | NE2 | 37.5-52.5 | 艮 | ken | Mountain Trigram |
| | 7 | | | | | |
| | 8 | | | | | |
| | 9 | | | | | |
| | 10 | SW2 | 217.5-232.5 | 坤 | k'un | Earth Trigram |
| ☽ | 13 | | | | | |
| ☿ | 12 | N1 | 337.5-352.5 | 壬 | jen/ren | Yang Water Stem |
| ☿ | 12 | N3 | 07.5-22.5 | 癸 | kuei | Yin Water Stem |
| ♀ | 14 | W1 | 247.5-262.5 | 庚 | keng | Yang Metal Stem |
| ♀ | 14 | W3 | 277.5-292.5 | 辛 | hsin | Yin Metal Stem |
| ☼ | 30 | | | | | |
| ♂ | 27 | S1 | 157.5-172.5 | 丙 | ping | Yang Fire Stem |
| ♂ | 27 | S3 | 187.5-202.5 | 丁 | ting | Yin Fire Stem |
| ♃ | 21 | E1 | 67.5-82.5 | 甲 | chia | Yang Wood Stem |
| ♃ | 21 | E3 | 97.5-112.5 | 乙 | yi | Yin Wood Stem |
| ♄ | 32 | Centre | – | 戊 &己 | wu & chi | Yin & Yang Earth Stems |
| ♈ | 15 | **N2** | 352.5-7.5 | 子 | **tzu** | Rat Branch |
| ♉ | 16 | NE1 | 22.5-37.5 | 丑 | ch'ou | Ox Branch |
| ♊ | 17 | NE3 | 52.5-67.5 | 寅 | yin | Tiger Branch |
| ♋ | 18 | **E2** | 82.5-97.5 | 卯 | **mao** | Rabbit Branch |
| ♌ | 19 | SE1 | 112.5-127.5 | 辰 | chen | Dragon Branch |
| ♍ | 20 | SE3 | 142.5-157.5 | 巳 | ssu | Snake Branch |
| ♎ | 22 | **S2** | 172.5-187.5 | 午 | **wu** | Horse Branch |
| ♏ | 24 | SW1 | 202.5-217.5 | 未 | wei | Sheep Branch |
| ♐ | 25 | SW3 | 232.5-247.5 | 申 | shen | Monkey Branch |
| ♑ | 26 | **W2** | 262.5-277.5 | 酉 | **yu** | Rooster Branch |
| ♒ | 28 | NW1 | 292.5-307.5 | 戌 | hsu | Dog Branch |
| ♓ | 29 | NW3 | 322.5-337.5 | 亥 | hai | Pig Branch |

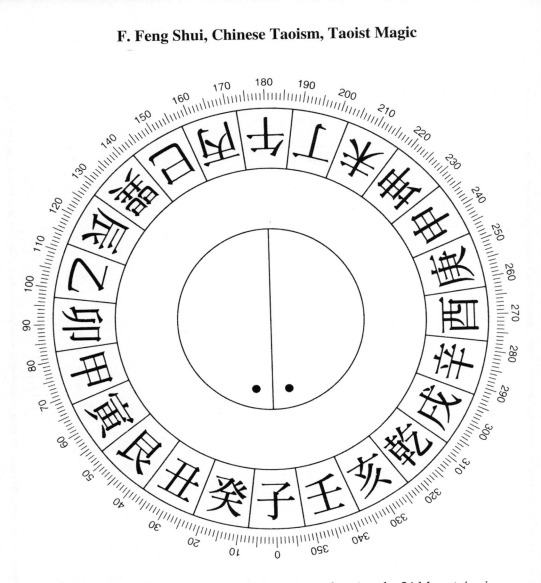

Figure 6: *Lo P'an* or Chinese feng shui compass showing the 24 Mountain ring (South is at the top).

# G. Geomancy

| Geomancy Order.[1] | | G1. Geomantic Binary Figures. | | G2. Traditional Meaning. | G3. Geomantic Elements. | G4. Geomantic Attributions to the Zodiac. | | | |
|---|---|---|---|---|---|---|---|---|---|
| | | | | | | Golden Dawn | Agrippa Esoteric | Gerard of Cremona | Christopher Cattan |
| ♋ | 18 | Populus | ⠿ | Crowd | Water | Cancer | Aquarius | Capricorn | Taurus |
| ♋ | 18 | Via | ⠇ | Road | Water | Cancer | Virgo | Leo | Cancer |
| ♍ | 20 | Conjunctio | ⠔ | Conjunction | Earth | Virgo | Libra | Virgo | Virgo |
| ♑ | 26 | Carcer | ⠢ | Prison | Earth | Capricorn | Pisces | Pisces | Aquarius |
| ♌ | 19 | Fortuna Major | ⠲ | Great Fortune | Fire | Leo | Taurus | Aquarius | Leo |
| ♌ | 19 | Fortuna Minor | ⠠ | Lesser Fortune | Air | Leo | Taurus | Taurus | Aries |
| ♐ | 25 | Acquisitio | ⠖ | Acquisition | Fire | Sagittarius | Aries | Aries | Pisces |
| ♉ | 16 | Amissio | ⠒ | Loss | Earth | Taurus | Sagittarius | Scorpio | Virgo |
| ♒ | 28 | Tristitia | ⠶ | Sorrow | Air | Aquarius | Sagittarius | Scorpio | Capricorn |
| ♓ | 29 | Laetitia | ⠆ | Joy | Water | Pisces | Gemini | Taurus | Sagittarius |
| ♏ | 24 | Rubeus | ⠦ | Red | Water | Scorpio | Cancer | Gemini | Scorpio |
| ♊ | 17 | Albus | ⠲ | White | Air | Gemini | Leo | Cancer | Pisces |
| ♎ | 22 | Puella | ⠒ | Girl | Air | Libra | Cancer | Libra | Libra |
| ♈ | 15 | Puer | ⠢ | Boy | Fire | Aries | Scorpio | Gemini | Aries |
| ☾ | 13 | Caput Draconis | ⠂ | Head of the Dragon | Earth | Caput Draconis | Libra | Virgo | Gemini |
| ☾ | 13 | Cauda Draconis | ⠄ | Tail of the Dragon | Fire | Cauda Draconis | Capricorn | Sagittarius | Aquarius |

---

[1] The 16 Figures of Geomancy cannot be easily accommodated in ZEP order as duplication occurs in the case of correspondences with the Sun and the Moon, so a 'Geomancy Order' is used throughout Table G. For the most complete text on the background, history and practice of geomancy see Stephen Skinner, *Terrestrial Astrology: Divination by Geomancy*, RKP, London, 1980 republished as *Geomancy in Theory & Practice*, Golden Hoard, Singapore, 2011.

# G. Geomancy

*Geomantic Figure Names in Various Languages*

| Geomancy Order. | | Geomantic Figures. | G5. Latin Names from Hugh of Santalla (fl. 1119-1157). | G6. Latin from *Geomantiae Nova* and *Estimaverunt Indi* (12th century). | G6a. Latin from Gerard of Cremona (1114-1187) |
|---|---|---|---|---|---|
| ♋ | 18 | Populus | Congregatio | Aggregatio | Populus, Aggregatio, Congregatio |
| ♋ | 18 | Via | Via | Via (Iter) | Via |
| ♍ | 20 | Conjunctio | Conjunctio | Coadunatio, Conjunctio | Conjunctio, Coadunatio, Associatio |
| ♑ | 26 | Carcer | Constrictus | Carcer | Carcer, Constrictus |
| ♌ | 19 | Fortuna Major | Auxilium intus | Tutela intrans | Fortuna Major, Auxilium Intus, Tutela Intrans, Omen Majus |
| ♌ | 19 | Fortuna Minor | Auxilium foris | Tutela exiens, Tutela Foris | Fortuna Minor, Auxilium Foris, Tutela Exiens, Omen Minus |
| ♐ | 25 | Acquisitio | Comprehensum intus | Comprehensum intus | Acquisitio, Comprehensum intus |
| ♉ | 16 | Amissio | Comprehensum foris | Comprehensum foris | Amissio, Comprehensum foris |
| ♒ | 28 | Tristitia | Transverses, Diminutus | Diminutus | Tristitia, Transversus, Caput Imum |
| ♓ | 29 | Laetitia | Barbatus | Barbatus, Ridens, Canus | Leticia, Barbatus, Caput Altum |
| ♏ | 24 | Rubeus | Rubeus | Rubeus | Rubeus, Ruffus |
| ♊ | 17 | Albus | Candidus | Candidus, Albus | Albus, Candidus |
| ♎ | 22 | Puella | Mundus facie | Mundus facie, Puella | Mundus facie, Puella |
| ♈ | 15 | Puer | Imberbis | Imberbis, Gladius erigendus, Flavus | Imberbis, Puer Flavus, Puella, Belliger |
| ☾ | 13 | Caput Draconis | Limen interius | Limen intrans, Intus | Caput Draconis, Limen intrans, Limen superius |
| ☾ | 13 | Cauda Draconis | Limen exterius | Limen exiens | Cauda draconis, Limen inferius |

# G. Geomancy

| Geomancy Order. | | Geomantic Figures. | G7. Traditional Arabic Names. | G8. Traditional Arabic Meanings. |
|---|---|---|---|---|
| ♋ | 18 | Populus | Jama'a | group of people, band, party, gang |
| ♋ | 18 | Via | Tariq | way, road, highway, trail |
| ♍ | 20 | Conjunctio | Ijtima | meeting, get together, gathering, social life, conjunction |
| ♑ | 26 | Carcer | 'uqla | prison, arrest, bond, tie |
| ♌ | 19 | Fortuna Major | El nusra el-dakila | interior, inside, inmost, hidden help or assistance (interior personal victory) |
| ♌ | 19 | Fortuna Minor | El nusra el-kharga | external, outer, outside, foreign, exterior, help, aid or assistance (exterior victory) |
| ♐ | 25 | Acquisitio | Qabd el-dakil | interior, grasping, taking possession, receiving, receipt (taken forcibly) |
| ♉ | 16 | Amissio | Qabd el-kharge | 'giving outside', to take outside, or give away |
| ♒ | 28 | Tristitia | Mankus el-kharga, ankis, rakiza kharga | change, turn, upside-down, to fall, inverted, reversed, relapsing or suffering a relapse |
| ♓ | 29 | Laetitia | El-dakila, janubi fariha | joy, southern happiness (happiness in the south?) rejoicing, gladness/bearded |
| ♏ | 24 | Rubeus | Humra | redness, red implying a bad omen, danger |
| ♊ | 17 | Albus | El-bayad | whiteness, or writing paper, or blank space in a manuscript, barren, desolate, wasteland |
| ♎ | 22 | Puella | Naqiy el-kadd | clear cheek (complexion), pure, clean, immaculate, unstained, free of dirt or impurity (young girl) |
| ♈ | 15 | Puer | Jud lahu, kausay | literally 'generosity is for him', openhandedness, *liberality/kausaj* is a swordfish/ beardless |
| ☾ | 13 | Caput Draconis | El 'ataba el-dakila | the interior threshold (the step to go inside) |
| ☾ | 13 | Cauda Draconis | El 'ataba el-kharga | the exterior threshold (the step to go out) |

# G. Geomancy

| Geomancy Order. | | Geomantic Figures. | G9. Arabic Names in Kordofan (Sudan). | G10. Divinatory Meaning in Kordofan (Sudan). |
|---|---|---|---|---|
| ♋ | 18 | Populus | Tiql | an ape, a man of empty talk |
| ♋ | 18 | Via | Tariq | a road, indicating a journey |
| ♍ | 20 | Conjunctio | Damir | a hungry man on a journey |
| ♑ | 26 | Carcer | Surra | a woman of good omen |
| ♌ | 19 | Fortuna Major | Rasn | a head-rope, indicating a journey |
| ♌ | 19 | Fortuna Minor | Jebbar | a powerful sheikh or notable |
| ♐ | 25 | Acquisitio | Qabid | indicating a successful seizure of an animal, etc. |
| ♉ | 16 | Amissio | Kharij | an indication of a journey, or selling, or loss of a stolen animal |
| ♒ | 28 | Tristitia | Jihin or abu heila | a fikih, red in colour *abu heila* |
| ♓ | 29 | Laetitia | Hurr | a tall yellow man with a fire-mark or pock-mark in mid forehead |
| ♏ | 24 | Rubeus | Humra' | a red woman, with red face markings, an indication of blood, a successful hunt |
| ♊ | 17 | Albus | Beyyad | a poor unimportant man |
| ♎ | 22 | Puella | Mahzum | a stouthearted man, the thief (if found in the enemy's houses), but weaker than jebbir |
| ♈ | 15 | Puer | Jodala | a woman of no importance |
| ☾ | 13 | Caput Draconis | Raiya | A tall woman, like a flag, full of words |
| ☾ | 13 | Cauda Draconis | Rakiza | a woman who brings news |

# G. Geomancy

| Geomancy Order. | | Geomantic Figures. | G11. Greek Geomantic Names – Pierre de Montdore, 1552-67. | G12. Greek Geomantic Names – Georges Midiates, 1462. | G13. French Provençale Names. |
|---|---|---|---|---|---|
| ♋ | 18 | Populus | (ν)τζαμαάτ τζμαάτης | | Poble |
| ♋ | 18 | Via | ταρίχ | | Via |
| ♍ | 20 | Conjunctio | ἰστιμᾰ(ς) (η) | | Conjunction |
| ♑ | 26 | Carcer | οὐχλᾰς ᾽ιουχλᾰ | φυλαχή | Carcer |
| ♌ | 19 | Fortuna Major | (ταρχάνα) νουσρατουλταχήλ | ἔξοδος τῆς δόξης | Aventura major |
| ♌ | 19 | Fortuna Minor | (σάμψαν) νουσρατουλχάριτζ | εἴσοδος τῆς δόξης | Aventura minor |
| ♐ | 25 | Acquisitio | β χαπδουλταχήλ | εἴσοδος τῶν χρημάτων | Aquisitio |
| ♉ | 16 | Amissio | β χαπδουλχάριτζ | εξοδς τῶν χρημάτων | Perda |
| ♒ | 28 | Tristitia | ἀγγής (ἀγχίς) (ἀγχῆς) | χατωφερές | Tristetia |
| ♓ | 29 | Laetitia | λαχιάμ λαχιάν | ἀνωφερές | Alegria |
| ♏ | 24 | Rubeus | χουμπρᾰ(ς) | ἐρυθροτής ἤγουν ὁ πόλεμος | Ros |
| ♊ | 17 | Albus | παγιάδ (θ) | λευχότης | Blancor |
| ♎ | 22 | Puella | ναχιουλχάτ | ἄνηδος ἤγουν ὁ ἀρσενιχός | Donzel |
| ♈ | 15 | Puer | φαρά(ρ)χ(ης) φαράχη φαράχ | σπανός, ἤγουν ὁ θηλυχός | Donzela |
| ☽ | 13 | Caput Draconis | χαιτ(σ)μᾰς | εἰσερχόμενον ἀνώφλιον | Portal alzat |
| ☽ | 13 | Cauda Draconis | (δαμσάπητα) θεπιτά(ς) | ἐξερχόμενον ἀνώφλιον | Portal reversat |

# G. Geomancy

| Geomancy Order. | | Geomantic Figures. | G14. Hebrew Names. | G15. Hebrew Names – Meaning. | G16. Hebrew Names – in Hebrew Characters. |
|---|---|---|---|---|---|
| ♋ | 18 | Populus | Kehila | Congregation | קהלה |
| ♋ | 18 | Via | Derech | Way | דרך |
| ♍ | 20 | Conjunctio | Chibur [Kibbutz] | Collective | חבור |
| ♑ | 26 | Carcer | Beit ha-sohar | Prison | בית הסהר |
| ♌ | 19 | Fortuna Major | Kabod nichnas | Honour or fortune comes | כבוד נכנס |
| ♌ | 19 | Fortuna Minor | Kabod yotze | Honour or fortune leaves | כבוד יוצא |
| ♐ | 25 | Acquisitio | Mamun nichnas | Incoming monetary fortune | ממון נכנס |
| ♉ | 16 | Amissio | Mamun yotze | Exiting monetary fortune | ממון יוצא |
| ♒ | 28 | Tristitia | Shefel rosh | Main humiliation | שפל ראש |
| ♓ | 29 | Laetitia | Nisho rosh | Main joy (wife) | נשוא ראש |
| ♏ | 24 | Rubeus | Ha-adom | Red one | ה אדום |
| ♊ | 17 | Albus | Ha-laban | White one | ה לבן |
| ♎ | 22 | Puella | Bar ha-lechi | Beautiful one | בר הלחי |
| ♈ | 15 | Puer | Nilcham | Fighter | נלחם |
| ☾ | 13 | Caput Draconis | Sof nichnas | Enters the threshold | סף נכנס |
| ☾ | 13 | Cauda Draconis | Sof yotze | Exits the threshold | סף יוצא |

# G. Geomancy

| Geomancy Order. | | Geomantic Figures. | G17. Malagasy Hova Interior Dialect Name. | G18. Malagasy Antanosy & Sakalava West Coast Name. | G19. Malagasy Name from Fort Dauphin Region. |
|---|---|---|---|---|---|
| | | | | | |
| ♋ | 18 | Populus | Jamà (or zomà) | Asombòla | Assomboulo |
| ♋ | 18 | Via | Taraiky | Taraiky | Tareche |
| ♍ | 20 | Conjunctio | Aditsimà (aditsimay) | Alatsimay | Alissima |
| ♑ | 26 | Carcer | Alokòla | Alikòla | Alocola |
| ♌ | 19 | Fortuna Major | Asòravàvy | Adabàra | Adabara |
| ♌ | 19 | Fortuna Minor | Asóralàhy | Asóralahy | Alaazadi |
| ♐ | 25 | Acquisitio | Vandal miòndrika (= Mòlahidy) | Alahòtsy | Alohotsi |
| ♉ | 16 | Amissio | Vandal mitsàngana (= Mikarija) | Adálo | Adalou |
| ♒ | 28 | Tristitia | Alikisy | Alikisy | Alinchissa |
| ♓ | 29 | Laetitia | Alàhizàny | Alizàha | Alihiza |
| ♏ | 24 | Rubeus | Alaimòra | Alihimòra | Alohomore |
| ♊ | 17 | Albus | Adibijàdy | Alabiàvo | Alibiauou |
| ♎ | 22 | Puella | Kizo | Alakaràbo | Al acarabo |
| ♈ | 15 | Puer | Adikasájy | Bètsivóngo | Alicozaza (Alimiza) |
| ☽ | 13 | Caput Draconis | Sàka | Alakaosy | Alacossi |
| ☽ | 13 | Cauda Draconis | Votsira (= Vontsira) | Karija | Cariza |

111

# G. Geomancy

| Geomancy Order. | | Geomantic Figures. | G20.Central African Tribal Name from Sara Madjingaye (South Chad). | G21.Central African Tribal Name from Sara Deme Figure (South Chad). | G22. Central African Name from Dakhel (North East Chad). |
|---|---|---|---|---|---|
| ♋ | 18 | Populus | jama'a – dead ancestors | tigil – (under the) shadow of a village tree | tigil – the crowd |
| ♋ | 18 | Via | tarik – little children | terek – all the men of the village | terik – exit, door, path, passage |
| ♍ | 20 | Conjunctio | danhur – meat | danhur – drink of bilibili (food) | dam'r – famine, lean person, empty stomach |
| ♑ | 26 | Carcer | sura – chiefs | sura – plenty of food | sura – small pregnant woman |
| ♌ | 19 | Fortuna Major | arshan – highways | rashan – all the young men of the village | rashan – wealth, assets, cattle |
| ♌ | 19 | Fortuna Minor | djobar – byways | djobar – weapons of the village | djabur – light colour and short hair (=enemy/infidel) |
| ♐ | 25 | Acquisitio | gab – objects of iron | gabat = qabdah – highway | gabat – strong and intelligent man, conqueror |
| ♉ | 16 | Amissio | harija – men of other villages | harija – war | harija – chiefs, men with authority and prestige |
| ♒ | 28 | Tristitia | djahiliti – death, foreign | djuhiliti – village hut | djuhiliti – a sign of bad omen, misfortune, lack of courage |
| ♓ | 29 | Laetitia | lahica – interior of huts, joys and possessions | pure – recovery from sickness | hurr – health |
| ♏ | 24 | Rubeus | homra – red | homra – people sleeping in huts | homra – red, blood, injury |
| ♊ | 17 | Albus | bahiti – world in the village, whiteness, death | bayada – injury | bayada – white, chance, joy, happiness |
| ♎ | 22 | Puella | metason – high place on the earth | madjum – anger of the village men, but not about hunger | mazum – ill men and women, suffering |
| ♈ | 15 | Puer | kosaje – shadow of a village tree | djoalla – thinking of something | djoalla – welcome during travel |
| ☽ | 13 | Caput Draconis | raya – men in the village | Raya – the bush or scrub outside the village | raya – beautiful man or woman |
| ☽ | 13 | Cauda Draconis | arkis – women of the tribe | rakis = kharija – men (servants?) of the village | rakis – woman with large buttocks, delay, expectation, deception |

# G. Geomancy

| Geomancy Order. | | Geomantic Figures. | G23. West African Tribal name from Dahomey. | G.24. Islamic Patriarchs – Bambara (Mali). |
|---|---|---|---|---|
| ♋ | 18 | Populus | yeku – west, night. | Moussa – Moses |
| ♋ | 18 | Via | gbe – life, east, day | Abachim |
| ♍ | 20 | Conjunctio | woli – ferocious animals, south | Ali |
| ♑ | 26 | Carcer | di – woman, copulation, north | Sulaymann – Solomon |
| ♌ | 19 | Fortuna Major | wele – illnesses | Nouhoun – Noah |
| ♌ | 19 | Fortuna Minor | loso – a hole, accident, misfortune | Kalantala – Muhammad |
| ♐ | 25 | Acquisitio | fu – white, maternal principle | Ousmane |
| ♉ | 16 | Amissio | ce – breakable, bad smell | Issa – Jesus |
| ♒ | 28 | Tristitia | akla – twins | Yacouba – Jacob |
| ♓ | 29 | Laetitia | abla – rope, duration, possessions | Adana – Adam |
| ♏ | 24 | Rubeus | ka– snake, filial piety, filial love | Amara – Amar |
| ♊ | 17 | Albus | turukpe – pregnancy, anything protruding | Idrissa – Idris |
| ♎ | 22 | Puella | tula – speech, mouths | Ladari (?) |
| ♈ | 15 | Puer | lete – earth, death | Jonas |
| ☾ | 13 | Caput Draconis | sa – black magic (ill-omen), feminine fire | Madi – the messenger |
| ☾ | 13 | Cauda Draconis | guda – sword, testicle, erection | Lassima al Houssein |

# G. Geomancy

*Dr Rudd's Geomantic Intelligences, etc.*

| Geomancy Order. | | Geomantic Figures. | G25. Dr. Rudd's Geomantic Intelligence – Hebrew. | G26. Dr. Rudd's Geomantic Intelligence – Transliteration. | G27. Dr. Rudd's Geomantic Intelligence – Translation.[2] |
|---|---|---|---|---|---|
| | | | **178** | | |
| ♋ | 18 | Populus | מוריאל | MVRIAL | Muriel |
| ♋ | 18 | Via | מוריאל | MVRIAL | Muriel |
| ♍ | 20 | Conjunctio | המליאל | HMLIAL | Hamaliel |
| ♑ | 26 | Carcer | הנאל | HNAL | Haniel |
| ♌ | 19 | Fortuna Major | ורכיאל | VRKIAL | Verachiel/Verakiel |
| ♌ | 19 | Fortuna Minor | אדוכיאל | ADVKIAL | Advachiel |
| ♐ | 25 | Acquisitio | אדוכיאל | ADVKIAL | Advachiel |
| ♉ | 16 | Amissio | אסמודאל | ASMVDAL | Asmodiel |
| ♒ | 28 | Tristitia | כאמבריאל | KAMBRIAL | Cambriel |
| ♓ | 29 | Laetitia | אמניציאל | AMNITzIAL | Amnitziel[3] |
| ♏ | 24 | Rubeus | ברכיאל | BRKIAL | Barachiel/Barakiel |
| ♊ | 17 | Albus | אמבריאל | AMBRIAL | Ambriel |
| ♎ | 22 | Puella | זוריאל | ZVRIAL | Zuriel |
| ♈ | 15 | Puer | מלכידאל | MLKIDAL | Malchidiel |
| ☾ | 13 | Caput Draconis | גבריאל | GBRIAL | Gabriel |
| ☾ | 13 | Cauda Draconis | גבריאל | GBRIAL | Gabriel |

---

[2] See also A40 for the use of this list as Zodiacal angels.

[3] Or Vakabiel וכביאל.

# G. Geomancy

| Geomancy Order. | | Geomantic Figures. | G28. Dr. Rudd's Enochian Letter Correspondence. | G29. Planetary Spirit.[4] | G30. Astrological Correspondence. |
|---|---|---|---|---|---|
| ♋ | 18 | Populus | Ω | Chasmodai | Moon in Cancer (waxing) |
| ♋ | 18 | Via | ꭒ | Chasmodai | Moon in Cancer (waning) |
| ♍ | 20 | Conjunctio | ꓶ | Taphthartharath | Mercury in Virgo |
| ♑ | 26 | Carcer | ꙅ | Zazel | Saturn in Capricorn |
| ♌ | 19 | Fortuna Major | ꭓ | Sorath | Sun in Leo (in Northern Declination) |
| ♌ | 19 | Fortuna Minor | ꝑ | Sorath | Sun in Leo (in Southern Declination) |
| ♐ | 25 | Acquisitio | ꓶ | Hismael | Jupiter in Sagittarius |
| ♉ | 16 | Amissio | ꭗ | Qedemel/Kedemel | Venus in Taurus |
| ♒ | 28 | Tristitia | Ɛ | Hismael | Saturn in Aquarius |
| ♓ | 29 | Laetitia | Ɛ | Hismael | Jupiter in Pisces |
| ♏ | 24 | Rubeus | Ͻ | Bartzabel | Mars in Scorpio [Pisces] |
| ♊ | 17 | Albus | ꭖ | Taphthartharath | Mercury in Gemini |
| ♎ | 22 | Puella | ꭉ | Qedemel/Kedemel | Venus in Libra |
| ♈ | 15 | Puer | V | Bartzabel | Mars in Aries |
| ☾ | 13 | Caput Draconis | ꜒ | Hismael and Qedemel/Kedemel | Caput Draconis |
| ☾ | 13 | Cauda Draconis | ꭍ | Zazel and Bartzabel | Cauda Draconis |

---

[4] See also Column M38.

# H. The Heavens and Astrology

*Planets*

| | | H1. The Ancient Greek Names of the (Wandering Stars or) Planets. | | | H1a. Egyptian Names of the Planets (and god). | H2. Sanskrit and Hindi Names of the Planets. |
|---|---|---|---|---|---|---|
| | | **Greek** | **Transliteration** | **Meaning** | | |
| ☾ | 13 | | | | | Chandra |
| ☿ | 12 | Στιλβων | *Stilbon* | Gleamer, Twinkler | Sebku (Set) | Hemnan, Budha |
| ♀ | 14 | ʽΕοσφοροσ, Φοσφοροσ, Εσπεροσ | *Phosphorus* | Herald of the Dawn, Light Bringer, Vesperine | Bennu-Asar Pi-Neter-Tuau Sbat Uatitha (eve) (Osiris) | Asphujit, Sukra |
| ☼ | 30 | | | | | Heli, Surya |
| ♂ | 27 | Πυροεισ | *Pyroeis* | The Fiery One | Heru-Khuti / Heru-Tesher (Ra) | Ara, Mangala, Kuja |
| ♃ | 21 | Φαεθων | *Phaethon* | The Luminous One | Heru-Ap-Sheta-Taui (n/a) | Jeeva, Brhaspati, Guru |
| ♄ | 32 | Φαινων | *Phainon* | The Shiner Brilliant One | Heru-Ka-Pet (Horus) | Kona, Sani |
| | | | | | | Rahu – North Node[1] |
| | | | | | | Ketu – South Node |

*Aspects between Planets*

| No. | H3. Planetary Aspects – Aspect. | H4. Planetary Aspects – Degrees Between Planets. | H5. Planetary Aspects – Influence of Aspect. |
|---|---|---|---|
| | | | |
| 1 | Conjunction | 0° | Combined influence |
| 2 | Opposition | 180° | Worst |
| 3 | Trine | 120° | Best |
| 4 | Square | 90° | Bad |
| 5 | Quintile | 72° | Good |
| 6 | Sextile | 60° | Good |
| 7 | – | | |
| 8 | Semisquare | 45° | Less Bad |
| 9 | Quincunx | 150° | Negative |
| 10 | Biquintile | 144° | Negative |

---

[1] The Nodes of the Moon are not Planets, but in Vedic astrology are treated as if they were.

# H. The Heavens and Astrology

## Planetary Dignities

| | | H6. Planets Ruling the Signs of the Zodiac. | H7. Planets Exalted in the Signs of the Zodiac. | H8. Planets Detriment in the Signs of the Zodiac. | H9. Planets Fall in the Signs of the Zodiac. |
|---|---|---|---|---|---|
| | | **138** | **139** | | |
| ♈ | 15 | ♂ – Mars | ☼ – Sun | ♀ – Venus | ♄ – Saturn |
| ♉ | 16 | ♀ – Venus | ☾ – Moon | ♂ – Mars | |
| ♊ | 17 | ☿ – Mercury | | ♃ – Jupiter | |
| ♋ | 18 | ☾ – Moon | ♃ – Jupiter | ♄ – Saturn | ♂ – Mars |
| ♌ | 19 | ☼ – Sun | | ♄ – Saturn | |
| ♍ | 20 | ☿ – Mercury | ☿ – Mercury | ♃ – Jupiter | ♀ – Venus |
| ♎ | 22 | ♀ – Venus | ♄ – Saturn | ♂ – Mars | ☼ – Sun |
| ♏ | 24 | ♂ – Mars | | ♀ – Venus | ☾ – Moon |
| ♐ | 25 | ♃ – Jupiter | | ☿ – Mercury | |
| ♑ | 26 | ♄ – Saturn | ♂ – Mars | ☾ – Moon | ♃ – Jupiter |
| ♒ | 28 | ♄ – Saturn | | ☼ – Sun | |
| ♓ | 29 | ♃ – Jupiter | ♀ – Venus | ☿ – Mercury | ☿ – Mercury |

## Zodiac

| | | H10. Dates of the Tropical Zodiac – Ptolemy. | H11. Dates of the Sidereal Zodiac – Vedic. | H12. Dates of the Astronomical Zodiac – when Sun actually enters the Constellation. |
|---|---|---|---|---|
| ♈ | 15 | March 21 | April 14 | April 19 |
| ♉ | 16 | April 21 | May 15 | May 14 |
| ♊ | 17 | May 22 | June 15 | June 21 |
| ♋ | 18 | June 22 | July 17 | July 21 |
| ♌ | 19 | July 24 | August 17 | August 11 |
| ♍ | 20 | August 24 | September 17 | September 17 |
| ♎ | 22 | September 24 | October 18 | October 31 |
| ♏ | 24 | October 24 | November 17 | November 23 |
| ♐ | 25 | November 23 | December 16 | December 18 |
| ♑ | 26 | December 22 | January 15 | January 19 |
| ♒ | 28 | January 21 | February 13 | February 16 |
| ♓ | 29 | February 20 | March 15 | March 12 |

# H. The Heavens and Astrology

| | | H13. Signs of the Zodiac – English. | H14. Greek Names of the Zodiac. | | H15. Greek Names of the Zodiac – Numeration. | H16. Zodiac – Hebrew Names. |
|---|---|---|---|---|---|---|
| | | **137** | | **Transliteration** | | |
| ♈ | 15 | Aries | ΚΡΙΟΣ, Κριος | Krios | 400 | Telah/Taleh |
| ♉ | 16 | Taurus | ΤΑΥΡΟΣ, Ταυροσ | Tauros | 1071 | Shor |
| ♊ | 17 | Gemini | ΔΙΔΥΜΟΙ, Διδυμοι | Didumoi | 538 | Thaumim/Teomim |
| ♋ | 18 | Cancer | ΚΑΡΚΙΝΟΣ, Καρκινος | Karkinos | 471 | Sartan/Sarton |
| ♌ | 19 | Leo | ΛΕΩΝ, Λεον | Leon | 885 | Aryeh/Ari |
| ♍ | 20 | Virgo | ΚΟΡΗ, Κορη<br>ΠΑΡΘΕΝΟΣ, Παρθενος | Kore,<br>Parthenos | 198<br>515 | Bethuleh |
| ♎ | 22 | Libra | ΖΥΓΟΣ, Ζυγος<br>ΧΗΛΑΙ, Χηλαι | Zugos,<br>Celae | 680<br>649 | Maznim/Moznain |
| ♏ | 24 | Scorpio | ΣΚΟΡΠΙΟΣ, Σκορπιος | Skorpios | 750 | Oqereb/Akrab |
| ♐ | 25 | Sagittarius | ΤΟΞΕΥΤΗΣ, Τοξευτης | Toxeutes | 1343 | Qesheth |
| ♑ | 26 | Capricorn | ΑΙΓΟΚΕΡΩΣ, Αιγοκερως | Aigokeros | 814 | Gedi |
| ♒ | 28 | Aquarius | ΥΔΡΧΟΟΣ, Υδρχοος | Hudrochoos | 1444 | Deli |
| ♓ | 29 | Pisces | ΙΧΘΥΕΣ, Ιχθυες | Ichthues | 1224 | Dagim |

| | | H17. Zodiac – Babylonian Names & Meanings. | H18. Zodiac – Akkadian Names & Meanings. | H19. Zodiac as specified by Marduk. |
|---|---|---|---|---|
| ♈ | 15 | Luhunga – a Hired Laborer | I-Ku-U – Prince | Nisannu – Labourer |
| ♉ | 16 | Gud-Annu – Heavenly Bull | Te Te – Bull of Light | Airu – the Star and the Bull of Heaven |
| ♊ | 17 | Mashtab-Bal-Gal-Gal – Great Twin | Do-Patkar – Two Figures | Simanu – the Faithful Shepherd of Heaven |
| ♋ | 18 | Allu – Crab | Nan-Guru – Solar North Gate | Duuzu – the Tortoise |
| ♌ | 19 | Urgula – Great Dog, Lion | Pap-Pilsag – Great Fire | Abu – the Great Lion/Dog |
| ♍ | 20 | Abshim – Spike of Corn | Khusak – Ear of Wheat<br>Bealtis – Wife of Bel | Ululu – virgin with ear of corn |
| ♎ | 22 | Zibanetum – Scales | Sugi – Chariot Yoke | Tashritum – balance scales |
| ♏ | 24 | Girtab – Scorpion | Girtab – Stinger | Arah Shamna – the Scorpion |
| ♐ | 25 | Pa-Bil-Sag – Overseer | Ban – Bow Star<br>Utukagaba – Smiting Sun Face | Kislimu – the god Enurta |
| ♑ | 26 | Sukhuyr-Mashu – Goat-Fish | Shahu – Ibex | Tebetum – the Goat-fish |
| ♒ | 28 | Gula – Giant | Ku-Ur-Ku - Flowing water Seat<br>Rammanu – God of Storms | Shabatu – the Great Star |
| ♓ | 29 | Shimmah – Great Swallow | Nunu – Fish<br>Zib – Boundary | Addaru – the Star and Fishes |

# H. The Heavens and Astrology

| | | H20. Zodiac Demotic – Egyptian Name & Meaning. | H20a. Zodiac – Zoroastrian. | H21. Zodiac – Arabic Names. | H22. Zodiac Names from the *Magical Calendar*. |
|---|---|---|---|---|---|
| ♈ | 15 | Pa-Yesu – Fleece | Varak – the Lamb | Hamal | Thaar |
| ♉ | 16 | Pa-Ka – The Bull | Tora – the Bull | Thaur | Pantheon |
| ♊ | 17 | Na-Hetru – Two Children | Do-patkar –Two figures | Jauza | Confor |
| ♋ | 18 | Pa-Gerhedj – Scarabaeus | Kalachang – the Crab | Saratan | Basan |
| ♌ | 19 | Pa-May-Hes – Fierce | Sher – the Lion | Assad | Corona |
| ♍ | 20 | Ta-Reply – a Female | Khushak – the Virgin | Sambula | Erim |
| ♎ | 22 | Ta-Akhet – Sunrise | Tarazhuk – the Balance | Mizan | Error (*sic*) |
| ♏ | 24 | Ta-Djel – Snake | Gazdum – the Scorpion | Aqrab | Zarnech |
| ♐ | 25 | Pa-Nety-Ateh – Arrow | Nimasp – the Centaur | Qaus | Hermon |
| ♑ | 26 | Pa-Her-Ankh – Goat-Face | Vahik (Capricorn) | Jady | Naim |
| ♒ | 28 | Pa-Mu – The Water | Dul – the Water-pot | Dalw | Saffor |
| ♓ | 29 | Na-Thebeteyu – Fish | Mahik – the Fish) | Hout | Elisan |

| | | H23. Zodiac – Hindu Names. | H23a. Zodiac Tibetan Names | H23b. Zodiac Tibetan Names - meaning | H24. Zodiac – Sanskrit Names. |
|---|---|---|---|---|---|
| ♈ | 15 | Kriya | Lug | Sheep/Ram | Mesha |
| ♉ | 16 | Tavura | gLang | Bull | Vrishabha |
| ♊ | 17 | Jituma | Kh'rig | Couple | Mithuna |
| ♋ | 18 | Kulira | Karta | Frog/crab | Karka |
| ♌ | 19 | Leya | Sengge | Snow-lion | Simha |
| ♍ | 20 | Pathona | Bhumo | Girl | Kanya |
| ♎ | 22 | Juka | Srang | Balance | Tula |
| ♏ | 24 | Kaurpi | sThrig | Scorpion | Vrishchika |
| ♐ | 25 | Taukshika | gShu | Bow & Arrow | Dhanus |
| ♑ | 26 | Akokera | Chusrin | Dragon head with fish tail | Makara |
| ♒ | 28 | Hridroga | Bhumpa | Water-Bearer | Kumbha |
| ♓ | 29 | Chettha | Nya | Fish | Meena |

# H. The Heavens and Astrology

*Elemental Qualities of the Zodiac*

| | | H25. The Quadruplicities of the Zodiac. | H26. The Triplicities of the Zodiac. | H27. The Sub-Elements of the Zodiac. | H28. Image of the Zodiac sign. |
|---|---|---|---|---|---|
| ♈ | 15 | Cardinal | Fire | Fire of Fire | Lightning |
| ♉ | 16 | Fixed | Earth | Air of Earth | Plains |
| ♊ | 17 | Mutable | Air | Water of Air | Vibrations |
| ♋ | 18 | Cardinal | Water | Fire of Water | Rain |
| ♌ | 19 | Fixed | Fire | Air of Fire | Sun |
| ♍ | 20 | Mutable | Earth | Water of Earth | Fields |
| ♎ | 22 | Cardinal | Air | Fire of Air | Wind |
| ♏ | 24 | Fixed | Water | Air of Water | Sea |
| ♐ | 25 | Mutable | Fire | Water of Fire | Rainbow |
| ♑ | 26 | Cardinal | Earth | Fire of Earth | Mountains |
| ♒ | 28 | Fixed | Air | Air of Air | Clouds |
| ♓ | 29 | Mutable | Water | Water of Water | Pool |

| | | H29. Elements Ruling. | H30. Elemental Qualities. | H31. The Elements and the 4 Humours. |
|---|---|---|---|---|
| | **1** | Root of Air | | |
| | **2** | Root of Fire | | |
| | **3** | Root of Water | | |
| | **4** | Water | | |
| | **5** | Fire | | |
| | **6** | Air [as Middle Pillar], Fire | | |
| | **7** | Fire | | |
| | **8** | Water | | |
| | **9** | Air [as Middle Pillar], Water | | |
| | **10** | Root of Earth | | |
| ⊛ | 31b | | | |
| **F** | 31 | Fire | Hot and Dry | Choleric – excess of yellow bile |
| **A** | 11 | Air | Hot and Moist | Sanguine – excess of blood |
| **W** | 23 | Water | Cold and Moist | Phlegmatic – excess of phlegm |
| **E** | 32b | Earth | Cold and Dry | Melancholic – excess of black bile |

# H. The Heavens and Astrology

*Houses of Heaven*

| | | H32. The Houses of Heaven. | H33. Ancient Name / Manilius' Temple Name. | H34. Subject of House. | H35. William Lilly's House Meaning. | H36. Modern House Meaning. |
|---|---|---|---|---|---|---|
| ♈ | 15 | 1st | The Horoscope The Star | Children, Home | Life | Personality and appearance |
| ♉ | 16 | 2nd | Gate of Hades Typhon's Throne | Fortune, estate, warfare, foreign travel | Riches and fortune | Money and possessions |
| ♊ | 17 | 3rd | Goddess [Luna] | Brothers, Business | Brothers, sisters, kin, short journeys | Knowledge, self expression, mental capabilities |
| ♋ | 18 | 4th | Lower Midheaven Daemonium | Parents, Law | Parents, lands, cities, hereditary, treasure | Childhood, family |
| ♌ | 19 | 5th | Good Fortune Daemonia | Children's health, marriage, friendships | Children, messengers | Children, love affairs, pleasure, risks |
| ♍ | 20 | 6th | Bad Fortune Gate of Toil | Health, prosperity | Sickness, servants | Health, work, service |
| ♎ | 22 | 7th | Occident Pluto's Portal | Legacies, dangers | Marriage, open enemies, lawsuits, controversies, contracts, wars, thefts | Love, marriage, business |
| ♏ | 24 | 8th | Beginning of Death Typhon's Throne | Death, class, rank | Death, dowry | Death, legacies |
| ♐ | 25 | 9th | God [Sol] | Vicissitudes, travels, Children | Religion, pilgrimage, long journeys, dreams | Philosophy, religion, travels, dreams |
| ♑ | 26 | 10th | Midheaven Fortune | Marriage, honours, character | Government, preferment, office, dignities, command | Career, responsibility, status, reputation |
| ♒ | 28 | 11th | Good Daemon Omen of Good Fortune | Friendships, health and sickness | Friends, hope, riches of kings | Friends, social life, hope, desire, ambition |
| ♓ | 29 | 12th | Evil Daemon Gate of Toil | Enemies, misfortune, success | Imprisonment, witchcraft, hidden enemies, labour, banishment | Enemies, limitations, secrets |

# H. The Heavens and Astrology

*Mansions of the Moon*

| | | Man-sion No. | H37. Mansions of the Moon – Hindu *Nakshatras*.[2] | | H37a. Mansions of the Moon – Hindu *Nakshatras* – Rulers. | | H38. Mansions of the Moon – Hindu *Nakshatras* – Corresponding Stars & Constellations. |
|---|---|---|---|---|---|---|---|
| | | | **Nakshatra** | **Translation** | **Ruler** | **God/Goddess** | |
| ♈ | 15 | 1 | Ashvinī | Horsewoman | Moon South Node (Ketu) | Ashvinis | β and γ Arietis |
| | | 2 | Bharanī | The Bearer | Venus (Shukra) | Yama | 35, 39, and 41 Arietis |
| ♉ | 16 | 3 | Krittikā | The Cutter | Sun (Ravi) | Agni | Pleiades |
| | | 4 | Rohinī | The Red One | Moon (Chandra) | Prajapati | Aldebaran |
| | | 5 | Mrighashīrsha | Deer's Head | Mars (Mangal) | Soma | λ, φ Orionis |
| ♊ | 17 | 6 | Ārdrā | Moist or Perspiring | Moon North Node (Rahu) | Rudra | Betelgeuse |
| | | 7 | Punarvasu | Good Again | Jupiter (Guru) | Adita | Castor and Pollux |
| ♋ | 18 | 8 | Pushya | Nourishing | Saturn (Shani) | Brihaspati | γ, δ and θ Cancri |
| | | 9 | Āshleshā | The Entwiner | Mercury (Budh) | Sarpas | δ, ε, η, ρ, and σ Hydrae |
| | | 10 | Maghā | The Mighty One | Moon South Node (Ketu) | Pitris | (α, λ, ε, ζ, η, μ Leonis – Regulus |
| ♌ | 19 | 11 | Pūrva Phalgunī | The Fig Tree | Venus (Shukra) | - | δ and θ Leonis |
| | | 12 | Uttara Phalgunī | The Latter Red One | Sun (Surya) | Bhaga | (β and 93 Leonis – Denebola) |
| ♍ | 20 | 13 | Hasta | Hand | Moon (Chandra) | Savitri | α to ε Corvi |
| | | 14 | Chitrā | Brilliant | Mars (Mangal) | Twastry | (Virgo – Spica) |
| ♎ | 22 | 15 | Svātī | The lead goat in a herd | Moon North Node (Rahu) | Vayu | (Bootes – Arcturus) |
| | | 16 | Vishākhā | Forked Branch | Jupiter (Guru) | Indra and Agni | α, β, γ and ι Librae |
| ♏ | 24 | 17 | Anūrādha | Success | Saturn (Shani) | Mitra | β, δ and π Scorpionis |
| | | 18 | Jyeshtha | Eldest | Mercury (Budh) | Indra | α, σ, and τ Scorpionis – Antares |
| | | 19 | Mūla | The Root | Moon South Node | Niritti | ε, ζ, η, θ, ι, κ, λ, μ and ν Scorpionis |
| ♐ | 25 | 20 | Pūrva Ashādhā | The Former Unsubdued | Venus (Shukra) | Apa | δ and ε Sagittarii |
| | | 21 | Uttara Ashādhā | The Latter Unsubdued | Sun (Surya) | Vishwadevas | ζ and σ Sagittarii |
| ♑ | 26 | 22 | Shravana | Ear of Hearing | Moon (Chandra) | The Maintainer | α, β and γ Aquilae – Altair |
| | | 23 | Shravishthā/ Dhanishtha | Wealth | Mars (Mangal) | Vasus | α to δ Delphinis |
| ♒ | 28 | 24 | Shatabhishaj | 100 Physicians | Moon North Node (Rahu) | Varuna | γ Aquarī |
| | | 25 | Pūrva Bhādrapada | Former Beautiful Foot | Jupiter (Guru) | Aja Ekapad | α and β Pegasi – Merkab |
| ♓ | 29 | 26 | Uttara Bhādrapada | Latter Beautiful Foot | Saturn (Shani) | Ahir Buhdnya | γ Pegasi and α Andromedae – Alpheratz |
| | | 27 | Revatī | Wealthy | Mercury (Budh) | Pushan | ζ Piscium |

---

[2] The 12 signs of the Zodiac are just an approximation, as they do not mesh exactly with the 27 Nakshatras, and therefore some Zodiac boundaries occur in mid-Nakshatra.

# H. The Heavens and Astrology

| Man-sion. | H39. The Mansions of the Moon – Abenragel. | H39a. The Mansions of the Moon – meaning. | H40. The Mansions – traditional first degree. | H40a. The Mansions – the first degree in 2000 CE. | H43. The Mansions of the Moon – Agrippa. |
|---|---|---|---|---|---|
| 1 | Alnath/Ilnath *Al Sharatain* | The Two Signals/signs | 0°0' 0" Aries (Ram's head) | 3° Taurus | Alnath, the Horns of Aries. His beginning is from the head of Aries of the eighth sphere. |
| 2 | Albethain *Al Butain* | The Little Belly | 12°11' 26" Aries | 18° Taurus | Allothaim or Albochan, the Belly of Aries. His beginning is from the 12° 51' 22" of the same sign. |
| 3 | Athoraie *Al Thurayya* | The Many Little Ones | 25°22' 52" Aries (Ram's belly) | 29° Taurus | Achaomazon or Athoray, Showering or Pleiades. His beginning is from 25° 42' 51" of Aries. |
| 4 | Addauennam *Al Dabaran* | The Follower | 8°34' 18" Taurus (Aldebaran) | 10° Gemini | Aldebaram or Aldelamen, the Eye or Head of Taurus. His beginning is from the 8° 34'17" of Taurus. |
| 5 | Alhathaya *Al Hak'ah* | The White Spot | 21°45' 44" Taurus (Orion's shoulder) | 24° Gemini | Alchatay or Albachay. The beginning of it is after the 21° 25' 40"of Taurus. |
| 6 | Alhana /Atabuen *Al Han'ah* | The Mark | 4°17' 10" Gemini | 9° Cancer | Alhanna or Alchaya, the Little Star of Great Light. Its beginning is after the 4° 17' 9"of Gemini. |
| 7 | Addirach *Al Dhira* | The Forearm | 17°36' 36" Gemini | 20° Cancer | Aldimiach or Alanach, the Arm of Gemini. It begins from the 17° 8' 34"of Gemini, and lasts even to the end of the sign. |
| 8 | Aluayra *Al Nathra* | The Gap | 0°0' 0" Cancer | 7° Leo | Alnaza or Anatrachya, Misty or Cloudy. |
| 9 | Attraaif *Al Tarf* | The Eyes | 12°11' 26" Cancer | 18° Leo | Archaam or Arcaph, the Eye of the Lion. |
| 10 | Algebhe *Al Jabhah* | The Brow | 25°22' 52" Cancer | 28° Leo | Algelioche or Albgebh, the Neck or Forehead of Leo. |
| 11 | Azobrach *Al Zubrah* | The Mane | 8°34' 18" Leo | 12° Virgo | Azobra or Arduf, the Hair of the Lion's Head. |
| 12 | Azarfa *Al Sarfah* | The Changer | 21°45' 44" Leo | 22° Virgo | Alzarpha or Azarpha, the Tail of Leo. |
| 13 | Aloce *Al Awwa* | The Wings | 4°17' 10" Virgo | 27° Virgo | Alhaire, Dog Star, or the Wings of Virgo. |
| 14 | Azimech *Al Simak* | The Unarmed | 17°36' 36" Virgo | 24° Libra | Achureth or Arimet, by others called Azimeth or Alhumech or Alcheymech, the Spike of Virgo, or Flying Spike (Spica). |

# H. The Heavens and Astrology

| Man-sion. | H39. The Mansions of the Moon – Abenragel. | H39a. The Mansions of the Moon – meaning. | H40. The Mansions – traditional first degree. | H40a. The Mansions – the first degree in 2000 CE. | H43. The Mansions of the Moon – Agrippa. |
|---|---|---|---|---|---|
| 15 | Algarf *Al Ghafr* | The Covering | 0°0' 0" Libra | 4° Scorpio | Agrapha or Algarpha, [the constellation] Covered, or Covered Flying. |
| 16 | Azebone *Al Jubana* | The Claws | 12°11' 26" Libra | 15° Scorpio | Azubene or Ahubene, the Horns of Scorpio. |
| 17 | Alidil *Iklil al Jabhah* | The Crown | 25°22' 52" Libra | 3° Sagittarius | Alchil, the Crown of Scorpio. |
| 18 | Alcalb *Al Kalb/ Al Qalb* | The Heart | 8°34' 18" Scorpio | 10° Sagittarius | Alchas or Altob, the Heart of Scorpio. |
| 19 | Yenla *Al Shaula* | The Sting | 21°45' 44" Scorpio | 24° Sagittarius | Allatha or Achala, by others called Hycula or Axala, the Tail of Scorpio. |
| 20 | Alimain *Al Na'am* | The Beam | 4°17' 10" Sagittarius | 13° Capricorn | Abnahaya, the Beam. |
| 21 | Albeda *Al Baldah* | The City | 17°36' 36" Sagittarius | 16° Capricorn | Abeda or Albeldach, a Defeat. |
| 22 | Sahaddadebe *Al Sa'dal Dhabih* | The Fortune of the Sacrificer | 0°0' 0" Capricorn | 4° Aquarius | Sadahacha or Zodeboluch or Zandeldena, a Pastor. |
| 23 | Zadebolal *Al Sa'dal Bula* | The Fortune of the Glutton | 12°11' 26" Capricorn | 12° Aquarius | Zabadola or Zobrach, Swallowing. |
| 24 | Zaadescod *Al Sa'dal Su'ud* | The Luckiest of the Lucky | 25°22' 52" Capricorn | 23° Aquarius | Sadabath or Chadezoad, the Star of Fortune. |
| 25 | Sadalabbia *Al Sa'dal Ahbiyah* | The Lucky Star of Hidden Things | 8°34' 18" Aquarius | 4° Pisces | Sadalabra or Sadalachia, a Butterfly, or a Spreading Forth. |
| 26 | Farg almocaden *Al Fargh al Mukdim / Awwal* | The Upper Spout | 21°45' 44" Aquarius | 23° Pisces | Alpharg or Phragol Mocaden, the First Drawing. |
| 27 | Alfarg amahar *Al Fargh al Thani* | The Lower Spout | 4°17' 10" Pisces | 9° Aries | Alcharya or Alhalgalmoad, the Second Drawing. |
| 28 | Bathnealoth *Al Batn al Hut* | The Belly of the Fish | 17°36' 36" Pisces | 22° Aries | Albotham or Alchalcy, Pisces. |

# H. The Heavens and Astrology

| Man-sion. | H41. The Mansions of the Moon according to Abenragel – Indian Interpretation. | H42. The Mansions of the Moon according to Abenragel – Dorotheos Interpretation. | H44. The Mansions of the Moon – Virtues – Agrippa. |
|---|---|---|---|
| | | | |
| 1 | Good for taking medicines, pasturing livestock, making journey, except second hour | Good for buying tame animals, for journeys, especially voyages, for making arms, planting trees, cutting hair or nails, putting on new clothes. Bad for contracting marriage (holds for Moon in Aries), making partnerships, or buying slaves, who will be bad, disobedient or run away. If captured, prison will be bad and strong. | It causes discords, and journeys. |
| 2 | Good for sowing and making journeys. | Bad for marriage, buying slaves, and for boats and prisoners similar to Alnath | It is conducive to the finding of treasures, and to the retaining of captives. |
| 3 | Good for trading and revenge on enemies; indifferent for travel. | Good for buying tame animals and hunting, for all matters involving fire, and for doing good. Bad for marriage, and making partnerships, especially with those more powerful. Bad for buying cattle or flocks, for planting trees, sowing or putting on new clothes. If captured, prison will be strong and long. Water journeys will bring fear and danger. | It is profitable to sailors, huntsmen, and alchemists. |
| 4 | Good for sowing, for putting on new clothes, for receiving women and feminine things, for demolishing a building or starting a new one, for making a journey, except for third part of day. | Good to build a house, which will be solid, and building in general, to dig a ditch, to buy slaves, who will be loyal and honest, and to buy livestock. Also good to be with kings and lords, for receiving power or honours. Bad to contract marriage, since woman will prefer another, or to enter partnerships, especially with those more powerful. Voyages will involve big waves. If captured, the captivity will be long but, if captured for skills, will be released through goodwill. | It causes the destruction and hindrances of buildings, fountains, wells, of gold mines, the flight of creeping things, and begets discord. |
| 5 | Good for contracting marriage, for putting boys to study laws, scriptures or writing, for making medicines, for making a journey. | Good for buying slaves, who will be good and loyal, for building, for travel by water, for washing head, indeed general washing, and cutting hair. Bad for partnerships. If captured, imprisonment will be long, unless captured for skills, when he will escape. | It helps the return from a journey, helps the instruction of scholars, it confirms edifices, and it gives health and good will. |
| 6 | Good for kings to declare war, enrollment of armies and cavalry, for knights seeking better pay, for the successful siege of a city, for smiting enemies and evildoers. Bad for sowing, seeking a loan, or burial. | Good for partnerships and ventures, associates will agree and be honest and loyal, for hunting, for journeys by water, though delays. Bad for taking medicine and for treating wounds. New clothes put on will soon tear. If captured, release within three days or very long imprisonment. | It is conducive to hunting, and besieging of towns, and revenge of princes, it destroys harvests and fruits and hinders the operation of the physician. |

# H. The Heavens and Astrology

| Man-sion. | H41. The Mansions of the Moon according to Abenragel – Indian Interpretation. | H42. The Mansions of the Moon according to Abenragel – Dorotheos Interpretation. | H44. The Mansions of the Moon – Virtues – Agrippa. |
|---|---|---|---|
| | | | |
| 7 | Good for ploughing and sowing, for putting on new clothes, for women's jewellery, for cavalry. Bad for journeys, except in last third of night. | Good for partnerships, which will be good and useful, with loyal and agreeable associates, for washing head, cutting hair and new clothes, for buying slaves and livestock, for smiting or making peace with enemies, for voyages towards destination, but delays on return. Bad for buying land, and for giving up medicine. If captured, unless he escapes in three days, he will die in prison. Likewise, if he has escaped something he fears, he will encounter it again. | It confers gain and friendship, it is profitable to lovers, it fears flies, and destroys magisteries. |
| 8 | Good for taking medicine, for cutting new clothes, for women's jewellery and putting it on. Rain will bring benefit not damage. Bad for travel, except for last third of night. | Good for voyages, swift on outward and return journeys. Marriages contracted will be harmonious for a while, then discordant. A slave bought will deceitful, accuse his master, and run away. A partnership started will involve fraud on either side. If captured, long imprisonment. | It causes love, friendship, and society of fellow travelers; it drives away mice and afflicts captives, confirming their imprisonment. |
| 9 | Bad for sowing, journeys, entrusting anything to anyone, or seeking to harm anyone. | Good for voyages, outward and return, for reinforcing doors and making locks, for making beds and putting up bed-curtains, for transplanting wheat. Bad for partnerships, which will involve fraud on either side. Bad for cutting hair, or new clothes. Putting on new clothes may lead to drowning in them. If captured, long imprisonment. | It hinders harvests and travelers, and puts discord between men. |
| 10 | Good for contracting marriage, for sugar and what is made with it. Bad for journeys and entrusting anything, for putting on new clothes or for women's jewellery. | Good for buildings, which will last, and for partnerships, benefiting all parties. If captured, at the command of a leader or because of great deed, and long, hard imprisonment. | It strengthens buildings, yields love, benevolence and help against enemies. |
| 11 | Good for sowing and planting, for besieging. Indifferent for trade and journeys. Bad for freeing captives. | Good for buildings and foundations, which will last, and for partnerships, from which associates will gain. Good for cutting hair. Bad for new clothes. If captured, at the command of a leader, and long imprisonment | It is good for voyages, and gain by merchandise, and for redemption of captives. |
| 12 | Good for starting all building, for arranging lands, sowing and planting, for marriage, for putting on new clothes, for women's jewellery, for making a journey in the first third of day. | Good for buying slaves and livestock, once the Moon is out of Leo, since the Lion is a great devourer. (If he eats a lot it leads to stomach pains, power, boldness and obstinacy.) What is lent will not be returned, or only with great effort and delay. Voyages will be long, hard and dangerous, but not fatal. | It gives prosperity to harvests, and plantations, but hinders seamen, but it is good for the bettering of servants, captives and companions. |

# H. The Heavens and Astrology

| Man-sion. | H41. The Mansions of the Moon according to Abenragel – Indian Interpretation. | H42. The Mansions of the Moon according to Abenragel – Dorotheos Interpretation. | H44. The Mansions of the Moon – Virtues – Agrippa. |
|---|---|---|---|
| | | | |
| 13 | Good to plough, sow, make a journey, marry, free captives. | Good to buy a slave, who will be good, loyal and honest, to start building, to give oneself to pleasures and jokes, to come before a king or famous man, to take medicines, to cut new clothes, to wash or cut hair. Not bad to marry a corrupted woman, and, if marrying a virgin, the marriage will last a while. A voyage undertaken will involve delay in return. If captured, he will be injured in prison, but captivity will end well. | It is prevalent for benevolence, gain, voyages, harvests, and freedom of captives. |
| 14 | Good for marrying a woman who is not a virgin, for medicines, sowing and planting. Bad for journeys or entrusting something to someone. | Good to start a voyage and a partnership, which will be profitable and harmonious, to buy a slave, who will be good, honest and respectful. Marriage with a virgin will not last long, and it is not bad to marry a corrupted woman. If captured, he will soon escape or be released. | It causes the love of married folk, it cures the sick, it's profitable to sailors, but it hinders journeys by land; and in these the second quarter of heaven is completed. |
| 15 | Good to dig wells and ditches, to cure illnesses to do with wind, but not others. Bad for journeys. | Good for moving house, for adapting or preparing a house, its owner and site. Good to seek to do a good deed, to buy and sell, but selling slaves not livestock, because Libra is a human sign. Bad for both land and sea journeys. Marriage will not last in harmony, or only for a while. Partnerships entered will lead to fraud and discord. Money lent will not be returned. Bad for cutting hair. | It's profitable for the extracting of treasures, for digging of pits; it helps forward divorce, discord, and the destruction of houses and enemies, and hinders travelers. |
| 16 | Bad for journeys, trade, medicines, sowing, women's jewellery, for cutting or putting on new clothes. | A slave bought will be good, loyal and honest. Bad for marriage, which will only last in harmony for a while, for partnerships, which will lead to dishonesty and mutual suspicion. If captured, he will soon be out of prison, if God wills. | It hinders journeys and wedlock, harvests and merchandise; it pre-vails for redemption of captives. |
| 17 | Good to buy flocks and livestock, to change their pasture, to put on new jewellery and besiege towns. | Good for starting building, which will be solid and durable, for settling a dispute between two people, to foster love, and love begun will be absolutely solid and last for ever. Good for all medicine. Voyages started will bring anxiety and sorrows, but he will survive. Partnerships started will bring discord, and he who marries, will find his wife impure. Bad for selling slaves or cutting hair. | It betters a bad fortune, makes love durable, strengthens buildings, and helps seamen. |

# H. The Heavens and Astrology

| Man-sion. | H41. The Mansions of the Moon according to Abenragel – Indian Interpretation. | H42. The Mansions of the Moon according to Abenragel – Dorotheos Interpretation. | H44. The Mansions of the Moon – Virtues – Agrippa. |
|---|---|---|---|
| | | | |
| 18 | Good for building, for arranging lands and buying them, for receiving honours and power. If it begins to rain, it will be wholesome, useful and good. Eastwards journeys are favoured. | Building undertaken will be solid. Good for planting and taking medicines. If a man gets married and the Mars is with the Moon here, he will find her not to be a virgin. If he enters a ship he will come out again. Bad for selling slaves, new clothes, cutting hair. Partnerships will result in discord. | It causes discord, sedition, conspiracy against princes and mighty ones, and revenge from enemies, but it frees captives and helps edifices. |
| 19 | Good for besieging towns and encampments, for disputing against enemies, for making a journey, for sowing and for planting trees. Bad for entrusting something to somebody. | If a man gets married, he will find her not to be a virgin. Bad for voyages, which will end in shipwreck, for partnerships, which will be discordant, for selling slaves, and very bad for a captive. | It helps in the besieging of cities and taking of towns; and in the driving of men from their places, and for the destruction of seamen, and perdition of captives. |
| 20 | Good for buying animals. Rain will be good and do no harm. Indifferent for journeys. | Good for buying small animals. Bad for partnerships and captivity. | It helps for the taming of wild beasts, for the strengthening of prisons, it destroys the wealth of societies, and it compels a man to come to a certain place. |
| 21 | Good for starting any building, for sowing, for buying lands or livestock, for buying and making women's jewellery and clothes. Indifferent for journeys. | A woman who is divorced or widowed will not marry again. Indifferent for slaves bought, since they will think much of themselves and will not humble themselves to their masters. | It is good for harvests, gain, buildings and travelers, and causes divorce; and in this is the third quarter of heaven completed. |
| 22 | Good for medicine and journeys, except for last third of day. Good for putting on new clothes. | Good for entering a partnership, which will bring profit and usefulness, and for entering a ship, though there will be great anxieties from a strong desire to return and the like. A man who becomes engaged will break the engagement before the wedding and die within six months, or the couple will be in conflict and live badly, with the wife mistreating the husband. Bad for buying slaves, who will do ill to their master, or run away, or be irksome or bad. If captured, he will soon gain freedom. | It promotes the flight of servants and captives, this they may escape, and helps in the curing of diseases. |
| 23 | Good for medicine, for putting on new jewellery and clothes, for a journey in the middle third of day. Bad to entrust something to someone. | Good for partnerships. Bad for marriage, since wife will mistreat husband and they will not be together much, for entering a ship, if a short voyage is wanted, for buying slaves. If captured, he will soon regain liberty. | It makes for divorce, liberty of captives and the health of the sick. |
| 24 | Good for medicine, sending out armies and soldiers. Indifferent for journeys. Bad for merchandise, jewellery, putting on new clothes, marrying. | A slave bought will be strong, loyal and good. Bad for partnerships, which will end in great harm and conflict, and for entering a ship. Marriage will only last a while. If captured, he will soon be free. | It is prevalent for the benevolence of married folk, for the victory of soldiers, it hurts the execution of government, and hinders that it may not be exercised. |

# H. The Heavens and Astrology

| Man-sion. | H41. The Mansions of the Moon according to Abenragel – Indian Interpretation. | H42. The Mansions of the Moon according to Abenragel – Dorotheos Interpretation. | H44. The Mansions of the Moon – Virtues – Agrippa. |
|---|---|---|---|
| | | | |
| 25 | Good for besieging towns and encampments, for going into a quarrel, for pursuing enemies and doing them harm, for sending messengers. Favours journeys southwards. Bad for marriage, for sowing, for merchandise, for buying livestock. | Good for buying slaves, who will be strong, loyal and good, for building, which will be solid and durable, and for voyages, though there will be delays. Marriage will only last for a while. Bad for partnerships, which will end badly and harmfully, and a slave will escape. | It helps besieging and revenge, it destroys enemies, makes divorce, confirms prisons and buildings, hastens messengers, it is conducive to spells against copulation, and so binds every member of man so that it cannot perform its duty. |
| 26 | Good for making a journey in the first third of the day, but the rest is good for neither journeys nor any other beginning. | Good for building, which will be solid and durable, for buying a slave, who will be loyal and good, for entering a ship, though there will be delays. Bad for partnerships. Marriage will not last. If captured, he will be in prison for a long time. | It makes for the union and love of men, for the health of captives, it destroys prisons and buildings. |
| 27 | Good for sowing, and useful for trading. Good for marriage. Indifferent for journeys, except for middle third of night when very bad. Bad for entrusting something to someone, or lending anything. | If starting a partnership, it will begin well but end in harm and conflict. Entering a ship will bring damage, dangers and travails. A slave bought will be bad. If captured, he will not leave prison. | It increases harvests, revenues, gain, it heals infirmities, but hinders buildings, prolongs prison sentences, causes danger to seamen, and helps to work mischief on whom you shall please. |
| 28 | Good for trade, sowing and medicines. Good for marriage. Indifferent for journeys, except for middle third of night when bad. Bad for entrusting something to someone, or lending anything. | A partnership started will begin well but end badly. A slave bought will be bad, irascible and very proud. If captured, he will not leave prison. | It increases harvests and merchandise, it secures travelers through dangerous places, it makes for the joy of married couples, but it strengthens prisons, and causes loss of treasures. |

# H. The Heavens and Astrology

| Man-sion. | H45. Images of the Mansions of the Moon – Magical Objectives. | H46. Images of the Mansions of the Moon – Magical Method. |
|---|---|---|
| 1 | For the destruction of someone | They made in an iron ring the image of a black man in a garment made of hair, and girdled round, casting a small lance with his right hand; they sealed this in black wax, and perfumed it with liquid storax, and wished some evil to come. |
| 2 | Against the wrath of the prince, and for reconciliation with him | They sealed in white wax and mastic, the image of a king crowned, and perfumed it with lignum aloes. |
| 3 | They affirmed that this gives happy fortune and every good thing | They made an image in a silver ring, whose table was square, the figure of which was a woman well clothed, sitting in a chair, her right hand being lifted up on her head; they sealed it and perfumed it with musk, camphire and *calamus aromaticus*. |
| 4 | For revenge, separation, enmity and ill wil | They sealed in red wax the image of a soldier sitting on a horse, holding a serpent in his right hand; they perfumed it with red myrrh, and storax. |
| 5 | For the favour of kings and officers, and good entertainment | They sealed in silver the head of a man, and perfumed it with sanders. |
| 6 | For to procure love betwixt two persons | They sealed in white wax two images embracing one another, and perfumed them with lignum aloes and amber. |
| 7 | For to obtain every good thing | They sealed in silver the image of a man well clothed, holding up his hands to heaven as it were praying and supplicating, and perfumed it with good odours. |
| 8 | For victory in war | They made a seal of tin, being an image of an eagle having the face of a man, and perfumed it with brimstone. |
| 9 | To cause infirmities | They made a seal of lead, being the image of a man wanting his privy parts, shutting his eyes with his hands; and they perfumed it with rosin of the pine. |
| 10 | To facilitate child-bearing, and to cure the sick | They made a seal of gold, being the head of a lion, and perfumed it with amber. |
| 11 | For fear, reverence and worship | They made a seal of a plate of gold, being the image of a man riding on a lion, holding the ear thereof in his left hand, and in his right, holding forth a bracelet of gold, and they perfumed it with good odours and saffron. |
| 12 | For the separation of lovers | They made a seal of black lead, being the image of a dragon fighting with a man, and they perfumed it with the hairs of a lion, and asafetida. |
| 13 | For the agreement of married couples, and for the dissolving of the charms against copulation | They made a seal of the images of both, of the man in red wax, of the woman in white, and caused them to embrace one another, perfuming it with lignum aloes and amber. |
| 14 | For divorce and separation of the man from the woman | They made a seal of red copper, being the image of a dog biting his tail, and they perfumed it with the hair of a black dog, and black cat. |

# H. The Heavens and Astrology

| Man-sion. | H45. Images of the Mansions of the Moon – Magical Objectives. | H46. Images of the Mansions of the Moon – Magical Method. |
|---|---|---|
| | | |
| 15 | For to obtain friendship and good will | They made the image of a man sitting, and indicting of letters, and perfumed it with frankincense and nutmegs. |
| 16 | For to gain much merchandising | They made a seal of silver, being the image of a man sitting upon a chair, holding a balance in his hand, and they perfumed it with well smelling spices. |
| 17 | Against thieves and robbers | They sealed with an iron seal the image of an ape, and perfumed it with the hair of an ape. |
| 18 | Against fevers and pains of the belly | They made a seal of copper, being the image of a snake holding his tail above his head, and they perfumed it with hartshorn, and reported the same seal to put to flight serpents, and all venomous creatures from the place where it is buried. |
| 19 | For facilitating birth and provoking the menstrual flow | They made a seal of copper, being the image of a woman holding her hands upon her face; and they perfumed it with liquid storax. |
| 20 | For hunting | They made a seal of tin, being the image of Sagittarius, half a man and half a horse, and they perfumed it with the head of a wolf. |
| 21 | For the destruction of somebody | They made the image of a man with a double countenance, before and behind, and they perfumed it with brimstone and jet, and did put it in a box of brass, and with it brimstone and jet, and the hair of him whom they would hurt. |
| 22 | For the security of runaways | They made a seal of iron, being the image of a man with wings on his feet, bearing a helmet on his head, and they perfumed it with argent vive. |
| 23 | For destruction and wasting | They made a seal of iron, being the image of a cat, having a dog's head, and they perfumed it with the hairs of a dog's head, and buried it in the place where they did pretend to hurt. |
| 24 | For the multiplying of herds of cattle | They took the horn of a ram, bull, or goat, or of that sort of cattle which they would increase, and sealed in it burning with an iron seal, the image of a woman giving suck to her son, and they hanged it on the neck of that cattle who was the leader of the flock, or they sealed it in his horn. |
| 25 | For the preservation of trees and harvests | They sealed in the wood of a figure, the image of a man planting, and they perfumed it with the flowers of the fig tree, and did hang it on the tree. |
| 26 | For love and favour | They sealed in white wax and mastic the image of a woman washing and combing her hairs, and they perfumed it with things smelling very well. |
| 27 | For to destroy fountains, pits, medicinal waters and baths | They made of red earth the image of a man winged, holding in his hand an empty vessel, and perforated, and the image being burnt, they did put in the vessel asafetida and liquid storax, and they did overwhelm and bury it in the pond or fountain which they would destroy. |
| 28 | For to gather fishes together | They made a seal of copper, being the image of a fish, and they perfumed it with the skin of a sea fish, and did cast it into the water, wheresoever they would have the fish to gather together. |

# H. The Heavens and Astrology

| Mansion. | H47. Mansions of the Moon – Chinese *hsiu*. | H48. Chinese *hsiu* (Wade-Giles). | H49. Chinese *hsiu* – English Translation. | H50. Chinese *hsiu* – Associated Planet. | H51. Chinese *hsiu* – Associated Animal. | H52. Number of Degrees Extent. | H53. Starting Point. |
|---|---|---|---|---|---|---|---|
| | | | | | | Basis 365.25° 'day degrees' | Basis 360° |
| 1 | 角 | Chiao | Horn | Jupiter | Scaly Dragon | 12.75 | 113.60 |
| 2 | 亢 | K'ang | Neck | Venus | Dragon | 9.75 | 103.98 |
| 3 | 氐 | Ti | Base/Root | Saturn | Marten | 16.25 | 87.96 |
| 4 | 房 | Fang | Room | Sun | Rabbit | 5.75 | 82.30 |
| 5 | 心 | Hsin | Heart | Moon | Fox | 6.00 | 76.38 |
| 6 | 尾 | Wei | Tail | Mars | Tiger | 18.00 | 58.64 |
| 7 | 箕 | Chi | Sieve/Winnowing basket | Mercury | Leopard | 9.50 | 49.28 |
| 8 | 斗 | Tou | Dipper Measure | Jupiter | Unicorn | 22.75 | 26.85 |
| 9 | 牛 | Niu | Ox herd boy | Venus | Ox | 7.00 | 19.96 |
| 10 | 女 | Nu | Maiden | Saturn | Bat | 11.00 | 9.11 |
| 11 | 虛 | Hsu | Void | Sun | Rat | 9.25 | 0.00 |
| 12 | 危 | Wei | Danger (Rooftop) | Moon | Swallow | 16.00 | 344.23 |
| 13 | 室火豬 | Shih | House | Mars | Pig | 18.25 | 326.24 |
| 14 | 壁 | Pi | Wall | Mercury | Porcupine | 9.75 | 316.63 |
| 15 | 奎 | K'uei | Astride | Jupiter | Wolf | 18.00 | 298.89 |
| 16 | 婁 | Lou | Mound/Tether | Venus | Dog | 12.75 | 286.32 |
| 17 | 胃 | Wei | Stomach | Saturn | Pheasant | 15.25 | 271.29 |
| 18 | 昂 | Mao | Pleiades constellation | Sun | Cock | 11.00 | 260.45 |
| 19 | 畢 | Pi | Conclusion or graduation | Moon | Crow | 16.50 | 244.19 |
| 20 | 觜 | Tsui | Beak/Turtle | Mars | Monkey | 0.50 | 243.69 |
| 21 | 參 | Shen | Crossing Mixture | Mercury | Ape | 9.50 | 234.33 |
| 22 | 井 | Ching | Well | Jupiter | Wild Dog | 30.25 | 204.51 |
| 23 | 鬼 | Kuei | Ghost | Venus | Sheep | 2.50 | 202.05 |
| 24 | 柳 | Liu | Willow | Saturn | Buck | 13.50 | 188.74 |
| 25 | 星 | Hsing | [Seven] Stars | Sun | Horse | 6.75 | 182.09 |
| 26 | 張 | Chang | Spread (e.g. of bow or net) | Moon | Deer | 17.75 | 164.60 |
| 27 | 翼 | I | Wings | Mars | Snake | 20.25 | 144.64 |
| 28 | 軫 | Chen | Carriage seat | Mercury | Worm | 18.75 | 126.16 |

# H. The Heavens and Astrology

*Decans and 'Faces'*

| | | H54. The 36 Decans with Planetary Rulers – Traditional. | | |
|---|---|---|---|---|
| | | **1st Decan** | **2nd Decan** | **3rd Decan** |
| ♈ | 15 | Mars | Sun | Venus |
| ♉ | 16 | Mercury | Moon | Saturn |
| ♊ | 17 | Jupiter | Mars | Sun |
| ♋ | 18 | Venus | Mercury | Moon |
| ♌ | 19 | Saturn | Jupiter | Mars |
| ♍ | 20 | Sun | Venus | Mercury |
| ♎ | 22 | Moon | Saturn | Jupiter |
| ♏ | 24 | Mars | Sun | Venus |
| ♐ | 25 | Mercury | Moon | Saturn |
| ♑ | 26 | Jupiter | Mars | Sun |
| ♒ | 28 | Venus | Mercury | Moon |
| ♓ | 29 | Saturn | Jupiter | Mars |

| | | H55. The 36 Decans with Planetary Rulers – Golden Dawn. | | |
|---|---|---|---|---|
| | | **1st Decan** | **2nd Decan** | **3rd Decan** |
| ♈ | 15 | Mars | Sun | Jupiter |
| ♉ | 16 | Venus | Mercury | Saturn |
| ♊ | 17 | Mercury | Venus | Saturn |
| ♋ | 18 | Moon | Mars | Jupiter |
| ♌ | 19 | Sun | Jupiter | Mars |
| ♍ | 20 | Mercury | Saturn | Venus |
| ♎ | 22 | Venus | Saturn | Mercury |
| ♏ | 24 | Mars | Jupiter | Moon |
| ♐ | 25 | Jupiter | Mars | Sun |
| ♑ | 26 | Saturn | Venus | Mercury |
| ♒ | 28 | Saturn | Mercury | Venus |
| ♓ | 29 | Jupiter | Moon | Mars |

# H. The Heavens and Astrology

| | | H56. Magical Images of the Ascendant Decans from the *Picatrix*. | H57. Magical Images of the Succedent Decans from the *Picatrix*. | H58. Magical Images of the Cadent Decans from the *Picatrix*. |
|---|---|---|---|---|
| | | **149** | **150** | **151** |
| ♈ | 15 | A tall, dark, restless man, with keen flame-coloured eyes, bearing a sword. | A green-clad woman, with one leg bare from the ankle to the knee | A restless man in scarlet robes, with golden bracelets on his arms |
| ♉ | 16 | A woman with long and beautiful hair, clad in flame-coloured robes. | A man of like figure (to the ascendant), with cloven hooves like an ox. | A swarthy man with white lashes, an elephantine body with long legs; with a horse, a stag and calf |
| ♊ | 17 | A beautiful woman with her two horses | An eagle-headed man, with a bow and arrow who wears a crowned steel helmet | A man in mail, armoured with bow, arrows, and quiver |
| ♋ | 18 | A man with distorted face and hands, a horse's body, white feet, and a girdle of leaves | A beautiful woman wreathed with myrtle. She holds a lyre and sings of love and gladness | A swift-footed person, with a viper in his hand, leading dogs |
| ♌ | 19 | A man in sordid raiment, with him a nobleman on horseback, accompanied by bears and dogs | A man crowned with a white myrtle wreath, holding a bow | A swarthy hairy man, with a drawn sword and shield |
| ♍ | 20 | A virgin clad in linen, with an apple or pomegranate | Tall, fair, large man, with him a woman holding a large black oil jar | An old man leaning on a staff and wrapped in a mantle |
| ♎ | 22 | A dark man, in his right hand a spear and laurel branch, and in his left a book | A man, dark, yet delicious of countenance | A man riding on an ass, preceded by a wolf |
| ♏ | 24 | A man with a lance in his right hand, in his left a human head | A man riding a camel, with a scorpion in his hand. | A horse and a wolf |
| ♐ | 25 | A man with 3 bodies – 1 black, 1 red, 1 white | A man leading cows, and before him an ape and a bear | A man leading another by his hair and slaying him |
| ♑ | 26 | A man holding in his right hand a javelin and in his left a lapwing | A man with an ape running before him | A man holding a book which he opens and shuts |
| ♒ | 28 | A man with bowed head and a bag in his hand | A man arrayed like a king, looking with pride and conceit on all around him | A small-headed man dressed like a woman, and with him an old man |
| ♓ | 29 | A man with two bodies, joined by their hands | A grave man pointing to the sky | A man of grave and thoughtful face, with a bird in his hand, before him a woman and an ass |

| | | H59. Magical Images of the 36 Faces of the Zodiac – Agrippa. | | |
|---|---|---|---|---|
| | | **1st Face** | **2nd Face** | **3rd Face** |
| ♈ | 15 | A black man, standing and clothed, in a white garment, girdled about, of a great body, with reddish eyes, and great strength, and like one that is angry; and this image signifieth and causes boldness, fortitude, loftiness and shamelessness. | A woman, outwardly clothed with a red garment, and under it a white, spreading abroad over her feet. This image causes nobleness, height of a Kingdom, and greatness of dominion. | A white man, pale, with reddish hair, and clothed with a red garment, who carrying on the one hand a golden Bracelet, and holding forth a wooden staff, is restless, and like one in wrath, because he cannot perform that good he would. This image bestows wit, meekness, joy and beauty. |
| ♉ | 16 | A naked man, an Archer, Harvester or Husbandman, who goes forth to sow, plough, build, people, and divide the earth, according to the rules of Geometry; | A naked man, holding in his hand a key; it gives power, nobility, and dominion over people. | A man in whose hand is a Serpent, and a dart, and is the image of necessity and profit, and also of misery & slavery. |
| ♊ | 17 | A man in whose hand is a rod, and he is, as it were, serving another; it grants wisdom, and the knowledge of numbers and arts in which there is no profit. | A man in whose hand is a Pipe, and another being bowed down, digging the earth: and they signify infamous and dishonest agility, as that of Jesters and Jugglers; it also signifies labours and painful searching. | A man seeking for Arms, and a fool holding in the right hand a Bird, and in his left a pipe, and they are the significations of forgetfulness, wrath, boldness, jests, scurrilities, and unprofitable words. |
| ♋ | 18 | A young Virgin, adorned with fine cloathes, and having a Crown on her head; it gives acuteness of senses, subtlety of wit, and the love of men. | A man clothed in comely apparel and woman sitting at the table and playing; it bestows riches, mirth, gladness, and the love of women. | A man, a Hunter with his lance and horn, bringing out dogs to hunt; the signification of this is the contention of men, the pursuing of those who fly, the hunting and possessing of things by arms and brawling. |
| ♌ | 19 | A man riding on a Lion; it signifieth boldness, violence, cruelty, wickedness, lust and labours to be sustained. | A man on whose head is a Crown; he hath the appearance of an angry man, and one that threatens, having in his right hand a Sword drawn out of the scabbard, & in his left a buckler; it hath signification upon hidden contentions, and unknown victories, & upon base men, and upon the occasions of quarrels and battles. | A young man in whose hand is a Whip, and a man very sad, and of an ill aspect; they signify love and society, and the loss of ones right for avoiding strife. |
| ♍ | 20 | A good maiden, and a man casting seeds; it signifieth getting of wealth, ordering of diet, plowing, sowing, and peopling; | A black man clothed with a skin, and a man having a bush of hair, holding a bag; they signify gain, scraping together of wealth and covetousness. | A white woman and deaf, or an old man leaning on a staff; the signification of this is to shew weakness, infirmity, loss of members, destruction of trees, and depopulation of lands. |

| | | 1st Face | 2nd Face | 3rd Face |
|---|---|---|---|---|
| | | H59. Magical Images of the 36 Faces of the Zodiac – Agrippa. | | |
| ♎ | 22 | An angry man, in whose hand is a Pipe, and the form of a man reading in a book; the operation of this is in justifying and helping the miserable and weak against the powerful and wicked. | Two men furious and wrathful and a man in a comely garment, sitting in a chair; and the signification of these is to shew indignation against the evil, and quietness and security of life with plenty of good things. | A violent man holding a bow, and before him a naked man, and also another man holding bread in one hand, and a cup of wine in the other; the signification of these is to shew wicked lusts, singings, sports and gluttony. |
| ♏ | 24 | A woman of good face and habit, and two men striking her; the operations of these are for comeliness, beauty, and for strife, treacheries, deceits, detractations, and perditions. | A man naked, and a woman naked, and a man sitting on the earth, and before him two dogs biting one another; and their operation is for impudence, deceit, and false dealing, and for to lend mischief and strife amongst men. | A man bowed downward upon his knees, and a woman striking him with a staff, and it is the signification of drunkenness, fornication, wrath, violence, and strife. |
| ♐ | 25 | A man armed with a coat of male [mail], and holding a naked sword in his hand; the operation of this is for boldness, malice, and liberty. | A woman weeping, and covered with clothes; the operation of this is for sadness and fear of his own body. | A man like in colour to gold, or an idle man playing with a staff; and the signification of this is in following our own wills, and obstinacy in them, and in activeness for evil things, contentions, and horrible matters. |
| ♑ | 26 | A woman, and a man carrying full bags; and the signification of these is for to go forth and to rejoice, to gain and to lose with weakness and baseness. | Two women, and a man looking towards a Bird flying in the Air; and the signification of these is for the requiring those things which cannot be done, and for the searching after those things which cannot be known. | A woman chaste in body, and wise in her work, and a banker gathering his money together on the table; the signification of this is to govern in prudence, in covetousness of money, and in avarice. |
| ♒ | 28 | A prudent man, and of a woman spinning; and the signification of these is in the thought and labour for gain, in poverty and baseness. | A man with a long beard; and the signification of this belongs to the understanding, meekness, modesty, liberty and good manners. | A black and angry man; and the signification of this is in expressing insolence; and impudence. |
| ♓ | 29 | A man carrying burdens on his shoulder, and well clothed; it hath his signification in journeys, change of place, and in carefulness of getting wealth and cloaths. | A woman of a good countenance, and well adorned; and the signification is to desire and put ones self on about high and great matters. | A man naked, or a youth, and nigh him a beautiful maid, whose head is adorned with flowers, and it hath his signification of rest, idleness, delight, fornication, and for the embracing of women. |

# H. The Heavens and Astrology

| | | H60. Egyptian Names of the Ascendent Decans. | H61. Egyptian Names of the Succedent Decans. | H62. Egyptian Names of the Cadent Decans. |
|---|---|---|---|---|
| | | **168** | **170** | **172** |
| ♈ | 15 | Assicean /Assican | Lencher / Senacher | Asentacer |
| ♉ | 16 | Asicath | Virvaso / Viroaso | Aharph |
| ♊ | 17 | Thesogar | Verasua | Tepistosoa |
| ♋ | 18 | Sothis | Syth | Thuismis |
| ♌ | 19 | Aphruimis / Afruimis | Sitlacer / Sithacer | Phuonidie / Fuonisie |
| ♍ | 20 | Thumis | Thopitius | Aphut / Afut |
| ♎ | 22 | Serucuth | Aterechinis | Arepien / Arpien |
| ♏ | 24 | Sentacer | Tepiseuth / Tepiseoth | Senciner |
| ♐ | 25 | Eregbuo | Sagen | Chenen |
| ♑ | 26 | Themeso | Epima | Homoth |
| ♒ | 28 | Oroasoer | Astiro | Tepisatras |
| ♓ | 29 | Archatapias | Thopibui | Atembui |

| | | H63. Egyptian Names of the Ascendant Decans – 2. | H64. Egyptian Names of the Succedent Decans – 2. | H65. Egyptian Names of the Cadent Decans – 2. |
|---|---|---|---|---|
| ♈ | 15 | Xont-Har | Xont-Xre | Si-Ket |
| ♉ | 16 | Xau | Arat | Remen-Hare |
| ♊ | 17 | Thousalk | Uaret | Phu-Hor |
| ♋ | 18 | Sopdet | Seta | Knum |
| ♌ | 19 | Xar-Knum | Ha-Tet | Phu-Tet |
| ♍ | 20 | Tom | Uste-Bikot | Aposot |
| ♎ | 22 | Sobxos | Tra-Xont | Xont-Har |
| ♏ | 24 | Spt-Xne | Sesme | Si-Sesme |
| ♐ | 25 | Hre-Ua | Sesme | Konime |
| ♑ | 26 | Smat | Srat | Si-Srat |
| ♒ | 28 | Tra-Xu | Xu | Tra-Biu |
| ♓ | 29 | Biu | Xont-Har | Tpi-Biu |

# H. The Heavens and Astrology

| | | H66. The Ptolemaic Egyptian Names of Ascendant Decans. | H67. The Ptolemaic Egyptian Names of Succedent Decans. | H68. The Ptolemaic Egyptian names of Cadent Decans. |
|---|---|---|---|---|
| ♈ | 15 | Tepa-Kenmut | Kenmut | Kher-Khept-Kenmut |
| ♉ | 16 | Ha-Tchat | Pehui-Tchat | Themat-Hert |
| ♊ | 17 | Themat-Khert | Ustha | Bekatha |
| ♋ | 18 | Tepa-Khentet | Khentet-Hert | Khentet-Khert |
| ♌ | 19 | Themes-en-Khentet | Sapt-Khennu | Her-Ab-Uaa |
| ♍ | 20 | Shesmu | Kenmu | Semtet |
| ♎ | 22 | Tepa-Semt | Sert | Sasa-Sert |
| ♏ | 24 | Kher-Khept-Sert | Khukhu | Baba |
| ♐ | 25 | Khent-Heru | Her-Ab-Khentu | Khent-Kheru |
| ♑ | 26 | Qet | Sasaqet | Art |
| ♒ | 28 | Khau | Remen-Heru-An-Sah | Metscher-Sah |
| ♓ | 29 | Remen-Kher-Sah | A-Sah | Sah               [37 = Septet] |

| | | H69. Graeco-Egyptian Gods of the Ascendent Decans. | H70. Graeco-Egyptian Gods of the Succedent Decans. | H71. Graeco-Egyptian Gods of the Cadent Decans. |
|---|---|---|---|---|
| | | **167** | **169** | **171** |
| ♈ | 15 | Aroueris | Anubis | Horus |
| ♉ | 16 | Serapis | Helitomenos | Apophis |
| ♊ | 17 | Taautus | Cyclops | Titan |
| ♋ | 18 | Apoltun | Hecate | Mercophta |
| ♌ | 19 | Typhon | Perseus | Nephthe |
| ♍ | 20 | Isis | Pi-Osiris | Chronus |
| ♎ | 22 | Zeuda | Omphta | Ophionius |
| ♏ | 24 | Arimanius | Merota | Panotragus |
| ♐ | 25 | Tolmophta | Tomras | Zeraph |
| ♑ | 26 | Soda | Riruphta | Monuphta |
| ♒ | 28 | Brondeus | Vucula | Proteus |
| ♓ | 29 | Rephan | Sourut | Phallophorus |

# H. The Heavens and Astrology

*Fixed Stars and Constellations*

| | | Name | Latin | Meaning | Some Stars |
|---|---|---|---|---|---|
| | | | | H72. The 48 Ptolemaic Constellations. | |
| | | Andromeda | Andromedae | The Daughter Of Cassiopeia | Alpheratz or Sirrah "the horse" or "navel" Mirach "the loins" |
| ♒ | 28 | Aquarius | Aquarii | The Water Carrier | Sadal Melik "lucky star of the king" Sadal Suud "luck of lucks" |
| | | Aquila | Aquilae | The Eagle | Altair "flying one" Alshain "falcon" |
| | | Ara | Arae | The Altar | Tchou "pestle" (Chinese) |
| | | Argo Navis | Argo Navis | Jason's ship Argo | Canopus, Menelaus' helmsman (2nd brightest star) |
| ♈ | 15 | Aries | Arietis | The Ram | Hamal "ram" Sheratan "the two signs" (Pisces & Aries) |
| | | Auriga | Aurigae | The Charioteer | Capella "she-goat" Prijipati "Lord of Creation" (Sanskrit/Pali) |
| | | Bootes | Bootis | The Oxherd | Arcturus "bear-guard" |
| ♋ | 18 | Cancer | Cancri | The Crab | Acubens "claw" |
| | | Canis Major | Canis Majoris | The Greater Dog | Sirius "scorching" (brightest star in sky) Mirzam |
| | | Canis Minor | Canis Minoris | The Lesser Dog | Procyon "before the dog" |
| ♑ | 26 | Capricorn | Capricorni | The Horned Goat | Al Giedi "goat" Dabih "slaughterer" Deneb Algiedi "tail of the goat" |
| | | Cassiopeia | Cassiopeiae | The Wife of Cepheus | Schedar or Shedir "breast" |
| | | Centaurus | Centauri | The Centaur | Rigel Kentaurus "foot of the Centaur" |
| | | Cepheus | Cephei | King of Ethiopia/Joppa | Alderamin "right forearm" |
| | | Cetus | Ceti | The Whale Menacing Andromeda | Menkar or Menkab "nostril" Diphda or Deneb Kaitos "frog" or "tail of Cetus" Baten Kaitos "belly of Cetus" |
| | | Corona Australis | Coronae Australis | The Southern Crown | |
| | | Corona Borealis | Coronae Borealis | The Northern Crown | Gemma or Alphecca "gem" or "the broken ring" Nusakan "the two series" |
| | | Corvus | Corvi | The Crow | Alchibah "tent" Gienah "wing" Algorab "raven" Minkar "beak" |
| | | Crater | Crateris | The Cup | Alkes "cup" |
| | | Cygnus | Cygni | The Swan | Deneb "tail of the hen" Albireo (from Ireus, a fragrant flower) |
| | | Delphinus | Delphini | The Dolphin | Al Dhanab al Dulfim "tail of the dolphin" |
| | | Draco | Draconis | The Dragon | Thuban "snake" Rastaban "head of the snake" Eltanin "snake" (Arabic name for Draco) Giauzar "dragon" (node of lunar orbit) |
| | | Equuleus | Equulei | The Little Horse | Kitalpha "part of the horse" |
| | | Eridanus | Eridani | The River | Achernar "end of the river" Cursa "chair/footstool of Orion" |
| ♊ | 17 | Gemini | Geminorium | The Twins, Castor and Pollux | Castor "beaver" Pollux "much wine" |

# H. The Heavens and Astrology

| | | Name | Latin | Meaning | Some Stars |
|---|---|---|---|---|---|
| | | | | | **H72. The 48 Ptolemaic Constellations.** |
| | | Hercules | Herculis | Heracles | Ras Algethi "head of the kneeling one"<br>Kornephoros "club-bearer" |
| | | Hydra | Hydrae | The Water Serpent | Alphard or Cor Hydrae "heart of the hydra"<br>Minhar al Shuja "the snake's nose" |
| ♌ | 19 | Leo | Leonis | The Lion | Regulus, Cor Leonis "heart of the lion"<br>Denebola "tail of the lion" |
| | | Lepus | Leporis | The Hare | Arneb "hare"<br>Nihal "camels quenching their thirst" |
| ♎ | 22 | Libra | Librae | The Scales | Zuben El Genubi "southern claw"<br>Zuben Eschamali "northern claw"<br>Zubenhakrabi or Zubanalakrab "scorpion's claw" |
| | | Lupus | Lupi | The Wolf | |
| | | Lyra | Lyrae | The Lyre | Vega "the swooping" (eagle)<br>Sheliak or Shelyak "harp"<br>Aladfar and Al Athfar "talons" (of the eagle) |
| | | Ophiuchus | Ophiuchi | The Snake Holder | Ras Alhague "head of the snake"<br>Cheleb or Celbalrai "dog of the shepherd" |
| | | Orion | Orionis | The Hunter | Betelgeuse "hand of Al-Jazwa"<br>Rigel "foot"<br>Bellatrix "warrioress" (west shoulder) |
| | | Pegasus | Pegasi | The Winged Horse | Markab or Marchab "shoulder" (from Mankib) |
| | | Perseus | Persei | The Rescuer of Andromeda | Mirfak or Marfak "elbow"<br>Algol "the ghoul" |
| ♓ | 29 | Pisces | Piscium | The Fish | Al Rescha or Rischa "rope"<br>Fum al Samakah "fish's mouth" |
| | | Piscis Austrinus | Piscis Austrini | The Southern Fish | Fomalhaut "mouth of the fish" |
| | | Sagitta | Sagittae | The Arrow | |
| ♐ | 25 | Sagittarius | Sagittarii | The Archer | [El] Nasl "arrowhead"<br>Nunki "of Enki" (Sumerian god of waters/Eridu) |
| ♏ | 24 | Scorpio | Scorpii | The Scorpion | Antares "anti-Ares", a rival of Mars<br>Graffias or Acrab "claws" or "scorpion"<br>Sargas "seizer/smiter" (Babylonian title; name of a weapon of the God of War) |
| | | Serpens | Serpentis | The Snake | Unuk Al Hay or Unukalhai "neck of the snake"<br>Chow "imperial dynasty" |
| ♉ | 16 | Taurus | Tauri | The Bull | Aldebaran "follower"<br>*The Pleiades* |
| | | Triangulum | Trianguli | The Triangle | Caput Trianguli "head of the triangle" |
| | | Ursa Major | Ursae Majoris | The Greater Bear/ Big Dipper | Dubhe "bear"<br>Merak "loins"<br>Phecda "thigh"<br>Megrez "insertion-point" (of the bear's tail)<br>Alioth "black horse/bull"<br>Mizar<br>Alcor<br>Alkaid or Benetnasch "daughters of the bier" |
| | | Ursa Minor | Ursae Minoris | The Lesser Bear | Polaris "pole star"<br>Kochab or Kokab "star"<br>Pherkab "calf" |
| ♍ | 20 | Virgo | Virginis | The Virgin | Spica or Azimech "ear of wheat"<br>Porrima (Roman goddess of childbirth)<br>Vindemiatrix "vine-harvestress" |

# H. The Heavens and Astrology

| No. | H73. The 15 Fixed Behenian Stars. | | H74. The 15 Fixed Behenian Stars – Images. | H75. The 15 Fixed Behenian Stars – Virtues and Magical Operations. | H76. The 15 Fixed Behenian Stars – Seals. |
|---|---|---|---|---|---|
| 1 | Head of Algol / Caput Algol | 26°07 Taurus | The head of a man with a bloody neck. | Bestows success on petitions, makes him who carries it bold and magnanimous, preserves the members of his body: helps against witchcraft, reflects evil endeavours and wicked incantations back upon our adversaries. | |
| 2 | Pleiades | 29°55 Taurus | A little virgin, or the figure of a lamp. | To increase the light of the eyes, to assemble spirits, to raise winds, to reveal secret and hidden things. | |
| 3 | Aldebaran / Aldaboram | 9°11 Gemini | The likeness of God, or of a flying man. | It gives riches and honour. | |
| 4 | Goat /Capella | 21°48 Gemini | Figure of a man willing to make himself merry with musical instruments. | It makes him who carries it acceptable, honoured and exalted before kings and princes; and helps the pain of the teeth. | |
| 5 | Greater Dog Star /Canis Major /Sirius | 14°03 Cancer | An hound and a little virgin. | It bestows honour and good will, and the favour of men, and aerial spirits, and gives power to pacify and reconcile kings, princes, and other men. | |
| 6 | Lesser Dog Star /Canis Minor / Procyon | 25°45 Cancer | A cock, or of three little maids. | It confers the favour of the gods, of spirits, and men; it gives power against witchcraft, and preserves health. | |
| 7 | Heart of Leo / Cor Leonis / Regulus | 29°47 Leo | A lion or cat, or the figure of an honourable person sitting in a chair. | It renders a man temperate, appeases wrath, and gives favour. | |
| 8 | Tail of Ursa Major /Akaid | 28°31 Virgo | A pensive man, or of a bull, or the figure of a calf. | It avails against incantations, and makes him who carries it secure in his travels. | |
| 9 | Wing of Corvus / Gienah | 13°23 Libra | A raven, or snake, or of a black man clothed in black. | This makes a man choleric, bold, courageous, full of thoughts, causes erotic dreams; drives away evil spirits and gathers them together; against the malice of men, devils and winds. | |
| 10 | Spica, the Spike | 23°47 Libra | A bird, or of a man laden with merchandise. | It confers riches, and makes one overcome contentions, it takes away scarcity and mischief. | |
| 11 | Alchameth / Arcturus | 24°11 Libra | A horse or wolf, or the figure of a man dancing. | It is good against fevers, it astringeth and retains the blood. | |
| 12 | Elphrya / Alphecca | 12°14 Scorpio | An hen, or of a man crowned and advanced. | It bestows the good will and love of men, and gives chastity. | |
| 13 | Heart of Scorpio / Antares | 09°43 Sagittarius | A man armed, and with a coat of mail, or the figure of a scorpion. | It gives understanding and memory, it makes a good colour, and aides against evil spirits, and drives them away, and binds them. | |
| 14 | Vulture cadens / Vega | 15°16 Capricorn | A vulture or hen, or of a traveler. | It makes a man magnanimous and proud, it gives power over devils and beasts. | |
| 15 | Tail of Capricorn / Deneb Algedi | 05°18 Pisces | An hart, or goat, or of an angry man. | It bestows prosperity, and increases wrath. | |

# H. The Heavens and Astrology

*Phases of the Moon*

| Cycle No. | H77. The Phases of the Moon – A Lunar Ephemeris. | | |
|-----------|-------------------------------------------------|------|------|
| | **Date of 1st New Moon of Year** | year | year |
| 1 | January 16 | 1999 | 2018 |
| 2 | January 6 | 2000 | 2019 |
| 3 | January 25 | 2001 | 2020 |
| 4 | January 14 | 2002 | 2021 |
| 5 | January 2 | 2003 | 2022 |
| 6 | January 21 | 2004 | 2023 |
| 7 | January 10 | 2005 | 2024 |
| 8 | January 29 | 2006 | 2025 |
| 9 | January 18 | 2007 | 2026 |
| 10 | January 7 | 2008 | 2027 |
| 11 | January 26 | 2009 | 2028 |
| 13 | January 16 | 2010 | 2029 |
| 13 | January 4 | 2011 | 2030 |
| 14 | January 23 | 2012 | 2031 |
| 15 | January 12 | 2013 | 2032 |
| 16 | January 1 | 2014 | 2033 |
| 17 | January 19 | 2015 | 2034 |
| 18 | January 9 | 2016 | 2035 |
| 19 | January 28 | 2017 | 2036 |

# H. The Heavens and Astrology

*Calendar Epochs*

| H78. Calendar Start Dates (Epochs). | | |
|---|---|---|
| **Calendar** | **Epoch (Gregorian equivalent)** | **Epoch (Julian equivalent)** |
| Julian Day number | November 24, -4713 | January 1, 4713 BCE |
| Hebrew | September 7, -3760 | October 7, 3761 BCE |
| Mayan | August 11, -3113 | September 6, 3114 BCE |
| Hindu (Kali Yuga start) | January 23, -3101 | February 18, 3102 BCE |
| Chinese | February 15, -2636 | March 8, 2637 BCE |
| Roman (AUC) | April 21, -753 | April 21, 753 BCE[3] |
| Julian | December 30, 0 | January 1, 1 CE |
| Gregorian (ISO) | January 1, 1 | January 3, 1 CE |
| Ethiopic | August 27, 7 | August 29, 7 CE |
| Coptic | August 29, 284 | August 29, 284 |
| Persian | March 22, 622 | March 19, 622 CE |
| Islamic (Hegira) | July 19, 622 | July 16, 622 CE |
| French Revolutionary | September 22, 1792 | September 11, 1792 CE |
| Baha'i | March 21, 1844 | March 9, 1844 |

---

[3] The exact date is subject to controversy.

# I. Islam

*Jinn*

| | | I1. Kings of the Jinn – Arabic. | I2. Kings of the Jinn – Transliteration. | I3. Kings of the Jinn – Meaning. |
|---|---|---|---|---|
| | | 47 | | |
| ☾ | 13 | الابيض | Al-Abeyadh | The White One |
| ☿ | 12 | برقان | Burqan | Two Thunders |
| ♀ | 14 | زوبعه | Zawba'ah | The Storm |
| ☼ | 30 | المذهب | Al-Mazhab | The Golden One |
| ♂ | 27 | الاحمر | Al-Ahmar | The Red One |
| ♃ | 21 | شمهورش | Shem huresh | The name Huresh |
| ♄ | 32 | ميمون | Maymon | Prosperous |

| | | I4. Kings of the Jinn Nicknames – Arabic. | I5. Kings of the Jinn Nicknames – Translation. | I6. Kings of the Jinn Nicknames – Meaning. |
|---|---|---|---|---|
| | | | | |
| ☾ | 13 | ابالنور | Abba Al-Nur | The Father of the Light |
| ☿ | 12 | ابو العجائب | Abbu Al-A'aja'eb | The Father of the Wonders |
| ♀ | 14 | ابو الحسن | Abba Al-Hassan | The Father of the Handsome |
| ☼ | 30 | اباديباج | Abba Deebaj | The Father of Silk Brocade |
| ♂ | 27 | ابو محرز | Abbu Mohrez | The Father of Attainer |
| ♃ | 21 | ابو الوليد | Abbu Al-Waleed | The Father of the new Born |
| ♄ | 32 | ابانوخ | Abba Nuch | The Father of Rest |

# I. Islam

*Hells and Heavens*

| | I7. The Seven Arab Hells. | I8. The Inhabitants of the Seven Arab Hells. | I9. The Sins associated with the Seven Arab Hells. | I10. The Koranic passage associated with the Seven Arab Hells. |
|---|---|---|---|---|
| | **125** | **126** | | |
| **1** | | | | |
| **2** | Hawijah / Hawiyah | Christians | Deceivers of the marketplace, hypocrites, liars | Koran 101:8 |
| **3** | | | | |
| **4** | Al-Jahim | Pagans or Idolaters | Those who deny Allah, the proud, blasphemers | Koran 2:113 |
| **5** | Sakar / Saqar | Gabars, Fire Worshippers of Persia | Those in theological error, fools | Koran 54:47 |
| **6** | Sa'ir | Sabians | Unjust and embezzlers of the innocents | Koran 4:11 |
| **7** | Al-Hutamah | Jews | [Unbelievers] | Koran 104:4 |
| **8** | Laza / Ladha' | Christians | Misers who turned their backs on Islam | Koran 98:5 |
| **9** | Jehannim / Jahannam | Muslims | Sinners who may one day be released from hell | Koran 19:72 |
| **10** | | | | |

| | I11. Seven Arab Heavens. | I12. Meaning of the Seven Arab Heavens. |
|---|---|---|
| | **127** | **128** |
| **1** | | |
| **2** | Dar al-Jalal | House of Glory, made of pearls |
| **3** | | |
| **4** | Dar as-Salaam | House of Rest or Peace, made of rubies and jacinths |
| **5** | Jannat al-Maawa | Garden of Mansions, made of yellow copper |
| **6** | Jannat al-Khuld | Garden of Eternity, made of yellow coral |
| **7** | Jannat al-Naim | Garden of Delights, made of white diamond |
| **8** | Jannat al-Firdaus | Garden of Paradise, made of red gold |
| **9** | Jannat al-'Adin or al-Karar | Garden of Eden, or Everlasting Abode, made of red pearls or pure musk |
| **10** | | |

# I. Islam

*Islamic Angels*

| No. | I13. Islamic Angels. | I14. Islamic Angels – Hebrew Equivalent. | I15. Islamic Angels – Rank. | I16. Islamic Angels – Attribute. | I17. Islamic Angels – Appearance. |
|---|---|---|---|---|---|
| 1 | Hamalat al-'arsh | | Throne-bearers | Carries God's Throne | There are 4 Bearers: Man & Bull & Eagle & Lion |
| 2 | [Kerubeem] | Cherubim | Cherubim | Praises God | |
| 3 | Jibril or Jibra'il | Gabriel | Archangel | Bearer of Revelations, who dictated the *Quran* | Has 600 Wings stretching from East to West; sitting on a Throne between Earth & Heaven |
| 4 | Mikal or Mika'il | Michael | Archangel | Providence, rewards of the just, thunder and lightning | Wings of emerald green |
| 5 | Azrail | Azriel | Archangel | Angel of Death | 4000 Wings; body formed from as many eyes & tongues as there are people |
| 6 | Israfil | Raphael | Archangel | Blows the Trumpet of Doom at the Last Judgement | Hairy body covered with mouths and tongues; 4 wings: one protects his body, one shields him from God, while the others extend from East to West |
| 7 | The hafazahs (or hafzas) | | Guardian Angels | Assigned to each imdividual | |
| 8 | Ridwan | | | Guards Heaven/Paradise | |
| 9 | Malikim | Malachim | | Guards Hell | |
| 10 | Munkar & Nakir | | | Questions the dead about their good and bad deeds | |
| 11 | Haaroot and Maaroot (or Harut and Marut) | | | Sent to Babylon to judge and teach men the sciences and magic (or *sihr*) | |

# J. Judaism

*Eden and Egypt*

| | | J1. The Four Rivers of the Garden of Eden. | J2. The Four Rivers of the Garden of Eden – English. | J3. The Four Rivers of the Garden of Eden – Numeration. |
|---|---|---|---|---|
| | | **56** | | |
| ✸ | 31b | | | |
| F | 31 | פישׁון | PIShVN – Pison | 446 or 1096 |
| A | 11 | חדקל | HDQL – Hiddekel (Tigris) | 139 |
| W | 23 | גחון | GHVN – Gihon | 64 or 714 |
| E | 32b | פרת | PRTh – Phrath (Euphrates) | 680 |

| | J4. The Ten Plagues (*Negeph*) of Egypt. | J5. The Ten Plagues of Egypt – Hebrew. | J6. The 10 Commandments of Moses. |
|---|---|---|---|
| | **122** | | |
| 1 | Death of the First-born (*Exodus* 12:12) | Malkath be-Koroth | Thou shalt have no other gods before me |
| 2 | Darkness  (*Exodus* 10:22) | Choshekh | Thou shalt not make unto thee any graven image |
| 3 | Locusts (*Exodus* 10:12) | Arbeh | Thou shalt not take the name of the Lord thy God in vain |
| 4 | Hail and Fire (*Exodus* 9:23) | Baradh | Remember the Sabbath day, to keep it holy |
| 5 | Boils (*Exodus* 9:9) | Shechin | Honour thy father and thy mother |
| 6 | Murrain (cattle disease) (*Exodus* 9:3) | Dever | Thou shalt not kill |
| 7 | Flies (*Exodus* 8:24) | Arov | Thou shalt not commit adultery |
| 8 | Lice (*Exodus* 8:17) | Kinnim | Thou shalt not steal |
| 9 | Frogs (*Exodus* 8:5) | Tzephardea | Thou shalt not bear false witness against thy neighbour |
| 10 | Water turned to Blood (*Exodus* 7:17) | Dam | Thou shalt not covet |

# J. Judaism

*Twelve Tribes*

| | | Direction (Masonic). | J7. The Twelve Tribes (Masonic). | J8. Direction (Agrippa). | J9. The Twelve Tribes (Agrippa). | J10. Direction (Biblical & Dee). | J11. The Twelve Tribes (*Numbers*). | J12. The Twelve Tribes (*Exodus*). | J13. The Twelve Tribes (Dee). |
|---|---|---|---|---|---|---|---|---|---|
| | | | 141 | | | | | | |
| ♈ | 15 | South | גד<br>Gad | North | Dan | East | Judah | Reuben | Naphtali |
| ♉ | 16 | West | אפראים<br>Ephraim | South | Reuben | East | Issacher | Simeon | Dan |
| ♊ | 17 | West | מנשה<br>Manesseh | East | Judah | East | Zebulun | Levi | Asher |
| ♋ | 18 | East | ישׁשׂכר<br>Issachar | West | Manasseh | South | Reuben | Judah | Gad |
| ♌ | 19 | East | יהודה<br>Judah | North | Asher | South | Simeon | Issachar | Reuben |
| ♍ | 20 | North | נפתלי<br>Napthali | South | Simeon | South | Gad | Zebulun | Simeon |
| ♎ | 22 | North | אשׁר<br>Asher | East | Issachar | West | Ephraim | Benjamin | Zebulun |
| ♏ | 24 | North | דן<br>Dan | West | Benjamin | West | Manasseh | Dan | Judah |
| ♐ | 25 | West | בנימן<br>Benjamin | North | Naphtali | West | Benjamin | Naphtali | Issachar |
| ♑ | 26 | East | זבולן<br>Zebulon | South | Gad | North | Dan | Gad | Ephraim |
| ♒ | 28 | South | ראובן<br>Reuben | East | Zebulun | North | Asher | Asher | Manasseh |
| ♓ | 29 | South | שמעון<br>Simeon | West | Ephraim | North | Naphtali | Joseph | Benjamin |

# J. Judaism

*Prophets and Judges*

| | | J14. The Major Hebrew Prophets (*nabi*). | | |
|---|---|---|---|---|
| | | **91** | | |
| 1 | | Messiah, son of David | | |
| 2 | | Moses | | |
| 3 | | Enoch | | |
| 4 | | Abraham | | |
| 5 | | Jacob, (Isaac) | | |
| 6 | | Elijah, (Jacob) | | |
| 7 | | Moses | | |
| 8 | | Aaron | | |
| 9 | | Joseph | | |
| 10 | | King David (Elisha) | | |

| | | J14a. The Minor Hebrew Prophets. | J15. The 12 Judges of Israel. | J16. The 12 Judges of Israel – Numeration. |
|---|---|---|---|---|
| ♈ | 15 | Malachi | Othniel | 561 |
| ♉ | 16 | Haggai | Ehud | 16 |
| ♊ | 17 | Zechariah | Shamgar | 543 |
| ♋ | 18 | Amos | Deborah | 217 |
| ♌ | 19 | Hosea | Gideon | 783 or 133 |
| ♍ | 20 | Micah | Tola | 506 |
| ♎ | 22 | Jonah | Jair | 221 |
| ♏ | 24 | Obadiah | Jephthah | 498 |
| ♐ | 25 | Zephaniah | Ibzan | 793 or 143 |
| ♑ | 26 | Nahum | Elon | 737 or 87 |
| ♒ | 28 | Habakkuk | Abdon | 782 or 132 |
| ♓ | 29 | Joel | Samson | 1346 or 696 |

# J. Judaism

*Psalter*

| | | **Purpose of Psalm** | **Hebrew/Protestant/KJV** | **Vulgate/Septuagint/Catholic** |
|---|---|---|---|---|
| | | J17. Magical Use of the Psalter. | | |
| | 1 | Used by Abramelin | 51, 130 | 50, 129 |
| | 2 | Consecration of the silk coverings | 8, 65, 72, 134 | 8, 64, 71, 133 |
| | 3 | To be said whilst putting on the vestments | 4, 9-10, 15, 51, 67, 68, 84, 102, 111, 114-115, 117, 119, 126, 127, 131, 137, 139 | 4, 9, 14, 50, 66, 67, 83, 101, 110, 113, 116, 118 (v.97-104), 125, 126, 130, 136, 138 |
| | 4 | To be used during ritual bathing | 14, 27, 53, 69, 103, 104, 106 | 13, 26, 52, 68, 102, 103, 105 |
| | 5 | Consecrating the iron instruments, burin, needle | 3, 7, 9, 31, 42, 51, 60, 130 | 3, 7, 9, 30, 41, 50, 59, 129 |
| | 6 | Constructing the floor Circle and Triangle | 2, 47, 51, 54, 67, 68, 113 | 2, 46, 50, 53, 66, 67, 112 |
| | 7 | Seven Penitential Psalms as used by Dr John Dee | 6, 32, 38, 51, 102, 130, 143 | 6, 31, 37, 50, 101, 129, 142 |
| | 8 | Consecrating the parchment | 72, 117, 124 | 71, 116, 123 |
| | 9 | Used in conjuration of spirits | 119 | 118 |
| | 10 | Consecration of the pentacles | 8, 19, 22, 27, 29, 32, 51, 54, 72, 134 | 8, 18, 21, 26, 28, 31, 50, 53, 71, 133 |
| ⊛ | 31b | Consecrating the Place of working | 2, 54, 67 | 2, 53, 66 |
| F | 31 | Consecrating the candles | 103, 117, 150 | 102, 116, 150 |
| A | 11 | Consecrating the quills and pen of Art | 117, 133 | 116, 132 |
| W | 23 | Consecrating the Water | 6, 51, 54, 102 | 6, 50, 53, 101 |
| E | 32b | Consecrating the wax discs or Earth | 8, 15, 22, 46, 47, 49, 50, 51, 53, 54, 68, 72, 84, 102, 113, 114-115, 126, 130, 131, 133, 139 | 8, 14, 21, 45, 46, 48, 49, 50, 52, 53, 67, 71, 83, 101, 112, 113, 125, 129, 130, 132, 138 |
| ☾ | 13 | Inscribed around ☾ pentacle | 107:16, 56:11, 40:13, 68:1 | 106:16, 55:11, 39:13, 67:1 |
| ☿ | 12 | Inscribed around ☿ pentacle | 24:7 | 23:7 |
| ♀ | 14 | Inscribed around ♀ pentacle | 22:14 | 21:14 |
| ☼ | 30 | Inscribed around ☼ pentacle | 13:3-4, 91:11-12, 69:23, 135:16, 116:16-17 | 12:3-4, 90:11-12, 68:23, 134:16, 114:16-17 |
| ♂ | 27 | Inscribed around ♂ pentacle | 77:13, 110:5, 91:13, 37:15, 105:32-33 | 76:13, 109:5, 90:13, 36:15, 104:32-33 |
| ♃ | 21 | Inscribed around ♃ pentacle | 112:3, 125:1, 112:3, 22:16-17, 113:7 | 111:3, 124:1, 111:3, 21:16-17, 112:7 |
| ♄ | 32 | Inscribed around ♄ pentacle | 72:8-9, 109:18, 18:7 | 71:8-9, 108:18, 17:7 |

*Old Testament Books*

| | J18. The Canonical Books of the Old Testament and their Authors. | | | | |
|---|---|---|---|---|---|
| **Category** | **Jewish** | **Roman Catholic** | **Greek Orthodox** | **Protestant (KJV)** | **Traditional Author** |
| Pentateuch/ Torah/ Tanakh | Genesis | Genesis | Genesis | Genesis | Moses |
| | Exodus | Exodus | Exodus | Exodus | |
| | Leviticus | Leviticus | Leviticus | Leviticus | |
| | Numbers | Numbers | Numbers | Numbers | |
| | Deuteronomy | Deuteronomy | Deuteronomy | Deuteronomy | |
| The Early Prophets (*Nevi*) | Joshua | Joshua | Josue | Joshua | Joshua |
| | Judges | Judges | Judges | Judges | Samuel |
| | I Samuel | I Samuel | I Kings | I Samuel | Samuel, then Gad or Nathan |
| | II Samuel | II Samuel | II Kings | II Samuel | |
| | I Kings | I Kings | III Kings | I Kings | Jeremiah |
| | II Kings | II Kings | IV Kings | II Kings | |
| The Writings (*Ketuvim*) | Ruth*[1] | Ruth | Ruth | Ruth | Samuel or Nathan |
| | I Chronicles | I Chronicles | I Paralipomenon | I Chronicles | Ezra |
| | II Chronicles | II Chronicles | II Paralipomenon | II Chronicles | |
| | Ezra | | | Ezra | |
| | Nehemiah | Nehemiah | II Esdras | Nehemiah | Nehemiah & Ezra |
| | Esther | Esther | Esther | Esther | Mordecai |
| | Job | Job | Job | Job | Job or Elihu |
| | Psalms | Psalms | Psalms | Psalms | David |
| | Proverbs | Proverbs | Proverbs | Proverbs | Solomon |
| | Ecclesiastes | Ecclesiastes | Ecclesiastes | Ecclesiastes | |
| | Song of Songs | Song of Songs | Canticle of Canticles | Song of Solomon | |
| The Later Prophets | Isaiah | Isaiah | Isaias | Isaiah | Isaiah |
| | Jeremiah | Jeremias | Jeremiah | Jeremiah | Jeremiah |
| | * Lamentations | Lamentations | Lamentations | Lamentations | Jeremiah |
| | Ezekiel | Ezekiel | Ezechiel | Ezekiel | Ezekiel |
| | * Daniel | Daniel | Daniel | Daniel | Daniel |
| The Twelve Minor Prophets | Hosea | Hosea | Osee | Hosea | Hosea |
| | Joel | Joel | Joel | Joel | Joel |
| | Amos | Amos | Amos | Amos | Amos |
| | Obadiah | Obadiah | Abdias | Obadiah | Obadiah |
| | Jonah | Jonah | Jonas | Jonah | Jonah |
| | Micah | Micah | Micheas | Micah | Micah |
| | Nahum | Nahum | Nahum | Nahum | Nahum |

---

[1] * = Considered to be a *ketuvim* rather than a prophet.

# J. Judaism

| | | J18. The Canonical Books of the Old Testament and their Authors. | | | |

| Category | Jewish | Roman Catholic | Greek Orthodox | Protestant (KJV) | Traditional Author |
|---|---|---|---|---|---|
| | Habakkuk | Habakkuk | Habacuc | Habakkuk | Habakkuk |
| | Zephaniah | Zephaniah | Sophonias | Zephaniah | Zephaniah |
| | Haggai | Haggai | Aggeus | Haggai | Haggai |
| | Zechariah | Zechariah | Zacharias | Zechariah | Zechariah & Jeremiah |
| | Malachi | Malachi | Malachias | Malachi | Malachi or Isaiah |
| Oral Law | Mishnah | | | | Moses |
| | Tosefta | | | | |
| Rabbinical Commentary | Midrash Halakha | | | | |
| | Midrash Aggada | | | | |
| | Talmud | | | | |
| | Gemara | | | | |
| | Meforshim | | | | |
| Kabbalah | Zohar | | | | Simeon ben Yohai/ Moses de Leon |
| Deutero-Canonical Apocrypha | | Tobit | Tobias (Tobit) | | |
| | | Judith | Judith | | |
| | | Wisdom | Wisdom of Solomon | | |
| | | Baruch | Baruch | | |
| | | I Maccabees | I Maccabees | | |
| | | II Maccabees | II Maccabees | | |
| | | additions to Esther | additions to Esther | | |
| | | Sirach/Ecclesiasticus | Ben Sirach | | |
| | | Prayer of Azariah[2] | Prayer of Azariah[1] | | |
| | | Book of Susanna[3] | Book of Susanna[2] | | |
| | | | Psalm 151 | | |
| | | | 1 Esdras | | |
| | | | 2 Esdras | | |
| | | | 3 Maccabees | | |
| | | | 4 Maccabees | | |
| | | | Psalms of Solomon | | |
| | | | Odes | | |
| | | | Letter of Jeremiah | | |
| | | | Prayer of Manasseh | | |

---

[2] Additional text in *Daniel*.
[3] Additional text in *Daniel* along with *Bel and the Dragon*.

# K. Kabbalah

*Tree of Life Layout, Spheres and Paths*

| GD Path Order | | K1. Hebrew Names of the 10 Sephiroth and 22 Hebrew Letters. | K2. Hebrew Names of the 10 Sephiroth and 22 Hebrew Letters – Transliteration. | K3. Hebrew Names of the 10 Sephiroth and 22 Hebrew Letters – Translated. | K4. Hebrew Names of the 10 Sephiroth and 22 Hebrew Letters – Meaning. | |
|---|---|---|---|---|---|---|
| | | **2** | | | **Cohen**[1] | **Traditional** |
| | 1 | כתר | KThR | Kether | | Crown |
| | 2 | חכמה | ChKMH | Chokmah | | Wisdom |
| | 3 | בינה | BINH | Binah | | Understanding |
| | 4 | חסד | ChSD | Chesed | | Mercy |
| | 5 | גבורה | GBVRH | Geburah | | Strength |
| | 6 | תפארת | ThPARTh | Tiphareth | | Beauty |
| | 7 | נצח | NTzCh | Netzach | | Victory |
| | 8 | הוד | HVD | Hod | | Splendour |
| | 9 | יסוד | ISVD | Yesod | | Foundation |
| | 10 | מלכות | MLKVTh | Malkuth | | Kingdom |
| A | 11 | אלף | ALP | Aleph | Avir, air | Ox |
| ☿ | 12 | בית | BITh | Beth | Hayim, life | House |
| ☽ | 13 | גמל | GML | Gimel | Shalom, peace | Camel |
| ♀ | 14 | דלת | DLTh | Daleth | Hokhmah, wisdom | Door |
| ♈ | 15 | הה / הא | HH/HA | He | Reyah, sight | Window |
| ♉ | 16 | וו | VV | Vau | Shemiyah, hearing | Nail |
| ♊ | 17 | זין | ZIN | Zayin | Reyhah, smell | Sword |
| ♋ | 18 | חית | ChITh | Cheth | Sihah, speech | Fence |
| ♌ | 19 | טית | TITh | Teth | Laytah, confusion | Serpent |
| ♍ | 20 | יוד | IVD | Yod | Miskab, lying down | Hand |
| ♃ | 21 | כף | KP | Kaph | Osher, wealth | Palm of hand |
| ♎ | 22 | למד | LMD | Lamed | Melakhah, work | Ox goad |
| W | 23 | מם | MM | Mem | Mayim, water | Water |
| ♏ | 24 | נון | NVN | Nun | Halokh, walking | Fish |
| ♐ | 25 | סמך | SMK | Samekh | Ruach, spirit | Prop |
| ♑ | 26 | עין | OIN | Ayin | Sehoq, laughter | Eye |
| ♂ | 27 | פא | PA | Peh | Zera, seed | Mouth |
| ♒ | 28 | צדי | TzDI | Tzaddi | Hirehur, suspicion | Fish-hook |
| ♓ | 29 | קוף | QVP | Qoph | Shinah, sleep | Back of head |
| ☼ | 30 | ריש | RISh | Resh | Hen, grace | Head |
| F | 31 | שין | ShIN | Shin | Aesh, fire | Tooth |
| ♄ | 32 | תו | TV | Tau | Memshalah, power | Tau cross |

---

[1] According to Rabbi Jacob Cohen (mid 13th century) in *Explanation of the Holy Name.*

# K. Kabbalah

| | K5. Magical Images of the Sephiroth. | K6. Other Names of the Sephiroth. |
|---|---|---|
| | **177** | |
| 1 | Ancient bearded king seen in profile | Concealed of the Concealed (TMIRA DTMIRIN Temira De-Temirin), Ancient of the Ancient Ones (OThIQA DOThIQIN Authiqa De-Authiqin) Most Holy Ancient One (OThIQA QDIShA Authia Qadisha) Ancient One (OThIQA Authiqa) Ancient of Days (OThIQ IVMIN Authiq Iomin) Primordial Point (NQDH RAShVNH Nequdah Rashunah) Smooth Point (NQDH PShVTh Nequdah Peshutah) White Head (RIShA HVVRH Risha Havurah) Inscrutable Height (RVM MOLH Rom Meolah) Vast Countenance Macroprosopus (ARIK ANPIN Arik Anpin) Small Point, Profuse Giver, Amen, Long Nose, Long Face, Existence of Existences, Most High, Hua, Head which is Not, Primal Glory, The Head, Lux Occulta, Mirum Occultum, Lux Simplicissima, Lux Interna, Hidden Intelligence, Supreme Crown (Kether Elyon), Will (Ratzon) |
| 2 | A bearded male figure | Father (AB, Ab) Abba, Supernal Father, Power of Yetzirah, Yod of Tetragrammaton, Tetragrammaton, Crown of Creation, Second Glory |
| 3 | A mature female figure | Dark Sterile Mother (AMA, Ama), Bright Pregnant Mother (AIMA, Aima), Throne (KVRSIA Korsia), Great Sea (Marah), Supernal Mother, Foundation of Primordial Wisdom, Creator of Faith, Palace, Womb Sanctifying Intelligence |
| 4 | A mighty crowned and enthroned king | Greatness (GDVLH Gedulah), Love, Liberality, Majesty, Grace, Cohesive or Receptive Intelligence |
| 5 | A mighty warrior in his chariot, armed for war | Fear (PChD, Pachad), Judgement or Rigour (DIN, Din), Justice, Strength, Rigour, Radical Intelligence |
| 6 | A majestic king, a child, a crucified/sacrificed god | Compassion (Rachamim), Lesser Countenance (ZOIR ANPIN, Zauir Anpin) [applies to Sephiroth 4-9], King (MLK, Melekh), Son (Ben), Adam, The Man, Blessed Holy One, Mediating Intelligence |
| 7 | A beautiful naked woman | Triumph, Lasting Endurance, Firmness, Occult Intelligence |
| 8 | An hermaphrodite | Praise [Fludd & Rosenberg], Splendour, Majesty, Absolute or Perfect Intelligence |
| 9 | A beautiful naked man, very strong | Foundation of the World (Yesod Olam), The Righteous One (Tzaddik), Establishment, Covenant, Righteous One, Pure Intelligence |
| 10 | A young woman crowned, enthroned and veiled | Kingdom, Shekinah (the Female part of Divinity), Inferior Mother (Matrona), Bride of Microprosopus (Kallah), Queen (Malkah), Diadem (Atarah), Virgin (Betulah), Daughter (Bot), Female (Nukvah) The Gate, Gate of Death, Gate of the Shadow of Death, Gate of Tears, Gate of Justice, Gate of Prayer, Gate of the Garden of Eden, Apple Orchard, Gate of the Daughter of the Mighty Ones, Resplendent Intelligence |

| GD Path Order. | Key Reference – Hebrew Letter. | K7. Position of the Paths on the Tree of Life – Golden Dawn. | K8. Corrected Astrological Attributions of *Sepher Yetzirah*. | K9. Lurianic Position of the Paths on the Tree of Life – Isaac Luria. | K10. Path Orientation: Horizontal, Vertical, Diagonal. |
|---|---|---|---|---|---|
| | | **12** | | | |
| 1 | | 1st Plane Middle Pillar | | 1st Plane Middle Pillar | |
| 2 | | 2nd Plane Right Pillar | | 2nd Plane Right Pillar | |
| 3 | | 2nd Plane Left Pillar | | 2nd Plane Left Pillar | |
| 4 | | 3rd Plane Right Pillar | | 3rd Plane Right Pillar | |
| 5 | | 3rd Plane Left Pillar | | 3rd Plane Left Pillar | |
| 6 | | 4th Plane Middle Pillar | | 4th Plane Middle Pillar | |
| 7 | | 5th Plane Right Pillar | | 5th Plane Right Pillar | |
| 8 | | 5th Plane Left Pillar | | 5th Plane Left Pillar | |
| 9 | | 6th Plane Middle Pillar | | 6th Plane Middle Pillar | |
| 10 | | 7th Plane Middle Pillar | | 7th Plane Middle Pillar | |
| A — 11 | **Aleph** | Path joins 1 – 2 | A | Path joins 4 – 5 | **H** |
| ☿ — 12 | *Beth* | Path joins 1 – 3 | ♄ | Path joins 2 – 4 | V |
| ☾ — 13 | *Gimel* | Path joins 1 – 6 | ♃ | Path joins 3 – 5 | V |
| ♀ — 14 | *Daleth* | Path joins 2 – 3 | ♂ | Path joins 1 – 6 | V |
| ♈ — 15 | He | Path joins 2 – 6 | ♈ | Path joins 1 – 2 | D |
| ♉ — 16 | Vav | Path joins 2 – 4 | ♉ | Path joins 1 – 3 | D |
| ♊ — 17 | Zayin | Path joins 3 – 6 | ♊ | Path joins 2 – 5 | D |
| ♋ — 18 | Cheth | Path joins 3 – 5 | ♋ | Path joins 4 – 6 | D |
| ♌ — 19 | Teth | Path joins 4 – 5 | ♌ | Path joins 2 – 6 | D |
| ♍ — 20 | Yod | Path joins 4 – 6 | ♍ | Path joins 6 – 7 | D |
| ♃ — 21 | *Kaph* | Path joins 4 – 7 | ☉ | Path joins 4 – 7 | V |
| ♎ — 22 | Lamed | Path joins 5 – 6 | ♎ | Path joins 8 – 9 | D |
| W — 23 | **Mem** | Path joins 5 – 8 | W | Path joins 7 – 8 | **H** |
| ♏ — 24 | Nun | Path joins 6 – 7 | ♏ | Path joins 7 – 9 | D |
| ♐ — 25 | Samekh | Path joins 6 – 9 | ♐ | Path joins 6 – 8 | D |
| ♑ — 26 | Ayin | Path joins 6 – 8 | ♑ | Path joins 3 – 6 | D |
| ♂ — 27 | *Peh* | Path joins 7 – 8 | ♀ | Path joins 5 – 8 | V |
| ♒ — 28 | Tzaddi | Path joins 7 – 9 | ♒ | Path joins 5 – 6 | D |
| ♓ — 29 | Qoph | Path joins 7 – 10 | ♓ | Path joins 3 – 4 | V |
| ☉ — 30 | *Resh* | Path joins 8 – 9 | ☿ | Path joins 6 – 9 | D |
| F — 31 | **Shin** | Path joins 8 – 10 | F | Path joins 2 – 3 | **H** |
| ♄ — 32 | *Tau* | Path joins 9 – 10 | ☾ | Path joins 9 – 10 | V |
| E — 32b | | | E | | |
| ✳ — 31b | | | ✳ | | |

| Connecting Sephiroth | | K11. The Paths of the Lightning Flash and the Serpent on the Lurianic Tree of Life. | K12. Sequential Numbering of the Paths following the Lightning Flash and the Serpent on the Lurianic Tree of Life. | |
|---|---|---|---|---|
| from | to | 9 | Path | |
| 1 | | Hilt of the Flaming Sword or Lightning Flash | | Creation |
| 1 | 2 | The zig-zags of the Lightning Flash The Creation, Emanation, and descent into matter | 11 | |
| 2 | 3 | | 12 | |
| 3 | 4 | | 13 | The Path across the Abyss |
| 4 | 5 | | 14 | |
| 5 | 6 | | 15 | |
| 6 | 7 | | 16 | |
| 7 | 8 | | 17 | |
| 8 | 9 | | 18 | |
| 9 | 10 | | 19 | |
| | 10 | The point of the Flaming Sword or Lightning Flash | | Full Manifestation in the Physical World |
| 10 | | Tail of the Serpent | | The point of Return and the First Initiation |
| 9 | 6 | Coils of the Serpent of Wisdom Initiation and return to Godhead | 20 | The first Path the Serpent crosses over, that has not already been traversed by the Lightning Flash |
| 7 | 6 | | 21 | Crosses over these Paths in turn ignoring the Paths it passes behind and the Paths already traversed by the Lightning Flash |
| 9 | 6 | | 22 | |
| 8 | 5 | | 23 | |
| 7 | 4 | | 24 | |
| 6 | 4 | | 25 | |
| 5 | 3 | | 26 | |
| 6 | 3 | | 27 | |
| 4 | 2 | | 28 | |
| 6 | 2 | | 29 | |
| 4 | 2 | | 30 | |
| 6 | 1 | | 31 | |
| 3 | 1 | | 32 | Completion, return to the Godhead |
| | 1 | Head of the Serpent | | Touches again on Path 11 suggesting a new beginning |

# K. Kabbalah

*The Four Worlds of the Kabbalah*

| | | K13. Letters of the Name IHVH. | K14. Four Worlds. | K15. The Four Worlds – Transliteration. | K16. Four Worlds – in English. | K17. Four Worlds – Meaning. | K18. Secret Names of the Four Words. | K19. Four Worlds – Secret Number | K20. Tetragrammaton revolved in the Four Worlds. |
|---|---|---|---|---|---|---|---|---|---|
| | | 54 | 63 | | | | 64 | 65 | 66 |
| | 1 | | | | | | | | |
| | 2 | י | אצילות | ATzILVTh | Atziluth | Archetypal World | | | |
| | 3 | | | | | | | | |
| | 4 | | | | | | | | |
| | 5 | ה | בריאה | BRIAH | Briah | Creative World | | | |
| | 6 | | | | | | | | |
| | 7 | | | | | | | | |
| | 8 | ו | יצירה | ITzIRH | Yetzirah | Formative World | | | |
| | 9 | | | | | | | | |
| | 10 | ה | עשיה | OShIH | Assiah | Material World | | | |
| ✹ | 31b | | | | | | | | |
| F | 31 | י | אצילות | ATzILVTh | Atziluth | Archetypal World | עב Aub | 72 | יוד הי ויו הי |
| W | 23 | ה | בריאה | BRIAH | Briah | Creative World | סג Seg | 63 | יוד הי ואו הי |
| A | 11 | ו | יצירה | ITzIRH | Yetzirah | Formative World | מה Mah | 45 | יוד הא ואו הא |
| E | 32b | ה | עשיה | OShIH | Assiah | Material World | בן Ben | 52 | יוד הה וו הה |

# K. Kabbalah

*Atziluth – the Archetypal World*

| | | K21. God-Names in Atziluth (Golden Dawn). | K22. God-Names in Atziluth – Transliteration. | K23. God-Names in Atziluth – English. | K24. God-Names in Atziluth – Numeration. |
|---|---|---|---|---|---|
| | | 5 | | | |
| | 1 | אהיה | AHIH | Eheieh | 21 |
| | 2 | יה | YH | Yah | 15 |
| | 3 | יהוה אלהים | IHVH ALHIM | Yahweh Elohim | 112, 672 |
| | 4 | אל | AL | El | 31 |
| | 5 | אלהים גבור | ALHIM GBVR | Elohim Gibor | 297, 857 |
| | 6 | יהוה אלוה ודעת | IHVH ALVH V-DOTh | Yahweh Eloah Va-Daath | 548 |
| | 7 | יהוה צבאות | IHVH TzBAVTh | Yahweh Tzabaoth | 525 |
| | 8 | אלהים צבאות | ALHIM TzBAVTh | Elohim Tzabaoth | 585, 1145 |
| | 9 | שדי<br>אל חי | ShDI<br>AL ChI | Shaddai<br>El Chai | 314<br>49 |
| | 10 | אדני מלך<br>אדני הארץ | ADNI MLK,<br>ADNI H-ARTz | Adonai Melekh,<br>Adonai Ha-Aretz | 155, 635<br>361, 1171 |
| ⊛ | 31b | יהשוה | YHShVH | Yeheshuah | 326 |
| F | 31 | אלהים | ALHIM | Elohim | 86, 646 |
| A | 11 | יהוה | IHVH | Yahweh | 26 |
| W | 23 | אל | AL | El | 31 |
| E | 32b | אדני הארץ | ADNI H-ARTZ | Adonai Ha-Aretz | 361, 1171 |
| ☾ | 13 | דה<br>אלים | DH<br>ALIM | Dah<br>Elim | 9<br>81, 641 |
| ☿ | 12 | אזבוגה | AZBVGH | Azbugah | 24 |
| ♀ | 14 | אהא | AHA | Aha | 7 |
| ☼ | 30 | אלה | ALH | Alah | 36 |
| ♂ | 27 | אדני | ADNI | Adonai | 65 |
| ♃ | 21 | אבא<br>אל אב | ABA<br>AL AB | Aba<br>El Ab | 4<br>34 |
| ♄ | 32 | אב<br>יה | AB<br>YH | Ab<br>Yah | 3<br>15 |

# K. Kabbalah

| Number of Letters. | K25. The Names of God of Various Numbers of Letters Used in Amulets – Hebrew. | K26. The Names of God of Various Length – Transliteration. | K27. The Names of God of Various Length – Translation. | K28. The Names of God of Various Length – Numeration. |
|---|---|---|---|---|
| 1 | ה or י | I or H | | 10 or 6 |
| 2 | יה or יי or אל | EL or II or IH | El or Yi or Yah | 31 or 20 or 15 |
| 3 | שדי or והו or יור or ייי | III or IVI or VHV or ShDI | III or Yvi or Vhu or Shaddai | 30, 25, 17, 331 |
| 4 | מצפץ יהוה | IHVH MTzPTz | Yahweh Matzpatz | 26 300/1110 |
| 5 | אליון or אלהים | ALHIM or ALIVN | Elohim or Elion | 86/646, 97/747 |
| 6 | אל גבור or אלוהים | ALVHIM or EL GBVR | Elohim or El Gibor | 92/652, 242 |
| 7 | אראריתא אשר אהיה | ARARIThA AShR AHIH | Ararita Asher Ehieh | 813 522 |
| 8 | יאהד ונהי אלוה ודעת יהוה ודעת | IAHD V-NHI ALVH V-DOTh IHVH V-DOTh | Yahd Ve-Nahi Eloha Ve-Daath IHVH Ve-Daath | 91 522 506 |
| 9 | יהוה צבאות יהוה צדקנו אלהים גיבר | IHVH TzBAVTh IHVH TzDQNV ALHIM GIBR | IHVH Tzabaoth IHVH Zidkenu Elohim Gibor | 525 276 301/861 |
| 10 | אלהים צבאות | ALHIM TzBAVTh | Elohim Tzabaoth | 585/1145 |
| 12 | הקדוש ברוך הוא אל אלהינו יהוה | H-QDVSh BRVK HVA[2] AL ALHINV IHVH | Ha-Qadosh Baruk Hua[2] El Elohinu IHVH | 655/1135 159 |
| 14 | רשלייודנגאיב יהוה אלהינו יהוה כוזו במוכסז כוזו | RShLIIVDNGAIB IHVH ALHINV IHVH KVZV BMVKSZ KVZV | IHVH Elohinu IHVH [A notariqon of the above] | 626 154 213 |
| 22 | אנקתם פסתם פספסים דיונסים יעקב יצחק אברהם ישרון שבטי | ANQThM PSThM PSPSIM DIVNSIM IOQB ITzChQ ABRHM IShRVN ShBTI | Anaqtam Pastam Paspasim Dionsim | 1681/3921 |
| 26 | יעקב אהליך תבו-מה ישראך משכנתיך | IOQB AHLIK ThBV-MH IShRAK MShKNThIK | | |
| 33 | אדני יהוה יה אהיה שדי אלהים אלוה אל צבאות | ADNI IHVH IH AHIH ShDI ALHIM ALVH AL TzBAVTh | Adonai YHVH Yah Eheieh Shaddai Elohim Eloah Al Tzabaoth | |
| 42[3] | אבגיתץ קרעשטן נגדיכש בטרצתג חקדרטנע יגלפזק שקוצית | ABGIThTz QROShTN NGDIKSh BTRTzThG ChQD[4]TNO IGLPZQ ShQVTzITh | Seven groups of 6 letters, one for each of the 7 days of the week, or the 7 Planets. | 506 + 729 387 + 704 241 + 230 + 906 = 3703 |

---

[2] The 11 letter name H-QDSh BRVD HVA is a corruption of this 12 letter name.
[3] An alternative 42 letter name is provided by Reuchlin in *De Arte Cabalistica*: ShGThBMO ShGThThKS MIThOTzB IMIPThA TzThGHPtZ ThGHtZMA TzATzPPSh which also has some useful properties.
[4] Or Beth כ instead of Daleth ד in some sources. The Gematria in the last column of this row assumes no final values.

# K. Kabbalah

*Briah – the World of Creation*

| | | | Testament of Solomon | Gnostics | Pope Gregory the Great | Pseudo-Dionysis | Geonic | Talismanic Magic | Janua Magica Reserata |
|---|---|---|---|---|---|---|---|---|---|
| | **Enoch I** | **Enoch III** | | | | | | | |
| | | | | | **K29. Comparative Table of Archangels in Briah.** | | | | |
| **1** | | | | | | | | | Mathraton |
| **2** | | | | | | | | | Raziel |
| **3** | Uriel | Mikael | Mikael | Michael | Michael | Michael | Michael | Zaphkiel | Zaphkiel |
| **4** | Raphael | Gabriel | Gabriel | Gabriel | Gabriel | Gabriel | Gabriel | Zadkiel | Zadkiel |
| **5** | Raguel | Shatqiel | Uriel | Raphael | Raphael | Raphael | Raphael | Camael | Samael |
| **6** | Michael | Baradiel | Sabrael | Uriel | Uriel | Uriel | Aniel | Raphael | Michael |
| **7** | Zerachiel | Shachaqiel | Arael | Barachiel | Simiel | Chamuel | Kafziel | Haniel | Anael / Haniel |
| **8** | Gabriel | Baraqiel | Iaoth | Sealtiel | Orifiel | Jophiel | Samael | Michael | Raphiel |
| **9** | Remiel/ Jeremiel | Sidriel | Adonael | Jehudiel | Zachariel | Zadkiel | Zadkiel | Gabriel | Gabriel |
| **10** | | | | | | | | | Soul of Messiah |

| | K30. Archangels of Briah. | K31. Archangels of Briah – Transliteration. | K32. Archangels of Briah – English. | K33. Archangels of Briah – Numeration. |
|---|---|---|---|---|
| | **99** | | | |
| **1** | מטטרון | MTTRVN | Metatron | 314, 964 |
| **2** | רזיאל / רציאל | RZIAL / RTzIAL | Ratziel / Raziel [or Iophiel] | 248/331 |
| **3** | צפקיאל | TzPQIAL | Tzaphkiel / Zaphkiel | 311 |
| **4** | צדקיאל | TzDQIAL | Tzadkiel / Zadkiel | 235 |
| **5** | כמאל | KMAL | Kamael / Camael | 91 |
| **6** | מיכאל | MIKAL | Michael [sometimes at 8] | 101 |
| **7** | דאוריאלף האניאל | HANIAL [AVRIAL] | Haniel / Hanael [or Auriel] | 97 [248] |
| **8** | רפאל | RPAL | Raphael [sometimes at 6] | 311 |
| **9** | גבריאל | GBRIAL | Gabriel | 246 |
| **10** | סנדלפון | SNDLPVN | Sandalphon [or 'Soul of the Messiah'] | 280, 930 |

# K. Kabbalah

*Yetzirah – the World of Formation*

| | Mishne Torah – Maimonides | Zohar | Maseketh Aziluth | Berith Menucha |
|---|---|---|---|---|
| | K34. The Orders of Angels in Yetzirah – Comparative Hebraic Sources. | | | |
| 1 | Chaioth ha-Qadesh | Malachim | Seraphim | Arelim |
| 2 | Auphanim | Erelim | Ophanim | Ishim |
| 3 | Aralim | Seraphim | Cherubim | Bene Elohim |
| 4 | Chashmalim | Hayyoth | Shinnanim | Malakim |
| 5 | Seraphim | Ophanim | Tarshishim | Hashmallim |
| 6 | Malachim | Hamshalim | Ishim | Tarshishim |
| 7 | Elohim | Elim | Hashmallim | Shinnanim |
| 8 | Bene Elohim | Elohim | Malakim | Cherubimn |
| 9 | Kerubin | Bene Elohm | Bene Elohim | Ophanim |
| 10 | Ishim | Ishim | Arelim | Seraphim |

| | St Ambrose | St Jerome | Gregory the Great | Thomas Aquinas | Isidore of Seville | Dante |
|---|---|---|---|---|---|---|
| | K35. The Orders of Angels in Yetzirah – Comparative Christian Sources. | | | | | |
| 1 | Seraphim | Seraphim | Seraphim | Seraphim | Seraphim | Seraphim |
| 2 | Cherubim | Cherubim | Cherubim | Cherubim | Cherubim | Cherubim |
| 3 | Dominations | Powers | Thrones | Thrones | Powers | Thrones |
| 4 | Thrones | Dominions | Dominations | Dominations | Principalities | Dominations |
| 5 | Principalities | Thrones | Principalities | Virtues | Virtues | Virtues |
| 6 | Potentates | | Powers | Powers | Dominations | Powers |
| 7 | Virtues | | Virtues | Principalities | Thrones | Archangels |
| 8 | Archangels | Archangels | Archangels | Archangels | Archangels | Principalities |
| 9 | Angels | Angels | Angels | Angels | Angels | Angels |
| 10 | | | | | | |

# K. Kabbalah

| | Choirs/Orders | Order | Description | Function | Source |
|---|---|---|---|---|---|
| | | | K36: Orders of Angels – Standard list of Dionysius the Areopagite. | | |
| 1 | Seraphim | First | Fiery with three pairs of red wings | Reflect the radiance of God, praise God | *Genesis* |
| 2 | Cherubim | | Single pair of blue wings, derived from Babylonian temple guardians. Guardians of Tree of Life east of Eden | Divine knowledge and wisdom | *Genesis* |
| 3 | Thrones | | Fiery wheels with eyes, or crystal thrones shining like the sun | Seat of God, steadfastness | *Ezekiel, St Paul's Colossians* |
| 4 | Dominations/ Dominions | Second | Enthroned like kings, on marble | | *St Paul's Colossians* |
| 5 | Virtues | | From *vir*, or virtue, meaning 'life force' | Infusing base matter with divine qualities. Caring for pilgrims and ships, performing miracles | |
| 6 | Powers | | Holding enchained demons | Embody laws of the cosmos and the workings of fate. Constrain demons or fallen angels | *St Paul's Colossians* |
| 7 | Principalities | Third | Benign princes, soldiers of God | | *St Paul's Colossians* |
| 8 | Archangels | | 7 Archangels in Christian tradition, 4 in Islam. Michael is depicted as a winged armed youth with lance and shield. | Driving rebel angels out of heaven, overseeing the cosmos, combating Satan | *Revelations, Book of Tobit, Apocrypha* |
| 9 | Angels | | Mostly looking human | Messengers to mankind | [Many] |
| 10 | | | | [Guardian angels] | *Psalm 91, St Matthew* |

| | K37. Orders of Angels in Yetzirah. | K38. Orders of Angels in Yetzirah – Transliteration. | K39. Orders of Angels in Yetzirah – English. | K40. Orders of Angels in Yetzirah – Meaning. | K41. Orders of Angels in Yetzirah – Numeration. |
|---|---|---|---|---|---|
| | **100** | | | **101** | |
| 1 | חיות הקדש | HIVTh H-QDSh | Chaioth ha-Qadosh | Holy Living Creatures | 833 |
| 2 | אופנים | AVPNIM | Auphanim | Wheels | 187, 747 |
| 3 | אראלים | ARALIM | Aralim | Thrones | 282, 842 |
| 4 | חשמלים | ChShMLIM | Chashmalim | Brilliant ones | 428, 988 |
| 5 | שרפים | ShRPIM | Seraphim | Fiery serpents | 630, 1190 |
| 6 | מלכים | MLKIM | Malakim or Malachim | Kings | 140, 700 |
| 7 | אלהים | ALHIM | Elohim | Gods | 86, 646 |
| 8 | בני אלהים | BNI ALHIM | Beni Elohim | Sons of the gods | 148, 708 |
| 9 | כרובים | KRBIM | Kerubim | Angels of Elements | 278, 838 |
| 10 | אשים | AShIM | Ashim or Ishim | Flames or Souls | 351, 911 |

# K. Kabbalah

| | K42. Orders of Angels in Yetzirah [non-standard attribution]. | K43. Orders of Angels in Yetzirah – Transliteration. | K44. Orders of Angels in Yetzirah – Translation.[5] |
|---|---|---|---|
| | **86** | | |
| 1 | שרפים | ShRPIM | Seraphim |
| 2 | אופנים | AVPNIM | Auphanim |
| 3 | כרובים | KRVBIM | Kerubim |
| 4 | שיננים | ShINNIM | Shinanim |
| 5 | תרשישים | ThRShIShIM | Tharshishim |
| 6 | חשמלים | ChShMLIM | Chashmalim |
| 7 | מלכים | MLKIM | Melakim |
| 8 | בני אלהים | BNI ALHIM | Beni Elohim |
| 9 | ישים | IShIM | Ishim |
| 10 | אראלים | ARALIM | Aralim |

*Assiah – the Material World*

| | K47. Angels of Assiah. | K48. Angels of Assiah – Transliteration. | K49. Angels of Assiah. – Translation. | K50. Angels of Assiah – Numeration. |
|---|---|---|---|---|
| | **85** | | | |
| 1 | יהואל | IHVAL | Yehuel | 52 |
| 2 | רפאל | RPAL | Raphael | 311 |
| 3 | כרוביאל | KRVBIAL | Kerubiel | 269 |
| 4 | צדקיאל | TzDQIAL | Tzadqiel | 235 |
| 5 | תרשיש | ThRShISh | Tharshish | 1210 |
| 6 | מתתרון חשמאל | MThThRVN HShMAL | Metatron Hismael | 1096, 1746 376 |
| 7 | וסיאל | VSIAL | Usiel | 107 |
| 8 | הסניאל | HSNIAL | Hisniel | 156 |
| 9 | יהואל זפניאל | IHVAL ZPNIAL | Yehuel Zephaniel | 52 178 |
| 10 | מיכאל | MIKAL | Michael | 101 |

---

[5] Tables K45 and K46 appeared in the First edition, but have been deleted from this edition as their content was essentially trivial, being simply a single Latin quote from von Rosenroth concerning the Seraphim, spread across nine of the Sephiroth.

# K. Kabbalah

| | | K51. The Heavens of Assiah (with Elements, Planets and Zodiac). | K52. The Heavens of Assiah (with Elements, Planets and Zodiac) – Transliteration. | K53. The Heavens of Assiah (with Elements, Planets and Zodiac) – English. | K54. The Heavens of Assiah (with Elements, Planets and Zodiac) – Numeration. |
|---|---|---|---|---|---|
| | | **6** | | **7** | |
| | 1 | ראשית הגלגלים | Rashith ha-Gilgalim | Sphere of Primum Mobile | 1032, 1592 |
| | 2 | מזלות | Mazloth | Sphere of the Zodiac | 483 |
| | 3 | שבתאי | Shabbathai | Sphere of Saturn | 713 |
| | 4 | צדק | Tzedeq | Sphere of Jupiter | 194 |
| | 5 | מאדים | Madim | Sphere of Mars | 95, 655 |
| | 6 | שמש | Shemesh | Sphere of Sol | 640 |
| | 7 | נגה | Nogah | Sphere of Venus | 58 |
| | 8 | כוכב | Kokab | Sphere of Mercury | 48 |
| | 9 | לבנה | Levanah | Sphere of Luna | 87 |
| | 10 | חלם יסודות | Cholem Yesodoth | 'Strong Foundations'[6] Sphere of the Elements | 564, 1124 |
| ✳ | 31b | א־ת | 'A-Th' | Spirit / Akasha | 401 |
| F | 31 | אש | Aesh | Fire | 301 |
| A | 11 | רוח | Ruach | Air | 214 |
| W | 23 | מים | Maim | Water | 90, 650 |
| E | 32b | ארץ | Aretz | Earth | 1101 |
| ☾ | 13 | לבנה | Levanah/Lebanah | Luna | 87 |
| ☿ | 12 | כוכב | Kokab | Mercury | 48 |
| ♀ | 14 | נגה | Nogah | Venus | 58 |
| ☼ | 30 | שמש | Shemesh | Sun | 640 |
| ♂ | 27 | מאדים | Madim | Mars | 95, 655 |
| ♃ | 21 | צדק | Tzedeq | Jupiter | 194 |
| ♄ | 32 | שבתאי | Shabbathai | Saturn | 713 |
| ♈ | 15 | תלה | Teleh | Aries ♈ | 435 |
| ♉ | 16 | שור | Shar | Taurus ♉ | 506 |
| ♊ | 17 | תאונים | Teonim | Gemini ♊ | 507, 1067 |
| ♋ | 18 | סרטן | Sarton | Cancer ♋ | 319, 969 |
| ♌ | 19 | אריה | Ari | Leo ♌ | 216 |
| ♍ | 20 | בתולה | Betulah | Virgo ♍ | 443 |
| ♎ | 22 | מאזנים | Moznaim | Libra ♎ | 148, 708 |
| ♏ | 24 | עקרב | Akrab | Scorpio ♏ | 372 |
| ♐ | 25 | קשת | Qesheth | Sagittarius ♐ | 800 |
| ♑ | 26 | גדי | Gedi | Capricorn ♑ | 17 |
| ♒ | 28 | דלי | Deli | Aquarius ♒ | 44 |
| ♓ | 29 | דגים | Dagim | Pisces ♓ | 57, 617 |

---

[6] Not 'Breaker of the Foundations' as it is sometimes incorrectly translated.

# K. Kabbalah

*Revolutions of the Divine Names*

| | | K55. The Revolutions of AHIH אהיה in Briah. | K56. The Revolutions of Eheieh in Briah – Transliterated. | K57. The Revolutions of IHVH יהוה in Yetzirah. | K58. The Revolutions of IHVH in Yetzirah – Transliterated. | K59. Twelve Banners or Zodiacal Permutations of IHVH. |
|---|---|---|---|---|---|---|
| | | 89 | | 96 | | 140 |
| | 1 | אהיה | AHIH | יהוה | IHVH | |
| | 2 | אההי | AHHI | יההו | IHHV | |
| | 3 | איהה | AIHH | יוהה | IVHH | |
| | 4 | חהיא | HHIA | הויה | HVIH | |
| | 5 | ההאי | HHAI | ההוי | HHVI | |
| | 6 | האהי | HAHI | ההוי | HHIV | |
| | 7 | האיה | HAIH | היהו | HIHV | |
| | 8 | היאה | HIAH | הוהי | HVHI | |
| | 9 | יאהה | IAHH | והיה | VHIH | |
| | 10 | יהאה. יחהא. אל. שדי | IHAH, IHHA El, Shaddai | וההי. ויהה. אל יהוה | VIHH, VHHI, AL IHVH | |
| | | | | | | |
| ♈ | 15 | | | | | IHVH |
| ♉ | 16 | | | | | IHHV |
| ♊ | 17 | | | | | IVHH |
| ♋ | 18 | | | | | HVHI |
| ♌ | 19 | | | | | HVIH |
| ♍ | 20 | | | | | HHIV |
| ♎ | 22 | | | | | VHIH |
| ♏ | 24 | | | | | VHHI |
| ♐ | 25 | | | | | VIHH |
| ♑ | 26 | | | | | HIHV |
| ♒ | 28 | | | | | HIVH |
| ♓ | 29 | | | | | HHVI |

| | K60. Revolutions of Adonai in Assiah. | | K61. Revolutions of Adonai in Assiah – Transliteration. | K62. Revolutions of the 42-fold Name in the Palaces of Yetzirah. | | K63. Revolutions of the 42-fold Name in the Palaces of Yetzirah – English. |
|---|---|---|---|---|---|---|
| | **102** | | | **90** | | |
| 1 | אדני | | ADNI | אב | | AB |
| 2 | אדינ | | ADIN | גי | | GI |
| 3 | אניד | | ANID | תץ | | ThTz |
| 4 | אינד | | AIND | קרעשטן | | QROShTN |
| 5 | אידנ | | AIDN | נגריכש | | NGDIKSh |
| 6 | דניא | | DNIA | בטרצתג | | BTRTzThG |
| 7 | דנאי | | DNAI | חקדטנע | | ChQD[7]TNO |
| 8 | דינא | | DINA | יגלפזק | | IGLPZQ |
| 9 | דיאנ | | DIAN | שקו | | ShQV |
| 10 | ינדא. אדני. דאני. אל | | DANI, ADNI, INDA, EL | צית | | TzITh |

*The Seven Palaces*

| | K64. The 7 Palaces of Briah. | K65. The 7 Palaces of Briah – Translation. | K66. The 7 Palaces of Briah – Latin. | K67. The 7 Palaces of Briah –English. | K68. The 7 Palaces of Briah – alternative version. |
|---|---|---|---|---|---|
| | **87** | | **88** | | |
| 1 | | | | | |
| 2 | | | | | |
| 3 | היכל קדוש קדשים | Hekel Qadosh Qadeshim | Palatium Sancti Sanctorum | Palace of the Holy of Holies | Kodesh Kedashim (Holy of Holies) |
| 4 | היכל אהבה | Hekel Ahbah | Palatium Amoris | Palace of Love | Ratzon (Desire/Will) |
| 5 | היכל זכות | Hekel Zakoth | Palatium Meriti | Palace of Merit | Ahavah (Love) |
| 6 | היכל רצון | Hekel Ratzon | Palatium Benevolentiae | Palace of Benevolence | Zekhut (Merit) |
| 7 | היכל עצם שמים | Hekel Etzem Shamaim | Palatium Substantiae Coeli | Palace of the Substance of the Heavens | Nogah (Lustre) |
| 8 | היכל נוגה | Hekel Nogah[8] | Palatium Serenitatis | Palace of Serenity | Etzem ha-Shamayim (Essence of Heaven) |
| 9 | היכל לבנת הספיר | Hekel Lebanath ha-Saphir | Palatium Albedinis Crystalinae | Palace of White Crystal (Sapphire Pavement) | Livnat ha-Sappir (Sapphire Pavement) |
| 10 | | | | | |

---

[7] Or Beth instead of Daleth, in some sources.
[8] Shown as Gonah in some sources.

# K. Kabbalah

*The Seven Heavens in the Seven Palaces*

| | K69. 7 Heavens in Seven Palaces. | K70. Seven Heavens in Seven Palaces. | K71. Seven Heavens in Seven Palaces – Latin. | K72. Seven Heavens in Seven Palaces – English. | K73. Seven Heavens in Seven Palaces – Contents. |
|---|---|---|---|---|---|
| | 93 | | 94 | | 95 |
| 1 | | | | | |
| 2 | | | | | |
| 3 | ערבות | Araboth | Planities | Plains | Righteousness, judgment and grace, life, peace and blessing, the souls of the spirits and souls which are about to be created, the dew with which the Holy One, is about to quicken mortals. Seraphs and holy beings, ministering angels and the throne of glory, the Living God. Ruled by the Messiah |
| 4 | מכון | Makon | Repositorium | Emplacement or Base | Hail, harmful dews, whirlwind, storm, the retreat of noisome vapours, snow, rain, spirit of life, blessings. Their doors are made of fire. Ruled by Moses |
| 5 | מעון | Ma'on | Habitaculum | Dwelling or Abode | Angels singing in the Divine Presence. Ruled by Abraham |
| 6 | זבול | Zebul | Habitaculum | Dwelling or Habitation | The heavenly Jerusalem, the Temple. The angel Michael offering the souls of the just. Ruled by Isaac |
| 7 | שחקים | Shechaqim | Locus Communicationis | Clouds/ Place of communication | Millstones where manna for the just is ground. Ruled by Jacob |
| 8 | רקיע | Raqia | Firmamentum | Firmament | Sol, Luna, planets, star constellations, and the 10 Sephiroth |
| 9 | תבל וילון שמים | Tebel Vilon Shamayim | Velum sive Cortina | Veil of the vault of Heaven | Has no specific use. Follows 390 heavens, and 18,000 worlds, Earth, Eden and Hell. It renews the work of Creation every day. |
| 10 | | | | | |

| | The Seven Heavens in Seven Palaces. | K74. The Seven Heavens in Seven Palaces – Angels from *Enoch 3, XVII, 1–3.* | K75. The Seven Heavens in Seven Palaces – Angels from *Pirqe Rabbi Ishmael.* | K76. The Seven Heavens in Seven Palaces – Angels from *Hekhaloth Zot.* |
|---|---|---|---|---|
| 1 | | | | |
| 2 | | | | |
| 3 | Araboth | Mikael | [none] | Mikael |
| 4 | Makon | Gabriel | Sandalphon | Gabriel |
| 5 | Ma'on | Shataqiel | Gabriel | Sodiel |
| 6 | Zebul | Shahaqi'el | Mikael | 'Akatriel |
| 7 | Shechaqim | Badariel | Shaphiel | Raphael |
| 8 | Raqia | Barakiel | Gallisur | Bodiel |
| 9 | Tebel Vilon Shamayim | Pazriel | Qemuel [and the angels of destruction] | Yomael |
| 10 | | | | |

# K. Kabbalah

| No. | K78. The Hierarchy of the Heavens before the Throne of Glory in order of Precedence – *Enoch 3* – Title. [9] | K79. The Hierarchy of Heaven before the Throne of Glory in order of Precedence – *Enoch 3* – Angel Names. |
|---|---|---|
| 1-4 | 4 Great Princes whose dwelling place is by the Throne of Glory, before the Judge | 2 'Irin & 2 Qaddishin |
|  | Prince who is appointed over the treasures of the books and Case of Writings | Radweriel [YHV]H' |
| 1 | Prince, wonderful, noble, great, honourable, mighty, terrible, a chief and leader, and a swift scribe, his body like an eagles body | Seraphiel |
| 2 | Great Prince, revered, high, lordly, fearful, ancient and strong, with 8466 eyes, 2116 on each side, appointed over the 'Ophannim | 'Ophphanniel [YHV]H' |
| 3 | Prince of highness and righteousness, at whose rebuke the *'Araboth* tremble…the bow of *Shekinah* is between his shoulders, royal diadem upon his skull, his body full of eyes, appointed over the chariot of the Kerubim | Kerubiel [YHV]H' |
| 4 | Prince, noble and revered, glorious and mighty, etc, who is able to swallow up the whole world in a moment, appointed over the 4 Holy Chayyoth | Chayyliel [YHV]H' |
| 5 | Prince, distinguished, honoured, noble, glorified, adorned, fearful, valiant, etc, in charge of the wheels of the *Merkabah* throne. | Rikbiel [YHV]H' |
| 6 | Two Great Princes, honoured, glorified, blameless, ancient and mighty, appointed over the books of death (he who kills) and the books of life (he who gives life) | Sopheriel [YHV]H' & Sopheriel [YHV]H' |
| 7 | Great Prince, glorified, revered, honoured, adorned, wonderful, exalted, beloved and feared among all who knows the mystery of the Throne of Glory | 'Azbuga [YHV]H' |
| 8 | Great Prince, the mighty, terrible and honoured one, glorified and feared in all the heavenly household | Zehanpuryu [YHV]H' |
| 9 | Great Prince, the mighty, terrible and honoured one who weighs all the merits of man in the balance in the presence of the Holy One | Shoqed Chozi |
| 10 | Prince, the great fearful and honoured one, keeper of the seals of the fiery river by the Throne of Glory | Sother 'Ashiel [YHV]H' |
|  | Prince who keeps the keys of the Heavenly Halls, who overshadows all the chambers of *Araboth Raqia* | 'Anaphiel [YHV]H' |
| 1 | Prince who is appointed to write down the merits of Israel on the Throne of Glory | Zakzakiel [YHV]H' |
| 2 | Prince who reveals all the secrets of the *Torah* | Gallishur [YHV]H' |
| 3 | Prince who presides in all the sessions of the children of Heaven | 'Ashruylu [YHV]H' |
| 4 | Prince | Araphiel [YHV]H' |
| 5 | Prince | Geburatiel [YHV]H' |
| 6 | Great Prince | Zazriel [YHV]H' |
| 7 | Great Prince | Sasnigiel [YHV]H' |
| 8 | Great Prince | Na'aririel [YHV]H' |
| 9 | Great Prince | Atrugiel |
| 10 | Great Prince | Tutresiel |
|  | Great Prince, fearful, honoured, pleasant and terrible one | Hamon [tumult] |
|  | Great Prince of 3 fingers (*sic*) in the heights of the Heaven *Araboth* | Barattiel |
|  | Prince at the head of all the children of Heaven | Tag'as |
| 1-4 | 4 Great Princes appointed over the 4 Camps of the *Shekinah* | Mikael, Gabriel, Uriel, Raphael |
| 1-7 | Doorkeepers of the 1st-7th Halls in the *Araboth Raqia* |  |
| 72 | 72 Princes of the [Earthly] Kingdoms |  |
| 1-7 | Princes of the 1st to 7th Heavens [lowest of the hierarchy] |  |

---

[9] Column K77 in the First Edition has now been amalgamated with Columns A10 and A11 in this edition.

# K. Kabbalah

*The Seven Earths in the Seven Palaces*

| | K80. Seven Earths in Seven Palaces – Hebrew. | K81. Seven Earths in Seven Palaces – Transliteration. | K82. Seven Earths in Seven Palaces – English (Crowley). | K83. Seven Earths in Seven Palaces – English (Rappoport from Godwin). | K84. Seven Earths in Seven Palaces (*Midrash Konen* from Godwin). | K85. Seven Earths in Seven Palaces (Godwin). |
|---|---|---|---|---|---|---|
| | **104** | | **105** | | | |
| **1** | | | | | | |
| **2** | | | | | | |
| **3** | ארץ | ARTz | Aretz (Earth – dry land) | Eretz ha-Tachtonah (Nethermost Earth) | Aretz (Earth) | Aretz (Earth) |
| **4** | אדמה | ADMH | Adamah (Red earth) | Adamah (Earth) | Adamah (Earth) | Adamah (Earth) |
| **5** | גיא | GIA | Gia (Undulating ground) | Arka (Earth) | Charabhah (Parched Land) | Gaye (Valley) |
| **6** | נשיה | NShIH | Neshiah (Pasture) | Ge (Valley) | Tziah (Dryness) | Neshiah (Oblivion) |
| **7** | ציה | TzIH | Tziah (Sandy desert earth) | Neshiah (Oblivion) | Yabbashah (Dry Land) | Tziah (Dryness) |
| **8** | ארקא | ARQA | Arqa (Earth) | Zija (i.e. Tziah) (Dryness) | Arqa (Earth) | Arqa (Earth) |
| **9** | תבל | ThBL | Tebhel (Wet earth) | Tebel (World) | Tebhel | Tebhel |
| **10** | [חלד] | [ChLD] | [Cheled (our world/Earth)] | | [Cheled (World)] | [Cheled (World)] |

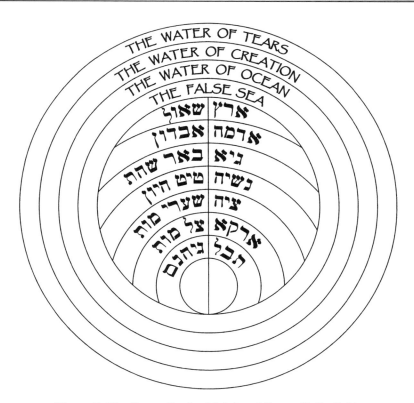

Figure 7: The Seven Earths (right) and Seven Hells (left).

169

# K. Kabbalah

## The Seven Hells in the Seven Palaces

| | K86. Seven Hells in Seven Palaces. | K87. Seven Hells in Seven Palaces – Transliteration. | K88. Seven Hells in Seven Palaces – Translation. | K89. Seven Hells in Seven Palaces – English. | K90. Seven Hells or Habitations of the Damned – Latin. |
|---|---|---|---|---|---|
| | 106 | | | 107 | |
| 1 | | | | | |
| 2 | | | | | |
| 3 | שאול | ShAVL | Sheol | Grave, Abyss | Fovea |
| 4 | אברון | ABDVN | Abaddon | Perdition/Destruction | Perdito |
| 5 | באר שחת | BAR ShChTh | Bar Shachath | Pit of Corruption/ Destruction | Puteus Inferitus |
| 6 | טיט היון | TIT HIVN | Tit ha-Yavon | Clay | Lutem fecis |
| 7 | שערי מות | ShORI MVTh | Shaare-Maveth | Gates of Death | Portae Mortis |
| 8 | צל מות | TzL MVTh | Tzal-Maveth | Shadow of Death | Umbra Mortis |
| 9 | גיהנם | GIHNM | Ge-Hinnom | Valley of Hinnom | Gehenna |
| 10 | | | | | |

## The Qliphoth

| | K91. Arch-Demons or Princes of the Qliphoth. | K92. Arch-Demons or Princes of the Qliphoth. | K93. Arch-Demons or Princes of the Qliphoth – Standard List (rulers of Column K97). | K94. Arch-Demons according to *Le Dragon Rouge*. |
|---|---|---|---|---|
| | | 108 | | |
| 1 | סטן מלך | Satan and Moloch | Satan and Moloch | Lucifer, Emperor |
| 2 | סמאל | Samael (father of Chioa, the Beast) | Beelzebub [or Belial] | Belzebut, Prince |
| 3 | אשת זנונים | Isheth Zenunim (mate of Samael, mother of the Beast) | Lucifuge [Lucifuge Rofocale] | Astarot, Grand Duke |
| 4 | – | Lucifuge | Ashtaroth | Lucifuge, Prime Minister |
| 5 | אשתרות | Ashtaroth | Asmodeus | Satanachia, Grand General |
| 6 | בלפגור חיא | Belphegor, Chioa (the Beast) | Belphegor | Agaliarept., General |
| 7 | אשמדאי | Ashmodai/Asmodeus | Baal [Chanan] | Fleurety, Lieutenant |
| 8 | בליאל אדרמלך | Belial Adramelek | Adrammelech | Sargatanas, Brigadier |
| 9 | לילית | Lilith (mate of Samael) | Lilith | Nebiros, Marshall de Camp |
| 10 | נעמה | Naamah[10] (mate of Samael, mother of Ashmodai) | Nahemah/Naamah | |

---

[10] The fourth mate of Samael was אגרת בת מחלת. Agerath bat Machalath.

| | | K95. Orders of Qliphoth. | K96. Orders of Qliphoth – Transliteration. | K97. Orders of Qliphoth – English. | K98. Orders of Qliphoth – Meaning. | K99. Orders of Qliphoth – Numeration. |
|---|---|---|---|---|---|---|
| | | 8 | | | 123 | |
| | 1 | תאומיאל | ThAVMIEL | Thaumiel | Twins Gods, Dual Contending Forces | 488 |
| | 2 | עוגיאל | OVGVAL | Augiel[11] | Hinderers | 120 |
| | 3 | סאתאריאל | SAThARIAL | Satariel | Concealers | 702 |
| | 4 | געשכלה | GOShKLH | Gasheklah[12] | Smiters | 428 |
| | 5 | גולחב | GVLChB | Golachab | Burners Flaming Ones | 49 |
| | 6 | תגרירון | ThGRIRVN | Thagiriron | Disputers/Hagglers | 869, 1519 |
| | 7 | ערב זרק | ORB ZRQ | Arab Zereq[13] | Ravens of Dispersion | 579 |
| | 8 | סמאל | SMAL | Samael | Poison of God | 131 |
| | 9 | גמליאל | GMLIAL | Gamaliel | Obscene Ones Obscene Ass | 114 |
| | 10 | לילית | LILITh | Lilith | The Evil Woman Queen of the Night | 480 |
| ☾ | 13 | גמיאל | GMIAL | Gamaliel | Obscene Ones Obscene Ass | 114 |
| ☿ | 12 | סמאל | SMAL | Samael | Poison of God | 131 |
| ♀ | 14 | ערב זרק | ORB ZRQ | Arab Zereq | Ravens of Dispersion | 579 |
| ☼ | 30 | תגרירון | ThGRIRVN | Thagiriron | Disputers/Hagglers | 869, 1519 |
| ♂ | 27 | גולחב | GVLChB | Golachab | Burners Flaming Ones | 49 |
| ♃ | 21 | געשכלה | GOShKLH | Gasheklah | Smiters | 428 |
| ♄ | 32 | סאתאריאל | SAThARIAL | Satariel | Concealers | 703 |
| ♈ | 15 | בעירירון | BOIRIRVN | Ba'airiron | Flock/Herd | 548, 1198 |
| ♉ | 16 | אדימירון | ADIMIRVN | Adimiron | Bloody Ones | 321, 971 |
| ♊ | 17 | צלילימירון | TzLILIMIRVN | Tzelilimiron[14] | Clangers | 476, 1226 |
| ♋ | 18 | שיחרירון | ShIChRIRVN | Shichiriron | Black Ones | 784, 1434 |
| ♌ | 19 | שלהבירון | ShLHBIRVN | Shalehbiron | Flaming Ones | 603, 1253 |
| ♍ | 20 | צפרירון | TzPRIRVN | Tzaphiriron | Scratchers | 636, 1286 |
| ♎ | 22 | עבירירון | OBIRIRVN | A'abiriron | Clayey Ones | 548, 1198 |
| ♏ | 24 | נחשתירון | NChShThIRVN | Necheshthiron | Brazen Ones | 1021, 1671 |
| ♐ | 25 | נחשירון | NChShIRVN | Necheshiron | Snakelike Ones | 624, 1274 |
| ♑ | 26 | דגדגירון | DGDGIRVN | Dagdagiron | Fishy Ones | 280, 930 |
| ♒ | 28 | בהימירון | BHIMIRVN | Bahimiron | Bestial Ones | 323, 973 |
| ♓ | 29 | נשימירון | NShIMIRVN | Nashimiron | Malign Woman | 666, 1316 |

[11] Also spelled Ogiel (Godwin), Ghagiel (Crowley), Chaigidel (Mathers), or Ghogiel (Regardie).
[12] Also spelled Gha'agsheblah by Crowley.
[13] Also spelled Oreb Zaraq (Godwin), A'arab Zaraq (Crowley), Harab Serapel (Mathers), or Gharab Tzerek (Regardie).
[14] Spelled צללדמירון, TzLLDMIRVN by Crowley. It may derive from צל, to (over) shadow, or צלה, to roast (in hell).

# K. Kabbalah

| | K100. The Kings [Melekh] of Edom. | K101. The Kings of Edom – Transliteration. | K102. The Kings of Edom – English. | K103. The Dukes [Aluph] of Edom. | K104. The Dukes of Edom – Transliteration. | K105. The Dukes of Edom – English. |
|---|---|---|---|---|---|---|
| | **109** | | | **109** | | |
| 1 | | | | | | Timnah |
| 2 | | | Bela son of Beor of Dinhabah | | | Alvah |
| 3 | | | | | | Jetheth |
| 4 | טע יובב בצרה | TO IVBB BTzRH | Jobab of Bozrah | אהליבמה | AHLIBMH | Aholibamah |
| 5 | חשם תימני | HShM ThIMNI | Husham of Temani | אלה | ALH | Elah |
| 6 | הדר עוית | HDD OVITh | Hadad of Avith | פינן | PINN | Pinon |
| 7 | שמלה משרקה | ShMLH MShRQH | Samlah of Masrekah | קנז | QNZ | Kenaz |
| 8 | שאול רחבית | ShAVL RHBITh | Saul of Rehoboth | תימן | ThIMN | Teman |
| 9 | בעל הנן | BOL HNN | Baal-Hanan | מבצר מגדיאל | MBTzR MGDIAL | Mibzar and Magdiel |
| 10 | הדר פעו | HDR POV | Hadar of Pau | עירם | OIRM | Eram |

| | | K105a. The Orders of Demon and their Princes. | | |
|---|---|---|---|---|
| | **Latin** | **English** | **Prince** | **Function** |
| 1 | Pseudotheoi | False gods | Beelzebub | Wish to be worshipped as gods |
| 2 | Spiritus Mendaciorum | Lying Spirits | Python | Deceives by oracles, divinations, and predictions |
| 3 | Vasa Iniquitas | Vessels of Iniquity [or Anger or Fury] | Belial | Mischief and all the wicked arts, who teach dice and cards |
| 4 | Ultores Scekorum | Revengers of wickedness | Asmodeus | Judgement |
| 5 | Praestigiatore | Tricksters, illusionists | Sathan | Seduce people with their miracles, serve the caco-magi |
| 6 | Aeriae Potestates | Arial Powers | Merizim | Corrupt the air, bring pestilence, thunder and lightning. Include the four Angels of the Apocalypse |
| 7 | Furiae | Furies | Apollyon [Abaddon] | Sowers of mischief, discord, war and destruction |
| 8 | Criminatores | Accusers | Astaroth [Diabolus] | Calumniator, accuser of the brethren |
| 9 | Tentatores Maligenii [Diaboli] | Tempters or bad Genii | Mammon | Infect the lower world |
| 10 | | | | |

# K. Kabbalah

*The Partzufim and the Body of God*

| | K106. The Ten Divisions of the Body of God – Latin. | K107. The Ten Divisions of the Body of God – English. | K108. The Countenances or *Partzufim*. | K109. The World Triads on the Tree. |
|---|---|---|---|---|
| | **103** | | | |
| 1 | Cranium | Skull | Macroprosopus, the Vast Countenance (Arik Anpin) | Intellectual World (OVLM MVShKL, Olahm Mevshekal) |
| 2 | Cerebrum dextrum | Right brain | Supernal Father (Abba) | |
| 3 | Cerebrum sinistrum | Left brain | Supernal Mother (Amma) | |
| 4 | Brachium dextrum | Right arm | Microprosopus, the Lesser Countenance (Zauir Anpin)<br><br>The Son (Ben) | Moral World (OVLM MVRGSh, Olahm Morgash) |
| 5 | Brachium sinistrum | Left arm | | |
| 6 | Totum corpus a gutture usque ad membrum sanctum | The whole body from the throat to the holy member (genitals) | | |
| 7 | Pes dexter | Right leg | | Material World (OVLM HMVTBO, Olahm Ha-Mevetbau) |
| 8 | Pes sinister | Left leg | | |
| 9 | Signum foederis sancti | Sign of the holy covenant | | |
| 10 | Corolla quae est in Jesod | Crown which is in Yesod | Bride of Microprosopus The Daughter (Bot) | |

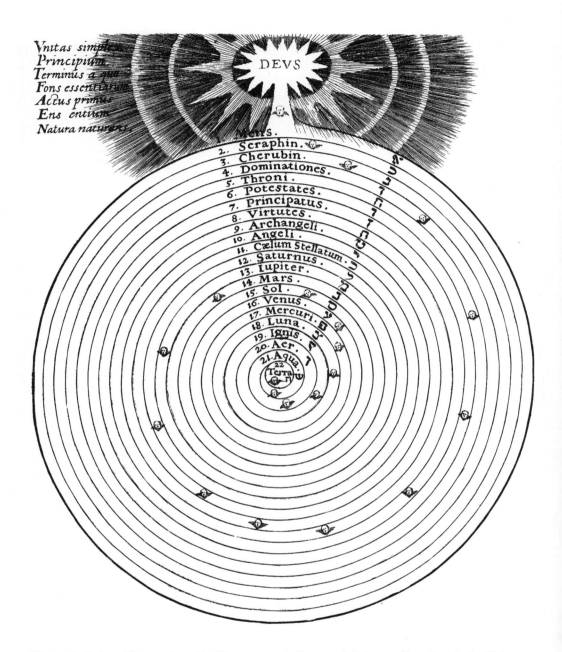

Figure 8: Robert Fludd's Angelic, Planetary and Elemental Spheres aligned with the Hebrew Alphabet.

# K. Kabbalah

## The Sepher Yetzirah

| | | K110. Elements and Directions. | | K111. The Four Quarters and Six Directions – Hebrew. | K112. The Four Quarters and Six Directions – Transliteration. | K113. The Four Quarters and Six Directions – English. |
|---|---|---|---|---|---|---|
| | | **110** | **Variant** | **57** | | |
| | 1 | | | | | |
| | 2 | Air | Beginning | א | A | |
| | 3 | Water and Earth | End | מ | M | |
| | 4 | Fire | South | ש | Sh | |
| | 5 | Height | North | מעלה | MOLH | Maalah (Above) |
| | 6 | Depth | East | מטה | MTH | Matah (Depth) |
| | 7 | East | Up | מזרח | MZRCh | Mezrach, East (Below) |
| | 8 | West | Down | מערב | MORB | Maareb, West (Behind) |
| | 9 | South | West | דרום | DRVM | Darom, South (Right) |
| | 10 | North | | צפון | TzPVN | Tzaphon, North (Left) |
| ✳ | 31b | | | | | |
| F | 31 | | | דרום | DRVM | Darom, South (Right) |
| A | 11 | | | מזרח | MZRCh | Mezrach, East (Below) |
| W | 23 | | | מערב | MORB | Maareb, West (Behind) |
| E | 32b | | | צפון | TzPVN | Tzaphon, North (Left) |

| | | Hebrew Alphabet. | K114. Planetary order in most versions of *Sepher Yetzirah.* | K115. Planetary order in Gra/Kaplan & Kalisch edition of *Sepher Yetzirah.* | K116. Planetary order only in Kircher *Sepher Yetzirah.* | K117. Planetary order only in Meyer version of *Sepher Yetzirah.* | K118. Planetary order in Shirat Yosef version of *Sepher Yetzirah.* | K119. Mathers' order. |
|---|---|---|---|---|---|---|---|---|
| ☽ | 13 | Gimel | **Jupiter** | Mars | Venus | Jupiter | Sun | Moon |
| ☿ | 12 | Beth | **Saturn** | Moon | Sun | Mars | Saturn | Mercury |
| ♀ | 14 | Daleth | **Mars** | Sun | Mercury | Saturn | Moon | Venus |
| ☼ | 30 | Resh | **Mercury** | Saturn | Jupiter | Venus | Jupiter | Sun |
| ♂ | 27 | Peh | **Venus** | Mercury | Saturn | Mercury | Mercury | Mars |
| ♃ | 21 | Kaph | **Sun** | Venus | Moon | Moon | Mars | Jupiter |
| ♄ | 32 | Tau | **Moon** | Jupiter | Mars | Sun | Venus | Saturn |

# K. Kabbalah

| GD Path Order | | K120. The Intelligences of the 32 Paths of the *Sepher Yetzirah* – Meaning. | K121. The Intelligences of the Paths of the *Sepher Yetzirah* – Aramaic. | |
|---|---|---|---|---|
| | | **13** | **Sekhel** | **Transliteration** |
| | 1 | Admirable/Hidden Intelligence | מופלא | Sekhel Mopla |
| | 2 | Illuminating/Shining Intelligence | מזהיר | Sekhel Mazohir |
| | 3 | Sanctified Intelligence | מקדוש | Sekhel ha-Qadesh |
| | 4 | Measuring/Cohesive/Settled Intelligence | קבוע | Sekhel Qavua |
| | 5 | Radical/Root Intelligence | נשרש | Sekhel Nesharash |
| | 6 | Intelligence of the Mediating Influence/ Transcendental influx | שפע נבדל | Sekhel Shepha Nivdal |
| | 7 | Hidden Intelligence | נסתר | Sekhel Nisetar |
| | 8 | Complete/Perfect Intelligence | שלם | Sekhel Shalem |
| | 9 | Pure or Clear Intelligence | טהור | Sekhel Tahur |
| | 10 | Resplendent Intelligence | מתנוצץ | Sekhel Mitnotzetz |
| A | 11 | Scintillating/Fiery Intelligence | מצוחצח | Sekhel Metzochtzoch |
| ☿ | 12 | Intelligence of Transparency/Light | בהיר | Sekhel Bahir |
| ☾ | 13 | Uniting/Inductive Intelligence | גמנהי האחדות | Sekhel Manhig ha-Achdoth |
| ♀ | 14 | Illuminating Intelligence | מאיר | Sekhel Meir |
| ♈ | 15 | Constituting/Standing Intelligence | מעמיד | Sekhel Maamid |
| ♉ | 16 | Enduring/Eternal Intelligence | נצחי | Sekhel Nitzchi |
| ♊ | 17 | Disposing Intelligence/ Consciousness of the Senses | ההרגש | Sekhel ha-Hergesh |
| ♋ | 18 | Intelligence of the House of Influence/Influx | בית השפע | Sekhel Beth ha-Shepha |
| ♌ | 19 | Intelligence of the Secret of all Spiritual Activities | סוד הפעולות הרות חניו כולם | Sekhel Sod ha-Pauloth ha-Ruach ha-Nioth Kolam |
| ♍ | 20 | Intelligence of Will/Desire | הרצון | Sekhel ha-Ratzon |
| ♃ | 21 | Intelligence of Conciliation/ Beseeched intelligence | החפץ והמבוקש | Sekhel ha-Chaphutz ve-ha-Mevukash |
| ♎ | 22 | Faithful Intelligence | נאמן | Sekhel Ne'eman |
| W | 23 | Stable/Sustaining Intelligence | קיים | Sekhel Qayyam |
| ♏ | 24 | Imaginative/Similar Intelligence | דמיוני | Sekhel Dimyoni |
| ♐ | 25 | Testing Intelligence | נסיוני | Sekhel Nisyoni |
| ♑ | 26 | Renewing Intelligence | מחודש | Sekhel Mechudash |
| ♂ | 27 | Exciting/Feeling Intelligence | מורגש | Sekhel Morgash |
| ♒ | 28 | Natural/Active Intelligence | מוטבע | Sekhel Motba |
| ♓ | 29 | Physical Intelligence | מוגשם | Sekhel Mughsham |
| ☼ | 30 | Collecting/General Intelligence | כללי | Sekhel Kelali |
| F | 31 | Perpetual Intelligence | תמידי | Sekhel Temidi |
| ♄ | 32 | Administrative/Lost Intelligence | נעבד | Sekhel Ne'evad |

# K. Kabbalah

*Sepher ha-Zohar*

| Sect-ion | K122. The Contents of the *Zohar*. | | | |
|---|---|---|---|---|
| | **Isaiah Tishby** | **Scholem** | **Mathers** [15] | **English** |
| 1 | i) *Zohar* on the *Torah*. The core commentary on the *Pentateuch*. | a) Untitled Commentary on the *Torah*. | [Simon and Sperling][16] | Commentary on the *Torah* |
| 2 | ii) *Zohar* on the *Song of Songs*. | n) *Zohar* to the *Song of Songs* | | Commentary on the *Song of Songs* |
| 3-6 | iii) *Midrash ha-Ne'elam* iv) *Midrash ha-Ne'elam* on *Song of Songs*. v) *Midrash ha-Ne'elam* on *Ruth*. vi) *Midrash ha-Ne'elam* on *Lamentations*. | r) *Midrash Ha-Neelam* s) *Midrash Ha-Neelam* on the *Book of Ruth* | | The Concealed Midrash [On the *Torah*, creation, the soul, the afterlife, and the Messianic age] |
| 7 | vii) *Sitrei Torah*, Secrets of the Torah. | l) *Sithre Torah* | | Secrets of the *Torah* |
| 8 | viii) *Matnitin* and *Tosefta* | m) *Mathnithin* | | *Mishnah* with Additions |
| 9 | ix) *Sava de-Mishpatim* | h) *Sava* | | The Old Man of Mishpatim |
| 10 | x) *Yanuka* | i) *Yenuka* | [Simon and Sperling] | The [Commentary of the] Child |
| 11 | xi) *Rav Metivah* | k) *Rav Methivtha* | | The Head of the Academy |
| 12 | xii) *Sifra di-Zeniuta* | b) *Sifra di-Tseniutha* | 1. *Siphra Dtzenioutha* | The Book of Concealed Mysteries |
| 13 | xiii) *Idra Rabba* or *Sefer ha-Zohar ha-Gadol*, the Great Zohar | c) *Idra Rabba*, Greater Assembly | 2. *Ha Idra Rabba Qadisha* | The Greater Holy Assembly |
| 14 | xiv) *Idra Zuta* | d) *Idra Zutta* | 3. *Ha Idra Zuta Qadisha* | The Lesser Holy Assembly |
| 15 | xv) *Idra de-Ve Mashkana* | e) *Idra di-be-Mashkana* | | Assembly of the Tabernacle |
| 16 | xvi) *Hekhalot* | f) *Hekhaloth* | | Halls or Palaces |
| 17 | xvii) *Raza de-Razin* | g) *Raza de-Razin* | | The Secret of Secrets. [On physiognomy and chiromancy] |
| 18 | xviii) *Sitrei Otiot* | p) *Sithre Othioth* | | The Secrets of the Letters. [On the 22 letters and IHVH] |
| 19 | xix) *Ma'amar Kav ha-Middah* | o) *Kav ha-Middah* | | The Mystical Standard of Measure |
| 20 | xx) Untitled | q) Untitled Commentary | | [Commentary on the symbolism of Ezekiel's Chariot] |
| 21 | xxi) *Raya Mehemna* | t) *Raya Mehemna* | | The Faithful Shepherd [Moses] |
| 22 | xxii) *Tikkunei ha-Zohar*. | u) *Tikkune Zohar* | | [Commentary on *Genesis*] |
| 23 | xxiii) Two items from the *Zohar Hadash*, the 'New' *Zohar* | v) Further additions to above | | [Further additions to above assembled later in Safed] |

[15] MacGregor Mathers in his *Kabbalah Unveiled* only translated Sections 12-14 from the Latin of von Rosenroth.
[16] The English translation of the *Zohar* by Simon and Sperling only includes Sections 1 and 9-11 with many omissions of difficult passages.

# K. Kabbalah

*De Arte Cabalistica*

| | K123. Hebrew Letters and their Secret Meanings from Reuchlin *De Arte Cabalistica.* | | | |
|---|---|---|---|---|
| | **Hebrew Letters** | | **Angel or Sphere** | **Nature** |
| **1** | א | Aleph | Hayoth ha-Kadesh | The Living Creatures of the Sanctuary who live directly below God. Aleph is the sign of the highest things |
| **2** | ב | Beth | Ophanim | 'Forms' or 'Wheels', angels second from God. |
| **3** | ג | Gimel | Aralim | 'Great, strong angels'. Angels out of the higher essences, illuminated by the power of God |
| **4** | ד | Daleth | Hasmalim | |
| **5** | ה | He | Seraphim | |
| **6** | ו | Vau | Malakhim | 'Angels' |
| **7** | ז | Zayin | Elohim | 'Gods'. Blessed higher spirits of the seventh emanation |
| **8** | ח | Cheth | Ben Elohim | 'Sons of gods'. Full of the power of El. |
| **9** | ט | Teth | Cherubim | |
| **10** | י | Yod | Ishim (אישים) | 'Nobles'. Those men so endowed are called AISh איש or 'men of noble intelligence'. Sekel ha Poel. Last sphere of the angelic world. |
| | כ | Kaph | Metatron | The first moveable after El Shaddai himself, and so it acts as if directly affected by the First Cause. Active Intellect of the sensible world, moved by and through the spirit of rational life |
| ⊛ | ך | Kaph final | Mazloth, the Zodiac | The ring of the fixed stars. This is called the second orb in relation to higher beings, but the eighth orb in relation to us. |
| ♄ | ל | Lamed | Shabatai, Saturn | First Sphere of the planets or 'wandering stars' or Leketh (לכת) or *Errones* (Latin) or *Planetas* (Greek) |
| ♃ | מ | Mem | Tzedek, Jupiter | |
| ♂ | ם | Mem final | Madim, Mars | |
| ☉ | נ | Nun | Shemesh, the Sun | The orb of Chamah (חמה), the 'right eye' of the world. |
| ♀ | ן | Nun final | Nogah, Venus | |
| ☿ | ס | Samekh | Kokab, Mercury | The 'doorkeeper' |
| ☾ | ע | Ayin | Lebanah, the Moon | Sometimes called Yareah (ירח). The 'left eye' of the world. Last orb of the stars/planets |
| | פ | Peh | | Intellectual soul, both particular and universal |
| | ף | Peh final | | Animal spirits which are ruled by the higher Intelligences |
| | צ | Tzaddi | | The material of the heavens (intelligible matter) and of the Elements (sensible matter) and mixed together |
| | ץ | Tzaddi final | | Forms of the Elements, Fire, Air, Water and Earth. |
| | ק | Qoph | | Inanimate things, minerals, 'mixed substances', things made of the Elements. |
| | ר | Resh | Ishim (אישים) | Vegetation, fruit, crops, things born of the earth |
| | ש | Shin | | Creatures that can crawl, move on the earth, fish of the sea, birds of the air, all irrational beings that possess movement and life |
| | ת | Tau | | Man and human nature, as the most perfect of created things |
| | | | | [The physical Earth] |
| | | | | [The Sprit of man] |

# L. Letters, Alphabets and Numerical Values

*Egyptian Hieroglyphic*

| | Path Order | L1. Egyptian Phonetic Hieroglyphic. | L2. Alternative Phonetic Hieroglyphic. | L3. Egyptian (non Phonetic) Hieroglyphic. |
|---|---|---|---|---|
| | | | | |
| A | 11 | *3 or 3* | | Ox |
| ☿ | 12 | b | | House |
| ☾ | 13 | g | | |
| ♀ | 14 | d | | Door |
| ♈ | 15 | h | ḥ | |
| ♉ | 16 | w | | Prop |
| ♊ | 17 | z | S | |
| ♋ | 18 | ẖ or kh | ẖ or ch | Courtyard, fence |
| ♌ | 19 | t | | |
| ♍ | 20 | ỉ | y | |
| ♃ | 21 | k | | |
| ♎ | 22 | | | |

179

# L. Letters, Alphabets and Numerical Values

| Path Order | | L1. Egyptian Phonetic Hieroglyphic. | L2. Alternative Phonetic Hieroglyphic. | L3. Egyptian (non Phonetic) Hieroglyphic. |
|---|---|---|---|---|
| | | | | |
| W | 23 | m | | Water |
| ♏ | 24 | n | | Snake |
| ♐ | 25 | ś | | |
| ♑ | 26 | ꜥ or 9 | | Eye |
| ♂ | 27 | p | f | |
| ♒ | 28 | ḏ or dj | | |
| ♓ | 29 | ḳ or q | | |
| ☼ | 30 | r | | Head |
| F | 31 | š or sh | | |
| ♄ | 32 | ṯ or tš | | Cross |
| E | 32b | | | |
| ⊛ | 31b | | | |

# L. Letters, Alphabets and Numerical Values

*Phoenician*

| | Path Order. | L4. Phoenician Alphabet. | L5. Phoenician Alphabet – English Equivalents. | L6. Phoenician Alphabet – Names. | L7. Phoenician Alphabet – Numeric Values. |
|---|---|---|---|---|---|
| | | | | | |
| | 1 | | | | |
| | 2 | | | | |
| | 3 | | | | |
| | 4 | | | | |
| | 5 | | | | |
| | 6 | | | | |
| | 7 | | | | |
| | 8 | | | | |
| | 9 | | | | |
| | 10 | | | | |
| A | 11 | 𐤀 | A | Aleph | 1 |
| ☿ | 12 | 𐤁 | B | Beth | 2 |
| ☾ | 13 | 𐤂 | G | Gimel | 3 |
| ♀ | 14 | 𐤃 | D | Daleth | 4 |
| ♈ | 15 | 𐤄 | H | He | 5 |
| ♉ | 16 | Y, 𐤅 | V | Waw | 6 |
| ♊ | 17 | Z | Z | Zayin | 7 |
| ♋ | 18 | 𐤇 | Ch | Heth | 8 |
| ♌ | 19 | | Th | Thet | 9 |
| ♍ | 20 | 𐤉 | I | Yod | 10 |
| ♃ | 21 | 𐤊 | K | Kaph | 20 |
| ♎ | 22 | 𐤋 | L | Lamed | 30 |
| W | 23 | 𐤌 | M | Mem | 40 |
| ♏ | 24 | 𐤍 | N | Nun | 50 |
| ♐ | 25 | 𐤎 | S | Samekh | 60 |
| ♑ | 26 | O | O | Ayin | 70 |
| ♂ | 27 | 7 | P | Pe | 80 |
| ♒ | 28 | 𐤑 | Ts | Sade | 90 |
| ♓ | 29 | 𐤒 | Q | Qoph | 100 |
| ☉ | 30 | 𐤓 | R | Resh | 200 |
| F | 31 | W | Sh | Sin | 300 |
| ♄ | 32 | 𐤕 | T | Taw/Tav | 400 |
| E | 32b | | | | |
| ✳ | 31b | | | | |

181

# L. Letters, Alphabets and Numerical Values

*Hebrew*

| | Path Order. | L8. Hebrew Letters. | L9. Hebrew Letters – English Equivalent. | L10. Hebrew Letters – Name. | L11. Numerical Value of the Hebrew Letters. | L12. Hebrew Massoretic Vowel Points and their Pronunciation. |
|---|---|---|---|---|---|---|
| | | **175** | | | **176** | |
| | 1 | | | | | Kamatz – ah, aw |
| | 2 | | | | | Patach – ah |
| | 3 | | | | | Tzerey – ay |
| | 4 | | | | | Segol – eh |
| | 5 | | | | | Shewa [none] |
| | 6 | | | | | Cholem – oh |
| | 7 | | | | | Chirek – ee |
| | 8 | | | | | Kibutz – u |
| | 9 | | | | | Shurek – oo |
| | 10 | | | | | |
| A | 11 | א | A | Aleph | 1, 1000 (large) | |
| ☿ | 12 | ב | B | Beth | 2 | |
| ☾ | 13 | ג | G | Gimel | 3 | |
| ♀ | 14 | ד | D | Daleth | 4 | |
| ♈ | 15 | ה | H | He | 5 | |
| ♉ | 16 | ו | V, U, O | Vav | 6 | |
| ♊ | 17 | ז | Z | Zayin | 7 | |
| ♋ | 18 | ח | Ch | Cheth | 8 | |
| ♌ | 19 | ט | T | Teth | 9 | |
| ♍ | 20 | י | I, Y, J | Yod | 10 | |
| ♃ | 21 | כ, ך | K, C | Kaph | 20, 500 | |
| ♎ | 22 | ל | L | Lamed | 30 | |
| W | 23 | מ, ם | M | Mem | 40, 600 | |
| ♏ | 24 | נ, ן | N | Nun | 50, 700 | |
| ♐ | 25 | ס | S | Samekh | 60 | |
| ♑ | 26 | ע | O, ' | Ayin | 70 | |
| ♂ | 27 | פ, ף | P, Ph | Peh | 80, 800 | |
| ♒ | 28 | צ, ץ | Tz | Tzaddi | 90, 900 | |
| ♓ | 29 | ק | Q | Qoph | 100 | |
| ☉ | 30 | ר | R | Resh | 200 | |
| F | 31 | ש | Sh | Shin | 300 | |
| ♄ | 32 | ת | Th | Tau | 400 | |
| E | 32b | | | | | |
| ⊛ | 31b | | | | | |

# L. Letters, Alphabets and Numerical Values

*Greek*

| Path Order. | | L13. The Greek Alphabet. | L14. The Greek Alphabet – English Equivalent. | L15. The Greek Alphabet – Name. | L16. Greek Alphabet – Numeration. | L17. Elements, Planets & Corresponding Vowels. |
|---|---|---|---|---|---|---|
| | | **53** | | | **185** | |
| | **1** | | | | | |
| | **2** | | | | | |
| | **3** | Ω, ω | Oo | Omega | 800 | Saturn |
| | **4** | ϒ, υ | U | Upsilon | 400 | Jupiter |
| | **5** | O, o | O | Omicron | 70 | Mars |
| | **6** | I, ι | I | Iota | 10 | Sun |
| | **7** | H, η | H | Eta | 8 | Venus |
| | **8** | E, ε | E | Epsilon | 5 | Mercury |
| | **9** | A, α | A | Alpha | 1 | Moon |
| | **10** | [vowels are also reflected below] | | | | |
| A | **11** | A, α | A | Alpha | 1 | Moon |
| ☿ | **12** | B, β | B | Beta | 2 | |
| ☾ | **13** | Γ, γ | G | Gamma | 3 | *Earth* |
| ♀ | **14** | Δ, δ | D | Delta | 4 | *Water* |
| ♈ | **15** | E, ε | E | Epsilon | 5 | Mercury |
| ♉ | **16** | F, ϝ | W | Digamma | 6 | |
| ♊ | **17** | Z, ζ | Z | Zeta | 7 | |
| ♋ | **18** | H, η | H | Eta | 8 | Venus |
| ♌ | **19** | Θ, θ | Th | Theta | 9 | *Ether* |
| ♍ | **20** | I, ι | I | Iota | 10 | Sun |
| ♃ | **21** | K, κ | K | Kappa | 20 | |
| ♎ | **22** | Λ, λ | L | Lambda | 30 | |
| W | **23** | M, μ | M | Mu | 40 | |
| ♏ | **24** | N, ν | N | Nu | 50 | |
| ♐ | **25** | Ξ, ξ | X | Xi | 60 | |
| ♑ | **26** | O, o | O | Omicron | 70 | Mars |
| ♂ | **27** | Π, π | P | Pi | 80 | *Fire* |
| ♒ | **28** | Ψ, ψ | Ps | Psi | 700 | |
| ♓ | **29** | ϙ | Q | Koppa/Qoppa | 90 | |
| ☼ | **30** | P, ρ | R | Rho | 100 | *Air* |
| F | **31** | Σ, σ | S | Sigma | 200 | |
| ♄ | **32** | T, τ | T | Tau | 300 | |
| E | **32b** | ϒ, υ | U | Upsilon | 400 | Jupiter |
| ⊛ | **31b** | ϡ | – | *Sanpi* | 900 | |
| | | Φ, φ | F | Phi | 500 | |
| | | X, χ | Kh | Chi | 600 | |

# L. Letters, Alphabets and Numerical Values

| Path Order. | | Greek Alphabet. | L18. The 24 Seniors/Elders or Angels. | L19. Magical Name of Letter – Greek. | L20. Magical Name of Letter – English. |
|---|---|---|---|---|---|
| A | 11 | Alpha | Achael | ΑΚΡΑΜΜΑΧΑΜΑΡΙ | Akrammachamari |
| ☿ | 12 | Beta | Banuel | ΒΟΥΛΟΜΕΝΤΟΡΕΒ | Boulmentoreb |
| ☾ | 13 | Gamma | Ganuel | ΓΕΝΙΟΜΟΥΘΙΓ | Geniomouthig |
| ♀ | 14 | Delta | Dedael | ΔΗΟΜΓΕΝΗΔ | Demogened |
| ♈ | 15 | Epsilon | Eptiel | ΕΝΚΥΚΛΙΕ | Enkyklie |
| ♉ | 16 | Zeta | Zartiel | ΖΗΝΟΒΙΩΘΙΖ | Zenobiothiz |
| ♊ | 17 | Eta | Ethael | ΗΣΚΩΘΩΡΗ | Eskothore |
| ♋ | 18 | Theta | Thathiel | ΘΩΘΟΥΘΩΘ | Thothoutthoth |
| ♌ | 19 | Iota | Iochael | ΙΑΕΟΥΩΙ | Iaeouoi |
| ♍ | 20 | Kappa | Kardiel | ΚΟΡΚΟΟΥΝΟΩΚ | Korkoounook |
| ♃ | 21 | Lambda | Labtiel | ΛΟΥΛΟΕΝΗΛ | Louloenel |
| ♎ | 22 | Mu | Merael | ΜΟΡΟΘΟΗΠΙΝΑΜ | Morothoepnam |
| W | 23 | Nu | Nerael | ΝΕΡΞΙΑΡΞΙΝ | Nerxiarxin |
| ♏ | 24 | Xi | Xiphiel | ΞΟΝΟΦΟΗΝΖΞ | Xonophoenax |
| ♐ | 25 | Omicron | Ouphiel | ΟΡΝΕΟΦΑΟ | Orneophao |
| ♑ | 26 | Pi | Pirael | ΠΥΡΟΒΑΡΥΠ | Pyrobaryp |
| ♂ | 27 | Rho | Rael | ΡΕΡΟΥΤΟΗΡ | Reroutoer |
| ♒ | 28 | Sigma | Seroael | ΣΕΣΕΝΜΕΝΟΥΡΕΣ | Sesenmenoures |
| ♓ | 29 | Tau | Tauriel | ΤΑΥΡΟΠΛΙΤ | Tauropolit |
| ☼ | 30 | Upsilon | Umnael | ΥΠΕΦΕΝΟΥΡΥ | Ypephenoury |
| F | 31 | Phi | Philopael | ΦΙΜΕΜΑΜΕΦ | Phimemameph |
| ♄ | 32 | Khi | Christuel | ΧΕΝΝΕΟΦΕΟΧ | Chenneopheoch |
| E | 32b | Psi | Psilaphael | ΨΥΧΟΜΠΟΙΑΨ | Psychompoiaps |
| ⊛ | 31b | Omega | Olithiel | ΩΡΙΩΝ | Orion |

| | Greek Vowels. | L21. Gnostic Heaven & Word of Power. | L22. Greek Vowels – Archangels. | L23. Greek Vowels – Directions. |
|---|---|---|---|---|
| 1 | | | | |
| 2 | | | | |
| 3 | Ω, ω | 7th – NARTORAK | Saraphuel | Centre |
| 4 | Υ, υ | 6th – ARTORAN | Anael | Up |
| 5 | O, o | 5th – ARTORE | Raguel | Down |
| 6 | I, ι | 4th – SEMIIAK | Suriel | South |
| 7 | H, η | 3rd – MIIAK | Raphael | West |
| 8 | E, ε | 2nd – EIIAK | Gabriel | North |
| 9 | A, α | 1st – EIA | Michael | East |
| 10 | | | | |

# L. Letters, Alphabets and Numerical Values

*Coptic*

| Path Order. | | L24. The Coptic Alphabet. | L25. Coptic Alphabet – English Equivalents. | L26. Coptic Alphabet – Name. | L27. Coptic Alphabet Numeration. |
|---|---|---|---|---|---|
| | | **51** | | | |
| | 1 | | | | |
| | 2 | | | | |
| | 3 | Ⲱ ⲱ | Õ, O | Omega | 800 |
| | 4 | | | | |
| | 5 | | | | |
| | 6 | | | | |
| | 7 | | | | |
| | 8 | | | | |
| | 9 | | | | |
| | 10 | | | | |
| A | 11 | Ⲁ ⲁ | A | Alpha | 1 |
| ☿ | 12 | Ⲃ ß | B | Veda/Vita | 2 |
| ☽ | 13 | Ⲅ ⲅ | G | Gamma | 3 |
| ♀ | 14 | Ⲇ ⲇ | D | Dalda | 4 |
| ♈ | 15 | Ⲉ ⲉ | E | Eje | 5 |
| ♉ | 16 | Ⲋ ⲋ | St, So | Sou [only as a number] | 6 |
| ♊ | 17 | Ⲍ ⲍ | Z | Zada/Zita | 7 |
| ♋ | 18 | Ⲏ ⲏ | Æ | Hada | 8 |
| ♌ | 19 | Ⲑ ⲑ | Th | Tutte | 9 |
| ♍ | 20 | Ⲓ ⲓ | I, y | Joda | 10 |
| ♃ | 21 | Ⲕ ⲕ | K | Kabba | 20 |
| ♎ | 22 | Ⲗ ⲗ | L | Lola/Laula | 30 |
| W | 23 | Ⲙ ⲙ | M | Mej | 40 |
| ♏ | 24 | Ⲛ ⲛ | N | Ni | 50 |
| ♐ | 25 | Ⲝ ⲝ | X/Ks | Xi/Eksi | 60 |
| ♑ | 26 | Ⲟ ⲟ | O | Ou | 70 |
| ♂ | 27 | Ⲡ ⲡ | P | Bej | 80 |
| ♒ | 28 | Ⲯ ⲯ | Ps | Ebsi/Psi | 700 |
| ♓ | 29 | Ⲫ ⲫ | F | Faj/Fai | 90 |
| ☼ | 30 | Ⲣ ⲣ | R | Rou | 100 |
| F | 31 | Ⲥ ⲥ | S | Samma/Sima | 200 |
| ♄ | 32 | Ⲧ ⲧ | T | Dav | 300 |
| E | 32b | Ⲩ ⲩ | Y, U | Ypsilon | 400 |
| ✳ | 31b | Ⲱ ⲱ | Sh | Shei/Saj | 900 |
| | | Ⲫ ⲫ | Ph | Fij/Phi | 500 |
| | | Ⲭ ⲭ | Ch/Kh | Kij/Khi | 600 |

# L. Letters, Alphabets and Numerical Values

*Arabic*

| Path Order. | | L28. The Arabic Alphabet. | L29. Arabic Alphabet – English Equivalents. | L30. Arabic Alphabet – Name. | L31. The Arabic Alphabet Numeration. | L31a. Associated Divine Attribute. | L31b. Meaning of Divine Attribute. |
|---|---|---|---|---|---|---|---|
| | | **52** | | | **184** | | |
| | 1 | Three Father Letters | | | | | |
| | 2 | | | | | | |
| | 3 | | | | | | |
| | 4 | ث | H | Tha | 500 | Thabit | Stable |
| | 5 | خ | Kh | Kha | 600 | Khaliq | Creator |
| | 6 | ذ | Dh | Dhal | 700 | Dhakir | He who remembers |
| | 7 | ض | Dha | Dhad | 800 | Dar | Chastiser |
| | 8 | ظ | Z/Dh | Zh/Dha | 900 | Dhahir | Apparent |
| | 9 | غ | Gh | Ghayin/Gha | 1000 | Ghafur | Indulgent |
| | 10 | | | | | | |
| A | 11 | ا | A | 'Alef | 1 | Allah | Allah |
| ☿ | 12 | ب | B | Ba | 2 | Baqi | He who remains |
| ☾ | 13 | ج | G, J | Jym/Jim | 3 | Jami | He who collects |
| ♀ | 14 | د | D | Dal | 4 | Dayan | Judge |
| ♈ | 15 | ه | H | Ha | 5 | Hadi | Guide |
| ♉ | 16 | و | W | Wa | 6 | Wali | Master |
| ♊ | 17 | ز | Z | Zayin | 7 | Zaki | Purifier |
| ♋ | 18 | ح | Ch, H | Ha | 8 | Haq | Truth |
| ♌ | 19 | ط | T | Tah | 9 | Tahir | Saint |
| ♍ | 20 | ي | Y | Yah | 10 | Yassin | Chief |
| ♃ | 21 | ك | K | Kaf | 20 | Kafi | Sufficient |
| ♎ | 22 | ل | L | Lam | 30 | Latif | Benevolent |
| W | 23 | م | M | Mym/Mim | 40 | Malik | King |
| ♏ | 24 | ن | N | Nun | 50 | Nur | Light |
| ♐ | 25 | س | S | Sin | 60 | Sami | Listener |
| ♑ | 26 | ع | A | 'Ayin | 70 | Ali | Raised up |
| ♂ | 27 | ف | F | Fa | 80 | Fatah | He who opens |
| ♒ | 28 | ص | S | Sad | 90 | Samad | Eternal |
| ♓ | 29 | ق | Q | Qaf | 100 | Qadir | Powerful |
| ☉ | 30 | ر | R | Ra | 200 | Rab | Lord |
| F | 31 | ش | Sh | Shin | 300 | Shafi | He who accepts |
| ♄ | 32 | ت | T | Ta | 400 | Tawab | He who restores to the good |

# L. Letters, Alphabets and Numerical Values

*Latin*

| | Path Order. | L32. Latin Alphabet Corresponding to the Hebrew Alphabet. | L33. Latin Alphabet – Numeration derived from Greek. | L34. Latin Alphabet with Pseudo–Pythagorean Numeration. |
|---|---|---|---|---|
| | 1 | | | |
| | 2 | | | |
| | 3 | | | |
| | 4 | | | |
| | 5 | | | |
| | 6 | | | |
| | 7 | | | |
| | 8 | | | |
| | 9 | | | |
| | 10 | | | |
| A | 11 | A | 1 | 1 |
| ☿ | 12 | B | 2 | 2 |
| ☽ | 13 | G | 3 | 7 |
| ♀ | 14 | D | 4 | 4 |
| ♈ | 15 | E | 5 | 5 |
| ♉ | 16 | [F], V | 6 | F=6, V=4 |
| ♊ | 17 | Z | 7 | 8 |
| ♋ | 18 | H | 8 | 8 |
| ♌ | 19 | Th | 9 | |
| ♍ | 20 | I, J | 10 | I=9, J=1 |
| ♃ | 21 | K, C | 20 | K=2, C=3 |
| ♎ | 22 | L | 30 | 3 |
| W | 23 | M | 40 | 4 |
| ♏ | 24 | N | 50 | 5 |
| ♐ | 25 | X | 60 | 6 |
| ♑ | 26 | O | 70 | 6 |
| ♂ | 27 | P | 80 | 7 |
| ♒ | 28 | | | |
| ♓ | 29 | Q | 90 | 8 |
| ☉ | 30 | R | 100 | 9 |
| F | 31 | S | 200 | 1 |
| ♄ | 32 | T | 300 | 2 |
| E | 32b | U [vowel] , V, W | 400 | U=3, V=4, W=5 |
| ✳ | 31b | | | Y=7, Z=8 |
| | | [Ph], F | 500 | F=6 |
| | | X, Kh | 600 | X=6 |

# L. Letters, Alphabets and Numerical Values

*Futhark*

| Serial Order. | L35. Runic – German Elder Futhark. | L36. Runic – German Elder Futhark – Transliteration. | L37. Runic – German Elder Futhark – Names. | L38. Runic – Anglo-Saxon Futhork. | L39. Runic – Anglo-Saxon Futhork – Transliteration. | L40. Runic – Anglo-Saxon Futhork – Names. |
|---|---|---|---|---|---|---|
| | | | | | | |
| 1 | | | | ᚨ | Ai | Ac |
| 2 | | | | ᚨ | Ae | Aesc |
| 3 | | | | ᛡ | Ye | Yr |
| 4 | | | | ✳ | Io | Ior |
| 5 | | | | ᛇ | Ea | Ear |
| 6 | | | | ᛢ | Q | Cweorp |
| 7 | | | | ᚴ | C | Calc |
| 8 | | | | ᛥ | St | Stan |
| 9 | | | | ᚸ | Gh | Gar |
| 10 | | | | | | |
| 11 | ᚠ | F | Fehu | ᚹ | F | Feoh |
| 12 | ᚢ | U | Uruz | ᚢ | U | Ur |
| 13 | ᚦ | Th | Thurisaz | ᚦ | Th | Thorn |
| 14 | ᚨ | A | Ansuz | ᚩ | O | Os |
| 15 | ᚱ | R | Raido | ᚱ | R | Rad |
| 16 | ᚲ | K | Kaunaz | ᚳ | K | Cen |
| 17 | ᚷ | G | Gebo | ᚷ | G | Gyfu |
| 18 | ᚹ | W | Wunjo | ᚹ | W | Wynn |
| 19 | ᚺ | H | Hagalaz | ᚻ | H | Haegl |
| 20 | ᚾ | N | Nauthiz | ᚾ | N | Nyd |
| 21 | ᛁ | I | Isa | ᛁ | I | Is |
| 22 | ᛃ | J | Jera | ᛄ | J | Ger |
| 23 | ᛇ | Ei | Eihwaz | ᛇ | E | Eoh |
| 24 | ᛈ | P | Perth | ᛈ | P | Peordh |
| 25 | ᛉ | Z | Algiz | ᛦ | Z | Eolh |
| 26 | ᛊ | S | Sowelu | ᛋ | S | Sigil |
| 27 | ᛏ | T | Teiwaz | ᛏ | T | Tir |
| 28 | ᛒ | B | Berkana | ᛒ | B | Beorc |
| 29 | ᛖ | E | Ehwaz | ᛗ | Eh | Eh |
| 30 | ᛗ | M | Mannaz | ᛗ | M | Mann |
| 31 | ᛚ | L | Laguz | ᛚ | L | Lagu |
| 32 | ◇ | Ng | Inguz | ᛟ | Ng | Ing |
| 33 | ᛥ | D | Dagaz | ᛟ | Oe | Ethel |
| 34 | ᛟ | O | Othila | ᛞ | D | Daeg |

# L. Letters, Alphabets and Numerical Values

*Enochian & Trithemius*

| Path Order. | | L41. The Enochian Alphabet. | L42. The Enochian Alphabet – English Equivalent. | L43. The Enochian Alphabet – Name. | L44. The Enochian Alphabet – Correct Numeration. | L45. Golden Dawn Cipher from Trithemius' *Polygraphiae*. |
|---|---|---|---|---|---|---|
| | 1 | | | | | |
| | 2 | | | | | |
| | 3 | | | | | |
| | 4 | | | | | |
| | 5 | | | | | |
| | 6 | | | | | |
| | 7 | | | | | |
| | 8 | | | | | |
| | 9 | | | | | |
| | 10 | | | | | |
| A | 11 | | A | Un | | ⊙ |
| ☿ | 12 | | B | Pa | 7 | |
| ☽ | 13 | | G | Ged | | |
| ♀ | 14 | | D | Gal | 3 | C |
| ♈ | 15 | | E | Graph | | |
| ♉ | 16 | | F | Or | | |
| ♊ | 17 | | Z | Ceph | | |
| ♋ | 18 | | H | Na | | ♀ |
| ♌ | 19 | | | | | |
| ♍ | 20 | | I, J, Y | Gon | | |
| ♃ | 21 | | K, C | Veh | | |
| ♎ | 22 | | L | Ur | 1 | |
| W | 23 | | M | Tal | 9 | e |
| ♏ | 24 | | N | Drux | 6 | |
| ♐ | 25 | | X | Pal | | |
| ♑ | 26 | | O | Med | 5 | |
| ♂ | 27 | | P | Mals | 8 | |
| ♒ | 28 | | | | | |
| ♓ | 29 | | Q | Ger | | |
| ☼ | 30 | | R | Don | | |
| F | 31 | | S | Fam | 4 | |
| ♄ | 32 | | T | Gisg | | |
| | | | U, V, W | Van | 2 | |

# L. Letters, Alphabets and Numerical Values

*Magical Scripts*

| Path Order. | | Reference Hebrew Alphabet. | L47. Celestial Characters. | L48. Crossing the River. | L49. Malachim Script. | L50. Alphabet of the Magi. | L51. AIQ BKR Cipher. |
|---|---|---|---|---|---|---|---|
| | 1 | | | | | | |
| | 2 | | | | | | |
| | 3 | | | | | | |
| | 4 | | | | | | |
| | 5 | | | | | | |
| | 6 | | | | | | |
| | 7 | | | | | | |
| | 8 | | | | | | |
| | 9 | | | | | | |
| | 10 | | | | | | |
| A | 11 | Aleph | | | | | |
| ☿ | 12 | Beth | | | | | |
| ☽ | 13 | Gimel | | | | | |
| ♀ | 14 | Daleth | | | | | |
| ♈ | 15 | He | | | | | |
| ♉ | 16 | Vav | | | | | |
| ♊ | 17 | Zayin | | | | | |
| ♋ | 18 | Cheth | | | | | |
| ♌ | 19 | Teth | | | | | |
| ♍ | 20 | Yod | | | | | |
| ♃ | 21 | Kaph | | | | | |
| ♎ | 22 | Lamed | | | | | |
| W | 23 | Mem | | | | | |
| ♏ | 24 | Nun | | | | | |
| ♐ | 25 | Samekh | | | | | |
| ♑ | 26 | Ayin | | | | | |
| ♂ | 27 | Peh | | | | | |
| ♒ | 28 | Tzaddi | | | | | |
| ♓ | 29 | Qoph | | | | | |
| ☉ | 30 | Resh | | | | | |
| F | 31 | Shin | | | | | |
| ♄ | 32 | Tau | | | | | |

| Path Order. | | Reference Latin Alphabet. | L46. Theban Alphabet. | L52. Royal Arch Masonic Cipher – version 1 | L53. Royal Arch Masonic Cipher – version 2 | |
|---|---|---|---|---|---|---|
| A | 11 | A | | | | |
| ☿ | 12 | B | | | | |
| | | C | | | | |
| ♀ | 14 | D | | | | |
| | | E | | | | |
| | | F | | | | |
| ☾ | 13 | G | | | | |
| ♈ | 15 | H | | | | |
| ♍ | 20 | I | | | | |
| | | J | | | | |
| ♃ | 21 | K | | | | |
| ♎ | 22 | L | | | | |
| W | 23 | M | | | | |
| ♏ | 24 | N | | | | |
| ♑ | 26 | O | | | | |
| ♂ | 27 | P | | | | |
| ♓ | 29 | Q | | | | |
| ☼ | 30 | R | | | | |
| ♐ | 25 | S | | | | |
| ♌ | 19 | T | | | | |
| ♉ | 16 | U | | | | |
| | | V | | | | |
| | | W | | | | |
| | | X | | | | |
| | | Y | | | | |
| ♊ | 17 | Z | | | | |
| | | Ω | | - | - | |
| ♋ | 18 | Ch | - | - | - | |
| F | 31 | Sh | - | - | - | |
| ♄ | 32 | Th | - | - | - | |
| ♒ | 28 | Tz | - | - | - | |

# M. Magic of the Grimoires – Angels, Demons and Spirits

*Testament of Solomon*

| | No. | M1. Demons Bound By Solomon. | M2. Demons – Appearance. | M3. Demons Bound By Solomon – Powers & Attributes. | M4. Demon Bound By or Constrained By. | M5. Demons Bound to Work. | M6. Demon Reside; or Child of |
|---|---|---|---|---|---|---|---|
| | | | | | | | |
| ♒ | 1 | Ornias | Assumes 3 shapes: a) man who craves the bodies of boys b) creature with wings, c) a lion | Strangles those whose sign is Aquarius because of their love of Virgo women. Plays with men in their sleep, steals money, and sucks the life out of them. Helped to bring other demons to Solomon | The name of the Archangel Ouriel/Uriel. He fears iron, as do many demons | Cuts Solomon's Temple stones transported from the Arabian sea | Resides in Aquarius. Offspring of archangel Uriel. |
| ♀ | 2 | Beelzeboul, the Prince or King of all Demons. | | Ruler of all Demons. Destroys Kings; Aids foreign tyrants; Sets demons up as gods; Instigates wars; Makes men envious & murderous & to commit sodomy; will Destroy the World | Almighty God; Patike (or *ho pater* – Father); Emmanouel (summing by isopsephy to 644); Eleeth; Elo-i | Cuts Theban marble for the Temple; Brings other demons | Highest ranking angel of those who fell. Resides in the Evening Star (Venus?) |
| ☾ | 3 | Onoskelis | A very beautiful fair woman with mule's legs, and changeable character | Strangles Men with a noose; Consorts with honey-coloured men; Travels by the full Moon | The name of the Holy One of Israel; and Solomon | Spins hemp for ropes | Lives in cliff, caves, ravines, or dens in the earth. Born of an echo of a black heaven |
| | 4 | Asmodeus | | Causes wickedness of men to spread. Plots against newly-weds so they are strangers; mars the beauty of virgins and makes their hearts grow cold; Spreads madness among women; Commits groups of murders | Liver and gall of the Sheatfish (a catfish found in Assyria) thrown on burning charcoal; Archangel Raphael; iron; 10 water jars encircling him; a storax branch | Molds clay and Carries Water. Has knowledge of the future | Son of the Great Bear, or Draco, or the Dipper constell-ation. Resides in Assyria |
| ☾ | 5 | Lix Tetrax or Tephras | Dust-devil / Whirlwind | Makes whirlwinds; Brings Darkness to Men; Sets Fields on Fire; Destroys Homesteads; Heals Hemitertian Fever | Archangel Azael; cures fever when invoked with the words "Baltala, Thallal, Melchal." | Raises Stones | Offspring of the Great One. Resides in the horn of the Moon in the South. Found in the *Ephesia Grammata* |

# M. Magic of the Grimoires – Angels, Demons and Spirits

| No. | M1. Demons Bound By Solomon. | M2. Demons – Appearance. | M3. Demons Bound By Solomon – Powers & Attributes. | M4. Demon Bound By or Constrained By. | M5. Demons Bound to Work. | M6. Demon Reside; or Child of |
|---|---|---|---|---|---|---|
| 6 | *Pleiades* 1st. Deception | | Deceives men & weave snares; plot & devise heresies | Bound by the Angel Lamechiel | | |
| 7 | *Pleiades* 2nd. Strife | | Brings clubs, pellets, swords & weapons | Angel Baruchiel | | |
| 8 | *Pleiades* 3rd. Fate | | Causes men to fight rather than make peace | Angel Marmaroth | | |
| 9 | *Pleiades* 4th. Distress | Seven Fair Women Bound hand & foot | Causes men to lack moderation & sobriety; Splits men into Factions | Angel Balthioul | All the Pleiades dig the foundations of the temple | All reside in Lydia or Olympus. |
| 10 | *Pleiades* : 5th. Error *(sic)* | | Leads men into error; Causes people to dig up graves and to stray from their religion | Angel Uriel/Ouriel | | |
| 11 | *Pleiades* : 6th. Power | | Deposes kings; Raises tyrants | Angel Asteraoth (perhaps the Canaanite goddess Astoreth) | | |
| 12 | *Pleiades* : 7th. [the worst equated with Hecate] | | Makes men worse; binds with the bonds of Artemis [desire] | A locust | | |
| 13 | Murder/Envy | Headless Man | Makes children dumb; steals heads; Emits fire; afflicts the limbs and feet; Inflicts sores | A fiery flash of lightning | Kept (chained) with Beelzeboul | |
| 14 | Rabdos (Sceptre) | Large dog | Was able to restrain the stars; deceives men who follow his star; Supplied emerald stone for the Temple | The great Briathos | Cuts marble | |
| 15 | Leontophoron (Lion-bearer) | Roaring Lion | Makes sick men weak; Rules the demons whose name is legion | Emmanouel; the name of three letters [IAO] | Carries wood, cuts kindling | Son of Araps |
| 16 | Head of the Dragons | 3-Headed Dragon spirit with awful skin | Blinds unborn children; bends their ears & makes them deaf & dumb; strikes men with seizures | The site of Golgotha; the Angel of the Wonderful Counsellor [Christ?] | Makes bricks | |
| 17 | Obyzouth, Obizuth | Woman with dishevelled hair, with a body of darkness | Divines the hour of birth; Strangles infants; injures eyes, mouths and minds; Makes bodies feel pain | Angel Raphael; writing 'Obyzouth' on papyrus | Bound by her hair and hung in front of the Temple | |
| 18 | Winged Dragon | Dragon with wings, human face & hands | Mates with fair women through the buttocks; causes wood to burn | The Angel of the Second Heaven, Bazazeth | Cuts marble | Constell-ation of Draco? |
| ☾ 19 | Enepsigos | Woman with heads and 2 arms on each shoulder. | Lives in the Moon; Invoked as Kronos; Foretold the downfall of Solomon's Temple & the Crucifixion | Angel Rathanael; must be chained with a triple link chain; can be conjured as Kronos | Imprisoned | Near the Moon |
| 20 | Kunopegos, Kunospaston | A horse's front with a fish's rear, or a man | Causes seasickness, and waves to sink ships and drown men, and receives their gold | Angel Iameth; fears lack of water | Imprisoned | |

|  | No. | M1. Demons Bound By Solomon. | M2. Demons – Appearance. | M3. Demons Bound By Solomon – Powers & Attributes. | M4. Demon Bound By or Constrained By. | M5. Demons Bound to Work. | M6. Demon Reside; or Child of |
|---|---|---|---|---|---|---|---|
|  |  |  |  |  |  |  |  |
|  | 21 | The lecherous spirit of a giant man | Man with gleaming eyes, carrying a sword | Lives in Cemeteries; ambushes men & either kills them or causes them to be possessed by a Demon | The Saviour; the Saviours mark [the cross] written on a forehead | Imprisoned | Inaccess-ible places |
|  | 22 | Ephippas (mentioned out of order) | Arabian wind demon | Sets Fires; Causes death; Moves mountains; Carry houses; Overthrows kings; Withers trees | Christ, "the one who is going to be born from a virgin and be crucified" | Carries Stone | Was bound in the abyss of the Red Sea. Arabia |
|  | 23 | Abezethibou (mentioned out of order) | Hostile demon, with one wing | Was the demon who helped the magicians of Egypt against Moses. Transported the pillar, with Ephippas, from the Red Sea to the Temple |  |  | Once resided in 1st Heaven called Amelouth. Now the Red Sea |
|  | 24 | *The 36 Decans - World Rulers of the night* |  |  |  |  |  |
|  | 25 | 1. Ruax |  | Causes headaches and throbbing temples | Say "Michael imprison Ruax" |  | 1st Decan |
| ♈ | 26 | 2. Barsafael |  | Causes headaches and throbbing temples | Say "Gabriel imprison Barsafael" |  | 2nd Decan |
|  | 27 | 3. Arotosael |  | Harms eyes | Say "Uriel/Ouriel imprison Aratosael" |  | 3rd Decan |
|  | 28 | 4. Oropel |  | Makes sore throats with much mucus | Say "Raphael imprison Oropel" |  | 4th Decan |
| ♉ | 29 | 5. Kairoxan-ondalon, Iudal |  | Blocked ears & deafness | Say "Uruiel/Ourouel imprison Kairoxanondalon/Iudal" | All 36 to do heavy work; or were imprisoned by Solomon. They also tend furnaces for metal-work | 5th Decan |
|  | 30 | 6. Sphendonael | All 36 with heads like formless dogs; humans, bulls, dragons | Tumours of the parotid gland and tetanic recurvation | Say "Sabael imprison Sphendonael" |  | 6th Decan |
| ♊ | 31 | 7. Sphandor |  | Weakens shoulders; deadens the nerves in the hand; paralyses limbs; damages necks | Say "Arael imprison Sphandor" |  | 7th Decan |
|  | 32 | 8. Belbel |  | Perverts the hearts & minds of men | Say "Karael imprison Belbel" |  | 8th Decan |
|  | 33 | 9. Kourtael |  | Bowel cholic | Say "Iaoth imprison Kourtael" |  | 9th Decan |
| ♋ | 34 | 10. Metathiax |  | Aching kidneys | Say "Adonael imprison Metathiax" |  | 10th Decan |
|  | 35 | 11. Katanikotael |  | Fights and feuds in men's homes | Write on 7 laurel leaves the Angel "Eae, Ieo, sons of Sabaoth, imprison Katanikotael"; Wash the laurel leaves in water and then sprinkle the water in your house |  | 11th Decan |

| | No. | M1. Demons Bound By Solomon. | M2. Demons – Appearance. | M3. Demons Bound By Solomon – Powers & Attributes. | M4. Demon Bound By or Constrained By. | M5. Demons Bound to Work. | M6. Demon Reside; or Child of |
|---|---|---|---|---|---|---|---|
| | 36 | 12. Saphathorael | | Dissension in the minds of men | Write on papyrus "Iae, Ieo, sons of Sabaoth" or "Ioelet Ithoth & Bae" then fold it and wear it [as an amulet] round your neck | | 12th Decan |
| | 37 | 13. Phobothel | | Loosens tendons | Say "Adonael/Adonai imprison Phobothel" | | 13th Decan |
| ♌ | 38 | 14. Leroel | | Shivering fits & sore throat | Say "Zoroel imprison Kumentael" | | 14th Decan |
| | 39 | 15. Soubelti | | Shivering and numbness | Say "Rizoel imprison Soubelti " | | 15th Decan |
| | 40 | 16. Katrax | | Incurable fevers | Chop up coriander and rub it on your lips then say "I adjure you by Zeus retreat from this image of God" | | 16th Decan |
| ♍ | 41 | 17. Ieropa, Ieropael | | Convulsions in the bath and fits on the road | Say into the right ear of the afflicted three times "Iouda Zizabou" or "Iudarize Sabune Denoe" | All 36 to do heavy work; or were imprisoned by Solomon. They also tend furnaces for metal-work | 17th Decan |
| | 42 | 18. Modebel | All 36 with heads like formless dogs; humans, bulls, dragons | Separates wives from husbands | Write down the names of the 8 Fathers [of the Ogdoad, or of Israel] "command thee to retire from this house in peace" and place them in the doorway, | | 18th Decan |
| | 43 | 19. Mardero | | Incurable fever | Write on the leaf of a book "Sphener Rafael retire, drag me not about, flay me not" and then tie it round your neck | | 19th Decan |
| ♎ | 44 | 20. Rhyx Nathotho | | Knees illness | Write on papyrus "Phounebiel depart " | | 20th Decan |
| | 45 | 21. Rhyx Alath | | Croup, coughing & breathing difficulties in infants | Write on papyrus "Rorex do thou pursue Alath" or "Rarideris do thou…" and fasten it round the neck | | 21st Decan |
| ♏ | 46 | 22. Rhyx Audameoth | | Heart pain | Write on papyrus "Raiouoth" | | 22nd Decan |
| | 47 | 23. Rhyx Manthado | | Aching kidneys and painful urination | Write on papyrus "Iaoth, Ouriel" or on a plate of tin "Iathoth Uruel Manthado" and fasten it round the loins | | 23rd Decan |

| | No. | M1. Demons Bound By Solomon. | M2. Demons – Appearance. | M3. Demons Bound By Solomon – Powers & Attributes. | M4. Demon Bound By or Constrained By. | M5. Demons Bound to Work. | M6. Demon Reside; or Child of |
|---|---|---|---|---|---|---|---|
| ♐ | 48 | 24. Rhyx Aktonme | | Aches in ribs | Write on a piece of wood from a ship that has run aground "Marmaraoth of mist" or engrave on copper taken from such a ship "Marmaraoth Sabaoth pursue Akton" and fasten it on your loins | | 24th Decan |
| | 49 | 25. Rhyx Anatreth | | Burnings & boilings in the entrails | Say "Arara, Arare" or "Arara Charara" | | 25th Decan |
| | 50 | 26. Rhyx Enenutha | | Steals men's minds and their hearts | Write "Kalazael" or "Allazool pursue Enenutha" and tie the papyrus round you | | 26th Decan |
| | 51 | 27. Rhyx Axesbuth | | Diarrhea & hemorrhoids | Say over wine "I exorcise thee by the eleventh Aeon to stop Rhyx Axesbuth" then drink it | | 27th Decan |
| | 52 | 28. Rhyx Harpax | All 36 with heads like formless dogs; humans, bulls, dragons | Insomnia | Write "Kok Phedismos" and bind it around your temples | All 36 to do heavy work; or were imprisoned by Solomon. They also tend furnaces for metal-work | 28th Decan |
| ♑ | 53 | 29. Rhyx Anoster | | Hysteria & pains in the bladder | Mash three seeds of laurel in pure oli, and smear it on saying "I exorcise thee Anoster, stop by Marmaraoth" | | 29th Decan |
| | 54 | 30. Rhyx Physikoreth | | Long term illness | Mix salt with pure oil and rub the body saying "Cherubim, Seraphim, help me" | | 30th Decan |
| | 55 | 31. Rhyx Aleureth | | Swallowing fish bones | Spike the breast with another bone from the same fish and cough | | 31st Decan |
| | 56 | 32. Rhyx Ichthuon | | Detached tendons | Say "Adonaeth/Adonai malthe/help!" | | 32nd Decan |
| ♒ | 57 | 33. Rhyx Achoneoth | | Sore throat and tonsilitis | Write on some ivy/fig leaves "'Leikourgos/ Lycurgos" removing one letter at a time and write it reversing the letters so "Lycurgos ycurgos kurgos yrgos gos os" | | 33rd Decan |
| | 58 | 34. Rhyx Autototh | | Jealousy & squabbles between lovers | Write on papyrus "Alpha and Omega" | | 34th Decan |
| ♓ | 59 | 35. Rhyx Phtheneoth | | Casts the evil eye on every Man | Draw the evil eye sign on papyrus | | 35th Decan |
| | 60 | 36. Rhyx Mianeth | | Destroys houses; Causes flesh to rot | Write on the front-door of the house "Melto Ardad Anaath" | | 36th Decan |

# M. Magic of the Grimoires – Angels, Demons and Spirits

*Liber Juratus, the Sworn Book of Honorius*

M7. The 100 Holy Names of God from *Liber Juratus*.

| Of Probable Hebrew Origin | Of Probable Greek Origin | | Possible Hebrew, Greek, or other Origins | |
|---|---|---|---|---|
| Admyhel 17 | Abdon 65 | Mesamarathon [Messaramathon] 21 | Abbadia 29 | Hospesk [Hofberk] 94 |
| Adonay 52 | Abracio [Abracon] 63 | Nomygon 88 | Achionadabir [Athionadabir] 53 | Ianemyer 8 |
| Agla 1 | Alpha & Omega 30 | Noymos 43 | Ely Deus [Elydeus] 4 | Lamyara [Lamiara] 7 |
| Baruch 69 | Amphynethon [Amphinethon] 6 | Occynnomos [Occymomos] 96 | Elscha [Escha] 28 | Leiste 31 |
| Elyorem [Elyoram] 97 | Anephenethon [Anepheneton] 64 | Occynoneryon [Occymomyon] 61 | Elzephares 36 | Maloht 26 |
| Emanuel 15 | Anethy [Anethi] 22 | Omytheon 54 | Fothon [Rothon] 49 | Melthe 66 |
| Genouem [Genonem] 71 | Archima [Archyna] 99 | Opiron [Opyron] 87 | Gelemoht 59 | Monon [Monhon] 2 |
| Messias [Messyas] 2 | Christus 93 | Orihel [Oryhel] 89 | Gelon 78 | Nothi [Nathi] 84 |
| Nathanathay [Nathanothay] 45 | Cirrhos [Cirhos] 86 | Orion 41 | Gofgar 95 | Nosulaceps [Nosulateps] 57 |
| On 16 | Egyrion [Egyryon] 37 | Oristion [Oristyon] 2 | Gogameli [Gofgameh] 14 | Ocleiste 5 |
| Rabur 100 | Ecthothas 62 | Pantheon 73 | Hofbor [Ofber] 34 | Pep [Pheb] 44 |
| Sabaoth 84 | Eryhona [Erihona] 23 | Paraclitus 60 | Hofga 55 | Porho 48 |
| Saday 25 | Eryon 42 | Pheta 38 | Hofob 20 | Rabarmas 75 |
| Sadyon 9 | Hel 79 | Porrenthimon [Porrenthymon] 12 | Hombona [Ombona] 39 | Sechce [Sechoe] 27 |
| Sellah [Sellaht] 85 | Heloy 98 | Sother 67 | Honzmorb 18 | Sporgongo 70 |
| Tetragramaton [Tetragrammaton] 3 | Hely 10 | Stimulamathon [Stymulamathon] 40 | Horha 92 | Techel [Rethel] 80 |
| Ya 91 | Ihelur 13 | Theon 46 | Horlon 11 | Zabuather 74 |
| | Ioht [Ioth] 19 | Theos 90 | | |
| | Iuestre 24 | Tutheon 58 | | |
| | Jeremon [Ieremon] 33 | Usirion [Usiyron] 68 | | |
| | Karex 83 | Ymeynlethon [Ymeynlethon] 82 | | |
| | Kyrios [Kyryos] 77 | Yschiros [Yskyros] 76 | | |
| | Letellethe [Lethellethe] 50 | Ysiston [Ysyston] 47 | | |
| | Leyndra [Leyndra] 56 | Ysmas 51 | | |
| | Merkerpon [Mercarpon] 35 | | | |

# M. Magic of the Grimoires – Angels, Demons and Spirits

| | | |
|---|---|---|
| | | M8. The Angels of the Days of the Week from *Liber Juratus*. |

| | Day & Planet | Angel |
|---|---|---|
| ♄ | Saturday – Saturn | Myraton, Pacrifon, Polypon, Capeiell, Eheniton, Alfiton, Cherion, Sandalson, Panion, Almion, Erpion, Paxon, Calirxon, Horrion, Melison, Unrion, Tonelin, Refaebilion, Moniteon, Bornailon, Paxilon, Lelalion, Onoxion, Quibon, Quiron, Vixasmion, Relion, Cassilon, Tifonion, Murion, Degion, Dapsion, Lenaion, Orleunion, Foilion, Monichion, Gabion, Paxonion, Pinsilon, Lepiron, Loeloon, Saron, Salion, Pion, Nargeron, Aaron, Selyypon, Pinmibron, Raconcall, Zelibron |
| ♃ | Thursday – Jupiter | Satquiel, Ahyell, Yebel, Aneniel, Jumiel, Juniel, Amiel, Faniel, Ramuel, Sanfael, Sacciniel, Galbiel, Lafiel, Maziel, Ymraell, Memiell, Pariel, Pamhiniel, Toupiel, Ambaniel, Omiell, Orfiell, Ael, Hearel, Memiel, Ynel, Syumeliel, Tranfiel, Mefeniel, Antquiel, Quisiell, Cumiriel, Rofiniel, Rubyeiel, Beell, Bariel, Cheduriel |
| ♂ | Tuesday – Mars | Samayelin, Tartalin, Doppeil, Racyelin, Farabin, Cabin, Asymolin, Mabareilin, Tralyeilin, Rubbelin, Marmarin, Tafanyelin, Fuheilin, Ruffar, Aneilin, Rabsilin,, Eralin,, Pyrteplin, Brofilin, Cacyrilin, Naffreinin, Nupurin, Raffilin, Nyrilin, Nyenyolin, Nybirin, Celabrill, Tubeilin, Haain, Vein, Paafirin, Cetenoilin, Letytyeilin, Rarafeill, Canueil, Bastailin, Costirin, Montyelin, Albilin, Parachbeill, Alyeill, Vaceill, Zalcicill, Amadiell, Vsararieill, Lyncodoneil, Daffripeil, Vnlilin, Carfzoneill, Gronieill, Gabrinin, Narbe |
| ☼ | Sunday – Sun | Daniel, Olyeill, Saffiell, Dargoyeill, Yelbrayeiell, Cemaguill, Gebarbaya, Faceyeill, Caram, Neyeill, Talgylueil, Bethtaez, Raneil, Salha, Hyeill, Armaquieyeill, Romail, Gybrill, Zemail, Mychaze, Zarsayeill, Amail, Antorayeill, Ronayeill, Reniayeill, Barhil, Marhill, Rarorhill, Merhill, Zarafill, Zaraill, An, Quyhim, Ceytatinin, Ezniah, Vehich, Dunedryneylin, Yedemkieil, Esmaadin, Elbedagrin, Zamaanel, Yocaleme, Detryeill, Aryeil, Arnaeill, Veremedin, Vnaraxi |
| ♀ | Friday – Venus | Hasuayeil, Barneyeil, Verday, Heill, Alzeyeill, Szeyeill, Bacapel, Zelfayeill, Morayeill, Borayeill, Alpheyeill, Arobilin, Canofilin, Ourilin, Zaryalin, Marilin, Bacoraye, Kolfayelin, Azrayeilin, Ambayeirin, Mayeilin, Cabueirin, Alseirin, Asueirin, Alneirin, Nenanrin, Rayorin, Orinin, Gedulin, Harerin, Namilin, Halilin, Hymeilin, Reffilin, Narraabilin, Hahyeilin, Landelin, Esfilin, Thefelin, Patnelin, Keyalin, Nailin, Leyraiell, Ablayeill, Talraylanrain, Barkalin, Bahorael |
| ☿ | Wednesday – Mercury | Michael, Beerel, Dafngel, Aryhyriel, Boel, Bariel, Meriel, Amiel, Aol, Semeol, Aaen, Berion, Sarinon, Keinerion, Feynon, Aneinin, Zamazinin, Cananin, Aall, Merygall, Pegal, Gabal, Veal, Aumeal, Faranyeal, Gebin, Caribifin, Autarilin, Metorilin, Nabyafsin, Fysfin, Barsslilin, Caruphilin, Danyturla, Fenyturla, Geumyturla, Amia, Alnamia, Tabinia, Nafia, Myacha, Tyagra, Bec, Alacaorinill, Benenonill |
| ☾ | Monday – Moon | Semhazylin, Semyhylim, Yasrozin, Agrasnydin, Aymsylin, Cathneylin, Alrasachysin, Abrachasin, Layralosin, Lang, Hasin, Anaenim, Niangarorin, Aezonin, Montazin, Labelas, Mafatin, Feya, Rachin, Cadanagin, Laeradonin, Caffrnbrin, Bachramin, Varthalin, Amnanyneylin, Hacoylin, Balganaychin, Aryeylin, Badeylin, Abranorin, Tarmanydin, Amdalysin, Sahgragynin, Adyanienin, Sacstoyein, Latebayfanisin, Caybeininin, Nabyalin, Cyzamanin, Abramacin, Laryagathin, Bofealyquin, Bayealadin, Gasorin, Asaphin, Daryenin, Macnayelin, Gomraorin, Marybin, Yebirin, Arilin, Faryelin, Nepenyelin, Banyelin, Astyeilin, Cerada |

# M. Magic of the Grimoires – Angels, Demons and Spirits

| | | Month | Ruler | Angels |
|---|---|---|---|---|
| ♈ | 15 | Nisan | Oriel | Oriel, Malaquiram, Acya, Zaziel, Paltifur, Yesmachia, Yariel, Araton, Robica, Sephatia, Anaya, Guesupales, Seniquiel, Sereriel, Malquia, Aricasom, Pacita, Abdiel, Ramasdon, Cafiel, Nascyasori, Sugni, Aszrus, Sornadaf, Admiel, Necamia, Caysaac, Benyh, Quor, Adziriell |
| ♉ | 16 | Iyar | Sasuyell | Safuelor, Sasnyeil, Santon, Cartemat, Aliel, Paltnia, Bargar, Galmus, Necpis, Aarom, Manit, Aadon, Quenanel, Quemon, Rasegar, Affrie, Absamon, Sarsall, Aspin, Carbiel, Regnia, Athlas, Nadis, Abitasi, Abitan, Pal |
| ♊ | 17 | Sivan | Amariel | Amariel, Tabriell, Casmuch, Nastifa, Almur, Naamab, Mamica, Zicaran, Samisarach, Naasein, Andas, Paltamus, Abris, Borzac, Saforac, Yayat, Dalia, Aziger, Nabsuf, Abuifor, Zenam, Dersam, Cefania, Maccasor, Naboon, Adiell, Maasiell, Szarzir, Tartalion, Adyysar |
| ♋ | 18 | Tammuz | Noriel | Noriel, Safida, Asaf, Mazica, Sarsac, Adryyaac, Nagron, Galuf, Galgal, Danroc, Saracu, Remafydda, Lulyaraf, Nedylar, Tyaf, Taanat, Lafayel, Genida, Nedir, Delqua, Maadon, Samiel, Amrael, Lezaydi, As, Ohoc, Nasyby, Razyarsady, Yadna, Caspa, Garitan, Elysafan, Pastama, Maday |
| ♌ | 19 | Av | Beraquiel | Beraquiel, Manhy, Amarya, Haya, Byny, Madrat, Aman, Tuliell, Cossuro, Fartis, Nactif, Nekyff, Pegner, Tablic, Manuat, Amasya, Guatiell, Reycat, Gnynzy, Paliel, Gadeff, Nesgnyraf, Abrac, Animiter, Carnby, Nachall, Cabake, Loch, Macria, Sase, Essaf |
| ♍ | 20 | Elul | Magnyuya | Manyny, Arabiell, Haniell, Nacery, Yassar, Rassy, Boell, Mathiall, Naccameryf, Zacdon, Nafac, Rapion, Saspy, Salhy, Rasersh, Malquiell, Sanytiell, Yoas, Gualaly, Danpy, Yamla, Golum, Zasziell, Satpach, Nassa, Myssyn, Macratyf, Dadiell, Carciell, Effygmato |
| ♎ | 22 | Tishri | Suriel | Surgell or Suriel, Sarycam, Guabryza, Szncariell, Sabybiall, Ytrnt, Cullia, Dadiel, Marham, Abercaysdon, Sacdon, Pagnlan, Arsabon, Asyramon, Agniel, Sastyracnas, Altym, Masulaef, Salamiel, Sascuniel, Barcaran, Yahnt, Alycas, Vlysacyaia, Abry |
| ♏ | 24 | Cheshvan | Barfiell | Barbits or Barfiell, Tylzdiell, Raamiell, Nehubaell, Alysaf, Baliel, Arzaf, Rashiel, Alson, Naspiell, Becar, Paliel, Elysu, Aiguap, Nacpas, Sansany, Aesal, Maarym, Sascy, Yalsenac, Mabint, Magdiell, Saneinas, Maaliel, Arsafael, Nanyseyorar, Becabalaf, Napybael, Suciel, Nabnell, Sariell, Sodiel, Marenell, Palytam |
| ♐ | 25 | Kislev | Adoniel | Edoniel, Radiel, Maduch, Racino, Hyzy, Mariel, Azday, Mandiel, Gumiel, Seriel, Kery, Sahaman, Osmyn, Sechiel, Pazehemy, Chalchyphay, Gey, Idael, Necad, Mynael, Arac, Ararygugel, Galnel, Gimon, Satuel, Elynzy, Baquylaguall |
| ♑ | 26 | Tevet | Anael | Anael, Amiel, Acior, Naclia, Rapines, Raacpel, Pacrel, Halion, Guanrynasnihe, Aslaom, Naspaya, Neapry, Sanihay, Hasasylgason, Gastaset, Yfaryamy, Man, Polimas, Sarananuf, Olyab, Sariel, Canel, Raziell, Pmla, Nisquem, Sarman, Malysan, Asyzat, Marimoe |
| ♒ | 28 | Shevat | Gabriel | Gabriel, Ysrael, Natriel, Gasziel, Nassam, Abrysaf, Zefaell, Zamiel, Mamiel, Taliel, Myriel, Sahiniel, Guriel, Samhiell, Dariel, Banorsasty, Satymn, Nasiel, Ransiel, Talguaf, Lebrachiel, Daliell, Gandriel, Sahuhaf, Myschiel |
| ♓ | 29 | Adar | Romiel | Romiel, Patiel, Guriel, Azriel, Paamiel, Cartiel, El, Anunalbeh, Parhaya, Ysael, Beriel, Laell, Tenebiel, Panten, Panteron, Faniel, Falason, Manciel, Pataron, Labiel, Ragael, Cetabiel, Nyazpatael |
| | | Büsextilis | Laciel | Laciel or Lantiel, Ardiel, Nosmiel, Ardiel, Celydael, Amiel, Malquiel, Gabaliel, Susuagos, Barylaguy, Yabtasyper, Magos, Sangos, Yayell, Yel, Yasmiel, Steluiel, Garasyn, Ceyabgos, Sacadiel, Garacap, Gabanael, Tamtiel |

M9. Angels of the Months from *Liber Juratus*.

# M. Magic of the Grimoires – Angels, Demons and Spirits

*Peter De Abano's Heptameron*

|  | M10. Angels of the Days of the Week from Peter de Abano's *Heptameron*. | | | | | | |
|---|---|---|---|---|---|---|---|
| **Day ->** | *Sunday* | *Monday* | *Tuesday* | *Wednesday* | *Thursday* | *Friday* | *Saturday* |
| *Implied Planet* | Sun | Moon | Mars | Mercury | Jupiter | Venus | Saturn |
| *Archangel* | Michael | Gabriel | Samael | Raphael | Sachiel | Anael | Cassiel |
| *Heaven [corrected]* | Machen [Zebul] | Shamaim | Machon [Ma'on] | Raquie | Zebul [Makon] | Sagun [Shechaqim] | – [Araboth] |
| *Heaven Number* | 4th | 1st | 5th | 2nd | 6th | 3rd | 7th |
| *Angels of Day* | Michael Dardiel Huratapal | Gabriel Michael Samael | Samael Satael Amabiel | Raphael Miel Seraphiel | Sachiel Castiel Asasiel | Anael Rachiel Sachiel | Cassiel Machatan Uriel |
| *Angels of the air – King* | Varcan | Arcan | Samax | Mediat or Modiat | Suth | Sarabotes | Maymon |
| *His Ministers* | Tus Andas Cynabal | Bilet Missabu Abuzaha | Carmax Ismoli Paffran | Suquinos Sallales | Maguth Gutrix | Amabiel Aba Abalidoth Flaef | Abumalith Assaibi Balidet |
| *Wind ruling* | North | West | East | South West | South | West [*sic*] | South West [*sic*] |
| *Sprit to be called from the East* | Samael Baciel Atel Gabriel Vionairaba | Gabriel Gabrael Madiel Deamiel Janael | Friagne Guael Damael Calzas Arragon | Mathlai Tarmiel Baraborat | [no angels or spirits of the air in this heaven] | Setchiel Chedusit-aniel Corat Tamael Tenaciel | [no angels of the air in this heaven] |
| *Sprit to be called from the West* | Anael Pabel Ustael Burchat Suceratos Capabili | Sachiel Zaniel Habaiel Bachanael Corabael | Lama Astagna Lobquin Soncas Jazel Isiael Irel | Jeresous Mitraton |  | Turiel Coniel Babiel Kadie Maltiel Huphaltiel |  |
| *Sprit to be called from the North* | Aiel Aniel or Aquiel Masgabriel Sapiel Matuyel | Mael Vuael Valnum Baliel Balay Humastrau | Rahumel Hyniel Rayel Seraphiel Mathiel Fraciel | Thiel Rael Jariahel Venahel Velel Abuiori Ucirnuel |  | Peniel Penael Penat Raphael Raniel Doremiel |  |
| *Sprit to be called from the South* | Haludiel Machasiel Charsiel Uriel Naromiel | Curaniel Dabriel Darquiel Hanun Anayl Vetuel | Sacriel Janiel Galdel Osael Vianuel Zaliel | Milliel Nelapa Babel Caluel vel Laquel |  | Porna Sachiel Chermiel Samael Santanael Famiel |  |
| *Perfume of the day* | Red Sandalwood | Aloes | Pepper | Mastick | Saffron | Pepperwort | Sulphur |

# M. Magic of the Grimoires – Angels, Demons and Spirits

| | | | Spring | Summer | Autumn | Winter |
|---|---|---|---|---|---|---|
| | | | | M10a. Angels of the Seasons from Peter de Abano's *Heptameron*. | | |
| | | Name of Season | Talvi | Casmaran | Ardarael | Farlas |
| | | Angels of Season | Caratasa, Core, Amatiel, Commissoros | Gargatel, Tariel, Gaviel | Tarquam, Guabarel | Amabael, Ctarari |
| | | Head of Sign | Spugliguel | Tubiel | Torquaret | Altarib |
| E | 32b | Earth in Season | Amadai | Festativi | Rabianara | Geremiah |
| ☼ | 30 | Sun in Season | Abraym | Athemay | Abragini | Commutaff |
| ☾ | 13 | Moon in Season | Agusita | Armatus | Matasignais | Affaterim |

*Codex Latinus Monacensis*

M11. List of Demons – from *Codex Latinus Monacensis*.

| No. | Name | Rank | Appearance | Function | Legions |
|---|---|---|---|---|---|
| 1 | Barbarus | Count and Duke | - | Discloses treasures not protected by magic | 36 |
| 2 | Cason | Duke | Seneschal | Responds about present, past, future, and hidden things; gives favour of friends and enemies; gives dignities (honours). | 45 |
| 3 | Otius | Preses and Count | Human with large teeth and 3 horns, sharp sword in hand. | Responds about present, future, and hidden matters; gives favour of friends and enemies. | 36 |
| 4 | Curson | King | Man, with crowned leonine face, viper in hand; rides horseback, trumpets preceeding. | Reveals present, past, future, hidden matters; reveals and opens treasures; assumes human and aerial body and responds about divine and hidden matters (including deity and creation of world); gives excellent familiars | 22 |
| 5 | Alugor | Duke | Splendid knight, with lance, banner; and sceptre | Responds about occult matters and duels; provides knights; gives favour of all kings, marquises, and knights. | 50 |
| 6 | Taob | Prince | Human | Excellent physician for women, making them burn with love for men, on request transforming them into another form until they come to their beloved; makes sterile. | 25 |
| 7 | Volach | President | Boy, with wings of angel; rides on dragon; has two heads. | Responds about hidden treasures; if serpents appear, gives over the serpents into the hands of exorcist. | 27 |
| 8 | Gaeneron | Duke | Beautiful woman, crowned, riding on camel. | Responds about present, past, and future matters, and hidden treasures; gives love of women, especially beautiful ones. | 27 |
| 9 | Tuveries | Marquis | Knight, riding on black horse. | Teaches the three subjects of the Trivium, reveals hidden treasures and other hidden things; causes person to cross seas and rivers quickly. | 30 |
| 10 | Hanni | President | Fiery flame, but takes human form | Teaches astronomy and other liberal arts; gives excellent familiars; gives favour with magnates and princes. | 30 |

# M. Magic of the Grimoires – Angels, Demons and Spirits

| | | Day | Angel | King | Spirits & co-adjutors | Suffumigations | Purpose | Image |
|---|---|---|---|---|---|---|---|---|
| ☽ | 13 | Monday | Gabriel | Almodab | Sylol, Millalu, Abuzaba | Aloes, anacap | Benevolence, concord, friendship | Gold or steel or white wax for concord |
| ☿ | 12 | Wednesday | Michael | Saba | Conas, Pactas, Sanbras | Altast | Enmity and hatred | Lead, for enmity |
| ♀ | 14 | Friday | Anael | Saabotes | Nassath, Ynasa | Almastic or lignum radim | Friendship | White wax, for love of a woman |
| ☼ | 30 | Sunday | Raphael | Saytam | Taatus, Candas, Vanibal | Yellow or red sandalwood | Binding tongues, otherwise binding people | Gold or yellow wax, for binding tongues |
| ♂ | 27 | Tuesday | Samael | Rex filius dyabuli | Carmath, Utanaual, Pascami | Pepper, abana, cyg | Illness and destruction | Red copper or red wax, for depopulating a house, causing bloodshed or illness, or other harm |
| ♃ | 21 | Thursday | Satquirel | Madrath, son of Arath | Hyrti, Ignaro, Quiron, Saalalebeth | Yellow incense | Peace | Yellow copper or yellow wax, for concord between man and woman |
| ♄ | 32 | Saturday | Captiel = Caffriel | Hayton, Assayby | Abimalyb, Haybalydoth, Yfla | Assandaron, sulphur | Binding locations | Pix clara, for binding tongues or places, for discord |

M12. Angels of the Days of the Week – from *Codex Latinus Monacensis*.

# M. Magic of the Grimoires – Angels, Demons and Spirits

| | | Hour | Hour Name | Function of Images made in the Hour | Angel |
|---|---|---|---|---|---|
| ♈ | 15 | 1st | Yayn | Binding tongues | Raphael |
| ♉ | 16 | 2nd | Yan, Or | Friendship, favour of potentates; Benevolence | Anael |
| ♊ | 17 | 3rd | Nassura | Hunting, fishing; Bring together birds and fishes | Michael |
| ♋ | 18 | 4th | Sala | Binding wild beasts; Dispelling beasts | Gabriel |
| ♌ | 19 | 5th | Sadadat | Binding beasts; Taming wild beasts | Gaffriel |
| ♍ | 20 | 6th | Tamhut | Freeing captives | Satquiel |
| ♎ | 22 | 7th | Caror | Peace between kings; Hunting and fishing | Samael |
| ♏ | 24 | 8th | Tariel | Discord; Destroying houses and other places | Raphael |
| ♐ | 25 | 9th | Karon | Travel, safe passage among robbers; Traveling without harm | Anael |
| ♑ | 26 | 10th | Hyon | Works with demons or demoniacs, foul wind, aid to ladies; Obtaining one's will with kings and princes | Michael |
| ♒ | 28 | 11th | Nathalon | Causing bleeding in women, binding men to women and vice versa; Concord | Gabriel |
| ♓ | 29 | 12th | Abat | Peace between men and women; Binding tongues | Cafriel |

M13. Angels of the Hours of the Day – from *Codex Latinus Monacensis.*

| | | Hour | Hour Name | Function of Images made in the Hour | Angel |
|---|---|---|---|---|---|
| ♈ | 15 | 1st | Leron | Working with demoniacs, foul winds; Illuminating dark places | Satquiel |
| ♉ | 16 | 2nd | Latol | Working with fish; knowing fortunes | Samael |
| ♊ | 17 | 3rd | Hami | Working with fire; Dispelling reptiles | Raphael |
| ♋ | 18 | 4th | Atyn | Destroying houses, expelling people; Destroying or depopulating villages; Causing enmity | Anael |
| ♌ | 19 | 5th | Caron | Asking questions of sleepers; Scattering armies | Michael |
| ♍ | 20 | 6th | Zaia | Working with fruit trees and other plants; Putting enemies to flight | Gabriel |
| ♎ | 22 | 7th | Nectius | Expelling people; causing sickness and death; Burning vegetation | Cafriel |
| ♏ | 24 | 8th | Tafat | Causing enmity; Gathering bees or birds | Satquiel |
| ♐ | 25 | 9th | Conassuor | Binding tongues; Entering before kinds and lords; Attracting and capturing birds | Samael |
| ♑ | 26 | 10th | Algo | Destroying evil speech or thought; Scattering besieging armies | Raphael |
| ♒ | 28 | 11th | Caltrua | Binding or catching birds; Not to be used for making images | Anael |
| ♓ | 29 | 12th | Salaij | Telling fortunes, disclosing theft or other crime | Michael |

M14. Angels of the Hours of the Night – *from Codex Latinus Monacensis.*

# M. Magic of the Grimoires – Angels, Demons and Spirits

| | | Rank | Metal | Binding Times | Incense | Number of Demons |
|---|---|---|---|---|---|---|
| | | | | M17. Ranks of the Demons of the *Goetia*.[1] | | |
| ☽ | 13 | Marquises | Silver | Ninth hour of day till compline, and compline till the end of the day [night?] (3pm – 9pm and 9pm – Sunrise)[2] | Jasmine | 12 |
| ☿ | 12 | Presidents | Mercury | Any hour of the day if his King is also invoked. But not twilight. | Storax | 12 |
| ♀ | 14 | Dukes | Copper | First hour of the day till noon. Sunrise – Noon (in clear weather) | Sandalwood | 22 |
| ☼ | 30 | King[3] | Gold | Third hour of day till noon and from ninth hour till evening (9am-Noon and 3pm– sunset) | Frankincense | 12 |
| ♂ | 27 | Earls (Counties/Counts) | Copper & Silver[4] | Any hour of the day (in a quiet place) | Dragon's blood | 7 |
| ♃ | 21 | Princes (& Prelates) | Tin | Any hour of the day | Cedar | 6 |
| ♄ | 32 | Knights | Lead | Dawn till sunrise and from Evensong till sunset. (Dawn – Sunrise and 4pm – Sunset) | Myrrh | 1 |
| | | *Total =* | | | | 72 |

---

[1] Note that in this edition Table M17 appears out of order before Table M15 so that the ranks of spirits in M15 are better able to be appreciated.
[2] The clock times are from Sloane MS 3825. It is more accurate to calculate the uneven planetary hours using the 'hour of the day' as drawn from Weirus.
[3] Ruling the 12 Zodiacal Signs.
[4] Instead of iron, which cannot be used with these demons.

*Goetia (Lemegeton I)*

| M15. Demons of the *Goetia* (*Lemegeton* Book I) – 1. | | | | | | |
|---|---|---|---|---|---|---|
| a. Wierus [Rudd 6482] | b. No. in Harley 6483 | c. Demon Name [alt. | d. Hebrew | e. Stead Ridden, Other Qualities | f. GD Decans | g. Ruling Angel Name (Rudd) |
| **♈** | | | | | | |
| 1 [11] | 1 | **Bael**[5] [Baell, Baël] | באל – בעל | Crocodile [Under Lucifer][6] [East] | Day 1♈ | Vehujah והויאה |
| 2 | 2 | Agares Agreas | אגאראש אגאר – | Order of Virtues Under Lucifer [East] | 2♈ | Jeliel יליאל |
| 0 | 3 | Vasago [Vassago] | ושאגו – | | 3♈ | Syrael שיראל |
| 46 [41] | 4 | Gamigin [Samigina, Gamygyn] | גאמיגין גמיגין כמיגין | | 1♉ | Elemiah אלאמיאה |
| 3 | 5 | Marbas [Barbas] | מארבש מארב – | [Under Lucifer] | 2♉ | Mahasaiah מהשיאה |
| 14 [59] | 6 | Valefar Valefor [Malaphar] | ואלפהר ואלפר ולפר | [Under Astaroth] | 3♉ | Jelahel ילאהל |
| **♉** | | | | | | |
| 5 | 7 | Amon [Aamon] | אמון אמון – | [Under Lucifer] | 1♊ | Achasiah אחאיה |
| 6 [12] | 8 | Barbatos | ברבטוש – – | Order of Virtues [Under Lucifer] [♐] | 2♊ | Cahatel כאהטל |
| 22 [55] | 9 | **Paimon** | פאימון פאימן פימון | Dromedary camel Order of Potestates [NW] Under Lucifer[7] | 3♊ | Hasiel האסיאל |
| 7 [22] | 10 | Buer | בואר – | [Under Belzebuth] [Sun in ♐] | 1♋ | Aladiah אלדיאה |
| 8 | 11 | Gusoin [Gusoyn, Gusoin] [Gorson?] | גוסוינ גוסין | [Under Belzebuth] | 2♋ | Laviah לאויאה |
| 21 [58] | 12 | Sitri [Sytry, Bitru] | שיטרי שיטרי שעטיר (?) | | 3♋ | Hahajah האחאיה |

---

[5] Kings are marked in bold. Bael is the major King ruling in the East. Maybe originally Ba'al, the Canaanite Thunder god.
[6] Where rulership is marked in square brackets, it is taken conjecturally from the *Grand Grimoire*. See Column M70.
[7] More accurately, northerly including NW. "More obedient unto Lucifer than other Kings". Attended by Bebal/Labal and Abalam/Abalim, two other Kings. Weir states he is of the Order of Dominations or of Cherubim.

# M. Magic of the Grimoires – Angels, Demons and Spirits

| | | | M15. Demons of the *Goetia* –1 (*continued*). | |
|---|---|---|---|---|
| **h. Rank** | **i. Planet** | **j. No. of Legions** | **k. Evoked Appearance** | **l. Powers & Attributes** |
| King | Sun | 66 | With three heads (toad, man and cat) or with each form separately. | Invisibility. |
| Duke | Venus | 31 | Old Man riding on a Crocodile, carrying a Goshawk on his fist. | Makes people run that stand still; returns Runaways. Teaches all languages, destroys dignities spiritual and temporal, causes earthquakes. |
| Prince | Jupiter | 26 | Good natured. | Declares things Past & Future; Discovers the Hidden & Lost. |
| Marquis | Moon | 30 | Little horse or ass, then as a human with a hoarse voice. | Teaches Liberal Sciences; Giveth Account of Dead causes Souls that died in Sin or drowned to answer questions. |
| President | Mercury | 36 | A mighty lion, human shape. | Reveals any hidden or secret things; Causes & cures diseases; Wisdom; knowledge of Mechanical Arts and handicrafts; Changes Men into other shapes. |
| Duke | Venus | 10 | Lion with man's head (a thief's head). | A good familiar, but he tempts the magician to steal, and may finally bring him to the gallows |
| Marquis | Moon | 40 | Wolf with serpent's tail vomiting fire, like a raven with dog's teeth. | Reveals things past, present and future; procures love; resolves controversies between friends and foes. |
| Duke & Earl | Venus | 300 [30] | Appears when Sun is in Sagittarius accompanied by 4 Kings & their Troops. | Teaches the language of birds, dogs & other creatures; breaks open hidden treasures enchanted by other magicians; Knows things past, present & future; Reconciles Friends with those in power. |
| King,[8] | Sun | 200+25 | Crowned man sitting upon a dromedary camel, with a host of musicians going before him. | Teaches all arts & sciences, the Elements & other secret things; he gives honours; he binds others to be obedient to the magician; gives good familiars. Of Angels & Potestates. Initially difficult to understand. |
| President | Mercury | 50 [40] | Appears when Sun is in Sagittarius. | Teaches Philosophy (moral & natural) & logic & the virtues of herbs and plants; heals illnesses; gives good familiars. |
| Duke | Venus | 40 [45] | Appears in the form of a Xenophilus.[9] | Reveals things past, present & future; answers all questions; reconciles friends; gives honours. |
| Prince | Jupiter | 60 | Leopard's face & Gryphon's wings, then very beautiful human. | Inflames men with woman's love and vice versa; Causes women to be luxurious and to go naked. |

---

[8] Arrives with 2 other Kings, Baball and Abalam.
[9] Maybe a *zenophali*. Not to be confused with the 4th century Pythagorean philosopher Xenophilus.

| | | | M15. Demons of the *Goetia* (*Lemegeton* Book I) – 2. | | | | |
|---|---|---|---|---|---|---|---|
| | **Wierus [Rudd 6482]** | **No. in Harley 6483** | **Demon Name [alt. spellings]** | **Hebrew** | **Stead Ridden, Other Qualities** | **GD Decans** | **Ruling Angel Name (Rudd)** |
| **II** | 20 [25] | 13 | **Beleth** [or Bilet, Byleth, Bileth] [S and E][10] | בלאת — — | Pale horse Order of Potestates | Day 1♌ | Jezalel יזאלאל |
| | 13 | 14 | Leraic [Leraye, Leraje, Leraika, Oray, Leraie][11] | לראיכ לראיך לריך | [Under Astaroth] [♐] | 2♌ | Mebahel מבאהל |
| | 12 | 15 | Eligos [Eligor, Abigor] | אליגוש — | [Under Belzebuth] | 3♌ | Haziel האזיאל |
| | 19 | 16 | Zepar | זאפר זפאר זפר | | 1♍ | Hakamiah האקמיאה |
| | 9 [19] | 17 | Botis [Otis] | בוטיש — | [Under Belzebuth] | 2♍ | Loviah לויאה |
| | 10 [16] | 18 | Bathin [Bathyn, Bathym, Marthim, Mathim] | באתינ באתין — | Pale horse [Under Belzebuth] | 3♍ | Caliel כאליאל |
| **♋** | 64 | 19 | Saleos [Sallos, Zaleos] | שאלוש — שלוש | Crocodile | 1♎ | Leuviah לוויאה[12] |
| | 11 | 20 | **Purson** [Pursan, Curson] | פורשונ פורשן פרשון | Bear [Under Belzebuth] Virtues & Thrones | 2♎ | Pahaliah פהליאה |
| | 15 | 21 | Morax [Marax, Foraii] | מאראם מאראץ מוראץ | [Under Astaroth] | 3♎ | Nelchael נלכאל |
| | 16 | 22 | Ipos [Ipes, Ayperos, Ayporos] | יפוש — — | [Under Astaroth] | 1♏ | Jejael ייאל |
| | 56 | 23 | Aim [Haborym, Haborim] | אים — אימה | | 2♏ | Melahel מלאהל |
| | 17 | 24 | Naberius [Naberus alias Cerberus] | נבריוש נבר — | [Under Astaroth] | 3♏ | Haiviah האיואה |

---

[10] Hoping to return to the 7th Throne.
[11] Or Loray, Lerajé, Leraika, or Leraie.
[12] Compare with number 17 which Rudd gives the same Hebrew spelling. See Column A24 for the correct Hebrew.

# M. Magic of the Grimoires – Angels, Demons and Spirits

| | | | | M15. Demons of the *Goetia* –2 (*continued*). | |
|---|---|---|---|---|---|
| **Rank** | **Planet** | **No. of Legions** | **Evoked Appearance** | **Powers & Attributes** |
| King | Sun | 85 | Rides a pale horse attended by trumpeters and musicians. Initially ill-tempered. | Causes love of man and woman. Of the Order of Powers, hoping to return in time to the 7th Throne. |
| Marquis | Moon | 30 | Archer clad in Green, carrying a bow and quiver. Sagittarius. | Causes wars & battles; putrefies wounds made by arrows. |
| Duke | Venus | 60 | Knight carrying a lance, ensign & serpent. | Discovers hidden things; Knows future things; Knowledge of Wars & how Soldiers will clash; Causes the love of Lords & great people. |
| Duke | Venus | 26 | Armed soldier clad in red. | Causes women to love men; can make women barren. |
| President & Earl[13] | Mercury | 60 | Ugly viper, then human with a great tooth & two horns, carrying a bright sword. | Reveals things past, present & future; Reconciles friends & foes. Understands the virtues of herbs and precious stones. |
| Duke | Venus | 30 | Strong man with serpent's tail, sitting upon a pale horse. | Gives Knowledge of herbs & precious stones; Transports people suddenly from one country to another. |
| Duke & Earl[14] | Venus | 30 | Soldier wearing a Duke's crown, riding a crocodile. | Causes men and women to love one another. |
| King | Sun | 22 | Man with lion's face, carrying a viper, riding on a bear, preceded by trumpeters. | Knows things hidden; Discovers treasure; Reveals the past, present & future; Answers truly things secret or divine; gives good familiars. |
| President & Earl | Mercury & Mars | 3 [30] | Bull with man's face. | Teaches Astronomy & all Liberal Sciences; Gives good wise familiars; Virtues of herbs & stones. |
| Prince & Earl | Jupiter & Mars | 36 | Angel with Lion's head, goose's feet, and a hare's tail. | Knows things past & future; Makes men witty & bold. |
| Duke | Venus | 26 | Man with 3 heads (serpent, man with two stars on forehead, cat), on a viper, with fire. | Set cities, castles and great places on fire; Makes people witty; Gives true answers to private matters. |
| Marquis | Moon | 19 | Black crow [or crane] fluttering round the circle, speaking with a hoarse voice. | Makes men cunning in all arts & sciences, especially rhetoric; Restores lost honours. |

---

[13] Under an Earl. Named as a Duke in Harley MS 6482 but this may be an error.
[14] Listed as an Earl in Weir.

| | | | M15. Demons of the *Goetia* (*Lemegeton* Book I) – 3. | | | |
|---|---|---|---|---|---|---|
| | **Wierus [Rudd 6482]** | **No. in Harley 6483** | **Demon Name [alt. spellings]** | **Hebrew** | **Stead Ridden, Other** | **GD Decans** | **Ruling Angel Name (Rudd)** |
| ♌ | 18 [40] | 25 | Glasya-La Bolas [Glasialabolas, Glacia La bolas][15] | גלאסיא לבולש<br>גלאם לבול<br>גלאס לבול | [Under Astaroth] | Day 1♐ | Nithhajah<br>ניתהיאה |
| | 24 [23] | 26 | Bune [Bimé, Bime, Bimé, Bim] | בימ<br>בים<br>— | | 2♐ | Haajah<br>האיאה |
| | 26 | 27 | Ronove [Roneve, Ronové] | רונוו<br>רינוו | | 3♐ | Jerathel<br>ירתאל |
| | 27 [21] | 28 | Berith [Beal, Beall, Beale, Berithi, Bolfry] | ברית<br>—<br>— | Red horse | 1♑ | Seechiah<br>שאחאה |
| | 28 [4] | 29 | **Astaroth** | אשטארות<br>אשתרות<br>עשתרת | Dragon | 2♑ | Reiajel<br>ריאיל (sic) |
| | 25 | 30 | Forneus [Forners] | פהורנארש<br>פורנאש<br>פרנאש | Order of Thrones and of Angels | 3♑ | Omael<br>ומאל |
| ♍ | 29 | 31 | Foras [Forras, Forcas] | פוראש<br>—<br>פראש | | 1♒ | Lectabal.<br>לאכתבל |
| | 35 [3] | 32 | **Asmoday** [Asmodai, Sydonay, Sidonay][East][16] | אסמודי<br>אסמודאי<br>אשמודאי | Under Amaymon | 2♒ | Vasariah<br>ואשריאה |
| | 36 [38] | 33 | **Gaap** [Gäap alias Tap] [Goap?][17] | גאאפ<br>געף<br>— | Under Amaymon. Order of Potestates | 3♒ | Jehujah<br>חויאה |
| | 30 | 34 | Furfur [Furtur] | פהור פהור<br>פורפור<br>— | | 1♓ | Lehahiah<br>לאההאה |
| | 31 [46] | 35 | Marchosias [Marchocias][18] | מרחושיאש<br>מרחוש | Order of Dominations | 2♓ | Chajakiah<br>חאיאקיאה |
| | 68 | 36 | Stolas [Stolus, Stolos] | שטולוש<br>שטוליש<br>צולם | | 3♓ | Manadel<br>מאנאדל |

---

[15] Alias Caacrinolaas or Caassimolar.

[16] See *Tobit* 3:8 and Column M1 (line 4) and Column M27 for more details.

[17] He "appeareth in a meridionall [southern] signe", i.e. a southerly Sign e.g. Libra, but also Libra through Pisces. Maybe a form of Goap, King of the South.

[18] He hopes, after 1200 years, to return to the 7th Throne.

| | | | M15. Demons of the *Goetia* –3 (*continued*). | |
|---|---|---|---|---|
| **Rank** | **Planet** | **No. of Legions** | **Evoked Appearance** | **Powers & Attributes** |
| President | Mercury | 36 | Dog with gryphon's wings. | Teaches all arts & sciences instantly; Bloodshed & manslaughter; Teaches all things, present & future; Causes love of friends & foes; Makes a man invisible. |
| Duke | Venus | 30 | Dragon with 3 heads (dog, gryphon, & man) speaking with a high-pitched voice. | Changes the places of the dead; Causes his spirits to gather on the sepulchers of the dead; Gives riches, wisdom & eloquence; Answers demands truly. |
| Marquis & Earl | Moon | 19 | Monster. | Teaches rhetoric and languages; Gives favour with friends or foes. |
| Duke | Venus | 26 | Soldier wearing red, riding a red horse, wearing a gold crown. | Reveals things past, present & future truely; Transmutes all metals to gold; gives honours and confirms them, but is a great liar, and not to be trusted. |
| Duke [& King][19] | Venus | 40 | Beautiful angel riding an infernal Dragon, carrying a viper, with dangerous and foul breath. | Gives true answers; Reveals things past, present & future and all secrets; Reveals how the angels fell; Gives knowledge of all Liberal Sciences. |
| Marquis | Moon | 29 | Great sea monster. | Teaches rhetoric; Causes men to have a good reputation; Teaches languages; Makes them loved by their foes and friends. |
| President | Mercury | 29 | Strong man. | Gives Knowledge of Herbs & Stones; Teaches Logic & Ethics; Makes Men Invisible & Long-lived & Eloquent. |
| King[20] | Sun | 72 | Man with 3 heads (bull, man, & ram), serpent's tail , goose's feet, on a dragon, with lance & flag. | Reveals the virtues of all herbs and stones; Teaches arithmetic, geometry, astronomy; Makes men invisible, witty, eloquent and long-lived; Finds things lost or hidden treasures. |
| President & Prince | Mercury & Jupiter | 66 | Man leading 4 mighty kings. Appears in the form of a doctor when he takes on human form. | Makes men knowledgeable in philosophy and all Liberal Sciences; Love & hatred; Delivers Familiars from other Magicians; Reveals things past, present & future; transports between Kingdoms. |
| Earl | Mars | 26 | Hart with Fiery tail. The form of an angel if in the Triangle. | Never speaks truly unless in the Triangle; Causes lightning & thunder; Answers things secret & divine. |
| Marquis | Moon | 30 | She-wolf with gryphon's wings & serpent's tail, breathing fire. Afterwards as a man. | Gives true answers to all questions & is very faithful to the Exorcist in doing his business. He is an excellent fighter. Was of Order of Dominations, hopes to return to heaven after 1200 years. |
| Prince | Jupiter | 26 | Raven, then in the form of a man. | Teaches astronomy; Gives knowledge of herbs & precious stones. |

---

[19] Should probably also be a King on the basis of his titles in other grimoires.
[20] Chief under Amaymon (East/Air).

| | | M15. Demons of the *Goetia* (*Lemegeton* Book I) – 4. | | | | |
|---|---|---|---|---|---|---|
| | **Wierus [Rudd 6482]** | **No. in Harley 6483** | **Demon Name [alt. spellings]** | **Hebrew** | **Stead Ridden, Other Qualities** | **GD Decans** | **Ruling Angel Name** |
| ♎ | 67 | 37 | Phenix [Phoenix, Phenex, Pheynix][21] | פאניס פאניך פניך | | **Night** 1♈ | Aniel אניאל |
| | 42 | 38 | Halphas [Malthas, Malthus or Malthous] | מאלתש האלף — | | 2♈ | Hamiah האמיאה |
| | 32 | 39 | Malphas[22] | מאלפש מאלף — | | 3♈ | Rehael רהאל |
| | 41 | 40 | Raum [Räum, Raim, Raym] | ראום רעם | Order of Thrones | 1♉ | Jejazel ייאזל |
| | 43 [36] | 41 | Focalor [Forcalor or Furcalor][23] | פהורכלור פוכלור — | | 2♉ | Hahahel הההל |
| | 33 | 42 | Vepar [Vephar, Separ] | ופאר — ופר | | 3♉ | Michael מיכאל |
| ♏ | 34 | 43 | Sabnock [Savnok, Sabnack, Sabnach, Sabnac, Salmac] | שבנוכ שבנוך — | Pale horse | 1♊ | Vevaliah וויליאה |
| | 37 | 44 | Shax [Shaz, Shass, Shan, Chax, Scox] | שאז שין — | | 2♊ | Jelahiah ילאהיה |
| | 44 | 45 | **Vine**[24] [Viné or Vinea] | וינא — | Black horse | 3♊ | Sealiah סאליאה |
| | 45 [18] | 46 | Bifrons [Bifrous, Bifrovs, Bifroüs] | ביפרונש ביפרו — | | 1♋ | Ariel אריאל |
| | 65 [61] | 47 | Vual [Uvall, Vuall, Voval] | ואל אואל ול | Order of Potestes | 2♋ | Alaliah אלאליאה |
| | 66 | 48 | Haagenti | האגנטי העגנת — | | 3♋ | Mihael מיחיאל |

---

[21] He hopes, after 1200 years, to return to the 7th Throne.
[22] The description is confused in the MS with the previous demon, Halphas.
[23] Hopes to return, after 1000 years, to the 7th Throne.
[24] Special numeration of 80.

| | | | M15. Demons of the *Goetia* – 4 (*continued*). | |
|---|---|---|---|---|
| **Rank** | **Planet** | **No. of Legions** | **Evoked Appearance** | **Powers & Attributes** |
| Marquis | Moon | 20 | Like a phoenix with a child's voice, then after as a man. | Speaks marvellously of all wonderful sciences; He hopes to return to the 7th Throne after 1200 years. |
| Earl | Mars | 26 | Stork dove, speaking with a hoarse voice. | Builds towers and furnishes them with ammunition & weapons; Sends warriors to their appointed places. |
| President | Mercury | 40 | Crow, then as a man speaking with a hoarse voice. | Builds houses & high towers; Brings craftsmen from all parts of the world; Gives good familiars; Imparts knowledge of enemy's desires & thoughts. |
| Earl | Mars | 30 | Crow, then as a man. | Steals treasures from king's houses; Destroys cities & honours of men; Reveals things past, present & future; Causes love between friends & foes. |
| Duke | Venus | 3 [30] | Man with gryphon's wings. | Kills & drowns men; Overturns ships of war; Power over seas and winds. |
| Duke | Venus | 29 | Mermaid. | Governs waters; Guides ships laden with armour & Munitions; Causes storms at sea [& Imaginary Fleets]; Kills men by causing worms to breed in them. |
| Marquis | Moon | 50 | Armed soldier with lion's head, riding a pale horse. | Builds high towers, castles & cities and furnish them with armour; Afflicts men with worms: Gives good familiars. |
| Marquis & Duke[25] | Moon | 30 | Stork dove, speaking with a hoarse and subtle voice. | Removes sight, hearing or understanding of any man or woman; Steals money out of king's houses; Fetches horses or any other thing; Discovers hidden things; Gives good familiars. Deceptive if not in the Triangle. |
| King & Earl | Sun & Mars | 36 | Lion [or man with lion's head] riding a black horse, carrying a viper. | Discovers things hidden, witches, and things past, present & future; Builds towers; Overthrows strong walls; Causes storms at sea. |
| Earl | Mars | 6 [60] [26] | Monster, but after as a man. | Knowledge of astrology & geometry & other arts & sciences; Teaches the virtues of stones & woods; Changes dead bodies, conveys them elsewhere, & lights [candles] upon their graves. |
| Duke | Venus | 37 | Dromedary but after as a man speaking imperfect Egyptian in a base voice. | Procures the special love of women; Reveals things past, present & future; Procures friendship between friends & foes. Was of the Order of Potestates. |
| President | Mercury | 33 | Bull with gryphon's wings, and after as a man. | Instructs men in many things; Transmutes all metals into gold; Changes wine to water and back again. |

---

[25] See the Latin of Weir.

| | | | | | | |
|---|---|---|---|---|---|---|
| | | | M15. Demons of the *Goetia* (*Lemegeton* Book I) – 5. | | | |

| | Wierus [Rudd 6482] | No. in Harley 6483 | Demon Name [alt. spellings] | Hebrew | Stead Ridden, Other Qualities | GD Decans | Ruling Angel Name (Rudd) |
|---|---|---|---|---|---|---|---|
| | 38 | 49 | Crocell [Crokel, Procel, Procell, Crokel] | כרוכל — | Order of Potestes | **Night** 1♌ | Vehuel והואל |
| | 38 bis[26] [37] | 50 | Furcas | פהורכש פורך | Pale horse[27] | 2♌ | Daniel דניאל |
| ♐ | 62 [17] | 51 | **Balam**[28] [Balaam] | באלאם בעלם בלעם | Bear Order of Dominations | 3♌ | Hahasiah חהשיאה |
| | 63 | 52 | Alloces [or Alocas, Allocer, Alocer, Alocas] | אלוכאם אלוך — | Gryphon | 1♍ | Imamiah ימאמיאה |
| | 40 [24] | 53 | Caim [Caym, Camio] | כאמיו כאין | Order of Angels | 2♍ | Nanael נאנאל |
| | 39 [52] | 54 | Murmur [Murmus, Murmux] | מורמוס מורם מערם | Gryphon Order of Thrones and Angels | 3♍ | Nithael ניתאל |
| | 57 | 55 | Orobas | ורובש אוראוב ערבם | | 1♎ | Nanael ננאל |
| | 50 [39] | 56 | Gemory [Gremory, Gamori, Gomory] | גמורי גמור — | Camel | 2♎ | Polial פוליאל |
| ♑ | 55 [54] | 57 | Ose [Oso, Osó, Oze, Voso] | ושז ושו — | | ♎3 | Nemamiah נמאמיאה |
| | 60 | 58 | Auns [Amy, Avnas] | אונש און — | Order of Angels and Potestates | 1♏ | Jejalel יאיאלאל |
| | 48 | 59 | Orias [Oriax][29] | וריאם וריאץ | Horse | 2♏ | Hazahel האזאהאל |
| | 58 | 60 | Napula [Nappula, Vapula, Naphula] | נפולא נפול נפל | | ♏3 | Mizrael מיזראל |

---

[26] Procell and Furcas are both numbered 38 in the *Pseudomonarchia Daemonum* as listed in Peterson's Appendix 2.
[27] Therefore possibly originally a Duke or Earl, with 'knight' being a description rather than a title.
[28] Was a Canaanite sorcerer.
[29] Maybe related to Ornias, the first demon in Column M1.

| Rank | Planet | No. of Legions | Evoked Appearance | Powers & Attributes |
|------|--------|----------------|-------------------|---------------------|
| | | | M15. Demons of the *Goetia* –5 (*continued*). | |
| Duke | Venus | 48 | Like an angel. | Speaks mystically of hidden things; Teaches geometry & liberal sciences; Makes the sound of running waters; Warms waters & baths. |
| Knight[30] | Saturn | 20 | Cruel old man with long beard & hoary head, riding a pale horse, carrying a sharp weapon. | Teaches practical philosophy, astrology, rhetoric, logic, chiromancy & pyromancy. |
| King | Sun | 40 | Man with 3 heads (bull, man, & ram), serpent's tail, flaming eyes, on a bear, with a goshawk. | Reveals true answers to things past, present & future; Makes men invisible & witty. Has a hoarse voice. |
| Duke | Venus | 36 [30] | Soldier riding a gryphon, wearing a Duke's crown, preceded by trumpeters. [see 54] | Teaches philosophy; Compels deceased souls to come before the magician to answer him.[see 54] |
| President | Mercury | 30 | A thrush, and afterwards a man carrying a sharp sword. | Teaches the language of birds, bullocks, dogs and other animals; Reveals truly future things. Answers in burning ashes. Was of the Order of Potestates. |
| Duke & Earl | Venus & Mars | 30 | Soldier riding a gryphon, wearing a Duke's crown, preceded by ministers with trumpets. | Teaches philosophy; Compels deceased souls to come before the magician to answer him. Was of the Order of Thrones and Angels. |
| Prince | Jupiter | 26 | Horse, then as a man. | Discovers things past, present & future; Gives honours & Prelacies, the favour of friends & foes; Gives true answers to divinity questions; Faithful to the magician. |
| Duke | Venus | 26 | Beautiful woman riding a camel, with a Duchess's crown around her waist. | Reveals things past, present & future & hidden treasures; Procures the love of women. |
| President | Mercury | 3 [30] | Leopard, afterwards pretending to be a man. | Makes men cunning in liberal sciences; Gives true answers to divinity & secret things; Changes a Man into any shape, and for an hour makes that man think that he is really that thing. |
| President | Mercury | 36 | Flaming fire, but after as a man. | Teaches astrology & all liberal sciences; Gives good familiars; Obtains treasures kept by spirits. |
| Marquis | Moon | 30 | Lion with serpent's tail riding a horse, holding 2 serpents in his right hand. | Teaches the virtues of the stars & mansions & virtues of planets; Transformation; Gives honours & prelacies, and the favour of friends & foes. |
| Duke & President | Venus & Mercury | 36 | Lion with gryphon's wings. | Teaches handicrafts, professions, philosophy & other sciences. |

[30] The only Knight amongst the whole 72 demons.

| | | | M15. Demons of the *Goetia* (*Lemegeton* Book I) – 6. | | | | |
|---|---|---|---|---|---|---|---|
| | **Wierus [Rudd 6482]** | **No. in Harley 6483** | **Demon Name [alt. spellings]** | **Hebrew** | **Stead Ridden, Other Qualities** | **GD Decans** | **Ruling Angel Name (Rudd)** |
| ♒ | 47 | 61 | **Zagan** [Zagam] | זאגאנ זאגן זגן | | **Night** 1♐ | Umabel ומבאל |
| | 49 [60] | 62 | Valac [Valu, Volac, Valak, Valac, Ualac] | ואלו ואל ולו | Two-headed dragon | ♐2 | Jahhael יהחאאל |
| | 53 | 63 | Andras | אנדראש אנדר אנדראש | Black wolf | 3♐ | Anavel אנאואל |
| | 61 | 64 | Flauros [Haures,Hauras, Hauros,Havres] | חאוראש חאור פלֿעֿר | | 1♑ | Mehiel מאהיאל |
| | 54 | 65 | Andrealphus [Androalphus] | אנדראלפחוש אנדראלף — | | ♑2 | Damabiah דמאביאה |
| | 59 [26] | 66 | Cimeries [Cimejes, Cimeies, Kimaris] | כימאריש כימאור כימער | Black horse | 3♑ | Marakel מאראקאל |
| ♓ | 52 | 67 | Amduscias [Amducias, Amdusias, Amdukias] | אמדוכיאש אמדוך — | Order of Virtues and Angels | 1♒ | Eiael איאל |
| | 23 [20] | 68 | **Belial**[31] | בליאל בליאל בליֿעל | Chariot Order of Vertues and Angels | 2♒ | Habujah חבויאה |
| | 51 | 69 | **Decarabi**a [Carabia] | דכארביא דכאוראב דכארביא | | 3♒ | Roehel רואהל |
| | 0 [20] | 70 | Seer [Seare, Seere, Sear, Seir] | שאר — — | Winged horse. Under Amaymon, King of the East | 1♓ | Tabamiah טבמיאה |
| | 0 | 71 | Dantalion [Dantaylion] | ראנטאליונ רנתאל רנתאליון | | 2♓ | Hajajel האיאיאל |
| | 0 | 72 | Andromalius | אנדרומליוש אנדרומאל — | | 3♓ | Mumiah מומייאה |
| | 4 | 0 | *Pruflas/Bufas*[32] | | *[Under Lucifer] Order of Thrones & Angels* | | — |

[31] One of the highest ranking Kings.
[32] Or Purflas. Only appears in Weir. Omitted from Scot's list and all the manuscript versions of the *Goetia*.

# M. Magic of the Grimoires – Angels, Demons and Spirits

| | | | M15. Demons of the *Goetia* – 6 (*continued*). | |
|---|---|---|---|---|
| **Rank** | **Planet** | **No. of Legions** | **Evoked Appearance** | **Powers & Attributes** |
| King & President | Sun & Mercury | 36 | Bull with gryphon's wings, and after a man. | Makes men witty; Turns Wine to Water and back again, and blood into wine; Transmutes all metals into coin of the realm; Makes fools wise. |
| President | Mercury | 30 | Boy with angel's wings, riding a 2-headed dragon. | Reveals Hidden Treasures truly & locations of serpents, which he will bring to the magician without compulsion. |
| Marquis | Moon | 30 | Angel with raven's head, riding a black wolf, flourishing a bright & sharp sword. | Sow discord; he may try to kill the magician and his assistants. |
| Duke | Venus | 3 [36] | Leopard, and after a man with fiery eyes and a terrible face. | Reveals things past, present & future, but lies if not in the Triangle; Teaches divinity & how the spirits fell; Destroys and burns enemies. |
| Marquis | Moon | 30 | Noisy peacock, but after as a human. | Teaches geometry, measurement & astronomy; Can transform a man into a bird. |
| Marquis | Moon | 20 | Soldier riding a black horse. | Rules over spirits in Africa; Teaches grammar, logic & rhetoric; Discovers treasures lost or hidden; Can make a man seem like a soldier. Rules parts of Africa. |
| Duke | Venus | 29 | Unicorn, and after as a man. | Causes musical instruments to be heard & trees to bend; Gives excellent familiars. |
| King, [33] | Sun | [more than] 80 [50, 30] | A beautiful angel sitting in a fiery chariot. | Distributes preferments of senatorship; Causes favour of friends & foes; Gives excellent familiars. But he must have offerings. |
| Marquis, King & Earl[34] | Moon | 30 | Star inside a Pentacle, but afterwards as a man. | Discovers the virtues of birds & precious stones; Creates the Illusion of tame birds singing and flying. |
| Prince | Jupiter | 26 | Beautiful man riding a winged horse. | Comes & goes; Brings things to pass suddenly; Carries things to & fro across the whole Earth instantly; Reveals Thefts & Hidden Treasures; Good natured. |
| Duke | Venus | 36 | Man with many faces (both men's and women's), carrying a book in his right hand. | Teaches all arts & sciences to anyone; Causes Love; Shows the true similitude of anyone wherever they are; [Declares secret counsels; Changes the thoughts of men & women?] |
| Earl | Mars | 36 | Man holding a serpent. | Returns thieves & stolen goods; Discovers wickedness & underhand dealings; Punishes thieves & wicked people; Discovers hidden treasures. |
| *Prince & Duke* | *Jupiter & Mars* | *26* | *The head of a night hawk.* | *Discord, war, quarrels, falsehood. Lives around the Tower of Babylon.* |

---

[33] He claims to have been created next after Lucifer
[34] Said to be a King and Earl in the Latin text of Weir, not found in Scot or any other version.

# M. Magic of the Grimoires – Angels, Demons and Spirits

M16. Powers and Specialties of the Demons of the *Goetia*.

| Speciality/Power | Demon |
|---|---|
| Alchemy | 28-Berith, 48-Haagenti, 61-Zagan |
| Animals | 24-Naberius, 53-Camio, 62-Valu, 69-Decarabia |
| Archery | 14-Leriac |
| Arithmetic | 32-Asmodai |
| Astrology | 21-Marax, 46-Bifrons, 50-Furcas, 58-Auns, 59-Orias |
| Astronomy | 21-Marax, 32-Asmodai, 36-Stolus, 50-Furcas, 59-Orias, 65-Andrealphus |
| Bravery | 17-Botis, 22-Ipos, 35-Marchosias |
| Builds Towers | 38-Malthas, 39-Malphas, 43-Sabnock, 45-Vine |
| Charisma, Wit, Humor | 22-Ipos, 23-Aim, 31-Foras, 51-Balam, 61-Zagan |
| Chiromancy or Palmistry | 50-Furcas |
| Demotion, Destruction of Honours | 2-Agares, 40-Raum |
| Destruction by Fire | 23-Aim |
| Destruction of Enemies | 40-Raum, 39-Malphas, 44-Shax, 45-Vine, 64-Haures |
| Divination | 3-Vassago, 7-Amon, 8-Barbatos, 11-Gusion, 15-Eligos, 17-Botis, 20-Purson, 22-Ipos, 25-Glasya-LaBolas, 26-Bime, 28-Berith, 29-Astaroth, 33-Gaap, 40-Raum, 45-Vine, 47-Vuall, 51-Balam, 55-Orobas, 56-Gemory, 64-Haures |
| Drowning | 41-Focalor, 42-Vepar |
| Earthquakes | 2-Agares |
| Ethics | 31-Foras |
| Familiar Spirits | 9-Paimon, 10-Buer, 20-Purson, 21-Marax, 33-Gaap, 39-Malphas, 43-Sabnock, 44-Shax, 52-Alloces, 58-Auns, 67-Amducias, 68-Belial |
| Flying | 18-Bathin, 33- Gaap |
| Friendships | 7-Amon, 8-Barbatos, 11-Gusion, 17-Botis, 25-Glasya-La Bolas, 27-Ronove, 30-Forners, 40-Raum, 47-Vuall, 55-Orobas, 59-Orias, 68-Belial |
| Geometry | 32-Asmodai, 46-Bifrons, 49-Crocell, 65-Andrealphus |
| Grammar | 66-Cimeries |
| Health & Healing | 5-Marbas, 10-Buer |
| Health, Ill-health | 14-Leraic, 43-Sabnock, 44-Shax |
| Herbs, Virtues of | 10-Buer, 17-Botis, 18-Bathin, 21-Marax, 31-Foras, 32-Asmodai, 36-Stolus, 46-Bifrons, 69-Decarabia |
| Honors, Promotions & Preferment | 9-Paimon, 11-Gusion, 15-Eligos, 24-Naberius, 28-Berith, 30-Forners, 55-Orobas, 59-Orias, 68-Belial |
| Immobility | 2-Agares, 31-Foras, 32-Asmodai |
| Infertility | 16-Zepar |
| Invisibility | 1-Bael, 25-Glasya-La Bolas, 31-Foras, 32-Asmodai, 51-Balam |
| Languages | 2-Agares, 8-Barbatos, 27-Ronove, 30-Forners, 53-Camio |
| Liberal Arts & Sciences | 4-Gamigin, 9-Paimon, 21-Marax, 24-Naberius, 25-Glasya-La Bolas, 29-Astaroth, 32-Asmodai, 33-Gaap, 37-Phenix, 46-Bifrons, 48-Haagenti, 49-Crocell, 57-Oso, 58-Auns, 60-Napula, 71-Dantaylion |
| Logic | 10-Buer, 31-Foras, 50-Furcas, 66-Cineries |

# M. Magic of the Grimoires – Angels, Demons and Spirits

M16. Powers and Specialties of the Demons of the *Goetia*.

| Speciality/Power | Demon |
|---|---|
| Longevity | 31-Foras, 32-Asmodai |
| Love | 7-Amon, 12-Sitri 13-Beleth, 14-Leraic, 15-Eligos, 16-Zepar, 19-Sallos, 32-Asmoday, 33-Gaap, 34-Furfur, 40-Raum, 47-Vuall, 56-Gemory, 71-Dantaylion, |
| Manslaughter | 25-Glasya-La Bolas, 41-Focalor, 42-Vepar, 64-Haures |
| Mechanical Arts & Handicrafts | 5-Marbas, 60-Napula |
| Mind Control | 71-Dantaylion |
| Money (see also Treasure) | 26-Bime |
| Music | 67-Amducias |
| Necromancy | 4-Gamigin, 24-Naberius, 26-Bime, 46-Bifrons, 52-Alloces, 54-Murmus, 58-Auns |
| Philosophy | 10-Buer, 33-Gaap, 50-Furcas, 52-Alloces, 54-Murmus, 60-Napula |
| Poetry | 37-Phenix |
| Pyromancy | 50-Furcas |
| Questions answered truthfully | 3-Vassago, 11-Gusion, 20-Purson, 23-Aim, 26-Bime, 29-Astaroth, 32-Asmodai, 34-Furfur, 35-Marchosias, 55-Orobas, 57-Oso |
| Rearranging graveyards | 26-Bime, 46-Bifrons |
| Retrieving things lost or stolen | 3-Vassago, 15-Eligos, 31-Foras, 32-Asmodai, 40-Raum, 44-Shax, 45-Vine, 70-Seer, 72-Andromalius |
| Returns runaways | 2-Agares |
| Rhetoric and Eloquence | 24-Naberius, 26-Bime, 27-Ronove, 30-Forners, 31-Foras, 32-Asmodai, 50-Furcas, 51-Balam, 66-Cineries |
| Secrets revealed | 5-Marbas, 15-Eligos, 20-Purson, 29-Astaroth, 34-Furfur, 57-Oso, 71-Dantaylion |
| Shipping | 41-Focalor, 42-Vepar |
| Stones, Virtues of | 17-Botis, 18-Bathin, 21-Marax, 24-Naberius, 31-Foras, 32-Asmodai, 36-Stolus, 46-Bifrons, 69-Decarabia |
| Teleportation | 18-Bathin, 33-Gaap, 39-Malphas, 70-Seer |
| Theology & Divinity | 20-Purson, 29-Astaroth, 34-Furfur, 55-Orobas, 57-Oso, 64-Haures |
| Things Past, Present & Future declared | 3-Vassago, 7-Amon, 8-Barbatos, 11-Gusion, 15-Eligos, 17-Botis, 20-Purson, 22-Ipos, 25-Glasya-La Bolas, 26-Bime, 28-Berith, 29-Astaroth, 33-Gaap, 40-Raum, 45-Vine, 47-Vuall, 51-Balam, 55-Orobas, 56-Gemory, 64-Haures |
| Transformations, Shape Shifting | 5-Marbas, 16-Zepar, 57-Oso, 59-Orias, 65-Andrealphus |
| Treasure Finding | 8-Barbatos, 20-Purson, 31-Foras, 32-Asmodai, 40-Raum, 44-Shax, 56-Gemory, 58-Auns, 62-Valu, 66-Cineries, 70-Seer, 72-Andromalius |
| War, Military & Death | 14-Leraic, 15-Eligos, 25-Glasya-La Bolas, 35-Marchosias, 38-Malthas, 39-Malphas, 41-Focalor, 43-Sabnock, 66-Cineries |
| Water into Wine | 48-Haagenti, 61-Zagan |
| Water, Controls | 45-Vine, 49-Crocell |
| Weather (Thunder, Lightning, Winds) | 34-Furfur, 41-Focalor, 42-Vepar, 45-Vine |
| Wisdom | 1-Bael, 5-Marbas, 6-Valefor, 25-Glasya-La Bolas, 26-Bime, 29-Astaroth, 48-Haagenti, 49-Crocell, 61-Zagan |

M18. Demons of the *Goetia* by Rank, Planet and Zodiacal Sign.[35]

| Rank | | Marquises | Presidents | Dukes | Kings | Earls (& Counts) | Princes (& Prelates) | Knights |
|---|---|---|---|---|---|---|---|---|
| | | per Sign | per Sign | 2 per Sign | per Sign | Per Planet | Planets exhalted in | |
| Planet > | | *Moon* ☾ | *Mercury* ☿ | *Venus* ♀ | *Sun* ☼ | *Mars* ♂ | *Jupiter* ♃ | *Saturn* ♄ |
| ♈ | 15 | 4-Gamigin | 5-Marbas | *2-Agares*[36]<br>6-Valefar | **1-Bael** | | 3-Vassago (☼) | |
| ♉ | 16 | 7-Amon | 10-Buer | *8-Barbatos*<br>*11-Gusion* | **9-Paimon** | (8-Barbatos)[37] | 12-Sitri (☾) | |
| ♊ | 17 | 14-Leraic | 17-Botis | 15-Eligos<br>16-Zepar<br>18-Bathin | **13-Beleth** | (17-Botis) | | |
| ♋ | 18 | 24-Naberius | 21-Marax | 19-Sallos<br>*23-Aim* | **20-Purson** | (19-Sallos)<br>(21-Marax)<br>(22-Ipos) | 22-Ipos (♃) | |
| ♌ | 19 | (27-Ronove)<br>30-Forneus | 25-Glasya-la Bolas | 26-Bime<br>*28-Berith*<br>(29-Astaroth) | **29-Astaroth**[38] | 27-Ronove | | |
| ♍ | 20 | 35-Marchosias | 31-Foras<br>(33-Gaap) | | **32-Asmoday** | 34-Furfur | (33-Gaap)<br>36-Stolas (☿) | |
| ♎ | 22 | 37-Phenex | 39-Malphas | 41-Focalor<br>42-Vepar | **33-Gaap**[39] | 38-Halphas<br>40-Raum | | |
| ♏ | 24 | 43-Sabnock<br>(44-Shax) | 48-Haagenti | 44-Shax<br>47-Vuall | **45-Vine** | (45-Vine)<br>46-Bifrons | | |
| ♐ | 25 | | 53-Camio | 49-Crocell<br>*52-Alloces*<br>54-Murmus | **51-Balam** | (54-Murmus) | 50-Furcas | (50-Furcas)[40] |
| ♑ | 26 | 59-Orias | 57-Ose<br>58-Auns<br>(60-Napula) | 56-Gemory<br>60-Napula | **69-Decarabia**[41] | | 55-Orobas (♂) | |
| ♒ | 28 | 63-Andras<br>65-Andrealphus<br>66-Cimeries | (61-Zagan)<br>62-Volac | 64-Haures | **61-Zagan** | | | |
| ♓ | 29 | (69-Decarabia) | | *67-Amducias*<br>71-Dantalion | **68-Belial** | 72-Andromalius<br>(69-Decarabia) | 70-Seer (♀) | |
| *Total*[42] *= 72* | | **12** | **12** | **22** | **12** | **7** | **7** | |

[35] Note that in this edition Table M17 appears out of order before Table M15.

[36] Italics indicates a Grand Duke, this title being drawn from other souces. In the *Goetia* he is simply listed as a Duke.

[37] Round brackets indicate a duplicated rank as originally found in the *Goetia*, with the demon thus appearing in two columns. The bracketed occurrence is the one I have chosen to ignore when it comes to totalling the demons in each column, to avoid double counting. The choice of which rank to ignore has been modified slightly since the First Edition.

[38] Astaroth has been given the additional title of King because he often has this rank in other sources. The three underlined Kings are all tentative placements.

[39] Gäap has many attributes with King-like qualities, in fact he guides "4 greate & mighty kings", so here he has tentatively been given the additional title of King.

[40] In Weir, Furcas is simply described as a *miles* or soldier which perhaps should *not* have been translated as 'knight'. If this is only a description not a title, then it is conceivable that Furcas might have been a higher rank or even a Duke, all of whom ride a horse or other mount, as does Furcas.

[41] Decarabia is usually listed as a Marquise. Only the Latin text of Weir shows him clearly as a King and Earl, something which is inexplicably left out of the translation in Scot. You might expect him to be the King in Pisces, but as this position was already occupied by Belial, I have tentatively moved him up two places to the only remaining slot, as King in Capricorn. Very interestingly, these two, Gäap and Decarabia, are directly opposite each other (if the 72 demons are laid out in a circlar fashion), and immediately adjacent to two other Kings, Asmoday and Belial respectively.

[42] The total in this row excludes the duplications in round brackets, which are not counted to avoid duplication.

| Legions | Marquises | Presidents | Dukes | Kings | Earls (& Counts) | Princes (& Prelates) | Knights |
|---|---|---|---|---|---|---|---|
| | | | M19. Demons of the *Goetia* by Title, Planet and Legion Numbers. | | | | |
| **Planet >** | *Moon* ☽ | *Mercury* ☿ | *Venus* ♀ | *Sun* ☉ | *Mars* ♂ | *Jupiter* ♃ | *Saturn* ♄ |
| 200 | | | | **9 – Paimon** | | | |
| 85 | | | | **13 – Beleth** | | | |
| 72 | | | | **32 – Asmoday** | | | |
| 66 | | | | **1 – Bael**<br>**33 – Gäap** | | | |
| 60 | | 17 – Botis | 15 – Eligos | | | 12 – Sitri | |
| 50 | 43 – Sabnock | 10 – Buer | | **68 – Belial** | | | |
| 48 | | | 49 – Crocell | | | | |
| 40 | 7 – Amon | 39 – Malphas | 11 – Gusoin | **51 – Balam**<br>**29 – Astaroth** | | | |
| 37 | | | 47 – Vuall | | | | |
| 36 | | 5 – Marbas<br>25 – Glasya La Bolas<br>58 – Auns | 52 – Alloces<br>60 – Napula<br>64 – Haures<br>71 – Dantalion | **45 – Vine** | 72 – Andromalius | 22 – Ipos | |
| 33 | | 48 – Haagenti | | **61 – Zagan** | | | |
| 31 | | | 2 – Agares | | | | |
| 30 | 4 – Gamigin<br>14 – Leraic<br>35 – Marchosias<br>59 – Orias<br>63 – Andras<br>65 – Andrealphus | 21 – Marax<br>53 – Camio<br>57 – Ose<br>62 – Volac | 8 – Barbatos<br>18 – Bathin<br>19 – Sallos<br>26 – Bime<br>41 – Focalor<br>44 – Shax<br>54 – Murmus | **69 – Decarabia** | 40 – Raum | | |
| 29 | 30 – Forneus | 31 – Foras | 42 – Vepar<br>67 – Amducias | | | | |
| 26 | | | 16 – Zepar<br>23 – Aim<br>28 – Berith<br>56 – Gemory | | 34 – Furfur<br>38 – Halphas<br>46 – Bifrons | 3 – Vassago<br>36 – Stolas<br>70 – Seer | |
| 22 | | | | **20 – Purson** | | | |
| 20 | 37 – Phenex<br>66 – Cimeries | | | | | 55 – Orobos | 50 – Furcas |
| 19 | 24 – Naberius | | | | 27 – Ronove | | |
| 10 | | | 6 – Valefar | | | | |
| **Totals = 72** | **12** | **12** | **23** | **12** | **6** | **6** | **1** |

# M. Magic of the Grimoires – Angels, Demons and Spirits

*Theurgia Goetia*

| No. | Emperors Ruling | Dukes | Direction | Commands | Some Spirits/Dukes Commanded |
|---|---|---|---|---|---|
| | | | | M20. Good and Evil Aerial Spirits (of the Compass) from *Theurgia Goetia* (*Lemegeton* Book II). | |
| 1 | Carnesiel | PAMERSIEL | E | 1000 Spirits for Day | Anoyr, Madriel, Ebra, Sotheans, Abrulges, Ormenu, Itules, Rablion, Hamorphiel, Itrasbiel, Nadres |
| 2 | | Padiel | E by S | 10000 Spirits for Day / 200000 Spirits for Night | [not given as 'Padiel rules all Spirits'] |
| 3 | | Camuel | SE | 10 Spirits for Day | Orpemiel, Omyel, Camyel, Budiel, Elear, Citgara, Pariel, Cariel, Neriel, Daniel |
| | | | | 10 Spirits for Night | Asimiel, Calim, Dobiel, Nodar, Phaniel, Meras, Azemo, Tediel, Moriel (s), Tugaros |
| 4 | | Aseliel | S by E | 10 Chief Spirits for Day | Mariel, Charas, Parniel, Aratiel, Cubiel, Aniel, Asahel, Arean, |
| | | | | 20 Chief Spirits for Night | Asphiel, Curiel, Chamos, Odiel, Melas, Sariel, Othiel, Bofar |
| 5 | Caspiel | BARMIEL | S | 10 Dukes for Day | Sochas, Tigara, Chansi, Keriel, Acteras, Barbil, Carpiel, Mansi |
| | | | | 20 Dukes for Night | Barbis, Marguns, Carniel, Acreba, Mareaiza, Baaba, Gabio, Astib |
| 6 | | Gediel | S by W | 20 Chief Spirits for Day | Coliel, Ranciel, Agra, Naras, Mashel, Anael, Sabas. Bariel, Aroan |
| | | | | 20 Chief Spirits for Night | Assaba, Reciel, Cirecas, Sariel, Sadiel, Aglas, Vriel, |
| 7 | | Asiriel/ Asyriel | SW | 20 Dukes for Day | Astor, Ariel, Maroth, Carga, Cusiel, Omiel, Buniel, Malguel, Budar |
| | | | | 20 Dukes for Night | Rabas, Amiel, Aspiel, Areisat, Cusriel, Faseua, Hamas |
| 8 | | Maseriel | W by S | 12 Dukes for Day | Mahue, Roriel, Zeriel, Atniel, Patiel, Assuel, Aliel, Espoel, Amoyr, Bachiel, Baras, Eliel, |
| | | | | 12 Dukes for Night | Vessur, Azimel, Chasor, Arach, Maras, Noguiel, Sarmiel, Earos, Rabiel, Atriel, Salvar |
| 9 | Amenadiel | MALGARAS | W | 30 Dukes for Day | Carmiel, Meliel, Borasy, Agor, Oriel, Misiel, Barfas, Arois, Raboc, Aspiel, Caron, Zamor, Amiel |
| | | | | 30 Dukes for Night | Casiel, Babiel, Cabiel, Udiel, Aroc, Dodiel, Cubi, Libiel, Aspar, Deilas, Basiel |
| 10 | | Darochiel | W by N | Dukes before Noon of the 24 Dukes for Day | Magael, Artino, Efiel/Artino, Maniel/Efiel, Suriel/Maniel, Carsiel/Suriel, Carsiel, Fubiel, Carba, Merach, Althor, Omiel |
| | | | | Dukes after Noon of the 24 Dukes for Day | Gudiel, Asphor, Emuel, Soriel, Cabron, Diviel, Abriel, Danael, Lomor, Casael, Busiel, Larfos |
| | | | | Dukes before Midnight of the 24 Dukes for Night | Nahiel, Ofisiel, Bulis, Momel, Darbari, Paniel, Cursas, Aliel, Aroziel, Cusyne, Vraniel, Pelusar |
| | | | | Dukes after Midnight of the 24 Dukes for Night | Pafiel, Gariel, Soriel, Maziel, Cayros, Narsiel, Moziel, Abael, Meroth, Cadriel, Lodiel |
| 11 | | Usiel | NW | 40 Dukes for Day | Abariel, Ameta, Arnin, Herne, Saefer, Potiel, Saefarn, Magni, Amandiel, Barfu, Garnasu, Hissam, Fabariel, Usiniel |
| | | | | 40 Dukes for Night | Ansoel, Godiel, Barfos, Burfa, Adan, Saddiel, Sodiel, Ofsidiel, Pathier, Marae, Asuriel, Almoel, Las Pharon, Ethiel |

# M. Magic of the Grimoires – Angels, Demons and Spirits

| No. | Emperors Ruling | Dukes | Direct-ion | Commands | Some Spirits/Dukes Commanded |
|-----|-----------------|-------|-----------|----------|------------------------------|
| | | | | M20. Good and Evil Aerial Spirits (of the Compass) from *Theurgia Goetia* (*Lemegeton* Book II). | |
| 12 | | Cabariel | N by W | 50 Dukes for Day | Satifiel, Parius, Godiel, Taros, Asoriel, Etimiel, Clyssan, Elitel, Aniel, Cuphal |
| | | | | 50 Dukes for Night | Mador, Peniel, Cugiel. Thalbos, Otim, Ladiel, Morias, Pandor, Cazul, Dubiel |
| 13 | Demoriel | RASIEL | N | 50 Dukes for Day | Baciar, Thoac, Sequiel, Sadar, Terath, Astael, Ramica, Dubarus, Armena, Albhadur, Chanael, Fursiel, Betasiel, Melcha, Tharas, Vriel |
| | | | | 50 Dukes for Night | Thariel, Paras, Arayl, Culmar, Lazaba, Aleasy, Sebach, Quibda, Belsay, Morael, Sarach, Arepach, Lamas, Thurcal |
| 14 | | Symiel | N by E | 10 Dukes for Day | Asmiel, Chrubas, Vaslos, Malgron, Romiel, Larael, Achot, Bonyel, Dagiel, Musor |
| | | | | 10 Dukes for Night | Mafrus, Apiel, Curiel, Molael, Arafos, Marianu, Narzael, Murahe, Richel, Nalael |
| 15 | | Armadiel | NE | 15 Dukes | Nassar, Parabiel, Lariel, Calvarnia, Orariel, Alferiel, Oryn, Samiel, Asmaiel, Jasziel, Pandiel, Carasiba, Asbibiel, Mafayr, Oemiel |
| 16 | | Baruchas | E by N | 15 Dukes | Quitta, Sarael, Melchon, Cavayr, Aboc, Cartael, Janiel, Pharol, Baoxas, Geriel, Monael, Chubo, Lamael, Dorael, Decaniel |

| | | Direction | Emperors | Commands | 12 Chief Dukes |
|---|-----|-----------|----------|----------|----------------|
| | | | | M21. Emperors of the Good and Evil Aerial Spirits from *Theurgia Goetia* (*Lemegeton* Book II). | |
| ✸ | 31b | | | | |
| F | 31 | South | Caspiel | 200 Great Dukes 400 Lesser Dukes 1,000,200,000,000 Ministering Spirits Attended by 2660 Lesser Dukes | Ursiel, Chariel, Maras, Femol, Budarim, Camory, Larmol, Aridiel, Geriel, Ambri, Camor, Oriel |
| A | 11 | East | Carnesiel | 1000 Great Dukes 100 Lesser Dukes 50,000,000,000,000 Ministering Spirits 60,000,000,000,000 attendant Dukes | Myrezyn, Ornich, Zabriel, Bucafas, Benoliam, Arifiel, Cumeriel, Vadriel, Armany, Capriel, Bedary, Laphor |
| W | 23 | West | Amenadiel | 300 Great Dukes 500 Lesser Dukes 40,000,030,000,100,000 Ministering Spirits Attended by 3880 Servants | Vadros, Camiel, Luziel, Musiriel, Rapsiel, Lamael Zoeniel, Curifas, Almesiel, Codriel, Balsur, Nadroc |
| E | 32b | North | Demoriel | 400 Great Dukes 600 Lesser Dukes 70,000,080,000,900,000 Servants Attended by 1140 Servants | Arnibiel, Cabarim, Menador, Burisiel, Doriel, Mador, Carnol, Dubilon, Medar, Churibal, Dabrinos, Chamiel |

# M. Magic of the Grimoires – Angels, Demons and Spirits

M20a. Good and Evil Aerial Spirits (the Wandering Princes) from *Theurgia Goetia* (*Lemegeton* Book II).

| No. | Emperor Ruler | Wandering Princes | Direction | Commands | Commands |
|-----|---------------|-------------------|-----------|----------|----------|
| 1 | Carnesiel Amenadiel Demoriel | Geradiel | ESE SE by E NNW NNE? | 18150 Servants | [not given] |
| 2 | Carnesiel Demoriel | Buriel | SE by S NNE NE by N | 12 Dukes for Night 880 Servants | Merosiel, Almadiel, Cupriel, Sarviel, Casbriel, Nedriel, Bufiel, Futiel, Drusiel, Carniel, Drubiel, Nastros |
| 3 | | Hidriel / Hydrial | SE by S SSE NE by N NE by E | 100 Great Dukes 200 Lesser Dukes | Mortaliel, Chalmoriel, Pelariel, Musuziel, Lameniel, Barchiel, Samiel, Dusiriel, Camiel, Arbiel, Lusiel, Chariel |
| 4 | Amenadiel | Pirichiel | NW by W NW by N | 8 Knights | Damarsiel, Cardiel, Almasor, Nemariel, Menariel, Demediel, Hursiel, Cuprisiel |
| 5 | | Emoniel | NW by N NNW | 20 Dukes | Ermoniel, Edriel, Carnodiel, Phanuel, Dramiel, Pandiel, Vasenel, Nasiniel, Cruhiel, Armesiel, Caspaniel, Musiniel |
| 6 | Carnesiel Caspiel Demoriel | Icosiel | SSE SSW NE by E ENE | 100 Dukes 300 Companions | Machariel, Psichiel, Thanatiel, Zosiel, Agapiel, Larphiel, Amediel, Cambriel, Nathriel, Zachariel, Athesiel, Cumariel, Munefiel, Heresiel, Urbaniel |
| 7 | | Soleviel | ESE SSW SW by S ENE | 200 Dukes 200 Companions | Inachiel, Praxeel, Moracha, Almodar, Nadrusiel, Cobusiel, Amriel, Axosiel, Charoel, Parsiel, Mursiel, Penador |
| 8 | Caspiel | Menadiel | SW by S SW by W | 20 Dukes 6 Chief Dukes 100 Companions | Larmol, Drasiel, Clamor, Benodiel, Charsiel, Samyel |
| | | | | 6 Lesser Dukes | Barchiel, Amasiel, Baruch, Nedriel, Curasin, Tharson |
| 9 | Caspiel | Macariel | SW by W WSW | 40 Dukes | Claniel, Drusiel, Andros, Charoel, Asmadiel, Romyel, Mastuel, Varpiel, Gremiel, Thuriel, Brufiel, Lemodac |
| 10 | Caspiel Amenadiel | Uriel | WSW WNW | 10 Dukes 100 Under Dukes | Chabri, Drabos, Narmiel, Frasmiel, Brymiel, Dragon, Curmas, Drapios, Hermon, Aldrusy |
| 11 | Amenadiel | Bidiel | WNW NW by W | 20 Chief Dukes 200 Other Dukes | Mudirel, Cruchan, Bramsiel, Armoniel, Lameniel, Andruchiel, Merasiel, Charobiel, Parsifiel, Chremoas |

Total = 4 Emperors + 11 Wandering Princes + 16 Aerial Spirits (Dukes) = 31 Spirits

# M. Magic of the Grimoires – Angels, Demons and Spirits

*Ars Paulina*

| Hr | Day Hour | Angel | Chief Dukes {Lesser Dukes} | Dukes & Servants |
|----|----------|-------|----------------------------|------------------|
| | | | **M22. Spirits of the Hours from *Ars Paulina* Part 1 – *Lemegeton* (Book III – 1).** | |
| 1 | – | Samuel [Samael] | Ameniel, Charpon, Darosiel, Monasiel, Brumiel, Nestoriel, Chremas, Meresyn | [10] Chief Dukes [100] Lesser Dukes 444 Servants each |
| 2 | Cevorym [Sevormi] | Anael | Menarchos, Archiel, Chardiel, {Orphiel, Cursiel, Elmoym, Quosiel, Ermaziel, Granyel} | 10 Chief Dukes 100 Lesser Dukes 330 Servants each |
| 3 | Dansor [Danzur] | Vequaniel | Asmiel, Persiel, Mursiel, Zoesiel, {Drelmech, Sadiniel, Parniel, Comadiel, Gemary, Xantiel, Serviel, Furiel} | 20 Chief Dukes 200 Lesser Dukes 1760 Servants |
| 4 | Elechym [Elechin] | Vathmiel [Vachmiel] | Armmyel, Larmich, Marfiel, Ormyel, Zardiel, {Emarfiel, Permiel, Queriel, Strubiel, Diviel, Jermiel, Thuros} | 10 Chief Dukes 100 Lesser Dukes 1550 Servants |
| 5 | Fealech [Tealech] | Sasquiel | Damiel, Araniel, Maroch, Saraphiel, Putisiel, {Jameriel, Futiniel, Rameriel, Amisiel, Uraniel, Omerach, Lameros, Zachiel, Fustiel, Camiel} | 10 Chief Dukes 100 Lesser Dukes 5500 Servants |
| 6 | Genapherim [Gebphorim] | Saniel [Samiel] | Arnebiel, Charuch, Medusiel, Nathmiel, Pemiel, {Gamyel, Jenotriel, Sameon, Trasiel, Xamyon, Nedabor, Permon, Brasiel, Camosiel, Evadar} | 10 Chief Dukes 100 Lesser Dukes 5500 Servants |
| 7 | Hamarym [Hemarim] | Barquiel | Abrasiel, Farmos, Nestorii, Manuel, Sagiel, {Harmiel, Nastrus, Varmay, Tulmas, Crosiel, Pasriel, Venesiel, Evarym, Drufiel, Kathos} | 10 Chief Dukes 100 Lesser Dukes 600 Servants |
| 8 | Jafanym [Jesamin] | Osmadiel | Sarfiel, Amalyn, Chroel, Mesial, Lantrhots, {Demarot, Janofiel, Larfuty, Vemael, Thribiel, Mariel, Remasyn, Theoriel, Framion, Ermiel} | 100 Chief Dukes 100 Lesser Dukes 1100 Servants |
| 9 | Karron [Carron] | Quabriel [Vadriel] | Astroniel, Charmy, Pamory, Damyel, Nadriel, {Kranos, Menas, Brasiel, Nefarym, Zoymiel, Trubas, Xermiel, Lameson, Zasnor, Janediel} | 10 Chief Dukes 100 Lesser Dukes 192980 Servants 650 Chief Servants |
| 10 | Lamarhon [Lamathon] | Oriel | Armosy, Drabiel, Penaly, Mesriel, Choreb, {Lemur, Ormas, Charny, Zazyor, Naveron, Xantros, Basilon, Nameron, Kranoti, Alfrael} | 10 Chief Dukes 100 Lesser Dukes 1100 Servants 5600 Spirits |
| 11 | Maneloym [Manelohim] | Bariel | Almarizel, Prasiniel, Chadros, Turmiel, Lamiel, {Menafiel, Demasor, Omary, Helmas, Zemoel, Almas, Perman, Comial, Temas, Lanifiel} | [10] Chief Dukes 100 Lesser Dukes 1100 Servants 5600 Spirits |
| 12 | Nahalon [Naybalon] | Beratiel [Beraliel] | Camaron, Astrofiel, Penatiel, Demarac, {Famaras, Plamiel, Nerastiel, Fimarson, Quirix, Sameron, Edriel, Choriel, Romiel, Fenosiel, Harmary} | [10] Chief Dukes [100] Lesser Dukes 1100 Servants 3700 Spirits |

# M. Magic of the Grimoires – Angels, Demons and Spirits

| Hr | Night Hour | Angel | Chief Dukes {Lesser Dukes} | Dukes & Servants |
|---|---|---|---|---|
| | | | M22. Spirits of the Hours from *Ars Paulina* Part 1 – *Lemegeton* (Book III – 1). | |
| 1 | Omalharien [Omalhavien] | Sabrathan [Sabrachon] | Domaras, Amerany, Penoles, Mardiel, Nastul, {Ramesiel, Omedriel, Franedac, Chrasiel, Dormason, Hayzoym, Emalon, Turtiel, Quenol, Rymaliel} | 1540 attendants [10] Chief Dukes [100] Lesser Dukes 2000 Servants |
| 2 | Panezur [Penazur] | Tartys [Taklis] | Almodar, Famoriel, Nedroz, Ormezyn, Chabriz, Praxiel, {Permaz, Vameroz, Emaryel, Fromezyn, Ramaziel, Granozyn, Gabrinoz, Mercoph, Tameriel, Venomiel, Jenaziel, Xemyzin} | 101550 attendants [10] Chief Dukes [100] Lesser Dukes 1320 Servants |
| 3 | Quabrion [Guabrion] | Serquanich [Sarquamech] | Menarym, Chrusiel, Penargos, Amriel, Demanoz, {Nestoroz, Evanuel, Sarmozyn, Haylon, Quabriel, Thurmytz, Fronyzon, Vanosyr, Lemaron, Almonoyz, Janothyel, Melrotz, Xanthyozod} | 101550 attendants 6 First Order Dukes 12 2nd Order Dukes 1320 Servants |
| 4 | Ramersy [Ramerzy] | Jefischa [Jefisiel] | Armosiel, Nedruan, Maneyloz, Ormael, Phorsiel, Rimezyn, {Rayziel, Gemezin, Fremiel, Hamayz, Japuriel, Jasphiel, Lamediel, Adroziel, Zodiel, Bramiel, Coreziel, Enatriel} | 101550 attendants 12 First Order Dukes 12 2nd Order Dukes 7260 Servants |
| 5 | Sanayfar [Sanaysor] | Abasdarhon [Abasdarho] | Meniel, Charaby, Appiniel, Deinatz, Nechorym, Hameriel, Vulcaniel, Samelon, Gemary, Vanescor, Sameryn, Xantropy, {Herphatz, Chrymas, Patrozyn, Nameton, Barmas, Platiel, Neszomy, Quesdor, Caremaz, Umariel, Kralym, Habalon} | 101550 attendants 12 First Order Dukes 12 2nd Order Dukes 3200 Servants |
| 6 | Thaazaron [Thaasoron] | Zaazenach | Amonazy, Menoriel, Prenostix, Namedor, Cherasiel, Dramaz, Tuberiel, Humaziel, Lanoziel, Lamerotzod, Xerphiel, Zeziel, {Pammon, Dracon, Gematzod, Enariel, Rudefor, Sarmon} | 101550 attendants 12 First Order Dukes 12 2nd Order Dukes 2400 Servants |
| 7 | Venaydor [Venador] | Mendrion | Ammiel, Choriel, Genarytz, Pandroz, Menesiel, Sameriel, Ventariel, Zachariel, Dubraz, Marchiel, Jonadriel, Pemoniel, {Rayziel, Tarmytz, Anapion, Jmonyel, Framoth, Machmag} | 101550 attendants 12 First Order Dukes 12 2nd Order Dukes 1860 Servants |
| 8 | Xymalim [Ximalim] | Narcoriel [Narcriel] | Cambiel, Nedarym, Astrocon, Marifiel, Dramozyn, Lustifion, Amelson, Lemozar, Xernifiel, Kanorsiel, Bufanotz, Jamedroz, {Xanoriz, Jastrion, Themaz, Hobrazym, Zymeloz, Gamisiel} | 101550 attendants 12 First Order Dukes 12 2nd Order Dukes 30200 Servants |
| 9 | Zeschar | Pamyel [Pamiel] | Demaor, Nameal, Adrapon, Chermel, Fenadros, Vemasiel, Comary, Matiel, Zenoroz, Brandiel, Evandiel, Tameriel, Befranzy, Jachoroz, Xanthir, Armapy, Druchas, Sardiel | 101550 attendants 12 First Order Dukes 12 2nd Order Dukes 1320 Servants |
| 10 | Malcho | Iassuarim [Jasguarim] | Lapheriel, Emarziel, Nameroyz, Chameray, Hazaniel, Uraniel | 100 Chief Dukes 100 Lesser Dukes 1620 Servants |
| 11 | Aalacho [Alacho] | Dardariel | Cardiel, Permon, Armiel, Nastoriel, Casmiroz, Dameriel, Furamiel, Mafriel, Hariaz, Damar, Alachuc, Emeriel, Naveroz, Alaphar, {Nermas, Druchas, Carman, Elamyz, Jatroziel, Lamersy, Hamarytzod} | [10?] Chief Dukes [100?] Lesser Dukes 420 Servants |
| 12 | Xephan | Sarandiel | Adoniel, Damasiel, Ambriel, Meriel, Denaryz, Emarion, Kabriel, Marachy, Chabrion, Nestoriel, Zachriel, Naverial, Damery, Namael, {Hardiel, Nefrias, Irmanotzod, Gerthiel, Dromiel, Ladrotzod, Melanas} | [10?] Chief Dukes [100?] Lesser Dukes 420 Servants |

# M. Magic of the Grimoires – Angels, Demons and Spirits

| | | 1° | 2° | 3° | 4° | 5° | 6° | 7° | 8° | 9° | 10° |
|---|---|---|---|---|---|---|---|---|---|---|---|
| ♈ | 15 | Biael | Gesiel | Hael | Vaniel | Zaciel | Cegnel | Japhael | Itael | Cakiel | Lariel |
| ♉ | 16 | Latiel | Hujael | Sachiel | Gneliel | Panael | Jezisiel | Kingael | Raphiel | Tezael | Gnakiel |
| ♊ | 17 | Latiel | Nagael | Sachael | Gnaliel | Paniel | Tzisiel | Kingael | Raphiel | Gnetiel | Bakiel |
| ♋ | 18 | Sachiel | Metiel | Asel | Sachiel | Mihel | Aniel | Sasael | Magnael | Aphiel | Sersael |
| ♌ | 19 | Mechiel | Satiel | Ajel | Mechiel | Sahel | Aniel | Masiel | Sengael | Aphiel | Metziel |
| ♍ | 20 | Celiel | Senael | Nasael | Sangiel | Gnaphiel | Parziel | Tzakiel | Kriel | Rathiel | Tangiel |
| ♎ | 22 | Ibajah | Chaiel | Sahael | Naviel | Saziel | Gnachiel | Patiel | Trajael | Kachiel | Baliel |
| ♏ | 24 | Teliel | Jeniel | Cesiel | Lengael | Naphael | Satziel | Gnakiel | Periel | Tzethiel | Rengliel |
| ♐ | 25 | Taliel | Janiel | Casiel | Langael | Naphael | Satziel | Gnakiel | Periel | Tzangiel | Jebiel |
| ♑ | 26 | Chushel | Temael | Jaajah | Cashiel | Lamajah | Naajah | Sasajah | Gnamiel | Paajah | Izashiel |
| ♒ | 28 | Chamiel | Tesael | Jaajeh | Camiel | Lashiel | Naajah | Samiel | Gnashiel | Paajah | Izamiel |
| ♓ | 29 | Lachiel | Neliel | Sanael | Gnasiel | Pangael | Tzapheal | Kphiel | Ratziel | Tarajah | Gnathiel |

M23. Angels of the Degrees of the Zodiac from *Ars Paulina* (Part 2) *Lemegeton* (Book III – 2).

| | | 11° | 12° | 13° | 14° | 15° | 16° | 17° | 18° | 19° | 20° |
|---|---|---|---|---|---|---|---|---|---|---|---|
| ♈ | 15 | Natheel | Sagnel | Gabiel | Pegiel | Gadiel | Kheel | Leviel | Hezael | Geciel | Betiel |
| ♉ | 16 | Beriel | Gethiel | Dagnel | Vabiel | Zegiel | Chadiel | Tahiel | Javiel | Chazael | Bachiel |
| ♊ | 17 | Geriel | Dathiel | Hegnel | Vabiel | Zagiel | Chadiel | Tahiel | Javiel | Chazael | Bachiel |
| ♋ | 18 | Makael | Ariel | Sethiel | Magnael | Abiel | Sagel | Madiel | Athiel | Savael | Maziel |
| ♌ | 19 | Sekiel | Ariel | Gnethiel | Sagiel | Abiel | Magiel | Sadiel | Athiel | Muviel | Saviel |
| ♍ | 20 | Gnasiel | Bagiel | Gediel | Dahiel | Hevael | Vaziel | Zachiel | Chetiel | Tiiel | Jechiel |
| ♎ | 22 | Tamael | Gnamiel | Bangiel | Gepheel | Datziel | Hekiel | Variel | Zethiel | Chengiel | Tibiel |
| ♏ | 24 | Rebiel | Tagiel | Gnadiel | Bevael | Geziel | Dachiel | Hephiel | Vagael | Zackiel | Chabiel |
| ♐ | 25 | Regael | Tediel | Gnaheel | Bevael | Geziel | Dachiel | Hephiel | Vagael | Zackiel | Chabiel |
| ♑ | 26 | Kmiel | Riajah | Tashiel | Gnamiel | Baajah | Gashiel | Dashiel | Haajah | Vashiel | Zamiel |
| ♒ | 28 | Kshiel | Raajah | Tamiel | Gnashiel | Baajah | Gashiel | Dashiel | Haajah | Vashiel | Zamiel |
| ♓ | 29 | Bengiel | Gebiel | Dagiel | Hadiel | Vahajah | Zavael | Chazael | Tachael | Jatael | Cajaiel |

M23. Angels of the Degrees of the Zodiac from *Ars Paulina* (Part 2) *Lemegeton* (Book III – 2) (*continued*).

| | | 21° | 22° | 23° | 24° | 25° | 26° | 27° | 28° | 29° | 30° |
|---|---|---|---|---|---|---|---|---|---|---|---|
| ♈ | 15 | Giel | Dachael | Habiel | Vagel | Zadiel | Chahel | Tavael | Jezel | Cechiel | Hetiel |
| ♉ | 16 | Getiel | Dajiel | Hachael | Vabiel | Zagiel | Chadiel | Gehiel | Javael | Chasiel | Sachael |
| ♊ | 17 | Getiel | Dajiel | Hachael | Vabiel | Zagiel | Chadiel | Tahiel | Daviel | Heziel | Vachael |
| ♋ | 18 | Achiel | Setiel | Maiel | Achael | Sabiel | Magiel | Adiel | Sahiel | Meviel | Aziel |
| ♌ | 19 | Achiel | Metiel | Siel | Achael | Mabiel | Sagiel | Adiel | Mahiel | Savael | Aziel |
| ♍ | 20 | Cabiel | Bagiel | Gediel | Dahiel | Hoviel | Vaziel | Zachiel | Chetivel | Tajael | Jachiel |
| ♎ | 22 | Jagiel | Cediel | Behel | Gevael | Daziel | Heckiel | Vatiel | Zajel | Chechiel | Tehiel |
| ♏ | 24 | Tagiel | Jadiel | Cahael | Baviel | Gezael | Dachael | Hatiel | Vajael | Zachiel | Chasiel |
| ♐ | 25 | Tagiel | Jadiel | Cahael | Baviel | Gezael | Dachael | Hatiel | Vajael | Zachiel | Chasiel |
| ♑ | 26 | Chael | Tashiel | Jashiel | Ciajah | Beshael | Gamael | Daael | Heshael | Vamiel | Zaajah |
| ♒ | 28 | Chael | Tashiel | Jashiel | Ciajah | Beshael | Gamael | Daael | Heshael | Vamiel | Zaajah |
| ♓ | 29 | Bachiel | Gabiel | Dagiel | Hediel | Vahejah | Zavael | Chazael | Tachiel | Jatael | Cajael |

**M23. Angels of the Degrees of the Zodiac from *Ars Paulina* (Part 2) *Lemegeton* (Book III – 2) (*continued*).**

*Ars Almadel*

**M24. Angels of The Altitudes (Choras) from *Ars Almadel – Lemegeton* (Book IV).**

| | | Chora | Colour | Angels | Appearance | God-Names |
|---|---|---|---|---|---|---|
| ⊛ | 31b | | | | | |
| F | 31 | **South** | Rose-red | Aphiriza Genon Geron Armon Gereimon | Young Child wearing Rose-red Satin & Crown of Gilly Flowers. | Helion Heloi Heli |
| A | 11 | **East** | Lily white | Alimiel Gabriel Barachiel Lebes Helison | Angel carrying Flag with White Cross wearing a Cloud & Crown of Roses. | Adonaij Helomi Pine |
| W | 23 | **West** | Green & whitish silver | Eliphaniasai Gelomiros Gedobonai Taranava Elomina | Children or Girls wearing Crowns of Bay Leaves. | Jod Hod Agla |
| E | 32b | **North** | Black & green | Barachiel Gediel Gedial Deliel Capitiel | Boys wearing Black & Green carrying Birds. | Tetragrammaton Shadai Jah |

*Key of Solomon – Clavicula Salomonis*

| | | Time | Hour Name | Sunday | Monday | Tuesday | Wednesday | Thursday | Friday | Saturday |
|---|---|---|---|---|---|---|---|---|---|---|
| | | | | M25. Hours of the Day and Night from *The Key Of Solomon*, and the Angels that Rule them. | | | | | | |
| ♈ | 15 | 1 am | *Yayn* | Raphael | Sachiel | Anael | Cassiel | Michael | Gabriel | Zamael |
| ♉ | 16 | 2 am | *Yanor* | Gabriel | Zamael | Raphael | Sachiel | Anael | Cassiel | Michael |
| ♊ | 17 | 3 am | *Nasnia* | Cassiel | Michael | Gabriel | Zamael | Raphael | Sachiel | Anael |
| ♋ | 18 | 4 am | *Salla* | Sachiel | Anael | Cassiel | Michael | Gabriel | Zamael | Raphael |
| ♌ | 19 | 5 am | *Sadedali* | Zamael | Raphael | Sachiel | Anael | Cassiel | Michael | Gabriel |
| ♍ | 20 | 6 am | *Thamur* | Michael | Gabriel | Zamael | Raphael | Sachiel | Anael | Cassiel |
| ♎ | 22 | 7 am | *Ourer* | Anael | Cassiel | Michael | Gabriel | Zamael | Raphael | Sachiel |
| ♏ | 24 | 8 am | *Thainé* | Raphael | Sachiel | Anael | Cassael | Michael | Gabriel | Zamael |
| ♐ | 25 | 9 am | *Neron* | Gabriel | Zamael | Raphael | Sachiel | Anael | Cassiel | Michael |
| ♑ | 26 | 10 am | *Yayon* | Cassiel | Michael | Gabriel | Zamael | Raphael | Sachiel | Anael |
| ♒ | 28 | 11 am | *Abai* | Sachiel | Anael | Cassiel | Michael | Gabriel | Zamael | Raphael |
| ♓ | 29 | **Noon** | *Nathalon* | Zamael | Raphael | Sachiel | Anael | Cassiel | Michael | Gabriel |
| ♈ | 15 | 1 pm | *Beron* | Michael | Gabriel | Zamael | Raphael | Sachiel | Anael | Cassiel |
| ♉ | 16 | 2 pm | *Barol* | Anael | Cassiel | Michael | Gabriel | Zamael | Raphael | Sachiel |
| ♊ | 17 | 3 pm | *Thanu* | Raphael | Sachiel | Anael | Cassael | Michael | Gabriel | Zamael |
| ♋ | 18 | 4 pm | *Athor* | Gabriel | Zamael | Raphael | Sachiel | Anael | Cassiel | Michael |
| ♌ | 19 | 5 pm | *Mathon* | Cassiel | Michael | Gabriel | Zamael | Raphael | Sachiel | Anael |
| ♍ | 20 | 6 pm | *Rana* | Sachiel | Anael | Cassiel | Michael | Gabriel | Zamael | Raphael |
| ♎ | 22 | 7 pm | *Netos* | Zamael | Raphael | Sachiel | Anael | Cassiel | Michael | Gabriel |
| ♏ | 24 | 8 pm | *Tafrac* | Michael | Gabriel | Zamael | Raphael | Sachiel | Anael | Cassiel |
| ♐ | 25 | 9 pm | *Sassur* | Anael | Cassiel | Michael | Gabriel | Zamael | Raphael | Sachiel |
| ♑ | 26 | 10 pm | *Agla* | Raphael | Sachiel | Anael | Cassael | Michael | Gabriel | Zamael |
| ♒ | 28 | 11 pm | *Cäerra* | Gabriel | Zamael | Raphael | Sachiel | Anael | Cassiel | Michael |
| ♓ | 29 | **Midnight** | *Salam* | Cassiel | Michael | Gabriel | Zamael | Raphael | Sachiel | Anael |

*Sacred Magic of Abramelin The Mage*

| Group | Ruled by | Spirits |
|---|---|---|
| | | **M26. The Servient Spirits from** *Abramelin*. |
| 1 | 111 [114] Spirits of the Four Quarters: *Common to* Oriens & Paimon & Ariton & Amaimon | Hosen Saraph Proxosos Habhi Acuar Tirana Alluph Nercamay Nilen Morel Traci Enaia Mulach Malutens Iparkas Nuditon Melna Melhaer Ruach Apolhun Schabuach Mermo Melamud Poter Sched Ekdulon Mantiens Obedama Sachiel Moschel Pereuch Deccal Asperim Katini Torfora Badad Coelen Chuschi Tasma Pachid Parek Rachiar Nogar Adon Trapis Nagid Ethanim Patid Pareht Emphastison Paraseh Gerevil Elmis Asmiel Irminon Asturel Nuthon Lomiol Imink Plirok Tagnon Parmatus Iaresin Gorilon Lirion Plegit Ogilen Tarados Losimon Ragaras Igilon Gosegas Astrega Parusur Igis Aherom Igarak Geloma Kilik Remoron Ekalike Isekel Elzegan Ipakol Haril Kadolon Iogion Zaragil Irroron Ilagas Balalos Oroia Lagasuf Alagas Alpas Soterion Romages Promakos Metafel Darascon Kelen Erenutes Najin Tulot Platien Atloton Afarorp Morilen Ramaratz Nogen Molin |
| 2 | 10 Spirits *Common to* Amaimon & Ariton | Hauges Agibol Rigolen Grasemin Elafon Trisaga Gagalin Cleraca Elaton Pafesla |
| 3 | 53 Spirits *Common to* Astarot & Asmodee | Amaniel Orinel Timira Dramas Amalin Kirik Bubana Buk Raner Semlin Ambolin Abutes Exteron Laboux Corcaron Ethan Taret Dablat Buriul Oman Carasch Dimurgos Roggiol Loriol Isigi Tioron Darokin Horanar Abahin Goleg Guagamon Laginx Etaliz Agei Lemel Udaman Bialot Gagalos Ragalim Finaxos Akanef Omages Agrax Sagares Afray Ugales Hermiala Haligax Gugonix Opilm Daguler Pachei Nimalon |
| 4 | 15 [12] Spirits *Common to* Asmodee & Magot | Toun Magog Diopos Disolel Biriel Sifon Kele Magiros Sartabakim Lundo Sobe Inokos Mabakiel Apot Opun |
| 5 | 65 Spirits of Magot | Nacheran Katolin Luesaf Masaub Urigo Faturab Fersebus Baruel Ubarin Butarab Ischiron Odax Roler Arotor Hemis Arpiron Arrabin Supipas Forteson Dulid Sorriolenen Megalak Anagotos Sikastin Petunof Mantan Meklboc Tigrafon Tagora Debam Tiraim Irix Madail Abagiron Pandoli Nenisem Cobel Sobel Laboneton Arioth Marag Kamusil Kaitar Scharak Maisadul Agilas Kolam Kiligil Corodon Hepogon Daglas Hagion Egakireh Paramor Olisermon Rimog Horminos Hagog Mimosa Amchison Ilarax Makalos Locater Colvam Batternis |
| 6 | 32 [31] Spirits of Astarot | Aman Camal Toxai Kataron Rax Gonogin Schelagon Ginar Isiamon Bahal Darek Ischigas Golen Gromenis Rigios Nimerix Herg Argilon Okiri Fagani Hipolos Ileson Camonix Bafamal Alan Apormenos Ombalat Quartas Ugirpen Araex Lepaca Kolofe |
| 7 | 16 [12] Spirits of Asmodee | Onei Ormion Preches Maggid Sclavak Mebbesser Bacaron Holba Hifarion Gilarion Eniuri Abadir Sbarionat Utifa Omet Sarra |
| 8 | 49 Spirits of Belzebud | Alcanor Amatia Bilifares Lamarion Diralisen Licanen Dimirag Elponen Ergamen Gotifan Nimorup Carelena Lamalon Igurim Akium Dorak Tachan Ikonok Kemal Bilico Tromes Balfori Arolen Lirochi Nominon Iamai Arogor Holastri Hacamuli Samalo Plison Raderaf Borol SorosmaCorilon Gramon Magalast Zagalo Pellipis Natalis Namiros Adirael Kabada Kipokis Orgosil Arcon Ambolon Lamolon Bilifor |
| 9 | 8 Spirits of Oriens | Sarisel Gasarons Sorosma Turitel Balaken Gagison Mafalac Agab |
| 10 | 15 Spirits of Paimon | Aglafos Agafali Dison Achaniel Sudoron Kabersa Ebaron Zalanes Ugola Came Roffles Menolik Tacaros Astolit Rukum |
| 11 | 22 Spirits of Ariton | Anader Ekorok Sibolas Saris Sekabin Caromos Rosaran Sapason Notiser Flaxon Harombrub Megalosin Miliom Ilemlis Galak Androcos Maranton Caron Reginon Elerion Sermeot Irmenos |
| 12 | 20 Spirits of Amaimon | Romeroc Ramison Scrilis Buriol Taralim Burasen Akesoli Erekia Illirikim Labisi Akoros Mames Glesi Vision Effrigis Apelki Dalep Dresop Hergotis Nilima |
| | *Total =* | *416 [411] Servient Spirits* |

# M. Magic of the Grimoires – Angels, Demons and Spirits

<table>
<tr><td colspan="6" align="center">M27. Hierarchy of the Abramelin Demons.</td></tr>
<tr><td></td><td></td><td colspan="2" align="center">Princes & Superior Spirits (4 Kings)</td><td colspan="2" align="center">Sub-Princes (8 Dukes)</td></tr>
<tr><td>F</td><td>31</td><td colspan="2">Lucifer</td><td rowspan="4" align="center">Demon Princes of the Four Quarters</td><td>Paimon/Paymon</td></tr>
<tr><td>A</td><td>11</td><td colspan="2">Satan</td><td>Oriens</td></tr>
<tr><td>W</td><td>23</td><td colspan="2">Leviathan</td><td>Ariton/Arito [or Egyn]</td></tr>
<tr><td>E</td><td>32b</td><td colspan="2">Belial</td><td>Amaimon/Amaymon</td></tr>
<tr><td></td><td></td><td colspan="2"></td><td rowspan="4" align="center">Traditional</td><td>Magot[h]</td></tr>
<tr><td></td><td></td><td colspan="2"></td><td>Astarot[h]</td></tr>
<tr><td></td><td></td><td colspan="2"></td><td>Asmodee/Asmodi</td></tr>
<tr><td></td><td></td><td colspan="2"></td><td>Belzebud/Beelzebub</td></tr>
</table>

## Magical Equipment Objectives and Abilities

<table>
<tr><td colspan="6" align="center">M27a. Grimoire Magical Equipment.</td></tr>
<tr><td></td><td></td><td align="center">Temple</td><td align="center">To be Worn</td><td align="center">Talisman making</td><td align="center">Rite specific</td></tr>
<tr><td></td><td>1</td><td>Holy Annointing Oil</td><td>Crown, Cap, Mitre, Magus-Band</td><td></td><td></td></tr>
<tr><td></td><td>2</td><td>Brass Vessel & Seal</td><td>Mantle</td><td></td><td></td></tr>
<tr><td></td><td>3</td><td>Trident of Paracelsus, Black hilted Knife</td><td>Long Robe, Linen Garment</td><td>Silk wraps</td><td></td></tr>
<tr><td></td><td>4</td><td>Sceptre</td><td>Ring of Solomon</td><td></td><td></td></tr>
<tr><td></td><td>5</td><td>Sword, Chain</td><td>Pentagram of Solomon</td><td>Engraver or burin</td><td></td></tr>
<tr><td></td><td>6</td><td>Dagger</td><td>Lamen, Angelic Breastplate Hexagram of Solomon</td><td></td><td></td></tr>
<tr><td></td><td>7</td><td>Oil Lamp, Candles</td><td>Girdle or Belt of lion skin</td><td>Colours</td><td></td></tr>
<tr><td></td><td>8</td><td>Wand, White hilted Knife, Table of Practice</td><td>Phylacteries</td><td>Pen or (crow) Quills, Inks, inkhorns</td><td>Liber Spirituum, Litanies</td></tr>
<tr><td></td><td>9</td><td>Magic (Black) Mirror, Glass Receptacle, Crystal</td><td></td><td></td><td>Seal of the Spirit</td></tr>
<tr><td></td><td>10</td><td>Circle & Triangle, Altar, Lecturn</td><td>Slippers or Sandals</td><td>Parchment, Metal discs</td><td>Pentacle, Almadel or Plate</td></tr>
<tr><td>F</td><td>31</td><td>Censer, Burner, Chafing Dish</td><td></td><td></td><td>Charcoal or specific woods</td></tr>
<tr><td>A</td><td>11</td><td>Bell, trumpet</td><td></td><td></td><td>Incense, Perfumes</td></tr>
<tr><td>W</td><td>23</td><td>Herb Aspergillum, Holy Water, Chalice</td><td></td><td></td><td>Fluid Condenser, Wine, Blood</td></tr>
<tr><td>E</td><td>32b</td><td>Salt, chalk, wax</td><td></td><td></td><td>Materia magica/ousia</td></tr>
</table>

# M. Magic of the Grimoires – Angels, Demons and Spirits

| | | M28. Abramelin Magical Operations (with Chapter Numbers). | M29. Magical Objectives and Abilities. |
|---|---|---|---|
| | | | **45** |
| ⊛ | 31b | IX – to transform men into animals, and vice versa <br> XXI – to transform oneself and take different forms | Invisibility, Transformations, Vision of the Holy Guardian Angel |
| F | 31 | III – to cause any Spirit to appear and take any form <br> V – to retain Familiar Spirits bond or free in any form | Evocation, Pyromancy |
| A | 11 | I – to know all manner of things past and future | Divination, Prophecy, Aeromancy |
| W | 23 | VIII – to excite tempests <br> XXV – to walk upon or operate under water | The Great Work, Crystal-gazing, Hydromancy |
| E | 32b | VI – to discover mines and help in working them <br> XVI – to find and take possession of hidden treasures | Alchemy, Geomancy, Making of Talismans |
| ☾ | 13 | IV – for diverse visions <br> XXVII – to cause visions to appear | White Tincture, Clairvoyance, Astral Travelling, the Evil Eye, Divination by Dreams, Visions |
| ☿ | 12 | II – to know all types of sciences, even doubtful ones <br> XVIII – to heal diverse maladies or illnesses | Alchemy, Healing, Gift of Tongues, Knowledge of all Sciences |
| ♀ | 14 | XIX – for every description of love and affection | Compounding of Love-philtres, Fascination |
| ☼ | 30 | XXVIII – to have as much gold and silver as desired | Red Tincture, Power of Acquiring Wealth & Fame, Invocation |
| ♂ | 27 | XXIX – to cause armed men to appear | Works of War, Wrath and Vengeance |
| ♃ | 21 | XII – to know the secrets of any person | Political and Religious Power |
| ♄ | 32 | XXII – for every kind of evil works | Works of Malediction and Death, Cursing |
| ♈ | 15 | XI – to cause (lost or stolen) books to be brought | Consecration |
| ♉ | 16 | XXIII – to demolish buildings and strongholds | Physical Strength |
| ♊ | 17 | XVII – to fly through the air, or travel to any place | Bi-location |
| ♋ | 18 | XV – for the spirits to bring food and drink | Casting Enchantments |
| ♌ | 19 | XXVI – to open any lock without a key or noise | Power of Training Wild Beasts |
| ♍ | 20 | XIV – to render oneself invisible | Invisibility, Parthenogenesis (creation of a homunculus) |
| ♎ | 22 | X – to hinder any necromantic or magical operations | Works of Justice and Equilibrium |
| ♏ | 24 | XIII – to revive a dead body by means of the spirits | Necromancy |
| ♐ | 25 | VII – to cause Spirits to perform metallurgic and alchemic work, and all necessary chemical operations | Transmutations |
| ♑ | 26 | XX – to excite hatred, enmity, discord and quarrels | The Witches' Sabbath so-called, Evil Eye |
| ♒ | 28 | XXIV – to discover any theft that has occurred | Astrology |
| ♓ | 29 | XXX – to cause comedies, operas or music to appear | Bewitchments, Casting Illusions |

*Franz Bradon - Practice of Magical Evocation*

| | | Claimed Nature | Seal Figures | Spirit Names | Actual Source |
|---|---|---|---|---|---|
| | | | | M30. Franz Bardon's Spirit Hierarchy from *Practice of Magical Evocation*. | |
| | 1 | Pluto | n/a | | – |
| | 2 | Uranus & Neptune | n/a | | – |
| | 3 | Saturn | see below | | |
| | 4 | Jupiter | see below | | |
| | 5 | Mars | see below | | |
| | 6 | Sun | see below | | |
| | 7 | Venus | see below | | |
| | 8 | Mercury | see below | | |
| | 9 | Moon | see below | | |
| | 10 | Earth-Girdling Zone (sub-Lunary intelligences) | 2/1 – 2/24 | Aschmunadai, Aladiah, Kolorum, Gibora, Siilla, Lilitha, Asamarc, Emuel, Ubiveh, Asael, Gojel, Armiel, Amuthim, Coel, [IHVH], Aeoiu, Juoea, Nahum, Immicat, Osrail, Ados, Sata-Pessajah, Laosa | Mixed sources |
| ✸ | 31b | | | | |
| F | 31 | Fire | 1/1 – 1/8 | Pyrhum, Aphtiph, Orudu, Itumo, Coroman, Tapheth, Oriman, Amtophul | |
| A | 11 | Air | 1/25 – 1/32 | Parahim, Apilki, Erkeya, Dalep, Capisi, Drisophi, Glisi, Cargoste | Abramelin: servants of Amaymon |
| W | 23 | Water | 1/9 – 1/16 | Amasol, Ardiphne, Isaphil, Amue, Aposto, Ermot, Osipeh, Istiphul | |
| E | 32b | Earth | 1/17 – 1/24 | Mentifil, Ordaphe, Orova, Idurah, Musar, Necas, Erami, Andimo | |
| ☾ | 13 | Moon | 4/1 – 4/28 | Ebvap, Emtircheyud, Ezhesekis, Emvatibe, Amzhere, Enchede, Emrudue, Eneye, Emzhebyp, Emnymar, Ebvep, Emkebpe, Emcheba, Ezhobar, Emnepe, Echotasa, Emzhom, Emzhit, Ezheme, Etsacheye, Etamrezh, Rivatim, Liteviche, Zhevekiyev, Lavemezhu, Empebyn, Emzhabe, Emzher | Supposedly the 28 Mansions of the Moon [but not Moon spirits] |
| ☿ | 12 | Mercury | 5/1 – 5/72 | Vehuiah, Jeliel, Sitael, Elemiah, Mahasiah, Lelahel, Achaiah, Kahetel, Aziel, Aladiah, Lauviah, Hahaiah, Jezalel, Mebahel, Hariel, Hakamiah, Lanoiah, Kaliel, Leuviah, Pahaliah, Nelekael, Jeiaiel, Melahel, Hahuiah, Nith-Haiah, Haaiah, Jerathel, Seeiah, Reiiel, Omael, Lekabel, Vasariah, Jehuiah, Lehahiah, Kevakiah, Menadel, Aniel, Haamiah, Rehael, Ieiazel, Hahahel, Mikael, Veubiah, Ielahiah, Sealiah, Ariel, Asaliah, Mihael, Vehuel, Daniel, Hahasiah, Imamiah, Nanael, Nithael, Mebaiah, Poiel, Nemamiah, Jeialel, Harahel, Mizrael, Umabel, Jah-Hel, Anianuel, Mehiel, Damabiah, Manakel, Eiaiel, Habuiah, Rochel, Jabamiah, Haiel, Mumiah | The 72 Shem ha-Mephorash angels OR Reuchlin's angels of Earth [not Mercury spirits] |
| ♀ | 14 | Venus | 6/1 – 6/90 | Omah, Oduja, Obideh, Onami, Osphe, Orif, Obaneh, Odumi, Orula, Osoa, Owina, Obata, Ogieh, Obche, Otra, Alam, Agum, Albadi, Aogum, Acolom, Achadiel, Adimil, Aser, Aahum, Acho, Arohim, Ardho, Asam, Astoph, Aosid, Iseh, Isodeh, Idmuh, Irumiah, Idea, Idovi, Isill, Ismee, Inea, Ihom, Iomi, Ibladi, Idioh, Ischoa, Igea, Orro, Oposah, Odlo, Olo, Odedo, Omo, Osaso, | 90 encoded names. Maybe drawn from Dr Franz Sättler Musallam's *Nekromantik* |

| | | Claimed Nature | Seal Figures | Spirit Names | Actual Source |
|---|---|---|---|---|---|
| | | | | M30. Franz Bardon's Spirit Hierarchy from *Practice of Magical Evocation*. | |
| | | | | Ogego, Okaf, Ofmir, Otuo, Phoah, Ocher, Otlur, Ogileh, Gega, Gema, Gegega, Garieh, Gesa, Geswi, Godeah, Guru, Gomah, Goldro, Gesdri, Gesoah, Gescheh, Gehela, Gercha, Purol, Podme, Podumar, Pirr, Puer, Pliseh, Padcheh, Pehel, Pomanp, Pitofil, Pirmen, Piomel, Piseph, Pidioeh, Pimel | [not Venus spirits] |
| ☼ | 30 | Sun | 7/1 – 7/45 | Emnasut, Lubech, Teras, Dubezh, Amser, Emedetz, Kesbetz, Emayisa, Emvetas, Bunam, Serytz, Wybiol, Lubuyil, Geler, Wybitzis, Wybalap, Tzizhet, Dabetz, Banamol, Emuyir, Dubek, Emtzel, Tasar, Fusradu, Firul, Ebytzyril, Lhomtab, Tzybayol, Gena, Kasreyobu, Etzybet, Balem, Belemche, Aresut, Tinas, Gane, Emtub, Erab, Tybolyr, Chibys, Selhube, Levum, Vasat, Ezhabsab, Debytzet | Arabic Names of the 45 Fixed Stars (enciphered) [not Sun spirits] |
| ♂ | 27 | Mars | Not given | ♈ - Rarum, Gibsir, Rahol,   ♉ - Adica, Agricol, Fifal, ♊ - Imini, Kolluir, Ibnahim,   ♋ - Ititz, Urodu, Irkamon, ♌ - Oksos, Otobir, Kutruc,   ♍ - Idia, Abodir, Idida, ♎ - Cibor, Asor, Abodil,   ♏ - Skorpia, Vilusia, Koroum, ♐ - Sagitor, Agilah, Boram,   ♑ - Absalom, Istriah, Abdomon, ♒ - Anator, Ilutria, Obola,   ♓ - Pisiar, Filista, Odorom | 36 Decan spirits / demons of the Picatrix [not Mars spirits] |
| ♃ | 21 | Jupiter | 8/1 – 8/12 | ♈ - Malchjdael [Malchidael], ♉ - Asmodel, ♊ - Ambriel, ♋ - Murjel [Muriel],   ♌ - Verchiel, ♍ - Hamaliel, ♎ - Zuriel,   ♏ - Carbiel, ♐ - Aduachiel, ♑ - Hanael,   ♒ - Cambiel, ♓ - Jophaniel | 12 zodiacal spirits [not Jupiter spirits] |
| ♄ | 32 | Saturn | n/a | Agiel, Arathron, Cassiel, Machatan, Uriel | From mixed sources |
| ♈ | 15 | Aries – Zone | 3/25– 3/54 | Morech, Malacha. Ecdulon, Lurchi, Aspadit, Nascela, Opollogon, Ramara, Anamil, Tabori, Igigi, Bialode, Opilon, Jrachro, Golog, Argilo, Barnel, Serpolo, Hyris, Hahadu, Oromonas, Bekaro, Belifares, Nadele, Yromus, Hadcu, Balachman, Jugula, Secabmi, Calacha | |
| ♉ | 16 | Taurus – Zone | 3/55– 3/84 | Serap, Molabeda, Manmes, Faluna, Nasi, Conjoli, Carubot, Jajaregi, Orienell, Concario, Dosom, Galago, Paguldez, Pafessa, Jromoni, Tardoe, Ubarim, Magelucha, Chadail, Charagi, Hagos, Hyla, Camalo, Baalto, Camarion, Amalomi, Gagison, Carahami, Calamos, Sapasani | |
| ♊ | 17 | Gemini – Zone | 3/85– 3/114 | Proxones, Yparcha, Obedomah, Padidi, Peralit, Isnirki, Morilon, Golema, Timiran, Golemi, Darachin, Bagoloni, Paschy, Amami, Pigios, Cepacha, Urgivoh, Amagestol, Debam, Kolani, Mimosah, Eneki, Corilon, Ygarimi, Jamaih, Bilifo, Mafalach, Kaflesi, Sibolas, Seneol | |
| ♋ | 18 | Cancer – Zone | 3/115 – 3/144 | Nablum, Nudatoni, Jachil, Helali, Emfalion, Pliroki, Losimon, Kiliki, Oramos, Tarato, Horomor, Tmako, Nimalon, Camalo, Nimtrix, Kalote, Ysquiron, Sikesti, Abagrion, Kibigili, Arakuson, Maggio, Dirilisin, Akahimo, Aragor, Granona, Zagol, Mennolika, Forfasan, Charonthona | Abramelin Spirits |
| ♌ | 19 | Leo – Zone | 3/145 – 3/174 | Kosem, Methaera, Jvar, Mahra, Paruch, Aslotama, Kagaros, Romasara, Anemalon, Tabbata, Ahahbon, Akanejonaho, Horog, Texai, Herich, Ychniag, Odac, Mechebbera, Paschan, Corocona, Rimog, Abbetira, Eralicarison, Golopa, Jgakys, Pagalusta, Ichdison, Takarosa, Andrachor, Carona | |
| ♍ | 20 | Virgo – Zone | 3/175 – 3/204 | Peresch, Bruahi, Moschel, Raschea, Girmil, Zagriona, Ygilon, Alpaso, Kirek, Buriuh, Yraganon, Argaro, Algebol, Karasa, Akirgi, Basanola, Rotor, Tigrapho, Cobel, Hipogo, Iserag, Breffeo, Elipinon, Naniroa, Olaski, Hyrmiua, Sumuram, Astolitu, Notiser, Regerio. | |

| | | M30. Franz Bardon's Spirit Hierarchy from *Practice of Magical Evocation*. | | | |
|---|---|---|---|---|---|
| | | **Claimed Nature** | **Seal Figures** | **Spirit Names** | **Actual Source** |
| ♎ | 22 | Libra – Zone | 3/205 – 3/234 | Thirana, Apollyon, Peekah, Nogah, Tolet, Parmasa, Gesegos, Soteri, Batamabub, Omana, Lagiros, Afrei, Rigolon, Riqita, Tapum, Nachero, Arator, Malata, Arioth, Agikus, Cheikaseph, Ornion, Gariniranus, Istaroth, Haiamon, Canali, Aglasis, Merki, Filakon, Megalogi | Abramelin Spirits |
| `♏ | 24 | Scorpio – Zone | 3/235 – 3/264 | Aluph, Schaluah, Hasperim, Adae, Helmis, Sarasi, Ugefor, Amillee, Ranar, Caraschi, Eralier, Sagara, Trasorim, Schulego, Hipolopos, Natolisa, Butharusch, Tagora, Panari, Nagar, Kofan, Schaluach, Sipillipis, Tedea, Semechle, Radina, Hachamel, Anadi, Horasul, Irmano | |
| ♐ | 25 | Sagittarius – Zone | 3/265 – 3/294 | Neschamah, Myrmo, Kathim, Erimites, Asinel, Geriola, Asoreg, Ramage, Namalon, Dimurga, Golog, Ugali, Elason, Giria, Hosun, Mesah, Harkinon, Petuno, Caboneton, Echagi, Batirunos, Hillaro, Ergomion, Ikon, Alosom, Gezero, Agasoly, Ekore, Saris, Elami, | |
| ♑ | 26 | Capricorn – Zone | 3/295 – 3/324 | Milon, Melamo, Porphora, Trapi, Jonion, Afolono, Paruchu, Pormatho, Ampholion, Kogid, Cemiel, Erimihala, Trisacha, Afimo, Garses, Masadu, Arabim, Amia, Kamual, Parachmo, Cochaly, Ybario, Lotifar, Kama, Segosel, Sarsiee, Kiliosa, Rosora, Ekorim, Ramgisa | |
| ♒ | 28 | Aquarius – Zone | 3/325 – 3/354 | Frasis, Pother, Badet, Naga, Asturel, Liriell, Siges, Metosee, Abusis, Panfodra, Hagus, Hatuny, Gagolchon, Bafa, Ugirpon, Capipa, Koreh, Somi, Erytar, Kosirma, Jenuri, Altono, Chimirgu, Arisaka, Boreb, Soesma, Ebaron, Negani, Nelion, Sirigilis | |
| ♓ | 29 | Pisces – Zone | 3/355 – 3/384 | Haja, Schad, Kohen, Echami, Flabison, Alagill, Atherom, Porascho, Egention, Siria, Vollman, Hagomi, Klorecha, Baroa, Gomognu, Fermetu, Forsteton, Lotogi,Nearah, Dagio, Nephasser, Armefia, Kaerlesa, Bileka, Ugolog, Tmiti, Zalones, Cigila, Ylemis, Boria | |

*Planetary Spirits and Intelligences*

| | | M31. Magical Squares of the Planets – Key Numbers. | | | | |
|---|---|---|---|---|---|---|
| | | | **Side of Square** | **Number of Squares** | **Sum of Row/Column** | **Sum of Whole Square** |
| ☾ | 13 | Moon | 9 | 81 | 369 | 3321 |
| ☿ | 12 | Mercury | 8 | 64 | 260 | 2080 |
| ♀ | 14 | Venus | 7 | 49 | 175 | 1225 |
| ☼ | 30 | Sun | 6 | 36 | 111 | 666 |
| ♂ | 27 | Mars | 5 | 25 | 65 | 325 |
| ♃ | 21 | Jupiter | 4 | 16 | 34 | 136 |
| ♄ | 32 | Saturn | 3 | 9 | 15 | 45 |

| | | M32. Intelligences of the Planets – Hebrew. | M33. Intelligences of the Planets – Transliteration. | M34. Intelligences of the Planets – English. | M35. Intelligences of the Planets – Numeration. |
|---|---|---|---|---|---|
| | | **78** | | **194** | |
| ☾ | 13 | מלכא ב-תרשישים ועד ב-רוח שהרים | MLKA B-ThRShIShIM V-OD B-RVH ShHRIM | Malkah Be-Tarshishim ve-ad be-Ruah Sheharim[43] | 3321 |
| ☿ | 12 | טיריאל | TIRIAL | Tiriel | 260 |
| ♀ | 14 | הגיאל | HGIAL | Hagiel | 49 |
| ☉ | 30 | נכיאל | NKIAL | Nakhiel | 111 |
| ♂ | 27 | גראפיאל | GRAPIAL | Graphiel | 325 |
| ♃ | 21 | יהפיאל/יופיל | YVPIL/YHPIAL | Yophiel | 136 |
| ♄ | 32 | אגיאל | AGIAL | Agiel | 45 |

| | | M36. Spirits of the Planets – Hebrew. | M37. Spirits of the Planets – Transliteration. | M38. Spirits of the Planets – English.[44] | M39. Spirits of the Planets – Numeration. |
|---|---|---|---|---|---|
| | | **79** | | **193** | |
| ☾ | 13 | חשמודאי שד ברשהמעת [ה]-שרתתן | ChShMVDAI ShD BRShHMOTh [H]-ShRThThN | Chasmodai Shad Barshehmoth [ha]-Sharthathan | 369 3321 |
| ☿ | 12 | תפתרתרת | ThPThRThRTh | Taphthartharath | 2080 |
| ♀ | 14 | קדמאל | QDMAL | Qedemel/Kedemel | 175 |
| ☉ | 30 | סורת | SVRTh | Sorath | 666 |
| ♂ | 27 | ברצבאל | BRTzBAL | Bartzabel | 325 |
| ♃ | 21 | הסמאל | HSMAL | Hismael | 136 |
| ♄ | 32 | זאל / זאזל | ZAZL | Zazel | 45 |

---

[43] Sheharim שהרים (Moon shaped talismans) enables the phrase to add correctly to 3321, rather than the usual word Shehaqim or Shechalim, which is quoted in most texts, and which fail to adds to the correct total. Tyson gives שחקים מלכא ב-תרשיתים עד ב-רוח which also adds correctly to 3321.

[44] See also Column G29.

| | | M40. The Familiar Shapes of the Planetary Spirits. |
|---|---|---|
| | | |
| ☾ | 13 | The Spirits of the Moon will for the most part appear in great and full body, soft and phlegmatique, of colour like a black obscure cloud, having a swelling countenance, with eyes red and full of water, a bald head, and teeth like a wilde boar. Their motion is as it were an exceeding great tempest of the sea. For their signe, there will appear an exceeding great rain about the Circle. |
| ☿ | 12 | The Spirits of Mercury will appear for the most part in a body of a middle stature, cold, liquid and moist, fair, and with an affable speech; in a humane shape and form, like unto a Knight armed; of colour clear and bright. The motion of them is as it were silver coloured clouds. For their signe, they cause and bring horror and fear unto him that calls them. |
| ♀ | 14 | The Spirits of Venus do appear with a fair body, of middle stature, with an amiable and pleasant countenance, of colour white or green, the upper part golden. The motion of them is as it were a most clear Star. For their signe, there will seem to be maids playing without the Circle, which will provoke and allure him that calleth them to play. |
| ☼ | 30 | The Spirits of the Sun do for the most part appear in a large, full and great body sanguine and gross, in a gold colour, with the tincture of blood. Their motion is as the Lightning of Heaven; their signe is to move the person to sweat that calls them. |
| ♂ | 27 | The Spirits of Mars appear in a tall body, cholerick, a filthy countenance, of colour brown, swarthy or red, having horns like Harts horns, and Griphins claws, bellowing like wilde Bulls. Their Motion is like fire burning; their signe is Thunder and Lightning about the Circle. |
| ♃ | 21 | The Spirits of Jupiter do appear with a body sanguine and cholerick, of a middle stature, with a horrible fearful motion; but with a milde countenance, a gentle speech, and of the colour of Iron. The motion of them is flashings of Lightening and Thunder; their signe is, there will appear men about the circle, who shall seem to be devoured of Lions. |
| ♄ | 32 | The Spirits of Saturn appear for the most part with a tall, lean, and slender body, with an angry countenance, having four faces; one in the hinder part on the head, one on the former part of the head, and on each side nosed or beaked: there likewise appeareth a face on each knee, or a black shining colour: their motion is the moving of the winde, with a kinde of earthquake: their signe is white earth, whiter then any Snow. |

| | | M41. The Visible Appearance of the Planetary Spirits. |
|---|---|---|
| | | |
| ☾ | 13 | A King like an Archer riding upon a Doe; a little Boy; a Woman-hunter with a bow and arrows; a Cow; a little Doe; a Goose; a Garment green or silver-coloured; an Arrow; a Creature having many feet. |
| ☿ | 12 | A King riding upon a Bear; a fair Youth; a Woman holding a distaffe; a dog; a she-bear; a magpie; a Garment of sundry changeable colours; a Rod; a little staff. |
| ♀ | 14 | A King with a Scepter riding upon a Camel; a Maid clothed and dressed beautifully; a naked maid; a She-goat; a Camel; a Dove; a white or green Garment; Flowers; the herb Savine. |
| ☼ | 30 | A King having a Scepter riding on a Lion; a King crowned; a Queen with a Scepter; a Bird; a Lion; a Cock; a yellow or golden Garment; a Scepter; Caudatus [Love-Lies-Bleeding plant]. |
| ♂ | 27 | A King armed riding upon a Wolf; a Man armed; a Woman holding a buckler on her thigh; a He-goat; a Horse; a Stag; a red Garment; Wool; a Cheeslip [Multiceps]. |
| ♃ | 21 | A King with a Sword drawn riding on a Stag; a Man wearing a Mitre in long raiment; a Maid with a Laurel-Crown adorned with Flowers; a Bull; a Stag; a Peacock; An azure Garment; a Sword; a Box-tree. |
| ♄ | 32 | A King having a beard riding on a Dragon; An Old man with a beard; An Old woman leaning on a staff; a Hog; a Dragon; An Owl; a black Garment [without wearer]; a [reaping] Hook or Sickle; a Juniper tree. |

*Olympic Spirits*

| | | M42. Olympic Spirits. | M43. Olympic Spirits – Greek Orthography. | M44. Olympic Spirits – Numeration. | M45. Olympic Spirits – Ministers. | M46. Olympic Spirits – Legions Commanded. | M47. Olympic Spirits – Provinces. |
|---|---|---|---|---|---|---|---|
| ♄ | 32 | Araithron | Αραιθρον | 341 = 11 x 31 | 49 Kings<br>42 Princes<br>35 Presidents<br>28 Dukes<br>21 Ministers<br>14 Familiars<br>7 Messengers | 36,000 Legions of Spirits | 49 = 7 x 7 |
| ♃ | 21 | Bethor | βεθορ | 186 = 6 x 31 | [49 ?][45]<br>42 Kings<br>35 Princes<br>28 Dukes<br>21 Counselors<br>14 Ministers<br>7 Messengers | 29,000 Legions of Spirits | 42 = 6 x 7<br>[not 32] |
| ♂ | 27 | Phaleg | φαλεκγ | 558 = 18 x 31 | – | – | 35 = 5 x 7 |
| ☿ | 30 | Och[46] | ευξ | 465 = 15 x 31 | – | 36,536 Legions of Spirits | 28 = 4 x 7 |
| ♀ | 14 | Hagith | ηαγιθ | 31 = 1 x 31 | 4 Kings<br>[at least] | 4000 Legions of Spirits [at least] | 21 = 3 x 7 |
| ☿ | 12 | Ophiel | οφιιλ | 620 = 20 x 31 | – | 100,000 Legions of Spirits | 14 = 2 x 7 |
| ☾ | 13 | Phul | φυλ | 930 = 30 x 31 | – | – | 7 = 1 x 7 |
| | | *Total =* | | *3131 = 101 x 31* | | | *196 = 28 x 7* |

---

[45] These ranks are in this order in the printed original, but have probably slipped one place down in transcription.

[46] In the First Edition, Och was transliterated as *οξ* = 130, and subject to a fudge to bring its numerology into line. Another possible transliteration of Och is *ωοξ* = 930 = (30 x 31).

| | | Olympic Spirits. | M48. Olympic Spirits – Powers & Attributes. | M49. Olympic Planetary Spirits – Days. | M50. Olympic Planetary Spirits – Years Ruled. |
|---|---|---|---|---|---|
| | | | | | |
| ♄ | 32 | Araithron | Converts Anything to Stone in a moment; Converts Treasures into coles [coals] and vice versa; Gives familiars with a definite power; Teaches Alchemy, Magic & Medicine; Reconciles Subterranean Spirits with Man [makes Earth Elementals and treasure guardians friendly to man]; Makes Hairy Men; Makes one Invisible; Makes the Barren Fruitful; Gives Long Life | First Hour of Saturday | 550 – 60 BC |
| ♃ | 21 | Bethor | Can confer titles and nobilities; Opens Treasures; Reconciles the Spirits of the Air that give true answers; Transports Precious Stones from place to place; Makes medicines work miraculously; Prolongs life to 700 years | First Hour of Thursday | 60 BC – 430 AD |
| ♂ | 27 | Phaleg | Gives great Honours in Warlike affaires | First Hour of Tuesday | 430 – 920 AD |
| ☉ | 30 | Och | Prolongs Life to 600 years with Perfect Health; Gives Great Wisdom; Gives excellent familiar spirits; Teaches perfect Medicine; Converts all Things into pure gold and precious stones; Gives gold, and a purse always filled with gold; Makes his Master to be worshipped as a Deity by the kings of the whole world [promotes intense admiration]. | First Hour of Sunday | 920 – 1410 |
| ♀ | 14 | Hagith | Governs venereal things [to do with love]; Makes People Fair & Beautiful; Converts Copper into Gold in a moment & back again; Gives familiar Spirits that faithfully serve their Masters. | First Hour of Friday | 1410 – 1900 |
| ☿ | 12 | Ophiel | Easily gives familiar Spirits; Teaches all Arts; Teaches the ability to, in a moment, convert Quicksilver (Mercury) into the Philosopher's Stone | First Hour of Wednesday | 1900 – 2390 |
| ☽ | 13 | Phul | Changes all Metals into Silver, in word and deed; Prolongs Life to 300 years; Heals Dropsy; Gives Familiar Spirits of Water, who serve in a visible form; Enables men to live 300 years. | First Hour of Monday | 2390 – 2880 |

# M. Magic of the Grimoires – Angels, Demons and Spirits

*Elementals*

| | | M51. Hebrew Name of Element. | M52. Bodily Humour & Elemental Qualities. | M53. Kings of the Elemental Spirits. | M54. The Rulers of the Elements. | M55. The Rulers of the Elements – English. | M56. The Rulers of the Elements – Numeration. |
|---|---|---|---|---|---|---|---|
| | | | | **62** | **60** | | |
| ⊛ | 31b | | | | | | |
| F | 31 | Aesch | Choler – Cold Dryness | Djin | שרף | ShRP – Seraph | 580 |
| A | 11 | Ruach | Phlegm – Heat Moisture | Paralda | אריאל | ARIAL – Ariel | 242 |
| W | 23 | Maim | Sanguine – Cold Moisture | Niksa | תרשים | ThRShIS – Tharsis | 970 |
| E | 32b | Aretz | Melancholy – Heat Dryness | Ghob | כרוב | KRVB – Kerub | 228 |

| | | M57. Angels of the Elements. | M58. Angels of the Elements – English. | M59. Angels of the Elements – Numeration. | M60. Traditional Names of the Elementals. | M61. Enochian Elemental Kings. |
|---|---|---|---|---|---|---|
| | | **61** | | | | **58** |
| ⊛ | 31b | | | | | |
| F | 31 | אראל | ARAL – Aral | 232 | Salamanders | Ohooohatan |
| A | 11 | חסן | ChSN – Chassan | 118, 768 | Sylphs | Tahoeloj |
| W | 23 | תליהד | ThLIHD – Taliahad | 449 | Undines, Limoniades, Mermaids, Naiads, Oceanids, Oreads, Potamides, Sea Maids, Water Sprites | Thahebyobeaatan |
| E | 32b | פורלאך | PVRLAK – Phorlakh | 337, 817 | Gnomes, Brownies, Dryads, Durdalis, Earth Spirits, Elves, Hamadryads, Pygmies, Sylvestres, Satyrs, | Thahaaotahe |

*Four Quarters and the Demon Kings*

| | | M64. Hebrew Demon Princes.[47] | M65. Cardinal Directions. | M66. Winds of the 4 Quarters. | M67. Rivers of Hell. | M68. The 4 Kerubs. |
|---|---|---|---|---|---|---|
| | | | | | | |
| F | 31 | Samael | South Meridionalis | Notus Auster | Phlegethon | Lion |
| A | 11 | Azazel | East Oriens | Eurus Subsolanus | Cocytus | Eagle |
| W | 23 | Azael | West Occidentalis | Zephyrus | Styx | Man |
| E | 32b | Mahazael | North Septentrionalis | Boreas | Acheron | Bull |

---

[47] Columns M62 and M63 appear expanded on the next page.

# M. Magic of the Grimoires – Angels, Demons and Spirits

| | | Cardinal Directions | M62. Demon Kings of the four Quarters.[48] | | | | | |
|---|---|---|---|---|---|---|---|---|
| | | | Agrippa[49] | Solomon[50] | Weirus[51] | Scott[52] | Abramelin[53] | Goetia[54] |
| | | | 1531 | c. 1550 | 1563 | 1583 | 1610 | 1641 |
| F | 31 | South | Amaymon | Amaymon | Ziminiar | Ziminiar | Amaymon | Goap |
| A | 11 | East | Oriens | Eggye | Amaymon | Amaymon | Oriens | Amaymon |
| W | 23 | West | Paymon | Paymon | Corson | Corson | Paimon | Corson |
| E | 32b | North | Egyn | Egyn | Goap | Goap | Ariton | Ziminiar |

| | | Cardinal Directions | M63. Traditional Demon Kings of the four Quarters.[55] | | | | |
|---|---|---|---|---|---|---|---|
| | | | Livre des Espiritz[56] | Honorius[57] | Pseudo-Moses[58] | Janua Reserata[59] | Clavis Inferni[60] |
| | | | 15th century | 1670 | 1734 | 17th century | 1757 |
| F | 31 | South | Aymoymon | Amaymon | Amaymon | Gäap/Goap | Maymon |
| A | 11 | East | Orient (sic) | Maimon | Oriens | Amaymon | Urieus/ Oraeus |
| W | 23 | West | Poymon | Paymon | Paymon | Corson | Paymon |
| E | 32b | North | Egin | Egin | Egyn | Ziminiar | Egyn |

---

[48] These variations are discussed at length in Skinner & Rankine, *Clavis Inferni,* Golden Hoard, Singapore, 2009, pages 22-23.
[49] *De Occulta Philosophia,* 1531.
[50] *Key of Solomon,* Additional MS 36,674, mid-Sixteenth century.
[51] *Pseudomarchia Daemonum,* 1563.
[52] *Discoverie of Witchcraft, 1583.*
[53] *The Sacred Book of Abramelin,* 1610.
[54] Sloane MS 3825, f. 111r.
[55] There are clearly two different traditions shown here: the majority arrangement represented by Agrippa, and a secondary arrangement by his pupil Weirus. The *Janua Reserata* arrangement has the least in common with the others.
[56] Trinity College, Cambridge MS 0.8.29, ff. 179-182v. 15th century.
[57] *Grimoire of Honorius,* 1670.
[58] *Sixth & Seventh Books of Moses,* 1734.
[59] *Janua Magica Reserata* from Sloane MS 3825. Reproduced in Skinner & Rankine, *Keys to the Gateway,* Golden Hoard, Singapore.
[60] *The Grimoire of St Cyprian: Clavis Inferni,* 1757[?], Golden Hoard, Singapore, 2009.

*Grimorium Verum*

| | | | |
|---|---|---|---|
| | | M69. Demons of the *Grimorium Verum*. | |

| Superior Demon | | Inferior Demons | | Appearance & Rulership |
|---|---|---|---|---|
| Lucifer | | | | As a fair boy, but red when angry. Rules Europe & Asia |
| | | Satanachia / Satanicae | Sergutthy | Power over maidens and wives |
| | | | Heramael | Healing, knowledge of cure of any illness. Virtues of plants |
| | | | Trimasael | Chemistry, alchemy, sleight-of-hand. |
| | | | Sustugriel | Magic, gives familiar spirits and mandragores |
| | | Agalierap | Elelogap | Matters connected with water. (Jointly ruled by Tarihimal) |
| Beelzebuth | | | | Monstrous, like a giant cow or a he-goat with a long tail. He vomits fire when angry. Rules Africa |
| | | Tarchimache | | |
| | | Fleruty | | |
| Astaroth | | | | In human shape. Rules America |
| | | Sagatana | | |
| | | Nesbiros / Nesbirots [Nebiros] | Hael | Any language, letter writing, hidden and secret things |
| | | | Sergulath | Speculation, gaming |
| Duke Syrach | 1 | Clauneck | | Riches, treasures, money |
| | 2 | Musisin | | Power over lords, knowledge of republics and allies |
| | 3 | Bechaud | | Storms, tempests, rain, hail and other natural forces |
| | 4 | Frimost | | Woman, girls, seduction |
| | 5 | Klepoth[61] | | Dreams and visions |
| | 6 | Khil | | Earthquakes |
| | 7 | Mersilde / Merfide | | Teleportation |
| | 8 | Clisthert / Clistheret | | Creates illusion of day or night |
| | 9 | Sirchade | | Natural and supernatural animals |
| | 10 | Segal | | Prodigies, illusions |
| | 11 | Hicpacth / Hiepacth | | Transport persons to your presence |
| | 12 | Humots | | Bring any book desired |
| | 13 | Frucissière | | Revives the dead |
| | 14 | Guland | | Causes all illnesses |
| | 15 | Surgat | | Opens every kind of lock |
| | 16 | Morail | | Can make anything invisible |
| | 17 | Frutimiere | | Prepares feasts |
| | 18 | Huictiigaras | | Sleep and insomnia |

---

[61] Rather suggestive of the Kabbalistic *kliphoth*. It is only after this name that corresponding sigils begin to appear in the text.

# M. Magic of the Grimoires – Angels, Demons and Spirits

| Superior Demon | | Inferior Demons | | Appearance & Rulership |
|---|---|---|---|---|
| | 1 | Proculo | | Causes sleep for 48 hours, knowledge of the spheres of sleep |
| | 2 | Haristum | | Pass through fire unscathed |
| | 3 | Brulefer | | To be beloved by women |
| | 4 | Pentagnony | | Invisibility, the love of great Lords |
| | 5 | Aglasis | | Teleportation |
| | 6 | Sidragosam | | Causes any girl to dance unclothed |
| | 7 | Minoson | | To win at any game |
| | 8 | Bucon | | Causes hate and jealousy between members of the opposite sex |
| Scyrlin[62] | | | | The messenger of all the others, but has the power of the 3 Emperors to make the the other spirits appear. He is therefore perhaps the most important spirit of all |

M69. Demons of the *Grimorium Verum*.

*Grand Grimoire*

M70. Demons of the *Grand Grimoire*.

| Principle Spirits | Superior Spirits[63] | Lesser Spirits[64] |
|---|---|---|
| Lucifer – Emperor | Lucifuge Rofocale[65] – Prime Minister Controls all the wealth and treasures of the world | Bael |
| | | Agares |
| | | Marbas |
| | Satanachia – Commander-in-Chief Power of subjecting all women and girls to his wishes | Pruslas |
| | | Amon |
| | | Barbatos |
| Belzebuth – Prince | Agaliarept – Another Commander Discovers arcane secrets in the courts of the world; unveils sublime mysteries | Buer |
| | | Gusion |
| | | Botis |
| | Fleurèty – Lieutenant-General Performs any labour over night; causes hailstorms | Bathin |
| | | Purson |
| | | Eligos |
| Astaroth – Grand Duke | Sargatanas – Brigadier-Major Makes any person invisible; transports them to any place; opens locks | Loray |
| | | Valefar |
| | | Foraii, or Morax |
| | Nebiros – Field-Marshal and Inspector General. Power to do evil to whoever he wills; reveals virtues of metals, minerals and vegetables | Ipos |
| | | Naberius |
| | | Glasya-Labolas |

[62] Suggestively similar to 'scrying'.
[63] Most of these 'Superior Spirits' are identical with the Inferior Demons of the *Grimorium Verum* in Column M69.
[64] The Lesser Spirits have obviously all been derived from the *Goetia*, see Column M15.
[65] Rofocale is probably an anagram of the *Goetia* demon Focalor. See Column M15.

# M. Magic of the Grimoires – Angels, Demons and Spirits

Faust - *Höllenzwang*

| | | Demon | Rank | |
|---|---|---|---|---|
| | 1 | Lucifer | Konig (King/Emperor) | |
| | 2 | Belial | Vice-Roi (Viceroy) | |
| | 3 | Satan | Gubernatores (Governors) | |
| | 4 | Belzebub | | |
| | 5 | Astaroth | | |
| | 6 | Pluto | | |
| | 7 | Abbadon | Grand-Ministers and secret Infernal Counsels | |
| | 8 | Chamus | | |
| | 9 | Milea | | |
| | 10 | Lapasis | | |
| | ? | Merapis | | |
| ⊛ | 31b | | | |
| F | 31 | | | |
| A | 11 | | | |
| W | 23 | | | |
| E | 32b | Milpeza | Secretarius | |
| ☽ | 13 | Marbuel | Gross-Fursten (Grand Dukes) | |
| ☿ | 12 | Ariel | | |
| ♀ | 14 | Anisel/Anael | | |
| ☼ | 30 | Aziel/Aciel | | |
| ♂ | 27 | Aniguel | | |
| ♃ | 21 | Mephistophilis | | |
| ♄ | 32 | Barfael/Barbuel/Barbiel | | |
| ♈ | 15 | Chinicham | Spiritus Familiares (Familiar Spirits) | |
| ♉ | 16 | Pimpam | | |
| ♊ | 17 | Masa | | |
| ♋ | 18 | Lissa | | |
| ♌ | 19 | Dromdrom | | |
| ♍ | 20 | Lomha | | |
| ♎ | 22 | Palasa | | |
| ♏ | 24 | Naufa | | |
| ♐ | 25 | Lima | | |
| ♑ | 26 | Pora | | |
| ♒ | 28 | Saya | | |
| ♓ | 29 | Wunsolay | | |

M71. Demons of Faust's *Dreifacher Höllenzwang*.

# M. Magic of the Grimoires – Angels, Demons and Spirits

Trithemius - *Steganographia*

| | | Angel | Spirts | |
|---|---|---|---|---|
| | | | M72. Planetary Angels and Spirits of the *Steganographia* Book III. | |
| ☾ | 13 | Gabriel | Remasiel | |
| | | | Tespiel | |
| | | | Theoriel | |
| ☿ | 12 | Raphael | Carmiel | |
| | | | Nabeyel / Nabyel | |
| | | | Pathiel | |
| ♀ | 14 | Anael | Zabdiel | |
| | | | Sacmiel | |
| | | | Adoniel | |
| ☼ | 30 | Michael | Laniel | |
| | | | Pasael | |
| | | | Vanriel | |
| ♂ | 27 | Samael | Amael | |
| | | | Asmael | |
| | | | Nebiel | |
| ♃ | 21 | Zachariel | Floriel | |
| | | | Ariel | |
| | | | Raphael | |
| ♄ | 32 | Orifiel | Sadael | |
| | | | Poniel | |
| | | | Morisiel | |

# M. Magic of the Grimoires – Angels, Demons and Spirits

*Papyri Graecae Magicae (PGM)*

<table>
<tr><td colspan="4">M73. Graeco-Egyptian Magic – headwords and types of magic</td></tr>
<tr>
<th>Code</th>
<th>Category of Rites<br>Procedure/Objective</th>
<th>Rubricated Greek Headwords<br>or key word</th>
<th>Literal Translation of Greek<br>Headwords</th>
</tr>
<tr>
<td>A</td>
<td>Amulets</td>
<td rowspan="2">πρὸς (pros)</td>
<td rowspan="2">for…</td>
</tr>
<tr>
<td>A2</td>
<td>Amulets personalised for named client</td>
</tr>
<tr>
<td>B</td>
<td>Evocationary Bowl Skrying/<br>Vessel Inquiry</td>
<td>λεκανομαντεία (lekanomanteia),<br>šn-hne (shen ben)</td>
<td>bowl skrying<br>vessel inquiry</td>
</tr>
<tr>
<td>C</td>
<td>Calendrical Considerations</td>
<td>κύκλος (kuklos)</td>
<td>circle/cycle<br>[of the heavens]</td>
</tr>
<tr>
<td>D</td>
<td>Defixiones</td>
<td>κατάδεσμος (katadesmos),<br>νεκυδαίμων</td>
<td>defixio,<br>ghost of a dead man</td>
</tr>
<tr>
<td>E</td>
<td>Evocationary Lamp Skrying</td>
<td>λύχνου (lychnou),<br>w<sup>c</sup> šn,<br>λυχνομαντείον (lychnomanteia),</td>
<td>lamp<br>lamp skrying</td>
</tr>
<tr>
<td>F</td>
<td>Face-to-Face Encounter with a God</td>
<td>αὔτοπτος (autoptos)</td>
<td>self-revealed (by the god)</td>
</tr>
<tr>
<td>G</td>
<td>God's Arrival</td>
<td>σύστασις (systasis), pḥ-nṯr<br>[Demotic]</td>
<td>god's arrival</td>
</tr>
<tr>
<td>G2</td>
<td>Invocation of a god</td>
<td>-</td>
<td>-</td>
</tr>
<tr>
<td>G3</td>
<td>Invocation of the Bear goddess</td>
<td>Ἀρκτικὴ (Arktikē)</td>
<td>Bear goddess/<br>asterism</td>
</tr>
<tr>
<td>H</td>
<td>Health</td>
<td>pḥre.t, mt.t a [Demotic]</td>
<td>prescription, magical formula</td>
</tr>
<tr>
<td>I</td>
<td>Invisibility</td>
<td>ἀμαύρωσις (amaurōsis)</td>
<td>darkening/<br>making invisible</td>
</tr>
<tr>
<td>J</td>
<td>Hymns (as integral parts of another rite)</td>
<td>ὕμνος</td>
<td>hymn or ode in praise of god</td>
</tr>
<tr>
<td>K</td>
<td>Foreknowledge and Memory</td>
<td>μνημονική (mnēmonikē)<br>πρόγνωσις (prognōsis)</td>
<td>memory<br>foreknowledge</td>
</tr>
<tr>
<td>L</td>
<td>Love Rites of Attraction or 'Love's Leash'</td>
<td>ἀγωγή (agōgē)</td>
<td>leading or drawing (love)</td>
</tr>
<tr>
<td>L2</td>
<td>Love Fetching</td>
<td>ἀγώγιμον (agōgimon)</td>
<td>Fetching the lover, or love tie</td>
</tr>
<tr>
<td>L3</td>
<td>Love Potions, worked at close quarters</td>
<td>φίλτρον (philtron)</td>
<td>love potions and salves</td>
</tr>
<tr>
<td>L4</td>
<td>Love Binding</td>
<td>φιλτροκατάδεσμος<br>(philtrokatadesmos)</td>
<td>love binding</td>
</tr>
<tr>
<td>L5</td>
<td>Love Enforced by hunger or insomnia</td>
<td>ἀγρυπνητικόν (agrupnētikon)</td>
<td>love enforced by<br>insomnia/hunger</td>
</tr>
<tr>
<td>L6</td>
<td>Love Separation</td>
<td>διάκοπος (diakopos)</td>
<td>separation of lovers/friends</td>
</tr>
<tr>
<td>L7</td>
<td>Other Love Rites</td>
<td>-</td>
<td>-</td>
</tr>
</table>

# M. Magic of the Grimoires – Angels, Demons and Spirits

| | M73. Graeco-Egyptian Magic – headwords and types of magic | | |
|---|---|---|---|
| Code | Category of Rites Procedure/Objective | Rubricated Greek Headwords or key word | Literal Translation of Greek Headwords |
| M | Mysteries and Initiation Rites | μυστήρια (*mystēria*), τελετή (*teletē*) | the Mysteries, initiation into the Mysteries |
| N | Necromancy | νεκυδαίμων (*nekudaimōn*) | ghost of a dead man |
| O | Homeric magic and divination | ὁμηρομαντεῖον (*homēromanteion*) | Homeric verses rite/oracle |
| P | *Paredros* or Assistant Daimon | πάρεδρος (*paredros*) | assistant daimon/ familiar spirit |
| Q | Daimonic Possession and Exorcism | δαίμονε (*daimone*) | daimon |
| R | Rings & Gemstones, Magical | δακτύλιον (*daktulion*), *wˁgswr* | [seal] ring |
| S | Statues, Magical | [στοιχεῖα (*stoicheia*)] | magical statue, shadow |
| T | Talismans, general | στήλη (*stēlē*), τέλεσμα (*telesma*) | lamella (or its text), talisman |
| T2 | Victory Talismans | νικητικὸν (*nikētikon*) | [talisman for] victory |
| T3 | Restraining Anger Talismans | θυμοκάτοχον (*thymokatochon*) | binding anger |
| T4 | Binding or Coercion Talismans | κάτοχος (*katochos*) | restraining, holding down |
| U | Phylacteries | φυλακτήριον (*phylaktērion*) | [magician's] phylactery |
| U2 | Phylacteries (as integral parts of another rite) | | |
| V | Visions and Dream Revelation | ὀνειραιτητόν (*oneiraitēton*) | dream revelation |
| V2 | Sending Dreams | ὀνειροπομπὸς (*oneiropompos*) | sending dreams |
| W | Prayers | εὐχή (*euchē*) | prayer |
| X | Other Magical Procedures | - | - |
| Y | Herbs and Plants | [βοτάνη (*botanē*)] | herbs/plants |
| Z | 'Evil Sleep,' Blindness and Death | *nktk bin* [Demotic only] | catalepsy and death |
| Ω | Composite Rites | - | - |

# M. Magic of the Grimoires – Angels, Demons and Spirits

| | M74. Graeco-Egyptian Magic – *nomina magica* | |
|---|---|---|
| **God, Daimon or Angel Name** | **Title/Ascription** | **Notes** |
| Aberamen thōou | | XXIII, 17[66] |
| Aberan nemane thōuth/ Aberamen thōou/ Aberamen thōouth lerth exanaxe threl thōouth enemareba | The god of the 3rd hour of the day, relating to Thoth. | |
| Abla | | VII, 33 |
| Ablanathanalba | A common palindrome, probably of Hebrew origin, which might be read as 'Abla Nathan Alba.' | I, 16 |
| Abrahme | Abraham, the Patriarch | |
| Abraōth | From Abra ('four') and Aōth, the four lettered supreme name. | |
| Abraxas/Arasax/ Abrasaks/Abrasax | The 'anguipede.' A solar god with snakes as legs, a cock's head, holding a whip and shield. Numerically equal to 365. The name of the Lord in 'Baboonic' [i.e. after the manner of the Gnostics. | XIII, 27; XXIII, 24; *PGM* XIII, 81-89 |
| Achramachamarei | The god of the heavenly firmaments.* See Akrammachamarei. | |
| Adōnai/Adōnaei/ Adonaiōs/Adonaēl | Hebrew אדני for 'the Lord,' often inflected in its Greek form, which form then assumes the role of a god. Also god of the 12th hour. | |
| Aerthoē | The god of the 12th hour of the day. | |
| Agathos daimon/ Agatha daimon | 'The good daimon' was originally invoked at Greek banquets, but in the *PGM* it becomes a god in its own right. | |
| Aiōn | The god of time or eternity. | |
| Akephalos | The Headless god. Sometimes identified with Besas. | |
| Akha-ghar-khan-grabynsa-nyni | | XVI, 16 |
| Akha-kha-nby | | VII, 6 |
| Akrammachamarei | The god of the 3rd hour of the day. See Achramachamarei. | |
| Akrourobore/Akryrobore | The ouroboros.[67] | VII, 26 |
| Aktiōphis/Aktiōphi | Form of Hekate. | XXIII, 16 |
| Aktiōphis Erescheichal Neboutosouant | The triple form of Hekate.* | |
| Albalal | The all-powerful god who is in the light of the skrying lamp. | *PGM* IV. 970. |
| Aldabiaeim/Aldabaeim | The magical name of nine (?) letters of the highest god. The name of the Lord in 'Egyptian' | *PGM* XIII, 81-89 |
| Amekranebecheo thōyth | The god of the 3rd hour of the day. | |
| Anoch (Aok) | "I am" used by magicians when self-proclaiming themselves as a god. | |
| Aōabaōth | The god of this day in which I bind.*[68] | |
| Aōnkreiph | The terrestrial…* | |
| Aōth | [The god] before whom every god prostrates himself and every daimon shudders, for whom every angel completes those things which are assigned. | *PGM* XII. 117 |

---

[66] Where '*PGM*' is not mentioned in the Notes column, the reference is to the demotic section and line number, in *PDM xiv,* as shown in the marginal note [ ] in Betz. These references should not be confused with *PGM* numbers. These numbers have been used to facilitate direct location in the demotic text.
[67] See also *PGM* I. 145-146; II. 32; IV. 337; IV. 2771ff; V. 424ff; VII. 680ff; VII. 895ff; XII. 203-4, 274-275; XIII. 923ff; XIXa. 12; XXXVI. 184; *DMP* vii, 25-26 for ouroboros formula.
[68] This one was the specific day on which the original talismanic binding was done.

# M. Magic of the Grimoires – Angels, Demons and Spirits

| | M74. Graeco-Egyptian Magic – *nomina magica* | |
|---|---|---|
| **God, Daimon or Angel Name** | **Title/Ascription** | **Notes** |
| Arai | The name of the Lord in 'birdglyphics' | *PGM* XIII, 81-89 |
| Arathy Adōnai | A god. | |
| Arbathiaō | Part of the formula/doxology of Echebykrōm of Helios. | *PGM* XIII. 80 |
| Arbrathiabri | The god of the 12th hour of the day. | |
| Arimouth | Called in Evocationary Lamp Skrying. One of the 11 Pillars in *Sepher Razim*. | |
| Archphēson (?) | The god of the underworld, the god who leads departed souls [like] holy Hermes.* | |
| Arourobaarzagran[69] | The god of Necessity.* | |
| Arpnophēr | Horus the son. | II. 118 VII. 362 |
| Arpōn/arepo (Latin) | Harpokrates. | IV. 2433 |
| Baalsamēs | Baal, Sun = Lord Sun | IV. 1019 |
| Bachachuch/Bakuksikhukh Bazachuch/Bchuch | A great daimon in Egypt.* See Bainchōōōch. | Lead tablet Carthage |
| Badētophōth zōthaxathōz | Secret name of Genna & Spora. | XIII. 176 |
| Bainchōōōch/ Bainchōōch | A daimon sometimes translated as 'Spirit of darkness,' or 'son of darkness.' | |
| Bainchōōōchōōōchniab | The great name in Egyptian to be carved on the chest of Apollo. | *PGM* XIII. 106 |
| Baisolbai | The god of the 6th hour of the day. | |
| Bakaxichuch/ Bakuksikhukh/ Bakaksikhekh/Baxyxsixyx/ Bakhykh-sikhykh | Prince of Daimones.[70] See Bainchōōōch. | VIII, 10; V, 8; VI, 25; XXVII, 31 |
| Balsames | Originally a Phoenician sun god. | |
| Barbathiaō | See Arbathiaō. | |
| Barzabouzath | | IV, 12 |
| Barzan | The great god | IV, 12 |
| Basma | In the name of… | IV. 1736 |
| Bathiabēl | The god of the 11th hour of the day. | |
| Bazētōphōth | The god of the 2nd hour of the day. | |
| Besbyki | The god of the 10th hour of the day. | |
| Bessyn berithen berio | Secret name of Phōs-Auge | XIII. 165 |
| Biaiothanatos | The spirit of one prematurely dead, utilised by *defixiones*. | |
| Biathiarbar berbir silatour bouphroumtrōm (the name of 36 letters) | Secret name of Kairos (Time). | *PGM* XIII. 190 |
| Biathiarbath | The name of the Lord in Hebrew. 'Anoch = I am | *PGM* XIII, 81-89 |
| Blableisphtheibal | The firstborn god of the Earth on which you lie.[71]* | |

---

[69] Variant of Oreobazagra.

[70] This name is glossed in Greek as ὁ τύραννος τῶν δαιμόνων (*o tyrannos tōn daimonōn*), Ruler (or prince) of Daimones, on an unpublished tablet in the Getty Museum. See Kotansky and Spier (1995), p. 319.

[71] Earth, meaning soil rather than the planet.

| | M74. Graeco-Egyptian Magic – *nomina magica* | |
|---|---|---|
| **God, Daimon or Angel Name** | **Title/Ascription** | **Notes** |
| Boel/Bouēl | The seventh saviour sitting on the throne of the first firmament. He is "the one who sits atop the world and judges everything." He is frequently called upon in Evocationary Lamp Skrying. | V, 19; VII, 8; VII, 14; XVI, 12-14; XVII, 1, 7, 10, 11, 27; XVIII, 3-5 |
| Bolbyel/Bolboel | *See* Boel. | *PGM* xiv. 126 |
| Bolchōsēth | Sacred name of the Egyptian god Seth. | XXIII, 15 |
| Bōrphorbabarbor | A supreme name sometimes associated with Hekate or Selene. | |
| Boubarzan | The great god. See Barzan | IV, 12 |
| Bouēl | *See* Boel | *PGM* IV. 972 |
| Chabaho | He of Eternity. = Tagrtat | V, 22; VII, 18; XVI, 11, 13; XVII, 10; XVIII, 4 |
| Cheaunxin | [The god] who granted as a favour to men, movement by the joints of the body.* | |
| CHI CHI CHI CHI CHI CHI CHI TIPH TIPH TIPH CHA CHA CHA CHA CHA CHA CHA | The name of the Lord in 'Falconic' [the language of Horus, the hawk] | *PGM* XIII, 81-89 |
| Chnoubis/Chnouphi/ Chnoub/Chnum | Chnum the Great. Lion-headed serpent god, a combination of Chnoum and Kneph. | *PGM* XIII. 1058 |
| Chōoichareamōn | The god who fashioned every kind of human being.* A form or title of Amoun. | |
| Chōouch | Darkness. | *PGM* VII. 361 |
| Chorborbath | The god of the 6th hour of the day. | |
| Damnameneus[72] | The goddess of the 4th hour of the day. Mentioned in the *Ephesia Grammata*. | |
| Danoup Chrator Berbali Barbith Iaō | Secret name of the strong man of the god's seventh breath (or 'laugh'). | *PGM* XIII. 197, 205 |
| Diatiphē | The god of the 8th hour of the day. | |
| Echebykrōm | A god: Echebykrōm of Helios. | *PGM* XIII. 80 |
| Ēchetarōpsieu | The god who granted vision to all men as a favour.* | |
| Echilatour Bouphroumtrom | The name of the Lord in Berbir [Berber] | *PGM* XIII, 81-89 |
| Eiau akri lyx… | The god of the 6th hour of the day. | |
| Elōaios | The Hebrew god El in Greek guise. One of the Gnostic Aeons. | |
| Enphanchouph | The god of the 5th hour of the day. | |
| Erbēth | Set.[73] | XXIII, 15 |
| Ereschigal[74] | Babylonian deity transformed into a daimon in the *PGM*. Often associated with Hekate. | VII, 26; XXIII, 16 |

---

[72] One of the constituents of the *Ephesia grammata*. See chapter 4.5 for an explanation of her nature, and a new tentative translation of the *Ephesia grammata*.

[73] See Iō Erbēth Iō Pakerbēth.

[74] See Akti[o]phi[s] Erescheichal Neboutosouant.

| M74. Graeco-Egyptian Magic – *nomina magica* | | |
|---|---|---|
| **God, Daimon or Angel Name** | **Title/Ascription** | **Notes** |
| Eschakleō | Name of the second god created. | XIII. 171 |
| Ēsthanchouchēn | See Enphanchouph. | |
| Harbathanōps Iaoai | Daimon who hymns the rising and setting sun. | *PGM* IV, 995 |
| Harpokrates/ Harpocrates | The young Horus with side-lock and finger to mouth. Especially significant for magicians. | |
| Harpon-knouphi | A form of Harpocrates-Chnoubis. [75] | |
| Hecate/Hekate | The tremor-bearing, scourge-bearing, torch-carrying, golden-slippered blood-sucking netherworldly and horse-riding one.* Liminal goddess. | |
| Heka/Hike | Egyptian god of magic. | |
| Iabaōth | Combination of IAŌ and Sabaoth | |
| Iaho | Derived from Iaō? | I, 15, 28; VII, 32, 33; VIII, 3,6; XXI, 6; XXVII, 9; XXVIII, 7 |
| Iaō | The god appointed over the giving of soul[s] to everyone.* The Greek transliteration of יהוה, IHVH. | X, 4, 5; XVI, 5 |
| Iaō iboēa | The god who lords over the heavenly firmaments.* | |
| Iaōth | A combination of IAŌ and Sabaoth | |
| Iarbatha | God, related to Helios. | *PGM* I. 142; XII. 94-95 |
| Ibas | A Samaritan form of IAŌ | |
| Illillou ilillou ilillou ilillou ithōr | Secret name of the Pythian serpent that arose after the god's creation of Psyche. (To be carved on the back of the statue of Apollo.) *See also* Marmaraugē… | *PGM* XIII. 109, 195 |
| Iō erbēth iō pakerbēth | Invocation of Set. [76] | |
| Iōna [77] | The god who established earth and heaven.* | |
| Ipos | A Samaritan form of IAŌ. | |
| Isos [78] | The god who has the power of this hour in which I bind you.* A god of the hour of the original operation. | |
| Ithuaō | The god of heaven.* | |
| Kentabaōth | Kenta (torments/rage?) + Sabaoth. | |
| Khnum (Chnum) | Egyptian ram god. | |
| Kmeph (Kneph/Kmēphis) | Egyptian serpent god. | |
| Korē | Proserpine, later a demon. | |
| Lailam | The god of winds and spirits.* The name of the Lord in hieroglyphics. [79] | *PGM* XIII, 81-89 |
| Lampsourē | Sun god. | V. 62 LXII. 27 |
| Lēmnei | The god of the 3rd hour of the day. | |
| Lion-Ram | | I, 12; VII, 30 |
| Lion-Ram-Lotus | | I, 12; IX. 6; XI, 8 |
| Lord of the Lands | | IX, 6 |
| Lord of Spirits | | XXVIII, 1 |

---

[75] See Harpon-Knouphi in *PGM* III. 435-6, 560-63; IV. 2433; VII. 1023-25; XXXVI. 219-20.
[76] See binding talisman of Sēth in *PGM* XXXVI. 1-34, which has the full formula.
[77] Possibly a form of IAŌ, as demiurge.
[78] Not Jesus as suggested by Gager (1992), p. 63.
[79] Not related to the Hebrew *le-olam,* forever, as has been suggested.

# M. Magic of the Grimoires – Angels, Demons and Spirits

| | M74. Graeco-Egyptian Magic – *nomina magica* | |
|---|---|---|
| **God, Daimon or Angel Name** | **Title/Ascription** | **Notes** |
| Lotus flower of stars | | IX, 6 |
| Marmaraugē phōchō phōbōch | The name to be carved around the Pythian serpent and tripod. *See also* Ililllou… | *PGM* XIII. 109, 195 |
| Marmariaōth/ Marmarauōth | The god of the second firmament who possesses power in himself.* | See also AŌTH. |
| Marmaripheggē | 'Marmari' followed by φέγγη, 'light, splendour and lustre.' | |
| Marmorouth | See Marmariaōth. | |
| Maskelli maskellō | A common formula.[80] | |
| Menchthōth | Thoth the beneficent. | II. 77 |
| Mene | Epithet of the Moon goddess Selene. | |
| Mene Phōiphōth | The name of the Lord in hieratic. | *PGM* XIII, 81-89 |
| Menebain | The god of the 1st hour of the day. | |
| Moirai | The Fates. | |
| Moltiēaiō | Protector (?).* | |
| Mormoth | The god of the 4th hour of the day. | |
| Mou rōph | The god of the 11th hour of the day. | |
| Nachar | The god who is the master of all tales.* | |
| Napupheraiō | Necessity (?)* | |
| Narzazouzan | | IV, 12 |
| Neboun | The god of the 2nd hour of the day. | |
| Neboutosoualēth[81] | Moon goddess. | IV, 11; XXIII, 16 |
| Negempsenpuenipē | The god who gives thinking to each person as a favour.* | |
| Neicharoplēx | The god who holds the power of the places down beneath [Underworld].* | |
| Nethmomaō | The god who has given you (the corpse [body]), the gift of sleep and freed you from the chains of life.* | |
| Nouphiēr | The god of the 5th hour of the day. | |
| Ōē Iao Eeēaph | The god of the air, the sea, the subterranean world, and the heavens, the god who has produced the beginning of the seas, the only-begotten one who appeared out of himself, the one who holds the power of fire, of water, of the earth and of the air.* | |
| Orbeēth | The god of the 7th hour of the day. | |
| Oreoba[r]zagra | See Arourobaarzagran. | XXVII, 22 |
| Osornouphe | Osiris the good. | VII. 444 |
| Osoronnophris | Osiris the beautiful. | |
| Ouēr/Ouēri | Great. | XII. 346 XIII. 1061 |
| Ouerto | The great one of earth. | XII. 265 |
| Oumesthōth | The god of the 7th hour of the day. | |
| Ouroboros | The serpent that swallows its tail, seen on phylacteries and also used as a protective floor circle. *See also* Akrourobore. | |
| Pakerbēth | Set. See Iō Erbēth Iō Pakerbēth. | XXIII, 15 |
| Panmōth | The god of the 8th hour of the day. | |
| Papipety Metybanes/ Papipetou Metoubanes | He who carried the mummy of Osiris to Abydos. | XV, 27-29 |

[80] In full it reads Maskeli Maskellō Phnoukentabaō Oreobazagra Rhēxichthōn Hippo-chthōn Pyripēganyx. Parts of this formula also appear as free-standing *nomina magica*.

[81] See also Akti[o]phi[s] Erescheichal Neboutosouant.

| M74. Graeco-Egyptian Magic – *nomina magica* | | |
|---|---|---|
| **God, Daimon or Angel Name** | **Title/Ascription** | **Notes** |
| Pharakounēth | The god of the 1st hour of the day. | |
| Phēous phōouth | The god of the 9th hour of the day. | |
| Phnou | The Abyss. | CVII. 1 |
| Phnouphoboēn | The Father-of-Father god (*sic*).* | |
| Phōiphōth | *see* Mene Phōiphōth | |
| Phōkengepseuaret-athoumisonktaikt | The god of the 5th hour of the day. | |
| Phōouth | The great snake. | IV. 1683 |
| Phōr | Short form for next two entries. | |
| Phorba | Short form for next entry. | |
| Phorbaborphorbabor-phororba | The true name that shakes Tartarus, earth, the [ocean] deeps and heaven.* | |
| Phrē | Egyptian Sun god Ra. | |
| Phrouer | The god of the 1st hour of the day. | |
| Pibēchis | The falcon. Also the name of a Theban magician. | IV. 3007 |
| Pnouthis | He of god.* | |
| Pōphopi | Apophis. | XIXB. 14 |
| Psinōth | Son of the female falcon (?) | VII. 316 |
| Psichom | The image/power. | VI. 711 |
| Ptah | Egyptian Creator god. | |
| Ra-Khepri-Atum | Triple form of the Sun god. | VI, 25; XI, 9 |
| Rabchlou | Master of Power, a Samaritan angel. | XXXVI. 175 |
| Rapōkmēph | The god who presides over all penalties of every living creature.* | |
| Sabaōth | The god who [brought] knowledge of all the magical arts.* Derived from the Hebrew Tzabaoth, the god of the angelic and spirit hosts specifically, rather than the usual mis-translation of 'god of armies.' | X, 4; XVIII, 3 |
| Saberra | Anubis. | XIa, 3 |
| Salbalachaōbrē | The god of the underworld who lords over every living creature.* | |
| Sarnochoibal | The god of the 10th hour of the day. | |
| Semea | Syrian goddess. Maybe also be associated with Shamash. Also addressed as a king. | III. 29 V. 429 III. 207 |
| Semeseilam | The god who illuminates and darkens the world.* Nous, Phrenes. | XIII. 174 |
| Senseggen bar pharaggēs (pharangēs) | A secret name for Harpocrates.[82] | |
| Senthenips (Sesenips) | The god of the 4th hour of the day. | |
| Set /Seth | Egyptian god opposed to Osiris, equated with Typhon by the Greeks. | XXIII, 13 |
| Sothon | Sothis? | X, 6 |
| Souarmimōouth | The god of Solomon.* | |
| Soumarta | | *PGM* IV. 946 |
| Souphi | The god of the 2nd hour of the day. | |
| Sthombloēn | The god who is lord over slumber.* | |
| Tabao/Ta-bao | | VII, 6; XVI, 16, 20 |

---

[82] See *PGM* II. 107. It has nothing to do with fig trees in ravines near Baaras, as has sometimes been claimed.

# M. Magic of the Grimoires – Angels, Demons and Spirits

| M74. Graeco-Egyptian Magic – *nomina magica* | | |
|---|---|---|
| **God, Daimon or Angel Name** | **Title/Ascription** | **Notes** |
| Tagrtat | He of Eternity = Chabaho | V, 22; VII, 18; XVI, 11, 13; XVII, 10; XVIII, 4 |
| Tat | A god. Son of Hermes. | II, 13; V, 11; XIV, 2; XVI, 13; XVII, 1, 11, 27; XVIII, 3 |
| Thōbarrabau | The god of rebirth.* | |
| Thoriobrititammaōrrangadō | Secret name of Moira. | XIII. 184 |
| Thymenphri | The god of the 9th hour of the day. | |
| Typhon | God. | XXIII, 13, 19 |
| Yaho | See Iaho | VI, 19; XIV, 27; XIX, 18, 39 |

# N. Natural Magic

*Animals*

| | | N1. Animals – Real. | N2. Animals – Imaginary and Legendary Orders of Being. | N3. Birds. |
|---|---|---|---|---|
| | | **38** | **183** | |
| | 1 | | | [Swan] |
| | 2 | Leopard | | [Phoenix] |
| | 3 | Seal | Dragon (Western) | Lapwing, [raven] |
| | 4 | Hart, eagle, lion (as Leontica) | Hippogriff | Eagle |
| | 5 | Horse, wolf, hawk, boar | Basilisk | Vulture, hawk |
| | 6 | Lion, child, lamb | Phœnix | Swan, pelican, peacock |
| | 7 | Man, goat, sow | Succubi | Dove, iynx (wryneck) |
| | 8 | Serpent, jackal, Cynocephalus ape, fox | Monoceros de Astris, unicorn, Caduceus serpents | Raven (as Corax), stork, ibis |
| | 9 | Cow, cat, elephant, toad, hounds, dog | Lares | Owl, stork, [vulture] |
| | 10 | Lamb, tortoise | Dweller on the Threshold, Sphinx | Mohr |
| ⊛ | 31b | | Sphinx (sword & crown) | |
| F | 31 | Lion as Kerub of Fire | Salamanders, phoenix | Stork |
| A | 11 | Man as Kerub of Air, dog, raven | Sylphs | Eagle |
| W | 23 | Eagle, snake, scorpion as Kerub of Water | Nymphs, undines, nereids, dragon (Eastern) | Dove, penguin |
| E | 32b | Bull as Kerub of Earth | Gnomes | Owl |
| ☾ | 13 | Seacat (catfish), cat, camel, frog, toad, baboon, crab, bat, hare, rabbit, otters, dog, sow | Lemures, ghosts, incubi | Owl, goose, swan, osprey |
| ☿ | 12 | Dog, mullet, monkey, jackal, Cynocephalus ape, civet cat, fox, weasel, bee, hybrids, fish | Caduceus serpents | Stork, ibis, swallow, cock, thrush, raven, peacock (in an alchemic sense) |
| ♀ | 14 | Goat, tithymallus (sea spurge), sow, dove | Succubi | Dove, swan, sparrow, turtledove, nightingale, wood-pigeon, pheasant, raven, duck |
| ☼ | 30 | Lion, seacalf (seal) | Will o' the Wisp | Swan, eagle, sparrow-hawk, falcon |
| ♂ | 27 | Horse, bear, wolf, boar, jaguar, panther, horse, pike, rhinoceros, dog | Furies, chimæras | Sparrow, cock, kite, hawk, screech owl, magpie, vulture |
| ♃ | 21 | Hart, dolphin | Hippogriff | Eagle, cuckoo |
| ♄ | 32 | Toad, bat, mole, cuttlefish, mice, crocodile, reptiles, goat, wolf, oysters, snakes, tortoise | Basilisk, ghouls, larvæ, corpse candles, ouroboros | Lapwing, owl, goose, vulture, crane, raven, crow |

# N. Natural Magic

| | | N1. Animals – Real. | N2. Animals – Imaginary and Legendary Orders of Being. | N3. Birds. |
|---|---|---|---|---|
| | | **38** | **183** | |
| ♈ | 15 | Ram | Mania, erinyes | Owl |
| ♉ | 16 | Ox, rhinoceros | Gorgons, minotaurs | Dove |
| ♊ | 17 | Dog | Banshees | Cock |
| ♋ | 18 | Crab, turtle, crablouse, snake | Vampires | Ibis, Heron |
| ♌ | 19 | Lion, cat, tiger, raven | Dragons, manticore | Eagle, vulture |
| ♍ | 20 | Virgin, any pure animal | Mermaids, banshees, unicorn | Sparrow, peacock |
| ♎ | 22 | Elephant | Fairies, harpies | Goose |
| ♏ | 24 | Scorpion, beetle, crayfish, bee, lobster, wolf, reptiles, spider | Lamiæ, stryges, Amphisbaena | Magpie |
| ♐ | 25 | Horse, dog | Centaur, hippogriff, unicorn, Cabeirian horses, Pegasus | Daw |
| ♑ | 26 | Goat, ass, fish | Satyrs, fauns, Indian cetea, hipocampus | Heron, lapwing, |
| ♒ | 28 | Man | Water nymphs, sirens, lorelei, Mermaids | Eagle, peacock |
| ♓ | 29 | Fish, dolphin, beetle | Phantoms, werewolves | Heron, swan |

*Plants*

| | | N4. Extended Plant Planetary Correspondences. |
|---|---|---|
| | | |
| ☾ | 13 | Crab-apple, hay, camphor, cucumber, poppy, pumpkin, gourd, lettuce, melon, nenuphar, water-melon, purslane, rampion, beetroot, reed, white sandalwood, tamaris, lime tree. |
| ☿ | 12 | Acacia, aniseed, beet, chamomile, honeysuckle, chicory, couch-grass, Milan kale, filbert-tree, wild rose, endive, madder, juniper, marshmallow, matricaria, mercury, yarrow, millet, hazelnut, sorrel, cinquefoil, sarsaparilla, savory, scabious, elder, tea, clover, privet, valerian. |
| ♀ | 14 | Almond tree, box, cassia, celandine, honeysuckle, lemon-tree, coriander, watercress, spinach, fuchsia, clover, mistletoe, iris, hyacinth, house-leek, purple lilac, lily, cherry-pie, medlar, forget-me-not, myrtle, Easter, daisy, pansy, periwinkle, plantain, apple tree, mignonette, rose, satyrion, wild thyme, colt's-foot, verbena. |
| ☼ | 30 | Angelica, balsam, corn, cinnamon, cardamom, caron, celandine, common cabbage, chrysanthemum, cyclamen, gentian, clove tree, heliotrope, laurel, lavender, lotus, marjoram, pimpernel, orange tree, barley, palm tree, primula, buttercup, polygonium, rosemary, saffron, red sandalwood, sage, tansy, thyme. |
| ♂ | 27 | Absinthe, acanthus, wild celery, agaric, garlic, wormwood, artichoke, arum, asparagus, burdock, basil, belladonna, briar, bryony, hemp, thistle, cibol, colocinth, bull's horn, cornel-tree, garden-cress, dog's tongue, euphrasy, bean, fern, gorse, gladiola, woad, hore-hound, mint, mustard, nutmeg, onion, auricula, nettle, poppy, leek, pepper-tree, blackthorn, horse-radish, wallflower, rhubarb, veronica, vine. |
| ♃ | 21 | Agrimony, aloe, amaranth, rest-harrow, daisy, beetroot, borage, bugloss, cedar, centaury, cherry tree, charm, red cabbage, quince, colchicum, sorb-apple, barberry, white fig tree, strawberry, germander, flax, mulberry, elm tree, poplar, peony, plane-tree, plum tree, buckwheat, sesame, violet. |
| ♄ | 32 | Aconite, agnus-castus, asphodel, cactus, hemlock, cocoa, cumin, cypress, datura, hellebore, spurge, fennel, black fig, male fern, stavesacre, lichen, mandragora, moss, parietary, lungwort, rue, soapwort, weeping willow, saxifrage, scrofulary, serpentine, tobacco plant. |

# N. Natural Magic

| | | N5. Plants. | N6. Vegetable and Synthetic Drugs. |
|---|---|---|---|
| | | **39** | **43** |
| | 1 | Almond in Flower | Soma, *Elixir Vitæ*, LSD |
| | 2 | Amaranth | Cocaine, Ether |
| | 3 | Cypress, Blue Lotus, White Lily, Yew, Pomegranate, Ivy | Belladonna, Soma, Ether |
| | 4 | Olive, Shamrock, Cedar, Oak | Opium |
| | 5 | Nettle, Hickory | Nux Vomica, Cocaine, Alcohol |
| | 6 | Sunflower, Acacia, Bay, Laurel, Gorse, Ash, Grape Vine, Rose, Lotus, Oak | Stramonium, Alcohol, Digitalis, LSD |
| | 7 | Rose, Honeysuckle, Damiana, Laurel, Peach | Damiana, Cannabis Indica, Anhalonium Lewinii, Mescaline, and all aphrodisiacs |
| | 8 | Moly (Alchemilla mollis), Ash | Coffee, Cocaine, Methedrine, Amphetamines |
| | 9 | Pomegranate, Banyan, Mandrake, Ginseng, Laurel, Lily, Willow, Mistletoe | Opium, Orchid Root, Hashish, Yohimba, LSD |
| | 10 | Ivy, Cereals, Olive, Oak, Mandrake, Vine | Hashish |
| ⊛ | 31b | Almond in Flower | Stramonium |
| F | 31 | Red Poppy, Hibiscus, Nettle | Ecstasy |
| A | 11 | Aspen, Peppermint, Lime, Linden, Pennyroyal | Pennyroyal |
| W | 23 | Lotus, Watercress, Banyan, all Water Plants | Blue Lotus |
| E | 32b | Oak, Ivy, Cereals, Corn, Thrift, Olive, Wheat | Hashish |
| ☾ | 13 | Almond, Mugwort, Hazel, Moonwort, Goosefoot, Apple Rannunculus, Alder, Pomegranate, Mistletoe, Peony | Juniper, all emmenagogues and ecbolics |
| ☿ | 12 | Nutmeg, Vervain, Ash, Herb Mercury, Majorlane, Palm, Arnica, Mullein, Cinquefoil | Amphetamines, and all cerebral excitants |
| ♀ | 14 | Myrtle, Rose, Clover, Peach, Fig, Apple, Woundwort | All aphrodisiacs |
| ☼ | 30 | Sunflower, Heliotrope, Knotgrass, Marigold | Alcohol |
| ♂ | 27 | Wormwood, Rue, Ribwort, Sulphurwort | Alcohol, Absinthe |
| ♃ | 21 | Hyssop, Oak, Poplar, Fig, Cedar, Agrimony | Cocaine |
| ♄ | 32 | Ash, Cypress, Hellebore, Yew, Nightshade, Elm, Amaranth, Sengreen/House leek | All soporifics |
| ♈ | 15 | Olive tree, Sanguinaria/Blood Root, Tiger Lily, Geranium, Asparagus | All cerebral excitants |
| ♉ | 16 | Myrtle tree, Upright Vervain, Mallow | |
| ♊ | 17 | Laurel, Bending Vervain, Hybrids, Orchids | |
| ♋ | 18 | Hazel, Comfrey, Lotus, Mangrove | |
| ♌ | 19 | Chestnut, Cyclamen/Sowbread, Aesculus, Lady's Seal, Sunflower | All tonics |
| ♍ | 20 | Pear, Calamint, Apple tree, Calamint, Snowdrop, Lily, Narcissus | All anaphrodisiacs |
| ♎ | 22 | Box tree, Mugwort/Artemisia vulgaris, Scorpion Grass, Aloe, garlic | All calmatives |
| ♏ | 24 | Dogwood, Scorpion grass/Forget-me-not, Basil, Wormwood, Cactus, Nettle, all poisonous plants | All poisons |
| ♐ | 25 | Palm tree, Pimpernel, Rush | |
| ♑ | 26 | Pine tree, Dock, Indian Hemp, Orchis Root, Thistle | Satyrion, Yohimba, Viagra, all aphrodisiacs |
| ♒ | 28 | Ramthorn, Dragonwort/Dracunculus vulgaris, Coconut | All diuretics |
| ♓ | 29 | Elm tree, Hartwort/Aristolochia clemantitis | Opium, all narcotics |

# N. Natural Magic

| No. | Latin Name | Common Name | Hebrew Name | Greek Name | Brief Uses |
|---|---|---|---|---|---|
| | | | | | **N7. The 16 Traditional Magical Plants of Albertus Magnus.** |
| 1 | Eliotropia | Marygold | Elios | Matuchiol | I–to discover immorality |
| 2 | Urtica: Uricacae | Nettle | Roibra | Olieribos | II–protects from fear & fantasy or vision<br>III– for catching fish |
| 3 | Virga Pastoris | Wild Teasel | Lorumboror | Allamor | IV– to make a beast or bird pregnant<br>V– to restore peace after argument or battle |
| 4 | Celidonia | Celindine | Aquillaris | Vallias | VI–to overcome all his enemies, and all matters in suit (legal case) and to cease all debate.<br>VII– placed on the head to test if an ill man will die: if yes he shall sing with a loud voice, if not he shall weep. |
| 5 | Provinca | Periwinkle | Iterisi | Vorax | VIII– induces love between man and his wife<br>IX – to turn blue |
| 6 | Mepeta | Calaminte, Peniroyale | Blieth | Ketus | X – causes a beast to give birth. Used in the nostrils will cause a person to fall to the ground as if dead; a little time after that they shall recover<br>XI – to attract bees, and to restore them if drowned |
| 7 | Lingua canis | Hounds tongue | Algeil | Orum | XII – to attract dogs; to keep all dogs silent with no power to bark<br>XIII – if put on the neck of a dog it will make him turn round till he fall to the ground as if dead. |
| 8 | Jusquianus | Henbane | Mansela | Ventosin | XIV – poisons mad dogs<br>XV – breaks silver cups to small pieces<br>XVI – attracts all hares |
| 9 | Lillium | Lillie | Ango | Amala | XVII – if prepared in a certain way causes insomnia<br>XVIII – if prepared in another way causes fever<br>XIX – can be used to cause all the cows to lose their milk |
| 10 | Usicus Querci | Mistletoe | Luperai | Assisena | XX – mixed with Martegon it opens all locks<br>XXI – attracts all birds within a space of five miles |
| 11 | Centaures | Century | Hiphilon | Digelon | XXII – makes men believe themselves to be witches; so that he thinks his head is in heaven and his feet on earth; make the stars to appear to run across the sky; if placed in the nostrils of any man he will flee |
| 12 | Salvia | Sage | Coloris or Colericon | Caramor | XXIII – causes a worm or bird to be engendered whose blood will cause a man to lose his sense or feelings for 15 days or more<br>XXIV – if this worm is put in a fire it will make a rainbow, and horrible thunder. |
| 13 | Verbena | Vervain | Olphantas | Hilirion | XXV – heals the 'falling sickness'<br>XXVI – can engender worms which, if they touch a man, he will die<br>XXVII – attracting doves; coloring the sun blue; causes strife among lovers |
| 14 | Milisopholos | Smallage | Celayos | Casini | XXVIII – after certain preparation makes the bearer gracious and able to vanquish his foes<br>XXIX – makes an ox obedient if bound to its neck |
| 15 | Rosa | Rose | Clerisa | Haphimus | XXX – used to make trees sterile<br>XXXI – gathers fishes; brings the magaris back to life; painted on a house makes it seem aflame |
| 16 | Serpentina | Snake Grass | Caturlin | Pentaphyllon | XXXII – engenders red and green serpents; on a lamp gives the illusion of serpents; if placed under a man's head he shall never dream of himself again<br>XXXIII – observation of the manner of working |

# N. Natural Magic

*Precious Stones and Metals*

| | | N8. Precious and Semi–Precious Stones. | N9. Metals and Minerals. |
|---|---|---|---|
| | | **40** | **44** |
| | 1 | Diamond | Aurum Potabile, Carbon as diamond |
| | 2 | Star Ruby, Turquoise | Phosphorus |
| | 3 | Onyx, Star Sapphire, Pearl | Lead, Silver |
| | 4 | Amethyst, Sapphire, Lapis Lazuli | Tin |
| | 5 | Ruby | Iron, Sulphur |
| | 6 | Carbuncle, Topaz, Yellow Diamond | Gold |
| | 7 | Emerald | Copper, Arsenic |
| | 8 | Achates, Opal, Alexandrite | Mercury |
| | 9 | Quartz, Moonstone, Pearl | Silver |
| | 10 | Rock Crystal | Magnesium Sulphate |
| ⊛ | 31b | Black Diamond | Carbon |
| F | 31 | Fire Opal | Nitrates |
| A | 11 | Topaz, Chalcedony | Oxides |
| W | 23 | Beryl, Aquamarine | Sulphates |
| E | 32b | Rock Crystal | Bismuth |
| ☾ | 13 | Moonstone, Pearl, Crystal, Chalcedony | Silver |
| ☿ | 12 | Achates, Opal, Agate | Mercury |
| ♀ | 14 | Emerald, Turquoise | Copper |
| ☼ | 30 | Carbuncle, Chrysolite, Pyrites (Fool's Gold), Aventurine, Sunstone | Gold |
| ♂ | 27 | Diamond, Ruby, any red crystal | Iron |
| ♃ | 21 | Sapphire, Amethyst, Lapis Lazuli | Tin |
| ♄ | 32 | Onyx, Jet | Lead |
| ♈ | 15 | Bloodstone, Topaz, Ruby | |
| ♉ | 16 | Sapphire, Garnet, Cornelian | |
| ♊ | 17 | Agate, Emerald, Topaz, Tourmaline | |
| ♋ | 18 | Emerald, Sapphire, Chalcedony, | |
| ♌ | 19 | Onyx, Diamond, Jasper, Cat's Eye | |
| ♍ | 20 | Carnelian, Zircon | |
| ♎ | 22 | Peridot, Agate | |
| ♏ | 24 | Aquamarine, Beryl, Amethyst, Snakestone | |
| ♐ | 25 | Yellow Topaz, Beryl | |
| ♑ | 26 | Ruby, Onyx, Chrysoprase, | |
| ♒ | 28 | Garnet, Jasper, Crystal | |
| ♓ | 29 | Amethyst, Ruby, Pearl | |

# N. Natural Magic

| | | N9a. Rocks, Metals and Semi–Precious Stones according to the *Picatrix*. |
|---|---|---|
| ☾ | 13 | Silver, silver coloured *marqashina*, small pearls, marble, azure lapis, onyx, sand coloured rocks |
| ☿ | 12 | *Idramus*, emery, emerald, mercury, chrysolite, tin, glass, marble |
| ♀ | 14 | Red brass, azure lapis, pearl, nacre, *dahnaj*, corals, sand coloured rocks, glass |
| ☼ | 30 | Gold, arsenic, sand coloured rocks, diamond, Pharaoh's glass, nacre, shiny rocks, *shadhanj*, emery, ruby |
| ♂ | 27 | Red brass, grey stone, suphur ores, *marqashina*, bloodstone, lodestone, glass, carbuncle, onyx, dark red rocks |
| ♃ | 21 | Diamond, sapphire, ruby, gold, crystal, shiny stones |
| ♄ | 32 | Iron, diamond, antimony, pure black onyx, jet, turquoise, lodestone, magnesium, gold, ruby, golden *marqashitha, shadhanj*, lead |

| | | | | N10. Stones of the High Priest's Breastplate. | | | |
|---|---|---|---|---|---|---|---|
| | | **Position** | **Stone** | **Colour** | **Hebrew** | **Translated** | **Tribe** |
| ♈ | 15 | 1 | Sardius or ruby | Red, with admixture of purple | אדם | Adem | Reuben |
| ♉ | 16 | 2 | Topaz or modern chrysolite | Pale green, with admixture of yellow | פטדה | Pithedah | Simeon |
| ♊ | 17 | 3 | Carbuncle | Fiery red | ברקת | Bareketh | Levi |
| ♋ | 18 | 4 | Emerald | A beautiful pure green | נפך | Nophech | Judah |
| ♌ | 19 | 5 | Sapphire or modern lapis lazuli | A deep blue, veined with white, and spotted with small golden stars | ספיר | Saphir | Issachar |
| ♍ | 20 | 6 | Diamond or sardonyx | Perfectly white | יהלם | Jahlom | Zebulun |
| ♎ | 22 | 7 | Ligure or hyacinth or jacinth | Dull red, mixed with yellow | לשם | Leshem | Dan |
| ♏ | 24 | 8 | Agate | Gray honey colour, spotted with different colours, chiefly of a dusky hue | שבו | Schebo | Naphtali |
| ♐ | 25 | 9 | Amethyst | Purple | אהלמה | Ahalamah | Gad |
| ♑ | 26 | 10 | Beryl or chrysolite | The modern aqua marina, bluish green | תרשיש | Tarshish | Asher |
| ♒ | 28 | 11 | Onyx | Bluish white | שהם | Shoham | Joseph |
| ♓ | 29 | 12 | Jasper | A beautiful green, sometimes clouded with white, red, or yellow | ישפה | Josepheh | Benjamin |

# N. Natural Magic

*Perfumes & Incenses*

| | | N11. Perfumes and Incenses. | |
|---|---|---|---|
| | | **42** | |
| | 1 | Ambergris | |
| | 2 | Musk | |
| | 3 | Myrrh, Bdellium, Civet | |
| | 4 | Cedar, Ammoniacum | |
| | 5 | Cinnamon | |
| | 6 | Olibanum, Frankincense | |
| | 7 | Benzoin, Rose, Red Sandal | |
| | 8 | Storax | |
| | 9 | White Sandalwood, Jasmine | |
| | 10 | Storax, Dittany of Crete, Oak Moss | |
| ⊛ | 31b | Mentha | |
| F | 31 | Dragon's Blood, Red Sandal, Petitgram, Cinnamon, Olibanum, and all fiery odours | |
| A | 11 | Galbanum, Pinus, Gum Arabic, Mastic, Anise and all fresh odours | |
| W | 23 | Camphor, Orris, Onycha, Clamus, Lotus, Myrrh, Guggul | |
| E | 32b | Storax, Black Copal, Vertivert and all dull and heavy odours | |
| ☾ | 13 | Camphor (as Ishtar), Aloes, Myrrh bark (as Diana), Jasmine, Willow, Black Copal (as lunar eclipse), all sweet virginal odours and odiferous roots | Camphor, Jasmine, White Sandalwood |
| ☿ | 12 | Mastic, Mace, Storax, Nutmeg, Euphorbium, Karaya and all fleeting odours | Cinnamon, Mace, Cloves, Narcissus, Storax |
| ♀ | 14 | Sandalwood, Myrtle, Musk, Patchouli, Jawee, Oak Moss, Rose Myrrh, and all soft voluptuous odours | Ambergris, Sandalwood, Musk, Benzoin, Pink Rose, Myrtle |
| ☼ | 30 | Olibanum, Frankincense, Cinnamon, Golden Copal, Sandrac, Amber, Elemi and all brilliant odours | Lign-Aloes, Saffron, Cinnamon, Myrrh, Cloves |
| ♂ | 27 | Red Sandal, Pepper, Dragon's Blood, Cape Aloes, all hot pungent odours | Benzoin |
| ♃ | 21 | Ammoniacum, Golden Copal, Mace, Balm of Gilead, Saffron, Ash, and all expansive odours | Nutmeg, Cinnamon, Cloves, Lign-Aloes, Balm |
| ♄ | 32 | Assafœtida, Scammony, Indigo, Sulphur and all dark or unpleasant odours | Civet, Musk |
| ♈ | 15 | Myrrh, Dragon's Blood, Star Anise | |
| ♉ | 16 | Costus, Storax | |
| ♊ | 17 | Mastic | |
| ♋ | 18 | Camphor, Onycha | |
| ♌ | 19 | Frankincense, Olibanum | |
| ♍ | 20 | Sanders | |
| ♎ | 22 | Galbanum | |
| ♏ | 24 | Opoponax, Siamese Benzoin | |
| ♐ | 25 | Lign-aloes or Oud | |
| ♑ | 26 | Asam, Gum Benjamin/Benzoin, Musk, Civet, Spikenard | |
| ♒ | 28 | Euphorbium, Galbanum | |
| ♓ | 29 | Armoniacum, Red storax, Ambergris | |

# N. Natural Magic

| | | N12. Zodiacal Perfumes (Ascendant Decans). | N13. Zodiacal Perfumes (Succedent Decans). | N14. Zodiacal Perfumes (Cadent Decans). |
|---|---|---|---|---|
| | | **152** | **153** | **154** |
| ♈ | 15 | Myrtle | Stammonia | Black Pepper |
| ♉ | 16 | Costum | Cardamom | Cassia |
| ♊ | 17 | Mastic | Cinnamon | Cypress |
| ♋ | 18 | Camphor | Succum | Anise |
| ♌ | 19 | Olibanum | Balsam | Muscador |
| ♍ | 20 | Oil of Sandalwood | Srorus | Mastic |
| ♎ | 22 | Galbanum | Bofor | Mortum |
| ♏ | 24 | Opoponax | Opoponax | Opoponax |
| ♐ | 25 | Lign-aloes or Oud | Fol Lori | Gaxisphilium |
| ♑ | 26 | Asafœtida | Colophonium/Colophony | Cubel Pepper/Jamaica Pepper |
| ♒ | 28 | Euphorbium | Stammonia | Rhubarb |
| ♓ | 29 | Thyme | Coxium | White Santal |

| | | N15. Planetary Perfume Compounds. |
|---|---|---|
| ☽ | 13 | Equal quantities of seed of white poppy, storax, benzoin, powdered camphor, frog's head, bull's eye. Prepare the paste with the blood of a frog, toad, crab, cat, osprey, bat, goose, swan, hare, rabbit, or preferably goose blood. |
| ☿ | 12 | Equal quantities of mastic, incense, cloves, cinquefoil, powdered agate. To be made into a paste with the blood of a cat, fox, magpie, swallow, monkey, linnet, weasel, thrush, or common green lizard, or preferably a fox. |
| ♀ | 14 | Equal proportions of musk, ambergris, aloe wood, red roses, powdered coral, to be made into a paste with the blood a turtledove, nightingale, wood-pigeon, dove, pigeon, goat, sheep, sparrow, pheasant, or preferably a dove. |
| ☼ | 30 | Equal quantities of saffron, aloe wood, balm, laurel seeds, cloves, myrrh, incense, musk, ambergris. The paste must be made into a paste and burned with incense and benzion, and the blood of an animal such as an eagles, goat, ram, canary, falcon, ibis, lion, or parrot. |
| ♂ | 27 | Equal quantities of spurge, cornel, ammonia, root of hellebore, powdered magnet, sulphur, gentian root. Make into a paste with the blood of a kite, cock, green woodpecker, horse, wolf, boar, dog, hawk, or in default of this with blood of any butcher's animal. |
| ♃ | 21 | Equal parts of seeds of ash, aloe wood, storax, benzoin, powdered azurite, powdered peacock feathers. Mix into a paste with the blood of a partridge. |
| ♄ | 32 | Equal parts of seed of poppy, seed of henbane, root of mandragora, powdered magnetic iron, powdered myrrh, made into a paste with the blood of a vulture, owl, toad, bat, great-owl, little owl, or mole, preferably a bat. |

# N. Natural Magic

| | | N16. Complete Perfumes from *Liber Juratus*. |
|---|---|---|
| | 1 | |
| | 2 | |
| | 3 | *Saturday* – all good smelling rottes [roots] such as costus and the herb thuris |
| | 4 | *Thursday* – all swete frutes as nuttmuges, cloves, the ryndes of orenges and citrynes drye and powdred with suche lyke of good odoure |
| | 5 | *Tuesday* – sanders the redd blake and white, and all swete woodes as lygnum aloes cipres, balsami and such lyke |
| | 6 | *Sunday* – masticke, muscus and suche lyke and all other good gumes of good odoure, as thus, beniamen, storax, labdanum, ambre, armoniacum, and such lyke |
| | 7 | *Friday* – mace roses violates and all other frutes or flowers of good odoure as crocus and such lyke |
| | 8 | *Wednesday* – the ryndes of all swete woodes, as cinamum, cassia, ligina corticus, lauri, and macis and all swete sedes |
| | 9 | *Monday* – folium mirti, and lawlri, and leves of good odor of all swet flowers |
| | 10 | |
| ✴ | 31b | |
| F | 31 | ambra, muscus, et alba cera |
| A | 11 | balsamus, camphora, et olium olmarum |
| W | 23 | algalya, almea, et tyryaca |
| E | 32b | lignum aloes, nux muscata, et maceys |
| ☾ | 13 | the heades of froges made of the aier which you may gather after some showers of raigne, with the eyes of a bull and the sede of whytt popye wt thure, and camphyre equall porcions, mixt all to gethere wt sangine menstruo, and the bloud of a whytt gander suche quantyte as yt may be verie odiferus |
| ☿ | 12 | mastike, thuer, cloues, the hearbe called sunckfoyle and of the stone in pouder called an agath, of equall porcions and mixt all thes to gethere, wt the braines of a fox and of a wesell, wt ye bloude of a pye called a hagester, suche a quantyte as shal be expedient, so yt it be verie odiferus |
| ♀ | 14 | muscke, ambre, lignum aloes, redd roses, and of the stone in pouder called corall, of yt whiche is redd equall porcions and mixt all thes to gethere, with the braines of sparowes male and female, and wt the bloude of a turcledour or of a howse doue being whytte, hauinge allwayes respect that it be odifirus |
| ☼ | 30 | saffrone, amber, muske, lignum aloes, lignum balsami, the frutte of laurell, wt cloues, mir, and thuer equall porcions so yt it be mixt all to gether after such manner yt it be veri swete of odour of the goumes aforsaide, put to this ye braines of an eygell and the bloude of an whytte coke suche quantite as yt may be verie odiferus as before sayde and make yt in lyttell balles or pylles and kepe yt verie close |
| ♂ | 27 | euphorbium, bedellium, armoniacum, the rottes of bothe ye hearbes called elleborus, of some yt is called bearfotte, wt the powder of the stone called magnes, and mirr, wt alyttell sulphuer, but of the other equall porcions, mixt all to gether wt the braines of a rauen, and humayne bloude wt the bloude of a blak catt suche a quantie as yt maye be verie odiferus |
| ♃ | 21 | the sede of a ayche tree, lignum aloes, storax, beniame and of the stone yt is called lapis lazuli, and the greate endes of the quiells of a pecoke equall porcions, and mixtall thes to gether wt the bloude of a storke, of a swalowe, and the braines of stagg called an hartte when he is kylled in the precens of the prince, the male or female will serve, but suche a quantite as yt may be verie odiferus |
| ♄ | 32 | the sedde of blake popye the sede of henbane, the rotte of mandragg, and of the stone in powder called magnes, and of mirr, equall porcions, mixt all thes togethers with the braines of a blake catt, and the bloude of backes called fluider myse, hauinge respecte to the quantite that it be odiferus |

# N. Natural Magic

| | | N16. Complete Perfumes from *Liber Juratus*. |
|---|---|---|
| ♈ | 15 | mir [myrrh] (2 parts); Scamonum (3 parts); pip nigrum |
| ♉ | 16 | costus (2 parts); cardamonum (3 parts); coprssum |
| ♊ | 17 | mastike |
| ♋ | 18 | camphyer, muscum |
| ♌ | 19 | lignum balsam (3 parts); mir muscata |
| ♍ | 20 | saunders (2 parts); crocum (3 parts); masticem |
| ♎ | 22 | galbanum (2 parts); ut almea (3 parts); garyophilum |
| ♏ | 24 | oponianac |
| ♐ | 25 | lingnum prima facies |
| ♑ | 26 | asam (2 parts); celephamam (3 parts); pip longum |
| ♒ | 28 | euphorbium (2 parts); ruberberum (3 parts); scamon |
| ♓ | 29 | armoniacum (2 parts); crocum (3 parts); sandalum album |

| | | N17. Perfumes of the Sub-Elements. | | | | |
|---|---|---|---|---|---|---|
| | | ✸ | Fire | Air | Water | Earth |
| ✸ | 31b | Ambergris | Civet | [Gall of the rukh] | Onycha | Musk |
| F | 31 | Saffron | Olibanum | Lign aloes or oud | Red sanders | Red Sandalwood |
| A | 11 | Lign aloes or oud | Olibanum | Galbanum | Mastic | Storax |
| W | 23 | Myrrh | Opoponax | Camphor | Siamese benzoin | Indigo |
| E | 32b | Dittany of Crete | Benzoin | Assafoetida | Clover | Storax |

# N. Natural Magic

| | | N18. Fumigations from the *Mystical Hymns of Orpheus*. | | N19. Incense from the *Greek Magical Papyri*. |
|---|---|---|---|---|
| | | **God or goddess** | **Fumigation or perfume** | |
| | 1 | | | |
| | 2 | | | |
| | 3 | Rhea & Juno, Tethys | Aromatics, Frankincense & Myrrh | Kronos = Styrax |
| | 4 | Jupiter | Storax, Frankincense and Manna | Zeus = Malabathron |
| | 5 | Vulcan | Frankincense & Manna | Ares = Kostos |
| | 6 | Apollo & Aurora, Bacchus & Iacchus & Misa, Adonis | Manna, Storax, Aromatics | Helios = Frankincense |
| | 7 | Victory | Manna | Aphrodite = Indian nard |
| | 8 | Hermes, Esculapius & Health | Storax, Manna | Hermes = Cassia |
| | 9 | Semele & Diana Prothyraea, Diana | Storax, Manna | Selene = Myrrh |
| | 10 | Ceres | Storax | |
| ⊛ | 31b | Ether | Saffron | |
| F | 31 | | | |
| A | 11 | Curetes & Boreas & Zephyrus | Frankincense | |
| W | 23 | Neptune, Nereus | Myrrh | |
| E | 32b | Earth | Every kind of seed except beans and aromatics | |
| ☾ | 13 | Moon | Aromatics | Selene = Myrrh |
| ☿ | 12 | Mercury | Frankincense | Hermes = Cassia |
| ♀ | 14 | Venus | | Aphrodite = Indian nard |
| ☼ | 30 | Sun | Frankincense and Manna | Helios = Frankincense |
| ♂ | 27 | Mars | Frankincense | Ares = Kostos |
| ♃ | 21 | Jupiter | | Zeus = Malabathron |
| ♄ | 32 | Saturn | Storax | Kronos = Styrax |
| ♈ | 15 | | | |
| ♉ | 16 | Protogonus | Myrrh | |
| ♊ | 17 | | | |
| ♋ | 18 | | | |
| ♌ | 19 | | | |
| ♍ | 20 | Vesta | Aromatics | |
| ♎ | 22 | Justice | Frankincense | |
| ♏ | 24 | | | |
| ♐ | 25 | | | |
| ♑ | 26 | | | |
| ♒ | 28 | | | |
| ♓ | 29 | | | |

# N. Natural Magic

| Perfume | Botanical Source |
|---|---|
| Armoniacum | Sap of Dorema Ammoniacum |
| Aspalathos | Root of Calycotome Villosa |
| Balsam | Both wood and sap of Commiphora opobalsamum |
| Bay or laurel | Laurus Nobilis |
| Bdellium | Gum resin from several species of Commiphora such as Commiphora Erythraea and Commiphora Africana |
| Benzoin | Gum resin from Styrax Benzoin |
| Black poppy | A variety of opium poppy, papaver somniferum |
| Bulrush | Species of Juncus such as Juncus Acutus and Juncus Maritimus |
| Camel grass (or Lemon grass) | Cymbopogon Citratus |
| Camphor | Cinnamomum Camphora |
| Cardamom | Eliettaria Cardamomum |
| Cassia | Cinnamomum Iners or Cinnamomum Cassia |
| Cedar | Cedrus Atlanticus |
| Cinnamon | Bark of the Cinnamomum Verum or Cinnamomum. Zeylanicum. |
| Citron | Citrus medica |
| Costus | The root of Costus Arabicus or Costus Speciosus |
| Cyperus (or Galingale) | Root of Cyperus Longus |
| Euphorbium | Sap of various species of Euphorbia such as Euphorbia Mauritanica, Euphorbia Officinalis, Euphorbia Resinifera |
| Frankincense (or Olibanum) | Gum resin from several species of Boswellia mainly Boswellia Cartierii. |
| Galbanum | Sap from Ferula Galbaniflua |
| Galingale | Root of Cyperus Longus |
| Gum Benjamin (Gum Benzoin) | Gum resin from Styrax Benzoin |
| Juniper | Dioscorides and Plutarch refer to two kinds of juniper: the minor is probably Juniper Oxycedrus. The major is probably Juniperus Phoenica (used in the Kyphi recipe in the Eber papyrus), or Juniperus Macrocarpa |
| Laurel (See Bay) | Laurus Nobilis |
| Lemon grass (See Camel grass) | Cymbopogon Citratus |
| Libomanum | Dioscorides mentions "Manna of Olibanum", probably a gum resin similar to olibanum |
| Lignum Aloes (see Oud) | Wood of Aquillaria Agallocha |

N20. Perfumes and their Plant Source.

# N. Natural Magic

### N20. Perfumes and their Plant Source.

| Perfume | Botanical Source |
|---|---|
| Lousewort | Delphinium straphis agria |
| Malabathron | Probably leaves of Cinnamomum Tamala or Cinnamomum. Albiflorum |
| Manna | Sap of Fraxinus Ornus |
| Mastic | Gum resin from Pistacia Lentiscus |
| Mint | Various species of Mentha such as Mentha Viridis and Menta Pulegium |
| Musk | Odoriferous substance from glands of the male Moscus Moschiferous |
| Myrrh | Gum resin from several species of Commiphora such as Commiphora Abyssinica, Commiphora Schimperi and Commiphora Momol |
| Myrtle | Myrtus Communis |
| Olibanum | Gum resin from several species of Boswellia mainly Boswellia Cartierii |
| Opium | Sap of Papaver Somniferum |
| Opoponax | Sap of Opopanax Orientalis |
| Oud | Oil derived from the wood of Aquillaria Agallocha |
| Peperwort | Lepidium Latifolium, a species of cress (Lepidium Sativum) |
| Pepper | Seeds of Piper Nigrum |
| Pine | Pinus Pinea or Pinus Halepensis |
| Red sanders or red sandalwood | Wood of Pterocarpus Santalinus |
| Red Storax | Gum resin from a variety similar to Styrax Officinalis. Usually applies to resin in lump form rather than tears of storax. |
| Saffron | Flower pistils from Crocus Sativus |
| Sage | Salvia Officinalis |
| Sandalwood (or Sanders) | Wood of Santalum Album |
| Sanders (see Sandalwood) | Wood of Santalum Album |
| Sesli | Could be Handquista Aegyptiaka, Buplerurum Fruticosum, or Tordylium Officinalis. |
| Spikenard | Nardostachys Jatarmansi |
| Stacte | According to Dioscorides, the oil produced from Myrrh |
| Storax | Gum resin from Styrax Officinalis |
| Sweet flag | Root of Acorus Calamus |

# N. Natural Magic

| | | | | |
|---|---|---|---|---|
| | | | | |

N21. Incenses in the *Book of Jubilees* and the *PGM*.

| Greek god/Planet | Incense | Botanical Source of the Resin | *Book of Jubilees* 160 BCE | *PGM* c. 100 CE[1] |
|---|---|---|---|---|
| Kronos Saturn | Storax Styrax | *Styrax officinalis* (Liquid *amber orientalis* tree) | Stacte[2] | Styrax |
| Zeus Jupiter | Tejpatra Tamaalpatra Indian Bay leaves | *Cinnamomum tamala or albiflorum* | Mixed spices | Malabathron[3] |
| Ares Mars | Costus Kostos | Root of *Costus Arabicus, Costus Speciosus, Saussurea lappa, Saussurea costus* | Costum | Kostos[4] |
| Helios Sun | Frankincense Olibanum (oil of Frankincense) | *Boswellia cartierii* & *Boswellia thurifera* | Frankincense | Frankincense |
| Aphrodite Venus | Spikenard | *Nardostachys grandiflora* or *Nardostachys jatamansi* | Nard | Indian nard |
| Hermes Mercury | Cassia Kasia | *Cinnamomum Cassia* | Galbanum | Cassia Galbanum |
| Selene Moon | Myrrh | *Balsamodendron myrrha, Commiphora myrrha* | Myrrh | Myrrh |

[1] *PGM* XIII. 16-22. These are the "secret incenses" of the planets. It adds "prepare sun vetch [Egyptian bean] on every occasion." They are listed in a different order, but without planetary correspondences in *PGM* XIII. 353-354.
[2] Stacte or στακτή is defined as 'oil of myrrh' by Dioscorides.
[3] Or Malabatrum. Leaves of *Cinnamomum tamala* or *C. albiflorum*. Liddell-Scott gives "the aromatic leaf of an Indian plant, the *betel* or *areca*." See also Dioscorides 1.12; Galen 12.66; Pliny HN12.129; Horace *Odes* 2.7.8. The word is probably derived originally from the Sanskrit *tamāla-pattra*.
[4] *Saussurea lappa* root.

# N. Natural Magic

| | |
|---|---|
| **N22. Magical Ingredient Codenames from the *PGM*.** | |

| Codename in the papyri | Actual ingredient |
|---|---|
| [blood] from the loins | camomile |
| blood [of a Titan] | wild lettuce |
| blood from a head | lupine |
| blood from a shoulder | bear's breach [a herb][5] |
| blood of a goose | mulberry tree's milk [sap] |
| blood of a hamadryas baboon | blood of a spotted gecko |
| blood of a hyrax | truly [blood] of a hyrax[6] |
| blood of a snake | hematite |
| blood of an eye | tamarisk gall |
| blood of Ares | purslane |
| blood of Hephaistos | wormwood |
| blood of Hestia | camomile |
| blood of Isis = *asphos* | black horehound = *ballota nigra* |
| blood of Kronos | [sap?] of cedar |
| bone of an ibis | buckthorn |
| crocodile dung | Ethiopian soil |
| dog testicles = *testiculus canis* | *Orchis militaris.* |
| eagle | wild garlic[7] |
| fat from a head | spurge |
| [fat] from the belly | earth-apple |
| [fat] from the foot | house leek |
| fox testicles = *testiculus vulpis* | *Orchis* |

[5] Scarborough (1991) suggests *Acanthus mollis L.* or *Helleborus foetidus L.*
[6] Scarborough (1991) suggests the rock hyrax, *Procavia capensis.*
[7] Scarborough (1991) suggests *Trigonella foenumgraecum* or *hellebore.*

# N. Natural Magic

<table>
<tr><td colspan="2" align="center">N22. Magical Ingredient Codenames from the PGM.</td></tr>
<tr><th>Codename in the papyri</th><th>Actual ingredient</th></tr>
<tr><td>hair of a lion</td><td>'tongue' of a turnip[8]</td></tr>
<tr><td>hairs of a hamadryas baboon</td><td>dill seed</td></tr>
<tr><td>heart of a hawk</td><td>heart of wormwood</td></tr>
<tr><td>Kronos' spice</td><td>piglet's milk</td></tr>
<tr><td>man's bile</td><td>turnip sap[9]</td></tr>
<tr><td>onion, wild</td><td>Asphodel or wild garlic[10]</td></tr>
<tr><td>physician's bone</td><td>sandstone</td></tr>
<tr><td>pig's tail</td><td>leopard's bane [a herb][11]</td></tr>
<tr><td>ram's horn</td><td>a herb like wild fennel</td></tr>
<tr><td>semen of a bull</td><td>egg of a blister beetle</td></tr>
<tr><td>semen of a lion</td><td>human semen</td></tr>
<tr><td>semen of Ammon</td><td>house leek</td></tr>
<tr><td>semen of Ares</td><td>clover</td></tr>
<tr><td>semen of Helios</td><td>white hellebore</td></tr>
<tr><td>semen of Hephaistos</td><td>fleabane</td></tr>
<tr><td>semen of Herakles</td><td>mustard-rocket[12]</td></tr>
<tr><td>semen of Hermes</td><td>dill</td></tr>
<tr><td>snake's 'ball of thread'</td><td>soapstone</td></tr>
<tr><td>snake's head</td><td>leech</td></tr>
<tr><td>tears of a hamadryas baboon</td><td>dill juice</td></tr>
</table>

[8] Scarborough (1991) suggests the taproot of a turnip.
[9] Scarborough (1991) suggests *Brassica napus l.*
[10] *PGM* xiv. 966-69.
[11] Scarborough (1991) suggests 'scorpion tail,' a variety of leopard's bane, or heliotrope.
[12] Scarborough (1991) suggests *Eruca sativa.*

# O. Orders, Grades and Officers

*Mithraic Grades*

| | O1. Mithraic Initiation Grades. | O2. Mithraic Initiation Grades – Translation. | O3. Mithraic Initiation Grades – Greek Numeration. | O4. Mithraic Grade Symbols. | O5. Mithraic Planetary Symbols. |
|---|---|---|---|---|---|
| **1** | | | | | |
| **2** | | | | | |
| **3** | 7 – Pater/Soter[n] | Father | 725 | Phrygian cap, *Patera*/libation dish, sceptre/staff, sickle, wand | Sickle |
| **4** | 4 – Leo/Leontica | Lion | 105 | Fire shovel, sistrum, thunderbolt wand (*dorje*) | Thunderbolt |
| **5** | 3 – Miles | Soldier | 285 | Lance, soldier's helmet, Persian cap, soldier's pack | Spear/lance |
| **6** | 6 – Heliodromus | Messenger of the Sun | 543 | Torch, 7–rayed crown/wreath, whip for Helios' horses | Whip |
| **7** | 2 – Nymphus/ Cryphius | Nymph/Hidden | 414 | Oil lamp, diadem/crown of Venus | Lamp |
| **8** | 1 – Corax | Raven | 234 | Raven, Caduceus, Cup with handle | Caduceus Wand |
| **9** | 5 – Perses | Persian | 596 | Sickle of Luna, Persian dagger, crescent moon with a star | Crescent |
| **10** | 0 – Mystes | | 854 | | |

| | | O5a. Mithraic Zodiacal and Elemental Animals and Symbols. | O5b. Mithraic Constellation. |
|---|---|---|---|
| ⊛ | 31b | | |
| **F** | 31 | Lion | |
| **A** | 11 | Dog, Raven | |
| **W** | 23 | Snake, Scorpion | |
| **E** | 32b | Bull, Wheat | |
| ♈ | 15 | Cautes, torchbearer | Aries, Spring Equinox |
| ♉ | 16 | Mithras, Bull | Perseus, Taurus |
| ♊ | 17 | Dog | Canis Minor |
| ♋ | 18 | Snake | Hydra |
| ♌ | 19 | Lion, Raven & Cup | Leo, Corvus & Crater |
| ♍ | 20 | Wheat | Spica |
| ♎ | 22 | Cautopates, torchbearer | Libra, Autumn Equinox |
| ♏ | 24 | Scorpion | Scorpius |
| ♐ | 25 | | |
| ♑ | 26 | | |
| ♒ | 28 | | |
| ♓ | 29 | | |

# O. Orders, Grades and Officers

*Hermetic Order of the Golden Dawn*

| | O6. Grades of the Hermetic Order of the Golden Dawn. | | O7. Cipher Manuscript Grades. | O8. Cipher Manuscript Grades – Hebrew. |
|---|---|---|---|---|
| | **121** | **Order** | | |
| 1 | [10°=1° Ipsissimus] | | | |
| 2 | 9°=2° Magus | 3rd Order | | |
| 3 | 8°=3° Magister Templi | | | |
| 4 | 7°=4° Adeptus Exemptus | | | |
| 5 | 6°=5° Adeptus Major | 2nd Order | | |
| 6 | 5°=6° Adeptus Minor | | | |
| 7 | 4°=7° Philosophus[1] | | Philosoph | פלסוף |
| 8 | 3°=8° Practicus | | Baal Omen | בעל אמן |
| 9 | 2°=9° Theoricus | 1st or Outer Order | Baal ha-Da'ath | בעל הדעת |
| 10 | 1°=10° Zelator | | Talmid [Student] | תלמיד |
| | 0°=0° Neophyte | | Mathchiel | מתחיל |

| | O9. Golden Dawn Passwords of the Grades – Hebrew. | O10. Golden Dawn Passwords – English. | O11. Golden Dawn Passwords – Numeration. | O12. Golden Dawn Passwords – Meaning. |
|---|---|---|---|---|
| | **114** | | **10** | |
| 1 | א | A | 1 | [Breathing] |
| 2 | אב | AB | 3 | Father |
| 3 | דב | DB | 6 | Bear |
| 4 | את | AT | 10 | Enchanter |
| 5 | יה | IH | 15 | First 2 letters of IHVH |
| 6 | אהיה | AHIH | 21 | I am |
| 7 | כח | KCh | 28 | Power |
| 8 | אלה | ALH | 36 | God |
| 9 | מה | MH | 45 | What |
| 10 | נה | NH | 55 | Ornament |

---

[1] Just below Dominus Liminus – Lord of the Paths of the Portal to the Vault of the Adepts

# O. Orders, Grades and Officers

| | O13. Pre-Golden Dawn Grades. | O14. Numbers Associated with Grade. | O15. Symbols by which a Lodge Superior knows his Inferior. | O16. Grade Name (used also in the Golden Dawn). | O17. Grade 'Consulates'. |
|---|---|---|---|---|---|
| 1 | | | | | |
| 2 | Magi | 7 | Equilateral triangle | Luxianus Renaldus de Perfectis | Hassan (Ispahan), Venice, etc |
| 3 | Magistri | 77 | (Geometric) compass | Pedemontanus de Reus | Naples |
| 4 | Adepti Exempti | 777 | Hitakel [Hiddekel] | Ianus de aure campis | Vienna |
| 5 | Majores | 788 | Prat[h] | Sphaere fontus a Sales | Prague |
| 6 | Minores | 799 | Pison | Hodus Chamlionis [sic] | Frankfurt-on-Oder |
| 7 | Philosophi | 822 | Gihon | Pharus illuminans | Dresden |
| 8 | Practici | 833 | Weth Aretz [Earth] | Monoceros de astris | Zurich |
| 9 | Theoretici | 844 | Maim [Water] | Porajus de Rejectus | Bergen-op-Zoom |
| 10 | Juniores | 909 | Aesch [Fire] | Pereclinus de Faustis | Innsbruck |

| | O18. Golden Dawn Temple Officers: Neophyte Grade. | O19. Female form of Officers' Title. | O20. Corresponding Egyptian God/Goddess. |
|---|---|---|---|
| 1 | | | |
| 2 | Secret Chiefs | | |
| 3 | | | |
| 4 | Praemonstrator: to instruct | | Isis |
| 5 | Imperator: to command | | Nephthys |
| 6 | Cancellarius: to record Hierophant | Hierophantria | Osiris, Thoth |
| 7 | Hierus, Dadouchos | Hiereia, Dadouche | Horus, Thaum-aesch-niaeth |
| 8 | Hegemon, Stolistes | Hegemone, Stolistria | Thmae-st, Aur-a-mo-ooth |
| 9 | Kerux | Kerukaina | Anubis |
| 10 | Sentinel, Neophyte | Phulax, Neophyte | Ano-oobi em-Pementte |

# O. Orders, Grades and Officers

*Masonic Grades*

| | O21. Officers in a Masonic Lodge. | O22. Masonic Grades – Relaxed Observance. |
|---|---|---|
| | **115** | |
| 1 | | Magus, or Knight of Splendour and Light |
| 2 | Past Master | Provincial Master of the Red Cross |
| 3 | | Sovereign Magus |
| 4 | Worshipful Master | Scottish Master |
| 5 | Senior Warden | Knight of the Eagle or Master Elect |
| 6 | Junior Warden | Knight of St Andrew |
| 7 | Senior Deacon | African Brother |
| 8 | Junior Deacon | |
| 9 | Inner Guard | as per Symbolical Masonry |
| 10 | Tyler (and Candidate) | |

| Grade order. | O23. Masonic Grades – Rite of Philalethes. | O24. Masonic Grades – Philosophic Scottish Rite. |
|---|---|---|
| 1 | Philalethes, or Searcher after Truth | Sublime Master of the Luminous Ring |
| 2 | Initiate | Grand Inspector, Grand Scottish Mason |
| 3 | Sublime Philosopher | Grand Inspector, Perfect Initiate |
| 4 | Unknown Philosopher | Knight of the Golden Fleece |
| 5 | Knight of the Temple | Knight of the Argonauts |
| 6 | Knight of the Rose Croix | True Mason |
| 7 | Knight of the East | Knight of Iris |
| 8 | Scottish Knight or Master | Knight of the Sun |
| 9 | Elect | Knight of the Phoenix |
| 10 | Master Mason | Knight of the Black Eagle or Rose Croix 3 |
| 11 | Fellow Craft | Knight of the Black Eagle or Rose Croix 2 |
| 12 | Entered Apprentice | Knight of the Black Eagle or Rose Croix 1 |

# O. Orders, Grades and Officers

| Grade Order. | O25. Masonic Grades – 33 degrees of the Scottish or Ancient and Accepted Rite. | | O26. Masonic Grades – 33 degrees of the Antient and Primitive Rite. |
|---|---|---|---|
| 1 | Craft Freemasonry | Entered Apprentice | Entered Apprentice |
| 2 | | Fellow Craft | Fellow Craft |
| 3 | | Master Mason | Master Mason |
| 4 | Lodge of Perfection | Secret Master | Discreet Master |
| 5 | | Perfect Master | Sublime Master |
| 6 | | Intimate Secretary | Sacred Arch |
| 7 | | Provost and Judge, or Irish Master | Secret Vault |
| 8 | | Superintendent of the Buildings, or Master in Israel | Knight of the Sword |
| 9 | | Master Elect of Nine | Knight of the Jerusalem |
| 10 | | Illustrious Master Elect of Fifteen | Knight of the Orient |
| 11 | | Sublime Knight, or Chevalier Elect of the Twelve | Rose Croix |
| 12 | | Grand Master Architect | Knight of the Red Eagle |
| 13 | | Knight of the Ninth Arch, or Royal Arch of Solomon | Knight of the Temple |
| 14 | | Grand Elect, Grand Scottish Chevalier of the Holy Vault, or of James VI | Knight of the Tabernacle |
| 15 | Chapter of Rose Croix | Chevalier / Knight of the East, or of the Sword | Knight of the Serpent |
| 16 | | Prince of Jerusalem, or Chief of the Regular Lodges | Knight Kadosch / Sage of Truth |
| 17 | | Chevalier of the East and West | Knight of the Royal Mystery / Hermetic Philosopher |
| 18 | | Sovereign Prince Rose Croix | Grand Inspector / Knight Kadosch |
| 19 | Council of Kadosh | Grand Pontiff, or Sublime Scottish Mason | Sage of Truth / Royal Master |
| 20 | | Venerable Grand Master of Symbolic Lodges | Hermetic Philosopher / Grand Intendant |
| 21 | | Noachite, or Prussian Chevalier | Grand Installator |
| 22 | | Prince of Lebanus, or Knight of the Royal Hatchet | Grand Consecrator |
| 23 | | Chief of the Tabernacle | Grand Eulogist |
| 24 | | Prince of the Tabernacle | Patriarch of Truth |
| 25 | | Chevalier of the Brazen Serpent | Patriarch of the Planispheres |
| 26 | | Scottish Trinitarian, or Prince of Mercy | Patriarch of the Sacred Vedas |
| 27 | | Knight Grand Commander of the Temple | Patriarch of Isis |
| 28 | | Chevalier of the Sun, or Prince Adept | Patriarch of Memphis |
| 29 | | Grand Scottish Chevalier of Saint Andrew of Scotland | Patriarch of the Mystic City |
| 30 | | Chevalier Kadosh | Master of the G.'. W.'. P.'. P.'. |
| 31 | Consistory of Sublime Princes | Grand Inspector Inquisitor Commander | Grand Defender of the Rite |
| 32 | | Sublime Prince of the Royal Secret | Sublime Prince of Memphis |
| 33 | Supreme Council | Sovereign Grand Inspector General | Sovereign Grand Conservator of the Rite |

# O. Orders, Grades and Officers

| Grade Order. | O27. Masonic Grades – Rite of Mizraim. | | |
|---|---|---|---|
| | **I – Symbolical Series** | **II – Philosophic Series** | **III – Mystical/ IV – Kabbalistic** |
| 1 | 1.  Entered Apprentice | 34. Knight of the Sublime Election | 67. Benevolent Knight |
| 2 | 2.  Fellow Craft | 35. Prussian Knight | 68. Knight of the Rainbow |
| 3 | 3.  Master Mason 2nd Class | 36. Knight of the Temple | 69. Knight Khanuka, Hynaroth |
| 4 | 4.  Secret Master | 37. Knight of the Eagle | 70. Most Wise Israelitish Priest |
| 5 | 5.  Perfect Master | 38. Knight of the Black Eagle | 71. Sovereign Princes Talmudim |
| 6 | 6.  Intimate Secretary | 39. Knight of the Red Eagle | 72. Sovereign Prince Zadkim |
| 7 | 7.  Provost and Judge or Irish Master | 40. White Knight of the East | 73. Grand Haram |
| 8 | 8.  English Master | 41. Knight of the East | 74. Sovereign Princes Haram |
| 9 | 9.  Elect of Nine | 42. Commander of the East | 75. Sovereign Princes Hasidim |
| 10 | 10. Elect of the Unknown | 43. Grand Commander of the East | 76. – |
| 11 | 11. Elect of Fifteen | 44. Architecture of the Sovereign Commanders of the Temple | 77. Grand Inspector Intendant Regulator, General of the Order Chief of the Third Order |
| 12 | 12. Perfect Elect | 45. Prince of Jerusalem | |
| 13 | 13. Illustrious Elect | 46. Sovereign Prince Rose Croix of Kilwinning and Heroden | 78. – |
| 14 | 14. Scottish Trinitarian | 47. Knight of the West | 79. – |
| 15 | 15. Scottish F.C. | 48. Sublime Philosopher | 80. – |
| 16 | 16. Scottish Master | 49. Chaos I. Discreet | 81. – |
| 17 | 17. Scottish Panisière | 50. Chaos II. Wise | 82. – |
| 18 | 18. Master Ecossais | 51. Knight of the Sun | 83. – |
| 19 | 19. Ecossais of the three J.J.J. | 52. Supreme Commander of the Stars | 84. – |
| 20 | 20. Ecossais of the Sacred Vault of James VI | 53. Sublime Philosopher | 85. – |
| 21 | 21. Ecossais of St Andrew | 54. First Degree of the Key of Masonry, Minor | 86. – |
| 22 | 22. Little Architect | 55. Second Degree, Washer | 87. Sovereign Grand Princes (1-3) |
| 23 | 23. Grand Architect | 56. Third Degree, Bellows Blower | 88. Sovereign Grand Princes (4-8) |
| 24 | 24. Architecture | 57. Fourth Degree, Caster | 89. Sovereign Grand Princes (9-13) |
| 25 | 25. Apprentice Perfect Architect | 58. True Mason Adept | 90. Absolute Sovereign Grand Master, Chief of the Fourth Series |
| 26 | 26. F.C. Perfect Architect | 59. Sovereign Elect | |
| 27 | 27. Master Perfect Architect | 60. Sovereign of Sovereigns | |
| 28 | 28. Perfect Architect | 61. Grand Master of Symbolic Lodges | |
| 29 | 29. Sublime Ecossais | 62. Most High and Most Powerful Grand Priest Sacrificer | |
| 30 | 30. Sublime Ecossais of Heroden | 63. Knight of Palestine | |
| 31 | 31. Grand Royal Arch | 64. Grand Knight of the White and Black Eagle | |
| 32 | 32. Grand Axe | 65. Grand Elect Knight Kadosh | |
| 33 | 33. Sublime Knight of Election Chief of the First Series | 66. Grand Inquiring Commander Chief of the Second Series | |

# O. Orders, Grades and Officers

| O27a. Masonic Grades – Oriental Rite of Memphis. | | |
|---|---|---|
| 1. Apprentice. | 34. Knight of the Temple, or Knight of the Red Eagle (1856), or Knight of Scandinavia (1862), or Knight Grand Inspector (Ragon). | 67. Guardian of the Three Fires, or Most Wise Mouni (1849), or Prince of the Sanctuary (1856), or Companion of the Luminous Ring (1862). |
| 2. Companion. | 35. Knight of Scandinavia, or Knight Master of Angels (1865), or Sublime Commander of the Temple (1862). | 68. Pontiff of Ogygia, or Grand Architect of the Mysterious City (1849), or Prince of the Temple of Truth (1856), or Companion of the Sacred Vedas (1862). |
| 3. Master. | 36. Knight Philalethes, or Knight of the Holy City (1856), or Sublime Negotiaie Commander of the Luminous Triangle (1862). | 69. Sovereign Grand Master of the Light, Chief of the Second Series, or Sublime Prince of the Sacred Courtine (1849), or Commander of the Second Series (1856), or Companion of the Sacred Name (1862). |
| 4. Discreet Master, or Secret Master (1862). | 37. Doctor of the Planispheres, or Knight Adept of Truth (1856), or Knight of Shota (1862). | 70. Doctor of the Sacred Fire, or Interpreter of Hieroglyphs (1849), or Orphic Sage (1856), or Companion of the Golden Fleece (1862). |
| 5. Perfect Master, or Master Architect (1849). | 38. Master of the Great Work, or Wise Siviast (1849), or Sublime Knight Elect of Truth (1856), or Sublime Elect of Truth or Philalethes (1862). | 71. Knight of the Luminous Triangle, or Orphic Doctor (1849), or Sage of Eleusis (1856), or Companion of the Lyre (1862). |
| 6. Sublime Master, or Intimate Secretary (1867). | 39. Prince of the Zodiac, or Knight Philalethes (1856), or Grand Elect of the Eons (1862). | 72. Theosophic Knight, or Guardian of the Three Fires (1849), or Companion of the Lybic Chain (1862). |
| 7. Just Provost, or Just and Perfect Master (1849), or Provost and Judge (1862). | 40. Sublime Hermetic Philosopher, or Doctor of the Planispheres (1856), or Wise Siviast, or Perfect Sage (1862). | 73. Sage of Heliopolis, or Guardian of the Incommunicable Name (1849), or Sage of Mithras (1856), or Companion of the Sanctuary (1862). |
| 8. Knight Intendant of the Building, or Knight of the Elect (1849) or Master in Israel (Ragon). | 41. Knight of the Seven Stars, or Wise Siviast (1856), or Knight of the Arch of Seven Colors (1862), or Knight or the Seven Stars (Ragon). | 74. Pontiff of Mithras, or Supreme Master of Wisdom (1849), or Sage of Delphos (1856), or Patriarch of Truth (1862). |
| 9. Knight Elect of Nine. | 42. Knight of the Arch of Seven Colors, or Hermetic Philosopher (1856), or Sublime Hermetic Philosopher (1862). | 75. Guardian of the Sanctuary, or Sovereign Prince of Senates of the Order (1849), or Sage of Samothrace (1856), or Sublime Master of the Secrets of the Order (1862). |
| 10. Illustrious Knight Elect of Fifteen. | 43. Knight Supreme Commander of the Stars, or Adept Installator (1856), or Doctor of the Planispheres (1862). | 76. Prince of Truth, or Sovereign Grand Master of Mysteries (1849), or Sage of Eleusis (1856), or Sage of Ellia (1862). |
| 11. Sublime Knight Elect. | 44. Grand Pontiff of Isis, or Adept Consecrator (1856), or Sublime Sage of the Zodiac (1862). | 77. Sublime Kavi, or Supreme Master of the Sloka (1849), or Sublime Sage of the Mysteries (1856), or Sage of Mithras (1862). |
| 12. Knight Grand Master Architect. | 45. Sovereign Master of the Mysteries, or Shepherd King of the Hutz (1849), or Adept Eulogist (1856), or Sublime Sage of Isis (1862). | 78. Doctor of the Sacred Vedas, or Doctor of the Sacred Fire (1849), or Sage of Wisdom (1856), or Sage of Delphi or Sacred Curtain (1862). |

| O27a. Masonic Grades – Oriental Rite of Memphis. | | |
|---|---|---|
| 13. Royal Arch. | 46. Sublime Prince of the Sacred Curtain, or Adept of Sirius (1856), or Sublime Pastor of the Hutz (1862). | 79. Most Wise Mouni, or Doctor of the Sacred Vedas (1849), or Sublime Sage of the Mysteries (1856), or Wise Theosopher (1862). |
| 14. Knight of the Sacred Vault, or Grand Scottish Elect (1862). | 47. Interpreter of Hieroglyphs, or Sage of the Pyramids (1849), or Adept of Babylon (1856), or Knight of the Seven Stars (1862). | 80. Knight of the Redoubtable Sada, or Sublime Knight of the Golden Fleece (1849), or Priest of the Sphinx (1856), or Sublime Sage of Symbols Interpreter of Hieroglyphs (1862). |
| 15. Knight of the Sword, or Knight of the Sword or East (Ragon), or Knight of the East (1862). | 48. Pastor-King of the Hutz, or Philosopher of Samothrace (1849), or Adept of the Rainbow (1856), or Sublime Guardian of the Sacred Mount (1862). | 81. Guardian of the Incommunicable Name, or Sublime Knight of the Luminous Triangle (1849), or Priest of the Phoenix (1856), or Sublime Sage of Wisdom (1862). |
| 16. Prince of Jerusalem. | 49. Prince of the Sacred Curtain, or Titan of the Caucasus, or Adept of the Seven Stars (1856), or Sublime Sage of the Pyramids (1862). | 82. Supreme Master of Wisdom, or Supreme Knight of the Redoubtable Sada (1849), or Priest of the Pyramids (1856), or Sublime Sage of the Mysteries (1862). |
| 17. Knight Prince of the East and West, or Knight of the East (1849), or Knight of the East and West (1862). | 50. Sage of the Pyramids, or Child of the Lyre (1849), or Commander of the Zodiac (1865), or Sublime Philosopher of Samothrace (1862). | 83. Grand Pontiff of Truth, or Sublime Knight Theosopher (1849), or Priest of Heliopolis (1856), or Sublime Sage of the Sphinx (1862). |
| 18. Knight Prince of the Rose of Heredom, or Knight of Rose Croix (1862). | 51. Philosopher of Samothrace, or Knight of the Phoenix, or Knight Banuka (1856), or Sublime Titan of the Caucasus (1862). | 84. Grand Inspector Intendant, or Sovereign Grand Inspector (1849), or Priest of On (1856). |
| 19. Knight Grand Pontiff of Jerusalem, or Knight Prince of the West (1849), or Grand Pontiff (1862). | 52. Prince of the Golden Fleece, or Sublime Scald (1849), or Knight of the Luminous Triangle (1856), or Sage of the Labyrinth (1862). | 85. Sovereign Prince of Masonry Chief of the Third Series, or Grand Defender of the Order (1849), or Priest of Memphis (1856). |
| 20. Knight Grand Master of the Temple of Wisdom, Chief of the First Series, or Grand Master of Lodges (1862), or Venerable Grand Master of all Lodges (Ragon). | 53. Titan of the Caucasus, or Knight of the Sphinx (1849), or Knight Zaradust (1856), or Sage of the Phoenix (1862). | 86. Sovereign Grand Master Constituent of the Order, or Sublime Master of the Luminous Ring (1849), or Pontiff of Serapis (1856). |
| 21. Knight Noachite, or Knight of the Tower, or Prussian Noachite (1862), or Master of the Key of Masonry (Ragon). | 54. Child of the Lyre, or Knight of the Pelican (1849), or Knight of the Luminous Ring (1856), or Sublime Scald (1862). | 87. Sovereign Prince General Ruler of the Order, or Regulator General of the Order (1849), or Priest of Isis (1856), or Pontiff of Isis (1862). |
| 22. Knight of Libanus, or Prince of Lebanon (1862), or Noachite Knight, or Knight of the Tower (Ragon). | 55. Knight of the Phoenix, or Sublime Sage of the Labyrinth (1849), or Prince Magus (1856), or Sublime Orphic Doctor (1862). | 88. Sovereign Grand Inspector-General Chief of the Supreme Representative Council of the Order, or Sublime Prince of Masonry (1849), or Priest of Knef (1856), or Pontiff of Knef (1862). |
| 23. Knight of the Tabernacle, or Chief of the Tabernacle (1862), or Knight Royal Axe, or Knight of Libanus (Ragon). | 56. Orphic Doctor, or Pontiff of Cadmea (1849), or Doctor of the Sacred Vedas (1856), or Sage of Cadmus (1862). | 89. Knight of the Knef Member of the Supreme Grand Council General, or Sublime Master of the Great Work (1849), or Pontiff of the Mystic City (1856). |

# O. Orders, Grades and Officers

| O27a. Masonic Grades – Oriental Rite of Memphis. | | |
|---|---|---|
| | | |
| 24. Knight of the Red Eagle, or Prince of the Tabernacle (1862), or Knight of the Tabernacle (Ragon). | 57. Sublime Scald, or Sublime Mage (1849), or Prince Bramin (1856). | 90. Prince of Memphis Member of the Sovereign Tribunal Defender of the Order, or Sublime Knight of the Knef (1849), or Perfect Prince Sublime Master of the Great Work (1856). |
| 25. Knight of the Brazen Serpent, or Knight of the Red Eagle, or Prince of the Tabernacle (Ragon). | 58. Knight of the Sphinx, or Prince Bramin (1849), or Sublime Scald (1856), or Wise Bramin (1862). | 91. Sovereign Patriarch Grand Commander of the Order: Grand Emperor, or Sovereign Prince of Memphis Chief of the Government of the Order (1849), or Past Grand Defender of the Rite (1856), or General Inspector of the Order (1862). |
| 26. Knight of the Holy City, or Scottish Trinitarian (1862), or Knight of the Brazen Serpent (Ragon). | 59. Perfect Master of the Sloka, or Pontiff of Ogygia (1849), or Scandinavian Knight (1856), or Sublime Sage of Ogygia (1862). | 92. Sovereign Prince of the Magi of the Sanctuary of Memphis, or Sublime Interpreter of Science and Hieroglyphs (1856), or Grand Defender of the Order (1862). |
| 27. Sovereign Grand Commander of the Temple, or Knight of the Holy City, or Prince of Mercy (Ragon). | 60. Knight of the Pelican, or Scandinavian Knight (1849), or Prince of the Sacred Name (1856), or Sublime Guardian of the Three Fires (1862). | 93. Grand Inspector Regulator of the Rite (1856), or Grand Regulator General of the Order (1862). |
| 28. Knight of Johan or of the Sun, or Grand Sublime Knight of St. Andrew of Scotland (1862). | 61. Sublime Sage of the Labyrinth, or Knight of the Temple of Truth (1849), or Prince of the Golden Fleece (1856), or Sublime Unknown Philosopher (1862). | 94. Sovereign Prince of Memphis (1856), or Sovereign Prince of Memphis or of Masonry (1862). |
| 29. Knight of St. Andrew, or Knight of Johan or of the Sun (1862). | 62. Pontiff of Cadmus, or Sage of Heliopolis (1849), or Prince of the Lyre (1856), or Sublime Sage of Eleusis (1862), or Sage of Heliopolis (Ragon). | 95. Sovereign Patriarchal Grand Conservator of the Rite (1856), or Sublime Prince of the Magi (1862). |
| 30. Knight Grand Kadosh Sovereign Grand Inspector, or Knight Kadosh (1862), or Knight of St. Andrew (Ragon). | 63. Wise Siviast, or Pontiff of Mithras (1849), or Prince of the Labyrinth (1856), or Adept of Sirius (1862). | 96. Sublime Magus (1856), or Sovereign Pontiff of Magi of the Sanctuary of Memphis (1862). |
| 31. Grand Inquisitor Commander, or Grand Master Commander (1862), or, Knight Grand Kadosh (Ragon). | 64. Grand Architect of the Mysterious City, or Guardian of the Sanctuary (1849), or Prince of the Lybic Chain (1856), or Adept of Babylon (1862). | 97. Grand Hierophant. |
| 32. Sovereign Prince of the Royal Mystery, or Prince of the Royal Secret (1862), or Grand Inquisitor Commander (Ragon). | 65. Sublime Magus, or Prince of Truth (1849), or Sublime Sage of Eleusis (1862). | |
| 33. Knight Grand Inspector General, or Grand Master General (1862), or Sublime Prince of the Royal Mystery (Ragon). | 66. Brahmin Prince, or Sublime Kavi (1849), or Prince of the Covenant (1956), or Companion Zaradust (1862). | |

# O. Orders, Grades and Officers

*Aleister Crowley's A.'.A.'. and O.T.O. Grades*

| | O28. Grades[2] and Magical Mottos personally adopted by Crowley. | | |
|---|---|---|---|
| | **Grade** | **Motto** | **Date conferred/adopted** |
| **1** | 10°=1□ Ipsissimus | | 23 May 1921- Feb 1924 |
| **2** | 9°=2□ Magus | To Mega Therion, The Beast 666 | 12 Oct 1915 |
| **3** | 8°=3□ Magister Templi | Vi Verum Vniversum Vivus Vici | 30 May 1907 - 3 Dec 1909 |
| | *Babe of the Abyss* | | |
| **4** | 7°=4□ Adeptus Exemptus | ΟΥ ΜΗ | 10 December 1906 |
| **5** | 6°=5□ Adeptus Major | Ol Sonuf Vaoresagi[3] | 10 April 1904 |
| **6** | 5°=6□ Adeptus Minor | Christeos Luciftias[4] | 16 Jan 1900 |
| | *Portal Grade* | | Dec 1899 |
| **7** | 4°=7□ Philosophus | | May 1899 |
| **8** | 3°=8□ Practicus | | Feb 1899 |
| **9** | 2°=9□ Theoricus | | Jan 1899 |
| **10** | 1°=10□ Zelator | | Dec 1898 |
| | 0°=0□ Neophyte | Frater Perdurabo | 18 Nov 1898 |
| | *Born Edward Alexander Crowley* | *Aleister Crowley* | *12 Oct 1875* |

---

[2] Golden Dawn format Grades rather than A.'.A.'.

[3] Enochian for 'I reign over you'. Soon after on 1 June 1905 Crowley adopted the name 'Baphomet' as his X° of the MMM.

[4] Crowley used 'Lucifer' in the same sense that Blavatsky used it when she named her Theosophical magazine after the Light Bringer. I also used it in that sense when I produced the counter-culture magazine *Lucifer* in Sydney in the 1960s. Crowley's motto could therefore be translated as 'the Anointed Light bringer' but is more likely to have also been adopted because of Crowley's lifelong anti-Christian sentiments. Maybe out of a desire not to upset his relationship, Crowley at one point told Gerald Yorke that his name for this Grade was 'Parzival' (a magical name later adopted by C S Jones) which has Christian Grail overtones.

# O. Orders, Grades and Officers

| | O29. Grades of the OTO – Crowley 1917. | Masonic equivalent | O30. Grades of the OTO – Modern. |
|---|---|---|---|
| 1 | X° - Supreme and Most Holy King | | X° - Rex Summus Sanctissimus |
| 2 | IX° - Illuminatus Perfectus | Illuminism | IX° -   Initiate of the Sanctuary of the Gnosis |
| 3 | VIII° - Oriental Templar | *Esoteric Rosicrucianism:* Illuminatus Princeps Adeptus Practicus | VIII° - Perfect Pontiff of the Illuminati, Epopt of the Illuminati |
| 4 | VII° - Mystic Templar | Grand Master of Light Magus of Light Theoreticus [*sic*] | VII° - Theoreticus [*sic*], Bishop of Ecclesia Gnostica Catholica |
| 5 | VI° - Historical Templar | Grand Inspector General Knight Kadosh, | VI° - Illustrious Knight of the Order of Kadosch, Companion of the Holy Graal |
| 6 | V° - Rose-Croix | Knight of Rose-Croix Knight of Pelican Knight of East & West | V° -  Sovereign Prince Rose-Croix, Knight of the Pelican & Eagle |
| 7 | IV° - Scotch Mason | Royal Arch Knight of St Andrew Scotch Mason | IV° - Perfect Magician & Companion of the Holy Royal Arch of Enoch |
| 8 | III° - Fellow Craft | Master Mason Fellow Craft Entered Apprentice | III° - Master Magician |
| 9 | II° - Minerval | Novices | II° -  Magician |
| 10 | I° - Probationer (0° - Neophyte) | | I° -  Man & Brother 0° - Minerval |

| | O31. The Grades of the A.'. A.'. | O32. The Order Divisions and Portal Grades of the A.'. A.'. | O33. Practices and Attainments for each A.'. A.'. Grade. |
|---|---|---|---|
| | **121** | | |
| 1 | 10°=1° Ipsissimus | | |
| 2 | 9°=2° Magus | [Inner] Order of the S.S. | Mastery of all magic |
| 3 | 8°=3° Magister Templi | | Tends his disciples and masters Samadhi |
| | Babe of the Abyss | | |
| 4 | 7°=4° Adeptus Exemptus | Order of the R.C. | Perfects all below |
| 5 | 6°=5° Adeptus Major | | Mastery of practical magic, Rosy Cross formula |
| 6 | 5°=6° Adeptus Minor | | Knowledge & Conversation of the HGA, Great Work |
| | Dominus Liminus | | Mastery of Pratyahara and Dharana |
| 7 | 4°=7° Philosophus | | Moral training and devotion to Order |
| 8 | 3°=8° Practicus | Outer Order of the G.D. | Completes intellectual study especially the Qabalah |
| 9 | 2°=9° Zelator | | Yoga Asana & Pranayama. Begins Rosy Cross |
| 10 | 1°=10° Neophyte 0°=0° Probationer Student | | Neophyte – Control of the Astral Plane Probationer – Begin practices and keep a record. Student – Intellectual knowledge of all practices |

# O. Orders, Grades and Officers

| | | O34. Magical 'Weapons' and Temple Equipment. | O35. Magical Formulae. |
|---|---|---|---|
| | | **41** | **187** |
| | 1 | Swastika or Fylfot Cross, Crown, Lamp | LAShTAL [=0], M....M [=0] |
| | 2 | Phallus/Lingam, Phallic Wand, Inner Robe of Glory | VIAOV = 93 |
| | 3 | Sickle, Cup/Chalice, Kteis/Yoni, Outer Robe of Concealment | BABALON = 806, VITRIOL = 726 |
| | 4 | Thunderbolt (*dorje*), Wand, Orb and Sceptre, Crook | IHVH = 26 |
| | 5 | Spear/Lance, Sword, Dagger, Scourge, Chain, Flail | AGLA = 35, ALHIM = 86 |
| | 6 | Whip, Lamen, Breastplate, Rosy Cross, Calvary Cross | ABRAHADABRA = 418, IAO = 81: INRI =270 |
| | 7 | Oil Lamp, Girdle of Venus | ARARITA = 813 |
| | 8 | Caduceus Wand, Barbarous Names, Versicles/Incantations, Apron | |
| | 9 | Crescent, Perfumes, Sandals, Magic Mirror, Cup/Chalice | ALIM = 81 |
| | 10 | Magical Circle and Triangle, Equal-armed Elementary Cross, Bread, Bitter Herbs, Consecrated Salt | VITRIOL = 726 |
| ⊛ | 31b | Breath | |
| F | 31 | Lamp, Pyramid of Fire, Thurible, Sword, Dagger | |
| A | 11 | Wand, Fan, Perfumes | |
| W | 23 | Cup/Chalice, Wine, Consecrated Water | |
| E | 32b | Pentacle, Talisman, Bread, Consecrated Salt | |
| ☽ | 13 | Crescent, Cup/Chalice | ALIM = 81 |
| ☿ | 12 | Caduceus Wand, Wand | |
| ♀ | 14 | Oil Lamp, Girdle of Venus | AGAPE = 93 |
| ☼ | 30 | Whip, Lamen | IAO = 81: INRI = 270 ABRAXAS = 365, MEITHRAS = 365 |
| ♂ | 27 | Spear/Lance, Sword, Dagger | |
| ♃ | 21 | Thunderbolt (*dorje*), Sceptre, Arrow | |
| ♄ | 32 | Sickle [Scythe] | |
| ♈ | 15 | Horns, Burin | |
| ♉ | 16 | Throne | |
| ♊ | 17 | Tripod | |
| ♋ | 18 | Cup | ABRAHADABRA = 418 |
| ♌ | 19 | Phoenix Wand | TO MEGA THERION = 666 |
| ♍ | 20 | Lamp | |
| ♎ | 22 | Cross of Equilibrium | |
| ♏ | 24 | Cilice Garter, Oath | AUMGN = 100 |
| ♐ | 25 | Bow and Arrow | ON = 120 |
| ♑ | 26 | Secret [Sexual] Force | ON = 120 |
| ♒ | 28 | Aspergillum | |
| ♓ | 29 | Magic Mirror | |

# P. Pagan Pantheons

*Middle Eastern*

| | | P1. Sumerian Gods. | P2. Akkadian, Assyrian, Mesopotamian Gods. | P3. Babylonian Planetary Gods. | P4. Planetary Gods Numeration. |
|---|---|---|---|---|---|
| | **1** | Abzu | Apsu | | |
| | **2** | Enki, An | Anu as sky, Ea as wisdom, Lumashi | | |
| | **3** | Ninurta, Ninmah | Adar, Ninurta, Nintu, Tiamat, Asherah | Adar | 4 |
| | **4** | Enlil (Ellil) | Marduk, Adad/Haddad, (Bel), Ashur | Marduk | 10 |
| | **5** | Inanna | Qingu, Nergal, Nanaja | Nergal | 8 |
| | **6** | Babbar, Utu, | Shamash | Shamash | 20 |
| | **7** | Inanna, Ishara, Irnini | Ishtar, Baalit | Ishtar | 15 |
| | **8** | Ninurta, Ninazu, Nisaba | Nebo/Nabu | Nebo | 12 |
| | **9** | Nannar, Ningal | Sin, Shahr | Sin | 30 |
| | **10** | Dumuzi, Abu, Enbilulu | Damkina as Earth mother, Tammuz, Nissaba, Kia, Ashnan | | |
| ⊛ | **31b** | | | | |
| **F** | **31** | | Ag, Gibil | Nusku, Gerra, Ishum | |
| **A** | **11** | Enlil | Adad, Enlil as Wind | | |
| **W** | **23** | Ninlil, Enki | Badur | | |
| **E** | **32b** | Enlil | Urash | | |
| **UW** | | Enmesharra, Ereshkigal, Nerigal, Ninazu, Ningishzida | Nergal, Ea, Mamitu, the Arallu | | |
| ☾ | **13** | | Sin | | |
| ☿ | **12** | | Gudud | | |
| ♀ | **14** | | Dlibat | | |
| ☼ | **30** | | Shamash | | |
| ♂ | **27** | | Mastabarru | | |
| ♃ | **21** | | Umunpaddu | | |
| ♄ | **32** | | Kaimanu | | |
| ♈ | **15** | | Agru | | |
| ♉ | **16** | | Kakkab U Alap Shame | | |
| ♊ | **17** | | (Viper) | | |
| ♋ | **18** | | Shittu (Snake) | | |
| ♌ | **19** | | Kalbu Rabu (Lakhamu) | | |
| ♍ | **20** | | Shiru (Whirland) | | |
| ♎ | **22** | | Zibanitum (Dog) | | |
| ♏ | **24** | | Akrabu (Scorpion-man) | | |
| ♐ | **25** | | Pa Bil Sag (Hurricane) | | |
| ♑ | **26** | | Suxur Mash (Fish-man) | | |
| ♒ | **28** | | Gula (Horned Beast) | | |
| ♓ | **29** | | Dilgan U Rikis Nini | | |

# P. Pagan Pantheons

| | | P5. Persian Gods. | P6. Phoenician and Canaanite Gods. | P7. Pre-Islamic Arabian Peninsular & Nabatean Gods. | P8. Syrian Gods. |
|---|---|---|---|---|---|
| | 1 | Ahura Mazda | Baal, [Pothos] | Allah, Al-Ilah | |
| | 2 | | El | | Hadad |
| | 3 | Zervan | Asherah/Asherat (as Sea) | Orotalt, Allat | Atargatis |
| | 4 | Ormazd | Adad/Hadad, Dagon | Dushara | Hadad, Rimmon (Jupiter Dolichenus) |
| | 5 | Tistrya | Resheph, Anath/Anat | Quam, Hubal? | |
| | 6 | Mithra | Adonis, Shamash, Shapash, Baal, Baal-Zebul, Moloch/Melech | Shams, Nabu/ Nebo, Dushara | Elagabalus |
| | 7 | Anahita/Anaitis | Anath, Astarte, Kadesh/Kedesh | Athar, Allat | Atargatis, Astarte |
| | 8 | | Eshmoun/Eshmun or Baalat Asclepius, Kothar, Kusor, Latpon | Kutbay | |
| | 9 | Tora | Kathirat, Yarikh, Sin, Tanith, [Lotan], Jarih/Erah | Sin, Allat | Atargatis, Semiramis |
| | 10 | | Melqart/Melkart, Baal-Hammon, Gea | | Adonis |
| ⊛ | 31b | | | | |
| F | 31 | | Reshef | | |
| A | 11 | | | | |
| W | 23 | Anahita | | | |
| E | 32b | | Asay | | |
| UW | | Angru Mainyu, Ahriman | Mot, Abaddon | | |
| ☾ | 13 | | Sin | | |
| ☿ | 12 | | Eshmoun/Eshmun, Malagbel | | |
| ♀ | 14 | | Anath | | |
| ☼ | 30 | | Shamash | | Elagabalus |
| ♂ | 27 | | | | |
| ♃ | 21 | | | | |
| ♄ | 32 | | Baal | | |
| ♈ | 15 | | | | |
| ♉ | 16 | Mithra | Ashteroth-Karnaim | | |
| ♊ | 17 | | | | |
| ♋ | 18 | | | | |
| ♌ | 19 | | | | |
| ♍ | 20 | | | | Atargatis |
| ♎ | 22 | | | Anbay | |
| ♏ | 24 | | | | |
| ♐ | 25 | | Reshef | | |
| ♑ | 26 | | | | |
| ♒ | 28 | | | | |
| ♓ | 29 | | | | |

284

# P. Pagan Pantheons

*Egyptian*

| | | P9. Egyptian Gods. | P10. Egyptian Gods as used ritually by the Golden Dawn. | P11. Egyptian Gods and the Bodily Attributes of the Perfected Man. |
|---|---|---|---|---|
| | | **19** | **20** | **21** |
| | 1 | Ptah, Osiris, Khnum/Kneph, Atum/Atem | Ptah | Disk of Ra – the face<br>Nu – the hair |
| | 2 | Amun, Nut/Nuit (as Zodiac) | Isis | [Daath: Assi – the neck] |
| | 3 | Mut/Mout, Isis, Nephthys, Tefnut, Nun, Nu, Naunet | Nephthys | Isis – neck<br>Mert – throat |
| | 4 | Amun, Isis, Hathor (as Nile goddess) | Amoun | Neith of Sais – the forearms |
| | 5 | Horus, Nephthys, Neith | Horus | Bab-neb-Tattu – the hands |
| | 6 | Osiris/Asar, Ra/Re, Kephra Harpocrates (Horus the child) | Ra | Mighty and Terrible One – the breast |
| | 7 | Hathor | Hathor | The Lords of Kher-aha – the kidneys |
| | 8 | Thoth, Anubis, Seshat/Sechat, Heka | Thoth | Nut – the hips and legs |
| | 9 | Shu, Min, phallic gods, the Djed, Bastet/Bast/Pasht/Bubastis | Shu | Osiris – phallus<br>Asar and Asi – the phallus and vulva.<br>Djed/Tet/Set – the spine.<br>Eye of Horus – anus |
| | 10 | Geb, Osiris, Isis, Nephthys. | Osiris | Ptah – feet |
| ✴ | 31b | | | |
| F | 31 | Horus, Renenutet, Sekhet | Canopic: Qebehsenuef/Kabexnuf (hawk), Thoum-Aesh-Neith, Kabeshunt, Tarpesheth, Mau | Serqet – the teeth |
| A | 11 | Shu, Tefnut | Canopic: Hapy/Ahephi (baboon/ape), Nu, Mout | Mighty and Terrible One – the breast/chest |
| W | 23 | Hapy (as Nile inundation), Nut, Ptah, , Heka, Isis, Hathor, Satet & Anuket | Canopic: Duamutef/Tmoumathph (jackal). Hesur, Tum-Athph-Auramoth, Ⲓⲥⲥⲅⲟⲟⲣⲉⲟ | Sekhet – the belly/kidneys and back |
| E | 32b | Geb, Nephthys, Aker, Bes | Canopic: Imsety/Ameshet (human), Satem, Ahapshi, Ⲥϥⲃⲁⲅⲟⲱⲟⲟ | Geb – the bones |
| UW | | Amentet, Anubis, Seth/Set, Sebek Apophis/Apep, Sokar/Seker | Apophrassz, Szathan Toophon, Bessz synthesised as Ommo-Szathan | Eye of Horus – the anus |
| ☽ | 13 | Khonsu/Khons | Chomse | Hathor – the left eye |
| ☿ | 12 | Thoth, Seshat, Imhotep deified | Thoth | Anpu – the mouth/lips |

# P. Pagan Pantheons

| | | P9. Egyptian Gods. | P10. Egyptian Gods as used ritually by the Golden Dawn. | P11. Egyptian Gods and the Bodily Attributes of the Perfected Man. |
|---|---|---|---|---|
| | | **19** | **20** | **21** |
| ♀ | 14 | Hathor | Hathor | Khenti-Khas – the left nostril |
| ☼ | 30 | Ra/Re, Ra-Horakhty, Aten, Harmachis, Horus | Ra | Hathor – the right eye |
| ♂ | 27 | Horus, Set/Seth, Onuris | Menthu | Khenti-Khas – the right nostril |
| ♃ | 21 | Amun-Ra | Amoun-Ra | Ap-uat – the left ear |
| ♄ | 32 | Sobek, Maga | | Ap-uat – the right ear |
| ♈ | 15 | Amun, Khnum, Heryshef/Arsaphes/ Harsaphes, Banebdjedet | Isis | |
| ♉ | 16 | Osiris/Asar, Imsety/Ameshet, Apis/Hapy/Seraphis as Bull, Menthi | Osiris | Uatchet – the shoulders |
| ♊ | 17 | Twin Deities | The twin Merti | |
| ♋ | 18 | Khephra/Khepri | Hormakhu | |
| ♌ | 19 | Sekhmet, Pakhet, Mahes/Mihos, Bast/Bastet/Pasht | Horus, Labo-Ae | Mighty and Terrible One – the breast/chest |
| ♍ | 20 | Isis (as Virgin) | Heru-pa-Kraath | |
| ♎ | 22 | Maat | Maat | |
| ♏ | 24 | Serqet/Serket, Wadjyt | Hammemit | Sekhet – the belly/kidneys and back |
| ♐ | 25 | Sati/Satet, Nephthys | Aroueris | |
| ♑ | 26 | Min, Seth/Set | Set | Osiris – the phallus |
| ♒ | 28 | Hapy/Ahephi, Aroueris | Nuit | The Lords of Kher-aha – the kidneys |
| ♓ | 29 | Hapy/Hapi (as Lord of the Fishes) | Anubis | |

# P. Pagan Pantheons

| | | | Symbol | Amulet use | Animal | Colour |
|---|---|---|---|---|---|---|
| | | | | P12. Egyptian Gods and their Attributes. | | |
| | 1 | Atum | Sacred stone | – | Ram, serpent, eel, cat, mongoose, lion, bull, ape | Gold |
| | | Ptah | Ptah sceptre, skull cap, straight beard | As a dwarf on Cippi, as a Djed pillar | Apis bull | Blue |
| | | Nefertem | Blue lotus, Khepesh sickle-sword, lotus headdress, perfume, silver | For childbirth | Lion | White |
| | 2 | Nut/Nuit | A 5-ponted star, sycamore, lapis lazuli | As a sow for fertility | Cow, sow | Blue and gold |
| | 3 | Isis | Ankh, Sirius, throne crown, uat sceptre, sycamore | Tyet | Kite, cow, scorpion, serpent, sow | White, blue |
| | | Neith/Neit | Bow, crossed arrows, harpoon, was sceptre | As crocodile headed woman, or nursing crocodiles | Crocodile, cow, serpent, bee | – |
| | | Mut | Twin crown of Upper and Lower Egypt, twin sceptre, vulture | As protective mother | Vulture, lioness, cat | Blue, red |
| | 4 | Amun | Twin plumed crown, ammonite | Eye ailments | Serpent, bull, ram, Nile goose, lion, bee | Blue, red |
| | 5 | Horus | Winged sun disk, Eye of Horus | Cippi amulet | Hawk, Falcon, falcon-headed crocodile | Gold, blue |
| | 6 | Ra/Re | Sun disk, Eye of Ra, mound, obelisk, cobra, pyramid, solar barque, flying vultures | For veneration and justice | Bull, cat, child, falcon, hawk, heron, lion, phoenix, ram, scarab, serpent, vulture | Gold, red |
| | 7 | Hathor | Horned solar disk, gold, mirror, myrrh, sistrum, turquoise, wine | Menat | Cow, serpent | Green, blue, red |
| | 8 | Thoth | Ibis, Moon, stylus | As ibis or baboon to aid in writing or magic | Ibis, baboon | green |
| | 9 | Bastet | Sistrum, uat sceptre, utchat eye | Menat | Cat, lioness | Green |
| | 10 | Osiris | Atef crown, crook and flail, djed pillar, (false) beard of kingship, corn | Djed pillar | Bull, wolf | Black, green, blue |
| ✳ | 31b | | | | | |
| F | 31 | Renenutet | Uraeus, royal headgear, cobra-shaped bowl | Cobra-headed woman with child | Cobra | – |
| A | 11 | Shu | Feather | Shown supporting Sun disk | Lion | – |
| W | 23 | Heka | Child with solar disk | – | Lion, serpent | – |
| | | Tefnut | Lion-headed serpent, Uraeus | – | Lioness, serpent, lion-headed serpent | – |
| E | 32b | Geb | Phallus, goose, vegetation | – | Goose, hare | Green |
| | | Bes | Knife, sa symbol, musical instruments | In childbirth and pregnancy | Lion | Black |

# P. Pagan Pantheons

| | | | P12. Egyptian Gods and their Attributes. | | | |
|---|---|---|---|---|---|---|
| | | | **Symbol** | **Amulet use** | **Animal** | **Colour** |
| UW | | Anubis | Embalming knife, imiut, Flail | Thread | Jackal, dog, cobra | Black, gold |
| | | Wepwawet/Up waut | Bow, mace, shedshed (royal placenta), tamarisk | – | Jackal | Grey |
| ☾ | 13 | Khonsu | Full moon disk, crescent shaped pectoral | – | Falcon, baboon | |
| ☿ | 12 | Seshat | 7-pointed star/rosette headdress, leopard skin, geometer's stake and mallet, stylus | – | Leopard | – |
| ♀ | 14 | Hathor | Horned solar disk, gold, mirror, myrrh, sistrum, turquoise, wine | Menat | Cow, serpent | Green, blue, red |
| ☼ | 30 | Ra/Re | Sun disk, Eye of Ra, mound, obelisk, cobra, pyramid, solar barque, flying vultures | For veneration and justice | Bull, cat, child, falcon, hawk, heron, lion, phoenix, ram, scarab, serpent, vulture | Gold, red |
| ♂ | 27 | Set/Seth | Ursa Major constellation, giant mace, iron, Set beast | To prevent miscarriage and heavy bleeding | Set beast, hippopotamus, fenekh fox, antelope, ass, bull, crocodile, leopard, oryx, panther, pig | Red |
| ♃ | 21 | Amun | Twin plumed crown, ammonite | Eye ailments | Serpent, bull, ram, Nile goose, lion, bee | Blue, red |
| ♄ | 32 | Sobek | Sun disk with horns and plumes, water | For fertility and protection | Crocodile | Green |
| ♈ | 15 | Khnum | Atef crown, potter's wheel | For childbirth | Ram, crocodile | Blue |
| ♉ | 16 | Apis | – | – | Bull | – |
| ♊ | 17 | The Merti | – | – | – | – |
| ♋ | 18 | Khephri | Scarab beetle | Scarab beetle, beetle-headed hawk | Scarab beetle | Black |
| ♌ | 19 | Sekhmet | Chariot, constellation of Leo, rosettes, seven arrows, sistrum, uat sceptre, Uraeus crown | Figure of Sekhmet | Lioness, cobra | Red |
| ♍ | 20 | Isis | Ankh, Sirius, throne crown, uat sceptre, sycamore | Tyet | Kite, cow, scorpion, serpent, sow | White, blue |
| ♎ | 22 | Maat | White feather, heart, balance | – | – | White |
| ♏ | 24 | Serqet/Serket | Scorpion | Scorpion amulet | Scorpion, crocodile, lioness, serpent | – |
| ♐ | 25 | Nephthys | Linen bandage | – | Kite | Black |
| ♑ | 26 | Min | Cos lettuce, Min emblem, phallus, flail | For male sexual potency | White bull, falcon, bee | Black |
| ♒ | 28 | Taweret/ Thooeris | Ankh, Sa symbol, flaming torch | For childbirth | hippopotamus | – |
| ♓ | 29 | Heket | Frog with knife | For pregnancy and childbirth | Frog | – |

# P. Pagan Pantheons

*Egyptian Gods in the PGM*

P12a. Egyptian Gods of the Hours of the Day from the *PGM*.

| Hour | Animal form | God of the Hour | God |
|------|-------------|-----------------|-----|
| 1st | Cat | PHARAKOUNĒTH | Bast |
| 2nd | Dog | SOUPHI | Anubis |
| 3rd | Serpent | AMEKRANEBECHEO THŌYTH | Apophis? |
| 4th | Scarab | SENTHENIPS | Khepera |
| 5th | Donkey/Ass | ENPHANCHOUPH | Typhon |
| 6th | Lion | BAI SOLBAI | Sekhmet |
| 7th | Goat | OUMESTHŌTH | Khnum |
| 8th | Bull | DIATIPHĒ | Apis |
| 9th | Falcon | PHĒOUS PHŌOUTH | Horus |
| 10th | Baboon | BESBYKI | Thoth? |
| 11th | Ibis | MOU RŌPH | Thoth |
| 12th | Crocodile | AERTHOĒ | Sobek |

P12b. The Gods of the Egyptian Months from the *PGM*.

| Zodiacal Sign | Egyptian Month | Egyptian god |
|---------------|----------------|--------------|
| Aries | 9. Pachōn | HAR-MONTH HAR-THŌCHE |
| Taurus | 10. Payni | NEOPHOBŌTHA THOPS |
| Gemini | 11. Epeiph | ARISTANABA ZAŌ |
| Cancer | 12. Mesore | PCHORBAZANACHAU |
| Leo | 1. Thōth | ZALAMOIR LALITH |
| Virgo | 2. Phaōphi | EILESILARMOU PHAI |
| Libra | 3. Athyr | TANTIN OURACHTH |
| Scorpio | 4. Choiak | CHORCHOR NATHI |
| Sagittarius | 5. Tybi | PHANTHENPHYPHLIA |
| Capricorn | 6. Mecheir | AZAZA EISTHAILICH |
| Aquarius | 7. Phamenōth | MENNY THYTH IAŌ |
| Pisces | 8. Pharmouthi | SERYCHARRALMIŌ |

*Gnostic*

| | | P13. Ophitic Gnostic Archons & Demiurges from *On the Origin of the World*. | P14. Gnostic Archons – Corresponding Meaning or 'Feminine Name.' | P14a. Alternative Ophite Archons Names. | P15. Gnostic Archons Numeration.[1] |
|---|---|---|---|---|---|
| | **1** | Chaos | | | 291 |
| | **2** | Pistis, Sophia, Acamoth | Faith, Wisdom, Wisdom | | 820, 780 |
| | **3** | Yaldabaoth/Ialdabaoth 'lion-like, androgynous, having great authority.' Also called Ariael. Father of Sabaoth | Pronoia (Foreknowledge) Sambathas, i.e. the Hebdomad | 1. Ialdabaoth, in the form of a lion | 128 |
| | **4** | Yao, IAO, first son of Yaldabaoth | Lordship | 3. Iaoth in the form of a scorpion or (amphibious) snake | 81, 811 |
| | **5** | Sabaoth, 'Lord of the powers/forces', son of Yaldabaoth | Divinity/Deity (wife = Zoe, daughter of Pistis). | 2. Sabaoth in the form of a bull | 283 |
| | **6** | Adonaios/Adonai, son of Yaldabaoth | Kingship | 4. Eloaios, in the form of an eagle | 406 |
| | **7** | Astaphaios, third son of Yaldabaoth | Sophia | 5. Thauthabaoth in the form of a bear | 1283, 1373 |
| | **8** | Eloai/Eloaio/Eloi, second son of Yaldabaoth | Envy/Jealousy | 6. Erathaoth, in the form of a dog or ape [Thoth] | 116, 186 |
| | **9** | Oraios/Ouraios, son of Yaldabaoth | Wealth | 7. Onoel or Thartharaoth, in the form of an ass | 451, 1181 |
| | **10** | Adam | | | 46 |
| ⊛ | **31b** | | | | |
| **F** | **31** | | | | |
| **A** | **11** | Adam & Eve | | | 46 & 406 |
| **W** | **23** | | | | |
| **E** | **32b** | | | | |
| ☾ | **13** | Oraios/Ouraios | | | |
| ☿ | **12** | Ailoaios, or sometimes Ailoein | | | |
| ♀ | **14** | Astraphaios | | | |
| ☼ | **30** | Adonaios | | | |
| ♂ | **27** | Sabaoth | | | |
| ♃ | **21** | Yao, IAO, Jah or Yahweh | | | |
| ♄ | **32** | Yaldabaoth, called "the Lion-faced", *leontoeides* | | | |

---

[1] Of the first name listed in Column P13.

# P. Pagan Pantheons

*European*

| | | P16. Greek Gods. | P17. Main Greek Gods – Greek.[2] | P18. Main Greek Gods – Numeration. |
|---|---|---|---|---|
| | | **34** | | |
| | 1 | Zeus | Ζευς | 612 |
| | 2 | Athena, Uranus/Ouranos, Metis | Αθηνη | 69 |
| | 3 | Demeter, Kronos, Cybele, Rhea, Hera, Tethys | Δημητηρ | 468 |
| | 4 | Poseidon , Zeus | Ποσειδων | 1289 |
| | 5 | Hephaestus, Ares, Athena | Ηφαιστος | 309 |
| | 6 | Apollo, Helios, Adonis, Dionysus, Bacchus, (Iacchus) | Απολλων | 1061 |
| | 7 | Aphrodité, Niké, Eros | Αφροδιτη | 993 |
| | 8 | Hermes, Aesculapius, Apollo Agyieus | Ερμης | 353 |
| | 9 | Artemis, Diana, Hekate, Selene, Mene | Αρτεμις | 656 |
| | 10 | Dionysus, Persephone, Psyche, Gaia, Pan, Ceres, Demeter, Kore | Διονυσος | 954 |
| ✳ | 31b | Iacchus, Zeus as Ether | | |
| F | 31 | Hestia, Prometheus, Ares as Fire | | |
| A | 11 | Boreas, Zeus, Dionysus as Air, Aeolus | | |
| W | 23 | Poseidon, Tethys, Amphitrite, Pontus, Nereus, the Nereids, Carmena | | |
| E | 32b | Demeter, Kore, Gaia | | |
| UW | | Persephone/Proserpine, Kore, Hades, Apollyon, Charon, Erebus, Pluto, Thanatos, Hecate/Hekate, Enodia, Demeter, Hermes Psychopompos, Adonis, Dionysus[3] | | |
| ☾ | 13 | Artemis, Hecate/Hekate, Selene, Hypnos | Αρτεμις | 651 |
| ☿ | 12 | Hermes, Asclepius, Eros | Ερμης | 353 |
| ♀ | 14 | Aphrodite, Hymenaios | Αφροδιτη | 993 |
| ☼ | 30 | Helios, Apollo | Ηλιος | 318 |
| ♂ | 27 | Ares | Αρησ | 309 |
| ♃ | 21 | Zeus | Ζευς | 612 |
| ♄ | 32 | Kronos, Erebus, Hecate/Hekate, Nyx | Κρονος | 510 |
| ♈ | 15 | Pallas Athena, Hermes (as god of flocks) | Παλλας Αθηνη | |
| ♉ | 16 | Hera, Cytherean Venus | Ηρα | 109 |
| ♊ | 17 | Kastor and Polydeukes, Apollo the Diviner, Phoebus | | |
| ♋ | 18 | Apollo the Charioteer | | |
| ♌ | 19 | Cybele (bourn by lions) | | |
| ♍ | 20 | Hera (renewed virginity), Daphne, Athena Parthenos | | |
| ♎ | 22 | Themis, Minos, Aeacus and Rhadamanthus, Dike | | |
| ♏ | 24 | Ares | | |
| ♐ | 25 | Apollo, Artemis (as hunters), Cupid | | |
| ♑ | 26 | Pan, Priapus, Phallic Hermes | | |
| ♒ | 28 | Ganymede | | |
| ♓ | 29 | Poseidon | | |

[2] The Twelve Olympian Gods in capitals.
[3] Dionysus according to Herodotus.

# P. Pagan Pantheons

| | | P19. The Orphic Theology. | P20. Greek Muse Governing. | P21. Greek Muses – Type of Lyric. |
|---|---|---|---|---|
| | | **Knowledge** | **Vivification** | |
| | 1 | Bacchus Eribromus / Bacchus Cribonius | Calliope | Eloquence and Heroic/Epic Poetry |
| | 2 | Pericionius | Urania | Astronomy and astrology |
| | 3 | Amphietus | Polymnia /Polyphymnia | Sacred Lyrics (and geometry) |
| | 4 | Sebazius | Terpsichore | Dancing and Choral Singing |
| | 5 | Bassarius / Bassareus Bacchus | Clio | History |
| | 6 | Trietericus Bacchus | Melpomene | Tragedy |
| | 7 | Lysius Bacchus | Erato | Lyrics and Love Poetry |
| | 8 | Bacchus Silenus | Euterpe | Music and Lyric Poetry |
| | 9 | Lyeus / Licniton Bacchus | Thalia | Comedy and Pastoral Poetry |
| | 10 | | | |
| ⊛ | 31b | | | |
| F | 31 | Phanes | Aurora | |
| A | 11 | Jove | Juno | |
| W | 23 | Ocean | Thetis | |
| E | 32b | Pluto | Proserpine | |
| ☾ | 13 | | | |
| ☿ | 12 | | | |
| ♀ | 14 | | | |
| ☼ | 30 | | | |
| ♂ | 27 | | | |
| ♃ | 21 | | | |
| ♄ | 32 | | | |
| ♈ | 15 | | | |
| ♉ | 16 | | | |
| ♊ | 17 | | | |
| ♋ | 18 | | | |
| ♌ | 19 | | | |
| ♍ | 20 | | | |
| ♎ | 22 | | | |
| ♏ | 24 | | | |
| ♐ | 25 | | | |
| ♑ | 26 | | | |
| ♒ | 28 | | | |
| ♓ | 29 | | | |

# P. Pagan Pantheons

| | | P22. Roman Gods. | P23. Etruscan Gods. |
|---|---|---|---|
| | | **35** | |
| | 1 | Jupiter | Tin/Tinia |
| | 2 | Janus, Coelus, Minerva | Uni, Menarva |
| | 3 | Saturn, Juno, Cybele, Hecate | Men |
| | 4 | Jupiter | Tin/Tinia |
| | 5 | Mars, Vulcan (as armourer), Bellona | Lar/Laran, Sethlans |
| | 6 | Apollo, Bacchus, Sol Invictus, Mithras | Cath/Cavtha, Usil, Fufluns, Apulu |
| | 7 | Venus | Turan |
| | 8 | Mercury, Asklepios, (Attis) | Turms, Nortia |
| | 9 | Diana (as Moon), Luna | Tiv, Artimi/Artumes/Artames |
| | 10 | Ceres, Flora, Lares & Penates | Cel, Aunis |
| ⊛ | 31b | | |
| F | 31 | Vulcan, Pluto | Velch/Velchans |
| A | 11 | Jupiter, Æolus, Juno (as humid air) | |
| W | 23 | Neptune, Neverita, Salacia, Fons | Neth or Nethuns |
| E | 32b | Ceres, Proserpina, Faunus, Fauna, Sylvanus, Tellus, Liber | Thanr, Calu |
| UW | | Proserpina, Dis Pater, Mors, Mania, Tarpeia, Labertina, Carna, (Lemures, Manes) | Vanth |
| ☾ | 13 | Diana, Luna, Juno | Tiv, Artimi/Artumes/Artames |
| ☿ | 12 | Mercury, Meditrina | Turms |
| ♀ | 14 | Venus | Turan |
| ☼ | 30 | Apollo, Sol Invictus | Cath/Cavtha, Usil, Apulu |
| ♂ | 27 | Mars, Bellona | |
| ♃ | 21 | Jupiter | Tin/Tinia |
| ♄ | 32 | Saturn, Lua | Vetis/Veive, Vediovis/Veiovis |
| ♈ | 15 | Mars, Pallas Minerva | |
| ♉ | 16 | Venus | |
| ♊ | 17 | Castor and Pollux, Janus | |
| ♋ | 18 | Mercury | |
| ♌ | 19 | Vulcan, Jupiter, Cybele (bourn by lions) | |
| ♍ | 20 | Ceres, Adonis, Vesta, Astræa, Pertunda, Cluerca | |
| ♎ | 22 | Justitia, Nemesis, Vulcan | |
| ♏ | 24 | Mars, Angitia | |
| ♐ | 25 | Diana (as Archer), Iris | |
| ♑ | 26 | Pan, Bacchus, Vesta | |
| ♒ | 28 | Juno | |
| ♓ | 29 | Neptune | |

# P. Pagan Pantheons

| | | P24. Celtic Gods. | P25. Celtic Gods – Ireland. | P26. Celtic Gods – Wales. |
|---|---|---|---|---|
| | 1 | | | |
| | 2 | | | Math, Nwyvre |
| | 3 | | Danu/Dana, Anu, Manannan | Don/Domnu, Arianrhod |
| | 4 | Taranis | Nuadha | |
| | 5 | Andraste, Camuos | Badb/Badhbh, Net, Morrigan, Macha, Scatha | Govannon/Gofannon |
| | 6 | Cernunnos/Herne | Bel/Belenus/Belinos/Beli Mawr | Lugh |
| | 7 | | Artio, Morrigan | Blodeuedd/Blodeuwedd/Blancheflor, Branwen |
| | 8 | | Diancecht, Oghma/Oghma | Gwydion, Math Mathonwy, Lugh |
| | 9 | | Brigid/Brigantia, Aine of Knockaine | Arianrhod, Ceridwen |
| | 10 | Sucellus, Abellio, Cernunnos/Herne | Anu/Anann/Dana | Amaethon |
| ⊛ | 31b | | | |
| F | 31 | | | |
| A | 11 | | | Amaethon |
| W | 23 | Nechtan, Fomorii | Lir, Manannan | Llyr |
| E | 32b | | Danu/Dana | |
| UW | | Cliodhna | Manannan | Arawn, Gwynn ap Nudd, Pwyll |
| ☽ | 13 | Arduinna | | Blodeuedd/Blodeuwedd/Blancheflor, Rhiannon |
| ☿ | 12 | Nuada, | Ogmios | Math Mathonwy |
| ♀ | 14 | Aine | | Branwen |
| ☼ | 30 | Mog Ruith | Bel/Belenus/Belinos/Beli Mawr | Lugh |
| ♂ | 27 | Neimain | | |
| ♃ | 21 | Taranis | | |
| ♄ | 32 | | | |
| ♈ | 15 | | | |
| ♉ | 16 | | | |
| ♊ | 17 | | | |
| ♋ | 18 | | | |
| ♌ | 19 | | | |
| ♍ | 20 | | | |
| ♎ | 22 | | | |
| ♏ | 24 | | | |
| ♐ | 25 | | | |
| ♑ | 26 | | | |
| ♒ | 28 | | | |
| ♓ | 29 | | | |

# P. Pagan Pantheons

| | | P27. Slavic Gods. | P28. Baltic Gods. | P29. Norse & Scandinavian Gods with Days of the Week. | |
|---|---|---|---|---|---|
| | | | | **33** | **Day** |
| | 1 | | | Wotan | Wednesday |
| | 2 | | | Odin | |
| | 3 | | | Frigga | |
| | 4 | Svarog, Herovit | Dievas | Thor | Thursday |
| | 5 | Perun | Perkunas | Thor, Tir, son of Odin | Tuesday |
| | 6 | Dazhbog, Hors | Saule | Baldr | |
| | 7 | Lel, Lada | Laima | Freya, Frigg (with Full, Gna, Hlin) | Friday |
| | 8 | Kozma, Demyan, Vels | Kalvaitis, Vels | Odin, Loki | |
| | 9 | | Meness | Loki | |
| | 10 | Mokos, Veles | Zermes-mate | Erd, Jord, Ymir | |
| ✷ | 31b | | | | |
| F | 31 | Svarogich | Gabie | | |
| A | 11 | Stribog | Vejapats | Njord | |
| W | 23 | | | Eagnor | |
| E | 32b | Mokos, Veles | Zermes-mate | Nerthus | |
| UW | | Veles | Vels, Sovius | Odin, Hel, Valkyries | |
| ☾ | 13 | | | | |
| ☿ | 12 | | | Loki | |
| ♀ | 14 | | | Freya | |
| ☼ | 30 | | | Baldr | |
| ♂ | 27 | | | Valkyries, Tir | |
| ♃ | 21 | | | Thor | |
| ♄ | 32 | | | | |
| ♈ | 15 | | | | |
| ♉ | 16 | | | | |
| ♊ | 17 | | | | |
| ♋ | 18 | | | | |
| ♌ | 19 | | | | |
| ♍ | 20 | | | | |
| ♎ | 22 | | | | |
| ♏ | 24 | | | | |
| ♐ | 25 | | | | |
| ♑ | 26 | | | | |
| ♒ | 28 | | | | |
| ♓ | 29 | | | | |

# P. Pagan Pantheons

*Asian*

|   |   | P30. Hindu Gods. | P31. Japanese Shinto Gods. |
|---|---|---|---|
|   |   | **22** |   |
|   | 1 | Parabrahm, Shiva, Brahma |   |
|   | 2 | Shiva, Vishnu (as avartar of Buddha), Lingam, Aditi | Izanagi |
|   | 3 | Bhavani (all forms of Sakti), Yoni, Kali, Durga | Izanami |
|   | 4 | Indra, Brahma, Shiva, Dyaush-pita | Asi-Suki-Taka-Hi-Kone, Kami-Nari |
|   | 5 | Vishnu, Varuna-Avatar, Mangala, Gokihar, Skanda, Rama | Kagu-Zuchi (fire god) |
|   | 6 | Vishnu, Krishna, Rama, Surya, Bagha | Amaterasu (sun goddess), Amo-No-Uzume (goddess of dawn), Wakahiru-me (rising sun) |
|   | 7 | Lakshmi, Lalita, Muspar, Bhavani, Savitri, Saraswati, Durga, Parvati, Amba | Kusa-nada-hime (?) |
|   | 8 | Hanuman, Visvakarman, Dhanvantari, Saraswati, the Buddhakapalini[4] | O-Kuni-Nushi (god of medicine & sorcery) |
|   | 9 | Chansra, Ganesh, Vishnu (Kurm), Surabhi, Soma | Tsuki-yomi (god of the Moon) |
|   | 10 | Rudra | Ninigi (god of the Earth) |
| ⊛ | 31b | [Akasa] |   |
| F | 31 | Agni [Tejas] | Kagu-Zuchi, Ho-Masubi |
| A | 11 | Maruts, [Vayu] | Shine-Tsu-Hiko |
| W | 23 | Soma, [Apas], Parjanya | O-Wata-Tsumi |
| E | 32b | Prisni, Prithivi Mata |   |
| UW |   | Yama, Mahakala, Rudra |   |
| ☽ | 13 | Chandra |   |
| ☿ | 12 | Hanuman, Vishnu (as Parasa-Rama) |   |
| ♀ | 14 | Lalita (sexual aspect of Sakti) |   |
| ☼ | 30 | Surya |   |
| ♂ | 27 | Karttikeya, Mangla |   |
| ♃ | 21 | Indra |   |
| ♄ | 32 | Brahma |   |
| ♈ | 15 | Shiva |   |
| ♉ | 16 | Shiva (as Sacred Bull) |   |
| ♊ | 17 | Aswini |   |
| ♋ | 18 | Krishna |   |
| ♌ | 19 | Vishnu (Nara-Singh Avatar) |   |
| ♍ | 20 | Gauri, the Gopi girls |   |
| ♎ | 22 | Yama |   |
| ♏ | 24 | Kundalini |   |
| ♐ | 25 | Vishnu (as horse Avatar) |   |
| ♑ | 26 | Lingam, Yoni |   |
| ♒ | 28 | Maruts |   |
| ♓ | 29 | Vishnu (Matsya Avatar) |   |

---

[4] The 6 goddesses of magic.

# P. Pagan Pantheons

| | | P32. Chinese Taoist Gods. | P33. Meditation Buddhas & Dakinis. |
|---|---|---|---|
| | 1 | Yu-Huang-Shang-Ti, Jade Emperor | |
| | 2 | T'ai I (High god), P'an Ku (Pangu) (as Cosmos) | |
| | 3 | Tou Mu/Dou Mu (North Dipper Mother), Kuan Yin/Guan Yin (Compassion) | |
| | 4 | Tai-yi (Sky), T'ien (Heaven), Hsuan Wu Ta Ti (Dark Lord of the North), Lei-Kung (thunder) | |
| | 5 | Yueh Fei (War), Kuan Yu (War), Guan Gong/Kuan Kung, Guan Di/Kuan Ti (War/Wealth), Chang Fei (War) | |
| | 6 | Shen Yi (Sun), Hou I (Archer) | |
| | 7 | Kuan Yin/Guan Yin, Songzi Niang Niang (Childbirth), Chuang-Mu | |
| | 8 | Chong-Gui/Zhong-Kui (Literature and Examinations), Yao Wang (Medicine), Wen Ch'ang Ta Ti (Literature), Yao Wang (Healing), Ts'ang-Chien | |
| | 9 | Heng-O, Heng E (Moon) | |
| | 10 | Choa Jun/Zao Jun (Kitchen), Fu-Lu-Shou (the 3 Household Gods) | |
| ✳ | 31b | | Vairocana, Akasa-Dhatesvari |
| F | 31 | Chu Jung | Amitabha, Pandarava-Sini |
| A | 11 | Feng-Po-Po | Amoghasiddhi, Tara |
| W | 23 | Lo Shen, Shui Khan | Aksobhya, Locana |
| E | 32b | Hou-T'u, Hou-Chi, T'u-ti | Ratnasambhava, Mamaki |
| UW | | Yen Wang Yeh/Yen Lo (Underworld Judge), Yama, Meng P'o | |
| ☾ | 13 | Heng-O, Heng E (Moon) | |
| ☿ | 12 | K'uei-Hsing, Shen Nung | |
| ♀ | 14 | Chuang-Mu | |
| ☼ | 30 | Shen Yi (Sun), Hou I (Archer) | |
| ♂ | 27 | | |
| ♃ | 21 | Tai Sui (counter–Jupiter) | |
| ♄ | 32 | | |
| ♈ | 15 | | |
| ♉ | 16 | | |
| ♊ | 17 | | |
| ♋ | 18 | | |
| ♌ | 19 | | |
| ♍ | 20 | | |
| ♎ | 22 | | |
| ♏ | 24 | | |
| ♐ | 25 | | |
| ♑ | 26 | | |
| ♒ | 28 | | |
| ♓ | 29 | | |

# P. Pagan Pantheons

*African & Voodoo*

|  |  | P34. Dahomean Gods. | P35. Yoruba Orishas. | P36. Santeria Gods. | P37. Voodoo Rada & Petra Loa Gods. | P38. Other African Gods. |
|---|---|---|---|---|---|---|
|  |  |  |  |  |  |  |
|  | 1 | Mawu | Olodumare Olorun |  | Dambhalah Wedo | Amma (Dogon), Akongo (Ngombe), Akuj (Turkana), Chuku (Ibo) |
|  | 2 | Afa | Orunmila | Obatala | Maraca |  |
|  | 3 |  | Yemoja Yemaya Oddudua | Oddudua Yemaya | Brigitte | Nana Buluku (Fon), Nzambi (Bankongo) |
|  | 4 | Heviosso, Xewioso, Danh | Shango | Orunla | Adoum-Guidi | Mulengi/Chiuta, En-Kai (Masai), 'Nenaunir (Masai), Wele (Bantu), Mungo (Giryama), Nyamia Ama (Senegal) |
|  | 5 | Egu/Gu | Ogun | Oggun | Ogou-Ferraille | Gu (Fon) |
|  | 6 | Fa |  | Chango Olofi | Ogou-Chango |  |
|  | 7 | Leza/Lisa | Ymoja | Oshun | Erzulie |  |
|  | 8 | Legba | Eshu, Babaluaiye | Eleggua | Legba | Anansi, Heitsi-Eibib (Hottentots) |
|  | 9 | Ge |  | Yemaya | Aido Wedo | Mawu (Fon), Ngami |
|  | 10 | Sakpata | Babaluaiye | Orish-Oko | Zaca | Asase Efua (Ashanti), Ala/Ale (Ibo) |
| ⊛ | 31b |  |  |  |  |  |
| F | 31 | Dan Sissinnon | Aganu |  |  |  |
| A | 11 | Aveji Da | Oya |  |  |  |
| W | 23 | Mami Wata | Oshun, Olokun, Yemoja | Oba |  | Behanzin |
| E | 32b |  |  |  |  |  |
| UW |  |  |  |  | Baron Samedi | Gauna (Bushmen), Jok Odudu (Alur) |
| ☾ | 13 |  |  |  |  |  |
| ☿ | 12 |  |  |  |  |  |
| ♀ | 14 |  |  |  |  |  |
| ☼ | 30 |  |  |  |  |  |
| ♂ | 27 |  |  |  |  |  |
| ♃ | 21 |  |  |  |  |  |
| ♄ | 32 |  |  |  |  |  |

# P. Pagan Pantheons

*Central American*

|  |  | P39. Aztec Gods. | P40. Inca Gods. | P41. Mayan Gods. |
|---|---|---|---|---|
|  | 1 |  | Virococha/Huiracocha as Creator | Hunab Ku |
|  | 2 |  |  | Ho as ancient god of interior Earth |
|  | 3 | Malinalxochitl, Tlalteutli, Coatlicue | Mama Cocha as Mother Sea |  |
|  | 4 | Chalchicehtlicue | Pachacamac as Supreme god | Ox as god of storms, Hurukan, Itzamna as sky god |
|  | 5 |  | Illapa as storm god | Ek Ahau, Ek Chuah, Hun Pic Tok |
|  | 6 | Xochipilli, Huitzilopochtli as Sun god | Inti, Apu Punchau as Sun god Manco Capac | Ca as god of sacrifice, Can as Sun god |
|  | 7 | Xochiquetzal as goddess of sexual love | Chasca | Lahca as sky (Venus), Ixtab as huntress |
|  | 8 | Yacatecuhtli as god of merchants | Virococha/Huiracocha as god of arts and civilization | Itzamna as god of writing, Kukulcan as god of learning |
|  | 9 | Centtzon Totochtin, Tlazolteotl, Chimalman, Xochiquetzal | Mama Quilla | Hun – Moon/Earth goddess, Ixchel as Moon, Ixchup |
|  | 10 | Chicomecoatl, Chantico, Xilonen as goddess of maize, Xipe Totec as god of agriculture | Pachamama as Earth Mother Pachacamac as Lord of the Earth | Uuc – jaguar god of Underworld, Uaxac – maize god Chac – as vegetation god Yum Caax – as god of maize |
| ⊛ | 31b |  |  |  |
| F | 31 |  | Pachacamac as god of fire | Masaya as goddess of volcanoes |
| A | 11 |  |  | Vac as god of wind, the Bacabs |
| W | 23 |  |  | Chac as rain god |
| E | 32b | Xipe Totec as god of agriculture | Pachamama as Earth Mother Urcaguary as god of underground treasure | Yum Caax as god of maize |
| UW |  | Xochiquetzal as goddess of Underworld, Xolotl as Lord of the Underworld | Supai as god of the Underworld | Ahpuch, Gucumatz |
| ☾ | 13 | Centtzon Totochtin, | Mama Quilla | Ixchel, Ixchup |
| ☿ | 12 |  |  |  |
| ♀ | 14 | Xolotl as the adverse Venus | Chasca | Kukulcan as Venus |
| ☼ | 30 | Huitzilopochtli as Sun god | Apu Punchau as Sun god | Tkinich Kak Mo as Sun god |
| ♂ | 27 |  |  |  |
| ♃ | 21 |  |  |  |
| ♄ | 32 |  |  |  |

299

*Knights of the Round Table*

| | | Q1. Knights on the Round Table at Winchester Castle c. 1270. | Q2. Knights of the Round Table – Mallory c. 1470. | Q3. Knights of the Round Table – Relationships. |
|---|---|---|---|---|
| | 1 | | The Grail | The Quest |
| | 2 | | Uther Pendragon | Arthur's father |
| | 3 | | Igraine | Arthur's mother |
| | 4 | | Sir Galahad | His seat was the *Siege Perilous* |
| | 5 | | Sir Lancelot du Lac | Arthur's champion |
| | 6 | Kyng Arthur | King Arthur | The King |
| | 7 | | Guinevere | Arthur's wife |
| | 8 | | Merlin | The Magician |
| | 9 | | Morgan le Fay | Arthur's half-sister who takes him to Avalon |
| | 10 | Sir Mordrede | Sir Mordred | Arthur's son, and destroyer of his kingdom |
| ♈ | 15 | Sir Gauen | Sir Gawain | Opponent of the Green Knight |
| ♉ | 16 | Sir Percyvale | Sir Percivale | Grail knight, son of Pellinore |
| ♊ | 17 | Sir Lyonell | Sir Lionel | Arthur gave him the throne of Gaul |
| ♋ | 18 | Sir Trystram Delyens | Sir Tristram de Lyoness | Champion of the King of Cornwall |
| ♌ | 19 | Sir Garethe | Sir Gareth | Son of the King of Lothian |
| ♍ | 20 | Sir Bedwere | Sir Bedivere | Brother of Lucan |
| ♎ | 22 | Sir Blubrys | Sir Bleoberis de Ganis | Became Duke of Poitiers |
| ♏ | 24 | Sir La Cote Male Tayle | Sir Bruin le Noire | The Knight of the ill-fitting Coat |
| ♐ | 25 | Sir Lucane | Sir Lucan | Brother of Bedivere, King Arthur's butler |
| ♑ | 26 | Sir Plomyde | Sir Palomides, or Palamedes | The Saracen |
| ♒ | 28 | Sir Lamorak | Sir Lamorak | Son of King Pellinore |
| ♓ | 29 | Sir Bors De Ganys | Sir Bors de Ganis | King of Gannes (Gaul) |
| | | Sir Safer | Sir Safir*[1] | Saracen brother of Sir Palomides |
| | | Sir Pelleus | Sir Pelleas | Enamoured of Ettard |
| | | Sir Kay | Sir Kay* | Half brother of Arthur |
| | | Sir Ectorde Marys | Sir Ector de Maris | Son of King Ban of Benwick |
| | | Sir Dagonet | Sir Dagonet* | The court jester |
| | | Sir Degore | Sir Tegyr* | Arthur's cupbearer |
| | | Sir Brumear | Sir Brunor the Black | One of the best knights |
| | | Sir Lybyus Dysconyus | Sir Guinglain*, Le Bel Inconnu | Sir Gawain's eldest son by a fairy named Blanchemal |
| | | Sir Alynore | Sir Alymere* | |

---

[1] Knights marked * are not found in Mallory, but have been extended into this column to show a more recent form or spelling. Interestingly the missing knights do not include any of the knights with zodiacal attributions, which are fully represented in Mallory.

# Q. Questing and Chivalry

*Chivalry*

<table>
<tr><th colspan="2"></th><th colspan="6">Q4. The Tinctures of Chivalry.</th></tr>
<tr><th></th><th></th><th>Blazon</th><th>Metal/Colour/<br>Fur</th><th>Stone</th><th>Virtue</th><th>Hatching</th></tr>
<tr><td>☾</td><td>13</td><td>Argent</td><td>Silver</td><td>Pearl</td><td>Innocency</td><td>Unhatched</td></tr>
<tr><td>☿</td><td>12</td><td>Purpure</td><td>Purple</td><td>Amethyst</td><td>Temperance</td><td>Diagonal /</td></tr>
<tr><td>♀</td><td>14</td><td>Vert or Sinople</td><td>Green</td><td>Emerald</td><td>Love</td><td>Diagonal \</td></tr>
<tr><td>☼</td><td>30</td><td>Or</td><td>Gold</td><td>Topaz</td><td>Faith</td><td>Dots</td></tr>
<tr><td>♂</td><td>27</td><td>Gules</td><td>Red</td><td>Ruby</td><td>Magnanimity</td><td>Vertical lines</td></tr>
<tr><td>♃</td><td>21</td><td>Azure</td><td>Blue</td><td>Sapphire</td><td>Loyalty</td><td>Horizontal lines</td></tr>
<tr><td>♄</td><td>32</td><td>Sable</td><td>Black</td><td>Diamond</td><td>Prudence</td><td>Cross-hatched vertical & horizontal</td></tr>
<tr><td></td><td></td><td>Ermine</td><td rowspan="4">Ermine fur</td><td></td><td></td><td>White with black spots</td></tr>
<tr><td></td><td></td><td>Ermines</td><td></td><td></td><td>Black with white spots</td></tr>
<tr><td></td><td></td><td>Erminois</td><td></td><td></td><td>Black spots on gold</td></tr>
<tr><td></td><td></td><td>Pean</td><td></td><td></td><td>Gold spots on black</td></tr>
<tr><td></td><td></td><td>Vair</td><td rowspan="3">Squirrel fur</td><td></td><td></td><td>Rows of bell shapes</td></tr>
<tr><td></td><td></td><td>Vairy</td><td></td><td></td><td>Rows of bell shapes coloured</td></tr>
<tr><td></td><td></td><td>Potent</td><td></td><td></td><td>Crutch shaped</td></tr>
</table>

# R. Rainbow Colour Scales

| | | R1. The King Scale of Colour (World of Atziluth) – *Yod.* | R2. The Queen Scale of Colour (World of Briah) – *Heh.* | R3. The Emperor Scale of Colour (World of Yetzirah) – *Vav.* | R4. The Empress Scale of Colour (World of Assiah) – *Heh* final. |
|---|---|---|---|---|---|
| | | **15** | **16** | **17** | **18** |
| | **1** | Brilliance | White brilliance | White brilliance | White flecked gold |
| | **2** | Pure soft blue | Grey | Blue pearl grey, like mother–of pearl | White, flecked red, blue, and yellow |
| | **3** | Crimson | Black | Dark brown | Grey flecked pink |
| | **4** | Deep violet | Blue | Deep purple | Deep azure flecked yellow |
| | **5** | Orange | Scarlet red | Bright scarlet | Red flecked black |
| | **6** | Clear pink rose | Yellow (gold) | Rich salmon | Gold amber |
| | **7** | Amber | Emerald | Bright yellow green | Olive flecked gold |
| | **8** | Violet purple | Orange | Red–russet | Yellow–brown flecked white |
| | **9** | Indigo | Violet | Very dark purple | Citrine flecked azure |
| | **10** | Yellow | Citrine, olive, russet, and black | Blank rayed with yellow, flecked gold | Black rayed yellow |
| ⊛ | **31b** | White, merging Grey | Deep purple (near black) | The 7 prismatic colours, the violet being outside | White, red, yellow, blue, black (the latter outside) |
| **F** | **31** | Glowing orange scarlet | Vermillion | Scarlet, flecked gold | Vermillion flecked crimson & emerald |
| **A** | **11** | Bright pale yellow | Sky blue | Blue emerald green | Emerald flecked gold |
| **W** | **23** | Deep blue | Sea–green | Deep olive–green | White flecked purple |
| **E** | **32b** | Citrine, russet, olive, and black (quartered) | Amber | Dark brown | Black and yellow |
| ☾ | **13** | Blue | Silver | Cold pale blue | Silver rayed sky–blue |
| ☿ | **12** | Yellow | Purple | Grey | Indigo rayed violet |
| ♀ | **14** | Emerald green | Sky blue | Early spring green | Bright rose of cerise rayed pale yellow |
| ☼ | **30** | Orange | Gold yellow | Rich amber | Amber rayed red |
| ♂ | **27** | Scarlet | Red | Venetian red | Bright red rayed azure or orange |
| ♃ | **21** | Violet | Blue | Rich purple | Bright blue rayed yellow |
| ♄ | **32** | Indigo | Black | Blue black | Black rayed blue |
| ♈ | **15** | Scarlet | Red | Brilliant flame | Glowing red |
| ♉ | **16** | Red orange | Deep indigo | Deep warm olive | Rich brown |
| ♊ | **17** | Orange | Pale Mauve | New yellow leather | Reddish grey inclined to mauve |
| ♋ | **18** | Amber | Maroon | Rich bright russet | Dark greenish brown |
| ♌ | **19** | Yellow, greenish | Deep purple | Grey | Reddish amber |
| ♍ | **20** | Green, yellowish | Slate grey | Green grey | Plum colour |
| ♎ | **22** | Emerald green | Blue | Deep blue–green | Pale green |
| ♏ | **24** | Green blue | Dull brown | Very dark brown | Livid indigo brown (like a black beetle) |
| ♐ | **25** | Blue | Yellow | Green | Dark vivid blue |
| ♑ | **26** | Indigo | Black | Blue black | Cold dark grey near black |
| ♒ | **28** | Violet | Sky blue | Blueish mauve | White tinged purple |
| ♓ | **29** | Crimson (ultra violet) | Buff, flecked silver–white | Light translucent pinkish brown | Stone colour |

# R. Rainbow Colour Scales

| | | R5. Mathers' Combined King & Queen Colour Scale. | R6. Rainbow Colours of the Zodiac. | R7. Rainbow Colours of the Zodiac – Wavelength median (x $10^{-9}$ metres). | R8. Rainbow Colours of the Zodiac – Frequency median (x $10^{12}$ Hz). |
|---|---|---|---|---|---|
| | | | | | |
| | 1 | White | | | |
| | 2 | Grey | | | |
| | 3 | Black | | | |
| | 4 | Blue | | | |
| | 5 | Red | | | |
| | 6 | Yellow | | | |
| | 7 | Green | | | |
| | 8 | Orange | | | |
| | 9 | Violet | | | |
| | 10 | Russet, olive, citrine, black | | | |
| ✴ | 31b | | | | |
| F | 31 | Red | | | |
| A | 11 | Yellow | | | |
| W | 23 | Blue | | | |
| E | 32b | | | | |
| ☾ | 13 | Blue | | | |
| ☿ | 12 | Yellow | | | |
| ♀ | 14 | Green | | | |
| ☉ | 30 | Orange | | | |
| ♂ | 27 | Red | | | |
| ♃ | 21 | Violet | | | |
| ♄ | 32 | Blue–Violet | | | |
| ♈ | 15 | Red | Red | 660 | 454 |
| ♉ | 16 | Red–Orange | Red–Orange | 625 | 467 |
| ♊ | 17 | Orange | Orange | 610 | 492 |
| ♋ | 18 | Yellow–Orange | Yellow–Orange | 590 | 504 |
| ♌ | 19 | Yellow | Yellow | 580 | 517 |
| ♍ | 20 | Yellow–Green | Yellow–Green | 565 | 536 |
| ♎ | 22 | Green | Green | 540 | 556 |
| ♏ | 24 | Blue–Green | Blue–Green | 520 | 597 |
| ♐ | 25 | Blue | Blue | 500 | 638 |
| ♑ | 26 | Blue–Violet | Blue–Violet | 485 | 660 |
| ♒ | 28 | Violet | Violet/Indigo | 440 | 682 |
| ♓ | 29 | Red–Violet | Dark Violet | 410 | 732 |

303

# R. Rainbow Colour Scales

## *Kabbalistic Colours*

|  | R9. Traditional Kabbalistic Colours. | R10. Rabbi Azriel's Colours. | R11. Dr Jellinek's Colours. |
|---|---|---|---|
|  |  |  | **111** |
| 1 | Blinding invisible white | Concealed Light | Concealed Light |
| 2 | White | Yellow | Sky blue |
| 3 | Yellow and green | Sky blue | Yellow |
| 4 | White and silver | White | White |
| 5 | Red and gold | Red | Red |
| 6 | Yellow and purple | White and red | White–red |
| 7 | Light pink | Whitish–red | Whitish–red |
| 8 | Dark pink | Reddish–white | Reddish–white |
| 9 | Orange | Mixture of 7 & 8 | Mixture of 6, 7 & 8 |
| 10 | Blue | White light containing all colours | White light containing all colours |

## *Tattwa Colours*

|  |  | R12. Tattwa Flashing Colours. | | |
|---|---|---|---|---|
|  |  | **Tattwa** | **Base Colour** | **Flashing Charge** |
| ✳ | 31b | Akasha | Violet-Black | White/light yellow |
| F | 31 | Tejas | Red | Green |
| A | 11 | Vayu | Blue | Orange |
| W | 23 | Apas | Silver | Violet |
| E | 32b | Prithivi | Yellow | Purple |

# S. Sacred Geometry

## Planetary Numbers

| | | S1. Planetary Equatorial Radius. | S2. Planetary Mass. | S3. Planetary Distance from the Sun. | S4. Planetary Sidereal Period of Rotation. | S5. Planetary Rotation on own axis. |
|---|---|---|---|---|---|---|
| | | metres x $10^6$ | kg x $10^{24}$ | metres x $10^{10}$ | days | days |
| E | 32b | 6.378 | 5.978 | 14.96 | 365.24 | 1.00 |
| ☾ | 13 | 1.738 | 0.073 | 14.96 | n/a | 27.32 |
| ☿ | 12 | 2.420 | 0.330 | 5.79 | 87.97 | 58.70 |
| ♀ | 14 | 6.085 | 4.869 | 10.82 | 224.70 | 243.00 |
| ☼ | 30 | 696.000 | 1,989,000.000 | n/a | n/a | 25.38 |
| ♂ | 27 | 3.375 | 0.642 | 22.79 | 687.00 | 1.03 |
| ♃ | 21 | 71.400 | 1899.000 | 77.83 | 4,331.77 | 0.41 |
| ♄ | 32 | 60.400 | 568.500 | 142.70 | 10,760.03 | 0.43 |

## Platonic Solids

| | | S6. The Platonic Solids. | S7. Number of Edges. | S8. Number of Planes. | S9. Number of Faces. | S10. Number of Vertices (Corners). |
|---|---|---|---|---|---|---|
| ✴ | 31b | Dodecahedron | 30 | 60 | 12 | 20 |
| F | 31 | Pyramid/Tetrahedron | 6 | 12 | 4 | 4 |
| A | 11 | Octahedron | 12 | 24 | 8 | 6 |
| W | 23 | Icosahedron | 30 | 60 | 20 | 12 |
| E | 32b | Cube/Hexahedron | 12 | 24 | 6 | 8 |
| | | Sphere | 1 | - | 1 | – |

| | | The Platonic Solids. | S11. Shape of Face. | S12. Surface Area. | S13. Volume. |
|---|---|---|---|---|---|
| ✴ | 31b | Dodecahedron | Pentagon | $15\Phi / (3- \Phi)$ or $3a^2\sqrt{(25 + 10\sqrt5)}$ | $5 \Phi^3/ (6-2\Phi)$ or $(1/4)a^3(15 + \sqrt5)$ |
| F | 31 | Pyramid/Tetrahedron | Triangle | $4 A$ | $1 / 3$ Ah |
| A | 11 | Octahedron | Triangle | $2a^2\sqrt3$ | $(1/3)a^3\sqrt2$ |
| W | 23 | Icosahedron | Triangle | $5a^2\sqrt3$ | $5 \Phi^5/ 6$ or $(5/12)a^3(3 + \sqrt5)$ |
| E | 32b | Cube/Hexahedron | Square | $6S^2$ | $S^3$ |
| | | Sphere | – | $4 \pi r^2$ | $4 / 3 \pi r^3$ |

# S. Sacred Geometry

| | | S14. Figures, Numbers, Platonic Solids and Perfect Geometric Shapes. | S15. Points of the Pentagram (Elements). | S15a. Points of the Hexagram (Planets). |
|---|---|---|---|---|
| | | **49** | **83** | **70** |
| | **1** | Point | | |
| | **2** | Line, the Cross | | |
| | **3** | Triangle, the Plane, the Diamond, Mandorla, Oval, Vesica Piscis (and other Yoni Symbols) | [Daath: Top point of Hexagram] | |
| | **4** | Square, Rhombus, Tetrahedron, Pyramid, Equal-armed Cross (a three dimensional figure) | Upper right point | |
| | **5** | Pentagram, Pentagon, Pentangle, Tesseract (or Hypercube) | Upper left point | |
| | **6** | Hexagram, Hexagon, Hexangle, Calvary Cross, Unicursal Hexagram, Cube, Truncated Pyramid | Centre point | |
| | **7** | Heptagram, Heptagon, Heptangle | Lower right point | |
| | **8** | Octagram, Octagon, Octangle | Lower left point | |
| | **9** | Enneagram, Enneagon, Enneangle | Bottom point | |
| | **10** | Decagram/Dekagram, Decagon/Dekagon, Decangle/Dekangle, Double Cube (of 10 faces) | | |
| ⊛ | **31b** | Dodecahedron | | Top point of Pentagram |
| F | **31** | Tetrahedron | | Lower right point |
| A | **11** | Octahedron | | Upper left point |
| W | **23** | Icosahedron | | Upper right point |
| E | **32b** | Square, Cube | | Lower left point |
| ☽ | **13** | Enneagram, Greek Cross | Bottom point of Hexagram | |
| ☿ | **12** | Octagram | Lower left point | |
| ♀ | **14** | Heptagram | Lower right point | |
| ☼ | **30** | Hexagram | Centre point | |
| ♂ | **27** | Pentagram | Upper left point | |
| ♃ | **21** | Square and Rhombus | Upper right point | |
| ♄ | **32** | Triangle | Top point | |

# S. Sacred Geometry

*Metrology*

S16. Sacred Geometry Conversion Factors.

| Measures covert to[1] | Imperial (inches) | Imperial (feet) | Metric (cm) | Metric (metre) |
|---|---|---|---|---|
| 1 Imperial Inch | 1 | 0.0833 | 2.540 | 0.0254 |
| 1 Imperial Foot | 12 | 1 | 30.48 | 0.3048 |
| 1 Imperial Rod[2] | 198 | 16.50 | 502.92 | 5.0292 |
| 1 Metric Centimetre | 0.3937 | 0.0328 | 1 | 0.01 |
| 1 Metric Metre | 39.37 | 3.28084 | 100 | 1 |
| 1 Megalithic Inch | 0.8166 | 0.06805 | 2.074164 | .02074164 |
| 1 Megalithic Yard | 32.664 | 2.722 | 82.96656 | .8296656 |
| 1 Megalithic Rod | 195.984 | 16.332 | 497.799 | 4.97799 |
| 1 Standard Cubit | 17.674 | 1.47283 | 44.893 | 0.44893 |
| 1 Royal Cubit | 20.620 | 1.7183 | 52.375 | 0.52375 |
| 1 Remen[3] | 29.156 | 2.429 | 74.069 | 0.74069 |
| 1 Roman Foot | 11.52 | 0.96 | 29.2608 | 0.292608 |
| 1 Greek Foot | 12 | 1 | 30.48 | 0.3048 |
| 1 Greek Stadia | 7200 | 600 | 18288 | 182.88 |
| 1 Greek Plethron | 1200 | 100 | 3048 | 30.48 |

[1] In each case the figure in the box is what you need to multiply the unit in the left hand column to get the measure listed across the top row.
[2] Imperial Rod = a Pole or Perch.
[3] Related to the Royal Cubit, being the length of the long side of a right angled triangle with other sides of one Royal Cubit.

# T. Tarot

*Major Arcana: Trumps*

| GD Path Order | | T1. Names and Numbers of the Tarot Trumps (Golden Dawn).[1] | T3. Titles of the Tarot Trumps (Golden Dawn). | T3a. Titles of the Tarot Trumps (Crowley). |
|---|---|---|---|---|
| | | **14 & 179** | **180** | |
| A | 11 | 0 – The Fool | The Spirit of Aether (*Αιθηρ*) | 0 - The Fool |
| ☿ | 12 | I – The Magician or Juggler | The Magus of Power | I – The Magus |
| ☽ | 13 | II – The High Priestess | The Priestess of the Silver Star | II – The Priestess |
| ♀ | 14 | III – The Empress | The Daughter of the Mighty Ones | III – The Empress |
| ♈ | 15 | IV – The Emperor | The Son of the Morning. Chief among the Mighty | IV – The Emperor |
| ♉ | 16 | V – The Hierophant [Pope] | The Magus of the Eternal | V – The Hierophant |
| ♊ | 17 | VI – The Lovers | The Children of the Voice: The Oracle of the Mighty Gods | VI – The Lovers |
| ♋ | 18 | VII – The Chariot | The Child of the Powers of the Waters: The Lord of the Triumph of Light | VII – The Chariot |
| ♌ | 19 | XI – Strength | The Daughter of the Flaming Sword | XI – Lust |
| ♍ | 20 | IX – The Hermit | The Prophet of the Eternal. The Magus of the Voice of Power | IX – The Hermit |
| ♃ | 21 | X – Wheel of Fortune | The Lord of the Forces of Life | X – Fortune |
| ♎ | 22 | VIII – Justice | The Daughter of the Lords of Truth. The Ruler of the Balance | VIII – Adjustment |
| W | 23 | XII – The Hanged Man | The Spirit of the Mighty Waters | XII – The Hanged Man |
| ♏ | 24 | XIII – Death | The Child of the Great Transformers. The Lord of the Gate of Death | XIII – Death |
| ♐ | 25 | XIV – Temperance | The Daughter of the Reconcilers The Bringer-forth of Life | XIV – Art |
| ♑ | 26 | XV – The Devil | The Lord of the Gates of Matter. The Child of the Forces of Time | XV – The Devil |
| ♂ | 27 | XVI – The Blasted Tower [of Babel] | The Lord of the Hosts of the Mighty | XVI – The Tower |
| ♒ | 28 | XVII – The Star | The Daughter of the Firmament. The Dweller between the Waters | XVII – The Star |
| ♓ | 29 | XVIII – The Moon | The Ruler of Flux and Reflux. The Child of the Sons of the Mighty | XVIII – The Moon |
| ☼ | 30 | XIX – The Sun | The Lord of the Fire of the World | XIX – The Sun |
| F | 31 | XX – The Last Judgement | The Spirit of the Primal Fire | XX – The Aeon |
| ♄ | 32 | XXI – The Universe | The Great One of the Night of Time | XXI – The Universe |

---

[1] Column T2 has been moved two pages forward, so that it falls in the Minor Arcana section.

| GD Path Order | | T4. Design of the Tarot Trumps. |
|---|---|---|
| | | **181** |
| **A** | 11 | A bearded Ancient seen in profile |
| ☿ | 12 | A fair youth with winged helmet and heels, equipped as a Magician, displays his instruments of art |
| ☾ | 13 | A crowned priestess sits before the veil of Isis between the Pillars of the Temple. She is reading a scroll or book |
| ♀ | 14 | Crowned with stars, a winged goddess stands upon the Moon. She bears a sceptre and shield, on which is a dove |
| ♈ | 15 | He is seated upon a cubical stone throne, whose sides show the alchemical Green Lion and White Eagle |
| ♉ | 16 | Between the Pillars sits a triple crowned and sceptred figure, with his hand in the sign of benediction. Four living creatures adore him |
| ♊ | 17 | A prophet, inspired by Apollo, young, and posed in the Sign of Osiris Risen. Represented by a boy with his bow and two women, a priestess and a harlot |
| ♋ | 18 | A young and holy king under a starry canopy. Before him goes the upright Egyptian Royal Uraeus serpent |
| ♌ | 19 | A smiling woman holds the open jaws of a fierce and powerful lion |
| ♍ | 20 | Wrapped in a cloak and cowl, an Ancient walks, bearing a lamp and staff |
| ♃ | 21 | A wheel of six spokes, whereon revolve the triad of Hermanubis, the Sphinx, and Typhon |
| ♎ | 22 | A conventional figure of Justice with scales and balance |
| **W** | 23 | The figure of a hanged or crucified man. From the gallows, shaped like a letter Tau hangs a young man by one foot. His other leg forms a cross with the vertical one. His arms form a triangle. |
| ♏ | 24 | A skeleton with a scythe mowing down men. His scythe handle is a Tau |
| ♐ | 25 | A winged and crowned goddess, with golden belt, stands and pours from her right hand a torch flame upon an Eagle, whilst her left hands pours water upon a Lion. Between her feet a silver cauldron smokes. |
| ♑ | 26 | The figure of Pan or Priapus depicted like Eliphas Levi's Baphomet |
| ♂ | 27 | A tower struck by forked lightning. The falling figure of a man takes the shape of the Hebrew letter *ayin.* |
| ♒ | 28 | A woman naked and kneeling on her left knee pours silver water from a vase in her right hand into a river, by which grow roses with butterflies. Her left hand pours golden water over her head and long hair. Above flames a great star of seven rays. Her positioning suggests a swastika |
| ♓ | 29 | The waning Moon below which a path leads between two towers, guarded by jackals, upon which is a scarabaeus beetle |
| ☼ | 30 | The Sun. below it a wall with two children embracing in front of it, in a fairy ring |
| **F** | 31 | Israfel (the Angel of Death) blowing the Last Trumpet, with a golden banner bearing a white cross. Below three dead rise from their tombs: a fair youth (with hands above his head like Shu), a fair woman (giving the sign of Water and an inverted triangle on her breast) and a dark man (with the sign of Fire on his forehead) |
| ♄ | 32 | A *vesica piscis* composed of 400 circles surrounding a naked woman, draped with a red scarf and holding two spiral wands. At the corners the four Kerubic animals: Man, Eagle, Bull and Lion. |

*Minor Arcana: Court Cards*

| | | Mathers/GD | Waite/Case | Crowley | Suit |
|---|---|---|---|---|---|
| | | T2. Court Cards and Suits of the Tarot Minor Arcana. | | | |
| F | 31 | 4 Kings | 4 Knights | 4 Knights | Wands/Staves |
| A | 11 | 4 Princes / Knights | 4 Kings | 4 Princes | Swords |
| W | 23 | 4 Queens | 4 Queens | 4 Queens | Cups |
| E | 32b | 4 Princesses | 4 Pages/Knaves | 4 Princesses | Coins/Pentacles/Disks |

| | | T5. The Titles of the Wands Court Cards. (Fire) | T6. The Titles of the Cups Court Cards. (Water) | T7. The Titles of the Swords Court Cards. (Air) | T8. The Titles of the Coins Court Cards. (Earth) |
|---|---|---|---|---|---|
| | | 71 | 72 | 73 | 74 |
| F | 31 | Lord of the Flame and the Lightning. King of the Spirits of Fire. | Lord of the Waves and the Waters. King of the Hosts of the Sea. | Lord of the Winds and the Breezes. King of the Spirits of Air. | Lord of the Wide and Fertile Land. King of the Spirits of Earth. |
| A | 11 | Prince of the Chariot of Fire. | Prince of the Chariot of the Waters. | Prince of the Chariot of Air. | Prince of the Chariot of Earth. |
| W | 23 | Queen of the Thrones of Flame. | Queen of the Thrones of the Waters. | Queen of the Thrones of Air. | Queen of the Thrones of the Earth. |
| E | 32b | Princess of the Shining Flame. Rose of the Palace of Fire. | Princess of the Waters. Lotus of the Palace of the Floods. | Princess of the Rushing Winds. Lotus of the Palace of Air. | Princess of the Echoing Hills. Lotus of the Palace of the Earth. |

| | T9. Titles of the Wands Suit. (Fire) | T10. Titles of the Cups Suit. (Water) | T11. Titles of the Swords Suit. (Air) | T12. Titles of the Coins Suit. (Earth) |
|---|---|---|---|---|
| | 133 | 134 | 135 | 136 |
| 1 | Root of the Powers of Fire | Root of the Powers of Water | Root of the Powers of Air | Root of the Powers of Earth |
| 2 | Lord of Dominion | Lord of Love | Lord of Peace Restored | Lord of Harmonious Change |
| 3 | Established Strength | Abundance | Sorrow | Material Works |
| 4 | Perfected Work (Completion) | Pleasure | Rest from Strife | Earthly Power |
| 5 | Strife | Loss in Pleasure | Defeat | Material Trouble |
| 6 | Victory | Pleasure | Earned Success | Material Success |
| 7 | Valour | Illusionary Success | Unstable Effort | Success Unfulfilled |
| 8 | Swiftness | Abandoned Success | Shortened Force | Prudence |
| 9 | Great Strength | Material Happiness | Despair and Cruelty | Material Gain |
| 10 | Oppression | Perfected Success | Ruin | Wealth |

*Astrological Dominion*

| | | T13. The Wands Court Cards of the Tarot, with their Golden Dawn Zodiacal Dominion. | T14. The Cups Court Cards of the Tarot, with their Golden Dawn Zodiacal Dominion. | T15. The Swords Court Cards of the Tarot, with their Golden Dawn Zodiacal Dominion. | T16. The Coins Court Cards of the Tarot, with their Golden Dawn Zodiacal Dominion. |
|---|---|---|---|---|---|
| | | **71** | **72** | **73** | **74** |
| **F** | 31 | Rules 20° ♏ to 20°♐, including part of Hercules. | Rules 20°♒ to 20° ♓, including most of Pegasus. | Rules 20°♉ to 20°♊ | Rules 20°♌ to 20°♍ |
| **A** | 11 | Rules 20° ♋ to 20° ♌ including most of Leo Minor. | Rules 20° ♎ to 20° ♏ | Rules 20° ♑ to 20°♒ | Rules 20°♈ to 20°♉ |
| **W** | 23 | Rules 20° ♓ to 20° ♈, including part of Andromeda. | Rules 20° ♊ to 20°♋ | Rules 20° ♍ to 20°♎ | Rules 20°♐ to 20°♑ |
| **E** | 32b | Rules 1st Quadrant of the Heavens around North Pole. | Rules 2nd Quadrant of the Heavens around North Pole. | Rules the 3rd Quadrant of the Heavens around North Pole. | Rules the 4th Quadrant of the Heavens around North Pole. |

| | T17. Zodiacal Attributions of the Wands Suit. | T18. Zodiacal Attributions of the Cups Suit. | T19. Zodiacal Attributions of the Swords Suit. | T20. Zodiacal Attributions of the Coins Suit. |
|---|---|---|---|---|
| | | | | |
| **1** | Fire | Water | Air | Earth |
| **2** | ♂ in ♈ | ♀ in ♋ | ☽ in ♎ | ♃ in ♑ |
| **3** | ☉ in ♈ | ☿ in ♋ | ♄ in ♎ | ♂ in ♑ |
| **4** | ♀ in ♈ | ☽ in ♋ | ♃ in ♎ | ☉ in ♑ |
| **5** | ♄ in ♌ | ♂ in ♏ | ♀ in ♒ | ☿ in ♉ |
| **6** | ♃ in ♌ | ☉ in ♏ | ☿ in ♒ | ☽ in ♉ |
| **7** | ♂ in ♌ | ♀ in ♏ | ☽ in ♒ | ♄ in ♉ |
| **8** | ☿ in ♐ | ♄ in ♓ | ♃ in ♊ | ☉ in ♍ |
| **9** | ☽ in ♐ | ♃ in ♓ | ♂ in ♊ | ♀ in ♍ |
| **10** | ♄ in ♐ | ♂ in ♓ | ☉ in ♊ | ☿ in ♍ |

# T. Tarot

*Tarot Shem ha-Mephorash Angels*

| | T21. Pairs of Angels Ruling Wands. | T22. Pairs of Angels Ruling Wands – Transliteration. | T23. Pairs of Angels Ruling Cups. | T24. Pairs of Angels Ruling Cups – Transliteration. |
|---|---|---|---|---|
| | 129 | | 130 | |
| 1 | *by Day - by Night* | *by Night - by Day* | *by Day - by Night* | *by Night - by Day* |
| 2 | רניאל וחואל | DNIAL, VHVAL | חבויה איעאל | HBVIH, AIOAL |
| 3 | עממיה החשיה | OMMIH, HChShIH | יבמיה ראהאל | IBMIH, RAHAL |
| 4 | ניתאל ננאאל | NIThAL, NNAAL | מומיה הריאל | MNMIH, HIIAL |
| 5 | יליאל וחואי | ILIAL, VHVAI | פהליה לוויה | PHLIH, LVVIH |
| 6 | עלמיה סיטאל | OLMIH, SITAL | ייאל נלכאל | YIIAL, NLKAL |
| 7 | ללהאל מהשיה | LLHAL, MHShIH | חחויה מלחסל | HHIH, MLHSL |
| 8 | האאיה נתחיה | HAAIH, NThHIH | ילחיה ווליה | ILHIH, VVLIH |
| 9 | שאחיה ירתאלן | ShAHIH, IRThALN | עריאל סאליה | ORIAL, SALIH |
| 10 | אומאל רייאל | AVMAL, RIIAL | מיהאל עשליה | MIHAL, OShLIH |

| | T25. Pairs of Angels Ruling Swords. | T26. Pairs of Angels Ruling Swords – Transliteration. | T27. Pairs of Angels Ruling Coins. | T28. Pairs of Angels Ruling Coins – Transliteration. |
|---|---|---|---|---|
| | 131 | | 132 | |
| 1 | *by Day - by Night* | *by Night - by Day* | *by Day - by Night* | *by Night - by Day* |
| 2 | מבחאל יזלאל | MBHAL, YZLAL | ושריה לכבאל | VShRIH, LKBAL |
| 3 | הקמיה הריאל | HQMIH, HRIAL | לההיה יחויה | LHHIH, IHVIH |
| 4 | כליאל לאויה | KLIAL, LAVIH | מנדאל הוקיה | MNDAL, HVQIH |
| 5 | חעמיה אניאל | HOMIH, ANIAL | פויאל מבחיה | PVIAL, MBHIH |
| 6 | ייזאל רהעאל | YIZAL, RHOAL | יילאל נממיה | YILAL, NMMIH |
| 7 | מיכאל חחהאל | MIKAL, HHHAL | מצראל הרחאל | MTzRAL, HRHAL |
| 8 | יהחאל ומבאל | IHHAL, VMBAL | כהיאל אכאיה | KHIAL, AKAIH |
| 9 | מחיאל ענואל | MHIAL, ONVAL | אלדיה חזיאל | ALDIH, HZIAL |
| 10 | מנקאל דמביה | MNQAL, DMBIH | חחעיה לאויה | HHTzIH, LAVIH |

# T. Tarot

*Tarot as Emblem Sets*

| | T29. Tarot of Mantegna – A. Astrology series. | T30. Tarot of Mantegna – B. Virtues series. | T31. Tarot of Mantegna – C. Liberal Arts series. | T32. Tarot of Mantegna – D. Nine Greek Muses series. [2] | T33. Tarot of Mantegna – E. Estates of Man (Strata of Society) |
|---|---|---|---|---|---|
| **1** | 50 Prima Causa – First Cause | 40 Fede – Faith | 30 Theologia – Theology | 20 Apollo – Patron of the Arts | 10 Papa – Pope |
| **2** | 49 Primo Mobile 48 Octava Spera | 39 Speranza – Hope | 29 Astrologia – Astrology | 19 Clio – History | 9 Imperator – Emperor |
| **3** | 47 Sarturno – Saturn | 38 Charita – Charity | 28 Philosofia – Philosophy | 18 Euterpe – Lyric poetry | 8 Re – King |
| **4** | 46 Jupiter – Jupiter | 37 Justica – Justice | 27 Poesia – Poetry | 17 Melpomene – Song | 7 Doxe – Doge |
| **5** | 45 Marte – Mars | 36 Forteza – Fortitude | 26 Musica – Music | 16 Talia – Idyllic Poetry and Comedy | 6 Chavalier – Knight |
| **6** | 44 Sol – Sun | 35 Prudencia – Prudence | 25 Arithmetrica – Arithmetic | 15 Polimnia – Sacred Music/ Hymns | 5 Zintilomo – Gentleman |
| **7** | 43 Venus – Venus | 34 Temperancia – Temperance | 24 Geometria – Geometry | 14 Erato – Erotic Poetry and mime | 4 Merchadante – Merchant |
| **8** | 42 Mercurio – Mercury | 33 Cosmico – Spirit of the Cosmos/ Cosmology | 23 Rhetorica – Rhetoric | 13 Terpsicore – Choral dance | 3 Artixan – Artisan or Goldsmith |
| **9** | 41 Luna – Moon | 32 Chronico – Spirit of Time/ Chronology | 22 Loica – Logic | 12 Urania – Astronomy | 2 Fameio – Servant or Valet |
| **10** | – | 31 Iliaco – Spirit of the Sun | 21 Grammatica – Grammar | 11 Caliope – Epic Poetry | 1 Misero – Beggar |

[2] Compare with Column P20 which uses a different order.

| | | T34. Tarot Emblems: Set 1 – The Estates of Man (Strata of Mediaeval society). | T35. Tarot Emblems: Set 2 – the 7 Planets & the Zodiac. | T36. Tarot Emblems: Set 3 – the 7 Virtues. | T37. Tarot Emblems: Set 4 – Christian Theology. |
|---|---|---|---|---|---|
| ⊛ | 31b | | XVII – The Stars – the Zodiac | | |
| F | 31 | | | | XX – The Last Judgment |
| A | 11 | 0 – The Fool or Knave or Juggler or Beggar | | | |
| W | 23 | | | | XII – The Hanged Man – Christ |
| E | 32b | | | | |
| ☾ | 13 | II – The High Priestess or Female Pope | XVIII – The Moon | | |
| ☿ | 12 | I – The Magician or Artisan or Merchant Trickster | Mercury | | |
| ♀ | 14 | III – The Empress | Venus | | |
| ☼ | 30 | | XIX – The Sun | | |
| ♂ | 27 | | Mars | | XVI – The Tower of Babel |
| ♃ | 21 | | Jupiter | | X – Wheel of Fortune – Luck or Fate |
| ♄ | 32 | | Saturn | | XXI – The World – the 4 Apostles |
| ♈ | 15 | IV – The Emperor | | | |
| ♉ | 16 | V – The Pope or Hierophant | | Faith | |
| ♊ | 17 | VI – The Lovers | | Hope | |
| ♋ | 18 | VII – The Chariot or Knight | | Charity[3] | |
| ♌ | 19 | | | VIII – Justice | |
| ♍ | 20 | | | | IX – Hermit – Father Time or St Anthony |
| ♎ | 22 | | | XI – Fortitude (Strength) | |
| ♏ | 24 | | | Prudence | XIII – Death |
| ♐ | 25 | | | XIV – Temperance | |
| ♑ | 26 | | | | XV – The Devil |
| ♒ | 28 | | | | |
| ♓ | 29 | | | | |

---

[3]As further proof of the existence of the Seven Virtues as a sub-set of Emblems within the 22 Trumps, the cards Faith and Charity are actually included as separate Trumps in the Cary-Yale-Visconti deck of circa 1428. It is quite revealing that Love was never listed by the Church as one of the Virtues.

*Tarot and Sepher Yetzirah*

| | | The Hebrew Letters. | T38. Planetary Attributions – *Sepher Yetzirah* Planetary Order. | T39. Tarot Trumps based on the usual *Sepher Yetzirah* Planetary Order. | T40. Planetary Attributions modified by Mathers for G.D. | T41. Tarot Trumps based on the Planetary Order as modified by Mathers for the G.D. |
|---|---|---|---|---|---|---|
| | | | | | | |
| | **1** | | | | | |
| | **2** | | | | | |
| | **3** | Beth ב | ♄ – Saturn | | | |
| | **4** | Gimel ג | ♃ – Jupiter | | | |
| | **5** | Daleth ד | ♂ – Mars | | | |
| | **6** | Kaph כ | ☼ – Sun | | | |
| | **7** | Peh פ | ♀ – Venus | | | |
| | **8** | Resh ר | ☿ – Mercury | | | |
| | **9** | Tau ת | ☾ – Moon | | | |
| | **10** | | | | | |
| | | | | | | |
| **F** | 31 | Shin | Fire | XX – The Last Judgement | Fire | XX – The Last Judgement |
| **A** | 11 | Aleph | Air | 0 – The Fool | Air | 0 – The Fool |
| **W** | 23 | Mem | Water | XII – The Hanged Man | Water | XII – The Hanged Man |
| **E** | 32b | | | | | |
| | | | | | | |
| | | Beth | ♄ **– Saturn** | XXI – The Universe | ☿ – Mercury | I – The Magician |
| | | Gimel | ♃ **– Jupiter** | X – Wheel of Fortune | ☾ – Moon | II – The High Priestess |
| | | Daleth | ♂ **– Mars** | XVI – The Tower | ♀ – Venus | III – The Empress |
| | | Kaph | ☼ **– Sun** | XIX – The Sun | ♃ – Jupiter | X – Wheel of Fortune |
| | | Peh | ♀ **– Venus** | III – The Empress | ♂ – Mars | XVI – The Tower |
| | | Resh | ☿ **– Mercury** | I – The Magician | ☼ – Sun | XIX – The Sun |
| | | Tau | ☾ **– Moon** | II – The High Priestess | ♄ – Saturn | XXI – The Universe |
| ♈ | 15 | Heh | ♈ – Aries | IV – The Emperor | ♈ – Aries | IV – The Emperor |
| ♉ | 16 | Vav | ♉ – Taurus | V – The Hierophant/Pope | ♉ – Taurus | V – The Hierophant |
| ♊ | 17 | Zain | ♊ – Gemini | VI – The Lovers | ♊ – Gemini | VI – The Lovers |
| ♋ | 18 | Cheth | ♋ – Cancer | VII – The Chariot | ♋ – Cancer | VII – The Chariot |
| ♌ | 19 | Teth | ♌ – Leo | XI – Strength | ♌ – Leo | XI – Strength |
| ♍ | 20 | Yod | ♍ – Virgo | IX – Hermit | ♍ – Virgo | IX – Hermit |
| ♎ | 22 | Lamed | ♎ – Libra | VIII – Justice | ♎ – Libra | VIII – Justice |
| ♏ | 24 | Nun | ♏ – Scorpio | XIII – Death | ♏ – Scorpio | XIII – Death |
| ♐ | 25 | Samekh | ♐ – Sagittarius | XIV – Temperance | ♐ – Sagittarius | XIV – Temperance |
| ♑ | 26 | Ayin | ♑ – Capricorn | XV – The Devil | ♑ – Capricorn | XV – The Devil |
| ♒ | 28 | Tzaddi | ♒ – Aquarius | XVII – The Star | ♒ – Aquarius | XVII – The Star |
| ♓ | 29 | Qoph | ♓ – Pisces | XVIII – The Moon | ♓ – Pisces | XVIII – The Moon |

# U. Uniform Timeline

*Magicians*

U1. Magicians Timeline.

| Magician | Dates | Reputation |
|---|---|---|
| King Solomon | 970-928 BC | Magician, compelled demons to help build his Temple in Jerusalem |
| Empedocles | 490-432 BC | Stated the Theory of Four Elements, reputed knowledge of magic |
| Abaris the Hyperborean | 550 BC fl. | Scythian magician, levitator, reputed to have taught Pythagoras |
| Pythagoras | 569-470 BC | Greek Philosopher reputed to be semi-divine and to have magical abilities and the gift of prophecy |
| Damigeron (translated by Evax) | 200 BC fl. | Magician and author of a lapidary |
| Simon Magus | 15 BC-33 AD | Magician mentioned in NT, did miracles in competition with St Peter |
| Apollonius of Tyana | 2-98 AD | Greek Magician: with well attested magical feats and miracles |
| Lucius Apuleius of Madaurus | 123-170 | Roman author of the *Golden Ass,* Isis/Dionysian initiate |
| Julian the Theurgist | 150 fl. | Magician to Marcus Aurelius and author of the *Chaldaen Oracles* |
| Plotinus | 205-270 | Neoplatonic Philosopher who discussed the nature of daemons |
| Iamblichus of Chalcis | 250-325 | Wrote the classic *On the Egyptian Mysteries*, theurgist |
| Chacidius | 300 fl. | Author of *On Demons* in *Commentarius* |
| Julian (the Apostate) | 331-363 | Not a magician, but the last pagan Emperor, a Neoplatonist. His death sadly marks the end of the pagan world |
| Proclus | 410-485 | Neoplatonist Philosopher, theurgist, magician. |
| Merlin | 500 fl. | British Arthurian magician |
| Maslama al-Majriti | c.940-1007 | Translated Ptolemy, probable author of the *Picatrix* |
| Pope Silvester II (aka Gerbert) | 950-1003 | Pope reputed to be a sorcerer |
| Pope Benedict IX | 1012-1065 | Reputed magician |
| Michael Psellus | 1018-1081 | Wrote on demons in *De Operatione Daemonum* |
| Robert Grossteste | 1170-1253 | English natural scientist and reputed magician |
| Michael Scot | 1175-1236 | Scottish magician and astrologer to Emperor Frederick II of Sicily. Introduced works of Aristotle to England |
| Gulielmus Parisiensis (William of Paris, William of Auvergne) | 1180?-1249 | Bishop of Paris, scholar, author of *De Universo,* his opinion on grimoires was quoted by Agrippa |
| Albertus Magnus, St | 1193-1280 | Bishop, Doctor of the Church and author of books on natural magic |
| Roger Bacon | 1214-1294 | Franciscan, scientist, magician |
| Peter de Abano | 1250-1317 | Physician, magician, astrologer, alchemist, author of the *Heptameron* |
| Zito | 1325 fl. | Magician to the court of King Wenceslas IV |
| Antonius de Monte Ulmi | c.1340-1400 | Italian astrological necromancer and magician |
| George Gemistos Plethon | 1355-1452 | Greek Neoplatonist Philosopher, pagan |
| Abraham ben Simeon of Worms | 1362-1458 | Probable author of the *Sacred Magic of Abramelin* [he took up its practice in 1409] |
| Rabbi Jacob ben Moses ha Levi Moellin (the MaHaRIL) | 1365-1427 | Possible author of the *Sacred Magic of Abramelin*. If Melin=Moellin then Abra Melin was his 'spiritual father' |
| Christian Rosenkreuz | 1378-1484 | Legendary founder of Rosicrucianism |
| Roger Bolingbroke | c.1400-1441 | English astrologer, magician |
| Marsilio Ficino | 1433-1499 | Translator of the *Corpus Hermeticum* |

# U. Uniform Timeline

U1. Magicians Timeline.

| Magician | Dates | Reputation |
|---|---|---|
| Johann Trithemius | 1462-1516 | Abbott, scholar, cryptographer, angel magician, key figure |
| Giovanni Pico, Count of Mirandola | 1463-1494 | Italian humanist, Platonist, magician, Kabbalist |
| Agostino Nifo of Sessa | 1473-1546 | Author of *De Demonibus* on demons |
| Dr Johannes Faustus | 1466-1538 | Archetypal pact orientated magician |
| Henry Cornelius Agrippa von Nettesheim | 1486-1535 | Author of *Three Books of Occult Philosophy*, the most influential book on western magic, magician |
| Paracelsus von Hohenheim | 1493-1541 | Revolutionary doctor, philosopher, alchemist |
| Georgius Sabellicus | 1500 fl. | The 'second Faustus', magician |
| Dr John Kaye (aka Dr Caius) | 1510-1573 | Scholar magician, physician to Edward VI and Mary |
| Johann Weyer (aka Johannes Wierus) | 1515-1588 | Agrippa's disciple, author of *Pseudomonarchia Daemonorum* |
| Pope Sixtus V | 1521-1590 | Reputed Papal sorcerer |
| Blaise de Vigenère | 1523-1595 | Skilled French angel magician, diplomat and cryptographer |
| Dr John Dee | 1527-1608 | British angel magician, mathematician, geometrician, geographer, antiquarian, cryptographer and advisor to Queen Elizabeth I |
| Abraham Colorno | 1530-c.1598 | Jewish engineer of Mantua who translated *The Key of Solomon* from Hebrew, and wrote on cryptography |
| Giovanni Battista della Porta | 1535-1615 | Italian writer on natural magic, cryptographer |
| Reginald Scot | 1538-1599 | British author of *Witchcraft* |
| Thomas Egerton Baron Ellesmere[1] | 1540-1617 | Probably an angel magician |
| Giordano Bruno | 1548-1600 | Neoplatonist, Hermeticist, magician |
| John Napier | 1550-1617 | Mathematician, inventor of logarithms, magician |
| Simon Forman | 1552-1611 | Astrologer, doctor, and magician |
| Edward Kelley | 1555-1595 | Dr John Dee's skryer, alchemist |
| Richard Napier | 1559-1634 | Rector of Great Linford, pupil of Simon Forman, magician |
| Tomasso Campanella | 1568-1639 | Planetary magician |
| Sir Robert Cotton | 1571-1631 | Collector of Dr John Dee's manuscripts |
| Abel l'Angelier | 1574-1610 | Editor of the works of Blaise de Vigenère |
| Robert Fludd | 1574-1637 | Philosopher, mystic and geomancer |
| Dr Thomas Rudd | 1583-1656 | British scholar-magician |
| Henry ('Wizard Earl') Percy | 1585-1632 | British magician, earl |
| Duc de Richelieu | 1585-1642 | French statesman, reputed magician |
| Jacques Gaffarel | 1601-1681 | French Kabbalist, librarian to de Richelieu |
| Elias Ashmole | 1617-1692 | English antiquary, collector of John Dee's manuscripts, angel magician, astrologer, herald, royalist, scholar |
| Robert Turner of Holshott | 1620-1665? | Translator of classics of magic including Agrippa's *Fourth Book* |
| John Aubrey | 1626-1695 | Transcribed and used the *Clavicula Salomonis* in 1674 |

---

[1] Lord Chancellor and Master of the Rolls.

# U. Uniform Timeline

U1. Magicians Timeline.

| Magician | Dates | Reputation |
|----------|-------|------------|
| Baron Somers of Evesham[2] | 1651-1716 | English aristocrat, angel magician, member of Parliament |
| Goodwin Wharton[3] | 1653-1704 | English aristocrat, angel and fairy magician, member of Parliament |
| Georg von Welling | 1655-1725 | Author of *Opus Mago-Cabbalisticum et Theosophicum* |
| Sir Hans Sloane | 1660-1753 | Antiquary, collector of manuscripts, angel magician |
| Sir Joseph Jekyll | 1663-1738 | Angel magician, lawyer and parliamentarian, Master of the Rolls. |
| Aptolcater, mage of Adrianople | 1724-c.1770 | Author of a curious grimoire which relies on magic squares |
| Johann Georg Schropfer | 1730-1774 | German necromancer, well attested practicing magician |
| Francis Barrett | 1770?-1806? | British author of *The Magus*, magician, balloonist |
| Percy Bysshe Shelley | 1792-1822 | British poet, romantic and Goetic sorcerer |
| Johannes Scheible | 1845 fl. | German compiler of grimoires in *Das Kloster* |
| Sir Edward Bulwer-Lytton | 1803-1873 | British novelist, author of *Zanoni* |
| Frederick Hockley | 1808-1885 | British skryer, angel magician, Freemason, mentor of Kenneth MacKenzie, writer of occult manuscripts, member Society of Eight |
| Eliphas Levi (Alphonse Louis Constant) | 1810-1875 | Romantic French writer on magic and the tarot, author of *Transcendental Magic, History of Magic* |
| Dr William Robert Woodman | 1828-1891 | Golden Dawn co-founder, Freemason, Supreme Magus of SRIA |
| Major Francis George Irwin | 1828-1893 | Society of Eight, Freemason, Chief Adept of the Bristol Soc. Ros. |
| Kenneth Robert MacKenzie | 1833-1886 | Freemason, Member of Society of Eight, author of *The Royal Masonic Encyclopedia*, co-founder SRIA (in 1866) |
| Robert Wentworth Little | 1840-1878 | British Freemason, co-founder and Supreme Magus of SRIA |
| Dr William Wynn Westcott | 1848-1925 | Freemason, Golden Dawn co-founder, Supreme Magus SRIA |
| Samuel Liddell MacGregor Mathers | 1854-1918 | Magician, Golden Dawn co-founder, member SRIA, translator of major grimoires and *Kabbalah Denudata*, occult scholar |
| Allan Bennett (Iehi Aour) | 1872-1923 | Magician, GD member, Aleister Crowley's mentor, Buddhist monk |
| Aleister Crowley | 1875-1947 | Magician, Golden Dawn member, mountain climber, poet, author of *Magick in Theory & Practice*, head of O.T.O and A.'.A.'. |
| Gerald Brosseau Gardner | 1884-1964 | Founder of modern witchcraft (wicca), expert in Malay magic & weapons |
| Dion Fortune (Violet M Firth) | 1890-1946 | Founder of the Society of Inner Light, author of many books |
| Walter Ernest Butler | 1898-1978 | Magician, student of Dion Fortune, author of *The Magician* |
| Dr Israel Regardie | 1907-1985 | Magician, Stella Matutina member, author of the *Golden Dawn* |
| Franz Bardon | 1909-1958 | Magician and author of *Initiation into Hermetics* |
| Cecil Hugh Williamson | 1909-1999 | Founder of the Witchcraft Research Center Boscastle, and the Museum of Witchcraft in Castletown, worked with Gerald Gardner |
| Dr Nicolas Tereshchenko | c.1917-2002 | Fourth Way devotee & Gurdjieff editor, Tarot scholar, magician, Praemonstrator of the Paris Golden Dawn Ahathoor Temple |
| Lewis de Claremont / Henri Gamache | 1935 fl. | Goetic magician, author, and source of some Hoodoo lore |
| Alex Sanders | 1929-1988 | Founder and populariser of modern 'Alexandrian' witchcraft |
| Francis X King | 1934-1994 | British author of many books on magic, occult historian |

---

[2] Lord Chancellor of England.
[3] Lord High Admiral of England.

# U. Uniform Timeline

## Kabbalists

U2. Kabbalists Timeline.

| Hebrew Kabbalist | Christian Kabbalist | Dates | Reputation |
|---|---|---|---|
| Rabbi Nehuniah ben Kana | | 1st century | Author/editor of the *Bahir* |
| Rabbi Shimon bar Yochai | | 135-161 fl. | Supposed author of *Sepher ha Zohar* |
| Aaron ben Samuel | | 850 fl. | Brought doctrines from Babylon to Italy |
| Saadiah Gaon | | 892-942 | Author of *Sepher Yerushot* |
| Solomon Ibn Gabirol | | c.1021-1058 | Moorish Jewish poet and philosopher. |
| Rabbi Yitzchaki (Rashi) | | 1040-1105 | Author of *Sepher ha-Pardess* |
| Isaac the Blind | | 1160-1235 | 'Father of the Kabbalah' |
| Eliezer of Worms | | 1165-1225? | Author of *Sepher ha-Ratziel* |
| Rabbi Azariel | | ?-1238 | Author of *Commentary on the Ten Sephiroth* |
| Moses Nachmanides | | 1194-1270 | Helped spread the Kabbalah |
| Moses de Leon | | 1240-1305 | Author/publisher of *Sepher ha Zohar* |
| Abraham Abulafia | | 1240-c.1292 | Founder of ecstatic Kabbalah |
| Rabbi Joseph ben Abraham Gikatilla | | 1248-1323 | Author of *Sha'are Orah*, pupil of Abulafia |
| Isaac of Acre | | 1250-1340 | Kabbalist, questioned de Leon's widow |
| – | Johannes Reuchlin | 1455-1522 | Author of *De Arte Cabbalistica* |
| – | Giovanni Pico, Count of Mirandola | 1463-1494 | Italian philosopher and classical scholar. Author of *Kabbalistic Conclusions* |
| – | Francesco Giorgio | 1466-1540 | Author of *De Harmonia Mundi* |
| – | Henry Cornelius Agrippa von Nettesheim | 1486-1535 | Author of *Three Books of Occult Philosophy*, Kabbalist, magician |
| – | Jerome Cardan | ?-1576 | Mathematician, physician, astrologer |
| – | Gulielmus Postellus | 1501-1581 | Translated *Sepher Yetzirah* into Latin |
| Rabbi Judah Loew ben Bezalel of Prague | | 1520-1609 | Rabbi of Prague reputed to have created the golem |
| Rabbi Moses Cordovero (the Ramak) | | 1522-1570 | Author of *Pardes Rimonim* (The Garden of Pomegranates) a key Kabbalistic book |
| Rabbi Isaac Luria (the Ari) | | 1534-1572 | Author of *Etz Chaim* |
| Rabbi Hayyim/Chaim Vital | | 1542-1620 | Key student of Luria |
| – | Johann Pistorius | 1546-1608 | Author of *Ars Cabalistica*, translator of *Sepher Yetzirah* |
| – | Giordano Bruno | 1548-1600 | Italian Neoplatonist, Kabbalist |
| Abraham Cohen de Herrera | | c.1570-1631/9 | Author of *Beth Elohim* |
| – | Robert Fludd | 1574-1637 | Speculative philosopher, Kabbalist |
| – | Athanasius Kircher | 1601-1680 | Polymath author of *Oedipus Aegyptiacus* |
| – | Henry More | 1614-1687 | Cambridge Platonist |
| – | Baron Knorr von Rosenroth | 1636-1689 | Translator of Kabbalah into Latin *Kabbalah Denudata* |
| Rabbi Israel Baal Shem Tov | | 1698-1760 | Founder of Hasidism |
| Rabbi Moshe Chaim Luzzatto (the RaMChal) | | 1707-1746 | Rational Kabbalist, alchemist |
| – | S L MacGregor Mathers | 1854-1918 | Translator of *Kabbalah Denudata* |
| Rabbi Yehuda Ashlag | | 1884-1954 | Isaac Luria's greatest modern disciple |
| Gershom Scholem | | 1897-1982 | Pre-eminent Kabbalah scholar |
| – | Robert Ambelain | 1907-1997 | French Kabbalist |

# U. Uniform Timeline

*Astrologers*

<table>
<tr><td colspan="4" align="center">U3. Astrologers Timeline.</td></tr>
<tr><th>Astrologer</th><th>Latin name</th><th>Dates</th><th>Reputation</th></tr>
<tr><td>Meton of Athens</td><td></td><td>c.432 BC</td><td>Propounded the Metonic 19-year eclipse cycle</td></tr>
<tr><td>Eudoxus of Cnidis</td><td></td><td>408-355 BC</td><td>Theorised about retrograde planets</td></tr>
<tr><td>Aristarchus of Samos</td><td></td><td>c.310-250 BC</td><td>Proposed a heliocentric solar system</td></tr>
<tr><td>Hipparchus</td><td></td><td>c.190-c.120 BC</td><td>Explained precession of the zodiac, and composed a star catalog of 1000 stars.</td></tr>
<tr><td>Marcus Manilius</td><td></td><td>c.10 AD</td><td>Wrote the Astronomica</td></tr>
<tr><td>Dorotheus of Sidon</td><td></td><td>1<sup>st</sup> Century</td><td>Oldest source for the triplicity rulership system. Author of Carmen Astrologicum</td></tr>
<tr><td>Claudius Ptolemy</td><td></td><td>100-178</td><td>Wrote the Tetrabiblos and the Almagest</td></tr>
<tr><td>Julius Firmicus Maternus</td><td></td><td>346 fl.</td><td>His work Matheseos covers late Hellenistic astrological techniques</td></tr>
<tr><td>Hephaistio of Thebes</td><td></td><td>380 fl.</td><td>Wrote Apotelesmatics</td></tr>
<tr><td>Theophilus of Edessa</td><td></td><td>c.695-785</td><td>The bridge between Greek and Arabic astrology</td></tr>
<tr><td>Masha'allah</td><td>Messahalla</td><td>c.740-c.815</td><td>Author of many works flourishing under the Caliphs al-Mansur and al-Mamun</td></tr>
<tr><td>Abû 'Alî al-Khayyât</td><td>Albohali Alchait</td><td>c.770-c.835</td><td>Author of The Judgments of Nativities and student of Masha'allah</td></tr>
<tr><td>Sahl ibn Bishr</td><td>Zahel ben Briz</td><td>c.786-845</td><td>One of the more Hellenistic of the Arabic astrologers</td></tr>
<tr><td>Ja'far ibn Muhammad Abû Ma'shar al-Balkhî</td><td>Albumasar</td><td>787/805-886</td><td>Major Arab astrologer. Author of De coniunctionibus.</td></tr>
<tr><td>Al-Kindi</td><td>Alkindus</td><td>c.796-873</td><td>Author of On the Stellar Ray, a seminal text for astral magic</td></tr>
<tr><td>Abu 'Abdallah Muhammad al-Khwarizmi</td><td>Algoritmi, Algaurizin</td><td>c.780 – c. 850</td><td>Introduced decimal positioning to the West. Source of word 'algorithm.' Revised Ptolemy's Geography.</td></tr>
<tr><td>Banu Musa ben Shakir</td><td>Filii Moysi filii Sekir</td><td>fl.830</td><td>The three children of Musa ben Shakir who worked as astronomers for al-Ma'mūn in the House of Wisdom in Baghdad translating Greek texts</td></tr>
<tr><td>Al-Farghani</td><td>Alfraganus</td><td>c.800-c.863</td><td>Wrote Elements, a non-mathematical summary of Ptolemaic astronomy</td></tr>
<tr><td>Ahmad ben Yusuf</td><td>Hametus filius Iosephi</td><td>c.839-912</td><td>Astronomical tables and mathematical works on ratio and proportion.</td></tr>
<tr><td>Qusta ibn Luqa of Baalbeck</td><td>Costa Ben Luca/ Quosti filius Luce</td><td>820-912</td><td>Wrote on astrology and astrolabes. Was adopted by W B Yeats as an inspiration for A Vision</td></tr>
<tr><td>Abu'l Hasan Thabit ibn Qurra' ibn Marwan al-Sabi al-Harrani</td><td>Thabit Benchorat</td><td>826-901</td><td>Author who came out of the Harranian tradition of magic, Neoplatonism and late Hermeticism</td></tr>
<tr><td>Abu Bakr Muhammad Ibn Zakariya Ar-Razi</td><td>Rhazes/Rasis</td><td>865-925</td><td>Physician and astrologer</td></tr>
<tr><td>Al-Battani</td><td>Albategni</td><td>882-900</td><td>A 'Sabian' born in Harran. Quoted by Tycho Brahe, Copernicus, Kepler and Galileo.</td></tr>
<tr><td>Al-Qabisi</td><td>Alchabitius Abdylaziz</td><td>c.895?-967</td><td>His Introduction to Astrology was one of the most popular works in Latin translation</td></tr>
<tr><td>'Alî ibn Ahmad al-'Imrânî</td><td>Haly Embrani</td><td>c.900-955/6</td><td>Author of Liber Electionum</td></tr>
<tr><td>Maslama al-Majriti or Abu al-Qasim al-Qurtubi al-Majriti</td><td>Abucasim</td><td>d.1007</td><td>Muslim astronomer falsely reputed to be the author of the Picatrix.</td></tr>
<tr><td>Muhammad ibn Ahmad al-Bîrûnî</td><td>Albiruni</td><td>973-1049</td><td>One of the most literate and skilled Arabic era astronomers</td></tr>
</table>

# U. Uniform Timeline

| | U3. Astrologers Timeline. | | |
|---|---|---|---|
| **Astrologer** | **Latin name** | **Dates** | **Reputation** |
| 'Alî ibn abî al-Rijâl, Abûl 'l-Hasan | Albohazen Haly Haly Abenragel | fl.1040 | Influential Arab era astrologer. Wrote an extensive treatise on astrology much used in the Middle Ages |
| Abu'l Hasan Ali ibn Ridwan Al-Misri | Haly Abenrudian | c.988-c. 1061 | Wrote a commentary on Ptolemy's *Tetrabiblos* |
| Abū Isḥāq Ibrāhīm ibn Yaḥyā al-Naqqāsh al-Zarqālī | Arzerchel | 1029–1087 | Muslim astrologer and instrument maker from Toledo |
| Abū Ḥāmid Muḥammad ibn Muḥammad al-Ghazālī | Algazel | c.1058–1111 | Muslim philosopher who wrote the *Incoherence of the Philosophers* and contributed to sufi doctrine |
| Abū Muḥammad Jābir ibn Aflaḥ | Gerber Aven Afflah | 1100–1150 | Made corrections to Ptolemy's *Almagest* |
| Abraham Ben Meir Ibn Ezra | Ibn Ezra Abenezra | 1092-1167 | Jewish scholar and influential Latin author |
| Hugo of Santalla | | 1119-1151 | Translations from Arabic notably books of Aristotle and an early geomancia |
| Adelard of Bath | | c.1125 | Translator of Arabic astrological texts |
| John of Seville | | c.1142 | Prolific translator from Arabic into Latin of astrology and geomancy texts |
| Micheal Scot | | 1175-1236 | Astrologer at Emperor Frederick II's court |
| Albertus Magnus | | 1193-1280 | Brought Aristotelianism into Western thought, wrote books on the virtues of stones and plants |
| Guido Bonatti | | c.1210-1290 | Author of *Liber Astronomiae* |
| Campanus of Novara | | c.1210-1296 | Campanus house system often attributed to him |
| Roger Bacon | | 1214-1294 | English Franciscan philosopher, magician, scientist |
| Leopold of Austria | | fl.1271 | Author of *Compilatio ... de astrorum scientia Decem continentis tractatus.* |
| John of Ashenden | | fl.1350 | Mainly devoted to political and mundane astrology |
| Marsilio Ficino | | 1433-1499 | Translator of *Corpus Hermeticum,* and Plotinus |
| Johannes Regiomontanus | | 1436-1475 | Wrote an epitome of Ptolemy's *Almagest* |
| Copernicus | | 1473-1543 | Rediscovered heliocentric astronomy |
| Philip Melanchthon | | 1497-1560 | Great patron of astrology |
| Michel Nostradamus | | 1503-1566 | The great prophet and astrologer who utilized the methods of the Greek Branchus oracle |
| Simon Forman | | 1552-1611 | Astrologer, physician and magician |
| Tycho Brahe | | 1546-1601 | Compiled the most accurate star catalog of his time |
| John Napier | | 1550-1617 | Inventor of logarithms, useful in astrology |
| Johannes Kepler | | 1571-1630 | Great astronomer and reformer of astrology |
| William Lilly | | 1602-1681 | Astrologer in the medieval tradition, interested in horary astrology and angel magic |
| Placidus de Titis | | 1603-1668 | Promoted the Placidian house system. |
| Elias Ashmole | | 1617-1692 | Astrologer, patron of astrologers, angel magician, founder of Ashmolean Museum at Oxford, herald, collector of Dee manuscripts |
| Nicholas Culpeper | | 1616-1654 | Wrote a classic astrological herbal, astrologer |

# U. Uniform Timeline

| | | | |
|---|---|---|---|
| | | U3. Astrologers Timeline. | |
| **Astrologer** | **Latin name** | **Dates** | **Reputation** |
| George Wharton | | 1617-1681 | Royalist astrologer and opponent of Lilly |
| John Gadbury | | 1628-1704 | Royalist and Catholic astrologer |
| John Heydon | | 1629-1667 | Author of *Theomagia*, geomancer, magician |
| John Partridge | | 1644-1715 | Rationalist who helped destroy mediaeval astrology |
| John Whalley | | 1653-1724 | Did first translation of Ptolemy into English |
| Ebenezer Sibley | | 1751-1799 | Wrote the most influential astrology text of the 18th Century, Solomonic magician, alchemist |
| – | | 1770 | Last academic course in astrology at the University of Salamanca. End of astrology as a recognized science |
| Raphael | | 1795-1832 | Early astrology reviver |
| Richard James Morrison | | 1795-1874 | Helped to revive astrology. Wrote under the pseudonym 'Zadkiel' |
| Alan Leo | | 1860-1917 | Important modern writer on astrology |
| Walter Gorn Old | | 1864-1929 | Wrote many books under pseudonym 'Sepharial' |
| Margaret Ethelwyn Hone | | 1892-1969 | Head of the Faculty of Astrological Studies |
| Dane Rudhyar | | 1895-1985 | Prolific writer on astrology, Theosophist, musician |
| Michael Erlewine | | 1941- | Pioneered the use of microcomputers in astrology, has revived many lost astrological arts |
| Tadd Mann | | 1943- | Researched a new theory of time and astrology, introduced more astronomical rigor into astrology |
| Robert Zoller | | 1947- | Re-introduced Medieval ways of looking at astrology. Translated Guido Bonatti |
| Christopher Warnock | | 1962- | Re-introducing Renaissance astrological magic |

# U. Uniform Timeline

*Alchemists*

U4. Alchemists Timeline.

| Alchemist | Dates | Reputation |
|---|---|---|
| Hermes Trismegistus | | Father of alchemy, Hermetics, magic. |
| Ko Hung  (Ge Hong) | 283-343 | Author of the *Pao Pu Tzu* (*Baopuzi*) of Chinese alchemy |
| Zosimus of Panopolis | 300 fl. | Author of one of the earliest mentions of 'alchemy' |
| Stephanus of Alexandria | 610-641 fl. | Best known Greek alchemist after Zosimus |
| Jabir Ibn Hayyan (Gerber) | c.721-c.815 | The "true Geber" |
| Abu Bakr Muhammad ibn Zakariyya (Al Razi/Rhazes) | 825-925 | Author of the *Book of the Secret of Secrets*. Interested in practical techniques of alchemy/chemistry |
| St Dunstan | 940-957+ | Abbot of Glastonbury, later Archbishop of Canterbury. Alchemist whose reputed book was later treasured by John Dee |
| Muhammad Ibn Umail | d. 960 | Author of the Arabic *Turba Philosophorum*, or 'Assembly of the Sages', probably translated into Latin in 12th century |
| Abu Ali al-Husain ibn Abdullah ibn Sina (Avicenna) | 980-1037 | Persian physician, most influential of all the Islamic philosopher-scientists. |
| Artephius Romanus | c.1119- | Wrote *The Secret Book*, possessor of a key alchemic secret. |
| Robert of Chester | 1144 fl. | Translated the first alchemy book from Arabic to Latin on 11 Feb 1144, *Liber de Compositione Alchimiae* or *The Composition of Alchemy*. Alchemy arrives in Europe |
| Michael Scot | 1175-1236 | Scottish alchemist and astrologer to Emperor Frederick II. |
| Vincent of Beauvais | c.1190-c.1264 | Alchemist and librarian and chaplain to Louis IX, author of *Speculum Maius* |
| Albertus Magnus, St | 1193-1280 | Bishop, alchemist and author of the *Book of Minerals* and the *Little Book of Alchemy* |
| Roger Bacon | 1214-1294 | English Franciscan alchemist, magician, scientist. Author of the *Mirror of Alchemy* |
| Raymund/Ramon Lully | 1235-1315 | Spanish Kabbalist, alchemist, seneschal of Majorca |
| Arnold de Villanova | 1235?-1313 | Spanish astrologer, alchemist, physician and alchemist |
| John Dastin | 1288-1342 fl. | Corresponded with Pope John XXII about alchemy |
| John of Rupescissa | c.1310 - c.1364 | Apocalyptic prophet, author of the *Quinte Essence* |
| Petrus Bonus | 1330 fl. | Author of the *New Pearl of Great Price* |
| Nicholas Flamel | 1330 -1418/9 | French alchemist claimed to have the Philosopher's Stone |
| Geoffrey Chaucer | c.1343-1400 | Wrote about alchemy in *Canon's Yeoman's Tale*, and probably practiced it |
| Basil Valentine | 1394-c.1450 | Author of *Triumphant Chariot of Alchemy* |
| Thomas Norton | c.1400-1477 | Author of *The Ordinall of Alchemy* |
| Isaac of Holland | 1415 fl. | Author of *Opera Mineralia sive de Lapide Philosophico* |
| Sir George Ripley | 1415-1490 | Important English alchemist, canon of Bridlington Cathedral |
| Salomon Trismosin | 1473 fl. | Author of *Splendor Solis* |
| Philippus Theophrastus Paracelsus von Hohenheim | 1493-1541 | Alchemist and physician. Applied the word 'spagyric' to his work. |
| William Holway (Holloway), last Prior of Bath Abbey | 1539 fl. | Hid the Red Elixir in the walls of the church, which may have been that Elixir subsequently found by Dee & Kelly. |

# U. Uniform Timeline

| Alchemist | Dates | Reputation |
|---|---|---|
| | | U4. Alchemists Timeline. |
| Thomas Charnock | 1526-1581 | Alchemist and author of *A Booke of Philosophie*, a pupil of William Holway |
| Leonhard Thurneisser zum Thurn | 1531-1596 | Aristocrat, alchemist, astronomer |
| Andreas Libavius | 1540-1616 | Alchemist and chemist, author of *Alchymia* |
| John Napier | 1550-1617 | Mathematician, inventor of logarithms, interested in alchemy |
| Alexander Seton | c.1550? -1604 | Alchemist reputed to have succeeded in projection, taught Sendivogius who published his *New Light on Alchemy*. |
| Edward Kelly | 1555-1597 | Skryer to John Dee, possessor of a key alchemic secret |
| John Pontanus | 1559?-1614 | Author of the *Epistle on the Secret Fire* |
| Heinrich Khunrath | 1560-1605 | Alchemist, author of *Amphitheatrum Sapientiae Aeternae* |
| Michael Sendivogius | 1566-1636 | Alchemist who performed projection, and may have identified oxygen |
| Michael Maier | 1568-1622 | Counselor to Rudolph II, author of *Atalanta Fugiens* |
| Johannes Battista van Helmont | 1577-1644 | Chemist and alchemist |
| Arthur Dee | 1579-1651 | The eldest son of Dr John Dee, physician to Tzar of Russia |
| Sir Kenelm Digby | 1603-1665 | Founder member of the Royal Society, alchemist |
| Benedictus Figulus | c.1608 | Author of the *Golden and Blessed Casket* |
| Elias Ashmole | 1617-1692 | Edited the *Theatrum Chemicum Britannicum*, and anthology of writings of the best of British alchemists |
| Thomas Vaughan (Eugenius Philalethes) | 1621-1666 | English alchemist, magician, Rosicrucian, author of *Lumin de Lumine, Anthroposophia Theomagica, Magia Adamica* |
| Johann Friedrich Schweitzer (Helvetius) | 1625-1709 | Alchemist, chemist and physician to the Prince of Orange, author of *Vitulus Aureus* |
| George Starkey (Eirenaeus Philalethes) | 1628-1665 | Physician and alchemist. *Ripley Reviv'd, Marrow of Alchemy, An Open Entrance to the Shut-Palace of the King,, Art of the Transmutation of Metals, Breviary of Alchemy* |
| Sir Isaac Newton | 1643-1727 | Physicist, alchemist, and 'the last of the magicians' |
| James Price (Higginbotham) | 1752-1783 | Alchemist, chemist and Fellow of the Royal Society who claimed transmutation, but committed suicide instead |
| Sigismund Bacstrom | 1770-1799 fl. | Scholar, Rosicrucian, translated alchemical texts |
| Rev. William Alexander Ayton | 1816-1909 | Alchemist and Golden Dawn member |
| Fulcanelli | c.1841-1926/32 | Mysterious French alchemist |
| Mary Ann Atwood (née South) | 1817-1910 | Author of *A Suggestive Enquiry into the Hermetic Mystery* |
| Francois Jollivet-Castelot | 1874-1937 | French alchemist |
| Archibald Cockren | c.1883-1950 | Practicing English alchemist |
| Eugene Canseliet | 1899-1982 | Fulcanelli's disciple, alchemist, who claimed transmutation |
| David Curwen (Lapidus) | 1893-1984 | Practicing English alchemist. Author of *In Pursuit of Gold* |
| Dr. Richard Albert Riedel (Frater Albertus) | 1911-1984 | American spagyricist associated with AMORC, the Paracelsus Research Society and plant alchemy |
| Adam McLean | 1948 - | Significant modern alchemical and magical scholar, author and publisher |

# U. Uniform Timeline

*Masters of the Knights Templar*

| No. | U5. Masters of the Knights Templar. | U6. Masters of the Knights Templar – years of rule. | U7. Alleged Masters of the *Prieure de Sion*. | U8. Alleged Masters of the *Prieure de Sion* – years of rule. |
|---|---|---|---|---|
| | | **Date** | | **Date** |
| 1 | Hugues de Payns | 1118-1136 | Jean de Gisors | 1188-1220 |
| 2 | Robert de Craon (Robertus Burgundio) | 1136-1146 | Marie de Saint-Clair | 1220-1266 |
| 3 | Everard des Barres (Ebrardus de Barris) | 1146-1149 | Guillaume de Gisors | 1266-1307 |
| 4 | Bernard de Tremelay | 1149-1153 | Edouard de Bar | 1307-1336 |
| 5 | André de Montbard | 1153-1156 | Jeanne de Bar | 1336-1351 |
| 6 | Bertrand de Blanchefort | 1156-1169 | Jean de Saint-Clair | 1351-1366 |
| 7 | Philippe de Milly (Philippus de Neapoli/ de Nablus) | 1169-1171 | Blanche d'Evreux | 1366-1398 |
| 8 | Odo (Eudes) de St Amand (Odon de Saint-Chamand) | 1171-1179 | Nicolas Flamel | 1398-1418 |
| 9 | Arnaud de Toroge (Arnaldus de Turre Rubea/de Torroja) | 1179-1184 | Rene d'Anjou | 1418-1480 |
| 10 | Gérard de Ridefort | 1185-1189 | Iolande de Bar | 1480-1483 |
| 11 | Robert de Sablé (Robertus de Sabloloi) | 1191-1193 | Sandro Filipepi | 1483-1510 |
| 12 | Gilbert Horal (Gilbertus Erail/Herail//Horal/Roral) | 1193-1200 | Leonardo de Vinci | 1510-1519 |
| 13 | Phillipe de Plessis (Plaissie / Plesse / Plessiez) | 1201-1208 | Connetable de Bourbon | 1519-1527 |
| 14 | Guillaume de Chartres (Willemus de Carnoto) | 1209-1219 | Ferdinand de Gonzague | 1527-1575 |
| 15 | Pierre (Pedro) de Montaigu (Petrus de Monteacuto) | 1219-1230 | Louis de Nevers | 1575-1595 |
| 16 | Armand de Périgord (Hermannus Petragoricensis) | 1232-1244 | Robert Fludd | 1595-1637 |
| 17 | Richard de Bures | 1245-1247 | Johannes Valentine Andrea | 1637-1654 |
| 18 | Guillaume de Sonnac (Guillelmus de Sonayo) | 1247-1250 | Robert Boyle | 1654-1691 |
| 19 | Renaud de Vichiers (Rainaldus de Vicherio) | 1250-1256 | Isaac Newton | 1691-1727 |
| 20 | Thomas Bérard | 1256-1273 | Charles Radclyffe | 1727-1746 |
| 21 | Guillaume de Beaujeu (Guillelmus de Belloico) | 1273-1291 | Charles de Lorraine | 1746-1780 |
| 22 | Thibaud Gaudin (Thiband Gandin) | 1291-1292 | Maximilien de Lorraine | 1780-1801 |
| 23 | Jacques de Molay last Master of the Templars | 1292-1314 | Charles Nodier | 1801-1844 |
| | | | Victor Hugo | 1844-1885 |
| | | | Claude Debussy | 1885-1918 |
| | | | Jean Cocteau | 1918-1963 |
| | | | Francois Ducaud-Bourget | 1963-1981 |
| | | | Pierre Plantard | 1981-1984 |

# U. Uniform Timeline

*Gnostic Movements and their Founders*

| | | | | |
|---|---|---|---|---|
| U9. Gnostic Movements and their Founders. | | | | |
| **Founder** | **Dates** | **Disciple of** | **Sect** | **Origin/Location/Comment/Books** |
| **John the Baptist** (bin Yahya) | c.6 BCE-30/36 CE | ? | Johannites → Mandaeans | *Samaritan*. Johannites still exist as a sect. John is still viewed as the Messiah by the Mandaeans. Buried in *Samaria* |
| Dositheos | d. 29 CE | John the Baptist | Dositheans | *Samaritan* magician, sometimes said to have come from Arabia |
| **Simon Magus** aka Faustus | 15 BCE-53 CE | Dositheos, Phillip | Simonians | *Samaritan* magician who levitated in front of the Emperor, and attempted to buy magical powers from the apostles. |
| **Jesus of Nazareth** | 6 BCE – 33 CE | John the Baptist | Nazarenes/ Christians | Said to be a *Samaritan*.[4] Not a Gnostic, but nevertheless the founder of a Jewish heresy that rejected Levite dietary laws, etc., but accepted the Jewish idea of a Messiah. |
| **Menander** | 35-117 | Simon | Menandrists/ Menandrians | *Samaritan* from Capparatea and Antioch. Probably a magician. Invented the 'bath of immortality.' |
| Cleobius | c. 50 | Dositheos | Cleobians | *Samaritan* associate of Simon. |
| Ebion[5] | c. 70 | Cerinthus | Ebionites | Jewish Christians in Pella, in *Samaria*. Arisen at the time of the destruction of the Second Temple (70 CE). |
| Simon of Gitta | c. 70 | | | *Samaritan* author of *Megale Apophasis*. Sometimes identified with Simon Magus. |
| Cerinthus | c. 70 | Menander? | Cerinthians | In Alexandria and Asia Minor. Predicted Christ's reign of 1000 years. Jewish-Christian. |
| Saturninus, Satornilus or Satornil | 90-150 | Menander | | Antioch. Founder of Syrian Gnosticism. Urged sexual restraint. Ascetic. |
| Carpocrates | 78-138 | Cerinthus, Saturninus | Carpocratians, Harpokratianoi | Probably a magician. In Alexandria and Antioch. Called themselves 'Gnostics.' Incorporated Egyptian Mysteries, Greek philosophy, reincarnation. Rejected Yahweh. *Secret Gospel of Mark, Gospel according to the Hebrews* |
| Cerdo | 135 fl. d. 143 | Simon Magus, Menander | Cerdonians | Syrian. Taught in Rome. Teacher of Marcion |
| **Basilides** | 85-145 | Matthias, Glaucias, Menander | Basilideans | Alexandria, Egypt and southern Europe. Abraxas. Author of the *Exegetica,* 24 books of commentary on the Gospels. |
| Isidorus | 125 fl. | Basilides | Basilideans | Son of Basilides |
| Marcellina | 145 fl. | Carpocrates | Carpocratians | Established in Rome |
| Euphrates | d. 160 | | Peratae | Worshipped the serpent which they identified with the brass serpent fashioned by Moses |
| **Marcion** | 90-165 | Cerdo | Marcionites | Wealthy ship owner who came to Rome in 140 and was excommunicated in 144 CE. Involved with astrology, symptomatic of Chaldaean roots. Rejected the OT and most of the NT. Later absorbed by Manicheans |

---

[4] Jesus was accused of being Samaritan and a magician by the Temple priests: "Then the Jews answered and said to Him, 'Do we not say well [true] that you are a Samaritan, and have a [tame] demon?'" in *John* 8:48. He was certainly pro-Samaritan, as shown by *Luke* 10:29-37.
[5] Maybe Ebion did not exist, but Ebionites simply derived their name from the Hebrew for "poor."

# U. Uniform Timeline

U9. Gnostic Movements and their Founders.

| Founder | Dates | Disciple of | Sect | Origin/Location/Comment/Books |
|---------|-------|-------------|------|-------------------------------|
| Theudas/Theodas | | St Paul | | A link in the Valentinian chain |
| **Montanus** | 110-172 | | Montanists / Cataphrygians | Pagan convert to Christianity, castrant from Phrygia. Montanus claimed to be the Paraclete. Sect founded in 156. Puritan, celebate, adventist, practised baptism for the dead (*vide* Mormons). Tertullian was a Montanist. |
| **Valentinus** | 110-175 | Basilides, Theodas | Valentinians | Alexandria, Rome. The most influential Gnostic teacher. Urged sexual freedom. *Gospel of Truth*. 'Mainstream' Gnosticism |
| Theodotus, the currier | 140-170 fl. | Valentinus | | *Excerpta ex Theodoto* |
| Marcus of Memphis | 150 fl. d. 175 | Valentinus | Marcosians / Marcians | Egyptian magician, taught in Asia Minor and Gaul. For him magic, Kabbalah and isopsephy (numerology) were important. |
| Alexander Abonouteichos, the Paphlagonian | c.105-180 | Apollonius of Tyana | Cult of Glycon | Alexander from Abonouteichos in Asia Minor, grandson of Asclepius. Maybe an indirect founder of the Ophites |
| Severus | d. 183 | Marcion | Encratites | Theology included Ialdabaoth |
| Apelles | 180 fl. | Marcion | Apelliasts | Taught in Rome and Alexandria. Used a skryer called Philumēnē. See *Mead (1960), 250-252* |
| Prodicus | 180 fl. | Carpocrates | | Persian. Alexandria to Carthage. |
| Ptolemaeus | 180 fl. | Valentinus | | Rome. Author of *Letter of Ptolmaeus to Flora*. See *Mead (1960), 383-390* |
| Justinus | c. 200 | | Ophites | Worshipped the serpent (*ophis*) of *Genesis,* and identified it with the brass serpent made by Moses. Justinus was not the founder of the Ophites, just an Ophite teacher. Primal power is Priapus. Author of *Book of Baruch* |
| Heracleon | 140-200 | Valentinus | Valentinians | Wrote commentary on St. John. "The most distinguished Valentinian." See *Mead (1960), 391-392* |
| Numenius of Apamea | 150-209 | Marcion | | 'Chaldaean' astrologer who influenced the neo-Platonist Plotinus |
| Axionicus | 220 fl. | Valentinus | | Antioch |
| **Bardesanes** | 154-222 | Valentinus | Bardaisanites | Assyrian from Edessa. Well educated from a wealthy family. Converted from Christianity. *Hymn of the Pearl*. Taught in Egypt, Syria, Asia Minor, Spain, Gaul. Contributed doctrinally to Manicheans, and probably to Cathars. See *Mead (1960), 392-405* |
| Plotinus | 204-270 | Numenius | | Philosopher and Neoplatonist, not a Gnostic |
| Priscillian | 340-386 | Marcus of Memphis | | Magician and Bishop of Avila, later excommunicated and executed for heresy, sorcery and studying magic, then later venerated as a martyr |

# V. Vedic and Hindu

*Tattwas*

| | | V1. Five Hindu Tattwas (Elements). | V2. Hindu Tattwas – Colour and Shape. | V3. Hindu Tattwas – Flashing Colour. | V4. Hindu Tattwas – Associated Sense. | V5. Nadas – Associated Internal Sounds. | V6. Observances – Niyama. |
|---|---|---|---|---|---|---|---|
| | | 75 | | | | | |
| ⊛ | 31b | Akasa | Black Egg | White | Hearing | Thunder Drums | Saucha – Cleanliness of Body and Mind |
| F | 31 | Tejas | Red Triangle or Pyramid or Cone | Green | Sight | Bees, Crickets | Tapas – Body Conditioning |
| A | 11 | Vayu | Light Blue Circle or Sphere | Orange | Touch | Flute | Prasadana – Purity of Mind, Attentiveness |
| W | 23 | Apas | Silver Crescent, horns upwards | Violet | Taste | Waterfall, Ocean | Swadhyaya – Study of Self |
| E | 32b | Prithivi | Yellow Square or Cube | Purple | Smell | Bell, Gong, Cymbal | Santosha – Contentment |

# V. Vedic and Hindu

*Chakras*

| | V7. Hindu Chakras. | V8. Hindu Chakras – Location in Body. | V9. Hindu Chakras – Interpretation. | V10. Hindu Chakras – Number of Petals. | V11. Hindu Chakras – Number of Rays. | V12. Tattwa Ruling this Chakra. |
|---|---|---|---|---|---|---|
| | **118** | | | | | |
| 1 | Sahasrara | Crown of the Head | The 1000–petaled lotus | 1000 | 360 | - |
| 2 | Ajna | Pineal Gland – between the eyebrows | Unlimited power | 2 | 64 | Manas, mental faculties |
| 3 | Visuddha | Larynx, throat | Pureness | 16 | 72 | Akasha |
| 4 | | | | | | |
| 5 | Anahata | Heart | Soundless sound | 12 | 54 | Vayu |
| 6 | | | | | | |
| 7 | Manipura | Solar Plexus – navel | City of jewels | 10 | 52 | Tejas |
| 8 | Svadisthana | Genitals – spinal region just above | Dwelling place of the self | 6 | 62 | Apas |
| 9 / 10 | Muladhara | Base of spine | Root entrance | 4 | 56 | Prithivi |

| | Hindu Chakras. | V13. Hindu Chakras – Shape of Mandala. | V14. Hindu Chakras – Bija syllable and its Vahana (carrier). | V15. Hindu Chakras – Devata. | V16. Hindu Chakras – Sakti of the Dhatu. | V17. Other Tattwas and organ of sense. |
|---|---|---|---|---|---|---|
| | | | | | | |
| 1 | Sahasrara | | | | Maha Shakti | |
| 2 | Ajna | | Om | Sambhu | Hakini | Mahat, Hiranyagarbha |
| 3 | Visuddha | Circle/Sphere | Ham on a white elephant | Sadasiva | Shakini | Sabda (sound), hearing |
| 4 | | | | | | |
| 5 | Anahata | Hexagon | Yam on an antelope | Isa | Kakini | Sparsa (feel), skin (organ of touch) |
| 6 | | | | | | |
| 7 | Manipura | Triangle/Cone | Ram on a ram | Rudra on a bull | Lakini | Rupa (form and colour), sight |
| 8 | Svadisthana | Crescent | Vam on the Makara | Vishnu on Garuda | Rakini | Rasa (taste), tongue |
| 9 / 10 | Muladhara | Square/Cube | Lam on the Airavata elephant | Brahma on Hamsa | Dakini | Gandha (smell), nose |

# V. Vedic and Hindu

*Yoga*

| | | V18. Hindu Meditations & Yoga Results. | V19. The Ten Traditional Yamas. | V20. The Ten Traditional Yamas – Meaning. | V21. The Ten Vayus. |
|---|---|---|---|---|---|
| | | **24** | | | |
| **1** | | Nerodha-samapatti, Nirvikalpa-samadhi (8) Atma darshana, Brahma darshana | Ahimsa | harmlessness, not causing of pain to any living creature in thought, word, or deed. | Vyana – in the whole body |
| **2** | | Shiva darshana | Satyam | truthfulness, word and thought in conformity with the facts | Kurmana – in the eyes |
| **3** | | Dhyana (7)[1] Mantra yoga | Asteya | non-stealing, non-coveting, non-entering into debt | Undana – in middle of the throat |
| **4** | | Dharana (6) | Brahmacharya | divine conduct, continence, celibate when single, faithful when married | Devadatta – causing yawning |
| **5** | | Pratyahara (5) | Kshama | patience, releasing time, functioning in the now | Samana – in the navel |
| **6** | | Pranayama (4) Vishvarupa darshana | Dhriti | steadfastness, overcoming, fear, and indecision; seeing each task through to completion | Prana – in the breast |
| **7** | | Yama (1) | Daya | compassion; conquering callous, cruel and insensitive feelings towards all beings | Kirkala – in the stomach |
| **8** | | Niyama (2) | Arjava | honesty, straightforwardness, renouncing deception and wrong doing. | Nag – producing vomiting |
| **9** | | Tantra yoga | Mitahara | moderation of appetite, neither eating too much nor too little, being vegetarian | Apana – in the excretory organs |
| **10** | | Hatha Yoga, Asana (3) | Shaucha | purity, avoidance of impurity in body, mind and speech | Dhananjaya – in whole body even after death |
| ✳ | 31b | Akasha-Bhawana | | | |
| **F** | 31 | Agni-Bhawana | | | |
| **A** | 11 | Vayu-Bhawana | | | |
| **W** | 23 | Apas-Bhawana | | | |
| **E** | 32b | Prithivi-Bhawana | | | |
| ☾ | 13 | Laya yoga Vision of Chandra | | | |
| ☿ | 12 | Jnana yoga | | | |
| ♀ | 14 | Bhakti yoga | | | |
| ☼ | 30 | Raja yoga Vision of Surya | | | |
| ♂ | 27 | Kriya yoga | | | |
| ♃ | 21 | Karma yoga | | | |
| ♄ | 32 | Hatha Yoga | | | |

---

[1] Numbers in brackets indicate the traditional Eight Limbs of Raja Yoga.

# W. Wheel of the Year, Seasons, Months and Hours

*Seasonal Quarters*

| | | W1. Seasonal Quarters of the Year – Pagan. | W2. Seasonal Quarters of the Year – Christian. | W3. Seasonal Quarters of the Year – Astronomic.[1] |
|---|---|---|---|---|
| ♈ | 15 | | | c. March 20 – Vernal Equinox |
| ♉ | 16 | April 30 – Walpurgis Night, Beltane | Roodmas, May Day Eve | |
| ♊ | 17 | | | |
| ♋ | 18 | | | c. June 21 – Summer Solstice |
| ♌ | 19 | August 1 – Lughnasadh | Lammas | |
| ♍ | 20 | | | |
| ♎ | 22 | | | c. September 23 – Autumnal Equinox |
| ♏ | 24 | October 31 – Samhain | Halloween, All Hallow's Eve, All Soul's Day | |
| ♐ | 25 | | | |
| ♑ | 26 | | | c. December 22 – Winter Solstice |
| ♒ | 28 | February 1 – Imbolg, Imbolc, Oimelc | Candlemass, St Bridget's Day, Lady Day | |
| ♓ | 29 | | | |

*Planetary Hours*

| | | W4. Genii of the Twelve Hours from the *Nuctameron*. | | | | | | |
|---|---|---|---|---|---|---|---|---|
| | | 173 | | | | | | |
| ♈ | 15 | Papus | Sinbuck | Rasphuia | Zahun | Heiglot | Mizkun | Haven |
| ♉ | 16 | Sisera | Torvatus | Nitibus | Hizarbin | Sachluph | Baglis | Laberzerin |
| ♊ | 17 | Hahabi | Phlogabitus | Eirneus | Mascarun | Zarobi | Butatar | Cahor |
| ♋ | 18 | Phalgus | Thagrinus | Eistibus | Pharzuph | Sislau | Schiekron | Aclahayr |
| ♌ | 19 | Zeirna | Tablibik | Tacritau | Suphlatus | Sair | Barcus | Camaysar |
| ♍ | 20 | Tabris | Susabo | Eirnils | Nitika | Haatan | Hatiphas | Zaren |
| ♎ | 22 | Sialul | Sabrus | Librabis | Mizgitari | Causub | Salilus | Jazar |
| ♏ | 24 | Nantur | Toglas | Zalburis | Alphun | Tukiphat | Zizuph | Cuniali |
| ♐ | 25 | Risnuch | Suclagus | Kirtabus | Sablil | Schachlil | Colopatiron | Zeffar |
| ♑ | 26 | Sezarbil | Azeph | Armilus | Kataris | Razanil | Bucaphi | Mastho |
| ♒ | 28 | Æglun | Zuphlas | Phaldor | Rosabis | Adjuchas | Zophas | Halacho |
| ♓ | 29 | Tarab | Misran | Labus | Kalab | Hahab | Marnes | Sellen |

---

[1] The dates of the Solstice and Equinox vary slightly from year to year. The above dates are for 2006. The seasonal references apply to the Northern Hemisphere.

# W. Wheel of the Year, Seasons, Months and Hours

| | | | | | | | | | |
|---|---|---|---|---|---|---|---|---|---|
| | | | W5. Table of Planetary Hours. | | | | | | |
| | Uneven Hours | For example... on the Equinox² | Sunday | Monday | Tuesday | Wednesday | Thursday | Friday | Saturday |
| **Hours of the Day** (Dawn to Sunset) | 1st | 6:00 AM | Sun | Moon | Mars | Mercury | Jupiter | Venus | Saturn |
| | 2nd | 7:00 AM | Venus | Saturn | Sun | Moon | Mars | Mercury | Jupiter |
| | 3rd | 8:00 AM | Mercury | Jupiter | Venus | Saturn | Sun | Moon | Mars |
| | 4th | 9:00 AM | Moon | Mars | Mercury | Jupiter | Venus | Saturn | Sun |
| | 5th | 10:00 AM | Saturn | Sun | Moon | Mars | Mercury | Jupiter | Venus |
| | 6th | 11:00 AM | Jupiter | Venus | Saturn | Sun | Moon | Mars | Mercury |
| | 7th | 12:00 PM | Mars | Mercury | Jupiter | Venus | Saturn | Sun | Moon |
| | 8th | 1:00 PM | Sun | Moon | Mars | Mercury | Jupiter | Venus | Saturn |
| | 9th | 2:00 PM | Venus | Saturn | Sun | Moon | Mars | Mercury | Jupiter |
| | 10th | 3:00 PM | Mercury | Jupiter | Venus | Saturn | Sun | Moon | Mars |
| | 11th | 4:00 PM | Moon | Mars | Mercury | Jupiter | Venus | Saturn | Sun |
| | 12th | 5:00 PM | Saturn | Sun | Moon | Mars | Mercury | Jupiter | Venus |
| **Hours of the Night** (Sunset till next Dawn) | 1st | 6:00 PM | Jupiter | Venus | Saturn | Sun | Moon | Mars | Mercury |
| | 2nd | 7:00 PM | Mars | Mercury | Jupiter | Venus | Saturn | Sun | Moon |
| | 3rd | 8:00 PM | Sun | Moon | Mars | Mercury | Jupiter | Venus | Saturn |
| | 4th | 9:00 PM | Venus | Saturn | Sun | Moon | Mars | Mercury | Jupiter |
| | 5th | 10:00 PM | Mercury | Jupiter | Venus | Saturn | Sun | Moon | Mars |
| | 6th | 11:00 PM | Moon | Mars | Mercury | Jupiter | Venus | Saturn | Sun |
| | 7th | 12:00 AM | Saturn | Sun | Moon | Mars | Mercury | Jupiter | Venus |
| | 8th | 1:00 AM | Jupiter | Venus | Saturn | Sun | Moon | Mars | Mercury |
| | 9th | 2:00 AM | Mars | Mercury | Jupiter | Venus | Saturn | Sun | Moon |
| | 10th | 3:00 AM | Sun | Moon | Mars | Mercury | Jupiter | Venus | Saturn |
| | 11th | 4:00 AM | Venus | Saturn | Sun | Moon | Mars | Mercury | Jupiter |
| | 12th | 5:00 AM | Mercury | Jupiter | Venus | Saturn | Sun | Moon | Mars |

---

² This column is only shown for the sake of illustration. In fact there will only be two dates in the year (the Equinoxes) when the Planetary hours are exactly an hour long. During Winter the hours of the day will be shorter and the hours of night longer. The reverse is true in Summer. You need to calculate the exact length of the hour using your local sunrise and sunset times on the day of the working itself, dividing the difference by 12. For example, sunrise at 6am and sunset at 8pm will give a daylight length of 14 hours or 840 minutes. The daylight hour will therefore by 840/12 = 70 minutes long.

# W. Wheel of the Year, Seasons, Months and Hours

*Months & Mini-Seasons*

| | | W6. Months of the Jewish Calendar – Hebrew. | W7. Months of the Jewish Calendar – Translation. | W8. Months of the Jewish Calendar – Commencement Dates. |
|---|---|---|---|---|
| ♈ | 15 | ניסן | 7 – Nisan | March 30, 2006 |
| ♉ | 16 | אייר | 8 – Iyar | April 29, 2006 |
| ♊ | 17 | סיון | 9 – Sivan | May 29, 2006 |
| ♋ | 18 | תמוז | 10 – Tammuz | June 27, 2006 |
| ♌ | 19 | אב | 11 – Av/Ab | July 26, 2006 |
| ♍ | 20 | אלול | 12 – Elul | August 25, 2006 |
| ♎ | 22 | תשרי | 1 – Tishri | October 4, 2005 |
| ♏ | 24 | חשון | 2 – Cheshvan/Marchesvan | November 3, 2005 |
| ♐ | 25 | כסלו | 3 – Kislev | December 2, 2005 |
| ♑ | 26 | טבת | 4 – Tevet/Tebeth | January 1, 2006 |
| ♒ | 28 | שבט | 5 – Shevet/Shebet | January 30, 2006 |
| ♓ | 29 | אדר | 6 – Adar | March 1, 2006 |

| | | W9. Months of the Egyptian Calendar[3]. | W10. Egyptian Mystery Celebrations. | W11. Months of the Egyptian Calendar – Theoretical Commencement Dates. |
|---|---|---|---|---|
| ♈ | 15 | 9. Pachon | Equinox – Isis | March 17 |
| ♉ | 16 | 10. Payni | | April 16 |
| ♊ | 17 | 11. Epiphi | | May 16 |
| ♋ | 18 | 12. Mesore | Solstice – Seraphis | June 15 |
| | | *5 epagomenal days* | Osiris, Horus, Set, Isis, Nephthys | July 15 |
| ♌ | 19 | 1. Thoth | | July 20 |
| ♍ | 20 | 2. Phaophi | | August 19 |
| ♎ | 22 | 3. Athyr | Equinox – Osiris | September 18 |
| ♏ | 24 | 4. Choiak | | October 18 |
| ♐ | 25 | 5. Tybi | | November 17 |
| ♑ | 26 | 6. Mecheir | Solstice | December 17 |
| ♒ | 28 | 7. Phamenoth | | January 16 |
| ♓ | 29 | 8. Pharmuthi | | February 15 |

---

[3] All months were exactly 30 days long. The month of Thoth was considered the first month.

# W. Wheel of the Year, Seasons, Months and Hours

| | | W12. Months of the Ancient Greek Lunar Civil Calendar. | | | |
|---|---|---|---|---|---|
| | | **Athens** | **Delos** | **Thessaly** | **Boetia** |
| ♈ | 15 | Hekatombaion (1) | Hekatombaion | Phyllikos | Hippodromios |
| ♉ | 16 | Metageitnion | Metageitnion | Itonios (1) | Panamos |
| ♊ | 17 | Boedromion | Bouphonion | Panemos | Pamboiotios |
| ♋ | 18 | Pyanepsion | Apatourion | Themistios | Damatrios |
| ♌ | 19 | Maimakterion | Aresion | Agagylios | Alalkomenios |
| ♍ | 20 | Poseideon | Poseideon | Hermaios | Boukatios (1) |
| ♎ | 22 | Gamelion | Lenaion (1) | Apollonios | Hermaios |
| ♏ | 24 | Anthesterion | Hieros | Leschanopios | Prostaterios |
| ♐ | 25 | Elaphebolion | Galaxion | Aphrios | Agrionios |
| ♑ | 26 | Mounychion | Artemision | Thuios | Thiouios |
| ♒ | 28 | Thargelion | Thargelion | Homoloios | Homoloios |
| ♓ | 29 | Skirophorion | Panamos | Hippodromios | Theilouthios |

| | | W13. Months of the Ancient Babylonian Calendar. | | W14. The 24 mini-Seasons of the Chinese Solar Calendar. | |
|---|---|---|---|---|---|
| | | **Sumerian** | **Month** | **Chi** | **Chieh** |
| ♈ | 15 | Bar | Nisannu | 4 Ch'un fen | 5 Ch'ing ming |
| ♉ | 16 | Gu | Ajjaru | 6 Ku yu | 7 Li hsia |
| ♊ | 17 | Sig | Simanu | 8 Hsiao man | 9 Mang chung |
| ♋ | 18 | Su | Du'uzu | 10 Hsia chih | 11 Hsiao shu |
| ♌ | 19 | Izi | Abu | 12 Ta shu | 13 Li ch'iu |
| ♍ | 20 | Kin | Ululu | 14 Ch'u shu | 15 Pai lu |
| ♎ | 22 | Du | Tesritu | 16 Ch'iu fen | 17 Han lu |
| ♏ | 24 | Apin | Arahsamnu | 18 Shuang chiang | 19 Li tung |
| ♐ | 25 | Gan | Kislimu | 20 Hsiao hsueh | 21 Ta Hsueh |
| ♑ | 26 | Ab | Tebetu | 22 Tung chih | 23 Hsiao han |
| ♒ | 28 | Ziz | Sabatu | 24 Ta han | 1 Li ch'un |
| ♓ | 29 | Se | Addaru | 2 Yu shui | 3 Ching chih |

# X. Cross-Reference to Isopsephy

## X1. Greek Isopsephy.

| Num | English | Greek | | Num | English | Greek |
|-----|---------|-------|---|-----|---------|-------|
| 6 | Father | Αββα | | 235 | Sacrifice, temple, ritual | Ιερον |
| 9 | Greek Earth goddess Gaea | Γεα | | 247 | The Beast (*Revelations* 13:11) | Θηριον |
| 11 | | Γη | | 251 | Thong, girdle of Venus | Ιμας |
| 15 | Goddess | Δεα | | 279 | Temple, altar; foundation | Εδος |
| 22 | Greek goddess Hestia | Εστια | | 281 | Goes, wizard | Γοης |
| 34 | Canaanite god Baal, 'Lord' | Βααλ | | 284 | God, deity | Θεος |
| 46 | Adam | Αδαμ | | 290 | Magi, magicians | Αοιδες |
| 60 | Magic | Μαγεια | | 291 | Chaos | Καος |
| 62 | Greek goddess Athena | Αθανα | | 301 | Greek goddess Selene, Moon | Σεληνη |
| 68 | Greek goddess Medea | Μηδεια | | 304 | | Σηληνη |
| 69 | Greek goddess Athena | Αθηνα | | 305 | Daimon (Socrates' genius) | Δαιμονιον |
| 76 | Goddess | Θεαινα | | 309 | Greek god Ares (Mars) | Αρης |
| 80 | Io [rapture cry] | Ιο | | 312 | Wizards | Θελγινες |
| 81 | IAO, Gnostic godname, [see also 811 IAO] | IAO | | 313 | Secret, unknown | Αδηλος |
| 88 | Greek goddess Nike, Victory | Νικη | | 314 | Magus | Μαγος |
| 93 | Love (see also 551) | Αγαπη | | 315 | Greek goddess Eris, discord | Ερις |
| 93 | Will (see also 551) | Θελημα | | 316 | Greek god Helios | Αελιοσ |
| 99 | Amen | Αμην | | 318 | | Ηλιος |
| 99 | Knowledge of the Mysteries | Μαθημα | | 320 | Greek goddess Iris | Ιρις |
| 101 | Egyptian Sun god Ra | Ρα | | 334 | Greek goddess Hecate | Εκατη |
| 106 | Greek goddess Rea | Ρεα | | 342 | Greek goddess Pallas (Athene) | Παλλας |
| 109 | Greek goddess Hera | Ηρα | | 343 | A spell | Γοος |
| 117 | Beast | Θηρ | | 353 | Greek god Hermes | Ερμης |
| 121 | Kore, Greek goddess of death or fate | Καρ | | 355 | Magician | Αοιδος |
| 128 | | Κηρ | | 359 | Angel, messenger | Αγγελος |
| 131 | Greek god Pan; all | Παν | | 360 | Roman/Persian god Mithras | Μιθρας |
| 135 | Splendor, glory, honor | Δοξα | | 365 | Abraxas, Abrasax | Αβραξας |
| 137 | Arcadia | Αρκαδια | | 365 | Roman/Persian god Meithras | Μειθρασ |
| 158 | Greek goddess Circe | Κιρκη | | 365 | River Nile | Νειλος |
| 179 | Ablanathanalba | Αβλαναθαναλβα | | 367 | Greek god Heracles | Ηρακλης |
| 184 | Orgia, secret rites | Οργια | | 373 | Logos; word | Λογος |
| 211 | Hail Pan! | Ιο παν | | 380 | Daimons | Δαιμονς |
| 213 | Hades | Αδησ | | 381 | To invoke | Επκαλεισθαι |
| 223 | | Αιδησ | | 387 | The Devil (the Adversary) | Διαβολος |
| 233 | Oracle | Λογιου | | 387 | Of the Beast | Θερος |

# X. Cross-Reference to Isopsephy

X1. Greek Isopsephy.

| Num | English | Greek | | Num | English | Greek |
|-----|---------|-------|---|-----|---------|-------|
| 388 | Sun (as salutation) | Ο ηλιος | | 510 | Greek goddess Nemesis | Νεμεσις |
| 390 | Mind, reason | Νοος | | 510 | Greek god Kronos | Κρονος |
| 396 | Horned | Κεραος | | 510 | Greek goddess Nyx, Night | Νυξ |
| 394 | Goetia | Γοετεια | | 510 | Will | Βουλη |
| 397 | | Γοητεια | | 518 | Gate, door (*Matthew* 7:13) | Πυλη |
| 397 | Serpent of Aesculapius (Asclepius) | Παρειας | | 518 | The Door (*John* 10:9) | η θυρα |
| 401 | Greek god Pan; all | Πανος | | 523 | Greek goddess Hestia | Εστιη |
| 406 | Eve | Ευα | | 551 | Will (see 93) | Βουλημια |
| 408 | Coitus | Κοιτη | | 551 | Love (see 93) | Θιλια |
| 413 | The spell | η γοος | | 552 | Satan | Σαταν |
| 417 | Mysteries, sacrifices, rites | Τα ιερα | | 555 | Necronomicon | Νεκρονομικον |
| 418 | Such are the words | Ειδε τα επη | | 560 | One who wills; a wizard | Θελητης |
| 418 | Foundation, base; shoe | Κρηπις | | 563 | *Poimandres* (from *Hermetica*) | Ποιμανδρης |
| 418 | Greek goddess Pallas Athene | Παλλας Αθηνη | | 580 | Conjuration (*orkismos*) | Ορκισμοσ |
| 418 | I am Hermes… | Ηρμες ειμι | | 585 | The god of oracles | η φαμαιθεια |
| 419 | Egyptian god Tuat, Thoth | Θυαθ | | 595 | Sirius, the dog-star | Σειριος |
| 420 | Egyptian goddess Isis | Ισις | | 596 | Graeco-Egyptian god Serapis (see also 666) | Σεραπις |
| 421 | A howling | Ιυγη | | 598 | Theurgia | Θεουργια |
| 443 | The Logos (as salutation) | Ο λογοσ | | 612 | Greek god Zeus | Ζευς |
| 445 | Divine being, genius | Δαιμονος | | 612 | Womb; belly | Γαστηρ |
| 450 | Egyptian goddess Nu | Νυ | | 617 | The Beast | Το θηριον |
| 450 | Offering, sacrifice | Θυμα | | 617 | Pangenetor (all-begetter) | Πανγγενετορ |
| 451 | Beetle | Κανθαρος | | 618 | Oracle | Ομφη |
| 454 | Greek goddess Demeter | Δαματηρ | | 626 | Egyptian god Keph-Ra | Κεφρα |
| 455 | Divine, god-like | Γαιμονιος | | 656 | Greek goddess Artemis | Αρτεμις |
| 460 | Gematria | Γεματρια | | 656 | Messiah | Μεσσιας |
| 460 | Horned | Κερεινος | | 656 | Initiation; the Mysteries | η τελετη |
| 461 | Greek goddess Demeter | Δημητρα | | 666 | The Great Beast | το μεγα θηριον |
| 461 | Temple of Hecate | Εκατειον | | 666 | Serapis (as salutation) | Ο σεραπις |
| 465 | Greek goddess Cybele | Κυβελη | | 666 | Titan | Τειταν |
| 469 | Egyptian goddess Nuit | Νυιθ | | 700 | *chi-rho*, Christ's symbol | ΧΡ |
| 473 | Spell, charm | Ιυγξ | | 733 | Egyptian god Anubis | Ανουβις |
| 474 | Sacrifice | Θυειν | | 741 | Spells, enchantments | Καταδεσις |
| 481 | IAOU, Gnostic name of God | ΙΑΟΥ | | 743 | Watcher, guardian | Εποπτης |
| 485 | | ΙΕΟΥ | | 753 | Satanas | Σατανας |

# X. Cross-Reference to Isopsephy

X1. Greek Isopsephy.

| Num | English | Greek | Num | English | Greek |
|-----|---------|-------|-----|---------|-------|
| 760 | Egyptian goddess Nuit | Νυιτ | 1090 | Secret | Μυστικον |
| 780 | Gnostic goddess Sophia | Σοφια | 1095 | Parthenon | Παρθενων |
| 800 | Lord; god | Κυριος | 1105 | Greek god Eros | Ερος |
| 810 | Io! [The rapture-cry] | Ιω | 1109 | Oannes | Ωαννησ |
| 811 | IAO, Gnostic name of God | ΙΑΩ | 1164 | Egyptian goddess Nephthys | Νεφθυς |
| 818 | Egyptian god Thoth | Θωθ | 1170 | Secret, hidden, occult | Κρυπτος |
| 820 | Pistis | Πιστις | 1170 | Egyptian god Horus | Ωρος |
| 822 | Spheres | Σφαιραι | 1178 | Secret rite, mystery | Μυστηριον |
| 861 | Aeon; eternity | Αιων | 1196 | Sorcery | Γοητευσις |
| 861 | Egyptian god Apophis | Αποφις | 1197 | Sorceress | Γοητευτρια |
| 888 | Jesus | Ιησους | 1219 | Icthus, Jesus Christ (Fish) | Ιχθυς |
| 890 | Olympus | Ολυμπος | 1219 | The Omega; the end | Το ωμεγα |
| 893 | Greek god Bacchus | Βακχος | 1219 | Greek god Poseidon | Ποσειδων |
| 897 | Incantation; spell | Επωδη | 1244 | Hierophant | Ιεροφαντης |
| 901 | Iacchus | Ιακχος | 1251 | Juggler; magician | Θαυματοποιος |
| 905 | Daimon (Guardian spirit) | Δαιμων | 1263 | Gnosis; wisdom | Γνωσις |
| 905 | Demiurge | Δημιουργος | 1264 | Geometry | Γεωμετρια |
| 908 | To call up, summon | Ανακαλεω | 1267 | Sorcerer | Φαρμακευς |
| 931 | Aeon (salutation) | Ο αιων | 1275 | Greek demi-god Orpheus | Ορφευς |
| 941 | Io Pan! Hail Pan! | Ιο Παν | 1285 | Babylon | Βαβυλων |
| 975 | Dragon (*Revelations* 12:9) | Δρακων | 1289 | Greek god Poseidon | Ποσειδων |
| 975 | Demiurge (as salutation) | Ο δημιουργος | 1289 | Greek god Hephaestus | Ηφαιστος |
| 979 | Thyrsus, staff of Bacchantes | Θυρσος | 1332 | Gnostic deity Chnoubis | Χνουβις |
| 993 | Greek goddess Aphrodite | Αφροδιτη | 1335 | Thaumaturgy | θαυματουργια |
| 1011 | Greek god Apollo (see 1061) | Απολλω | 1352 | Teletarchs | Τελεταρχαι |
| 1018 | Greek goddess Persephone | Περσεφονη | 1429 | Pleroma | Πληρωμα |
| 1049 | Thyrsus, staff of Bacchantes | Ο Θυρσος | 1461 | Apollyon | Απολλυων |
| 1059 | Mysteries | Μυστηρια | 1484 | Simon Magus | Σιμων ο Μαγος |
| 1060 | Zion | Σιων | 1500 | Egyptian god Horus | Ωρυσ |
| 1060 | Philtron (spell) | φιλτρον | 1525 | Synoches, Chaldaean gods | Συνοχες |
| 1060 | Priests of Zeus | Τομουροι | 1560 | Perfection | Τελειωσις |
| 1061 | Greek god Apollon (see 1011) | απολλων | 1708 | Greek god Pluto | Πλουτων |
| 1065 | Semitic/Greek god Adonis | Αδωνις | 2050 | Typhon | Τυφων |
| 1085 | IAO SABAO, God of Hosts | ΙΑΩ ΣΑΒΑΟ | 2220 | Osoronnophris | Οσοροννωφρις |
| 1090 | Greek god Chronos | Χρονος | 3663 | Bainchoooch, soul of darkness | Βαινχωωωχ |

# Y. Yi Jing or I Ching

| Hexagram Number | Lower Trigram | Upper Trigram Number | Upper Trigram | Hexagram in Wade-Giles | Hexagram in Pinyin | Hexagram Meaning in English | Other Hexagram Meanings |
|---|---|---|---|---|---|---|---|
| 1 | | 9 | Heaven | Ch'ien | qian | Heaven | Active, creative |
| 43 | | 4 | Lake | Kuai | quai | Resolution | Decision |
| 14 | | 3 | Fire | Ta yu | da you | Great possession | To have abundance |
| 34 | 9 Ch'ien Heaven ☰ | 8 | Thunder | Ta Chuang | da zhuang | Great strength | Great power |
| 9 | | 2 | Wind | Hsiao ch'u | xiao chu | Small accumulation | A small (animal) offering |
| 5 | | 7 | Water | Hsu | xu | Needing | Calculated inaction, waiting |
| 26 | | 6 | Mountain | Ta ch'u | da chu | Great accumulation | Great nourisher, restraint |
| 11 | | 1 | Earth | T'ai | tai | Tranquillity | State of calm, peace, self possession |
| 10 | | 9 | Heaven | Lu | lu | Treading carefully | Careful conduct |
| 58 | | 4 | Lake | Tui | dui | Lake | Enjoyment, joy |
| 38 | | 3 | Fire | K'uei | kui | Estrangement | Separation |
| 54 | 4 Tui Lake ☱ | 8 | Thunder | Kuei mei | gui mei | Marriageable maiden | Nubile girl |
| 61 | | 2 | Wind | Chung fu | zhong fu | Central truth | Inner confidence and sincerity |
| 60 | | 7 | Water | Chieh | jie | Restraint | Limitation |
| 41 | | 6 | Mountain | Hsun | xun | Loss | Loss, reduction, decrease |
| 19 | | 1 | Earth | Lin | lin | To approach | Overlooking |

# Y. Yi Jing or I Ching

Y1. The 64 Hexagrams in the Order of their Position on the *San Yuan lo p'an.*

| Hexagram Number | Lower Trigram | Upper Trigram Number | Upper Trigram | Hexagram in Wade-Giles | Hexagram in Pinyin | Hexagram Meaning in English | Other Hexagram Meanings |
|---|---|---|---|---|---|---|---|
| 13 | | 9 | Heaven | T'ung jen | tong ren | Fellowship | People like us |
| 49 | | 4 | Lake | Ko | ge | Revolution | Transformation, skin, leather |
| 30 | | 3 | Fire | Li | li | Fire | Shining, brightness |
| 55 | 3 Li Fire ☲ | 8 | Thunder | Feng | feng | Abundance | Greatness, rich |
| 37 | | 2 | Wind | Chia jen | jia ren | Family | People in same home |
| 63 | | 7 | Water | Chi chi | ji ji | Already accomplished | Already fulfilled |
| 22 | | 6 | Mountain | P'i | bi | Adornment | Decoration, elegance |
| 36 | | 1 | Earth | Ming I | ming yi | Brightness dimmed | Brightness obscured |
| 25 | | 9 | Heaven | Wu wang | wu wang | Without wrongdoing | Without absurdity, integrity |
| 17 | | 4 | Lake | Sui | sui | Following | Obedient participation |
| 21 | | 3 | Fire | Shih ho | shi he | Biting through | Gnawing, bite |
| 51 | 8 Chen Thunder ☳ | 8 | Thunder | Chen | chen | Thunder | Arousing, shaking |
| 42 | | 2 | Wind | I | yi | Increase | Gain, profit |
| 3 | | 7 | Water | Chun | tun | Initial difficulties | Storing up, sprouting |
| 27 | | 6 | Mountain | I | yi | Nourishment | Literally jaws |
| 24 | | 1 | Earth | Fu | fu | Turning back | Return, consider it again |

# Y. Yi Jing or I Ching

Y1. The 64 Hexagrams in the Order of their Position on the *San Yuan lo p'an*.

| Hexagram Number | Lower Trigram | Upper Trigram Number | Upper Trigram | Hexagram in Wade-Giles | Hexagram in Pinyin | Hexagram Meaning in English | Other Hexagram Meanings |
|---|---|---|---|---|---|---|---|
| 44 | 2 Hsun Wind | 9 | Heaven | Kou | gou | Meeting | Encountering, coitus |
| 28 | | 4 | Lake | Ta kuo | da guo | Great Test | Strained to the breaking point, excess |
| 50 | | 3 | Fire | Ting | ding | Metal cauldron | Three legged bronze vessel |
| 32 | | 8 | Thunder | Heng | heng | Perseverance | Constancy, Long lasting |
| 57 | | 2 | Wind | Hsun | sun | Wind | Penetrating |
| 48 | | 7 | Water | Ching | jing | Well | Well |
| 18 | | 6 | Mountain | Ku | gu | Poison | Poisoning illness or bewitchment |
| 46 | | 1 | Earth | Sheng | sheng | Ascending | Promotion |
| 6 | 7 K'an Water | 9 | Heaven | Sung | song | Conflict | Dispute, arguments |
| 47 | | 4 | Lake | K'un | kun | Exhaustion | Weary, trapped, distress |
| 64 | | 3 | Fire | Wei ch'i | wei ji | Not yet completed | Prior to completion |
| 40 | | 8 | Thunder | Hsieh | jie | Release | Loosen, liberate |
| 59 | | 2 | Wind | Huan | huan | Dispersal | Disintegration, scattering, overflowing |
| 29 | | 7 | Water | K'an | kan | Water | Watery depths, abyss, pit |
| 4 | | 6 | Mountain | Meng | meng | Immaturity | Child, uncultivated |
| 7 | | 1 | Earth | Shih | shi | Multitude | Many people, the army |

# Y. Yi Jing or I Ching

Y1. The 64 Hexagrams in the Order of their Position on the *San Yuan lo p'an*.

| Hexagram Number | Lower Trigram | Upper Trigram Number | Upper Trigram | Hexagram in Wade-Giles | Hexagram in Pinyin | Hexagram Meaning in English | Other Hexagram Meanings |
|---|---|---|---|---|---|---|---|
| 33 | | 9 | Heaven | Tun | dun | Withdrawal | Running away, yielding |
| 31 | | 4 | Lake | Hsien | xian | Mutual attraction | Moving emotion, influence |
| 56 | | 3 | Fire | Lu | lu | Traveller | Wanderer, exile |
| 62 | 6 Ken Mountain | 8 | Thunder | Hsiao kuo | xiao guo | Small test | Small error or weakness |
| 53 | | 2 | Wind | Chien | jian | Developing gradually | To advance slowly |
| 39 | | 7 | Water | Chien | jian | Obstruction, trouble | Walking with difficulty, trouble |
| 52 | | 6 | Mountain | Ken | ken | Mountain | Keeping Still, ceasing action |
| 15 | | 1 | Earth | Ch'ien | qian | Modesty | Respectful |
| 12 | | 9 | Heaven | P'i | pi | Stagnation | Obstruction, the nadir |
| 45 | | 4 | Lake | Ts'ui | cui | Gathering of people | Assembly |
| 35 | | 3 | Fire | Chin | jin | Progress | Proceeding Forward, advance |
| 16 | 1 K'un Earth | 8 | Thunder | Yu | yu | Pleasure | Pleased |
| 20 | | 2 | Wind | Kuan | guan | Observation | Looking |
| 8 | | 7 | Water | Pi | bi | Unity | Binding together, to follow |
| 23 | | 6 | Mountain | Po | bo | Stripping away | Peeling off |
| 2 | | 1 | Earth | K'un | k'un | Earth | Female, receptive, acquiescing |

# Y. Yi Jing or I Ching

| Y2. King Wen's Sequence of the Hexagrams. | | | |
|---|---|---|---|
| **Lower Canon - Humanity** | | **Upper Canon - Heaven** | |
| 32–Endurance/Constancy | 31–Feeling/move away | | |
| 34–Great Force | 33–Retreat/hide from force | **2–Earth** | **1–Heaven** |
| 36–Darkening | 35–Advance/increase | 4–Unknowing/Youthfulness | 3–Difficulty |
| 38–Opposition/strangers | 37–Family | 6–Conflict/Dispute | 5–Waiting (before action) |
| 40–Release (from hardship) | 39–Hardship | 8–Closeness/Union | 7–Army/Multitude |
| 42–Increase | 41–Decrease | 10–Treading (on tiger's tail) | 9–Little Taming/offering |
| 44–Encounter/meet a problem | 43–Breakthrough/solve | 12–Stagnation/stopped | 11–Peace/Prosperous |
| 46–Rising/ascending | 45–Gathering together | 14–Great Possessions | 13–Fellowship/sharing |
| 48–The Well | 47–Impasse/distress | 16–Enthusiasm/pleasure | 15–Modesty |
| 50–Cauldron/the State | 49–Revolution/change | 18–Spoilage/poisonous | 17–Following |
| **52–Keeping Still/Mountain** | **51–Shock/Thunder** | 20–Viewing from a distance | 19–Approach/arrive |
| 54–Maiden marrying | 53–Development/Advance | 22–Grace/decorate | 21–Biting |
| 56–Traveller (without possessions) | 55–Fullness/Abundance | 24–Renewal/return | 23–Splitting/stripping |
| 58–The Joyous/Lake | 57–The Gentle/Wind | 26–Great Taming/offering | 25–Innocence/No error |
| 60–Limitation/Regulation | 59–Dispersion | 28–Excess | 27–Nourishment |
| 62–Getting By | 61–Inner Sincerity | **30–The Clinging/Fire** | **29–The Abysmal/Water** |
| **64–Not-Yet-Across** | **63–Already Across** | | |

| Y3. Eight Trigrams or *pa kua*. | | | | | |
|---|---|---|---|---|---|
| **Kua** | **Trigram** | **Element** | **Natural Phenomena** | **Season** | **Family Member** |
| ☰ | Ch'ien | Metal | Heaven | Late Autumn | Father |
| ☷ | K'un | Earth | Earth | Late Summer | Mother |
| ☳ | Chen | Wood | Thunder | Spring | Eldest Son |
| ☵ | K'an | Water | Moon/Water | Winter | Middle Son |
| ☶ | Ken | Earth | Mountain | Early Spring | Youngest Son |
| ☴ | Hsun | Wood | Wind | Early Summer | Eldest Daughter |
| ☲ | Li | Fire | Sun/Lightning | Summer | Middle Daughter |
| ☱ | Tui | Metal | Lake | Mid Autumn | Youngest Daughter |

*Parts of the Body*

| | | Z1. The Human Body. | Z2. The Members of the Body of Terrestrial Man. | Z3. *Sepher Yetzirah* [Long version] Body Attributions. | Z4. Typical Diseases. |
|---|---|---|---|---|---|
| | | **182** | | | **186** |
| | 1 | Spirit | Brain | | Death |
| | 2 | Brain | Lungs | | Insanity |
| | 3 | Spleen | Heart | | Dementia (especially Amnesia) |
| | 4 | Liver | Stomach | | Dropsy |
| | 5 | Gall | Liver | | Fever |
| | 6 | Heart | Gall | | Heart Disease |
| | 7 | Kidneys | Reins (kidneys) | | Skin Troubles |
| | 8 | Lungs | Reins (kidneys) | | Nerve Troubles |
| | 9 | Genitals | Vitals (genitals) | | Impotence |
| | 10 | Womb or Matrix | Womb | | Sterility |
| ⊛ | 31b | Organs of Intelligence | | | Death |
| F | 31 | Organs of Circulation | | | Fever |
| A | 11 | Respiratory Organs | | | Fluxes |
| W | 23 | Organs of Nutrition | | | Chills |
| E | 32b | Excretory Organs, Skeleton | *Sepher Yetzirah* [Short]: | *Sepher Yetzirah* [Long]: | Sluggishness |
| ☾ | 13 | Lymphatic Systems | Mouth | Left ear | Menstrual disorders |
| ☿ | 12 | Cerebral and Nervous Systems | Left nostril | Right ear | Ataxia |
| ♀ | 14 | Genital System | Right nostril | Left nostril | Syphilis, Gonorrhoea |
| ☼ | 30 | Circulatory System | Left ear | Right nostril | Repletion |
| ♂ | 27 | Muscular System | Right ear | Left eye | Inflammation |
| ♃ | 21 | Digestive System | Left eye | Right eye | Gout |
| ♄ | 32 | Excretory System | Right eye | Mouth | Arteriosclerosis |
| ♈ | 15 | Head and Face | Right hand | Liver | Apoplexy |
| ♉ | 16 | Throat, Neck | Left hand | Gall | Indigestion |
| ♊ | 17 | Arms, Lungs | Right foot | Spleen | Tuberculosis, Pneumonia |
| ♋ | 18 | Stomach, Breast | Left foot | *Massas* | Rheumatism |
| ♌ | 19 | Heart, Spine | Right kidney/testicle | Right kidney/testicle | Heart conditions, low blood pressure |
| ♍ | 20 | Belly, Intestines | Left kidney/testicle | Left kidney/testicle | Spinal weakness, Paralysis |
| ♎ | 22 | Kidneys, Liver | Liver | *Korkeban* | Kidney disorders |
| ♏ | 24 | Genitals | Spleen | *Kivah* | Cancer |
| ♐ | 25 | Hams, Hips and Thighs | Gall | Right hand | Apoplexy, Thrombosis |
| ♑ | 26 | Knees | Intestines, *massas* | Left hand | Arthritis |
| ♒ | 28 | Legs | Bladder, genitals, *kivah* | Right foot | Cystitis |
| ♓ | 29 | Lower legs and Feet | Rectum, bowels, *korkeban* | Left foot | Gout |

| | | Z5. Chinese Acupuncture Meridians. | | Z6. Chinese Acupuncture Meridians – Element. | Z7. Chinese Acupuncture Meridians – origin *hsueh*. | Z8. Chinese Acupuncture Meridians – which run via… | Z9. Chinese Acupuncture Meridians – terminus *hsueh*. |
|---|---|---|---|---|---|---|---|
| | | | | | | | |
| ☾ | 13 | 任脈 | Conception Vessel | Six Yin | Pelvic cavity, in the center of the perineum | Midline of the abdomen, through the chest and throat to the mandible | Two front teeth, between the lower lip and gums |
| ☿ | 12 | | | | | | |
| ♀ | 14 | | | | | | |
| ☼ | 30 | 督脈 | Governing Vessel | Six Yang | In the pelvic cavity between the tip of the coccyx and anus | Middle of spinal column, over the skull | Two front teeth, between the upper lip and gums |
| ♂ | 27 | | | | | | |
| ♃ | 21 | | | | | | |
| ♄ | 32 | | | | | | |
| ♈ | 15 | 手太陰肺經 | Lung | Yin Metal | Near armpit, between second and third ribs | Upper and lower arms | Inside of thumb at the root of the nail |
| ♉ | 16 | 手陽明大腸經 | Large Intestine | Yang Metal | Base of index fingernails | Up inner side of the arms | Sides of the nostrils |
| ♊ | 17 | 足陽明胃經 | Stomach | Yang Earth | Just under the eye | Down the body and legs | Root of the second toenail |
| ♋ | 18 | 足太陰脾經 | Spleen | Yin Earth | The root of the nail of the big toe | Up the inside of the legs and torso | Below the armpit |
| ♌ | 19 | 手少陰心經 | Heart | Yin Fire | Base of the armpit | Down inner side of arm | Base of the little fingernail |
| ♍ | 20 | 手太陽小腸經 | Small Intestine | Yang Fire | Base of the little fingernail | Up the arm and side of face | Just in front of each ear |
| ♎ | 22 | 足太陽膀胱經 | Bladder | Yang Water | The inside corner of the eye | Over the skull, down the spinal column | Base of the little toenail |
| ♏ | 24 | 足少陰腎經 | Kidney | Yin Water | Soles of feet | Up the inside leg, through the center of the body | Below the collar bone between the clavicle and the first rib |
| ♐ | 25 | 手厥陰心包經 | Heart Governor | Yin Fire | The chest muscle area | Down the arms | Base of the middle fingernail |
| ♑ | 26 | 手少陽三焦經 | Triple Heater | Yang Fire | The ring finger, on the little finger side | Up the arm to the head | Near the eye, under the eyebrow |
| ♒ | 28 | 足少陽膽經 | Gall Bladder | Yang Wood | Outer corner of the eye | Several points on the head | The second joint of the fourth toe |
| ♓ | 29 | 足厥陰肝經 | Liver | Yin Wood | Base of the nail of the big toe | Up the inside of the leg | Near the nipple |

# Z. Zones of the Body, Mind & Spirit

*Parts of the Soul*

| | Z10. The Kabbalistic Parts of the Soul. | Z11. The Kabbalistic Parts of the Soul – English. | Z12. Kabbalistic Parts of the Soul – Meaning. | Z12a. The Esoteric Makeup of Man. |
|---|---|---|---|---|
| | **67 & 97** | | **98** | |
| 1 | יחידה | Yechidah | The Self | The Pleroma, The Monad The Overself |
| 2 | חיה | Chiah | The Life Force | Ego - assertive |
| 3 | נשמה | Neshamah | The Intuition | Soul - receptive |
| 4 | | | | Memory |
| 5 | | | | Will |
| 6 | רוח | Ruach | The Intellect | Consciousness – Self the controlling 'I' |
| 7 | | | | Desire |
| 8 | | | | Reason |
| 9 | נפש | Nephesh | The Animal Soul. | Animal Soul Image-ination |
| 10 | גנ | Guph | The Body | Physical body |

| | Z13. Egyptian Parts of the Soul (Crowley). | Z14. Egyptian Parts of the Soul (Crowley – Whitcombe). | Z15. Egyptian Parts of the Soul (Wallis Budge & Florence Farr). | Z16. Egyptian Parts of the Soul. |
|---|---|---|---|---|
| | **116** | | | |
| 1 | Hammemit (0) Kha or Yekh | Khabs | Hammemit, unborn soul | Akhu/Khu, the immortal part |
| 2 | Khai, or Ka | Khu | Khu, magical powers | Ka, life force |
| 3 | Ba, or Baie | Ab | Ba, penetrating mind | Ba, human headed bird, true personality |
| 4 | | Sekhem | Ka, ego | Ren, the true name |
| 5 | | | Aib, will | Sekhem, personification of the life force |
| 6 | Aib | | Hati, instinct, heredity | Ab, heart centre |
| 7 | | Ba | Khaibt, aura | Tet, spiritual body |
| 8 | | | Tet, spiritual body | Sahu, vessel of the spiritual body |
| 9 | Hati | | Sahu, astral body | Khaibt, the shadow |
| 10 | Kheibt, Khat, Tet, Sahu | Khat | Khat, body | Khat, body |

# Z. Zones of the Body, Mind & Spirit

| | Z17. Hindu Parts of the Soul (Theosophy). | Z18. Raja Yoga divisions of the Soul. | Z19. Lower Worlds of Theosophy. | Z20. The Planes – Golden Dawn and Case derived from Theosophy. |
|---|---|---|---|---|
| | **117** | | | |
| 1 | Atma | Atma | Atala (Death & Rebirth) | Spiritual Plane |
| 2 | Buddhi | Ananda Mayakosa | Vitala (Separation of Higher from Lower) | Causal Plane |
| 3 | Higher Manas | Vijnana Mayakosa | | |
| 4 | Lower Manas | Mano Mayakosa | Sutala (Mind struggling with desire) | Higher Mental Plane |
| 5 | | | | |
| 6 | | | Talatala (Lower Mind) | Egoic Plane |
| 7 | Kama | Prana Mayakosa | Rasatala (Desire) | Lower Mental Plane |
| 8 | Prana | | | |
| 9 | Linga Sharira | | Mahatala (Astral body) | Astral Plane |
| 10 | Sthula Sharira | Anna Mayakosa | Patala (Physical body) | Physical Plane |

| | | Z21. The Five Hindu Khandas/Skandhas making up Self. | Z22. The Five Hindu Khandas/Skandhas making up Self – English. |
|---|---|---|---|
| | | **76** | |
| ✴ | 31b | Vinnana/Vijnana | Consciousness or cognition |
| F | 31 | Sanna/Samjna | Perception or recognition |
| A | 11 | Sankhara/Samskara | Will, intention (mental reactions) |
| W | 23 | Vedana | Feeling or sensation |
| E | 32b | Rupa | Body corporeality |

*Senses and Bodily Functions*

| | | Z23. The Senses. | Z24. The Body. | Z25. Bodily Functions. |
|---|---|---|---|---|
| | | **55** | **188** | **189** |
| ✴ | 31b | Hearing | Semen, Marrow | Generating |
| F | 31 | Sight | Blood | Moving |
| A | 11 | Smell | Breath | Speaking, Thought |
| W | 23 | Taste | Chyle, Lymph | Holding, Nutrition |
| E | 32b | Touch | Bones, Tissues | Excreting |

# THE COMMENTARY

Figure 9: Angel from the fourteenth century *De Lisle Psalter*

# Table A. Angels – Biblical, Apocryphal and Gnostic

Angels have become a very popular New Age commodity, but originally they were simply considered as the messengers of God, from the Greek word *angelos* or messenger. The word probably derives ultimately from the Sanskrit *angiras,* a divine spirit, or from Persian *angaros,* a messenger or courier. Even ordinary kings had such messengers. The Hebrew equivalent is מלאך *malak.* In early Christian usage the terms angel and *daimon* (or demon) were interchangeable, as in the writings of the Apostles Paul and John.

Contrary to popular opinion, named angels are rare in the Old Testament, the only ones being Michael and Gabriel, who were probably inherited from Babylonian mythology during the time of the captivity. These archangels are associated with fire and water respectively. Raphael appears later in the apocryphal *Book of Tobit.* The last angel that makes up the well known four angels of the Elements or quarters of the compass is Uriel, and he appears in *Enoch I* and *2 Esdras.* Uriel is often associated with fire or the sun, despite his Golden Dawn attribution to Earth. The most fruitful books of the Bible for the description of Angels are *Genesis, Isaiah* and *Ezekiel.* In the New Testament, Thrones, Dominions, Principalities and Powers are briefly mentioned by St Paul in his *Epistle to the Colossians,* and these are later seized upon by Dionysius and made into angel categories. Angelology reached its peak in terms of numbers of angels under Christianity in the 11th-13th centuries. Beyond the *Bible,* the various books of *Enoch* have many more angelical names and descriptions, which incidentally is why Dee associated the language of the angels with Enoch.

Perhaps the most famous angels of the past 400 years were the angels that Dr John Dee spoke to through the agency of his skryer Edward Kelley. In fact they have been so influential that they have here been given their own section (see Table D). Essentially angels were part of the cosmology of the three Middle Eastern monotheistic religions, Judaism, Christianity and Islam. Most angels have come from the Hebraic tradition, filtered through Christian thought. Polytheistic religions don't really need angels as part of their theurgic structure.

From a Christian point of view, angels divide into fallen and unfallen. Those who 'fell' from heaven became demons, so you should also look to the section on the Magic of the Grimoires (Table M) for more angels, mostly of the fallen kind, and the section on the Kabbalah (Table K). At one point the term 'Intelligence', meaning a carrier of news or information (think 'Intelligence Agency'), was interchangeable with 'angel'. In the Hebraic tradition God is referred to as the 'Lord of Hosts', the heavenly Hosts being the angels.

One of the oldest stories of the interaction between angels and mankind is that of the *Grigori,* a story investigated in Andrew Collins' *From the Ashes of Angels.*

## Angels of Enoch

### Column A1-A4: Watchers or *Grigori* - Aramaic Names.

These Columns list the Nephilim or 'Watchers' who rebelled against God by mating with the daughters of men and producing a race of troublesome giants. They are also called the *Grigori*, although there is some confusion between these terms. The unfallen Nephilim are said to reside in the 5th Heaven, the fallen ones in the 3rd Heaven (or in hell, depending upon which authority you consult). They are listed in *Enoch I*, 6 and 69. In this list of 21 angels, Turel is repeated twice, and so is Azazel, so the list effectively shows only 19. Column A4 shows what useful, and especially what warlike arts, they are supposed to have taught mankind.

As the lists of names do not quite agree, I have included the three main sources: Column A1 is from the book of *Enoch* from Qumran, Column A2 is from *Enoch I*, 6 and Column A3 is from *Enoch I*, 69:1-3.

### Column A5-A7: Earliest Names of the Archangels

One of the earliest mentions of the 7 Archangels is in *Enoch I*, 20. See Column K29 in the Kabbalah Table for a comparative listing of the names of the 7 Archangels from various sources, but Column A5 is probably one of the earliest. Columns A5-A6 are drawn from *Enoch I*, 20. Column A7 is from *Enoch I*, 40.

### Column A8-A9: Names of the Fallen Angels or 'Satans' – Aramaic

Another listing of the fallen angels, this time from *Enoch* I, 69:4-15. It is interesting that the term 'Satan' is in the plural, suggesting that originally the term was a status (fallen angel) rather than a specific personage. It is also interesting that the Beni Elohim (or 'sons of gods') are spoken of as having bodies.

### Column A10-A11: The Angel Prince Rulers of the Earth

This list from *Enoch 3*, shows the angelic Rulers of Earth with their responsibility for a type of weather, or part of the heavens. These Rulers are drawn from *Enoch 3*, XIV, 4-5 and XVII, 4-7. These angels are said to belong to the Second Heaven, Raqia. Their description includes significant numbers associated with the Planets. For example 365,000 myriad is a direct reference to the 365 days in the year. The attribution of 72 great angels to the Constellations suggests a possible link with the Shem ha-Mephorash angels generated from the Name of 72 characters (see Column A24).

### Column A12-A13: The Sarim or Angel Princes

These are the Angel Princes who are responsible for the Heavens and Earth. As they are in charge of various Orders of Angels, like the Seraphim,

Cherubim, Powers, and Thrones, in a sense they equate with the Archangels. In fact traditional Archangels, like Gabriel, Metatron, Sandalphon, Michael, Uriel and Raphael are listed amongst their number. There also appears to be some overlap with Column A10 and A11. They do not appear to be in hierarchical order, so the numbering column is for convenience only. Column A12 lists their names, and Column A13 their functions and attributes.

## Column A14: The 64 Angel Wardens of the 7 Celestial Halls

The Halls or *Hekhaloth* equate with the 7 Heavens which in turn equate with the 7 Planetary Spheres, but each at a different level. This Column lists the Wardens of each Hall. See the Kabbalah section on the Seven Palaces, columns K64 to K90 for other material associated with the *Hekhaloth*.

## Column A15-A18: The Archangels of the Four Quarters

These are the standard four Archangels of the 4 Quarters and the 4 Elements. Column A18 contains the numerical sum of their names. See also Column K29 for a comparative listing of other Archangels.

## *Gnostic Angels*

## Column A19-A22: The 30 Gnostic Aeons

The Gnostics favoured an emanational view of creation just as did the Kabbalists. Accordingly it is important to identify the order of emanation or generation. The generation numbers show that the primary group of Aeons is the Ogdoad (an 8-fold group) although there is some difference of opinion as to the exact order of generation within the Ogdoad mapped on to the 7 Planets plus one higher Sphere. This is followed by the Decad (10-fold grouping) and Dodecad (12-fold grouping). The Decad can be mapped onto the 10 Sephiroth and the Dodecad onto the 12 Zodiacal signs.

## *Shem ha-Mephorash Angels*

Shem ha-Mephorash (שם ה-מפרש) literally refers to the name of God of 72 letters contained in three verses of *Exodus*. The Shem ha-Mephorash angels are a very important set of angels. Their names are generated from three verses in the Bible, specifically *Exodus* 14:19-21. Each verse has exactly 72 Hebrew letters. The procedure for generating the names of the 72 angels is to write the three verses, one on top of the other on three lines. The trick however is to write the top line from right to left (the normal Hebrew writing direction), the second line from left to right, and the third line from right to left. This order is called *boustrophedon*, which literally means 'ploughed like a field', first one way then another. Then you read each group of three Hebrew letters vertically, so that you derive 72 three-letter root words (these roots are listed in Table A24). To each of these Hebrew roots you add a suffix, either אל - AL or יה – IH. The resultant 72 five-letter names are the names of the 72 Shem ha-Mephorash angels.

The expression Shem ha-Mephorash also refers to the simple combinations of the four letters of the Name IHVH, and Franz Bardon passes it off as this, although he definitely knew the more complete meaning, explained above.

Then, because written Hebrew does not have vowels (except in the very restricted sense of ו and י) these names need to be rounded out with vowels to pronounce them, or to write them in English. It is this rounding-out process which is responsible for much of the apparent differences in the Shem ha-Mephorash Angel names from one authority to another. In Hebrew the names are cut and dried, but the spelling in English varies considerably. There are many English spelling versions of the 72 Shem ha-Mephorash angels. Basically, this is because Hebrew letters like ו *Vav* can be transliterated as 'V' (consonant), 'U' (vowel) or even 'O'. *Yod* י corresponds with the English 'I' (vowel), 'Y' (vowel or consonant) and 'J' (consonant), hence words containing either of these letters are open to many transliterations. All Shem ha-Mephorash angel names contain one or other of these letters.

The only way to get a 'correct' version is to go back to the original Hebrew which is what I have done here, and having added one of the two possible suffixes, you end up with a correctly spelled angel name in Hebrew. From this you can with certainty derive the numerical value. But then to transliterate them into English is either a matter of taste or tradition.

This leads to issues of the correct pronunciation of these names. One way is to go back to the traditional Hebrew rules and associate a particular vowel sound with each one of the consonants. There is a precise formula described by Abraham Abulafia in *Chayey ha-Olam ha-Bah* for adding vowels to the Hebrew, but it produces some rather strange sounding angel names, with spellings that include difficult groups of letters like 'aaa' or 'aae'. It is in fact probably this sort of formula that Mathers applied to the pronunciation of Enochian, which distorted the pronunciation of that language for almost a century.[1]

I have however applied common sense to the spellings, which make for more readable angel names. Each Hebrew word is only 5 letters long, so transliteration should not be too complex. Agrippa's spelling is logical, with the possible replacements of his Germanic 'jah' endings with 'iah'. Also I prefer to use 'Y' rather than 'I' or 'J' where *Yod* is the first letter of a name. How anyone can, for example, seriously propose an English spelling such as 'Ngnaneauel' for the 63rd angel Anueil, I do not know. The final test of course is to see if these

---

[1] Since the publication of Dr Donald Laycock's *Complete Enochian Dictionary* we now have a much clearer idea of the correct pronunciation of Enochian.

pronunciations work in practice when invoking the angels – but that is material for another book.

Note that Blaise de Vigenère, Lenain, Mathers and Robert Ambelain all give a series of 72 sigils associated with these angels. I think that these sigils may be demonic and not at all angelic, and so should be used with caution.

## Column A23: Ambelain's Table of the 72 Shem ha-Mephorash Angels

Robert Ambelain in *La Kabbale Pratique* lists the 72 Shem ha-Mephorash angels in a novel way, and divides them into 9 groups. These groupings are according to the hierarchy of Dionysius the Areopagite. Ambelain refers to his diagram as the Tree of Life in Yetzirah. This arrangement appears to be unique to Ambelain, so don't take the lateral correspondences with the Sephiroth 2 to 9 too seriously, although Ambelain appears to map these angels precisely on to those Sephiroth. In fact the most interesting division in this arrangement is the ordering of these angels under the 9 different orders of angels: Seraphim, Cherubim, Thrones, Powers, Dominations, Virtues, Principalities, Archangels and Angels. It is a view, but only one man's view. I have retained Ambelain's spelling of the angel names for this Column, but have rectified the spelling in the following columns.

## Column A24: The 72 Shem ha-Mephorash Angels, their Hebrew Root, Name, Degrees and Nature

This column gives the 3-letter Hebrew root of each angel, with a rectified English spelling that can be easily verified against it. The Hebrew root is taken vertically from the three *Exodus* verses. To this must be added either אל –AL (-el or –iel) or יה –IH (-yah or -iah) to make the full angel name.

This Table also shows the degrees of the Zodiac which correspond to each of these angels. If you divide the 360° of the Zodiac by 72 you get a rulership of 5° for each angel. There has been a controversy as to where these degrees start, either at 0° Aries (conventional Tropical Zodiac, as suggested by most French authorities) or 0° Leo (Sidereal Zodiac as supported by the Golden Dawn). I have simply listed the degrees from 0° to 360°, so they can be commenced at either point. If you subscribe to the 0° Leo starting point then simply add 120° to the degrees listed, to move the commencement point from 0° Aries to 0° Leo. If the answer comes to more than 360°, then subtract 360° from the answer.

Mathers wanted to tie the Shem ha-Mephorash angels to the Decans, so that he could match them up with both the Enochian system and the Tarot. See Columns T21-T28 for Mathers' attribution of these angels to the Tarot.

Mathers started the angels at Leo, as this coincides with the beginning of the Egyptian Decanal year. I am not convinced that these angels are necessarily attributable to the Decans anyway, and prefer to just consider them in terms of the compass degrees, which gives them a suitable facing direction for invocation.

The last Column has a description of their particular virtues and spheres of influence, although this is a relatively modern attribution, and maybe of minor value, but is put here for the sake of completeness.

Robert Ambelain attributes a secondary angel to each of these Shem ha-Mephorash angels, for example Chontare with Vehuiah. These are a mixture of Greek and Roman names attributed to the Decans, and are not very reliable (leaving aside the question of relevant Decanal starting point) and therefore have not been listed here. He also gives an associated planet, the time of the day, days of the year, season and godname, all of which I have also omitted from these tables, as they appear to be fairly recent additions to the basic angel list, however the full list may be seen in his *Practical Kabbalah*.

### Column A25: The 72 Shem ha-Mephorash Angels with their corresponding Invocatory Psalm

This column supplies the appropriate invocatory Psalm in both Latin and English, for use in a practical context. Note that the Psalm numbers are from the KJV *Bible* which differs slightly from the Hebrew version of the *Bible*, the *Tanakh*. For further details of Psalm numbering see Column J17, and for the corresponding demons of the *Goetia* see Table M15.

## Astrological Angels

### Column A26-A27: Angels Ruling the Astrological Houses

These are the angels of the fixed Houses of Heaven. Note that the Zodiac scale on the left is just a convenient way of marking the 12 Houses, which are usually simply labelled 1 to 12. There is no *direct* connection between the two.

### Column A28-A29: The Lesser Assistant Angels in the Zodiacal Signs

These are the Lesser Assistant angels ruling the 12 Zodiacal signs.

### Column A30-A33: Angel Lords of the Elemental Triplicities in the Signs

The Triplicities of the Zodiac are formed by dividing up the 12 Zodiacal Signs into four groups according to their ruling Element. The angels who rule the three Zodiacal Signs that make up each Triplicity are:

| | |
|---|---|
| Michael | Fiery Triplicity |
| Raphael | Air Triplicity |
| Gabriel | Water Triplicity |
| Uriel | Earth Triplicity |

These are then further divided into Night and Day Triplicities.

# Commentary

## Column A34-A39: Angels of the 36 Decans

Each of the 12 Zodiacal signs is divided into three Decans. The first of these in each sign is the Ascendant Decan, the second is the Succedent Decan (the one that follows it) and the third is called the Cadent Decan. For further information on the Decans themselves and their attributions refer to Columns H54-H71.

## Column A40 Angels of the Zodiacal Signs

These are drawn from Francis Barrett's *The Magus*. The overall angel of the Zodiac is Masleh (probably derived from *mazloth* the Hebrew word for Zodiac).

## *Yezidi and Persian Angels*

## Column A41: Yezidi Angels

The supreme angel of the Yezidi is the Peacock Angel, Melek Ta'us. Even as recently as 20 years ago, you could still hear the cry of captive peacocks in villages inhabited by the Druse and the Yezidi, although they are unhappy to talk with strangers about this bird and the strange and beautiful angel it symbolises. In the modern world, people still honour the name of their angel in more subtle ways, such as in the naming of a company, or use in its logo. The Yezidi see no dichotomy, and do not believe, as do Christians, that there is a spiritual adversary opposing God. The Peacock Angel's supporting Archangels appear in this table. This Yezidi hymn rather beautifully sums it up.

> Oh my Lord, you are the angel of men and jinns,
> Oh my Lord, you are the angel of the Throne and the Seat,
> Oh my Lord, you are the angel of the Bull and the Fish,
> Oh my Lord, you are the angel of the world and what is holy.
>      - from *Qewlê Tawûsî Melek*, 'The Hymn of Melek Ta'us'

## Column A42-A43: The 7 Amesha Spentas

The 7 Amesha Spentas or Amenta Spentas of the Persians are benign immortals which may be the forerunners of the Archangels. They are the messengers of the Zoroastrian Ahura Mazda. There are some interesting parallels between their names and with the Hindu caste system of India, as in the case of Khshathra Vairya which parallels the name of the Hindu warrior caste.

The following Tables are all new additions to the Third edition.

## *Key of Solomon Angels*

## Column A44: Archangels and Angels of the Days from the *Key of Solomon*

Simple angelic and archangelic correspondences for the Planets and the days of the week from the *Key of Solomon* [1] primarily use in the creation of talismans.

---

[1] Skinner & Rankine. *The Veritable Key of Solomon*, SWCM Vol. 4, Golden Hoard, Singapore, 2008.

## Sepher Raziel Angels

The following tables are taken from Sloane MS 3826 entitled *Sepher Raziel* which dates from 1564.[1] This consists of eight Treatises: the *Clavis* on the astrological conditions for practice; *Ala* on the virtues of stones, plants and animals, and their use in magic; *Tractatus Thymiamatus* on the uses of incenses in ritual; a Treatise on timing; *Samaim* on the angels; and the *Book of Virtues* on the art of magic.

**A45. The Angels of the 12 Hebrew Months in *Sepher Raziel*.**

**A46. Angels of the 7 Days of the Week in *Sepher Raziel*.**

**A47. Names of the Planets by the Elements, with their Angels in *Sepher Raziel*.**

**A48. Names of the 4 Elements and the Lowlands [Underworld] in the 4 Seasons in *Sepher Raziel*.**

**A49. The 7 Heavens and the Angels ruling in each of their Directions in *Sepher Raziel*.**

**A50. Names of Heavens, and the names of the Directions, distributed over the 4 Seasons from *Sepher Raziel*.**

**A51. Angel Names for the Semiforas from *Sepher Raziel*.**

**A52. Names of the Angels ruling over the 4 Elements in *Sepher Raziel*.**

**A53. Name of the Planets, and their Angels, in the 4 Seasons, in *Sepher Raziel*.**

**A54. Angels ruling over 7 Heavens in *Sepher Raziel*.**

**A55. Names of Angels having power in each Direction in *Sepher Raziel*.**

## Planetary Angels

**A56. Angels of the Planets.**

**A57. Angel and Demons of the Days of the Week in the *Hygromanteia*.**

The *Hygromanteia* is the true ancestor of the *Key of Solomon*. Manuscript copies of the *Hygromanteia* date back to at least 1440, well before any extant manuscript of the *Clavicula Salomonis*.[2] This grimoire contains many tables showing the rulership of every hour of every day of the week, which are too large to be reproduced here.

---

[1] See Karr & Skinner, *Sepher Raziel*, Golden Hoard, SWCM Volume 7, Singapore, 2010 for the source of the Tables A45 – A55.

[2] See Ioannes Marathakis, *The Magical Treatise or Hygromanteia*, SWCM Volume 8, Golden Hoard, Singapore, 2011.

# Table B. Buddhism

Buddhism was founded in India by prince Gautama Buddha in the fifth century BC and has subsequently spread into China, Sri Lanka, Burma, Thailand, Vietnam, Tibet, Nepal, Bhutan Laos and Cambodia. Although much of this material is not part of mainstream Western magical practice, it is useful to see parallel systems of magic and mysticism correlated with Western theory and practice.

### Column B1-B2: The Noble Eightfold Buddhist Path

These stages on the Path are appropriately attributed to the Sephiroth, not as Crowley did (probably for typographical convenience) to the Paths of the Tree.

### Column B3-B4: Buddhist Courts of Hell

Buddhist Courts of Hell, with their direction in respect of Mount Meru and the President of each Court. These hells were originally Indian, but adopted by Chinese Buddhists. The lowest is numbered as 1, and corresponds to Malkuth. The forecourt to these hells is the 'Hall of Oblivion' or *Meng po*, where the entrant forgets the events of his recently concluded life. The 10th hell is where his next incarnation is decided upon. These hells are supposed to be situated 20,000 *yoganas* (180,000 miles) below the Great Sea at the foot of Mount Meru in the Himalayas. Each hell is said to measure 5,000-8,000 feet on each side. Their cardinal points do not fit comfortably on the Tree.

### Column B5-B6: The Ten Fetters of Buddhism

These are the 10 fetters that bind one to the cycle of rebirth and stand in the way of Enlightenment.

### Column B7: The Four Noble Truths of Buddhism

### Column B8: The Forty Buddhist Meditations

The 40 classical Buddhist Meditations have been attributed in ZEP order, following their division into the 10 Recollections (Sephiroth), 10 Impurities (Zodiac), 10 Kasinas (5 colours relating to 5 Elements), and 4 Brahmaviharas (Sublime States). The 4 Arupa-dhyanas relate to Ain Soph Aur. This differs slightly from Crowley's attributions, particularly with regard to the 7 Planets.

### Column B9: Twelve (Chinese) Buddhist Teachers

### Column B10-11: Buddhist Animals and Symbols

The animals, basically borrowed from Hinduism, and the four symbols.

### Column B12-B15: Forms of the Buddhas

The forms include the eight Buddhas (peaceful and terrifying) and the Dakini consorts of Tantric Buddhism. Akshobya and Vairocana (in the East and Centre) are sometimes interchanged.

# Table C. Christianity

It may seem strange to include a Christian section amongst these tables, but many of the practices and practitioners of magic in Europe, for the last two millennium, were of course Christian. Many of the saints and Doctors of the Church (listed in Column C18) have contributed extensively to the literature of demonology and angelology and even of magic.

## Virtues and Sins

### Column C1: Western Virtues

These are the conventional virtues plus devotion/accomplishment of the Great Work. Crowley lists Pyrrho-Zoroastrianism in row 1 of his column 50 (which he called Transcendental Morality) which hardly qualifies as a virtue. In the same column he also lists the four parts of Eliphas Levi's injunction 'To know, dare, will and to keep silence' four verbs which he associated with the four Elements (in Latin *Noscere, Audere, Velle, Tacere*), but as these are not really virtues either, but injunctions, they have not been included here.

### Column C2: Western Mysticism – Visions

The major visions are here listed correlated with their appropriate Sephiroth.

### Column C3-C4: The 7 Deadly Sins

The 7 Deadly Sins which are not Biblical, but have been around as a list since the time of St Gregory, are listed with their usual order of seriousness from Pride (the most serious) to Lust (the least serious). These 7 can more sensibly be mapped on to the Sephiroth rather than the planets. A few additional sins like Hypocrisy (a very Jovial sin) and Dishonesty (a sin against truth) might have been included in Chesed and Hod respectively.

## Apostles

### Column C5-C8: The Twelve Apostles - Greek

Column C6 gives the emblem or instrument of martyrdom usually associated with each Apostle, which are useful if you are trying to identify a particular figure in a painting or emblem. For example the scallop shell of St James the Elder, which later became the most easily recognisable symbol for Christian pilgrims, also appears in some alchemic engravings. Columns C7-C8 gives the Greek version of their name and its corresponding numeration. Although the Apostles would have had Aramaic/Hebrew names originally, the details of their lives were recorded in Greek in the gospels and so the Greek numeration of their names might well have been as important.

# Commentary

## Column C9-C13: The Twelve Apostles - Hebrew

There are several versions of the Apostles names in Hebrew with correspondingly different numerations. Column C9-C11 showed Agrippa's. In the First Edition, Column C12-C13 showed Dr Rudd's orthography as used in Harley MS 6482. However as there were only three differences, which may have been simply errors by Rudd, they have been moved here in this edition:

| Simon Peter | שמעון כבפי | 1228 |
|---|---|---|
| Andrew | אלקוזי | 154 |
| Jude or James/Thaddeus | חטיפאא | 105 |

The different numerations show the dangers of non-Hebraic writers trying to reverse engineer Hebrew/Aramaic spelling. The same thing happened with Crowley and Rudd's attempts to reverse engineer the Hebrew names of the Goetic demons: both generated spellings that would never have occurred.

## Theology and Hell

### Column C14: Christian Hell – the levels of Dante's *Inferno*

As a lot of literature about demons talks about hell, it seems appropriate to tabulate its environs according to its most popular recorder, Dante Alighieri (1265-1321) who copied from the *Aeneid* of Virgil. The levels are shown in descending order from the comparative comfort of good pagans, unbaptised souls, ancient philosophers, poets, and Old Testament Patriarchs to the deepest damnation of traitors.

### Column C15: Christian Theology

Christ, plus the other two persons of the Trinity, attributed to various Sephiroth. The Trinity appears vertically on the Middle Pillar as God the Father (Kether), God the Son (Tiphareth) and God the Holy Ghost/Spirit (in Yesod), closest to man in Malkuth. The Christian Kabbalists, following Reuchlin, would have attributed the Trinity to the three Supernal Sephiroth: Father (Kether), Son (Chokmah) and Holy Ghost (Binah), but I think a 'descent into matter' scenario works better. The feminine principle in the form of the Virgin Mary, (and some would add Mary Magdalene) appears in Binah. The missing element from this theology is Chokmah (Wisdom) which in the Gnostic Christian view would be associated with Sophia (Wisdom).

### Column C16: The 7 Early Churches of Asia Minor

Early Christianity spread northwards from Jerusalem through Turkey and into the Greek world initially. The early churches were all located in this region, which is why it is strange that the Roman church, rather than the Byzantine church, triumphed in the end. The 7 churches are defined in *Revelations* 1:11:

"What thou seest, write in a book, and send it unto the seven churches which are in Asia [Minor]; unto Ephesus, and unto Smyrna, and unto Pergamos, and unto Thyatira, and unto Sardis, and unto Philadelphia, and unto Laodicea."

Missed from this list are churches at Jerusalem, Rome, Galatia, Corinth, and Antioch.

## Doctors of the Church

### Column C17: The Doctors of the Catholic Church

These are the Catholic theologians who have had perhaps most input into shaping or misshaping Christian theology over the years. There are now officially thirty-three Doctors of the Church, of whom eight were from the Eastern church (Byzantium) and twenty-four from the Western church (Rome). They are most interesting in that they sometimes recorded at length the doctrines of various heresies which they sought to suppress.

They include two Carmelites, two Jesuits, three Dominicans, three Franciscans, a Redemptorist, and five Benedictine monks. The eight marked in italics are considered the greatest Doctors of the Church, four from the Eastern, and four from the Western church. Thomas Aquinas was also very important in his pronouncements about demons and other spiritual creatures, and St Albertus Magnus has more than a passing interest for those interested in magic.

## Saints

### Column C18: A Selection of Saints

If you consider prayers to a saint a form of invocation, then this table has a place in this book. There are over 10,000 named saints and *beati* from history, the Roman martyrology and Orthodox sources, but no definitive 'head count'. Only the better known or more interesting saints, like St. Albertus Magnus and Saint Cyprian of Antioch,[1] have been included.

According to some writers the origin of beatification and canonisation in the Catholic Church can be traced back to the ancient pagan procedure *apotheosis*, although in his classic work on the subject, Pope Benedict XIV refutes this view.[2]

*Apotheosis* literally means 'to make a god', and the ancient Romans as well as the Chinese, often promoted their heroes to the status of a god. Often the decree embodying this elevation was based solely on the statement that an eagle (in the case of the emperors), or a peacock (Juno's sacred bird, in the case of their consorts), was seen to carry the spirit of the departed heavenward.[3] *Apotheosis* was awarded to many members of the imperial family, with little regard to their actual virtues or remarkable achievements.

---

[1] Skinner & Rankine. *The Grimoire of St Cyprian: Clavis Inferni*, Golden Hoard, Singapore, 2009.
[2] *De Servorum Dei Beatificatione et Beatorum Canonizatione.*
[3] Livy, *History of Rome*, I, xvi; Herodian, *History of Rome*, IV, ii, iii.

# Commentary

## Table D. Dr John Dee's Angels

"To someone living in the latter part of the sixteenth century, the possibility that one could have a conversation with an angel or demon was pretty much taken for granted. That John Dee was able to communicate with an otherworldly being through the use of simple ritual (prayer) and a shewstone was not a matter for debate; it was only a question of whether he was communicating with angels or demons. Modern scholars, even those promoting the notion of Renaissance Hermeticism, have found the angelic operations of sixteenth-century England's foremost natural philosopher hard to swallow. "

- Frank Klaassen

Dr John Dee (1527-1608) was mathematician and astrologer to Queen Elizabeth I. His interests were very wide ranging, from the geometry of Euclid through optics and astrology to the reform of the calendar, alchemy, the improvement of navigational equipment, and espionage. But his greatest love was magic, particularly angel magic. During the 1580s and 1590s, he and his skryer Edward Kelley derived and recorded several systems of magic, which are now categorised under the general description of Enochian magic.

Enochian magic is considered by modern commentators to be one of the most powerful systems of magic. However there is little difference between it and the other grimoire magic of the same period, except that it is perhaps better documented. Generated by Dr John Dee and Edward Kelley's skrying, it passed through the hands of a succession of angel-magicians of the 17th and 18th century.

Dee's system was utilised by angel magicians during the 17th and 18th centuries, then re-discovered in the late 19th century by MacGregor Mathers who elaborated it considerably making it part of the practice of the Hermetic Order of the Golden Dawn.

Mathers however, although aware of some of the work done on it by the likes of Dr Thomas Rudd in the 17th century, used just a small part of the system. It is only now that the history of this system and its use by angel magicians of the 17th to 19th century is coming to light with the publication of important manuscripts of that period.[1]

These Tables list the names of just some of the most important angels in the system, categorising them according to their source amongst Dee's manuscripts. Details of the orthography and value of the Enochian letters used in the skrying sessions will be found in Columns L41-L44.

---

[1] See Skinner & Rankine, *Practical Angel Magic of Dr John Dee's Enochian Tables*, Golden Hoard, London & Singapore, 2004.

## *Liber Scientiae Auxilii et Victoriae Terrestris*

## Column D1-D10: The Angels of the 91 Parts of the Earth

These Columns show Dee's attribution of the 91 countries (of the then known world) to their ruling planet, zodiacal sign, angel and Aether.

The Roman numbers in the second header row reflect the column numbers used in Dee's original manuscript, Sloane MS 3191 in the British Library. Two of the original manuscript columns (IV and X) are missing from this Table, for the reasons given below. Dee's column IV contains the 91 sigil characters which are the visual key to the *Clavicula Tabularum Enochi* (see Column D17) indicating by their shape the letters of angelic names which are listed here anyway.

This Table is most important as it ties together Agrippa (Column D2-D4), Dee's *Tabularum Bonorum* (Column D5), Dee's 30 Aethers and their Calls from LIL to TEX (Column D6), the Kings ruling these (Column D9) and the 12 Tribes of Israel (Column D10) which Dee considered very important for their indications of the 12 directions (springing from the 4 points of the compass) and the shape of the New Jerusalem.

Columns D2-D3 (Planets and Zodiacal Signs) are drawn from Agrippa (Chapter XXXI) and do not appear in Dee's manuscript, although Dee would have been well aware of them and utilised them in drawing up this table. The country names are ancient, and are essentially derived from Ptolemy via Agrippa. Dee did not add in the lands of the New World (America) as might have been expected of someone so keen on navigation, discovery and Empire. Where the Planet and Zodiacal sign are missing it has not been possible to match Dee's countries exactly with Agrippa's list.

Dee's missing column X is abbreviated in Column J10 and J13 of the present volume, where it can be easily compared with Column J8-J9, which is the original arrangement of the Tribes as recorded in the *Bible*.[1] Robert Turner has something quite interesting to say about Dee's column X, which adds another layer of complexity, and another reason for not just simply transcribing Dee's column here:

> "The zones of the world assigned to the Twelve Dispersed Tribes of Israel do not (as certain commentators have indicated) represent the usual points of the compass: North, South, East, West, North N-W, East N-E, etc. The key to Dee's intended directions can be clearly found in the second diagram he appends to his manuscript... The diagram is representative of the order of the Tribes at their dispersal (and indeed in 1585) drawn within the walls of the Holy City. To interpret Dee's intentions it is necessary to imagine oneself viewing a particular wall of the city from the *outside*. Then following the directive with reference to the

---

[1] *Numbers* 2:3-31.

relevant diagram the meaning becomes obvious. E.g. 'On the East side, to the right-hand = NAPHTALI (Dee: Oriens-dexter = Nephthalim); on the West side, to the left-hand = ISSACHAR (Dee: Occidens-sinister = Isacaraah); to the North = MANASSEH (Dee: Aquilonaris = Manasse) etc.' Therefore in each instance the direction in which one is facing (i.e. towards a particular wall of the city) would be geographically opposite the Cardinal point named in this column (X)."[1]

Column D6 are the 30 Aethers, from LIL to TEX, worked by Aleister Crowley in *The Vision and the Voice.* Column D8 is essentially the total of each group of three Servant numbers in Column D7.

## Column D11: Zodiac Mapped on to the Geography of the Ancient World.

This column shows other views on the geographic distribution of the 12 Signs of the Zodiac. Manilius in his *Astronomica* proposed a Zodiacal rulership of the countries of the then known world (90 BC). This was later adopted by Agrippa in his list of the Zodiacal rulership of 91 countries. Dee went a step further and devised/discovered their angelic rulership (see Columns D6-D9). Amongst Kabbalistic sources, *Sheshem Chanokol* states:

> "Saturn, Jupiter, Mars, Sun, Venus, Mercury and the Moon...in these seven Heavens are the Spirits of the seventy nations, ten nations under each Planet, and the twelve [Zodiacal] constellations give abundance unto them."

The 70 nations were later changed to 72 to match with the angels of the Shem ha-Mephorash and the divisions of the Zodiac, by the addition of two more Prince-Angels, Michael (angel of Israel) and Gabriel (angel of all nations).

## *De Heptarchia Mystica*

## Column D12: John Dee's 49 *Bonorum Angelorum*

This Column lists Dee's 49 Good Angels from his grimoire *De Heptarchia Mystica,* as well as the Kings and Princes from the same seven-fold book. The best translation of the title *De Heptarchia Mystica* is 'Of the Mysteries of the Sevenfold Kingdom' of the Watchtowers. Although most commentators have looked to Latin for its meaning, 'heptarchy' was in fact an accepted English word by the twelfth century, when it came to refer to the seven separate kingdoms that made up Anglo-Saxon England in the 9th century. The names are taken from Dee's manuscript circular table of the 49 Good Angels.

## Column D13-D15: The Heptarchical Kings and Princes

In this table the initial letter 'B' has been removed leaving perhaps the real names. The system of *De Heptarchia Mystica* is keyed especially into the 7 Planets and the 7 days of the week.

---

[1] Robert Turner, *Elizabethan Magic: the Art of the Magus,* Element, Longmead, 1989, pages 48-49.

## Sigillum Dei Aemeth

### Column D16: John Dee's *Sigillum Dei Aemeth*

These are the names used in the construction of Dee's key sigil *Sigillum Dei Aemeth,* shown in Figure 4. This sigil is also found in *Liber Juratus,* which was probably Dee and Kelley's source, and later in a slightly different form in Athanasius Kircher. The names of the 4 Great Elemental Kings appear in Table D22.

## Clavicula Tabularum Enochi

### Column D17: *Clavicula Tabularum Enochi*

This is the version of the Four Great Elemental Tables that was rectified by the angel Raphael on April 20, 1587. The numbering down the side columns enabled Dee to allocate a number between 1 and 624 to identify every letter. This is the key to one of Dee's substitution ciphers. Note the reversed and deformed letters at locations 120, 312, 619, 620, 481 and so on, which indicate table 'entry points' for reading off certain names.

### Column D18: The Tablet of Union

This Table is found at the centre of the Four Great Elemental Tables. Note that for consistency, the order of the names has been changed to match the standard Column order of the Elements. In Dee's original table the order was:

e x a r p

h c o m a

n a n t a

b i t o m

### Column D19-D21: Directions and Colours of the Watchtowers

The colours attributed to Dee's four Watchtowers or Elemental squares. Note that the Golden Dawn 'rectified' the colours.

### Column D22: The Kings and Seniors of the *Tabularum Enochi*

These are attributed to the 4 cardinal directions. All these Kings and Seniors are derived from Column D17.

### Column D23: Angels of the *Tabularum Enochi*

These are divided by Element and direction, and then subdivided into four sub tables, each with its own Name of God, Divine Name, and angel name derived by tracing out specific squares in the main table shown in Column D17.

# Commentary

## Table E. Emblems and Alchemy

The art of alchemy and the art of emblems have been inextricably linked. Emblems presented an ideal way for alchemists to conceal their ideas from all but the most perceptive. Emblems were of course part of the symbolical mindset of the Renaissance, and any cultured man or woman would have been aware of many of the hidden jests and classical references embedded in emblems. Nowadays these are no longer part of our education and so emblems are looked upon as mere curios rather than as a very rich symbolic language. Magic and alchemy both use symbols, and so emblems and their meaning are an important part of their study.

The Tarot is a case in point. As it was made up of a handful of broken emblem sets, it would not have been a mystery to any cultured man of its period. It is only a mystery when these meanings are lost, when we no longer know, for example, that there actually was a female Pope Joan. Books like Andreas Alciati's *Book of Emblems*, published in 1531 or Junius' *Emblemata* would have been read by many, and made the study of contemporary alchemical works a lot easier. To study alchemy effectively it is necessary to re-absorb the culture of emblems, so that at least basic interpretation becomes possible. This section is brief because there are others, such as Adam McLean or Gary Nottingham, who are much better fitted to interpret this imagery. Because the practitioners of alchemy and magic often overlapped, so the vocabulary of one may well help with the language of the other.

### Golden Dawn and Chemistry

### Column E1-E2: Alchemical Elements on the Tree of Life

These two possible sets of attributions were derived by Mathers from the *Aesch Mezareph* as translated by W Wynn Westcott from the Latin of Knorr von Rosenroth. Note that these do not mesh in any way with the standard Planetary attributions of metals to the Sephiroth.

### Column E3: Chemical Elements (Golden Dawn)

A simple listing probably originally drawn up by the chemist Julian Baker.

### Column E4: Chemical Symbol and Latin Names of Planetary Metals

The modern chemical symbol is often derived from the Latin name of the element.

### Column E4a: Periodic Table for Planetary Metals: Number, Row & Column

Note that on the Periodic Table the alchemic metals are located very near each other. Most suggestively, Mercury (Hg) which was one of the metals most significant in alchemy, is right next to Gold (Au). Gold is in the same column as Silver (Ag) and Copper (Cu). Antimony (Sb), one of the possible starting points in the alchemic process, is adjacent to Tin (Sn) which is in turn adjacent to Lead (Pb). Although metals are grouped together anyway, such close proximity of the significant alchemic metals is quite suggestive, especially their row and column numbers in the Periodic Table.

### Column E5: Alchemical Processes

These are the twelve basic processes of alchemy matched with the zodiac according to Pernety and the modern English alchemist Lapidus. As you can see in the next column, there is some agreement with Ripley's twelve stages.

## *Ripley and Lapidus*

### Column E6: Ripley's Twelve Gates.

This is another attribution of the twelve basic alchemical processes by George Ripley (1415-1490). These fit only approximately on to the Zodiacal signs.

## *Emblems*

The remaining columns in this Table are concerned with the iconography and imagery of alchemy, one of its richest aspects.

### Column E7-E8: *Splendor Solis* Emblems

This manuscript by Salomon Trismosin is perhaps the most gorgeously illustrated and symbolically explicit of all alchemic manuscripts. Each illustration is set in a frame, with images often painted outside that frame so the description is divided into two parts. In the case of the planetary images, an explicit portrayal of typical planetary activities confirms the planet.

Emblems 1 to 11 are allegorical.
Emblems 12 to 18 are Planetary (here listed with their order reversed).
Emblems 19 to 22 are strangely domestic.

### Column E9: *Book of Lambspring* Emblems

Lambsprink's *De Lapide Philosophico* is book of fifteen typical emblems which was published in 1625 by Lucas Jennis (the step-nephew of Theodore de Bry who engraved the *Magical Calendar)* and might as easily be part of an emblem book as a book specifically on alchemy. The text first appeared in 1599.

### Column E10: *The Twelve Keys* of Basil Valentinus Emblems

Basil Valentinus (1394-c.1450) was famous for his championing of antimony in the alchemical process.

### Column E11: *Atlanta Fugiens* Emblems
This sequence of 50 Emblems designed by Michael Maier (1568-1622) takes in music, famous Hermetic sayings, Classical Greek mythology, country scenes and a whole host of other things, meant to be obscure even at the time it was engraved in 1618 by Johann Theodore de Bry (engraver of the *Magical Calendar).*

# Commentary

## Table F. Feng Shui, Chinese Taoism and Taoist Magic

There were three main religions in pre-Revolutionary China, Taoism, Buddhism and Confucianism. The second of these was an import from India, and did not take root till 500 years after it was founded. The third is more a system of ethics and social behaviour than a true religion. Taoism however has its roots deep in China's culture. One of the traditional practices based on Taoist cosmology is feng shui, a practice that is concerned with the disposition and ordering of *ch'i* in our living spaces to the best advantage of the occupants. It has been recently rather trivialised in the West, but still has deep roots in Chinese culture, particularly in Taiwan, Hong Kong and Singapore.

In this table I have used Wade-Giles transliterations rather than *pinyin*, as the former is still more frequently found in serious traditional feng shui books in English.

### Taoism and Trigrams

### Column F1-F3: Taoism and the Trigrams of the Former Heaven Sequence

The relationship of the Taoist system and the trigrams of the *I Ching* (see also Table Y for the relationship of the trigrams to each other and their union in the hexagrams).

Although Crowley put the Tao on the zero row as Ain Soph, it is much more appropriate to identify the undifferentiated *wu chi* as Ain Soph. The Tao more correctly aligns with Kether. Crowley also puts Shang Ti, the supreme Taoist divinity in his Taoist Cosmology column, but Shang Ti is a Taoist god (Column P32) rather than part of cosmology.

Furthermore Crowley's attribution of the trigrams to the Tree of Life does severe damage to Chinese metaphysics, and has therefore not been utilised here. There are several ways to arrange the trigrams, but the simplest and most direct method has been used, which is to associate the trigrams with the Sephiroth via the Elements and their associated Planets, so that for example:

*Li* = Fire = 'Fire Star' = Mars = Geburah, and
*K'an* = Water = 'Water Star' = Mercury = Hod

This procedure can then be extended to the Elements and Planets upon the Paths, but not to the Zodiacal Signs which have a different system of attributions dependant instead upon the 12 Chinese Earthly Branches.

In Columns F1-F2 the Trigrams *Ch'ien* and *K'un* pair as the opposites Heaven and Earth, and therefore fit on Kether and Malkuth respectively. However these two also pair with pure Yang and Yin, laterally across Chokmah and Binah. *Tui* is not water in the normal sense, but means lake or swamp, and therefore is part of the important pair Mountain-Lake axis, which is also reflected in the pairing of the Sun and the Moon. Hence the attribution of *Tui* has to be more subtly done than Crowley's simplistic association of it with Water.

### Column F4-F5: The Five Chinese Planets

These Columns are an analysis of Taoist cosmology which fits the Tree of Life very comfortably, by using the Element of each of the 5 Chinese planets (called *hsing* or stars) as the criterion. Using these attributions, plus the natural places of the Sun and Moon at Sephiroth 6 and 9 respectively, it is then easy to map the trigrams correctly on to the Tree of Life, rather than using the rather contorted logic that Crowley employed.

## *Five Chinese Elements*

### Column F6-F10: Attributions of the Five Chinese Elements

These are key tables for basic feng shui being the attributions of colour, season and directions to the 5 Elements. Column F10 lists the traditional association of the Elements with the reigns of five of the classical Emperors. For example, the reign of Huang-Ti, the Yellow Emperor is obviously ruled by yellow Earth.

### Column F11-F14: Feng shui and the Five Chinese Elements

Column F11 lists the five locations which should be considered for a traditional feng shui reading. This list presupposes a traditional Chinese courtyard house. The most important point for growth (or *sheng ch'i*) is the main door through which comes the most influential *ch'i*. The stove and its positioning is most important, especially if it burns with real fire. The courtyard in the middle is like the middle of the *lo shu*, devoted to Earth. The street gate, if it is a house in a compound is another important location. Also the exact positioning of the pond at the front is a very important influence. These incidentally are the main locations where offerings would be made if the occupants were Taoist. The five *shen* in Column F12 relate to the previous column. Lastly the *lo shu* (Column F13) and *Ho t'u* (Column F14) numbers are those used to represent the 5 Elements, and to do feng shui calculations such as 'flying the stars'.

### Columns F15-F19: Traditional Attributions of the Five Chinese Elements

Tones, tastes, odours and so on can be used to diagnose the lack, presence or excess of one or more of the five Chinese Elements. These tastes and odours are also very relevant to Traditional Chinese Medicine.

## *Heavenly Stems*

### Column F20-25: The 10 Heavenly Stems

The 10 Heavenly Stems and 12 Earthly Branches are indispensable to understanding Chinese metaphysics, cosmology and feng shui. These are amongst some of the most ancient Chinese cosmological terms, and are found inscribed on very ancient oracle bones. Columns F20-F21 show the 10 Heavenly Stems, while Column F22 shows their yin/yang qualities, and Column F23 their Element. You can see that the 10 Heavenly Stems are actually just the yin and yang qualities of the 5 Elements. Column F24-F25 are a rather specialised Taoist use of the Heavenly Stems.

## *Earthly Branches*

### Column F26-F34: The 12 Earthly Branches

Columns F26-F27 list the 12 Animal signs of popular Chinese astrology. These are not a zodiac as is popularly thought, but are listed against the Western zodiac for convenience. Column F28 to F29 lists the 12 Earthly Branches which are associated with these Animal Signs. Columns F30-F31 show the yin/yang and Element qualities of each of the 12 Earthly Branches. Finally Columns F32-F34 illustrate some of the relationships which exist between the 12 Earthly Branches.

## *Flying Stars*

### Column F35-F38: The Nine Flying Stars

The nine stars of the *pei tou*, Northern Ladle or Big Dipper constellation are very important to Taoist cosmology, and are the key to many feng shui formula. The Nine Flying Stars or *fei hsing* are made up of the 7 stars from this constellation plus two 'Assistant' stars. Column F35 to F37 show them attributed to the Sephiroth with regard to their titles and essential natures. For example *Wu ch'u* or Military Career is attributed to Geburah/Mars for obvious reasons. Column F38 then shows them in the traditional Chinese order, this time *not* correlated with the Sephiroth. Note that the two Assistant stars are sometimes listed together as one star (called *Fu Pi*) an arrangement used to facilitate an exact correspondence between the 9 stars and the 8 trigrams. The Pole Star (or the Dark Emperor who resides there, and about whom the other Stars revolve) naturally fits in Kether.

### Column F39-F45: The Nine Flying Stars, Names, Directions and Elements

Apart from their position in the Heavens the Nine Flying Stars are also used in Flying Star feng shui where their respective Elements, *lo shu* numbers, directions and corresponding trigrams are used to draw up a map of the subtle energies present in any building at any point in time.[1] Their secret and talisman names are also used in a specialised branch of Taoist magic.

## *Immortals and Spirits*

### Column F46-48: Eight Taoist Immortals

The Eight Immortals have not as far as I know ever been correlated with the Sephiroth. The reasons for the attributions are based on their descriptions and attributes as follows:

---

[1] See Stephen Skinner, *Flying Star Feng Shui*, Tuttle, Boston, 2003.

*Chesed*:   Han Hsiang-tzu because of his statesman like behaviour.
*Geburah*:  Lu Tung-pin because of his magic sword and warlike behaviour.
*Tiphareth*: Ts'ao Kuo-Chiu because 'the heart is in the sky, the sky is in the Way.'
*Netzach*: Chung-Li Ch'uan because he transmuted copper (Venus) into silver.
*Hod*:      Lan Ts'ai-Ho because she was a trickster and possibly hermaphrodite. Also Li T'ieh-Kuai, because of his magic gourd and medicines.
*Yesod*:    Ho Hsien-Ku because of her virginity and mother-of-pearl association.
*Malkuth*: Chang-Kuo Lao because of his skill at necromancy (bringing back souls from the other side implies a function as a psychopomp), and his fertility enhancement and matrimonial skills.

### Column F49-F52: The 12 *Shen* and *Ting-Chia* spirits

These 12 are simply allocated in order, rather than having a particular claim on a particular Zodiacal Sign. The first 6 are *ting shen* or spirits of the *ting* cycle, and the second 6 are *chia shen*. *Chia* is the first of the 10 Heavenly Stems while *ting* is the 4th Heavenly Stem. Here the *ting* Heavenly Stems combines with the first six Earthly Branches, and then the *chia* Heavenly Stems combines with the last six Earthly Branches. These spirits are important in Taoist magic.

## The 60-Year Cycle

### Column F53: Chinese Animal and Element 60-Year Cycle

The combination of the 12 Animal or Earthly Branches with the yin and yang versions of the 5 Elements (the 10 Heavenly Stems) creates a cycle of 60 which is used to mark and determine the quality of each year. If the calendar used is lunar, the starting point of each new year fluctuates between mid-January and mid-February. However for feng shui calculations, the solar calendar is used, and the starting point of each year is always 4th/5th February.

### Column F54: Start of the Chinese Lunar New Year

This column gives the actual dates of the start of the Chinese Lunar Year through to 2020. The Solar Year starts on the 4th/5th of February regardless.

### Column F55: Chinese Animal and Element Year Vitality, Destiny and Luck Cycles

These cycles are based on a Tibetan version of T'ang dynasty Chinese Element divination. More details on how to use them will be found in my book.[1]

## Lo P'an

### Column F56: The 24 Mountains of the *lo p'an* or Chinese compass

The main ring of the *lo p'an* categorised into Stems, Branches and Trigrams. The 12 Earthly Branches have arbitrarily been matched against the Western zodiac for convenience, beginning with Rat = Aries.

---

[1] See Stephen Skinner, *Tibetan Oracle*, Carroll & Brown, London, 2005.

# Commentary

# Table G. Geomancy

Geomancy is one of the four main Western systems of divination. In the 14th century it came a close second to astrology, but then fell out of use till its revival at the end of the 19th century. I have traced the development of geomancy from North Africa through Greece and Spain to Northern Europe, and then to the Americas with the slave trade, as well as south into Equatorial Africa.[1] The tables confirm this transmission, with the equivalents of the names of the 16 geomantic figures shown in a range of languages over this spectrum starting from its Arabic roots into Europe and Africa.

I would like to emphasise, from a position of detailed knowledge of both systems, that geomancy is *not* in any way related to, or utilised like, feng shui (see Table F). This confusion arose because Reverend Yates, a Victorian missionary, used the word 'geomancy' (the Western meaning of which he did not understand) in the late 19th century to mis-translate the Chinese characters 'feng shui.' As a result, many New Age writers have on this basis ever since been futilely trying to connect these vastly different practices.

Although the geomantic figures can be related to the Paths on the Tree of Life, and were so attributed by the Golden Dawn, the fit is not at all comfortable. For example there are four figures which relate to the Moon alone, Via, Populus, Caput Draconis and Cauda Draconis. Consequently the Columns in this Table are simply arranged using the order of the geomantic figures, which is repeated on every page of Table G for ease of reference. All of Table G is therefore sorted according to Geomancy Order rather than either Path or ZEP order (which is used in most of the Tables in this book).

## *Astrological Attributes*

## Column G1: Geomantic Binary Figures

This Column shows the actual figures of geomancy which are made up of four 'layers', each layer containing either a single 'point' or two points. There are therefore $2^4$ or 16 such possible combinations.

## Column G2: Traditional Meaning

These are the meanings which have become standardised by Golden Dawn use.

## Column G3: Geomantic Elements

There are several differing Elemental attributions, but I here use those of John Heydon's *Theomagia*, which were used by the Golden Dawn, which are the most commonly used.

---

[1] In Stephen Skinner, *Terrestrial Astrology: Divination by Geomancy*, RKP, London, 1980, now reprinted as *Geomancy in Theory and Practice*, Golden Hoard, Singapore, 2011.

### Column G4: Geomantic Attributions of the Zodiac

The 16 figures of geomancy do not map conveniently on to the 12 Zodiacal signs, and there are at least five variant arrangements, however I have shown the four most traditional here.

## Geomantic Figure Names in Various Languages

### Column G5-G23: Latin, Arabic, Greek, French, Hebrew & African Names

These columns show the names and (slightly different) meanings of the 16 geomantic figures in various languages and areas of the Arab world (where they originated), and in Africa and Europe, including Latin, Arabic, Greek, Hebrew, Provençale French, and various African and Malagasy (Madagascar) dialects. Additional Latin Columns have been added to the Third edition.

### Column G24: Islamic Patriarchs

This column further confirms geomancy's Arab roots by showing the attribution of the Islamic patriarchs to each geomantic figure. Note that Noah and Muhammad are attributed the Major and Minor Fortunes, but Jesus is associated with Amissio or 'loss', a further confirmation of the Islamic origins of geomancy.

## Dr Rudd's Geomantic Correspondences

### Column G25-G27: Dr Rudd's Geomantic Intelligences - Enochian Letter

These are listed by Dr Rudd in Harley MS 6482 as 'Geomantic Intelligences'. Crowley uses the same description, although he does not make a clear tabular link between them and specific geomantic figures. Here they are arranged in Geomantic Order. The same Geomantic Intelligences are also shown in Francis Barrett's *The Magus*, where they are listed as purely Zodiacal angels (see Table A40) without any reference to geomancy.

### Column G28: Dr Rudd's Enochian Letters

The attribution by Dr Thomas Rudd of John Dee's Enochian letters to the 16 figures of geomancy in the same Harley manuscript is very significant. This column is very important because it enabled MacGregor Mathers to link John Dee's Enochian system with geomancy, and thence to astrology, and from there with Hebrew and finally the other Western esoteric tradition attributions like the Tarot, enabling him to build up his 'Concourse of the Forces'.

### Column G29: Planetary Spirit

These are the traditional Planetary Spirits (see also Column M38) but here they are associated with the Geomantic figures rather than the planets.

### Column G30: Astrological Correspondences

Zodiacal signs follow Golden Dawn attributions as shown in Column G4.

# Table H. The Heavens and Astrology

Astrology is an integral part of magic, and it is only in recent times that it has been looked on *solely* as a means of determining individual fortune and character. Astrology (and indeed astronomy as well) is all about dividing up the sky so that the position and import of various heavenly bodies can be measured. The most obvious divisions are those of the path of the Sun (the 12 divisions of the Zodiac) and the path of the Moon (the 28 Mansions of the Moon). Both divisions are found in almost every culture in the world, but the Mansions of the Moon are now rather neglected in modern Western astrology and astronomy. They were and are however very important in magic.

There are finer divisions of the night sky, of which the most obvious is the division of the Zodiac into 36 Decans. The earliest record of the Decans has been found inside coffin lids dating from the Tenth Egyptian Dynasty which means around 2100 B.C. Decans are also mentioned in the Babylonian *Enuma Anu Enil*, which dates approximately four centuries later. The root of the word 'Decanate' is Greek in origin and means 'ten days apart.'

An even finer division of the Decans is the 72 Quinances (each extending over 5 degrees). These divisions have been of specific interest to magicians in the past, and are often associated with the 72 angels of the Shem ha-Mephorash or the demons of the *Goetia*, as there are 72 each of these.

Lastly there is the fixed grid of the 12 Houses which depends upon the position of the horizon rather than the layout of the stars for its measurement. The Houses determine the 'action' of each Planet in the various departments of life.

Once the dome of the sky has been divided up, then comes the analysis which depends upon which of these divisions the 'wanderers' or Planets have fallen into, and their mutual relation one to another: for it is the Planets that are the key.

## *The Planets*

### Column H1: The Ancient Greek Names of the Planets

The Planets are the most important part of astrology, as it is these 'Wandering Stars', set against the background of the Fixed Stars, which are the main players in astrology. This Table shows the original Greek names of the Planets.

### Column H2: The Sanskrit and Hindi Names of the Planets

This Table shows the Sanskrit and Hindi names of the Planets.

### Column H3-H5: Aspects between Planets

This is a simple table of the effect of angular aspects between different planets. It is helpful to realise the number of degrees involved in these aspects are quite significant numbers in themselves. These do not relate directly to the

Tree of Life or the Sephiroth and have just been laid out on the standard table for convenience. Their interpretation depends upon which two planets make the actual aspect.

## Column H6-H9: Planetary Dignities (the Relationship of Planets to Zodiac)

These Columns show the Essential Dignity of a planet, or how each planet is affected, according to which of the 12 Zodiacal signs it falls into. This effect ranges from Rulership and Exaltation to Detriment and Fall.

A planet is strengthened (dignified) if it falls within the sign that it rules. If a planet falls in the sign opposite that which it rules, it is said to be weakened (in its detriment).

A planet is also strengthened when it is in its sign of Exaltation. For example, the Moon in Cancer is considered "strong" (well-dignified), while in Taurus the Moon is said to be in its Exaltation. In traditional horary astrology, Exaltation denotes a level of dignity somewhat exaggerated compared to rulership.

Seventeenth century astrologer William Lilly compared rulership (e.g. Moon in Cancer) to a king on his throne, with considerable dignity. Exaltation was considered to give the planet (or what it signified in a horary chart) less dignity, or using the metaphor of an honoured guest – one who is the centre of attention but with limited ability to actually act.

A planet in the sign opposite to its position of Exaltation, is said to be in its Fall (e.g. Moon in Scorpio), and thus weakened, more so than when it is in its Detriment.

The relatively recently discovered planets beyond Saturn like Uranus, Neptune and Pluto are not recognised by Indian Astrology, nor do they have any importance in the tabulation of angels, demons and spirits, and so I will not attempt to include them in this Column.

For those who are interested in the trans-Saturnian Planets (those beyond Saturn in the solar system) the following are their rulerships. The usually assigned rulers are the positive rulers (left). There is also a negative rulership (right), of which Pluto's rulership is the only one commonly agreed upon:

| | | |
|---|---|---|
| *Uranus* | Aquarius | Capricorn |
| *Neptune* | Pisces | Sagittarius |
| *Pluto* | Aries | Scorpio (or Aries) |

Many modern, psychologically-oriented astrologers contend that Uranus is the ruler of Aquarius instead of Saturn; Neptune is the ruler or co-ruler of Pisces instead of Jupiter, and that Pluto is the ruler or co-ruler of Scorpio instead of Mars.

## *The Zodiac*

### Column H10-H12: The Dates of the Zodiac

These Columns show the dates upon which the Sun enters each sign. Three dates are listed for each sign. The first date is the usual date that you will see in popular Western astrology columns across the world, as was determined by Ptolemy according to the Tropical Zodiac. The dates fluctuate from year to year by as much as two days. The second column shows the dates as calculated by Vedic astrology according to the Sidereal Zodiac.

Because of the precession of the Zodiac over the centuries, the actual stars making up a sign will have moved on slightly from the position they were in when measured by Ptolemy. Accordingly (although not used by astrologers) the third column shows the date the Sun actually enters each Zodiacal constellation in the sky (as measured in 1977, although little has changed since then). There is however an argument for using the third column for the timing of some magical work.

### Column H13: The Signs of the Zodiac

The basic familiar list of Zodiacal signs.

### Column H14-H15: Original Greek Names of the Zodiac

The Greek origin of the Zodiacal names as we know them, together with their Greek numeration. The later is provided because the numbers of the Planets (in the Babylonian tradition at least) were very significant, and so the Greek numeration of the Zodiacal names might also prove of use.

### Column H16. Zodiac – Hebrew Names

### Column H17: Zodiac - Babylonian Names and Meanings

### Column H18: Zodiac - Akkadian Names and Meanings

### Column H19: Zodiac as specified by Marduk[1]

### Column H20: Zodiac Demotic Egyptian Name and Meaning

### Column H20a. Zodiac – Zoroastrian

### Column H21: Zodiac - Arabic Names

### Column H22: Zodiac Names from the *Magical Calendar*

### Column H23: Zodiac – Hindu Names

### Column H23a-H23b. Zodiac Tibetan Names

### Column H24: Zodiac - Sanskrit Names

---

[1] In David Conway, *Magick of the Gods and Goddesses,* Crossing Press, Berkeley, 2003, page 136.

## Elemental Qualities of the Zodiac

### Column H25-H26: Triplicities and Quadruplicities

The Triplicities and Quadruplicities are something that every good astrologer should know. The Cardinal Zodiac sign represents the birth of the Element, the Kerubic or Fixed sign its maturity, and its Mutable sign represents its subsequent cyclical decline. The Triplicities are simply the 12 signs grouped according to the four Elements.

### Column H27-H28: Sub-Elements, Image of the Sign

These are combinations of the Elements, taken two at a time, with an image encapsulating the nature of each sign.

### Column H29: Elements Ruling

Crowley lists out ruling Elements for each of the Sephiroth, but this is rather oversimplified, just allocating Fire, Air [Middle] and Water to the three Pillars of the Tree. From this you get nonsensical attributions of Air to both Yesod and Tiphareth, when it is very plain that Luna/Yesod is really a Water Sphere, and Sol/Tiphareth a Fire Sphere. I have also included the 4 Elemental Roots on the Tree.

### Column H30: Elemental Qualities

The Qualities of the Elements themselves are the standard combinations. These are also applied by Ptolemy to the Planets, but they do not quite agree with modern practice, especially in the case of Mercury, so are omitted.

### Column H31: Elements and the 4 Humours

The 4 Humours were very important in the Middle Ages as the essential bridge between astrology and medicine.

## Houses of Heaven

### Column H32-H36: The Houses of Heaven and their Meanings

The Houses are not part of the night sky but are a geometric division. The 12 Houses divide the sky into 12 sectors counting from the Eastern horizon, and include not just the 180 degrees of the visible sky, but the full 360 degrees. The House structure provides the astrologer with categories or aspects of life, which are interpreted in terms of the presence of which planets fall in that House. Houses without a Planet present have no effect. In this Column the 12 Zodiacal signs have been used as a convenient parallel, but are not the same as the 12 Houses. The names of the 12 Houses are not standardised like the signs, and so they are often just referred to by number. Manilius in his *Astronomica* lists the aspects of life governed by the Houses, and he poetically refers to them as 'Temples'.

# Commentary

## *Mansions of the Moon*

The Mansions of the Moon divide the course of the Moon in the sky into 28 segments. The Mansions of the Moon were particularly important in Arab astrology, and in the Mediaeval world, and therefore in magic, but have fallen out of common use in astrology today.

### Column H37-H38: Mansions of the Moon – Hindu *Nakshatras*

Although the 28 Mansions of the Moon seem to form part of every culture, their method of calculation differs somewhat from one culture to another. The Indian tradition is different from the Arab Mansions, and measures the movement of the Moon by two possible methods.

The most common method measures the movement of the Moon around the Zodiac, and this yields a cycle of approximately 27 days and 7 ¾ hours. Based on this, the Zodiac was divided into 27 *Nakshatras* (of 13° 20′). The 7¾ hour shortfall in a sidereal lunar cycle is made up by a short intercalary *Nakshatra* which makes the '28th' *Nakshatra*.

The *Nakshatra* in which the moon lies at the time of sunrise of any day is defined as the *Nakshatra* ruling that day

There are various types of approximation designed to synchronize the two rotational periods of the Sun and Moon, the Solar Year and the Lunar Month, but none of them very elegant. The history of the calendar is in fact the history of the attempts by various astronomers, astrologers, priests and mathematicians to perform the ultimate magic of synchronising the Solar and Lunar periods. In these tables I have simply delineated the most commonly accepted limits of the *Nakshatras*, and the main fixed stars in each.

### Column H39-H42: The Mansions of the Moon according to Abenragel

The coincidence of the twenty-eight letters of the Arabic alphabet and the 28 days of the cycle of the Moon, together with the symbolic significance of the crescent Moon in Islam, gives the Mansions of the Moon a particular significance in Arabic astrology and magic. This table dates from circa 1040 AD.

It is through Islamic culture that Hellenistic astrology (including the Gnostic and Hermetic Corpus), Indian astrology, and the decimal number system were transmitted to Europe during the late Middle Ages. In fact Arab culture preserved much of the culture of Greece as well, that might otherwise have been obliterated forever by the over-zealous Christian heresy hunters.

During the great efflorescence of Islamic translation and science, roughly from the ninth to the thirteenth centuries AD, much of this material was translated from Arabic into Latin in Spain. Amongst the alchemy texts and the classics of Greek philosophy, there were many writers in Arabic on astrology. Many of these with their Latinised names and dates will be found in Table U.

The most frequently cited authors include Messahalla, Albumasar, Al-Kindi (Alkindus), Alfraganus, Haly Abenragel, and Alberuni, to give them all their Latinised names. See Column U3 for their full Arabic names and dates.

Almost all of these writers include some treatment of the lunar Mansions. These treatments of the lunar Mansions often derive ultimately from the Hellenistic system of Dorotheus Sidonius (first century AD), with some additional influences imported from the Indian *Nakshatras*.

Also from Spain, during this period of cultural interchange came one of the most famous sources of magical lore. The *Ghâyat al-Hakîm fi'l-sihr*, or *The Goal of the Wise*, was known in Europe by the name of its supposed author, Picatrix. It is one of the largest and most comprehensive of the handbooks of magic, focussing on astrological images, the Mansions of the Moon, etc. There are Latin, French, German and Arabic editions, and finally a complete edition in English.[1] The author is sometimes (possibly erroneously) identified as the Andalusian mathematician al-Majriti (c.940-1007 AD). The Latin translation, which dates from 1256 AD and the court of Alphonso the Wise, king of Castille, has exerted a considerable influence on the evolution of Western magic.

Column H39 summarises the list of the Mansions of the Moon given by Haly Abenragel circa 1040 AD, from the Latin translation of the book by Abenragel called *Libri de Judiciis Astrorum...per Antonium Stupam*, published in Basel in 1551. Recommended times derived from these Mansions vary from the most important actions to the most trivial, from marriage to when to put on new clothes, rather like Chinese Almanacs of the current period. Certain activities are favoured and others cautioned against depending on the Mansion currently occupied by the Moon. Of course for this to work, the Moon must also be free from making any bad aspects with other planets. In Europe these restrictions were adopted more for magical operations and the making of talismans rather than for day to day events like the cutting of hair.

### Column H43-H44: The Mansions of the Moon and their Virtues - Agrippa

This lists the virtues of each of the Mansions of the Moon according to Agrippa.[2]

### Column H45-H46: Images of the Mansions of the Moon and their Magical Uses

The magical uses of the Mansions of the Moon with their seals and procedures used.

### Column H47-H53: The Mansions of the Moon – Chinese *Hsiu*

The Chinese also have a system of 28 Mansions of the Moon, or *hsiu*, but the

---

[1] John Michael Greer & Christopher Warnock, *Picatrix: the Classic Medieval Handbook of Astrological Magic*, Adocentyn, Iowa, 2010.
[2] *Three Book of Occult Philosophy*, Llewellyn, St Paul, 1993, Book II, Chapter XXXIII.

difference is that these are of widely different sizes, ranging from half a degree in extent (*Tsui* – the Beak) to 30.25 degrees in extent (*Ching* – the Well). These divisions are very ancient and appear on the penultimate ring of most feng shui compasses or *lo p'ans*. Column H52 shows the extent of each *hsiu* in days taken by the moon to traverse it. Column H53 shows the starting point of each *hsiu* based on a 360 degree circle counting from *Hsu*, the Void.

## Decans and 'Faces'

The Decans are a traditional division of each of the 12 Zodiac signs into 3 parts, making a total of 36 Decans, each 10 degrees in extent.[1] Agrippa and some of the older authorities refer to them as 'Faces' although there is a slight technical difference between the two terms. Each Zodiacal sign is divided into:

| | |
|---|---|
| Ascendant Decan | from 0-10° |
| Succedent Decan | from 11-20° |
| Cadent Decan | from 21-30° |

There has been a lot of controversy as to whether the Decans begin at 0° Aries or 0° Leo, particularly with regard to the attribution of the *Goetic* demons. If you go back to the Egyptian origin of the Decans, you will discover that the Decans commence precisely on the heliacal rising of Sirius, in other words the date on which Sirius is first observable rising over the horizon at dawn.[2] This is close to 0° degrees of Leo. The date of the heliacal rising of Sirius changes very slowly from period to period. It is even different at different latitudes.[3] Except in Egypt (where the atmosphere is very dry and clear) this date can even differ according to different atmospheric conditions.

To determine the current starting point of the Decan divisions we could take the date from the heliacal rising of Sirius in Egypt in 2005. In 2005 the exact heliacal rising of Sirius in Egypt was 4th August 2005 at 05:03 am. The Decans therefore currently commence from 12° of Leo. The tables for 2005 should show the 1st Decan spanning 12° Leo to 21° Leo, and the second from 22° Leo to 1° Virgo, and so on. This confirms the correctness of the Golden Dawn usage of 0° Leo, as that would have been approximately the case 100 years ago.

For the sake of consistency with the Golden Dawn you could read the Decans from Leo, but where you start makes no difference to the actual images listed

---

[1] Where the Decans are correlated with the days of the year, 36 Decans make up 360 days, and a 37th represents the remaining 5.25 days of the year. This difficulty also arises in Chinese feng shui where a *lo p'an* ring is sometimes divided into 360 degrees, but more often into 365.25 'Chinese day degrees' each of which correlates exactly with a day of the year. Very precise feng shui compasses will even show the odd quarter degrees.

[2] Neugebauer, *The Exact Sciences in Antiquity*, Dover, New York, 1969, page 83.

[3] For a demonstration of the effect of the curvature of the Earth on heliacal rising, note that in the same year Sirius was not visible in London (51 degrees latitude) till 25th August 2005.

for specific Decans. The ancient Egyptians adjusted the position of the Decans to follow the actual rising of Sirius, so if you are doing precise practical work that depends upon this, remember to move the Decans forward by 12° degrees. However I have listed the Decans in the usual Zodiacal order starting with Aries, as that is how they are shown in European sources like Agrippa.

Having established that, this still does not answer the question concerning the starting point for the cycle of the 72 *Goetic* demons. If these demons are *not* tied to the Decans, which is my view, they start their cycle at 0° Aries (see Columns M15-M19), especially as Decans are not mentioned at all in that grimoire, but divisions by planet and Zodiacal sign are often mentioned.

### Column H54-H55: The 36 Decans with Planetary Rulers

The Planets expressed as rulers of each of the 36 Decans. The astrological interpretation of the Decans is based upon a system of Planetary rulership, of which there are two in common use. The traditional method ascribed Mars to the first Decan of Aries and then carries forward a fixed series throughout the 36 Decans, coming full cycle with Mars also ruling the third Decan of Pisces. The sequence is Mars, Sun, Venus, Mercury, Moon, Saturn, and then Jupiter.

The Golden Dawn method shown in Column H55 employs the Ruler of the Sign as the Ruler of the First Decan, with the Second and Third Decans associated with the Rulers of the other two Signs in the same Elemental triplicity. Thus the First Decan of Aries is ruled by Mars; the Second Decan by the Sun; and the Third Decan by Jupiter.

### Column H56-H58: Magical Images of the Decans

There are several sets of magical images corresponding to the Decans. This set is drawn from the *Picatrix*.

### Column H59: Magical Images of the 36 Faces of the Zodiac

The second more detailed set is drawn from Agrippa Book II, Chapter XXVII. Here 'Face' is equivalent to Decan.

### Column H60-H68: Egyptian Names of the Decans

Lenain and others see the names in H60-H62 as the names of spirits of the Decans. Column H66-H68 is derived from Budge.[1]

### Column H69-H71: Egyptian Gods of the Decans

These form an interesting mixture of mostly rather obscure gods, plus a few mainstream Egyptian gods. The most interesting row is that of Leo in the first set which contains Typhon, Perseus (who here may here have a Mithraic connotation) and Nephthe.

---

[1] Wallis Budge, *The Gods of the Egyptians*, Dover, New York, 1969, Vol.2, page 304-308.

Figure 10: The Classical Constellations of the Northern Hemisphere.

Figure 11: The Classical Constellations of the Southern Hemisphere

## Fixed Stars and Constellations

The fixed stars cycle overhead each night (and also during the day but then we can't see them because they are obscured by the light of the sun). Although they appear to move, it is in fact the Earth's rotation that causes this appearance. The fixed stars retain the same relative position to each other, and therefore can act as reference points for all other heavenly bodies. They act, if you like, as a backdrop to the movements of the Sun, Moon and planets.

### Column H72: The 48 Ptolemaic Constellations

The constellations are figurative groupings of the fixed stars. There are 88 modern Western constellations (as defined by the IAU) which cover every part of the sky, and enable all of the sky, or celestial sphere, to be mapped. These 88 are based on the 48 classical constellations of the Greek astronomer Claudius Ptolemy, which only cover certain key areas of the sky. These include 21 Northern and 15 Southern Hemisphere constellations.

Along the ecliptic lie the remaining 12 constellations which are most important as they make up the Zodiac, and these are marked in the first two columns. One large Ptolemaic constellation, Argo Navis, does not appear anymore on modern sky maps, as it was broken down into several smaller ones.

### Column H73-H76: The 15 Fixed Behenian stars

From these 48 classical constellations, magicians singled out 15 particularly significant stars. These are not popular with modern astrology, but once were of great significance to Mediaeval magicians. They still have an importance to magic in that they are involved in generating certain types of talisman. Just to give one example of the assigned qualities which show agreement over a number of cultures:[1]

> "Algol is a white variable star that brightens and dims, making it very conspicuous in the northern heavens. The Arabs call it the Blinking Demon. The Hebrews named it Satan's Head and Lilith, after the demon lover of Adam. The Chinese called it the Piled-up Corpses [Star]. It was everywhere regarded as violent, dangerous, and highly unlucky."

The Behenian fixed stars are a selection of just fifteen specific stars considered especially useful for magical applications. Their name derives from the Arabic *bahman*, or 'root,' as each was considered a source or root of the astrological power for one or more planets. Each is also connected with a gemstone and plant that would be used in rituals meant to draw down the star's influence [2]. When a planet was within six degrees of its Behenian star, this influence was is strong.

---

[1] Agrippa *Occult Philosophy*, Book II, Chapter XXXI, footnote by Donald Tyson page 363.
[2] Magical sigils associated with these stars can be found in a manuscript dating back to 1300 Royal MS 12 E XXV, folio 164.

## Phases of the Moon

### Column H77: The Phases of the Moon – a Lunar Ephemeris

The Moon is key for the timing of many magical actions. The cycle of the Moon's waxing and waning can be measured in several different ways, each giving a different length:

Synodic – from New Moon to New Moon = 29 days, 12 hours, 44 minutes, 2.7 seconds

Sidereal – against the backdrop of the fixed stars = 27 days, 7 hours, 43 minutes, 11.5 seconds

Anomalistic – movement from one perigree to another = 27 days, 13 hours, 18 minutes, 37.5 seconds

Draconic – by succeeding conjunctions with *Caput Draconis* = 27 days, 5 hours, 5 minutes, 35.8 seconds

This makes calculations involving the Moon quite complex. As it is impractical to publish a whole lunar ephemeris in the space of one table, so I have contented myself with a table of the dates of the first New Moon of each year for the next 48 years. These are derived from the cycle of Meton who deduced that the dates of the Moon's phases will only coincide with the solar calendar once every 19 years. To calculate any other new Moon during any given year, simply add the required number of lunar months to the first New Moon of the year as given below.

To find subsequent New Moons in any year just alternatively add 30 and 29 till you reach the New Moon you require. Thus for

| First New Moon | | = read direct from Column H68 |
|---|---|---|
| 2nd New Moon | add 30 days | = +30 days |
| 3rd New Moon | add 29 days | = +30+29 = +59 days |
| 4th New Moon | add 30 days | = +30+29+30 = +89 days |
| 5th New Moon | add 29 days | = +30+29+30+29 = +118 days |

And so on. This Column is thus a perpetual Moon calendar. Having said that, very occasionally the date will be out by just one day.

## Calendar Epochs

### H78. Calendar Start Dates (Epochs).

Every calendar has a starting date, usually the date of an important historical event, such as Muhammad's flight to Medina, or the birth of Jesus, or the supposed founding date of an empire or a city. So to find out the date in any of the calendars listed simply subtract the Epoch date (in Gregorian format) from the present date to get the year as measured by that calendar. The exact day might be a bit more difficult to work out. Note, the Epoch is *not* the date the calendar was invented.

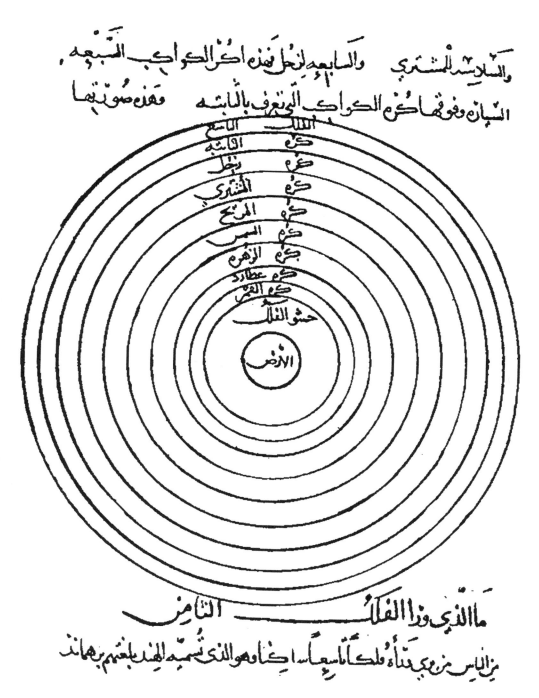

Figure 12: Islamic Cosmology showing the Nine Spheres with Earth in the centre then Moon, Mercury, Venus, Sun, Mars, Jupiter, Saturn, the Sphere of the Fixed Stars, as derived from Ptolemy. Thabit ibn Qurra of Harran (d. 901) added a ninth Sphere beyond the fixed stars called *falak al-falak* which houses the machinery which handles the 'peturbation of the equinoxes.'

# Table I. Islam

Although much of the cultural heritage of Western Europe derives from Greece and Rome, it is not acknowledged as often as it should be that it was Islam that preserved and passed on to Europe much of its Greek heritage in the form of astronomy, philosophy and geometry, that would otherwise have been lost. Much more magic theory and practice derive from Greece, that land of supremely logical thinkers, than has ever been realised. Much of this magic from Greece reached the Latin West via Islamic sources. It is not for nothing that the *Thousand and One Nights* is one of the greatest storehouses of magical lore. The Burton translation (which fascinated Crowley) contains a lot of detailed magical and sexual lore that graces the pages of the original, although the bowdlerised versions read to children have not got much of the real magic left.

*Jinn*

Islam defines 'jinn' as a separate supernatural and invisible race of beings, below angels in status, but with more powers than humans. Most often they were defined as being made from fire, and usually look like humans or animals. If they appear in human form then they are gross, or will have some animal quality, like a paw or a tail. They are said to dwell in desolate places or in caverns or trees, and may sometimes possess small animals like black dogs and black cats. There are good and bad jinn, but all are long lived, and all will supposedly be judged on Judgment Day.

Incidentally 'genii' is not a Westernised version of 'jinn' but is a totally different word, which instead derives from the Greek word 'genius'.

### Column I1-I6: Kings of the Jinn

There is an elaborate hierarchy of jinns, divided up by the 4 Elements. The Water jinn, called *marids,* thought by some to be the most powerful, are intimately involved in the stories of brass vessels being cast into the sea or retrieved by fishermen. King Solomon is said to have sealed up a number of demons or evil spirits in a brass vessel and flung it into the sea or a lake near Babylon. This vessel was subsequently retrieved by some fishermen who opened it, hoping to find treasure, thereby freeing the demons. A list of these demons will be found in Column M1, and the technique for the use of this brass vessel will be found in the commentary to *Dr Rudd's Goetia*.[1]

The Fire jinns, supposedly the most arrogant, are called *ifreets.* They were reputedly created before Adam, and have therefore always been jealous of mankind because, although they were the firstborn they were (under certain conditions) made subject to man. Most important are the kings of the jinn listed here with their 'nicknames'.

---

[1] Stephen Skinner & David Rankine, Golden Hoard Press, London & Singapore, 2007.

# Commentary

## *Hells and Heavens*

### Column I7-I10: The Traditional Islamic Hells.

In Islam hell is *an-nar* or 'the fire'. As in Christianity, it is supposed to be the abode of sinners, and has seven layers. The disposition and contents of Islamic Hells vary from sect to sect. It is interesting that in the particular arrangement listed in these Columns, sinful Muslims occupy the lowest or easiest hell, whilst the worst punishments are reserved for Christians. With his tongue in his cheek, Crowley would have relished the association of 'Hypocrites' and Christians as the occupants of *hawijah*, which would have agreed with his view of Victorian Christianity, particularly the 'fire and brimstone' Plymouth Brethren variety of his childhood days.

### Column I11-I12: The Traditional Islamic Heavens.

It has been said that Islam accepts that members of other monotheistic religions have a greater claim on Paradise than polytheistic believers, and the *Quran* (2:62) states:

> "Indeed, those who have believed [in the Prophet] and those who became Jews and Christians and the Sabians who [truly] believe in God and the Day of Judgment and do good deeds, they shall have their reward with their Lord and they shall neither have fear [for the future] nor any remorse [for the past]."

The Gabars were probably Zoroastrians, or fire worshippers. The Sabians, who came from an area near Petra, are particularly interesting as they were reputed to have long preserved ancient pagan and magical practices up to at least the 10th century AD, making it a sort of latter day Alexandria.

The *Ikhwan al-Safa* (or Brethren of Purity) relied upon the Sabians for much of their astral (astronomical and astrological) and magical knowledge. This is an area which deserves more research. Seyyed Hossein Nasr gives an excellent account of this and of the Islamic development of Hellenistic cosmology and astrology in general. [1]

## *Islamic Angels*

### Column I13-I17: Traditional Islamic Angelology

You can see the similar derivation of many of the angel names in both the Hebraic and Arabic traditions. Compare these with angel names in Columns K29-K32 and in Column A5.

---

[1] In Nasr, *An Introduction to Islamic Cosmological Doctrines: Conceptions of Nature and Methods Used for its Study by the Ikhwan al-Safa', al-Biruni, and Ibn Sina,* University of New York Press, Albany, 1978, Part I.

# Table J. Judaism

Although often seen as at odds with Islam, in fact Judaism, Christianity and Islam stand shoulder to shoulder as the three great monotheistic religions of the world, all of which were generated within the relatively small and barren, but extraordinarily spiritually fertile triangle of desert that stretches between Egypt, Palestine, and Mecca. Judaism is also the fertile soil from which the Kabbalah arrived, and which has been influential in magic since the Renaissance. Judaism is also the root-stock of Christianity, and therefore culturally influenced Christian thinking on theology, religion and magic.

## Eden and Egypt

### Column J1-J3: The four Rivers of Eden

The four rivers of Eden figure in Kabbalistic speculation, and in the rituals of the Golden Dawn, as well as the Bible.

### Column J4-J5: The Ten Plagues of Egypt

These were an extraordinary feat of magic by the leaders of the exiting Hebrew population of Egypt, particularly Aaron. His competition with the magicians of Egypt who also turned their staffs into snakes is one of the most explicit mentions of magic in the *Bible* in *Exodus* 7:10-12.

### Column J6: The Ten Commandments of Moses

Taken from *Exodus* 30:3-7, the 10 Commandments fit easily on to the 10 Sephiroth.

## Twelve Tribes

### Column J7-J13: The Twelve Tribes of Israel

This list is complicated by the fact that the descriptions of the distribution of the twelve tribes are not consistent in the *Bible*. The distribution of the tribes of Israel fascinated Renaissance magicians, especially Dr John Dee. He also used their disposition as a clue to the angelic rulership of the various countries of the Earth, using the compass direction of each tribe's encampment as the key.

Column J7 contains the Masonic order taken from Albert Pike's *Morals and Dogma*, and in turn used by the Golden Dawn. Column J11 is drawn from *Numbers* 2:3-33 [7.10]. Column J13 is John Dee's arrangement made in 1585. See also Column D10 for details of Dr. John Dee's usage.

## Prophets and Judges

### Column J14-J16: The Hebrew Prophets and Judges of Israel

The major prophets of Israel have been mapped on to the 10 Sephiroth, and the lesser ones on the 12 Zodiacal signs, in accordance with Agrippa's usage.

# Commentary

## *Psalter*

### Column J17: The Magical Psalter

The magical use of the Psalms has a long history, and is perhaps most familiar from their use in the grimoire *The Key of Solomon*. They are to be said, sung, or engraved on talismans. Abramelin recommends that all the Psalms of David be recited at least twice every week. Not all Psalms are of equal efficaciousness, and the 'Seven Penitential Psalms' are thought to be especially effective. These Psalms 6, 32, 38, 51, 102, 130, 143 were used frequently by Dee.

Psalms were used for magical purposes, specifically the purification of various pieces of magical equipment from ancient times through the Middle Ages, right down to relatively modern grimoire style texts like the so called *Sixth and Seventh Books of Moses*.

The numbering of the Psalms is a little vexing, and differs from the Catholic (which follows the *Vulgate* and *Septuagint* versions of the Bible) and Protestant (which follows the Hebrew numbering) sources. So be careful to identify your source before selecting the correct Psalm. The Psalm numbers correlate as follows:

| *Hebrew/King James Version* Protestant | *Septuagint/Vulgate Version* Catholic |
|---|---|
| 1-8 | 1-8 |
| 9-10 | 9 |
| 11-113 | 10-112 |
| 114-115 | 113 |
| 116 | 114-115 |
| 117-146 | 116-145 |
| 147 | 146-147 |
| 148-150 | 148-150 |

The task for which a large number of Psalms are recommended is the putting on of robes or vestments. The other task for which a wide range of Psalms is recommended is the consecration of 'Earth and of the wax disks', which is interesting in the light of Dr John Dee's magical use of wax disks, or maybe the phrase just refers generally to talismans.

The Planetary rows indicate the Psalm and verse of the inscription set around pentacle of each particular planet as they appear in MacGregor Mathers' edition of *The Key of Solomon*.[1]

## *Old Testament Books*

### J18. The Canonical Books of the Old Testament

---

[1] Skinner, Stephen & Rankine, David. *The Veritable Key of Solomon*, SWCM Volume 4, Golden Hoard Press, London & Singapore, 2008.

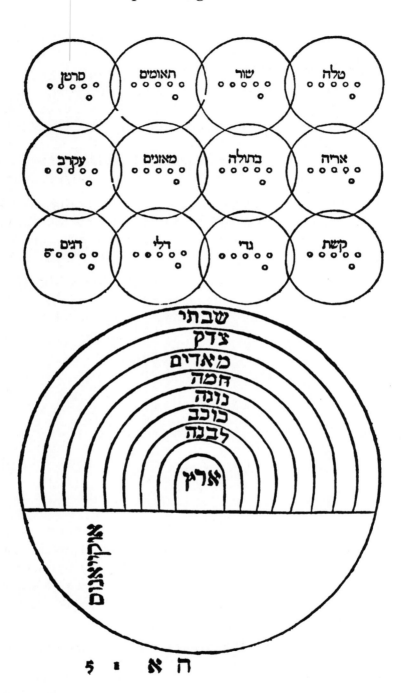

Figure 13: The Kabbalistic Earth and Heavens. The smaller circles at the top of the illustration contain the Hebrew names of the 12 Zodiacal Signs. The centre of the lower half-circles contains the word 'Aretz', or Earth, surrounded by the 7 Planets radiating out from LBNH, *Levanah* (the Moon) to ShBThI, *Shabbathai* (Saturn). The large half-circle is the location of the sub-lunary world of spirits and demons, so important to magic.

# Commentary

## Table K. Kabbalah

In a real sense this section follows directly from the previous section; as the Kabbalah is at root one of the mystical systems of Judaism. Although often thought of as the foundation of Western magic, the Kabbalah is also still part of a living mystical tradition within Judaism. Its recent and probably transient incarnation as a popular media phenomena is just one symptom of its underlying durability and strength. Most importantly just one diagram drawn from it, the Tree of Life, provides the theological structure upon which many topics in this book, from angelology to grimoire magic, have been hung.

Kabbalah or קבלה (QBLH) in Hebrew is transliterated in a number of different ways. This word can be transliterated as Kabbalah, Cabalah or Qabalah. I have consciously used 'Kabbalah' in this section to indicate the traditional Rabbi driven mystical, magical and interpretative philosophy and practice rooted in Judaism and in books like the *Sepher Yetzirah,* the *Bahir* and the *Zohar.*

The spelling 'Cabalah' most often indicates the Christian Renaissance usage of these doctrines by writers like Reuchlin and Pico della Mirandola, often as a form of doctrinal support for Christianity. 'Qabalah' has been appropriated as a label to indicate the 20th century use of it as a magical classification and meditative system, as utilised by the Golden Dawn, although Mathers certainly would not have used that spelling.

The traditional texts of the Kabbalah are insistent that there are 10 Sephiroth not 11 Sephiroth. However from the end of the 13th century there arose the idea of an 11th Sephirah just below Chokmah and Binah. As a result 20th century occultists, including Crowley, have portrayed this Sephirah Daath as a kind of Abyss. In fact there is a line often drawn between the three Supernal Sephiroth and the rest of the Tree. Daath is not the Abyss, but a kind of balancing unity achieved after the outflow from God of the three Supernals, specifically a balance between and below Chokmah and Binah, a hesitation before emanation continued with the seven lower Sephiroth. Because it is a sort of overflow, there is also a tendency to confuse it with the Qliphoth and the Abyss. More accurately it should be seen as a reflection or pre-figuring of the reflection of Kether into the seven lower Sephiroth.

The attributions of Crowley's zero row representing the Unmanifest are the three Veils of Negative Existence, Ain, Ain Soph and Ain Soph Aur, comment on which is beyond the scope of this book. The three veils are:

אין Ain - Nothingness

אין סוף Ain Soph - Limitlessness

אין סוף אור Ain Soph Aur – Limitless Light

391

## *The Tree of Life Layout, Spheres and Paths*

### Column K1-K4: Hebrew Names of the 10 Sephiroth and 22 Hebrew Letters

These Columns are made up of two different series. The numbers 1-10 are the Hebrew names of the 10 Sephiroth of the Tree of Life. A separate series is the numbers 11-32, which are the letters of the Hebrew alphabet attributed to the Paths of the Tree of Life. To find the Hebrew letter, look at the first Hebrew letter (the rightmost) in each case in Column K1. These Hebrew letters will be repeated by themselves in the Letters and Alphabet Column L8. The difference is that here the letter is spelled out in full, for example אלפ, Aleph is spelled out as 'ALP', rather like spelling out 'Z' as 'zee' or 'zed'.

Column K4 (Traditional) has a translation of the Sephiroth names in the first 10 rows, and then the item associated with each of the 22 Hebrew letters in the next 22 rows. These items are a bit like children learning the Latin alphabet by saying 'A for Apple', so not too much should be read into these 22 items. Column K4 (Key) has more appropriate correspondences.

Despite 20th century practice, it is going a step too far to identify a camel with the High Priestess Tarot card, just because 'camel' happens to be mnemonic for the letter Gimel. Rather like using the Latin alphabet to associate apple with Air, because of the child's alphabet learning sequence 'A is for apple'.

### Column K5: The Magical Images of the Sephiroth

These images are very useful anthropomorphic characterisations of the Sephiroth, and were used by the Golden Dawn for meditation, amongst other things.

### Column K6: Other Names of the Sephiroth

Collectively the Sephiroth are sometimes called 'the King's faces', an indication that they are not separate but an integral part of God. These names are taken from the Kabbalistic texts translated in MacGregor Mathers' *Kabbalah Unveiled*, and reveal aspects of each Sephirah rooted in traditional texts.

It is interesting that Rahamim (Compassion) is in fact a more common name in Hebrew Kabbalistic texts for the sixth Sephirah than the usual Tiphareth (Beauty). Compassion associates rather well with the identification of Christ and Tiphareth.

### Column K7: Position of the Paths on the Tree of Life

There is more than one way to place the Paths (and the Hebrew letters) on the Tree of Life. Columns K7 and K9 show the location of each of the 22 Paths on two of the main versions of the Tree of Life diagram. This will come as a surprise to those who have only ever seen the Golden Dawn model of the Tree of Life (as fixed by the Jesuit Athanasius Kircher), and assumed it was the only model. The Golden Dawn Path arrangement is shown in Figure 3.

# Commentary

## Column K8: Corrected Astrological Attributions of the *Sepher Yetzirah*

This shows the attribution of the 7 Planets adjusted to the configuration as shown in most versions of the *Sepher Yetzirah*, as distinct from the GD arrangement.

## Column K9: Lurianic Position of the Paths on the Tree of Life

One of the most respected Kabbalists was Rabbi Isaac Luria (1534-1572), nicknamed the 'Ari' who founded Lurianic Kabbalah. Column K9 shows the Path connections which follow Isaac Luria's Tree structure (see Figures 4 and 14), and the most usual *Sepher Yetzirah* attributions as shown in Column K8.

The most obvious visual differences between the two Tree structures are that the connecting Paths between Malkuth (10) and Hod (8) or between Malkuth (10) and Netzach (7) are not present in the Lurianic Tree. Instead two additional Paths connect Chokmah (2) and Geburah (5) and also connect Binah (3) and Chesed (4), which means that this arrangement still has 22 Paths. This makes the upper part of the Tree more symmetrical, and leaves Malkuth as a 'pendant' connected to the rest of the Tree by only one Path (32), reflecting the idea of the Fall. Indeed this is how a lot of early Kabbalistic texts (including the *Bahir*) describe Malkuth, as a pendant. Of course, as a result, the Path numbering is also completely different.

This means that the attribution of the Planets and Zodiac and Elements to the letters of the Hebrew alphabet may still be the same, but the attribution of the letters to the Paths, and the actual location of these Paths upon the Tree, is different. This difference is fundamental, and it is one of the reasons why the Tables in the present book are grouped by ZEP order (Zodiac, Element and Planet), rather than by numerical Path order, which as we have just seen, can vary.

In the Lurianic version, the Path numbers assume a delightful graphical symmetry that does not exist in the Golden Dawn version of the Tree. In fact this format groups the Elements, Planets, and Zodiac together (using the inherent grammatical structure of the Hebrew alphabet) rather than dispersing them across the Paths of the Tree, apparently at random. Under the Lurianic arrangement (following the Hebrew letters) the Paths group nicely as:

| | | |
|---|---|---|
| The 3 Mother Letters = | the horizontal Paths = | the 3 Elements.[1] |
| The 7 Double Letters = | the vertical Paths = | the 7 Planets |
| The 12 Double Letters = | the diagonal Paths = | the 12 Zodiac signs. |

The three Mother letters are particularly suggestive representing the Elements:

א Aleph – Air

מ Mem – Water

ש Shin – Fire

---

[1] Air, Water and Fire, excluding Earth which is attributed to Malkuth.

The Elemental letters thus split the Tree into three Elemental layers. The use of the Hebrew letter ת Tau (which is not a Mother letter) to represent Earth is essentially a fudge. As you can see from this layout the Element Earth is the pendant Sephirah Malkuth and *not* one of the Paths at all. Crowley did not find that convenient, and so introduced the self-confessedly clumsy 32-bis numeration. I have retained these numbers in the second column of each table, in order to make the material in these tables backwardly compatible with the Tree of Life structure which was commonly used throughout the 20th century.

It is interesting that the ancient Hebrew interpretation was of 3 Elements, whilst the Greek view was of 4 Elements, while Chinese cosmology posits 5 Elements.

### Column K10: Path Orientation

The geometric orientation of each Path, as we have seen, is very significant on the Lurianic Tree as:

a)   the 3 Elements are all *horizontal* Paths
b)   the 7 Planets are all *vertical* Paths
c)   the 12 Zodiacal signs are all *diagonal* Paths

This seems very appropriate as the 3 Elements are mentioned in the *Sepher Yetzirah* as the initial agents of Creation, and appropriately they hold the opposing Pillars of the Tree together at each plane. The fact that the 7 Planetary paths are all vertical also reflects the universal magical/mystical practice of Rising on the Planes, where each level is ruled by one of the Planets. This well-worn theme of the Planets laid out vertically recurs throughout Mesopotamian, Orphic, Kabbalistic, Merkabah, Gnostic and Renaissance cosmology. All of these traditions have diagrams which show the Planets ranging from the sphere of the Moon up to the sphere of Saturn, *in that order*, in concentric spheres around the Earth reaching up to God. This is exactly reflected in the Lurianic Tree.

This structure is also much more intellectually satisfying than the apparently random scattering of Elements, Planets and Zodiacal signs on to the Paths of the Golden Dawn Tree of Life.

This is not to say that something which is more intellectually satisfying is necessarily spiritually more correct. But, practice indicates that in many cases Path workings done with the Lurianic structure (in the correct order) are a lot more vivid and do not seem to suffer from the 'dead end concentration lapses' which sometimes afflict Path workings done using the Golden Dawn Tree format.

Let us now look at how the Paths of the Lurianic Tree are numbered. In the next Column we are here just concerned simply with the *numbering*, not with the Hebrew letters or with other attributions, which remain unchanged. The numbering is the key to meditational order, and effective Rising on the Planes.

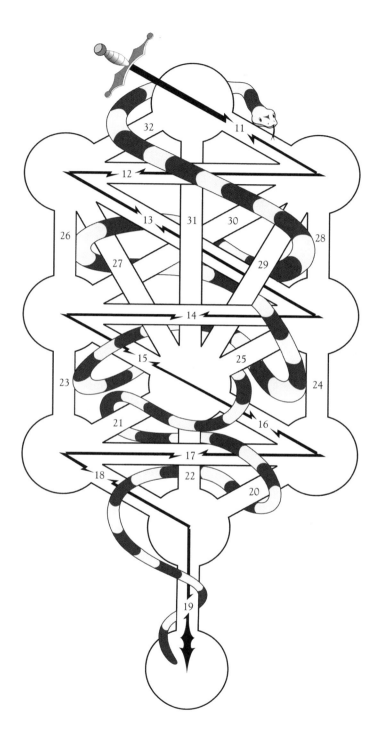

Figure 14: The Lightning Flash and Serpent on the Lurianic Tree of Life showing the correct sequential numbering of the Paths.

## Column K11-K12: The Paths of the Lightning Flash and the Serpent

The Paths of the Golden Dawn Tree of Life are well enough known and appear to the left of Column K1. Column K11 and K12 show the Path order of the Lightning Flash (Emanation) and Serpent of Wisdom (Initiatory) on the Lurianic Tree of Life.

Apart from the attribution of the Hebrew letters to the 22 Paths, there is also the question of how the Paths should be numbered. The Golden Dawn attribution of Path *numbers* was achieved by a simple 'down and sideways' allocation, but this is definitely just convenient, and not traditional. The real key to the numerical ordering of the Paths is the Lightning Flash and Serpent diagram (Figure 14). There are few glyphs in the Kabbalistic writings, and therefore those that do exist should be taken very seriously. The illustration of the Lightning Flash and the Serpent on the Tree of Life is often given in books on the Kabbalah, but to my knowledge its real purpose has never been explained in English. It is indeed a key glyph.

First it gives the correct order of the 9 Paths of descent or Emanation, in numerical order from 11 to 19. Kabbalistic texts often speak of the Lightning Flash of creation. This is not just a literary device, portraying the suddenness of Emanation, but a direct reference to this glyph which shows the correct downward numerical Path sequence.

Secondly this glyph helps to validate the Lurianic Tree, which *does* have a Path from Binah to Chesed. This glyph suggests very strongly that there has to be a Path between Binah and Chesed.

The coiled Serpent of Wisdom also has a very concrete purpose. On the Tree its shape is very convoluted, and not at all natural looking. Why? Because the coils cross over each Path in turn on their return to the Godhead, *in a very specific order*. The Serpent is truly the symbol of Wisdom and Initiation. In *Genesis* the serpent is not portrayed on the ground, or in a hole, as would be natural, but it is shown on the Tree. The use of this glyph is to show the correct order of the Paths of redemption, or of return to the Godhead, the Paths 20 to 32. The Serpent shows the *numeric* Path of return.

The correct numbering of all the Paths on the Tree is thus shown by this glyph, rather than the speculative numbering of the Golden Dawn. The Path of the Serpent is also immensely practical as it shows the order in which the Tree should be ascended – in short, the correct practical meditational order.

It is typical of the Kabbalah that such details should be clearly shown in a diagram, with only an oral explanation as to how it works.

The mechanics of following the Lightning Flash and the Serpent is as follows. The path of the Lightning Flash exactly falls on the first 9 Paths as it descends.

# Commentary

Where it crosses the Abyss (on the Lurianic Tree) from Binah (3) to Chesed (4) it definitely follows a Path (number 13). The Golden Dawn Tree does not have a Path connecting these two Sephiroth. The fudge used by the Golden Dawn Tree to allow the Lightning Flash to cross the Abyss, was to use the Path between Kether and Tiphareth to replace the missing Path between Binah and Chesed. It is unthinkable that the Lightning Flash finds itself unable to cross the Abyss, dithers around, returns to Kether and then crosses the Abyss via the Path from Kether to Tiphareth. But this compromise is exactly how the Lightning Flash is explained in terms of the Golden Dawn Tree of Life.

Of course the problem does not arise with the Lurianic Tree as the Path Binah-Chesed already exists. It is also noteworthy that on the Lurianic Tree, the Lightning Flash in its descent takes in *all* the Elemental Paths, Aleph (Air), Mem (Water) and Shin (Fire), listed as an essential part of the process of Creation in the *Sepher Yetzirah*. Two of these Elemental Paths are *missed completely* by the Lightning Flash on the Golden Dawn format Tree of Life.

Let us now look at the Path of Return. Anyone who wished to make an artistic design of a Serpent on the Tree, would certainly not have disported the coils in the traditional fashion. Therefore there must be some significance in the coils, and indeed there is. The rules for determining which Paths the Serpent crosses in its upwards journey, and in what order are simple:

    a. Only consider the Paths that the Serpent crosses *over*. The ones it passes behind do not count.
    b. If the Path that the Serpent crosses already has been traversed by the Lightning Flash, then ignore that Path.

The Serpent then clearly marks out the sequence of Path numbers for the return from Malkuth to Kether, and these are shown in Column K12 and Figure 14. When you have so numbered the Paths a number of other obscure Kabbalistic references suddenly become clear, and Rising on the Planes becomes a lot easier.

*Four Worlds of the Kabbalah*

## Column K13-K20: The Four Worlds of the Kabbalists

This Column is the key to Columns K21 to K54, which are grouped according to the Four Worlds, beginning with Atziluth, the highest of the Four Worlds. The Four Worlds can be seen to have an entire Tree of Life in each, or they can be seen as a division of one Tree. Both interpretations are valid. Column K20 contains the secret 'revolutions' of IHVH in each of the Four Worlds (these are not correct in *Liber 777*). Column K19 contains the Gematria totals of the Hebrew in Column K20, and acts as a sort of 'check digit' to its correctness. Column K18 is simply the Hebrew letters which express these numbers in Column K19, for example 72 = Ayin (70) + Beth (2). This is why בנ is spelled with an ordinary נ, not a final Nun ן which would not then have added to 52.

### Column K21-K24: God-Names in Atziluth

For some reason Crowley lists these Godnames as being in Assiah, when clearly both traditional Kabbalistic sources and the Golden Dawn ascribe them to Atziluth. Their Gematria totals are listed in Column K24.

### Column K25-K28: The Names of God of Various Length

These are the names of God (in addition to the previous group of Columns) most frequently used on Kabbalistic amulets, and are, if you like, the most 'practical' Godnames. The most famous Godname of 72 letters is treated at length in Columns A23 to A25 (along with it derivative angels). The Name of 42 letters appears in various forms – here I have used Hebraic sources rather than the Golden Dawn or Crowley spelling. There are also several names of 12, 14, and 22 letters, as you would expect.

### Column K29: Comparative Table of Archangels in Briah

The second World of the Kabbalists is called Briah. This Column is a comparative list drawn from various sources, so that you can see how the ordering and constituents of this most important list of Archangels has changed over time.

### Column K30-K33: Archangels in Briah

For some reason Crowley lists the Archangels also as being in Assiah, when clearly both traditional sources and the Golden Dawn put them in the World of Briah. The most contentious ascription is that of Michael and Raphael to Tiphareth and Hod. These are sometimes reversed. The reasoning is that as Raphael is Archangel of Air he should be in Tiphareth as a point of balance. I believe he should be in Hod because his name means 'Medicine of God'. Also as Michael is God's soldier, I feel it is more appropriate that Michael falls into Tiphareth. One temptation is to resolve this by using the positions in the Lesser Banishing Ritual of the Pentagram, but this does not work as its Archangel ascriptions are not the traditional ones anyway.

### Column K34: Orders of Angels in Yetzirah – Comparative Hebraic sources

This is a comparative table drawn from various sources so that you can see how the Hebraic ordering and constituents of this list has changed over time.

### Column K35: Orders of Angels in Yetzirah – Comparative Christian sources

This is a comparative table drawn from various sources so that you can see how the Christian ordering and constituents of this list has changed over time.

### Column K36: Orders of Angels – Standard list of Dionysius the Areopagite

This list, drawn up by Dionysius the Areopagite in *The Celestial Hierarchies,* has become the *de facto* standard amongst Christian commentators, and was the first clear attempt to categorise the different Choirs/Orders of angels. This table also shows Dionysius' sources for the different types of angel making up

# Commentary

his Nine Choirs. Guardian angels are not part of the Choirs, but have been listed under Malkuth, for completeness, as they are closer to mankind.

## Column K37-K44: Orders of Angels in Yetzirah

For some reason Crowley lists these Orders (or Choirs) of Angels as also being in Assiah, when clearly both traditional sources and the Golden Dawn put them in the Yetziratic World. The standard attributions are shown in Columns K37-K41. The Choirs shown in K37 are according to the Golden Dawn, Tycho Brahe and Francis Barrett. A non-standard variant is shown in Columns K42-K44.

## Column K45-K46: Angelic Descriptions in the World of Yetzirah

These trivial Columns, present in the First Edition, have been omitted from this edition.

## Column K47-K50: The Angels of Assiah

For some reason Crowley lists these Angels as being in Briah, when clearly both traditional sources and the Golden Dawn put them in Assiah. The source of this Column is Maimonides, otherwise known as Rabbi Moses ben Maimon.

## Column K51-K54: The Heavens of Assiah

The standard list of Hebrew names for the Zodiac, Elements, and Planets with their translation, meaning and numeration. This is a key Column and maybe should have been put at the front of the Kabbalah Table, but is instead placed here in its traditional place in the World of Assiah.

## Revolutions of the Divine Names

## Column K55-K63: Revolutions of the Divine Names

These Columns show the permutations of the Divine Name in three of the Four Worlds, and provide some useful formulae. See also Column K20 for the overall Revolution of IHVH in the Four Worlds. Note that in K59 the sixth and twelfth banners have been interchanged, correcting an error that appears in Agrippa and was repeated by Crowley.

## The Seven Palaces

The Seven Palaces or *hekel* (plural *hekhaloth*) are also called Halls or Chambers. They are to be found in the *Sepher Yetzirah* 4:15. This chapter deals with the 7 Double letters of the Hebrew alphabet. With them are associated Seven Heavens, Earths, Seas, Rivers, Deserts, Days, Weeks, Years, Sabbaticals and Jubilees. We are only concerned with the first few of these categories in the following Tables.

One way of looking at the Seven Palaces is to see them in the Four Worlds, as follows:

| World of Briah | The 7 Palaces or Halls | Columns K64-K68 |
|---|---|---|
| World of Yetzirah | The 7 Heavens | Columns K69-K73 |
| | angels of the 7 Heavens | Columns K74-K79 |
| World of Assiah | The 7 Earths | Columns K80-K85 |
| | The 7 Hells | Columns K86-K90 |

When they are placed on the Tree of Life it has sometimes been customary to amalgamate the first three Sephirah and also the last two Sephiroth, to achieve just 7 Palaces. However, as the root of these 7 Palaces are the Spheres of the 7 Planets, I believe that they should just be associated with the 7 planetary Sephiroth, 3-9, and not be attributed to Sephiroth 1,2 or 10 at all.

### Column K64-K68: The Seven Palaces

The Seven Palaces range from the holiest in Binah, to the Palace of the Moon in Yesod. Kaplan in his edition of the *Sepher Yetzirah* gives a slightly different order and transliteration (Column K68) of which Netzach=Nogah (Venus) is the most immediately recognisable. I have not used this order, but simply listed it in Column K68 for completeness.

### *The Seven Heavens in Seven Palaces*

### Column K69-K73: The Seven Heavens in Seven Palaces

The Seven Heavens are related to the Seven Earths (Columns K80-K85) and the Seven Hells (Columns K86-K90). The terms Palaces and Halls (*Hekhaloth*) may be interchangeable. Traces of this system can be found in early grimoires, like de Abano's *Heptameron* (see Column M10 where his slightly corrupt usage of the Heavens has been corrected).

The attributions of the Heavens are drawn from the *Zohar*. Crowley gives the Hebrew and Latin one row out of step. Godwin, in his excellent book,[1] suggests that the *Zohar* is out by one line, with Araboth equated with Chesed, and Vilon equated with Malkuth, but I think this is a misreading of the passage, and that the *Zohar* agrees quite well with Column K69.

Originally the archangels of each of the seven Heavens were archangels of the 7 planetary Spheres, therefore the Heavens are an extension of the 7 planetary Spheres. So when attributing the Heavens to the Tree of Life they should exclusively be attributed to Binah (Saturn) through to Yesod (Moon), and not include Kether, Chokmah or Malkuth in their dominion, especially not the latter.

The Latin of the 1st Heaven *Velum sive Cortina* has an interesting possible double meaning, as this may literally also be read as the 'veil of the oracular cauldron' in the sense of the oracle at Delphi.

---

[1] In David Godwin, *Cabalistic Encyclopedia*, Llewellyn, St Paul, 2004, page 138.

# Commentary

### Column K74-K76: Angels of the Seven Heavens in Seven Palaces

These angels are taken from *Enoch 3*, *Pirqe Rabbi Ishmael* and *Hekhaloth Zot*. Each Angel is said to be accompanied by 496,000 myriads of ministering angels.

### Column K77: Princes in the Second Heaven of Raqia

The contents of this Column have in this edition been transferred to Column A10.

### Column K78-K79: The Hierarchy of Heaven

This Column is taken from a series of chapters in *Enoch 3*, XVIII-XXI and ties together a number of angels and hierarchies in the Heavens. This is listed as if it was just one continuous hierarchy from the bottom to the top, but it is obviously made up of a number of other series. It is tempting to think that it is the hierarchy spread across all Four Worlds, but it is unfortunately not that neat. The numbers down the left column are suggestive rather than definitive.

*The Seven Earths in the Seven Palaces*

### Column K80-K85: The Seven Earths in Seven Palaces

These are related to the Seven Heavens and the Seven Hells. The Seven Earths are seen as 'stacked' one beneath the other. The Earth corresponding to Malkuth, Cheled, is our own planet, and not strictly one of the Seven Earths. Arqa in Hod also in one sense contains the Seven Hells. The other Earths are populated by men who are said not to have Adam as their ancestor, and therefore are not exactly human. This makes them sound rather like Middle Earth, suggesting a rather Tolkeinesque vision of the occupants of the other Earths. Figure 7 shows the list of the Seven Earths and Seven Hells in Hebrew circumscribed by the Four Waters, which links neatly with the next section.

*The Seven Hells in the Seven Palaces*

### Column K86-K90: The Seven Hells in Seven Palaces

The Seven Hells are related to the Seven Heavens and the Seven Earths. There are several variant orders of these Hells, and Crowley lists their translation out of order. Gehenna has been used to describe a metaphysical Hell, but its origin is the graveyard, burning ground and rubbish dump just outside Jerusalem where those who could not afford a burial were unceremoniously dumped, a literal hell indeed. The Latin is from Rabbi Joseph Castiliensis in *Hocto Nucis*.

## The Qliphoth

### Column K91-K94: Arch-Demons or Princes of the Qliphoth

The standard list (Column K93) are the rulers of the Orders of the Qliphoth (Column K97) whilst Column K92 includes the wives and children of Samael as recorded in the *Zohar*. Column K94 is drawn from a French grimoire.

## Column K95-K99: Orders of the Qliphoth

Crowley allocates three Orders of the Qliphoth to the Unmanifest Ain Soph Aur. This cannot be metaphysically correct as the Qliphoth are the shells created by the unbalanced forces generated as each of the Sephiroth were created. As Ain Soph Aur is the state/potentiality before any Sephiroth were created, it follows that they cannot have Orders of the Qliphoth attributed to them. But for the sake of completeness however I list these three Orders of the Qliphoth below:

Qemetial -     the Crowd of gods (more appropriate as an obverse of Kether)
Belia'al –     Worthlessness (in reality found lower down the Tree)
A'athiel –     Uncertainty (a state generated by the need to attribute these Orders somewhere!). Traditionally these 3 were attributed to Kether, Chokmah and Binah respectively, not to Ain Soph Aur.

## Column K100-K105: The Kings and Dukes of Edom

Crowley in *Liber 777* put both of these categories in the same column, and then used the planetary sign for the Sun to indicate Kings and the planetary sign for Venus to indicate Dukes, which seems an unnecessary complication.

The source of these Dukes and Kings is *Genesis* 36:31-43 where these worthies are given in a straightforward manner with geographical locations and partial genealogy, suggesting that they were originally *real* kings (whose lands the Israelites probably took by force of arms) and whose names were later appropriated by the Kabbalists to label something altogether different.

## Column K105a: The Orders of Demons and their Princes

### *The Partzufim and Body of God*

## Column K106-K107: Ten Divisions of the Body of God

This is a piece of Kabbalistic anthropomorphism. There is nothing sinister about the Latin word *sinistrum* or *sinister*: it simply means 'left', and does not imply the evil side of the Tree as some writers have suggested.

## Column K108: The Countenances or *Partzufim*

*Partzuf* literally means 'face' so this section is about the Kabbalistic division of the Countenance of God into different 'faces'. The divisions of Macro- and Micro-prosopus are well delineated in MacGregor Mathers' *Kabbalah Unveiled*.

## Column K109: The World Triads on the Tree

This division into three Worlds is not the same as the Four Worlds.

### *Sepher Yetzirah*

## Column K110: Elements and Directions from the *Sepher Yetzirah*

These directions are quite important and bear upon the distinction between a two dimensional Tree of Life (as is usually shown) and a three dimensional Cube of Space (as Carlos Suares suggests). These directions however vary from one edition of the *Sepher Yetzirah* to another. The second column shows the directions according to Isaac Luria and from the *Pardes Rimmonim*.

## Column K111-K113: The Four Quarters and Six Directions

An important part of the structure of the *Sepher Yetzirah* that has been made much of by Carlos Suares and Paul Foster Case who uses it to illustrate the 'Cube of Space'.

## Column K114-K119: The Planetary Order in the *Sepher Yetzirah*

These key columns show the main variant attributions of the Planets to the Hebrew letters plus MacGregor Mathers' attribution which comes from no version of the *Sepher Yetzirah* known to me. These Columns provide background information for some of the discussion in the Introduction.

## Column K120-K121: The Intelligences of the Paths of the *Sepher Yetzirah*

This Column is drawn from a list called 'The Thirty-two Paths of Wisdom' added as a 17th century appendix to an edition of the *Sepher Yetzirah*. These are designated as *sehkel*, 'Intelligences'. The word 'intelligence' meant in the 17th century a spiritual creature (such as an angel) rather than a measure of IQ. These names are supposed to describe the Sephiroth and Paths on the Tree, but they may have been, at one time, a set of qualifying phrases or powers attached to a now missing list of angels. Alternatively the Intelligence may have been the guardian of a particular Path or Sphere. However this is just an hypothesis and depends upon finding the matching list of 32 angels or Intelligences for it to be proven.

The attributions to the Paths follow Golden Dawn protocols, but I believe that there is a different, more correct attribution, which can be derived by using the Path numbers on the Lurianic Tree of Life as shown in Figure 14 and in Columns K11-K12.

## *Sepher ha-Zohar*

## Column K122: The Contents of the *Zohar*

This Column has been added to the Second Edition, as the *Zohar* and especially MacGregor Mathers' translation of Knorr von Rosenroth's Latin has been the source of much of the material in this Table. Several new translations of the *Zohar*, specifically those of Isaiah Tishby and Daniel C Matt supplement Mather's work which only included a small part of the *Zohar*. The English translation by Sperling and Simon, has to a large extent been superseded.

## *De Arte Cabalistica*

## Column K123: Hebrew Letters and their Secret Meanings from Reuchlin's *De Arte Cabalistica*.

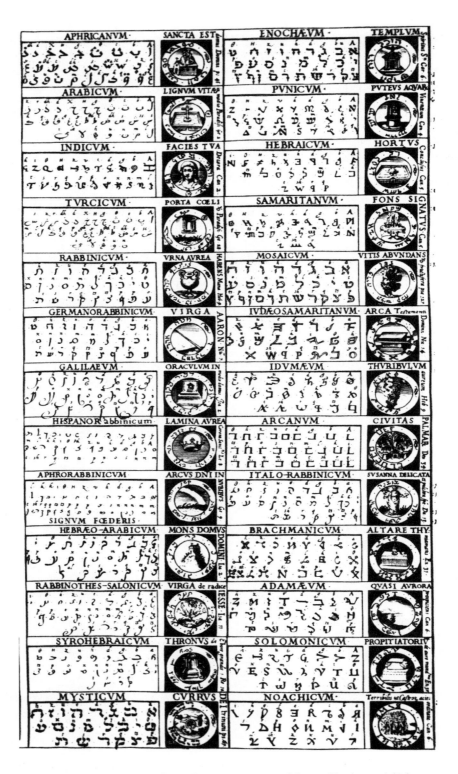

Figure 15: Alphabets from the *Virga Aurea* of James Hepburn, 1616.

# Commentary

# Table L. Letters Alphabets & Numeric Values

An important part of magical knowledge is the scripts in which many magical formulae are written: these can be the letters of a real language like Greek or Hebrew, or solely magical alphabets used for no other purpose. Writing divides into alphabetic and ideographic scripts. Alphabetic scripts (like Latin, Greek or Coptic) have a limited number of characters (typically around 25 characters) which have a specific sound. Words are formed from combinations of these characters or letters. Ideographic scripts (like ancient Egyptian or Chinese) have a huge number of characters (typically measured in the thousands) with each representing an idea or a word. In this Table we will be looking at only one ideographic language, Egyptian in Column L1-L3, and isolating a few phonetic characters – but on the whole the writing of ancient Egyptian cannot be directly compared with any alphabetic language.

The alphabet in its various guises sprang essentially from Early Phoenician, which has in turn spawned Hebrew, Greek, Arabic, Persian, Coptic, Cyrillic, (extended to 36 letters) and of course the Latin alphabet used by English. Apart from the fact that much of the roots of magic are to be found in these languages, we are interested in them because of *Isopsephy*.

Isopsephy is the Greek name given to the practice of equating numeric values with individual letters, and therefore being able to total them to give a numeric value for any word written in any language which sprang from Early Phoenician. This practice was very common in Greek, and so the names of gods and other spiritual creatures written in that language will often have a significant numerical value, from which legitimate deductions about that entity can be made. A selection of significant isopsephy is to be found in Table X.

More famously, this practice is common in Hebrew where the Kabbalistic practice of Gematria has been used to associate many words with a common numeric value. Some might say that this technique has been stretched to the limit by some modern writers who feel that any coincidence of sound or number is sufficient to draw a precise equivalence. Although such coincidences can appear very magical, I feel that we are only on safe ground where whole systems of significant numbers mesh (as with the Mithraic temple grades). When a series of key words are made up from the same multiples or differences (such as the names of the Olympic Spirits), then the use of Isopsephy or Gematria in deductive reasoning is vindicated, but where just a single example is observable, then you should be very wary of coincidence and its seductive traps. Accordingly in this volume, I have provided Columns of numeric values only where they are most likely to be significant. Alphabetic scripts, particularly Hebrew and Greek, lend themselves to numerical equivalents, as indeed both these alphabets have been used as numbers, on a day to day basis.

## *Egyptian Hieroglyphics*

### Column L1-L3: Egyptian Hieroglyphics

Ancient Egyptian is, like Chinese, a language in which specific glyphs stand for whole words or ideas. It is therefore not alphabetic (except in a limited phonetic sense), and so does not stand direct comparison with alphabetic languages. However a limited number of its symbols also have a phonetic value, so I have listed these here because of the interest in Egyptian magic.[1] It is not possible to tabulate the many hundreds of other Egyptian glyphs. The phonetic symbols shown here should *not* be equated with the letters on the same row in the alphabetic columns, as alphabetic languages are not directly comparable with hieroglyphic languages. Non alphabetic scripts like Egyptian, Mayan and Chinese have completely different roots and structure. Column L3 shows Hieroglyphics which do not have the phonetic value but have a correlation in meaning to specific Phoenician/Hebrew characters.

## *Phoenician*

### Column L4-L7 Phoenician Alphabet and Numeration

Phoenician is the root of most of the important cultural alphabets of the Middle East and Europe, including Hebrew, Greek, Latin, Coptic and obviously the English alphabet. Numeric values given for this are the same as the Hebrew values. There are no 'final' letter forms in Phoenician as in Hebrew.

## *Hebrew*

### Column L8-L11: Hebrew Alphabet and Numeration

This is one of the most important tables in this book for the purposes of practical Kabbalah, especially Gematria. Too much has been written about this to require further comment.

### Column L12: Hebrew Masoretic Vowel Points and Pronunciation

Hebrew is written with only consonants, although a few consonants like *Vav* did duty as both consonants and vowels. While Hebrew was a living language, scholars knew how to pronounce the words, so vowels were not thought necessary. About the 7th century AD a system was introduced by the Massoretes in the interest of preserving what they considered was the correct pronunciation. These were marked in 'points' or dots and bars above or below the consonants. It is just as well they did, because gradually Hebrew ceased to be a spoken language, until its recent revival in the mid 20th century. This Column shows the vowel 'pointings' and their pronunciation, although most Kabbalah books in English ignore these altogether. The pointings do not have a numeric value of their own.[2]

---

[1] See David Rankine, *Heka: The Practices of Ancient Egyptian Ritual & Magic*, Avalonia, 2006.
[2] The attribution of the points to the Sephiroth comes from the *Tikuney Zohar* 70, 129a, b.

# Commentary

## *Greek*

### Column L13-L16: Greek Alphabet and Numeration

It is useful to note that the attribution of the Planets and Elements to the Greek letters is quite different to the attribution of these to the Hebrew alphabet. So although Greek and Hebrew, as alphabets, had a common ancestor in Phoenician, they have developed their own Planetary and Elemental attributions. One of the reasons for this is that as a written language Hebrew is basically consonantal, whereas Greek has a strong emphasis upon vowels. The Greeks attributed their vowels to the Planets. Therefore do not mix up these different attributions.

### Column L17: Elements and Planets Corresponding to Greek Letters

### Column L18: The 24 Elders or Seniors

Column L18 includes a Senior or Elder (or angel) for each Greek Letter. These 24 Elders are mentioned in the *Book of Revelation* as surrounding the throne of God. From these Dr John Dee took his term for the 'Seniors' on his Enochian tables. Seniors is exactly the same Greek word as rendered 'Elders' in the Bible. The names are drawn from a Coptic Gnostic manuscript.[1] In the Gnostic context they became identified as heavenly powers that could be appealed to. They may also map onto the Zodiac signs, but are here mapped on to the more obvious key, the Greek letters which begin each of their names.

### Column L19-L20: Magical Name of the Greek letters

Secret names or words of power associated with each letter.

### Column L21: Gnostic Heaven and Word of Power

Important words of power associated with each of the seven Gnostic Heavens.

### Column L22-L23: Greek Vowels

These Columns focus on the extension of the Greek cult of the vowel into Gnostic theology. Here we see associated Archangels and directions.

## *Coptic*

### Column L24-L27: Coptic Alphabet and Numeration

The Coptic alphabet is basically the Greek alphabet adapted to the needs of Ptolemaic Egypt, after its conquest by Alexander the Great. Additional letters had to be created to accommodate additional sounds. As such the numeration is very similar. The Copts however altered the Greek numbering system for values above 100. In some texts they simply add the letter *rho* (100) after another letter to indicate 'hundreds', so *beta rho* equals 2 x 100 = 200.

---

[1] From Berlin MS 11347.

In addition to the letters already in this table there are a further five letters that have no numeric value:

| H | *Hori* |
|---|---|
| Ch, H | *Haj* |
| Sz, C | *Sima/Chima* |
| J, G | *Djanda/Ganga* |
| Tt | *Dij* |

These therefore have no isopsephy or Kabbalistic import, and should not be arbitrarily allocated to the Sephiroth for convenience, as is sometimes done.

## *Arabic*

### Column L28-L31: The Arabic Alphabet and Numeration

Arabic has the same roots as Hebrew. Arabic is written right to left and has 28 basic letter forms. The use of 'alphabetic numerals' by the Arabs was introduced in imitation of Hebraic usage for the first 22 letters (i.e. up to 400) by the Jewish and Gnostic communities of Syria and Palestine, and then from the Greeks for the remaining six letters (500 to 1000). Although the numerical values agree for the most part across the whole Islamic world, there are some differences in the usage in the Maghreb (Islamic north Africa, including Morocco, Algeria, Tunisia and Libya), primarily in letters corresponding to English 'S' and 'D', and these are listed below.

| *Letter* | *East Arabic value* | *Maghreb value* |
|---|---|---|
| Sin | 60 | 300 |
| Sad | 90 | 60 |
| Shin | 300 | 1,000 |
| Dhad | 800 | 90 |
| Dha | 900 | 800 |
| Ghayin | 1,000 | 900 |

The usual order of the Arabic alphabet is different from Hebrew, but has here been re-ordered in order to align it with the numeric values. This particular numerical order was called *abjad*, a term which is familiar from the Kabbalah of the nine chambers, showing that *abjad* was originally probably just an ordering mnemonic. The Arabic equivalent of Gematria is called *khisab al jumal* ('calculating the total') or *huruf al jumal* (or 'totals by means of letters'). Following the Arab conquest of Egypt, Syria and Mesopotamia, numbers were often spelled out in full or written in borrowed Greek characters, showing their partial dependence on Greek isopsephy.

In Arabic, as in Hebrew, vowels are not letters, only signs added to the letter preceding them. In most cases the vowels are not written, so that the name

# Commentary

'Muhammad' for example, is just written 'mhmd'. The vowels are normally only indicated in special cases, like where there is doubt about the correct meaning of the word, and in reading books for school children, and have no effect on the numeration of the words.

## Column L31a-b: Associated Divine Attribute and Meaning

### *Latin*

## Column L32-L33: The Latin Alphabet Corresponding to Hebrew

This column shows the Latin or English alphabet in relation to Hebrew. Some letters in the English alphabet are relatively recent, so that 500 years ago for example U,V, and W ('double U') were the same letter, with 'u' being used inside a word (medially) as a vowel, but the other form 'v' being used at the beginning of a word or as a consonant.

Likewise I, J and Y are essentially the same letter, so that the number 4 could be written 'iiii' or more often as 'iiij'. Also 'x' is an import (from Greek) as can be seen by the limited number of words which begin in English with that letter. There is no 'x' in Hebrew. So excluding 'x' and the duplicated letters, the Latin alphabet was effectively one of 22 letters.

Unfortunately these 22 letters do not map exactly on to the 22 Hebrew letters, as the latter language has few vowels. For example, there is also no 'e' in Hebrew. Also in Hebrew there are two 't' characters, Teth (transliterated here as 'T') and Tav (shown here as 'Th'). Likewise there are two 's' letters, Samekh (shown as 'S') and Shin (shown as 'Sh'). These things prevent a one-to-one correspondence, however this column shows the Latin alphabet in Hebraic order.

## Column L34: Latin Alphabet Numeration

There is a lot of controversy about allocating numeric values to the Latin alphabet. Only I, V, X, L, C, D and M were ever used specifically as numbers by the Romans, unlike Greek and Hebrew where *every* letter was used as a number. So the number column for Latin should only show these values. However, in order to utilise numerical values for the whole alphabet, in more recent times, the numbers 1 to 9 have simply been allocated in sequence to the letters, as shown in Column L34.

### *Futhark*

## Column L35-L40: Runic Alphabet

Although there are a number of different types of runes, I have only included the German elder futhark and the Anglo-Saxon futhork [*sic*]. I do not believe there is a provable numeration for these letters, apart from a simple sequence counting from the beginning, despite various modern attempts to provide one, and so there is no numeration column.

## Enochian & Trithemius

### Column L41-L43: Enochian Alphabet

This is the alphabet that was transmitted through the skrying of Edward Kelley to Dr John Dee in the 1580s. It purports to be the alphabet of the language spoken by the angels, but in fact is very like the alphabet to be found in *Voarchadumia*, a book that was owned by Dee at the time of the skrying.

### Column L44: Enochian Alphabet - Numeration

The key to the numeration of Enochian was first demonstrated by Dr Donald Laycock in *The Complete Enochian Dictionary*. The basic 1-9 numeric values were all established by him except for 7 which Robert Turner very reasonably pointed out probably corresponds with 'B', because this letter is the recurring initial letter of the angel names in Dee's *De Heptarchia Mystica* ('Of the Sevenfold Mystery').

An objective confirmation of the correctness of these number-letter correspondences is arrived at by placing the letters corresponding to the numbers 1 to 9 in sequential order. If you place these in a row you get:

```
1 2 3   4 5 6   7 8 9
LUD  SON  BPM
```

The phrase 'Lud Son' leaps off the page. Lud's son in the *Bible* was of course Enoch, after which these Enochian letters are named. Either this is a confirmation of the innate angelic intelligence behind the generation of these letters, or an indication that Kelley used the phrase as a crib mnemonic. I prefer the first explanation, but either way it confirms the validity of these numeric correspondences. The next three letters BPM yield an even more interesting key, the explanation of which lies in the 49 Good Angels.

Enoch was the son of Lud, who was son of Shem who was the son of Noah. Enoch supposedly lived 365 years, a symbolic number which is suggestive of a solar god. Enoch is also called Idris in the *Koran*, and Idris was reputed to be the inventor of geomancy (see Table G). It was through Dr Rudd's attribution of Enochian letters to geomantic figures, that Mathers was able to tie together all of the symbolism used by the Golden Dawn into his Concourse of the Forces.

A further interesting coincidence is that King Lud (whose name is celebrated in the famous pub of the same name near Lud's Circus in the city of London) was an ancient British god who John Dee researched at some length. It has been suggested that the 'London Stone' is now all that remains of an ancient stone circle that once stood at the top of Ludgate Hill on the same site now occupied by St Paul's Cathedral. King Lud lived in the city around 73 BC and expanded it considerably. London was for a while even known as 'Caer-Ludd' (Lud's Town). When Lud died he was buried at what was believed to be the highest point in London, now known as Ludgate. Dee was fascinated by King Lud and the supposed powers of his London Stone, and for a while was supposed to have lived nearby. Although the story of King Lud was probably invented by Geoffrey of Monmouth, this does not diminish the significance of Dee's interest.

## Column L45. The Golden Dawn Cipher from Trithemius

The Golden Dawn Cipher manuscript was allegedly the source of the First Order rituals and some of the knowledge lectures of the Golden Dawn, and as such might be considered an important source of the material in the present volume. This column shows the magical script in which this very important Cipher manuscript was written.

The Cipher Manuscripts have been published several times but most completely by Darcy Kuntz.[1] These are written in a simple letter for letter cipher derived from Trithemius' *Polygraphiæ*, which was printed in Paris in 1561 but written half a century before. This cipher is shown in Column L45.

The Cipher manuscript contains some Hebrew, but seemingly not written by someone accustomed to writing Hebrew. Otherwise it is in ciphered English, but written backwards in imitation of Hebrew. It is therefore almost certainly written by a native born English speaker, possibly in the form of a summary or notes taken during or after a ritual.

It has been suggested that the Cipher manuscript came from German sources, specifically Fraulein Anna Sprengel. No German appears in the manuscript, and folio number 59 (which contains the only reference to her) although in cipher, is badly written in a different hand using a different pen, in the opposite direction (from left to right, instead of right to left). It is obvious therefore that folios 55, 57-59 and probably 60 are written by a different person, and added later. It seems to me that the Sprengel letters were added to the Cipher manuscript to help provide a link to the supposed provenance, rather than allowing it to stand on its own merits.[2]

The suggestion that the Cipher manuscript was picked up from a Farringdon Road book stall is also inherently unlikely, as anyone wishing to get this manuscript into what turned out to be the right hands would not have taken the

---

[1] Darcy Kuntz, *The Complete Golden Dawn Cipher Manuscript*, Holmes Publishing, 1996. With an introduction by R A Gilbert. Limited to 200 copies.

[2] It may be a coincidence, but Gershom Scholem mentions a Frankfurt Jewish Masonic lodge founded in 1807 with a name identical to the Hebrew name of the Golden Dawn, except for the order of the words. The founders of this lodge were connected with the Rite of Strict Observance of the Baron von Hund. One of von Hund's adherents was Christian von Sprengeisen, an interesting family name that might later have been shortened, or Anglicized, to Sprengel. Interestingly Sprengeisen died in 1809, the possible date of manufacture of the paper used by the author of the Cipher manuscript.

risk of leaving it for sale, because the manuscript might have been bought by someone else simply as a curio.

Although the paper dates from 1809 or maybe 1780/1790, I think it was probably (from the contents, which include post 1860 material) written after 1860. This period has been referred to as the 'Golden Age of English Fringe Masonry' by Darcy Kuntz, and therefore it is not surprising that the Cipher manuscript, which in essence is a series of Masonic style rituals, was penned during this period. In fact it is very much concerned with (Masonic) Temple arrangement, for the second folio is not a general introduction, or theory, as you might expect, but immediately states with 'where members ought to sit in the Temple'. The emphasis upon badge and insignia design, even to the point of crude designs for them, strongly suggests that the writer was certainly a Mason rather than a Rosicrucian or a ritual magician.

The first folio gives the name of the rite or Order, and it is not expressed as the Hermetic Order of the Golden Dawn, which seems to have been a later title. The initial title is in Hebrew and is "חברת "זרח אור בקר. Interestingly this piece of Hebrew is the only one with vowel pointing to indicate the pronunciation, which is Chebrat "Zeracha Aur Beqor." The root of Chebrat is ChBR which means to join together (as in a Society). It also has a fascinating secondary meaning of 'to enchant, charm, or by incantations to collect serpents...without harm.' Aur means 'light' and Zerach means 'to dawn'. Beqir also means the dawn, but has an interesting secondary meaning of Ox with its implication of the yoke of fellowship. Gustav Meyrink in his novel *The Golem* writes of a seal which bears the name Chabrath Zereh Aour Boqer.

Other features in the Cipher manuscript are mentions of the Tarot cards, which are very interesting, because they are already set out in the sequence later adopted by Mathers, rather than in Eliphas Levi's Tarot trump order of 1860. Folio 35 shows a later alteration, with a cross edit arrow indicating the swap between the cards Strength and Justice (which Mathers has been credited with) whilst a little later on folio 38 this change is included without comment or alteration. Therefore it must have been a new change, and one just familiar to the writer of the manuscript at the time he was writing it.

Another most interesting point is the inclusion of Enochian in several of the rituals without comment. This proves the writer was familiar with Dr John Dee's system, and must have had access to Dee's papers in the British Museum or copies thereof.

Lastly there is nothing Rosicrucian about the manuscript, and the word itself is not used, so it would seem that the original intention was completely Masonic and Kabbalistic and not at all Rosicrucian. The drawing of the 'Jewel of the Adepts' which later became known as the Rosy Cross, only appears in folio 57, amongst the rather suspect later additions to the manuscript, and

# Commentary

anyway the reference to it as a 'jewel', which is a completely Masonic term. The Rosicrucian elements of the Second Order were the product of MacGregor Mathers' scholarship. It therefore seems likely that Mathers was *not* the author of the Cipher manuscript, as it does not contain any overt Rosicrucian references. If Mathers had originally authored the manuscript then there probably would have been a Rosicrucian flavour from the beginning.

This makes it pretty certain that the writer was not Mathers, nor a German or a French author, but an English Mason with access to the British Museum, probably writing after 1860, who had just recently adopted the idea of a Strength-Justice Tarot card swap.

## *Magical Scripts*

### Column L46: The Theban Alphabet

The Theban alphabet relates directly to the Latin alphabet, as distinct from the following alphabets which relate to the Hebrew alphabet. Unlike Celestial, Malachim, and Crossing the River, Theban has one letter for each letter of the Latin alphabet and is similar to Trithemius' cryptographic system, although no connection has been positively established.

### Column L47-L50: Magical Scripts relating to Hebrew

Various classical magical alphabets were often used in the composition of sigils and talismans. Many are to be found in Agrippa[1]. As these scripts correlate with Hebrew, they may have come to Europe from Hebrew sources, or via the Arab world. Agrippa's alphabets, known as Malachim, Celestial Writing, and Crossing the River are all similar in terms of shape and style. All feature unusual serifs, with shape borrowings from Greek and Hebrew characters. Many of the characters are roughly similar to Hebrew, for example, in Celestial Script, the Aleph is a very simplified version of the Hebrew Aleph. The Shin letter is roughly similar to the Hebrew Shin. Greek is also represented. The Celestial Yod is a simple triangle, similar to the Greek Delta. However, nothing more than a superficial analysis can be made between these alphabets since there is no definitive evidence for where Agrippa derived them.

### Column L51-L53: AIK BKR Cipher, Royal Arch Masonic Cipher

The AIK BKR (איק בכר) cipher is loosely based on the Kabbalah of Nine Chambers, with its name based on the letters in the first two chambers. The chambers contain the 22 letters of the Hebrew Alphabet, plus the 5 final forms, yielding 27 letters, three in each square. Details are to be found in chapter XXX of Agrippa. Two versions of the Royal Arch Masonic cipher resemble this, but are based on the English alphabet instead.

---

[1] *Three Books of Occult Philosophy*, Llewellyn, St Paul, 1993, Book III, Chapter XXX.

Figure 16: Angel with the Keys of Hell releasing a demon, by Albrecht Durer.

# Commentary

## Table M. Magic of the Grimoires

The grimoires are the basic texts of practical magic, the books of the sorcerers, and the catalogues of spirits, angels and demons that they contain is the subject matter of Table M. In assembling this Table it became apparent where a lot of individual spirit names came from. With the exception of the *Goetia*, this tabulation of the demons of the classical grimoires has never been done before.

First let us consider the derivation of the word 'demon.' The word comes from *daimon* which was characterised by Homer as a divine being, but somewhat below a *theos* or god. Many Christian theologians have likewise looked upon demons as simply fallen angels.

Each person was thought to be allocated a Holy Guardian Angel at birth, so *daimons* were often associated with an individual, as in the case of Socrates' *daimon* who accompanied him during his lifetime. From the 5th century BC, this function was linked with luck, and so the lucky person was called *eudaimon* (i.e. with a good *daimon*) whilst the unlucky person was referred to as *kakodaimon* (that is, with a bad *daimon*). The Neoplatonists like Porphyry and Iamblichus accepted the existence of both good and bad *daimons*. Early Christian theologians tended to see good *daimons* as angels, and bad *daimons* as demons, the embodiment and provocation of evil. After the Middle Ages, in Europe *daimon* or demon was seen universally as bad, and the original meaning lost to sight. This view was finally fixed with the translation of the King James version of the Bible, in which all sorts of spiritual entities of quite different categories were simply rendered as 'devil'.

In this section I have drawn material from grimoires in roughly chronological order, so that the earlier tables are the oldest material. There is some duplication because each grimoire is based on the ones that have gone before. I have resisted the temptation of synthesising the correspondences, and have preferred to leave them in such a way that the historical development can still be plainly seen, and readers will be encouraged to consult such source texts as have been already printed.

I had intended to add in a table for the grimoire of *Armadel* which was translated by Mathers from manuscript Science et Arts 88, in the Bibliotheque de l'Arsenal in Paris, and published by Francis King in 1980. However on closer inspection this manuscript is so corrupt, and collated in a completely scrambled order, as to be worse than useless. Its contents derive from older grimoires which have already been documented, and so it does not contribute anything to our knowledge to tabulate it here. In fact it is likely to have been one of the forefather manuscripts of the grimoires used by Henri Gamache to generate those very scrambled Hoodoo classics, the *Sixth, Seventh and Eighth Books of Moses* so popular still in Nigeria, Ghana and Louisiana.

## *Testament of Solomon*

### Column M1-M6: Demons Bound by Solomon

This is one of the oldest spirit catalogues or grimoires, probably dating from the 3rd century AD. The Greek title of this oldest of grimoires calls the book:

> "The testament of [King] Solomon, Son of David, who reigned in Jerusalem, and subdued all the spirits of the air, of the earth, and under the earth; through (which) he also accomplished all the magnificent works of the Temple; what their authority [powers] are against men; and by what angels these demons are thwarted [bound]."

The demons referred to are the demons bound by King Solomon to help him in the construction of his famous temple. This construction is also the setting of the most important story of Freemasonry, that of Hiram Abif its Tyrian architect. Hiram would certainly have needed to know how to work alongside these demons. The most interesting Column is M4, as it shows the exact means of constraining each of the demons. This demonstrates the magical principle, which seems to have been mostly lost sight of, that the magician, of himself, cannot constrain such creatures. He needs to invoke another spiritual creature (such as an angel) and use that spiritual creature's authority to bind or constrain the demon. Once the demon is bound, then a contract or covenant can be negotiated with the demon to make it much easier for the magician next time.

Such a covenant is of the same nature as the covenant between Yahweh and Israel, although at a much lower level, rather than the one sided soul-hocking pact of popular Faustian demonology. The list of demons is an interesting mix of well known and very obscure names. The demons naturally fall into the following groups:

1-21 Demons forced by Solomon to work on the Temple, or simply imprisoned by him, some of which are named, some simply described. These include classical demons like Asmodeus who also appears in many later grimoires. Of these, numbers 6-12 are the demons of the seven stars of the constellation Pleiades, one of the 15 important magical constellations near Taurus (see Column H73).

22-23 Ephippas and Abezethibou, two very powerful demons that Solomon used to transport a great pillar from the Red Sea, the latter being the demon that also aided Pharaoh's magicians Jambres and Jannes against Aaron and Moses.

24-60 The demons of the 36 Decans. These are obviously from a different source, as they are mostly sickness demons, rather than the earlier ones who had more wide-ranging powers. See Columns H54 to H71 for more details of the Decans.

## Liber Juratus or the Sworn Book of Honorius

### Column M7: The 100 Holy Names of God

*Liber Juratus*, *Liber Sacer* (the 'Sacred Book') or as it is better known, the *Sworn Book* of Honorius of Thebes dates from around 1225 AD. This table is very interesting, not so much for the names of God *per se*, but because in analysing the names into their language of origin, it became obvious that the majority of the god names in this grimoire are from Greek roots, rather than Latin, Egyptian or even Hebraic roots. This confirms that the Thebes spoken of in the preamble to this grimoire as the home town of the author is Thebes in Greece rather than Thebes in Egypt. The mix of names also includes Christian ones like Paraclitus and pagan common nouns like Pantheon. The Names are meant to provide a wide selection for the use of the magician to enforce his commands to the angels or spirits. The number after each Name of God indicates the order they fall in the original Latin text. The orthography is that of Gösta Hedegård's Latin edition. The name in brackets is the variant found in Daniel Driscoll's edition of the *Sworn Book*.

### Column M8: The Angels of the Days of the Week

This Column give the names of the angels for each day of the week (and hence for each Planet) drawn from *Liber Juratus*.

### Column M9: The Angels of the Months

This Column gives the names of the angels for each month of the year drawn from *Liber Juratus*. Interestingly the months quoted are Hebraic months, and hence only approximate to the Zodiacal signs.

## Heptameron

### Column M10: Angels of the Days of the Week

This complex Column summarises the various angels of Peter de Abano's *Heptameron*. Interestingly, Abano correlates the angels with the 7 Heavens (see K69-K70). The 7-fold Planetary/day structure of this grimoire is echoed later in Dr Dee's *De Heptarchia Mystica*, both titles incorporation 'hepta-' or 'sevenfold'. It is often said that the *Heptameron* could not have been written by de Abano, because he was interested in 'proper' subjects like medicine. This is said by commentators who do not understand the mediaeval mindset where magic is as serious a part of the world view as astronomy or herbal medicine.

## Codex Latinus Monacensis

These tables are drawn from a nameless early 15th century Latin grimoire (manuscript CLM 849) edited by Richard Kieckhefer.[1]

---

[1] *Forbidden Rites: a Necromancer's Manual of the Fifteenth Century*, Sutton, Stroud, 1997.

## Column M11: List of Demons

An interesting list of spirits described as Kings, Dukes, Presidents, Marquises and Princes, a few of which, such as Volach and Curson/Purson, re-occur in the *Goetia*.

## Column M12: Angels of the Days of the Week

An 'heptarchical' listing of Angels and their Kings for every day of the week.

## Column M13-M14: Angels of the Hours of the Day and of the Night

A similar listing for angels designed to be evoked on particular Planetary hours.

## *Lemegeton*

The following set of tables are drawn from perhaps the best known grimoire of all, the *Lemegeton*. There are many editions of this work, but the most accurate, and thorough edition is that edited by Joseph Peterson.[1] The edition of Dr Rudd's copy of the *Goetia* contains much of the actual techniques of evocation.[2]

The *Lemegeton* (or *Lesser Clavicule of Solomon*) is divided into five parts:

  I)   *Goetia*
  II)  *Theurgia Goetia*
  III) *Pauline Art (Parts 1 & 2)*
  IV)  *Almadel*
  V)   *Ars Notoria* [not the *Ars Nova*]

The last part V may not always be present in copies of the *Lemegeton*. The following tables are drawn only from the first four books of the *Lemegeton*.

### *Goetia (Lemegeton Book I)*

## Column M15: Demons of the *Goetia*

This Column is drawn from the *Goetia*, the first of the books of the *Lemegeton*, which contains a catalogue of 72 demons. This material was shown in a much less organised and sketchy form in Crowley's *Liber 777*, in columns 155-166.

Column M15 spans both pages, and is organised by Zodiacal sign. The 72 demons are attributed in sequential order to the 12 Signs of the Zodiac in the first sub-column. When this is done, all of the Solar Kings fall neatly into one Zodiacal Sign each. The attribution of the 72 demons to the 12 Zodiacal signs seems most naturally to start at Aries, despite the Golden Dawn preference for Leo (examined in Table H). This attribution of the Kings to each sign of the Zodiac is also summarised in Column M18. Column M15 is divided into twelve sub-Columns as follows:

---

[1] Joseph Peterson, *The Lesser Key of Solomon*, Weiser, York Beach, 2001.
[2] Skinner & Rankine, *Dr Rudd's Goetia*, Golden Hoard Press, London & Singapore, 2007.

# Commentary

a. **Number.** The number of the demon in Weirus' list in *Pseudomonarchia Daemonum* (taken from Peterson's Appendix 2, rather than his Appendix 3 where the numbering differs in the case of demons 23-37 and 68). The number in square brackets is the number in Rudd's list in Harley MS 6482, ff. 28v-38.

b. **Number.** The standard numbering of the demon in Harley MS 6483, and also in all printed editions of the *Goetia*.

c. **Demon Name.** The demon's name with alternative spellings from various sources.

d. **Hebrew.** This is a very contentious and important facet, as the numerical value derived from these names may be of practical use in working with the demon, and in deciding its exact nature. The demon names listed here have been rendered into Hebrew by three different authorities. The first line in the Column is that of Dr Rudd. He used a rather simplistic letter for letter translation, for example, 'פה' has been used when 'פ' would have been more correct and perfectly adequate to render 'ph'. Note that Hebrew final letter forms were not generally used by Rudd, evidence of his lack of facility. The second version is that of Mathers as listed by Crowley, a version that also shows a lack of familiarity with that language. The third version is that favoured by the Aurum Solis. Where the versions agree a dash has been used to indicate this. Any attempt to reverse engineer the Hebrew names of the Goetic demons is fraught with pitfalls. Any numeration derived from these attempts is therefore *very* speculative, and so has not been included in the Third Edition.

In the manuscripts of the *Goetia* the demons' names are written in Latin characters, and so there is no certainty (except in a few cases) that they all had Hebrew equivalents. Some might in fact have been derived from Greek. Some may have originated in Latin. In one version of the *Goetia* it says at the end that:

> "These Books were first found in the Chaldee and Hebrew Tongues at Jerusalem by a Jewish Rabbi; and by him put into the Greek language and thence into Latin."

Assuming, for the moment, that this is true, it might make more sense to seek out orthography for each demon according to whether the name had Greek, Latin or Hebrew roots. This approach may be more reasonable than forcing Greek names into a Hebrew mould or vice versa. Certainly many of the names have Latin endings like Naberius or Andrealphus. Other like Ipos (Ayperos), Halphas, or Bathym are probably of Greek derivation. Others like Astaroth, Asmoday, Balam, and Bael are obviously of Hebraic, 'Chaldee', or Phoenician origin.

e. **Stead Ridden, Other Qualities.** This is important as senior demon rank is often indicated by the fact that the demon rides. Also included is the Ruling demon where known, the direction from which the demon will come, and the Sign (if mentioned in the text) which usually does not agree with either the first sub-column or GD Decanal attribution.

f. GD Decans. I do not believe that there is a clear association of the 72 demons with the 36 Decans of the Zodiac, at least not in the way Crowley and the Golden Dawn mapped it. There is no mention of this division in the original grimoire, and so this Decan correspondence is not certain. To make the 72 demons fit into the 36 Decans, they were rather clumsily repeated twice over by the Golden Dawn and most modern writers. Thus demons 1-Bael through to 36-Stolas were attributed to the day Decans of the 12 Zodiacal signs, beginning with Aries. Then demons 37-Phenex to 72-Andromalius were attributed to the 36 Decans of the night. This 'solution' seems to have been devised by Mathers for the Golden Dawn. The Aurum Solis proposed a different system using the Quinances and starting with Leo. But neither is a part of the original *Goetia* system. I have included the Golden Dawn Decan attribution in this sub-Column only for completeness, but I do not believe it is correct.

g. Ruling Shem ha-Mephorash Angel Name. In practice each demon needs to be considered alongside its corresponding Shem ha-Mephorash angel. These connections between angel and demon have been long standing, but they were probably first clearly documented, outside of Hebrew texts as matching pairs by Blaise de Vigenère and later Dr Thomas Rudd. [1] The Hebrew orthography used here is that of Rudd. This column uses Rudd's spelling for both the English and the Hebrew. It therefore does not quite agree with my standardised spelling of these angel names in Columns A24-A25.

h. Rank. There are at least seven demons with dual ranks in the *Goetia*. This leads me to believe that some confusion of rank has been introduced by copyists, and that there was originally probably one King for each Zodiacal Sign. There are however only 9 Kings (demons attributed to the Sun) clearly marked as such in the *Goetia*. One demon not marked as a King, but by any other criterion should rank as one, is Astaroth. Astaroth is most certainly a major ruling demon, as documented in many other sources, so I have added the title of King to his existing title of Duke. Decarabia is listed as a King in the original Latin text of Weir, but this title has not survived translation, accordingly I have revived it in this Column. Finally Gäap is shown with many kingly qualities, and in fact leads 4 kings. His name is also suspiciously close to Goap, King of the West, so I have added the title of King to his existing titles. All three 'new Kings' are marked in Column M18 by underlining. This then creates exactly one King per Zodiacal Sign. You can see easily how the rationale of this minor restoration works out in Column M18.

i. Planet. The attribution of the demons to the 7 Planets is quite clear in the *Goetia* as this is implied in their titles and also in the metals associated with these titles.

---

[1] Full instructions for utilising the Shem ha-Mephorash angels in Goetic evocations are given in Skinner & Rankine, *Dr Rudd's Goetia*, Golden Hoard Press, London and Singapore, 2006.

# Commentary

j. Number of Legions governed by each demon. See also Column M19.

k. Evoked Appearance. Crowley refers to the description of these demons very misleadingly (in his *Liber 777* columns 156-166) as 'Magical Images', as if they were similar to the Magical Images of the Decans. In fact they are not at all, for these descriptions are the usual initial evoked appearance of the 72 demons of the *Goetia*. These are listed so that the karcist may recognise a specific demon upon its arrival. Many of the descriptions state clearly that the demon will then change into a more suitable semi-human form if requested to do so.

l. Powers and Attributes. Lastly the powers and attributes of each demon are listed. These also appear in Column M16 ordered by power.

## Column M16: Powers and Specialities of the Demons of the *Goetia*

This Column lists the 72 Demons by their specialities and abilities, and should be useful in working out which demon to evoke for a particular purpose. This list was first compiled by Idries Shah in his *Secret Lore of Magic* many years ago, but has been here amplified considerably by returning to manuscript sources.

## Column M17: Ranks of the Demons of the *Goetia*

Note that in this edition Table M17 appears out of order before Table M15. M17 shows the correlation between demon Rank, Planet and metal. The metals corresponding to each Rank are shown clearly in the *Goetia*. It is interesting that Earls and Counts, who correspond with Mars do not have iron as their metal. This is because traditionally such demons fear that metal, and we are all familiar with the use of the iron sword to threaten demons, or to safely pass something beyond the circle bounds. In the past iron chains were sometimes used to form circles. See also M65 for Kings of the 4 Quarters.

## Column M18: The Demons of the *Goetia* by Rank, Planet and Zodiacal Sign

This key Column shows the individual demons of the *Goetia* according to their rank or Planet tabulated against the division by the 12 signs of the Zodiac. There are exactly 6 demons per Zodiacal Sign.

What shows up clearly are the 7 demons which originally have two ranks each in the text of the *Goetia*, together with the three demons now restored to dual rank. Where this occurs, one occurrence has been enclosed in brackets so as not to be included in the totals count at the bottom.

If we count Furcas as a Duke, that would result in 24 Dukes, giving exactly two Dukes per Sign. If that were the case, then the apportionment of spirits to planets would be somewhat more rational in Table M18: giving 24 Dukes (Venus), 12 Kings (Sun), 12 Marquises (Moon), 12 Presidents (Mercury), and with the remaining 12 made up of the other ranks (Mars & Jupiter). The attribution of these spirits in multiples of 12 now makes attribution to the 12 Zodiacal Signs, as well as to the planets, much more likely.

This correlation with the Zodiacal Signs definitely makes more sense than the Golden Dawn or Aurum Solis use of Decans and Quinances.

### Column M19: Demons of the *Goetia* by Title, Planet and Legion Numbers

The number of legions commanded by the demon may be just that, or it may have a numerical significance relating to the nature of the demon. It is interesting that most of the Marquises have 30 legions, whilst most of the Kings have large legions. Gaap with 66 legions, was therefore a likely candidate for Kingship.

*Theurgia Goetia (Lemegeton Book II)*

### Column M20-M21: Good and Evil Aerial Spirits of the Compass

This Column is drawn from the second of the books of the *Lemegeton*, the *Theurgia-Goetia*. These spirits are in turn derived from Book I of Trithemius' *Steganographia*, where the invocations contain the names of the lesser spirits listed in the last sub-column of Column M20. The order the spirits are listed in is however subtly changed. The emphasis here is upon compass direction, which is shown in the fourth sub-column of Column M20. The Emperors of the Good and Evil Aerial Spirits are listed in Column M21, where they rule the four cardinal points of the compass and vast numbers of Dukes, ministering spirits and servants.

These Columns will also act as a key to Book I of Trithemius' *Steganographia*.

*Ars Paulina (Lemegeton Book III)*

### Column M22: Spirits of the Hours from *Ars Paulina (Lemegeton III - 1)*

This Column is drawn from the third book of the *Lemegeton*, the *Ars Paulina*, and lists the spirits of the hours. The first 12 are spirits of the day, the second 12 are spirits of the night. There is no consistency in numbers of Dukes named. In each case the Lesser or Second degree Dukes are marked out by curly braces. This Column will also act as a key to Book II of Trithemius' *Steganographia*.

### Column M23: Angels of the Degrees of Zodiac from *Ars Paulina (Lemegeton III - 2)*

This Column is also drawn from the third of the books of the *Lemegeton*, the *Ars Paulina*, and lists the spirits of each degree of the Zodiac. The numbers along the second header row are degrees, and are to be read in conjunction with the Zodiacal signs down the left hand edge of the Table.

*Ars Almadel (Lemegeton Book IV)*

### Column M24: Angels of the Altitudes (*Choras*)

This Column is drawn from the fourth of the books of the *Lemegeton*, the *Ars Almadel*. I have not derived any tables from Book V of the *Lemegeton*.

# Commentary

## Key of Solomon

### Column M25: Hours of the Day and Night from *Key of Solomon*

Simple angel, day and hour correspondences from the *Key of Solomon* and Trithemius' *Art of Drawing Spirits into Crystals.*

## Sacred Magic of Abramelin the Mage

Mathers did the occult world a great service by discovering the French manuscript, and translating it into English at the end of the nineteenth century. However a hundred years later it has been realised that the French manuscript was incomplete, particularly in the matter of the completeness of its all-important magical squares, and earlier and more complete German manuscripts have been uncovered and published in German. A new edition of this important grimoire was published in English in 2006. [1]

### Column M26: Servient Spirits from *Abramelin*

This Column list the spirits conjured by Abramelin according to their ruler. The publication of the Dehn version drawn from German manuscript sources helps to show the logic behind these grouping. The spirits have been divided according to their ruler. Before reading this column you should look at Column M27. In the light of this, the groups have been divided by slightly bolder horizontal rulings. The first two groups are concerned solely with the rulership of the Princes of the 4 Quarters, and groups 9-12 take each Prince of the Quarters individually. Groups 5-8 are purely the province of the 4 non-directional Princes, and groups 3-4 are the same Princes but in combination.

Strangely the Greek goddess of the underworld, Koré, was introduced as a ruler into the fifth group, by Mathers. In fact she is just one of the ordinary spirits in Magot's group, and should not have been shown by Mathers as ruling.

With regard to the number of spirits listed, there is a discrepancy between the total listed by Mathers of 416 and the total listed by Dehn of 411. The numbers in square brackets are Dehn's totals, where they differ from Mathers. The Dehn arrangement has not been separately tabulated. These totals may be random, but are more likely to betray the existence of an underlying structure in the source from which Abramelin drew his information. For example in the first row of Column M26 you find 111 (114 in Dehn) spirits ruled jointly by the 4 Sub-Princes of the 4 Quarters, this suggests that it may originally have been a system grouped by the 28 Mansions of the Moon, as 4 x 28 = 112. Likewise, the 49 spirits of Belzebud (*sic*) may have originally been 7 x 7 planetary spirits, an Heptarchical system, and the 12 spirits of Astaroth may have been zodiacal.

---

[1] Georg Dehn (translated by Steven Guth), *The Book of Abramelin*, Ibis, Lake Worth, 2006.

### Column M27: Hierarchy of the Abramelin Demons

The structure is more clearly laid out in the Dehn version. The Princes are called Kings in the Dehn version: Lucifer, Leviathan, Satan, and Belial. The Sub-Princes are called Dukes in the Dehn version, and fall into two categories. The first four Dukes are Astaroth, Asmodi, Magoth and Beelzebub. The second four Dukes are the four traditional demon Princes which rule the four Quarters of the world: Oriens, Ariton, Paymon, and Amaymon.

The attribution of the Elements to the Kings and Dukes is tentative, and does not specifically appear in Abramelin.

*Magical Equipment Objectives and Abilities*

### Column M27a: Grimoire Magical Equipment

A more practical listing of the equipment of evocation than Column O34.

### Column M28: Abramelin Magical Operations

This shows the various types of operations outlined by Abramelin categorised by Zodiac, Element and Planet. This table also gives the chapter numbers in the Mathers' edition for ease of reference.

### Column M29: Magical Objectives and Abilities

This division is fairly tentative, and many other magical skills could have been added in. Some attributions are very apt like the compounding of Love-philtres to Venus, or works of wrath to Mars, but some are less so, like the tongue-in-cheek attribution of Invisibility to Virgo.

*Franz Bardon – Practice of Magical Evocation*

### Column M30: Franz Bardon's Spirit Hierarchy

Bardon drew many of his spirit names silently and without acknowledgement from the German text of Abramelin edited by Peter Hammer,[1] specifically his Zodiacal Spirits and his Spirits of Air. His other spirits he drew from Agrippa, the list of the fixed stars, and the Shem ha-Mephoresh angels, sometimes encoding them with a simple alphabet replacement code, sometimes just copying them as they appear in the original source. 'Mars spirits' for example were actually spirits of the Decans, and you can easily verify this by looking for example at Skorpia (which is the spirit of the first Decan of Scorpio, or Sagitor (which is the spirit of the first Decan of Sagittarius): from their names they obviously relate to the Zodiacal signs Scorpio and Sagittarius. Neither of them are Mars spirits by any stretch of the imagination. The perplexing thing is

---

[1] Peter Hammer, *Die egyptischen großen Offenbarung, in sich ...* Köln 1725. Reprinted by J. Scheible, Stuttgart, ca. 1850.

that although Bardon undoubtedly knew their origins, he mixed up their planetary attributions, so one use of this Table is to show where he really derived his spirit names from. An example of this is his use of the 12 Zodiacal spirits as 'Jupiterian' spirits. Or his use of the names of the Fixed stars in an enciphered form as 'Spirits of the Sun.' He attributed the 72 Shem ha-Mephoresh angels to Mercury. His source for these was *Die Adonistich Denurische Kabbalistik* by 'Rah Omir',[1] a text promoting a new Adonis-centred religion. However his instructions in practical evocatory technique are amongst the clearest written in the 20th century.

## Planetary Spirits & Intelligences

### Column M31: Magical Squares of the Planets – Key Numbers

The magic squares of the Planets are most important as they are the means of generating various sigils. As these squares are already tabular, I have contented myself with simply listing the number of squares, sides and rows in each square, in summary form. These numbers are in themselves suggestive, the number of squares being obviously the square of the number of the corresponding Sephiroth of the Planet in question. In the column showing the sum of all the numbers in the square the most striking is 666 shown as the sum of the numbers in the square of the Sun, but the other numbers also have a numerological significance. The number 666 is famous from *Revelations* chapter 13:18 where St John writes:

> "Here is wisdom. Let him that hath understanding count the number of the Beast: for it is the number of a man; and his number is Six hundred three score and six."

I am sure that Aleister Crowley would have noticed the Kabbalistic implications:

> "Here is Wisdom (Chokmah = 2). Let him that hath Understanding (Binah = 3) count the number of the Beast (2 x 3 = Tiphareth = 6): for it is the number of a man (111) ; and his number is Six hundred three score and six (6 x 111 = 666)."

### Column M32-M35: Intelligences of the Planets

These Intelligences are benevolent, as opposed to the Spirits of the Planets, who may act malevolently as well. The correct numeration of these creatures is important, and it is derived from the numbers of the Kameas. Intelligence is an old term which was equivalent to 'angel', as well as implying a cogent deductive faculty.

The Hebrew words for the Intelligence of the Intelligences of the Moon have provoked a number of possible interpretations. The Hebrew orthography is usually shown as מלכא ב-תרשישים ועד ב-רוח שחקים but this only adds to

---

[1] Friedrich Wilhelm Quintscher, (1883-1945).

3221, which then has to be fudged. But with just one letter changed the correct Luna total of 3321 is reached with מלכא ב-תרשישים ועד ב-רוח שהרים. The pronunciation then becomes Malkah Be-Tarshishim ve-ad be-Ruah Sheharim.

The revised word 'sheharim' means *lunulas* or round ornaments like little moons. The whole name now roughly translates as the 'Queen of Chrysolite and watery moon discs' which has a much more relevant meaning than other suggested translations. Of course to support this reading MLKA would have to be read as MLKH, Queen. Note how the numeration of the Hebrew in Columns M35 and M39 ties in with the arithmetic of Column M31.

### Column M36-M39: Spirits of the Planets

These spiritual creatures may act malevolently or neutrally. The correct numeration of these creatures is important. The most famous is perhaps the Mercurial spirit called Taphthartharath, who was subject to a full invocation by Golden Dawn members including Allan Bennett, Florence Farr, F L Gardner and other leading lights of that organisation, and which was written up in Crowley's *Equinox* Vol. 1, No. 3.

### Column M40: The Familiar Shapes of the Planetary Spirits

This and the next Column are important traditional tables drawn from Agrippa.[1]

### Column M41: The Visible Appearance of the Planetary Spirits

These descriptions are useful in determining if the right spirit has responded, and in deciding its rank. For example Crowned spirits are usually Kings, those with a crest or a plume are Dukes, those with a horn are Earls (sometimes quaintly expressed as 'Country'), whilst other ranks hold sceptres, swords or forked wands. Those spirits riding on an animal, like a bear or a dromedary, usually have a higher rank than those on foot. These attributions helped to discover spirits whose rank has changed due to transcriptional errors, for example Decarabia.

### *Olympic Spirits*

### Column M42-M47: Olympic Spirits

The Olympic Spirits come from the *Arbatel*[2], although their origin considerably predates that book. They are primarily Planetary Spirits. These are quite important spirits and were a much stronger part of the German magical tradition than the English magical tradition. The clue to their nature is in the word 'Olympic' meaning from Olympus (nothing to do with games). They are in fact Greek Planetary spirits. Several writers have attempted to put their

---

[1] Agrippa, *Fourth Book of Occult Philosophy*, Ibis Press, Berwick, 2005, pages 30-34.
[2] Published in Agrippa, *Fourth Book of Occult Philosophy*, Ibis Press, Berwick, 2005, page 145-153.

names into Hebrew with little success, as cursory inspection will show that they are obviously Greek names. I have accordingly restored their Greek names. Their numeration is as follows:

| | | |
|---|---|---|
| Hagith = | 31 = | 1 x 31 |
| Bethor = | 186 = | 6 x 31 |
| Och = | 465 = | 15 x 31 |
| Araithron = | 341 = | 11 x 31 |
| Phaleg = | 558 = | 18 x 31 |
| Ophiel = | 620 = | 20 x 31 |
| Phul = | 930 = | 30 x 31 |

Immediately a pattern becomes obvious, confirming the accuracy of the orthography. All the names are based on 31 or αλ 'AL' in Greek, and are therefore a carefully constructed formula, not just random mediaeval names, as most people previously assumed. Even the grand total of all the values comes to 3131. The Greek names of the Olympic Spirits also form a key to Crowley's *Liber AL vel Legis*, although one of which Crowley was perhaps not aware, a key that I do not believe has been published by anyone else to date. I intend to postpone the explanation of that material to a later time. Suffice it to say that they are a significant key to *Liber AL vel Legis*.

Furthermore, the multiples of 31 are in themselves significant. Apart from the factors 15, 20, and 30, the remaining factors form a significant Middle Pillar formula:

1 + 6 +11 = 18, can be interpreted as Kether + Tiphareth + Daath = *ih* (10 + 8) or Arrow (in Greek). The path so traced out is indeed the Path of the Arrow. The key numbers for these Spirits are therefore:

| | | | |
|---|---|---|---|
| Hagith = | 1 | Och = | 15 |
| Bethor = | 6 | Ophiel = | 20 |
| Araithron = | 11 | Phul = | 30 |
| Phaleg = | 18 | | |

## Column M48-M50: Olympic Spirits – Powers & Attributes, Days & Years

These Columns come from the *Arbatel* in Agrippa's *Fourth Book of Occult Philosophy.*

### *Elementals*

The last category of spirits listed here are the Elementals. Franz Bardon gives excellent instruction in the method of their use.

## Column M51: Hebrew Names of the Elements

## Column M52: Bodily Humours and Qualities

## Column M53-M56: Traditional Kings and Rulers of the 4 Elements

### Column M57-M59: Angels of the 4 Elements

### Column M60: Traditional Names of the Elementals

Names to be principally found in folktales and fairytales, but nonetheless valid.

### Column M61: Enochian Elemental Kings

Drawn from Dr John Dee's Tables. See also Table D.

## Four Quarters and the Demon Kings

### Column M62-M64: Demon Kings and Princes of the 4 Elements

There is some difference of opinion about the directional attribution of these Kings, and these have been laid out according to the source.

### Column M65-M66: Cardinal Directions and Winds of the 4 Quarters

### Column M67: Rivers of Hell [1]

### Column M68: The 4 Kerubs

These were used to represent the 4 Apostles in Christian art of the Middle Ages

## Grimorium Verum

### Column M69: Demons of the Grimorium Verum

The earliest edition of the Grimorium Verum is dated 1517, but is more likely to have been actually printed in 1617.

## Grand Grimoire

### Column M70: Demons of the Grand Grimoire[2]

Other derivative grimoires include the Secret Grimoire of Turiel (which was taken from de Abano's Heptameron) and the Grimoire of Armadel, which was translated by MacGregor Mathers and later edited by Francis King. The Armadel, despite its nice coloured seals, is however hopelessly scrambled. The Sixth and Seventh Books of Moses (1849) were drawn from Das Kloster. Henri Gamache's Mystery of the Long Lost 8th, 9th and 10th Books of Moses, are still popular grimoires amongst the Hoodoo and Afro-Caribbean communities.

## Faust – Höllenzwang

### Column M71: Demons of Faust's Dreifacher Höllenzwang.

The Faustian cycle of grimoires and demons never really became popular in the English speaking world, despite E. M. Butler's excellent study.

---

[1] See also Column C14.
[2] See Darcy Kuntz, The Grand Grimoire, Holmes, 2005.

## *Trithemius - Steganographia*

### Column M72: Planetary Angels and Spirits of the *Steganographia* Book III.

## *Papyri Graecae Magicae (PGM)*

The following columns are drawn from Skinner, *Techniques of Graeco-Egyptian Magic,* Golden Hoard, 2014.

### Column M73: Graeco-Egyptian Magic – headwords and types

These are the 40+ categories into which the operations recorded in the *PGM* can be divided, along with the specific Greek headwords used to make this division.

### Column M74: Graeco-Egyptian Magic - *nomina magica*

This is a selection of *nomina magica* from the *PGM*. They are not, as many modern commentators suggest, just nonsense words. Most of the *nomina magica* recorded in this table are actually the names of daimones or gods.

# Table N: Natural Magic

This Table contains the magic of correspondences between natural things, the magic of Albertus Magnus, della Porta and Agrippa. The correlation between naturally occurring substances, like roots, leaves and stones (semi-precious or otherwise) under the headings of the Zodiac, Elements and Planets is at the root of all sympathetic magical correspondences. The ZEP order is very important in understanding the grouping of this Table. It is impossible in the space to justify every single attribution, and so only a few random highlights have been picked out.

## Animals

### Column N1: Animals – Real

The first animal listed against each of the ten Sephiroth is the attribution given by Agrippa, who is on the whole more reliable than Crowley in matters of symbolic animals. Of these only the bull for Yesod is contentious, although that has been rectified by replacing it with the cow.

Crowley, in his notes to *Liber 777*, attributes Draco the dragon to the Unmanifest row zero. I have instead placed the dragon amongst imaginary animals (Column N2), and as a constellation in Table H72.

The hawk, as the highest flying animal has some claim to being placed in Kether. Among Egyptian gods, the Horus hawk could be considered the symbol of the highest manifestation of Godhead, but it fits more comfortably as a symbol of Horus in Geburah. The crocodile is obviously Saturnian, as it is a devourer of corpses, but the attribution is more appropriate to the Underworld, or the Path of Saturn, rather than to the Sephiroth.

The horse is sacred to Mars on account of its use in war. The bear is martial because of its great strength and savagery. The wolf is sacred to Mars also because of his savage nature, and its suckling of Romulus and Remus, the founders of Rome, whose devotion to Mars is well known.

The lion is a typically solar animal and hence suitable for Tiphareth. Crowley places the spider in Tiphareth, as he visualised it geometrically in the centre of the web of the Tree of Life, but this is an overly-intellectual association and out of tune with the actual nature of Tiphareth. Like the bee (in its capacity as a stinging insect) the spider is more appropriate to Scorpio. The lamb pertains to Tiphareth as the sacrificed god, Christ, Attis or Osiris, but also to Malkuth in the pastoral sense.

The sow is appropriate to Venus as it is the female opposite of the boar of Mars. The boar is martial, as shown in the legend of Adonis. Mercury has an hermaphrodite nature, but listing the hermaphrodite as an 'animal' of

# Commentary

Mercury makes little sense. The jackal is the sacred animal of Anubis and so fits here. Mercury and medicine are symbolised by the double serpent Caduceus wand. The bee is associated with sweetness and honey and so might be appropriate to Venus, but the bee is also a Rosicrucian symbol for stored up wisdom, and in this capacity is appropriate to Mercury. As a stinging creature it also fits with Scorpio, but this is less important. The ape is sacred to Thoth and hence also to Mercury. The fox fits on Hod because of its sagacity. All fish are sacred to Mercury because of the iridescent mercurial colours of their scales, but at the level of a Path rather than the Sephirah Hod.

The dog is the companion of the huntress Artemis, and hence fits with both the Moon and Yesod. The elephant is sacred to Ganesha, the god who breaks down obstacles. The elephant, in the sense of holding the world on its back, is also a fit symbol of Yesod (the Foundation) with the tortoise supporting it in Malkuth. The tortoise also fits Saturn because of its Chinese *lo shu* magical square association. The toad fits with Yesod and the moon because of its witchcraft and lunar astral associations.

The four Kerubs are the four animals of the Elements: Lion for Fire, Man for Air, Bull for Earth. The Eagle-Snake-Scorpion Kerub resonates with Water.

Of the Zodiacal signs, the most obvious associations are the animals of the signs themselves, so the ram is the symbol of Aries, the crab is the symbol of Cancer and so on.

The lion is the typical animal of Sol, and via its rulership, and its image, is most appropriate to Leo. The cat and tiger likewise happily fit on Leo.

In the Chinese twelve Animal cycle, the ox is sometime replaced by the rhinoceros, so this animal fits in Taurus. It was often portrayed as if its skin was made of armour (by Durer) and so it may also be attributed to Mars.

The elephant may be appropriate to Libra because of its stability and equilibrium, but is much more relevant as the foundation in Yesod.

Scorpio means scorpion and so that creature, plus all stinging creatures go with that sign. The Khephra beetle is also attributed to Scorpio on account of it association with transmutation and putrefaction. All reptiles, the spider and the bee, may be placed here because of their venomous sting. The lobster and crayfish are sometimes placed here because they are superficially 'water scorpions'.

Capricorn is portrayed as a goat with a fish's tail, so both these animals are associated with this sign. The goat, the ass and the oyster are traditionally associated with libidinous behaviour, and so they all fit well under Capricorn.

Pisces is obviously the fish. The dolphin, an aquatic mammal also pertains to Pisces.

## Column N2: Animals - Imaginary and Legendary Orders of Being

As a joke Crowley attributed God to row 1, and Man and Woman to lines 2 and 3. This only really works in the context of the Garden of Eden, and would only be complete if the Serpent and the Angel with the Flaming Sword were also included in this table.

The Unicorn is only Jupiterean via its connection with the horse of Sagittarius, and so this is too fragile a correspondence. It is more significant as an heraldic animal or in its Romance connection. *Monoceros de Astris*, the 'Unicorn from the Stars,' is given as the symbolical title of a Practicus Grade which corresponds with Hod, so this is where it has been placed. It also has a place in Virgo, because of its associations with virginity.

Succubi are appropriate to Venus because of their sexual proclivities, although they could also be attributed to the Moon for the same reason.

The centaur, half-horse half man, is traditionally connected with archery and hence Sagittarius. The hippogriff also has some of the eagle of Jupiter about it, as it is the offspring of a griffin (part eagle) and a mare, so it has also been placed in Chesed.

## Column N3: Birds

The basic list of Zodiacal birds is drawn from Agrippa whose attributions have been given more prominence[1]. The pelican is an alchemic and Rosicrucian symbol, feeding its children with its own blood.

The peacock might be referred to Tiphareth (or even to Mercury) on account of its plumage. The vision of the Universal Peacock is also connected with the Beatific Vision, in which the Universe is perceived fractally as a whole in every part.

The swallow for its swiftness is associated with Mercury. The ibis is sacred to Thoth and hence to Mercury. The hawk is solar as all-seeing like the sun. The eagle is the sacred bird of Jupiter.

The sparrow, swan and dove are particularly sacred to Venus. The iynx or wryneck is connected with Aphrodite. Iynx used magic to make Zeus fall in love with her. Hera was furious and transformed her into the wryneck bird. This bird was also used in early Greek love-magic. The raven and carrion birds should not be attributed to Venus just because Netzach translates as 'Victory', but there is a case for attributing the raven to Saturn following Edgar Allen Poe. More importantly the raven was the symbol of the Mithraic grade of Corax which corresponds to Mercury.

The white stork is associated with childbirth in fairy tales and so goes with Yesod. The owl is sacred to Aries as the bird of Minerva.

---

[1] Agrippa, *Three Books of Occult Philosophy*, Llewellyn, St Paul, 1993, pages 274-5, 296-7.

# Commentary

## *Plants*

### Column N4: Extended Plants Planetary Correspondences

This is a fuller and less selective listing of plant associations than Column N5. It is useful in understanding early herbal medicine, the Doctrine of Signatures especially, which influenced early herbal medicine and the attribution of individual plants.

### Column N5: Plants

The first plant listed for each of the 12 Zodiacal signs is the attribution given by Agrippa, on the whole more reliable than Crowley in matters of symbolic plants.[1] Other plants listed amongst the Zodiacal signs are quoted by Agrippa from Apuleius. The rest are more speculative, and only a few highlights will be commented upon.

Crowley attributed the lotus and rose to the Unmanifest on very shaky grounds. The rose fits in Tiphareth because of the Rosicrucian symbolism. The lotus Crowley puts in Water and Cancer, but its Buddhist symbolism of enlightenment (with its roots in the earth, body in the water, and flower in the air) clearly makes it a Middle Pillar plant. I have placed it in Tiphareth for this reason. The grape also goes here for its Bacchic qualities.

The peach belongs to Netzach and Venus because it is a Chinese symbol for the female sex organ.

The mistletoe fits in Yesod and the Moon for its druidic associations. For the same reason the oak is attributed to Tiphareth. The oak is also Jupiterian. The vine goes into Malkuth, for no matter how high it climbs it is still rooted in earth.

### Column N6: Vegetable and Synthetic Drugs

LSD is attributed to Sephiroth on the Middle Pillar for its ability to induce a rising on the planes trip, and finally to Kether because of its ability to induce complete ego loss. LSD is capable of giving visions of the direct path, the flight up the Middle Path passing through Yesod and Tiphareth to Daath and the complete ego loss of Kether.

I feel that Crowley attributes hashish far too high up the tree, and a 'widening of mental horizons' philosophic drug like ether is more appropriate there.

Coffee as an intellectual stimulant and fits easily in Hod rather than Tiphareth. Cocaine, methedrine and caffeine also fit in Hod in their most intellectual and incisive modes. Anhalonium Lewinii is too rich and visual a drug to fit anywhere but Yesod or Netzach.

---

[1] Agrippa, *Three Books of Occult Philosophy*, Llewellyn, St Paul, 1993, page 296-7.

Cannabis is appropriate to the lunar dreams of Yesod, and in a sense also belongs to Malkuth for its effect upon the sensual appetites.

### Column N7: The 16 Traditional Magical Plants of Albertus Magnus.

These are listed because they form a list of the fundamental herbs of the period, with their name in four languages as understood in the late Middle Ages. The 33 magical properties of each herb is listed as a very condensed indication only, and it omits the precise procedure and preparation.

## Precious Stones and Metals

### Column N8: Precious and Semi-Precious Stones

The first stone listed for each of the 12 Zodiacal signs is the attribution given by Agrippa, on the whole more reliable than Crowley in matters of symbolic stones. Crowley's attribution in his notes attributes the Star Sapphire (because of its Islamic reputation) and the Black Diamond to row zero, but these seem altogether too bold. In the Zodiacal section the first two stones are the traditional Zodiacal gems. The first named is found in ancient Hebrew, Roman or Arabic lists. Stones with rather too far-fetched connections, such as the attribution of jacinth to Sagittarius, have been omitted.

### Column N9: Metals and Minerals

Crowley allocates Carbon to the zero row, in the sense that carbon might be the basis of all life. Kether is a possible position on the Tree for that element, both in its guise as a diamond, and as pitch black coal.

*Aurum Potabile* is the drinkable gold of the alchemists which is supposed to be a universal medicine, hence its attribution to Kether.

Strangely Crowley attributes lead to Luna, but a much more convincing attribution is lead to its own planet Saturn. Silver is obviously more appropriate for the Sphere of the Moon. See also the alchemy Column E4.

### Column N9a Rocks, Metals and Semi-precious stones according to the *Picatrix*.

This is a new Column, which did not appear in the First Edition.

### Column N10: The Stones of the High Priest's Breastplate

This device was a lamen studded with 12 precious stones, representing the 12 tribes of Israel. Its prime function was to protect the High Priest from the sometimes deadly energies of the Ark of the Covenant. It is interesting that the covenant between god and the Hebraic people was so central to their faith that it was preserved in such splendour.

The first three stones formed the top row (counting left to right), stones 4-6 formed the second row, and so on. Some authorities suggest that the emerald and the carbuncle should be reversed. The details of the Breastplate's construction are clearly set out twice in *Exodus* 28:13-30 and 39:8-21.

On a much smaller scale is the Breastplate used by 17th century magicians such as Dr Thomas Rudd to protect themselves against the 72 demons of the *Goetia*. The modern and pale reflection of both of these is the parchment lamen worn on the chest and sometimes held before the eyes to provide similar protection during evocation. The stones of the High Priests Breastplate are therefore of more than historical interest to the practicing magician. There are many ways of listing them, and many interpretations of what the stones are in modern nomenclature. The attribution to the Tribes is one of several attributions. Even the *Bible* has different orderings and is not internally consistent.

## Perfumes & Incenses

### Column N11: Perfumes and Incenses

The heady suffumigations of ceremonial magic should be chosen with care, and matched with the type of force being invoked or evoked. Unfortunately modern man no longer has a nose for the subtle distinction between these incenses and perfumes, or a sensitivity to exactly what magical environment will be created by the heating of a particular resin. Such an appreciation is important to magic. A reading of J K Huysmans *A Rebours (Against Nature)* or Patrick Suskind's *Perfume* may do something to rectify this lack of appreciation. Note that different modes of heating (burning, melting, steaming or boiling) a particular resin or oil give very different results.

Despite Crowley's attribution of tobacco to Geburah, I do not feel that tobacco is a perfume in any sense, but should instead be listed under drugs. Cinnamon has the biting quality of Geburah and Dragon's Blood its colour. Nor is menstrual blood, attributed to the Moon by Crowley, a perfume in the same sense as the other perfumes in this Column. Wormwood is not a perfume either, but a herb or a drug.

In the list of 12 Zodiac signs, the first perfume listed is the most important attribution, being drawn from Agrippa and *Liber Juratus*. The second part of this Column are planetary incenses suggested by David Conway.

### Column N12-N14: Zodiacal Perfumes of the Decans

The Decans are divided into Ascendant, Succedent and Cadent Decans. For more information on the Decans, see Table H54-H71.

### Column N15: Planetary Perfume Compounds

These are the traditional mediaeval recipes for the most important planetary incenses. Although there are many proprietary brands of planetary incense, few actually include all the ingredients as prescribed, and will substitute other things, often just simple church incense, so it is good to either compound it yourself, or to buy from a reliable supplier such as Peacock Angel.

Traditionally an animal's blood was introduced to bind the incense. This also then acted as a sort of sacrifice – something no longer considered acceptable today. Remember that Jewish practice, as documented in the *Bible*, involved extensive sacrifice of animals in the temple, and so it was only natural that this procedure also found a place in magic.

Strangely these Biblical passages remain un-excised, whilst orthodox practice no longer countenances such sacrifices. I would not like to encourage cruelty or the senseless killing of innocent animals, and suggest some other binder in the form of a liquid resin is used. I strongly suggest that you do not use your own blood for this purpose, as has been suggested by various writers, because of the implications of sacrificing yourself to the entity being invoked.

### Column N16: Complete Perfumes from *Liber Juratus*

This duplicates some of the material in Column N11, but it is included to demonstrate the range of perfumes, antiquity and consistency of these recipes. This example is drawn from *Liber Juratus*, a grimoire of the early 13th century. The spelling has deliberately not been modernised, so you get the full impact of reading an early grimoire.

### Column N17: Perfumes of the Sub-Elements

These are the perfumes of the combinations of one of the five Elements with each of the others as listed by Crowley. The Element listed in the column on the left is the base Element, and the Element listed across the top is the sub or tincture Element. It is suggestive to select one Element and read its full column and its full line together. The 'gall of the rukh' is a fictional perfume suggested by Crowley, designed to suggest the ultimate in Air, based on the huge fictional bird in the story of *Sinbad the Sailor* from the *1001 Arabian Nights*.

### Column N18: Fumigations from the *Mystical Hymns of Orpheus*

This Table lists the perfumes that were regularly used for ancient Greek Orphic rites as listed in Thomas Taylor's translation of the *Mystical Hymns of Orpheus*. Very useful if invoking the Greek gods.

### Column N19: Incense from the Greek Magical Papyri

This Column, taken from *PGM* XIII lines 17-22, contains very traditional incenses.

### Column N20: Perfumes and their Associated Plants

This column is a key to interpreting traditional perfumery names, which are here shown with their botanical source. This is useful in tracking them down.

### Column N21: Incenses in the *Book of Jubilees* and the *PGM*.

### Column N22: Magical Ingredient Codenames from the *PGM*.

Figure 17: Masonic Grades: York and Scottish Rites in 19th century US.

# Table O. Orders, Grades and Officers

This Table shows the various grade structures used by a selection of religious, occult, Masonic and magical groups, from early Mithraic grades in use two millennium ago to the most modern magical fraternity of the 21st century. Freemasonry columns predominate, because of the close connection between Freemasons and founders of magical fraternities like the Golden Dawn. From this Table you can see how the vividly inflated titles of Freemasonry have rubbed off on the occult tradition.

## *Mithraic Grades*

### Column O1-O5a: Mithraic Initiation Grades and their Greek Numeration

As far as I know, nobody has noticed the regularity of the numeration of the Grade names in the Mithraic initiations. In listing these, I have corrected a few of Walter Moeller's numerations.[1] I have used Leo rather than Leontica, and Sotern rather than Pater. The results are extraordinary and will repay further research.

The key is the number 129, which might well be a secret numeration of Mithra. It is certainly the key to Mithraic planetary initiation grades. The arithmetic difference between the numerations of many of the Grades, well beyond the level of coincidence, comes out again and again to this figure, for example:

| | | | | |
|---|---|---|---|---|
| Mercury – Jupiter | = | Corax – Leo | = 129 |
| Mars – Venus | = | Miles – Nymphus | = 129 |
| Sol – Venus | = | Heliodromus – Nymphus | = 129 |
| Saturn – Moon | = | Pater/Sotern – Perses | = 129 |
| Earth – Saturn | = | Mystes - Pater/Sotern | = 129 |

This is not just fantasy, as it can be clearly seen from the fact that these otherwise disparate and unconnected words were used specifically on account of their Greek numeration. It also explains why such strange Grade names were used, as they do not appear to make up a logical set.

It is such patterns as this, where Gematria can be used to validate ancient terminology, that are a much more valid and wide-ranging use of Gematria than the modern penchant for idly equating two words together which just happen to have the same numeration. For numerations to be usable they need to be either well attested in ancient authorities, or be part of a pattern as they are here.

Another example validating the Mithraic numeration of 129 is as follows. The constellation of the Bull (Taurus) corresponds to the Greek letter *digamma*. This letter is obsolete, or hidden if you like. If you add Mithra to the Bull (129 + 6) you get *doxa* or 'glory and honour' very important concepts in the context

---

[1] *Etudes Preliminaires aux Religions Orientales dans L'Empire Romain*, Tome 38, 1973.

of Mithraism, which mainly appealed to, and was spread by, the Roman legions. Another clue to the real identity of Mithra is that grade 'Perses' is not just any 'soldier'. He is specifically the son of Perseus, the hero. This is the name given to the constellation in the sky just above Taurus the Bull. You may remember that the key story about Mithras is that he slayed the bull, so here in the sky is the constellation of Perseus 'kneeling on' the Bull, whilst together their numeration equates with the soldierly qualities of 'glory and honour'.

For another example of the serious use of Gematria to reconstruct ancient mysteries, look at Columns M42-M47 on the Olympic Spirits, which have now been proven (using this technique) to be a definite and coherent series of planetary spirits of Greek origin, not just some arbitrary invention of some 16th century writer.

The Mithraic images of dog, snake, lion, raven, cup, snake and the two torchbearers in Column O5a, are very clearly associated with constellations closer to the horizon, but adjacent to the familiar twelve Zodiac signs. Interestingly the last four signs of the Zodiac are not represented at all in the Mithraic mythos. This imagery does not rely upon speculative modern written sources, but can be readily seen in actual Mithraeums throughout Europe.

The contrast between Fire (Leo) and Water (Nymphus) formed an integral part of the rites. The Miles (Mars - soldier degree) emphasises the coming forth into light. The Moon (Perses) is also contrasted with the Sun (Heliodromus). The 'Persian dagger' used to symbolise Perses is the curved sword (or *harpe*) that Perseus used to decapitate the Gorgon.

## Hermetic Order of the Golden Dawn

### Column O6-O8: Grades of the Hermetic Order of the Golden Dawn

The Golden Dawn grades divide into three separate Orders, a pattern that Crowley followed in the A.'.A.'. The First Order was all that was outlined in the Golden Dawn Cipher manuscript, and these relied upon the Kabbalah. Mathers was responsible for writing the Second Order rituals, and these had a significant Rosicrucian content. The Third Order was made up of 'Secret Chiefs'.

### Column O9-O12: Passwords of the Grades of the Golden Dawn

The passwords are no longer valid, in the sense that they are changed regularly by working lodges, but it is useful to see what they were and how they were obviously selected on the basis of their numeration, rather than for their literal sense.

### Column O13-O17: Pre-Golden Dawn Grades

Less known, are the alternate titles of the Golden Dawn initiation Grades, e.g. 'Monoceros de Astris' and so on. These alternate titles were taken from old Masonic/Rosicrucian 'brotherhood names', pass-words of a sort, intended to change periodically. The Golden Dawn used some of them for permanent grade titles.

These grades listed in Kenneth Mackenzie's *Royal Masonic Cyclopaedia* show where the Golden Dawn got its grade structure.[1] The numbers associated with each grade are significant, and *777* equates with Adeptus Exemptus. Column O16 lists the lovely poetic Latin names of the grades. Hodos Chameliontos (a slightly different spelling from that used by Mackenzie), or the Path of the Chamelion was an image used by W B Yeats to great effect in his poetry.

The 'Consulates' shown in Column O17 were probably a piece of fantasy, but may also indicate the addresses of other adepti in communication with Kenneth Mackenzie, or the founders of the Golden Dawn.

Column O15 contains the Hebrew words for three of the Elements, and Hiddekel, Phrath, Pison and Gihon which are the four rivers of the Garden of Eden, which were associated with Golden Dawn grades.

### Column O18-O20: Golden Dawn Temple Officers

These are the titles of various officers in a working temple of the Golden Dawn. Female equivalents of the officer's titles were obviously important in the Golden Dawn. The corresponding Egyptian godform is that which would be visualised and then assumed by the officer concerned.

### *Masonic Grades*

Note that Columns O23 to O27a are numbered in Grade order. No attempt has been made to correlate them with the Spheres and Paths of the Tree of Life.

### Column O21: Officers in a Masonic Lodge.

This is the standard list of Freemasonic officers.

### Column O22-O27a: Masonic Grades of various Rites

These are the grade structures of some of the more important Masonic bodies with an interest in esoteric work. They are also amongst those organisations that Crowley claimed to have subsumed in his OTO, although their respective governing bodies might well not agree.

### Column O22: Masonic Grades – Relaxed Observance

This degree was originated by Baron von Cavin and Dr August von Starck in Vienna in 1767. This particular strand of Freemasonry had a Templar flavour, and concerned itself with magic, alchemy and the Kabbalah.

---

[1] See Kenneth Mackenzie's *Royal Masonic Cyclopaedia*, London 1877, and Manly Palmer Hall's *Codex Rosae Crucis*, 1938, page 13.

### Column O23: Masonic Grades – Rite of Philalethes

'Philalethes' is Greek for 'Lover of Truth'. This Rite was founded in Paris in 1773, and is allied with the principles of Martinism, and its members specialised in the study of occult science. The principle members included Prince Friedrich Ludwig of Hesse-Darmstadt, and Court de Gebelin, who was responsible for foisting the theory that the Tarot sprang from Egyptian roots onto an unsuspecting world. Cagliostro may also have been connected with the sponsoring society, under his alias of St Germain.

### Column O24: Masonic Grades – Philosophic Scottish Rite

This Rite was established in Paris in 1776 being founded on Dom Pernety's 'Rite of the Hermetic Sublime Masters of the Luminous Ring' which was heavily concerned with alchemy. Initiates were assumed to be Master Masons already.

### Column O25: Masonic Grades – Scottish or Ancient & Accepted Rite

In 1761 it is said that the 'Council of Emperors of the East and West' granted a patent to spread the Rite of Perfection in America. The Ancient & Accepted Rite descends from this, and although one of the most popular rites, and by some considered 'standard Freemasonry', it in fact only dates from about 1802.

### Column O26: Masonic Grades - Antient & Primitive Rite

This rite (with is antique spelling) was established at Montauban in 1815.

### Column O27: Masonic Grades – Rite of Memphis and Mizraim

'Mizraim' or 'Misraim' is the Hebrew word for Egypt. This Freemasonic Rite derives from Count Alessandro Cagliostro (1743-1795) an Italian and self-styled Rosicrucian, who intrigued the courts of Europe with his tales. He was born Giuseppe Balsamo of a poor Palermo family, but initiation into the Knights of Malta and then into Freemasonry allowed him to move up in society. Despite being accused of theft and fraud, and being imprisoned by the Inquisition, he managed to found, or at least transmit, one of the most famous Rites, which subsequently had links with various magical fraternities. Some of its elaborate grades and titles were also adopted by these fraternities, hence their relevance here. The Rite was especially celebrated at the equinoxes. In 1862 the Rite of Memphis was admitted as a subordinate Masonic system of the Grand Orient Lodge of France. Note the division into four Orders, particularly the Mystical (III) and Kabbalistic (IV) Orders.

### O27a: Masonic Grades – Oriental Rite of Memphis.

## Aleister Crowley's A.'.A.'. and O.T.O. Grades

### Column O28: Grades and Magical Mottos personally adopted by Crowley

This is not a grade list as such but a biographical list of the dates on which Crowley reached, or claimed to have reached, various grades, with the motto he adopted.

## Column O29-O30: Grades of the OTO

Column O29 is the grade structure of the OTO as given in the 'Synopsis of Degrees' attached to the OTO manifesto of 1917. As you can see the OTO was designed to embrace and include grades and teachings from Masonry, Rosicrucianism, the Templars and Illuminism. This early formulation was subsequently modified by Crowley, who added a O° which he entitled 'Minerval', a title which was previously the second degree title. Column O30 shows the expanded 21st century grade structure, although there are a number of more recently developed grades and titles not shown on this abbreviated version.

The Ordo Templi Orientis was founded by a wealthy paper chemist, Carl Kellner (1851-1905). Kellner was a student of the occult and believed that he had discovered a 'Key' to the symbolism of Freemasonry and to the Mysteries of Nature. Along with Theodore Reuss (1855-1923), he decided to call his order the OTO. In 1902, Reuss, with the occult writer Franz Hartmann and Henry Klein, purchased the rights to perform the Scottish, Memphis and Mizraim rites of Freemasonry (see Columns O25 and O27), the authority for which was confirmed in 1904 and again in 1905. These rites, along with the Swedenborgian Masonic Rite, formed the core of the newly established Order. When Kellner died in 1905, Reuss assumed full control, becoming the first Outer Head of the Order.

The OTO became famous through its association with Aleister Crowley. Reuss met Aleister Crowley and in 1910 admitted him to the three degrees of the OTO. Only two years later, Crowley was placed in charge of the OTO for Great Britain and Ireland, and was advanced to the X°. The appointment included the operation of the ordinary Masonic degrees of the OTO, and an inner division which was called the Mysteria Mystica Maxima. Within a year Crowley had written the Manifesto of the M.'.M.'.M.'. which described a basic ten-degree system, which was still principally Masonic, with Kellner's three degree of Academia Masonica forming the VII°, VIII° and IX° of the OTO.

After Crowley's death, the baton passed to Karl Germer, who with the assistance of Gerald Yorke, moved the activities of the OTO to America.

Under Germer, OTO activity diminished to little more than an association in name alone, and Germer died in 1962 without naming a successor. It was not until 1969 that anyone stepped into the void and Grady McMurtry invoked an old authorization from Crowley to form a 'camp' and assumed the title of Caliph. He began performing OTO initiations the following year. The OTO was not incorporated under the laws of the State of California till 1979. When Grady McMurtry died in 1985, his position passed by election to William

Breeze who, together with Bill Heidrick, has breathed life into the organisation, and increased its membership and level of activity considerably.

## Column O31-O32: Grades of the A.'. A.'.

The grades of Crowley's order, the A.'.A.'., as shown in *Magick in Theory and Practice* in 1929. Note the two grades between the three sub-Orders, following the Golden Dawn structure. 'Babe of the Abyss' corresponded to Daath as a link grade and 'Dominus Liminus' corresponded to the Veil Paroketh, just below Tiphareth, also as a link grade.

## *Magical 'Weapons' and Equipment*

## Column O33: Practices and Attainments for each Grade

Crowley's list of magical attainments required by each grade.

## Column O34: Magical 'Weapons' and Temple Equipment

This table is an attribution of the various pieces of magical equipment to the Tree of Life. This Column differs from Crowley in a few important respects, notably the return to the grimoire attributes for the four Elements, specifically Wand = Air and Sword = Fire. The correctness of this revision is reflected in Crowley's own attribution of Sword = Mars which equals Fire, and Wand = Mercury which equals Air. There is no dispute about Cup = Water or about Coins = Earth.

Planetary equipment attributions are in line with the planetary natures, but Crowley's Zodiacal attributions are forced and artificial. The reason for this is obvious: magical equipment is used to invoke the planets, but the Zodiacal signs are not usually invoked. Therefore the astrological attributions have only been shown to support the positioning of the magical Formulae in the next column.

Crowley attributes the Bow and Arrow to Path 13 and Path 25, because of the image of the arrow passing up the Middle Pillar fired from the bow Qesheth (the rainbow), and not because of any intrinsic correspondence to these Paths. The Furnace is an unlikely (sexual) attribution to Path 18, and it has been replaced by magical equipment more in tune with Cancer. The Wand was only appropriate to Virgo in the phallic sense of semen retained.

## Column O35: Magical Formulae

The formula were primarily god names, but by dint of using Gematric analysis, have been applied as mnemonics for organising ritual. Some of these like Abraxas are ancient Gnostic formulae, some are Hebraic like ALHIM, and others are Crowley's version of traditional formulae like Abrahadabra, which differs by one letter from the conventional spelling. You may regard such changes as restoration of the original word, corruption of the original word, or an extension of the original meaning. Much of this material will be found in Crowley's *Magick in Theory & Practice* (especially Chapters II to VII).

## Table P. Pagan Pantheons

The nature of the gods changes over time, so trying to categorise them is a risky business. In every culture certain archetypes or styles of god or goddess will be found repeated again and again. The nature and attributes of the gods are not arbitrary. This is either because man creates the gods the same way, no matter what his race or culture, or alternatively the gods really exist, and they are just given different names in different cultures. It does not really matter if the gods exist or not, as 'the universe behaves as if they do'.

Accordingly it is important for us to categorise them and see the many parallels that exist between one culture's gods and the next. For those readers who are hardened monotheists, I suggest they view the various gods as different facets of the same divinity. For those readers who are comfortable with a polytheistic outlook on life, I suggest that there is but one Creator God: as the universe is too well made to have been constructed by a committee.

In analysing the gods, the clearest associations are those with the 7 Planets. If this identification can be made, then this also allows us to place them within the 10 Sephiroth. The 4 Elements are also useful in placing water or fire gods, although the gods of earth have a competing allegiance in Malkuth, and so sometimes appear in both places. In some cases, where a god has changed in quality over time, or has widely varying functions, they appear in more than one row.

One category which is not well provided for on the Tree of Life is the Underworld. In Classical times this was not seen as hell, and it is not appropriate to equate it with the Qliphoth. As a compromise, gods like Hades have in the past been attributed to Saturn or Earth on the 32nd path. This might be partially justified in terms of where the soul goes after death when it leaves Earth or Malkuth, but it is still a compromise. The god Hades (as distinct from his domain) for example was seen as 'that other Zeus' and as powerful in the Underworld as was Zeus in the land of the living, so placing him on the 32nd path does not really do him any justice.

Gods were referred to as *chthonian* if they were connected to the lower worlds, and the obvious Greek chthonian gods were Persephone, Demeter, Hekate, Pluton and Hades. To facilitate categorisation of these gods of an Underworld that has no exact correspondence in the Kabbalah, I have added an Underworld 'UW' row, but only in the Pagan Pantheons Table P, to accommodate these gods.

In the Middle Ages, Ovid and Virgil were widely read, and formed the main source for classical myths in Western Europe. During the Renaissance a large number of Greek and Hermetic texts again became available, but detailed knowledge of the Egyptian gods had to wait for the interpretation of

# Commentary

hieroglyphics by Champollion (1790-1832). Having said that, there was a certain amount of information about the Egyptian gods available from Greek sources, like Herodotus, some of which was thought to be myth but is only now proving to be in many cases literally correct. I await with interest, confirmation that the descriptions that Herodotus gave of the elaborate chambers and passages under the pyramids of Cheops (Khufu) are in fact true.

Why is it instructive to compare the gods of different pantheons, looking for common qualities and comparing their myths? Crowley[1] had some interesting comments:

> "Priests, to propitiate their local fetish [god], would flatter him with the title of creator; [but] philosophers, with a wider outlook, would draw identities between many gods in order to obtain a unity. Time and the gregarious nature of man have raised gods as ideas grew more universal; sectarianism [on the other hand] has drawn false distinctions between identical gods for polemical purposes."

His key distinction was between priests and philosophers. It is certainly one of the jobs of a priest to build up the reputation of the god he serves. It is likewise the job of a philosopher to see parallels and connections on a universe wide scale. Using the Kabbalistic Tree of Life it is possible to analyse these various themes. There have been other attempts to categorise the multiplicity of gods by their qualities:

Solar    Martial    Earthly    Paternal    Lunar    Beautiful    Stellar    Sapiential

This division is of course directly based on the planetary Sephiroth, as follows:

| Tiphareth | Geburah | Malkuth | Chesed | Yesod | Netzach | Binah | Hod |
|-----------|---------|---------|--------|-------|---------|-------|-----|
| Sun | Mars | Earth | Jupiter | Moon | Venus | Saturn | Mercury |

These gods can then be categorised as either masculine or feminine, thereby opening up twice as many categories. Some Sephiroth, such as Netzach, still however have only one sex gods (female). Further divisions of the gods and goddesses can be by quality, occupation, or reputation.

At this point the theory runs into trouble, and some of the resulting categorisations demonstrate the difficulty of dealing with the gods, and the danger of using modern psychological theory to divide them up. It is important, but not sufficient, to just play with the archetypes. The real key is to understand the myths, and to know which aspect of the universe that a particular god most fully reveals if invoked.

Of all the tables, the pantheons of which little is known are perhaps the most controversial. For the gods of Greece and Rome there is much known, and much still practised. The Roman gods were definitely not far away when the

---

[1] In his Preface to *Liber 777*, page xii.

445

present author witnessed by moonlight a full dress Latin invocation in one of the still standing temples of ancient Pompeii, which could have been a direct successor to the Mysteries once held there, and which had none of the self-consciousness of so many modern magical ceremonies. Unfortunately much of the newly awakened New Age celebration of the ancient gods seems to leave out the necessary elements of awe and respect, substituting instead an overly familiar and patronising attitude, as if the gods and goddesses were so many wilful pets, rather than potent, and sometimes dangerous, entities.

For example, the Scandinavian gods have a level of real violence which is alien to many of us brought up in softer cultures. For Egypt there are masses of (predominantly funeral) texts, but their gods were never part of the mainstream European/Anglo-Saxon culture. For those of African descent, the gods of that continent might be much closer, either in their original guise or in the guise of the Voodoo *loa*. The African Columns could have been much larger, but I have just picked out a few key gods and goddesses.

Finally you might ask why it is important to know the gods and their attributes. One of the early members of the Golden Dawn, J W Brodie-Innes, a lawyer, put it rather well when he said 'Whether the Gods...really exist is comparatively unimportant; the point is that the universe behaves as though they do.'

## Middle Eastern Gods

### Column P1-P4: Sumerian, Akkadian, Assyrian, Mesopotamian & Babylonian Gods

Most people have only a hazy notion of the history and mythology of the area between and around the Tigris and Euphrates rivers, modern day Iraq. To put it in a simplified form the ancient name of Mesopotamia (given by Alexander the Great and subsequently used by the Romans) encompasses Assyria in the north and Sumer in the marshy south of the region. Babylonia was named after Babylon and located as a city state near modern day Baghdad. The gods of this region with minor name changes have been shared by all those living in that region. The Mesopotamian pantheon is rather tangled because it stretches over such a long time period, and varies according to which part of 'the land between the rivers' was in the ascendancy at the time. About 50 of the 1000+ gods of this region were considered main gods, especially the seven planetary gods which are listed separately in Column P3.

The names listed in Column P2 against the Zodiac are in fact just the names of these constellations as rendered by Wallis Budge.

Column P3-P4 lists the Babylonian gods representing the planets, with their corresponding numeration. This column is interesting as it indicates derivable numerical relationships between the gods and planets.

# Commentary

For example Mars (8) + Mercury (12) = Sun (20). Other combinations and ratios suggest themselves. The sum total of all the planets is 99.[1]

### Column P5: Persian Gods

Persia is the source of much of the dualistic religion in the Middle East.

### Column P6: Phoenician and Canaanite Gods

This Column is important, especially for those interested in the pagan roots of Judaism.

### Column P7: Pre-Islamic Arabian Peninsular & Nabatean Gods

This Column is important, especially for those interested in the pagan roots of Islam.

### Column P8: Syrian Gods

## Egyptian Gods

### Column P9: Egyptian Gods

As Egyptian gods evolved over a long period of time, and were sometimes merged with each other, their qualities and hence their attributions changed. For this reason, sometimes the same god will appear in several places in the Column.

Crowley placed Harpocrates, Amoun, and Nuith on the zero row. Amoun is so listed in his form as the 'Concealed One.' However as they are gods of *this* universe with shrines and devotees, they are here attributed to Kether.

Crowley also added in relatively minor gods from the *Book of the Law* into his Egyptian tables, but I have stuck to the main gods of the Egyptian pantheons and not including these. He also used what is now rather outdated spelling, such as Asar-un-Nefer as the perfected Osiris in Kether. Asar was just a Victorian spelling of Osiris, and Nefertum was 'the god of the lotus'. It was only in comparatively late times that Osiris was called Un-nefer. Asar Un-nefer was just the first name in Budge's list of over 172 names of Osiris.[2]

In Egypt magic and religion were more closely entwined than in any other culture. Ritner (1993, 247) convincingly argues that Egyptian magic was the:

> "'technique' or 'mechanics' of Egyptian religion it was the 'cultic manipulation' of the dynamic, divine creative force 'by recitation, substance, and ritual'."

Mathers and his fellow Golden Dawn members like Florence Farr, and the scholar Wallis Budge had a particular fondness for the Egyptian gods

---

[1] See David Hulse, *The Eastern Mysteries,* Llewellyn, St Paul, 2004, p.11.
[2] Wallis Budge, *The Gods of the Egyptians,* Dover, New York, 1969, Vol.2, page 176.

precisely because of their overt magical connections.

The equivalences between Egyptian and Greek gods are very useful in placing the Egyptian gods correctly. This is not just modern speculation but was made by the Greeks of the Ptolemaic period. Herodotus has clearly made the connections between Egyptian gods and Greek gods in a time when both sets of gods were still worshipped, so it is worth our while just looking at what he says. He identified Dionysus (Osiris = 6) and Demeter (Isis = 3) as the parents of Apollo (Horus = 5) and Artemis (Bast = 9). To quote him:[1]

"In Egyptian, Apollo is Horus, Demeter is Isis, and Artemis is Bubastis."

## Column P10: Egyptian Gods as used ritually by the Golden Dawn

This table shows the practical temple use made of the Egyptian gods in the rituals of the Golden Dawn. The spelling of some of the gods in this column are in the form used by the Golden Dawn, and hence a little obsolete by modern Egyptological standards. They derive from Wallis Budge, and from Kabbalistic manipulation of Coptic, and have been preserved unchanged, so that they may more readily be identified in Golden Dawn rituals. The Underworld row contains Apophrassz, Szathan Toophon, and Bessz synthesised as Ommo-Szathan. These are non-standard Golden Dawn spellings used ceremonially for the 'Stations of the Evil One'.

## Column P11: Egyptian Gods and the Bodily Attributes of the Perfected Man

These are primarily derived from the *Papyrus of Ani*. I have not followed Crowley's placement of Nu (as the hair) on the zero row. The 7 planets are all associated with parts of the face, and therefore Anpu/Anubis is associated with the Opening of the Mouth ceremony, not the hips. The Zodiacal attributions run in order down the body.

## Column P12: Egyptian Gods and their Attributes

These attributions include the appropriate amulet, animal, colour, function and symbols of the main gods and are therefore very practical. They are derived from David Rankine's very logically presented book on Egyptian magic.[2]

## *Egyptian Gods from the PGM*

### Column P12a: Egyptian Gods of the Hours of the Day from the *PGM*

The animal form associated with the hour is derived from *PGM* IV. 1596-1715. The God of the Hour is to be found in *PGM* IV. 1596-1715 and in *PGM* XXXIX. 1-21. This is in a sense the secret name of the god of the hour.

---

[1] Herodotus, *Histories*, 2:156.
[2] David Rankine, *Heka*, Avalonia, London, 2006.

# Commentary

## Column P12b: Egyptian Gods of the Zodiac from the *PGM*

The Egyptian names of the months are not in the original papyrus, but inserted here for convenient reference. Instead the papyrus has the Greek names of the 12 signs of the zodiac. The gods' attributions are logical: for example Horus-Montu, the Egyptian god of war, is attributed to Aries. See Preisendanz (1931), Vol. 2, pp. 35-36 for their sigils.

## *Gnostic*

## Column P13-P15: Gnostic Gods & Demiurges

Although many Gnostic accounts of creation and the intermediate gods tend to be fragmentary, the account given in the Nag Hammadi codex *On the Origin of the World* is fairly complete. This Sephirothic rows of this Column represents an attempt to fit this theology on to the 10 Sephiroth. The positions of Pistis, Sophia, Yaldabaoth (the Demiurge), and Adonaios are fairly certain, but the other sons of Yaldabaoth are not so certainly placed.

In this third edition, Sophia has been moved up one line and joined with Pistis, as Sophia = Wisdom = Chokmah. Yaldabaoth is also said to have generated his own mother, Achamoth. Sabaoth is also identified with Jesus Christ, but partakes of some of his heavenly Father's qualities. He is described as riding a chariot called Cherubin (*sic*), attended by dragon-angels called Seraphin (*sic*). The same codex goes on to describe both the Greek Eros-Psyche myth and the Hebraic Adam-Eve Tree of Life story, showing that Gnosis has roots in both Hebraic and Greek cultures. Interestingly Eve is portrayed as promiscuously having children by all seven of Yaldabaoth's sons, as well as Adam.

Gnostic eschatology considered as the soul's struggle with hostile archons in its ascent, may be looked at in terms of rising on the planes through the realms of the seven planets, as in Babylonian astrology. This arrangement is therefore reflected in the Planetary rows at the bottom of Column P13. Another column, P14a has been introduced to accommodate Archon names from the so-called 'Diagram of the Ophites' mentioned by Celsus and Origen.

The Gnostics were a bridge between Judaism and Hellenic culture, and the emerging mix of these two, Christianity, and so it is appropriate that this Column falls between Middle Eastern and European god Columns.

## *European Gods*

## Column P16: Greek Gods

Of all the Hellenic gods there are twelve who were recognised all over the Greek world, and these were the twelve Olympians, all parts of the family of Zeus. These are (according to Thucydides) Zeus, Hera, Poseidon, Demeter, Apollo, Artemis, Hephaestus, Athena, Ares, Aphrodite, Hermes and Dionysus.

Because their histories are well known from the works of Homer and Hesiod, or later Apollodorus, it is relatively easy to place them on the Tree. Of course each god has various facets, each of which might serve to categorise him. For example Hades is obviously a god of the Underworld, but he was often referred to as the 'the other Zeus' or the 'chthonian Zeus' giving him a right to a position alongside Zeus.

Regarding the Greek god Aion and Iao, a Greek form of Jehovah:

> 'The highest god and creator of the world is called by many names. One of his names is Aion. When the vowels were rearranged, the name of the one Jewish God, Iao, was produced. While Aion, the great god that lived in Alexandria, was Greek, [he] was Iao himself to the many Jews in [Egypt]'.

### Column P17-P18: The Main Greek Gods and their Numeration

Seven of the most important Greek gods are here listed in Greek with their numeration.

### Column P19-P20: Orphic Theology

This Column is extracted from *Theologia Platonica* by Marsilio Ficino, published around 1482.[1] Ficino was key in introducing Hermetic philosophy to Europe, and helping to launch the Renaissance. Orphic theology considers two categories of power in both souls and the celestial orbs, and they are here separated into two Columns, being those gods concerned with knowledge and those gods concerned with the vivifying power and governance of the Planetary orbs and their souls. This list is very useful in understanding many Renaissance Hermetic allusions.

Athanasius Kircher published a different order, shown on the following illustration (Figure 18):

| | |
|---|---|
| Saturn | – Polyhymnia |
| Jupiter | – Euterpe |
| Mars | – Erato |
| Sun | – Melpomene |
| Venus | – Terpsichore |
| Mercury | – Calliope |
| Moon | – Clio |
| Earth | – Thalia |

The *Orphic Rhapsodies* put Chronos in the place of origin of all. From Chronos is generated Aither (Ether) and Chaos, who together form an egg or shining cloud, from which springs Phanes, the winged bisexual and self-fertilizing god who is the ultimate creator of the cosmos, and who gives

---

[1] See Donald Tyson's edition of Agrippa, *Three Books of Occult Philosophy*, footnote 1 on Book II, Chapter LVIII, page 424.

birth to the first generation of the gods. In the Orphic theology, Chronos, Aither and Chaos could be attributed to the Ain, Ain Soph and Ain Soph Aur of the Kabbalah.

Alternatively, if we identify Kronos with Chronos, then this god could hold its usual place at Binah, with Aither and Chaos falling in Daath and Phanes being attributed to Chesed, as Father of the gods.

## Column P21: Greek Muse Governing Type of Lyric

The Greek Muses are part of the Ophic theology, and their lyrical associations are listed in Column P21. This is how they have come down to us, as an important part of the study of the Liberal Arts in the Renaissance (see also Column T32 where they are listed in yet another order).

Surprisingly, amongst subjects like lyric poetry or dance are also to be found geometry and astronomy, as if they were art-forms that needed a muse to inspire them.

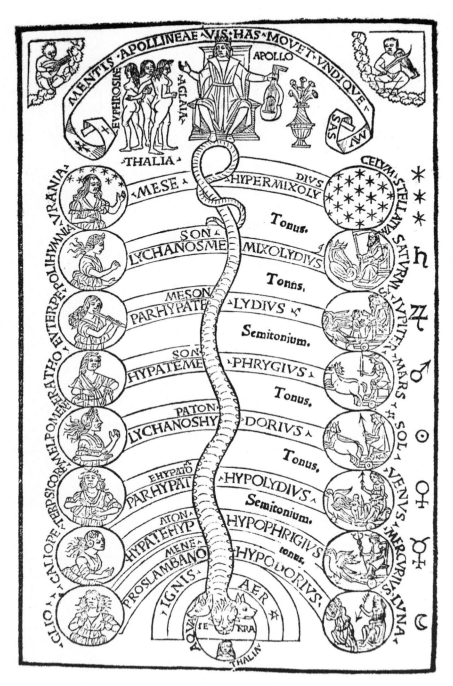

Figure 18: The Nine Spheres ascending from Earth to Heaven, each with its own representative of the Nine Muses, through the 7 Planets from Clio (Moon - Histories) to Polyhymnia (Saturn – Sacred Song) and Urania (the fixed stars), with Apollo enthroned above. Thalia is usually depicted as Earth. From *De Harmonia Musicorum Instrumentorum Opus* by Franchino Gaffurio, Milan, 1518.

# Commentary

## Column P22: The Roman Gods.

The Roman gods were mainly derived from Greek gods and the indigenous and the highly developed Etruscan civilisation which existed in Italy before the rise of Rome.

The main group of twelve gods was called the *Dii Consentes* and includes Jupiter, Juno, Minerva, Vesta, Ceres, Diana, Venus, Mars, Mercurius, Neptunus, Volcanus, and Apollo. These are listed by the poet Ennius about the 3rd Century BC. Six were male and six were female, and their golden statues stood in the Forum.

The number 12 may have been taken from the Etruscans, who also worshipped a main pantheon of 12 gods. The *Dii Consentes* were not identified with Etruscan deities but rather with the Greek Olympian gods.

Roman household or family cult gods were called the *Dii Familiaris*. Of these, the *Lar Familiaris* (guardian spirit, or *genius*, of the family), the *Lares Loci* (guardian spirits of the place where the house is built), the *Genius Paterfamilias* (House-Father), the *Dii Penates* (gods of the storeroom), the *Dii Manes* (spirits of the ancestors) and other domestic deities were given offerings daily by the members of the family. The household cult is reflected in the state cult (which had a *Lar Praestites* and *Penates Publici*).

Other important Roman gods include Janus, Saturnus, Quirinus (adopted from the Sabines), Volturnus, Pales, Furrina, Flora, Carmenta, Pomona, Portunus, Fontanus. There is also a group of mysterious deities formed by native tutelary deities, river gods or deified heroes from Latium which are collectively called *Dii Indigites* (for example the hero Aeneas, Faunus, Sol Indiges, Jupiter Indiges, and Numicus). Other tutelary deities representing Rome and its river (like Roma, Tiberinus), native Latin deities (Bellus, Bellona, Liber, Libera), and abstract concept deities such as Fortuna (Fate), Concordia (Concord), Pax (Peace), Iustitia (Justice), were worshipped.

The *Dii Inferni*, or gods of the Underworld (or Infernus) held a special place, and include Dis/Orcus and Proserpina, who equated respectively to the Greek gods Hades/Plouton (Pluto) and Persephone.

Trade and conquest brought new cults to Rome, and these were democratically adopted and permitted to set up their temples in Rome. These foreign deities were called the *Dii Novensiles*, and include Bacchus/Dionysus, Sol Invictus, Elagabalus, Isis, Serapis, Cybele, Attis, Mithras and many others.

## Column P23: Etruscan Gods

The religious practices of the Etruscans are to be found in the *Etrusca Disciplina*, which included the *Libri Haruspicini, Fulgurales* and *Rituales*. Divination seems to have been of overwhelming importance to the Etruscans. Their holy books were closely tied up to the practice of haruspices, inspecting the entrails of sacrificial animals, especially the sheep's liver, for predictions. The parts of the liver corresponded with the abodes of the gods in the sky, and hence to the gods, and so summed up their pantheon. The Etruscan word for god is *ais*, and there were a large number of such *aiser*. Those with the most clearly defined functions are listed here.

### Column P24 – P26: Celtic Gods

Most Celtic religion was passed on verbally and not recorded in writing. There are four main sources for Celtic religion: Romano-Celtic iconography, classical Roman descriptions, and recorded Irish and Welsh literature, the later having passed through the filter of monastic scriptoriums. Druids were virtually eliminated by the Romans in Britain and displaced by Christianity in Ireland. The [o]vates and bards however survived into the late Middle Ages in Ireland and Wales. They are the source of much of our knowledge about the Celtic gods.[1]

Even between these two areas there is not a lot of consistency. For example, the horse goddess Epona is roughly equivalent to the Welsh Rhiannon, the 'divine queen' or the Irish Macha.

### Column P27: Slavic Gods

### Column P28: Baltic Gods

These gods are from the area around Latvia, Lithuania and the Baltic Sea.

### Column P29. Norse and Scandinavian Gods

Thor as god of lightning is attributed to Chesed (Jupiter). Tiw as a warrior god fits (with Thor) on Geburah. The Valkyries belong with Mars on the battlefield, or in the Underworld, not with the Element Air, as Crowley suggests, just because they fly. Loki is the archetypal Mercurial trickster, but he also has some affinity with the Moon.

## *Asian Gods*

### Column P30: Hindu Gods

Crowley attributes AUM to his zero row, which seems appropriate, as the ground of all creation. There is such a plethora of Hindu gods that this column could have been infinitely extended.

### Column P31: Japanese Shinto Gods

The main Shinto gods are Izanagi (first god of earth who created the world) and Izanami (the first goddess of the earth). Other gods include Kagu-Zuchi

---

[1] For information about the whole range of Celtic gods and goddesses, see Rankine, David & Sorita D'Este. *The Isles of the Many Gods*. Avalonia, London, 2007.

# Commentary

(the fire god), Amaterasu (the Sun goddess and ruler of heaven), and Tsuki-yomi (God of the moon).

As well as these Kami there are local gods often tied to a specific village. Tengu are sometimes spiteful spirits inhabiting trees in mountainous areas, reputed for their martial arts ability. Oni are fierce, cruel and lecherous horned devils, often gigantic, and sometimes with three eyes, and Kappas are scaly vampiric river or pond spirits.

### Column P32: Chinese Taoist Gods

This is only a small selection of the huge possible range of Taoist gods.

### Column P33: Meditation Buddhas & Dakinis

Primarily the figures of Tantric Buddhism attributed to the Elements.

## African & Voodoo Gods

These include African derived pantheons like the Voodoo pantheon with its admixture of Catholic saints and local spirits. The basic voodoo split is between Petra Loa which tend to be the older gentler gods of Africa, and the Rada Loa, the rather more boisterous and historically more recent gods.

### Column P34: Dahomean Gods

### Column P35: Yoruba Gods

### Column P36: Santeria Gods

### Column P37: Voodoo Rada & Petra Loa

A more detailed study would separate these two types of loa, one brought over from Africa, and the other generated in the Caribbean.

### Column P38: Other African Gods

Because of the diversity of religion in Africa, just a small selection are included here from other African cultures and regions.

## Central American Gods

### Column P39: Aztec Gods

### Column P40: Inca Gods

### Column P41: Mayan Gods

I would like to conclude with a quote from Edward Moore about the relationship between man and his gods which contrasts the pagan and Christian approaches:

> "The purpose of Iamblichean theurgy, then, is not to supplicate the gods and ask them to pardon one's sinfulness, but rather to purify the soul so that it may consort with the gods, on an equal footing. The theurgist, unlike the Christian priest, does not debase himself before his God; instead, he raises himself up to communion with the divinity."

Figure 19: King Arthur's Round Table in Winchester.

This 13th century Round Table was probably made for Edward I, nicknamed 'Longshanks,' a known Arthur enthusiast. The main repainting was done in the 1520s (probably following the lines of the original design). The kingly figure might have been a portrait of Henry V, as the red rose (symbol of the Tudor dynasty) is shown in the centre.

# Commentary

# Table Q: Questing and Chivalry

## *Knights of the Round Table*

### Column Q1-Q3: The Knights of the Round Table

The classic tale of such quests is that of King Arthur. There are many books that have gone into creating the chivalric story of King Arthur (c.500-c.550) and the Knights of the Round Table. The Arthurian literature had its heyday in the 13th and 14th centuries, but has never lost its grip on the popular imagination since then. To place each knight on the Tree is a difficult job, especially as there were so many. In the simpler versions there are just twelve knights, plus Arthur, reflecting the numbers present at the Last Supper. Varying numbers of knights are included in different sources listed below:

13 knights in the *Didot-Perceval* (c.1225)
50 knights in Robert De Boron's *Merlin* (c.1195)
60 knights in Jean D'Ouremeuse's *Ly Myreur des Histors* (c.1350)
130 knights in the English ballad, *The Legend of King Arthur* (16th century)
140 knights in Hartmann Von Aue's *Erec* and *Iwein* (late 12th century)
150 knights in the Vulgate *Lancelot* (c.1220)
250 knights in the Vulgate *Merlin* (c.1225)
1,600 knights in Layamon's *Brut* (late 12th century)

I have opted to just place the better known knights, and have used as my main source the best known image of the Round Table a painting of which hangs in Winchester Castle. This large painted circular wooden table (shown in Figure 19) was previously thought to be a Victorian construction, but the wood has now been carbon dated to the 13th century. If the painted text is similarly old, then it is amongst the earliest sources. This version has 25 knights, which are perhaps the best known, so these have been used here as the basic list. The key players have been speculatively allocated to the Sephiroth, and the next 12 to the Zodiac. Column Q2 gives more up to date names from Mallory's *Morte d'Arthur*, written 200 years later. Column Q3 gives a short description of each.

## *Chivalry*

### Column Q4: The Tinctures of Heraldry

This table is useful in determining the meaning of heraldic and even alchemic emblems. The planetary part is drawn from Sir John Ferne's *The Glory of Generositie,* 1586, and would have been the standard for heraldic symbolism during Dr John Dee's life and during the high point of alchemical engraving in the 17th century. The conventions for depicting colours and metals in black and white drawings is useful, as a knowledge of heraldry, classical mythology and the symbolism of emblem books goes some way to elucidating much of the symbolism of alchemy.

# Table R. Rainbow Colour Scales of the Tree of Life

Colour is an important part of magical symbolism from the use of the colours of the 7 Planets for talismans, to the complex Zodiacal and Sephirothic colour scales devised by Moina Mathers for the Hermetic Order of the Golden Dawn. The First Edition listed these in Path order, but this edition has been adjusted to ZEP order.

## *King, Queen, Emperor and Empress Scales*

### Column R1-R4: The Four Colour Scales

These four scales are attributed to the Four Worlds of the Kabbalists as follows:

> *King Scale*     Atziluth
> *Queen Scale*    Briah
> *Empress Scale*  Yetzirah
> *Emperor Scale*  Assiah

In addition to the 10 Sephiroth and 22 Paths, Daath (which is sometimes incorrectly referred to as the '11th Sephirah') has the following colour attributes: *King Scale* – Lavender; *Queen Scale* - Grey-white; *Empress Scale* - Pure violet; *Emperor Scale* - Grey flecked with gold

### Column R5: Mathers' Combined King & Queen Scale[1]

This is a nice compromise devised by Mathers and very suitable for practical work. The Sephirothic colours derive from the Queen scale, the Elemental colours from the Tattwas, and the Zodiacal colours from the rainbow spectrum.

### Column R6-R8: Rainbow Colours of the Zodiac with Frequencies

This table is an attempt to update the magical colour scales in the light of what physics has discovered about colour in the last few centuries. The numerical frequencies are interesting, for the same reason that Aristotle was interested in frequencies, for the ratios between the lengths of strings producing different notes. In both cases these numbers allow you to examine ratios between different notes or different colours.

## *Kabbalistic Colours*

### Column R9-R11: Traditional Kabbalistic Colours

Column R9 comes from Shadrach (2004); Column R10 from Rabbi Azriel (1160-1238 CE) and Column R11 from the Kabbalistic scholar Dr. Jellinek.

## *Tattwa Colours*

### Column R12: Tattwa Flashing Colours

These were an important aid to Golden Dawn skrying practice.

---

[1] With acknowledgements to David Hulse, *Eastern Mysteries*, Llewellyn, St Paul, 2004, page 142.

# Table S. Sacred Geometry

The ancient Greeks, in the person of Euclid (325-265 BC), formalised and proved most of the geometry we know today, more than two thousand years ago. Geometry is perhaps the only subject which is equally true today as it was two thousand years ago. The ancient Greeks considered the subject, because of the purity of its logic, to be sacred. But ironically it is also such a practical subject that it forms the basis for many sciences and trades today, and particularly for architecture. Sacred Geometry is geometry applied to the architecture of temples, the proportions of the human body, the ratios of natural growth, the intervals of the musical scale, or numbers such as the Fibonacci series. It is a subject whose horizons have been expanded considerably in the last 50 years to include:

1      *Noumenal* – the geometry behind physical matter, the geometry used by the Great Architect of the Universe to create the universe.

2      *Natural* – the discovery that geometry lies behind the structure of the solar system, the pattern of sunflower seeds, the structure of a snowflake, the geometry used by a nautilus bivalve to build its shell, or the form of a beehive.

3      *Manmade* – the use of specific lengths and special ratios like *phi* in the building of the pyramids, megalithic stone circles, the Parthenon, the Gothic cathedrals of the Middle Ages, and the great buildings of the Renaissance.

In order to pursue any of these branches of Sacred Geometry it is useful to know certain basic dimensions and ratios which are the subject of the following Columns.[1]

## *Planetary Numbers*

### Column S1-S5: Planetary Data

Based on Pythagoras' theory of the universal application of numbers, Kepler discovered numeric relationships between the orbits and periods of the planets, hence these figures are listed here as one of the many applications of Sacred Geometry and arithmetic to the physical universe.

## *Platonic Solids*

### Column S6-S10: The Platonic Solids

The five Platonic solids were considered to be, along with the sphere, the only perfect 3-dimensional objects, and representative of the five basic Elements that make up the universe. The numerology of the Platonic solids is therefore basic to understanding Greek philosophical and geometric thought.

---

[1] For more information see Stephen Skinner, *Sacred Geometry*, Gaia/Hamlyn, London, 2006.

You can relate all the figures in these four Columns together by using the very useful formula:

Number of edges + 2 = Number of faces + Number of vertices.

### Column S11-S13: The Platonic Solids Formulae

These Columns give the formulae for calculating the surface areas and volumes of each of the Platonic solids.

### Column S14: Figures, Numbers, Platonic Solids and Perfect Geometric Shapes

As well as being basic to ancient Greek geometry, the standard Platonic Solids and regular geometric figures were an important Renaissance study, and part of the knowledge lectures of the Golden Dawn.

Crowley places the Circle in row zero. This is not appropriate as the circle has a definite boundary, but the Unmanifest does not. In the same column (his column 49) he mixes up geometry with geomancy. In an adjacent column (48) he mixes geometry with temple furniture like the *menorah* or seven-branched candlestick, the Calvary Cross, and the Table of Shewbread, although admittedly the latter has some geometric significance.

Here we consider geometry by itself. For the most part the number of sides of the figure relates to the number of the Sephiroth or corresponding planet. There is a lot more that could be said about the relationship of geometry to cosmology than is encapsulated in this Column. Even more esoteric are the formulas which govern the geometric relationships between magic and geometry, why for example the pentagram is used for one type of magical operation, but the hexagram for another, or the special geometry required to constrain certain types of spiritual creature.

### Column S15 & S15a: Points of the Hexagram and the Pentagram

These attributions are not really a part of sacred geometry, as they are more correctly ritual correspondences, but are listed here because of their geometric content. These are simply the attributions of the five Elements to the five points of the pentagram, and the seven planets to the six points of the hexagram, with the sun as the middle point. The hexagram attributions fit on the Tree of Life centred on the sun at Tiphareth, with the lowest vertex in Yesod, and the topmost vertex in Daath (symbolised by Saturn, which is 'borrowed' from Binah for that purpose).

These correspondences are necessary to determine the starting point for ritual inscription of either of these figures. Of course part of the Lesser Banishing Ritual of the Pentagram is the visualisation of the four traditional Archangels at the four quarters. According to the Golden Dawn, these directions are set out as follows:

| In front of me | Raphael |
|---|---|
| On the right hand | Michael |
| Behind me | Gabriel |
| On the left hand | Uriel |

It is interesting in relation to the Lesser Banishing Ritual of the Pentagram to read the *Ma'ase Merkaba*[1] where it talks of the Shekinah:

> "the Princes of the four camps of the Shekinah are: Mikael, Gabriel, Uriel and Raphael, standing to the right, to the left, in front of, and behind the Throne of Glory respectively."

This order is exactly repeated in a number of other Kabbalistic texts, and is:

| In front of me | Uriel |
|---|---|
| On the right hand | Michael |
| Behind me | Raphael |
| On my left hand | Gabriel |

David Rankine noted in his recent book on the Kabbalah[2] a traditional Jewish prayer said at night before retiring which echoes the same directions:

> "In the name of YHVH The God of Israel: At my right hand Michael. At my left Gabriel. Ahead of me Oriel [Uriel]. Behind me Raphael. Above my head the Shekinah of God!"

Mathers appears to have changed this traditional order simply to match the Enochian Elemental directions, which seems a bit unnecessary. It may be more consistent to use the traditional order when performing the Lesser Banishing Ritual of the Pentagram.

## *Metrology & Measurement*

### Column S16: Sacred Geometry Conversion Factors

Metrology is the study of different systems of measurement, and how they relate to each other. Such studies are very important when measuring ancient structures, because if you can determine the units used by the original architects, then the main dimensions are likely to resolve themselves as whole numbers, or even very significant whole numbers. For example, a temple might measure 182.88 metres along one side. This number holds no significance until we realise that the temple is exactly one Greek *stadia* long. By determining the original units of measurement we get an insight into the thinking of the architect.

This Column shows the conversions between modern Metric and Imperial measures and Roman feet, Greek stadia, Egyptian cubits and Megalithic yards.

---

[1] British Library Additional MS 26,922.
[2] David Rankine, *Climbing the Tree of Life*, Avalonia, London, 2005.

# Table T. Tarot

The Tarot is a pack of playing cards that has been extant for about 600 years. For only 225 of those years has it been anything other than a game, and been associated with the occult. The pack of Tarot cards usually consists of 22 trump or illustrated cards, 16 court cards and 40 pip cards numbered 1 to 10 in 4 suits, a total of 78 cards. There have been variations, but that is the basic structure.

Since 1781 this card pack has been first associated with the 22 letters of the Hebrew alphabet, and then with the 22 Paths of the Tree of Life. Finally a little over 100 years ago, MacGregor Mathers wove a complete occult synthesis around the pack, and since then over a thousand books have been written about these associations. However if we go back before 1781 there is not a shred of occult mystery clinging to the cards. The cards would have simply been seen as obvious emblems (including social archetypes like Emperor and Pope) to those who played with them.

In this Table, I have listed the rich correspondences that were woven around the Tarot by Mathers. The first 28 Columns (T1-T28) show conventional 20th century Golden Dawn Tarot attributions. Incidentally, I have not adopted the swap later recommended by Crowley of the Emperor and the Star trumps (on the basis of a passage in his *Book of the Law*) but have preferred to retain the original Golden Dawn ordering which Crowley initially endorsed.

Columns T34 to T41 however demonstrate that the Tarot as we know it today is:

a) Made up of four broken Mediaeval emblem sets (Columns T34-T37).
b) Has its 7 Planetary Trumps misaligned with the Hebrew letters due to Mathers' ignoring the traditional *Sepher Yetzirah* ascriptions (Columns T38-T41).

Columns after T33 show material that is completely new, and show the real origin and attributions of the Tarot, for which both the Golden Dawn Strength-Justice swap and the Crowley Emperor-Star swap are both irrelevant.

Column T38-T41, and K114-K119 show how Mathers ignored the planetary correspondences clearly shown in the *Sepher Yetzirah* (in the earliest, and in most of its variant versions) in preference to a scheme which was in fact just a later Greek-inspired revision of the original Hebraic order. In Columns T38-T39, I have re-asserted the original *Sepher Yetzirah* Hebraic Planetary order.

## Origins and Symbolism

But first we need to look at a little history. The oldest surviving reference to Tarot cards was a ban imposed upon them and on playing cards in general, in 1367. This ban and many later references simply objects to them because they encouraged gambling. In this period the cards were used predominantly for gambling, not for divination or philosophic speculation. The oldest surviving card fragments date from 1392 with packs made for the amusement of Charles

# Commentary

VI of France. Later in 1450 more 'instructive' decks were created for the Italian Visconti and Sforza families. The current pack printed from the Visconti-Sforza cards is the oldest and probably the most authentic pack in current circulation.[1] These were soon followed by the conceptually very important Mantegna pack of 1465. It was however not until 1540 that Marcolino mentioned the Tarot as a divination system – before that it had been purely a game.

The Tarot has laboured for many years under a fake history which gave its purported origins as ancient Egypt. This supposed origin has been completely discredited, but was believed up until very recently. Even in the 20th century Crowley, who should have know better, called his book on the Tarot *The Book of Thoth*, although he well knew that the cards did not in fact originate in Egypt, not even in inspiration. There have even been modern 'reconstructed' packs whose aim is to re-Egyptianise the cards, a pointless exercise as they were never Egyptian in the first place. Anyone familiar with the iconography of ancient Egypt can easily see that there is no connection, except of course the basic human symbol-making faculty that is common to all mankind.

This false history was first proposed in 1781 by Court de Gebelin in his huge book *Le Monde Primitif* ('The Primitive World'). He was probably thinking of some of the hieroglyph 'meanings' of the imaginative Horapollo when he suggested that the Tarot dated back to ancient Egypt. Remember that, although French society in this period was all agog with interest in the ancient civilisation of the Nile valley, it was not till 40 years later, in 1822 that Champollion even began to understand how to actually translate hieroglyphics. [2] De Gebelin was in fact just guessing. Unfortunately his guesses were enthusiastically taken up and expanded by 'Etteilla' (whose real name was Alliette) later in that century.

In fact the Tarot cards are of purely Mediaeval, and predominantly of Christian origin, although that statement will no doubt upset a number of New Age writers. In the Middle Ages, because of the low level of general literacy, symbols were very important. For example all public house signs would be graphically signposted like the 'Elephant & Castle' or 'Rose & Crown', two popular English pub names. Anyone could give street directions to someone to find a particular place, even if they were illiterate and could not read street signs. Anyone who has travelled in China, or a country where the Latin alphabet is not used on street signs will know the importance of these

---

[1] Two of the Trumps in this pack are speculative restorations – but they do not invalidate what follows.

[2] I am aware that one London researcher claims that hieroglyphs had been decoded hundreds of years earlier by an Arabic alchemist, Abu Bakr Ahmad Ibn Wahshiyah, but this is not directly relevant to the present discussion, as the French occult world was not aware of that.

kind of directions. Not just pubs, but virtually every trade and business had an emblem. Of course pubs have retained these emblems, at least in the UK, whilst virtually every other business has moved on from emblems, to printed signs, in the present era of almost universal literacy.

However whilst our ancestors were attuned to emblems, we are not. Emblems were a part of everyday life, and there was a proliferation of emblem books which helped artists identify and copy particular standard symbols. Anyone who has spent any time studying a range of emblem books will realise that in fact the Tarot is just an emblem book printed on separate cards.

If you look carefully at Mediaeval illuminated manuscripts, or old emblem books, you will very soon realise that these emblems came in sets. There was a set of heraldic animals (lion, unicorn, etc) a set of symbolic plants (thistle, sunflower etc). There were sets of symbolic animals like the bee and the pelican (later taken up by the Rosicrucians). There were also sets of theological emblems used to teach Christianity and theology, and amongst these the most popular were the 7 virtues (originating with St. Gregory). This set included Temperance, Fortitude, Hope, and so on. For astronomy and astrology and indeed alchemy there were emblem sets for all the planets and the stars of the Zodiac, of which the Sun and the Moon were the most popular emblems. Amongst the emblems used to convey the concepts of Christianity were the Tower of Babel, Death, the Devil, and the Last Judgement. Then there were sets depicting the 'Estates of Man' (different strata of society) spanning the range from Pope, Emperor, Empress down to the vagabond or Fool. You might have noticed that in the last five sentences I have mentioned more than half the Tarot Trumps.

These origins are clearly shown in Columns T34-T37 where the four Emblem sets that contributed to the structure of the modern Tarot are shown. The emblems with Roman numbers are the present day Tarot Trumps, the ones without numbers, like 'Hope' are those emblems that were discarded. You can see at a glance that these sets have not been drawn upon equally, and that material from the same set is grouped together in the same part of the pack, helping to confirm their origin. In addition some of the missing members of these emblem sets which occur commonly, but which were not selected to form part of the current Tarot pack are also shown, without trump numbers, so you can see that indeed the Tarot is made up of parts of other whole sets.

About one third of the emblems that make up the pack are of direct Christian theological extraction, and in fact the most heavily represented set is the one which was used in the Middle Ages to teach basic Christian doctrine. Three trumps are emblems from the 7 Virtues, three are drawn from the emblems of Astrology, and at least three trumps are representatives of various social stratum. This leaves *no* cards that might be of pagan origin, or likely to have come from outside of Mediaeval Europe, and there are definitely no emblems from Egypt. Tarot iconography is a recognised sub-discipline in the Italian art history world today, and despite the attention of many careful scholars, no image has yet been found which comes from outside of European culture.

The Tarot is in fact just a specific selection of emblems taken from a number of Mediaeval emblem sets. This is further readily confirmed if one looks at some of the early Tarot packs, for example the Mantegna pack of 1465 which are listed in full in Columns T29-T33.[1]

In the 1465 Mantegna pack there are five individual *complete* sets, each of 10 emblems taken from the following categories:

> A – Astrological
> B – Christian Virtues
> C – Liberal Arts Curriculum
> D – Greek Muses
> E – Estates of Man (Strata of Society)

These Columns show that the Mantegna pack uses *all* of five distinct emblem sets with 50 Trumps. However what has come down to us with the modern Tarot is just 22 Trumps which belong to four partial sets.

Let us look at the Mantegna pack and take just the third Set, the 7 Virtues of Pope Gregory. They are usually listed in this order:

> Faith
> Hope
> Charity
> Fortitude or Strength
> Justice
> Prudence
> Temperance

Reading down Column T36 you can see that these virtues also follow in the same order in the Tarot pack. But wait a minute you say, what about Strength (Fortitude) and Justice? Of course these two trumps were swapped by Mathers to sensibly match up with their corresponding Zodiacal signs. I have merely put them back to the pre-1890 order for the purpose of this demonstration of the origins of the Tarot trumps. Only subsets of each of the four emblem sets in Columns T34-T37 were taken into account by the creators of the modern Tarot pack, as follows:

> Estates of Man (Strata of Mediaeval Society)  – 8 cards
> Biblical Emblems  – 8 cards

---

[1] David Hulse in his *Western Mysteries* utilises this pack to discuss A E Waite's designs for the suit of Pentacles, rather than using them as a real key to the structure of all the Tarot Trumps.

| | |
|---|---|
| The 7 Planets and Zodiac | – 3 cards |
| The 7 Christian Virtues | – 3 cards |

If 8 cards had been fashioned from each emblem set, we would today have had a 32 Trump Tarot pack.

Further evidence of these emblem sets being of different origin can be seen if you examine the Cary-Yale/Modrone deck which has additional trumps, including the three missing theological virtues Faith, Hope, and Charity.

In the Visconti-Sforza pack (probably the earliest complete pack we have) you can see distinct similarities between the artistic style of individual Trumps drawn from the same origin emblem set. For example the designs of all the Trump cards are based on grass, except four. These four are seated on a low platform. These happen to be the most important cards from the Estates of Man emblem set, (forming two matching pairs), confirming their shared set origin.

I imagine that the revelation of the multi-emblem set origin of the Tarot (and the Christian origins of at least two of these sets) may disquiet many people who have got used to seeing the Tarot as a complete, ancient, and perfect unity. The Tarot is indeed a sublime set of symbols which appeal to us at a very visceral level, but we should not let that blind us to their true origin. The reason they appeal to us is that they are made up from existing and deeply rooted archetypal emblem sets that, although not used any longer, form a part of the cultural inheritance of Europe, and are so still very important, both magically and psychologically. As such the Tarot emblems are of course still very valuable as divinatory and meditative images.

It would be most enlightening to have a pack (closer in concept to the Mantegna set) which contains full runs of each of the major emblem sets, so that a completer range of archetypes was represented. However, you say, that would ruin the one to one correspondence of the Trumps with Hebrew letters. That is not a problem, as there never was such a correspondence till 1781, and the cards' attribution to the Tree of Life is even more recent than that.

### The Tarot and the Tree

You can see that the symbols of the Tarot do not form such an ancient centre piece of esoteric though as they were previously painted. Their attribution to the Paths of the Tree of Life is an even more recent affair. For example, it is only in an essay by Comte De Mellet (included in de Gebelin's book in 1781), that the happy coincidence of their numerical correspondence to the 22 letters of the Hebrew alphabet was mentioned in print. Nobody took much notice of that till 1856 when Eliphas Levi stated it more romantically. Before that date, the Tarot was *not* generally thought of as a part of the Kabbalah, even in its Christian guise. It is only after Levi's identification that the Tarot trumps came to be placed on the Tree of Life. I have treated them in Columns T1 to T28 using the same Golden Dawn categorisation by Path, because the Tree of Life is capable of categorising anything, but *not* because they were originally intrinsically part of that Tree.

That Levi was a bit of a romantic is obvious to anyone who has read his books: they certainly fired my imagination when I first read them at the age of thirteen. Building on de Gebelin, he was the first writer to popularise this connection that we now all take for granted. As well as romanticising magic, it is universally acknowledged that Levi deliberately introduced various 'blinds' into his writings, or in other words, deliberate mistakes designed to trap the unwary or the unworthy.

Mathers was aware of Levi's tendency, so he 'rectified' Levi's attributions when he incorporated them into the Golden Dawn knowledge lectures. Mathers modified Levi's deliberately blinded scheme, moving the zero trump the Fool from the second last position to the first position in the scheme, plus making several other eminently sensible changes. Mathers swapped the cards Strength and Justice on the very reasonable grounds that Justice should be associated with Libra, and Strength with Leo (the card shows a lion).

In 1887 Mathers drew together the various strands which created the Tarot in the form it is recognised today and set them out in *Book T*, of which the present Table T is a tabular summary. Every later commentator including A E Waite, Aleister Crowley, Israel Regardie, Paul Case, Stuart Kaplan, even P D Ouspensky and Salvador Dali, all rely upon Mathers' synthesis.

I would like to examine this synthesis. Mathers made the bridge between the Tarot and the Kabbalah by uniting two sets of correspondences:

a.      the connection between the Hebrew letters of the Paths of the Tree and their astrological attributions, all of which can be found clearly laid out in the *Sepher Yetzirah*. Mathers and Westcott based a lot of the Kabbalah of the Golden Dawn on just this text, and Westcott even edited one of the first English editions of the *Sepher Yetzirah*.

b.      the connection between the Hebrew letters and the Tarot trumps, which, as we have seen, is a fairly recent and romantic notion promoted by De Mellet and Levi.

The history of Mathers' integration of these two things, the attribution of the Zodiac, Planets, and Elements to the Paths, and the attribution and rectification of the Tarot attribution to the Paths has been excellently told by David Hulse.[1]

What Hulse does not quite make clear, although he is undoubtedly aware of it,

---

[1] In the Addendum 'Mather's Qabalistic Proof of the Tarot' in *The Western Mysteries*, p.344-351.

is that to make if all fit, Mathers not only changed two of the attributions of the Tarot to the Astrological signs, but he also changed the attributions of the 7 Planets to seven of the Hebrew letters which he found in the *Sepher Yetzirah*. This later change is silent however, and much less excusable.

The first use of the word Sephirah (plural Sephiroth) is in the *Sepher Yetzirah*, which probably dates from around the 3rd century AD. Obviously if this is the first mention of the Sephiroth it must also be the first mention of the Paths between them and their attributions to the 22 Hebrew letters, the Planets, Elements and the Zodiac. Therefore the *Sepher Yetzirah* must be considered the earliest and therefore probably the most definitive text on these attributions, as it is the first text to speak about them.

On the face of it, it should have been sufficient for Mathers to adjust the modern and speculative attributions of the Tarot, whilst leaving untouched the ancient and very clearly documented Hebrew attributions of the *Sepher Yetzirah*. In fact he changed the Hebrew letter and Path positions of the Planets to match the Tarot, rather than the other way around.

Because of this anomaly I have decided to add a set of Columns (T38-T41) which shows the differences between the traditional Kabbalistic and Mathers' attributions, which only applies to the 7 Planetary rows.[1] I have therefore reproduced the Tarot-Path correspondences from the Order papers of the Luculentus Astrum as Column T39, because they have preserved the *Sepher Yetzirah* Planetary correspondences intact. This is contrasted with Mathers' Tarot trump attributions to the Hebrew letters, and hence the Paths on the Tree.

Having said this, all Columns up to and including T28 follow Mathers' Golden Dawn attributions.

## *Major Arcana: Trumps*

### Column T1: Names and Numbers of the Tarot Trumps.

The Tarot Trumps showing the traditional Golden Dawn title and numbering. Column T2 has been moved to after Column T4.

### Column T3-T3a: Titles of the Tarot Trumps

Titles in T3 are as used by the Golden Dawn, and T3a are those used by Crowley.

### Column T4: The Design of the Tarot Trumps

This Column follows the Golden Dawn designs of the Tarot cards, but does not take into account the design innovations made by Crowley and Lady Frieda Harris in their *Thoth Pack*.

---

[1] If you wish to go in more detail into the question of Planet to Hebrew letter attribution in the *Sepher Yetzirah*, then consult Columns K114-K119.

# Commentary

In the last Trump, The World, despite the fact that the central figure is a woman, Crowley strangely suggests that the scarf hides male genitals, and is shaped like the Hebrew letter Kaph. There is no question of the figure being hermaphrodite.

## *Minor Arcana: Court Cards*

The 4 suits, Staves, Swords, Cups, and Coins are attributed to the 4 Elements. In old packs the fourth suit is clearly made of gold coins with recognisable coinage stampings on them. In Victorian times the name of the fourth suit was changed to 'Disks' or 'Pentacles' (in an effort to make the pack look more magical). The first suit, even in Waite's pack, is very obviously a walking stave, but it was changed to 'Wands'.

The four suits were originally the four things that any mediaeval traveller would have taken with him, a walking stave, a sword for protection, his own cup to drink from, and coins to pay for food and lodging. This does not invalidate the more magical interpretation, but it explains why I have used the term 'Coins' instead of 'Pentacles' or the meaningless 'Disks' in these Tables.

Note that the ascriptions of Staves/Wands to Fire and Swords to Air are the Golden Dawn attributions. Their original grimoire associations were:

Wands, which were cut at one stroke from a living tree at the stirring of the first breeze of dawn, and therefore = Air.

Swords, forged in the heat of Vulcan's furnace, and used to threaten recalcitrant spirits with burning in hell, and therefore = Fire.

## Column T2: Court Cards and Suits of the Tarot Minor Arcana.

Golden Dawn titles for the 16 Court Cards. There is some controversy about the personages of the four sets of court cards. The Golden Dawn usage was:

| | |
|---|---|
| Fire | King |
| Air | Prince |
| Water | Queen |
| Earth | Princess |

Other commentators introduced Knights and Pages, and even female Knights and female Pages occurred in the older packs. This ascription of the Elements to the Suits dates from recent times.

## Column T5-T8: Titles of the Tarot Court Cards

## Column T9-T12: Titles and Attributions of Pip Cards

The Minor Arcana has 40 pip cards which can be attributed to the 10 Sephiroth. The Golden Dawn titles or divinatory meaning of the 10 numbered or 'pip' cards for each suit (including the 4 Aces) are outlined in these Columns.

## Astrological Dominion

### Column T13-T20: Astrological Attributions of Minor Arcana

The Astrological attributions are from MacGregor Mathers' inventive projection of the cards onto the heavens in his Concourse of the Forces.

## Tarot Shem ha-Mephorash Angels

### Column T21-T28: Pairs of Angels Ruling Court Cards

Pairs of angels rule each of the 36 pip cards (numbers 2 to 10), one by day and one by night.

## Tarot as Emblem Sets

### Column T29-T33: Tarot of Mantegna

The complete 50 Trumps from the Mantegna Tarot, demonstrating what a pack with 5 complete sets of emblems looks like. This is in contrast to the modern Tarot trumps which are made up of four partial or broken emblem sets. Let us look at each of these sets in detail:

### Column T29: Tarot of Mantegna – Astrology series

This shows the traditional 10 Spheres of the cosmos according to the Ptolemaic view. Lines 3 to 9 contain the 7 Planets in traditional order. The Prime Cause or God is ascribed to Kether. Between this and Saturn are squeezed in both the eighth (*Octava Spera*) and ninth Spheres.

### Column T30: Tarot of Mantegna – Virtues series

The Virtues are a set of seven, so to make up the series of ten, the artist (who probably was not Mantegna) creatively added in three 'Spirits': The Spirits of Cosmology, Chronology and Astronomy.

### Column T31: Tarot of Mantegna – Liberal Arts series

The Liberal Arts were divided into the Trivium ('the three roads') and the Quadrivium ('the four roads').

**The Trivium** consisted of verbal and thinking skills:

    a.      Grammar
    b.      Rhetoric
    c.      Logic

**The Quadrivium** consisted of mathematical skills:

    d.      Geometry – Number in space
    e.      Arithmetic – Number in itself
    f.      Music, Harmonics, or Harmonic Theory – Number in tune
    g.      Astronomy or Cosmology – Number in space and time

# Commentary

Although this looks from our perspective to be a bit dry and just a small subset of a possible curriculum, in fact it is in some ways rather better balanced than any modern university course. In the Trivium, the student is taught to write properly and compose correct sentences (Grammar), to think logically, develop an argument, and test each statement (Logic) and then to speak clearly, and deliver his thoughts in a persuasive manner (Rhetoric). Knowing the ins and outs of the latest version of Windows, or the short-lived theories of yet another economist or politician, is no substitute for being able to think and express yourself logically.

The mediaeval Quadrivium followed the division of mathematics made by the Pythagoreans. Recently, mathematics has been defined as 'the study of patterns in space and time,' which very much resembles the ancient Pythagorean understanding of mathematics. The study of geometry is the study of the patterns behind everything, and something which has engaged the finest minds for thousands of years. In fact, with the exception of the *Bible*, versions of Euclid's *Elements of Geometry* have sold more copies than any other book up until the late twentieth century, when it was eclipsed by the magical writings of Tolkien and J K Rowling. Music is no longer considered a science, now that the physics of the spectrum of frequencies has replaced simple musical ratios. Astronomy remains in the curriculum.

Theology and Philosophy were often envisioned as uniting all branches of knowledge, nourishing the Seven Liberal Arts. Poetry was added to make up the numbers.

## Column T32: Tarot of Mantegna – Nine Greek Muses series

The nine Muses, with the god Apollo at their head. See also P20-P21 and Figure 18.

## Column T33: Tarot of Mantegna –Estates of Man series

This Column shows the strata of society as it was in the Late Middle Ages, with the Pope at the top, above the (Holy Roman) Emperor who ruled the Kings of smaller countries who in turn had Dukes or Doges ruling provinces or semi-independent cities (like Milan or Venice). Below that were the gentleman, the merchant, and at the bottom the servants and beggars or fools.

## Column T34-T37: Standard Tarot Analysed into its Separate Symbol series

Here the 22 modern Tarot Trumps are analysed into 4 of their emblem sets, with some of the missing emblems shown. The fact that cards drawn from the same set are mostly sequentially grouped together is further proof of this.

## *Tarot and Sepher Yetzirah*

## Column T38-T41: Planetary Attributions and Tarot Trumps

Column T38-T39 shows the original planetary attributions of the *Sepher Yetzirah*, and the Tarot if it followed these. Column T40-T41 shows Mathers' attributions.

# Table U. Uniform Timeline of Magicians, Kabbalists, Astrologers, Alchemists & Masters

These Columns list some of the most historically important practicing Magicians, Kabbalists, Astrologers and Alchemists together with masters of the Knights Templar and the shadowy Prieure de Sion. The list does not include some of the figures who often feature in popular histories of magic such as Comte de St Germain, Cagliostro (who were both pseudo-aristocratic adventurers) or Giles de Retz (a titled sadistic psychopathic serial killer, who was duped by his priest) who were peripheral to the actual development and practice of magic. More attention has been given to scholar-magicians and practitioners who actually experimented with magic or alchemy, and who passed on the working tradition. Living persons are deliberately excluded to avoid controversy, except for a few notable modern astrologers. There is some slight overlap between lists as skill or reputation in one of these subjects often meant interest in another.

### Column U1: Magicians

This list of magicians and sorcerers also includes philosophers like Pythagoras who at one time or another were rumoured to have exercised magical powers.

### Column U2: Kabbalists

Jewish Kabbalists have been separated from their Christian colleagues who developed the Kabbalah in a rather different direction.

### Column U3: Astrologers

Many of these were Arab astrologers, but when their work was translated into Latin, their names were also simplified, so both their Latin name and their Arabic name are shown to enable them to be more easily identified.

### Column U4: Alchemists

Undoubtedly some important names have been left out from the list of alchemists, for example the Chinese alchemists.

### Column U5-U6: Masters of the Knights Templar

Falsely accused of heresy and blasphemy, the immensely rich Knights Templar may in some sense have been the predecessors of the Freemasons. They were certainly obsessed with the architecture of King Solomon's Temple (on the ruins of which they built their headquarters in Jerusalem). Significantly their fifth Master, André de Montbard was the uncle of St. Bernard of Clairvaux, who preached in favour of the Crusades, and drew up the Templar rules.

# Commentary

## Column U7-U8: Alleged Masters of the *Prieure de Sion*

This column lists the Masters of the *Prieure de Sion* according to the 'Dossiers Secrets' probably drawn up by Henri Lobineau, promoted by Pierre Plantard, and recorded by Michael Baigent.[1] The suspicious inclusion of well known figures, like Newton and da Vinci leaves this list open to considerable doubt. One of the most interesting entries is Charles Nodier who was a librarian at the Arsenal Library in Paris, which contained manuscripts of some of the most interesting grimoires, including the French version of the *Book of Abramelin* later translated by Mathers.

## *Gnostic Prophets*

## Column U9: Gnostic Movements and their Founders

Gnosticism is not a single religion but a term used to embrace a collection of Jewish heresies which also intermixed with Christianity (another Jewish heresy) from the 1st to the 5th century CE. Common elements across the many Gnostic sects, include the rejection of the Creator god (Yahweh or Ialdabaoth), the worship of the serpent who offered knowledge, or *gnosis*, in the Garden of Eden. This serpent appears in a Greek (Abraxas) and Egyptian (Chnoubis) guise. Gnosticism was essentially a revolt against Yahweh, a Jewish heresy, initiated by Samaritan magicians. Where it entwined with Christianity it was simply one Jewish heresy interacting with another, in an era when even the Fathers of the Church flirted with heresies or converted from one to another.

Gnosticism was founded in its early years predominantly by Samaritans. The first eight Gnostic teachers were either Samaritans or lived and taught in Samaria, the most notable of which was Simon Magus. Even Jesus Christ was pro-Samaritan. Most of these teachers were also magicians, including Jesus, who used magic/miracles to impress his converts and draw disciples.

One hallmark of almost all of the Gnostic sects was an admixture of magic. Prophets were expected to do miracles. Nascent Christianity was no exception, as Jesus performed many miracles, and was in his day regularly acclaimed as a magician or wonder-worker.[2] This provided later Christians with an ongoing dilemma as to how to distinguish magic from miracle.

Gnosticism was not initially nor essentially Christian, because the basic premises (such as the evil demiurge, the snake and the rebellion against an evil Creator god) were all very clearly Jewish concerns not Christian ones. Gnosticism is therefore not a source of magical techniques, but an utiliser.[3]

---

[1] In Baigent, Leigh and Lincoln, *The Holy Blood and the Holy Grail*, BCA, London, 1982, p. 101.

[2] See Morton Smith, *Jesus the Magician*.

[3] Efforts by writers such as Thomas Churton, to label certain modern movements as 'gnosticism,' is really just playing with the term adjectively, rather than identifying genuine Gnostic movements.

# Table V. Vedic and Hindu

## *Tattwas*

### Column V1-V2: Hindu Tattwas

The Tattwas are a basic part of Hindu philosophy but they were appropriated by Western occultism over a century ago. They date back to Kapila's Sankhya system which divided the universe into the five basic Elements, the Tattwas, each with its own distinctive shape and colour. The Tattwas became closely linked to yoga *pranayama* techniques and the system of the seven subtle body Chakras (see Columns V7-V12). Tibetan Buddhism also imported the Tattwas from India. In the late 19th century H P Blavatsky utilised esoteric Tibetan Buddhism and chakra symbolism in the structure of her Theosophical Society. Mathers discovered the Tattwas in Rama Prasad's book *Nature's Finer Forces*, and successfully incorporated them into the skrying practices of the Golden Dawn, from where they have become part of the western occult tradition.

### Column V3: Hindu Tattwas - Flashing colours

These are the complementary colours to be used as background or 'charge' colours with the Tattwa symbols. See also Column R12.

### Column V4-V6: Hindu Tattwas – Sense, Sounds & Observances

These are the associations of the Tattwas, and can be used as meditational checks to see if a Tattwa meditation is going particularly well.

## *Chakras*

### Column V7-V17: Hindu Chakras

Chakra literally means 'wheel' but refers to the 7 whirling centres of etheric energy in the body which are affected by various yoga and Tantric practices. They have little to do with what is now commonly purveyed as New Age chakras.

## *Yoga*

### Column V18: Hindu Meditation & Yoga Results

This list is not exhaustive. These results are appropriate to correlate with the Sephiroth, their Planets and the four Elements, but not with the Zodiacal signs.

### Column V19-V20: The Ten Traditional Yamas

A *yama* is a 'restraint' or rule for living virtuously. Ten *yamas* are codified in numerous authorities, including the *Varaha Upanishads*, the *Hatha Yoga Pradipika* by Swatmarama (pupil of Gorakshanatha), and the *Tirumantiram* of Tirumular. Patanjali lists five *yamas* in his *Yoga Sutras of Patanjali*.

### Column V21: The Ten Vayus

# Table W. Wheel of the Year, Seasons, Months and Hours

Timing is very important for the performance of both religious and magical rituals, so as to take advantage of the predominant seasonal or astrological influences. Calculations particularly of the hour, and the lunar month, are important in the timing of magical rituals. It is useful to know the date in different calendars, so I list here the year numbers corresponding to 2006:

| | | |
|---|---|---|
| 5766/7 = Hebrew | 5107/8 = Hindu Kali Yuga | 4702/3 = Chinese |
| 2759 = Roman *Ab Urbe Condita* | 2755 = Egyptian | 2084 = Hindu Saka |
| 2061/2 = Vikram Samvat | 2006 = MMVI Gregorian | 1998/9 = Ethiopian |
| 1995 = Taiwanese | 1928/9 = Shaka Samvat | 1722 = Coptic |
| 1455 = Armenian | 1427/8 = Islamic | 1384/5 = Persian |

## *Seasonal Quarters*

### Column W1-W2: Seasonal Quarters of the Year – Pagan and Christian

The four great northern European pagan festivals, which are now marked and honoured by modern witchcraft. Column W2 gives the Christian names for these festivals which were also subsumed into the calendar of the church.

### Column W3: Seasonal Quarters of the Year – Astronomic

The dates fluctuate each year, and fall between the 20th and 23rd of the month concerned.

## *Planetary Hours*

### Column W4: Genii of the Twelve Hours from the *Nuctemeron*

This list is supplied by Eliphas Levi as a translation from the *Nuctemeron*, said to have been written by Apollonius of Tyana. It is unlikely to have been written by Apollonius and is included here simply for the sake of completeness. One interesting item however is the first Genii of Aries, Papus, which was the pen-name adopted by Dr Gerald Encausse when writing about the Tarot and similar subjects. In *Ritual Magic* Butler expresses her views on Levi's accuracy:

> "Levi seems to be writing with his tongue in his cheek, moved to saturnine mirth by the imbecilities he was describing or inventing or embellishing. Certain it is that his works on magic belong more truly to literature than to the science of the occult; his poetic enthusiasms, his riotous imagination, his vivid style make his books the despair of serious students and the delight of amateurs..."

### Column W5: Table of Planetary Hours

Sunset marks the start of the 12 night hours, and sunrise marks the start of the 12 day hours. This means that night hours may be longer or shorter than day hours, depending on the season. Planetary hours are of elastic length, and depend upon sunset and sunrise times. If you want to be very precise about them, you can check the official time in your local newspaper, or you can check sunset yourself by using the test 'as soon as three stars become visible'.

The determination of Planetary hours is most important for any magical operation. The length of the Hours of the Day are determined by dividing the time between dawn and sunset into 12 equal parts. Likewise the Hours of the Night are derived by dividing the time from sunset to sunrise into 12 equal parts. Obviously as the seasons change so will the length of these hours, so that in winter the Hours of the Night are longer and in summer the Hours of the Day are longer. Only on two nights of the year will all the hours be of equal length and 60 minutes in duration, and this is at the time of the Equinox (which literally means 'equal night'). So bear in mind that the column 'Uneven Hours' means precisely that. The next sub-column which commences at 6.00 AM is there just by way of example, and will only be true twice a year.

## Months

### Column W6-W8: Months of the Jewish Calendar

The current definition of the Jewish calendar is generally said to have been set down by the Sanhedrin president Hillel II in approximately 359 AD. The original details of his calendar are, however, uncertain. The Jewish calendar is both solar and lunar based. The beginning of the year, or *Rosh HaShanah,* falls on the new Moon of 1st Tishri, which will vary from year to year but is approximately mid September to early October. This day is a celebration of the creation of the world and marks the start of a new calendar year. The dates in Column W8 are only approximate, being correct for 2006 only.

Hebrew months, which are lunar based, appear in grimoires alongside the names of angels of the month, indicating the source of a lot of Mediaeval magic.

Years are counted since the creation of the world, which is assumed to have taken place in 3761 BC. In that year, Anno Mundi (AM = Anno Mundi = year of the world) numbering commenced. Therefore the year 2006 will be the Jewish year AM 5766.

### Column W9-W11: Months of the Egyptian Calendar

All Egyptian months were exactly 30 days long. The 5 epagomenal days left over at the end of the year were dedicated to the 5 gods: Osiris, Horus, Set, Isis and Nephthys and were declared holidays. The Egyptian calendar is perhaps the simplest and most straightforward that man has ever devised, but it fell backwards by a day every four years. The year began at the heliacal rising of the star Sothis, and this has been taken in this table for convenience as 20th July, and coincides with the beginning of the Nile floods.

# Commentary

## Column W12: Months of the Ancient Greek Lunar Civil Calendar

Ancient Greek calendars are particularly complex. They are lunar and hence can have 12 months to the year but with a 13th inserted in some years. But, the various city states of ancient Greece did not agree when this event should occur, or even which was the first month of the year. Even odd days were inserted when convenient for religious or political ends. Consequently I have just contented myself with listing their names, rather than attempting to precisely correlate their dates with the Zodiac, which is an impossible task as it varied year to year and state to state, so the left two columns are very rough. The principle use of this table is to be able to recognise ancient Greek month names in Greek texts. The first month of each year is indicated by '(1)'.

## Column W13: Months of the Ancient Babylonian Calendar

The Babylonian year begins with the new Moon of Spring, and the year contains either 12 or sometimes 13 lunar months. The first column is the simple Sumerian ideogram, while the second column is the actual month name. If you look at the first month Nisannu you can see that it is the obvious source of the first Hebraic month of Nisan, which in turn appears in Mediaeval grimoires.

## Column W14: The mini-Seasons of the Chinese Solar Calendar

Legend has it that the Emperor Huang Ti invented the calendar in 2637 BC. The Chinese calendar is based on exact astronomical observations of the sun and the phases of the moon. Chinese years are also denoted in terms of Emperor reign years, and measured in terms of the 60 Sexagenary characters, which cycle round every 60 years. These are made up of combinations of the 10 Heavenly Stems and the 12 Earthly Branches, which are listed in Table F.

There are two calendars, one Solar and one Lunar.

a. The Solar Calendar, also called the farmers' calendar, agricultural calendar, or Hsia calendar. This is based on the Sun and the cycles of the seasons, and in some ways is more accurate than the western Gregorian calendar. This is divided into 24 *ch'i/chieh* periods or mini seasons tabulated here. The numbering begins with Li Ch'un, or the beginning of Spring on 4/5th February. The dates barely change from year to year, and then only by a day or so (a fluctuation caused by the Western device of leap years rather than by any inherent errors in the Hsia calendar). This is the calendar used for feng shui calculations.

b. The Lunar calendar, which determines most Chinese religious festivals. This can have either 12 or 13 months, which is why the Chinese Lunar New Year celebration moves its date each year between January and February. This calendar is usually what people are referring to when they give the year an animal name. For the dates of the next 15 lunar years see Column F54.

# Table X: Cross-Reference to Greek *Isopsephy*

*Isopsephy* is the Greek equivalent of Hebrew *Gematria*, the addition of the numerical values of the constituent letters of a word to give a total which then in a way represents the essence of that word. It has been claimed that Greek isopsephy predates the Hebrew practice. It is certainly true that many mystical Greek and Gnostic words have actually been devised with an eye to their numerical value, and as we have seen with the Mithraic mysteries and with the Olympic spirits, there is often a patterning of the numbers which does not occur nearly so frequently in Hebrew Gematria. In fact *deliberate* isopsephy is much more common than deliberate Gematria.

There is a fundamental difference between these two cultures. The Greek approach is often to specifically choose words for their numeric totals, whilst the Hebrew approach is to see what total the word happens to have, and to use that number as an aid to its interpretation or exegesis.

It is true to say that often single Gematria equivalences are false or coincidental, but where a whole set of words have the same multiplier or differences, or have common significant totals, then we are on much firmer ground.

## Column X1: Greek Isopsephy

This table contains a selection of only the more important Greek isopsephy equivalences, particularly the isopsephy of the major Greek gods. Apart from these, a number of Gnostic words of power have been included. Also abstract nouns like 'love' and 'will' are quite instructive in the light of isopsephy. For example, it is very revealing that the last two words both add to 93, and Aleister Crowley chose to base his theology on both 'Will' and 'Love'. As further confirmation of the connection between these two words, even their alternative Greek spelling also adds to the same number, 551.

There are also Gematria and isopsephy keys buried in the structure of the present book. In the Subject Listing of Tables, for example, the sections listed under Magic are Tables ADGM NOT. The numeric total of ADGM is 48, the numeration of כוכב Kokab, the Sphere of Mercury, god of Magic. Its Greek numeration is also 48, the numeration of μη or 'not', confirming the word NOT that follows. That word NOT adds to an isopsephy total of 420, Ισις or Isis. It also equates with Ζησες, 'arise and live again'.

For this section I am indebted to Kieren Barry's brilliant book[1] which goes a long way towards adjusting the cultural balance and showing that we have to thank the Greeks as much as the Hebrews for the subtle and sometimes magical links between numbers and words. Note that there are sometimes two different Greek spellings of the same word, especially where *epsilon* and *eta* are interchangeable.

---

[1] *The Greek Qabalah*, Weiser, York Beach, 1999.

# Table Y. *Yi Jing* or *I Ching*

The *I Ching* is one of the oldest and most respected of the Chinese classics. It is considered both as a work of philosophy and as a stand alone divination system. It is in the later capacity that it has been seconded to Western occultism, where it stands alongside astrology, geomancy and the Tarot as one of the four main systems of divination currently practiced in the West. The 1960s saw a rapid increase in its use and appreciation in the West. Divination usually proceeds by casting three coins six times and using these casts to determine if each of the six lines of the hexagram is either yin or yang.

The resulting hexagram (and the hexagram that it may transmute into) is then looked up in the *I Ching*, and the text there found applied oracularly to the situation being enquired about. It is only now that some of the more advanced systems of divination, based solely on numerical and trigram analysis rather than the text are making themselves felt in the West as well.

The arrangements of the constituent trigrams on the Tree of Life are shown in Columns F1-F3. Those arrangements are completely new, and arranged in accordance with the Chinese view of the trigrams, rather than an attempt to force these symbols into an arbitrary Western mould which ignores their real meaning.

### Column Y1: The 64 Hexagrams

The 64 hexagrams are formed from the eight trigrams, combined in pairs. The resultant hexagrams (grouped by their generating trigrams) are shown in Column Y1. The sequence used follows their arrangement on any traditional San Yuan feng shui *lo p'an*, and also in classic Chinese editions of the *I Ching*.

### Column Y2: King Wen's Sequence of the Hexagrams.

This revealing layout has been suggested by Denis Mair's work, and relies upon each pair of hexagrams being the reverse of its adjacent partner. This Column is very useful in understanding the true nature of each of the hexagrams, as analysed through their pairing.

### Column Y3: Eight Trigrams or *pa kua*.

The Trigrams or *kua* are one of the basic constituents of Chinese philosophy and cosmology and also the root of the *I Ching*.

# Table Z. Zones of Body, Mind and Spirit

This Table looks at how the mind, body and spirit of man have been analysed from time immemorial, from the many division of the soul discerned by the Egyptians and Chinese which are considerably more complex than the comparatively simple divisions of modern psychology.

Esoteric anatomy runs the gamut from the purely symbolical astrological equivalents of the body, to the semi-physical etheric parts of the body as described by the Hindu chakras (see Columns V8-V12) and the Chinese acupuncture meridians (Columns Z5-Z9).

## *Parts of the Body*

### Column Z1: The Human Body

The attributions for rows 1-10 are derived from Agrippa.[1]

### Column Z2: The Members of the Body of the Terrestrial Man

These attributions are according to Basnage's tables of 'Rabbinical Significations of the Sephiroth', which in some ways are more logical than Agrippa's more well known attributions.

The lower half of this Column comes from the Short version of the *Sepher Yetzirah.*.

### Column Z3: *Sepher Yetzirah* Body Attributions

The attributions in this Column come from the Long version of the *Sepher Yetzirah*. This also agrees with Scholem and the arrangement by the Ramak in *Pardes Rimonim*. See Column Z2 for the Short version attributions. There are many other variations, another of which appeared in this Column in the First Edition. However, bodily part attributions to the Hebrew letters and hence to the Zodiacal signs and planets are not nearly as critical as for example, the astrological identification of the Hebrew letters.

### Column Z4: Typical Diseases

This list predominantly follows astrological considerations.

### Column Z5-Z9: Chinese Acupuncture Meridians

The main groupings of six Yin and six Yang meridians are attributed to the Moon and Sun respectively. The rest are *jing* meridians attributed on the basis of equating the 12 Chinese Earthly Branches with the 12 Western Zodiacal signs. The connection with the Earthly Branches is fully justified, but their association with the 12 Zodiacal signs is just a convenience, so do not try to extrapolate these correspondences any further than that.

---

[1] Agrippa, *Three Books of Occult Philosophy*, Llewellyn, St Paul, 1993, pages 288-9.

# Commentary

## Parts of the Soul

### Column Z10-Z12: Kabbalistic Parts of the Soul

Crowley allocates the 'Parts of the Soul' to the 5 Elemental Paths as well as the Sephiroth. The correct place for these however is just on the 10 Sephiroth, as shown in this column.

### Column Z13-Z16: Egyptian Parts of the Soul

There is no universal agreement on the attribution of the Egyptian parts of the soul, except that they are numerous, so four possible attributions have been listed. The last Column is my own view. The parts of the soul are:

* Akhu (Akh, Khu, Ikhu) - The immortal part, the radiant and shining being that lived on in the Sahu, the intellect, will and intentions of the deceased that lives with the gods or the imperishable stars. The Akhu came in to being after the deceased passed post-mortem judgement, and the Ka and Ba were united.
* Ka - The double that lingered in the tomb inhabiting the body or even statues of the deceased, independent of man and could move, eat and drink at will.
* Ba - The human headed bird that flitted around in the tomb during the day bringing air and food to the deceased, but travelled with Ra on the Solar Barque at night.
* Ren - The true name, a magical part that could be used to destroy a man if his name was obliterated, or could give a magician power over the man.
* Sekhem - The incorporeal personification of the life force of man, which lived in heaven with the Akhu after death.
* Ab - The heart, the source of good and evil within a person, the centre of thought that could leave the body at will, and live with the gods after death, or be eaten by Ammut at the final death, if it failed to weigh against the feather of Ma'at.
* Sahu - The incorruptible spiritual body of man that could dwell in the heavens, appearing from the physical body after the judgement of the dead was passed, with all of the mental and spiritual abilities of a living body.
* Khaibt - The shadow of a man that could partake of funerary offerings and was able to detach itself from the body and travel at will, but stayed near the Ba.
* Khat - The mortal physical form, the body that could decay after death, unless preserved by mummification.

### Column Z17-Z20: Hindu Parts of the Soul

The Theosophical Planes are grouped with Hindu categories as that is where they were ultimately derived from.

### Column Z21-Z22: The Five Hindu Khandas

Sometimes these are referred to as Skandas, which are the subtle parts of the body making up the Self.

## Senses and Bodily Functions

### Column Z23-Z25: The Senses, Body and Bodily Functions

These are a bit speculative, and are predominantly based on astrological considerations.

# REFERENCE

# Biography

This section is a quick look at the biographies of the writers whose works have contributed most to these tables. In almost every case there is a direct connection between each person and the next name of this list, as the magical tradition has clearly passed from one hand to another down the centuries.

### Honorius of Thebes (fl. 1225)

Author of *Liber Sacer*, the 'Holy Book', also know as *Liber Juratus* or *The Sworn Book*, the most influential grimoire of the early 13th century.

### Peter de Abano (1250-1317)

Peter de Abano was one of the most important scholars of his day. His *Heptameron* was also one of the most influential grimoires, and his correlation of angels and days of the week prevails to this day.

### Johannes Trithemius (1462-1516)

Trithemius was an Abbott and key exponent of both cryptography and angel magic. He obviously had a keen sense of humour, for in his most famous work, the *Steganographia*, he utilised one dangerous subject (cryptography) in the service of another dangerous subject (magic). He used De Abano's work, and was a teacher and mentor to both Agrippa and Paracelsus.

### Francesco Giorgio (1466-1540)

He was a Venetian monk, fascinated by correspondences and sacred geometry, the author of an enormous Pythagorean treatise called *De Harmonia Totius Mundi* (1525) 'The Harmony of all the World'. He was an early 'Christian Kabbalist' and was responsible for recommending the use of a geometry derived from Plato's *Timaeus* in the building of a church. See Figure 18 for an example of the correspondences which he saw in the Nine Muses of Greek myth, planets and musical notes. He also constructed lists of correspondences between animals, plants, minerals and the planets.

### Henry Cornelius Agrippa (1486-1535)

Agrippa's *Three Books of Occult Philosophy* published in 1533 was the standard work of the period on magic, upon which John Dee and later commentators, right up to the present day, drew heavily.

### Dr John Dee (1527-1608)

Key scholar-magician, and centre of many of the intellectual movements of his day, from introducing the geometry of Euclid to the English speaking world in a practical format, to devising the navigational methods and charts which underpinned Elizabethan England's exploration and colonisation of much of the world. He is also credited, with good reason, with being a precursor of the Rosicrucian movement. His main sources were grimoires such as the *Heptameron* and *Liber Sacer*, and Agrippa.

### Tycho Brahe (1541-1601)

This famous astrologer and astronomer was a key figure whose precise observations of the planets enabled Kepler to construct his famous laws of circumsolar planetary motion. Both also cast horoscopes. Brahe was in touch with John Dee, and in 1590 Brahe[1] wrote that he was sending his latest book to the 'most noble and illustrious John Dee' for his opinion. Brahe is credited with devising the format of the *Magical Calendar*, the archetypal single page tabular summary of magical knowledge published in 1620, although its actual author is listed as Johan Baptista Großschedel ab Aicha. It is interesting that Brahe whose standards of factual observation were so high, felt that tables of magical correspondences were also worthy of his serious attention.

### Dr Thomas Rudd (1583-1665)

Rudd was a key angel magician of the 17th century who met Dee, and was responsible for developing his angel magic. His work is in the course of being published by the Golden Hoard Press.

### Christian Knorr von Rosenroth (1636 - 1689)

During his lifetime von Rosenroth was reputed to be the most profound Christian scholar of the Kabbalah, and was in touch with Leibniz, Henry More and Van Helmont. Von Rosenroth's *Kabbalah Denudata*, or the 'Kabbalah Revealed' which was published in Latin in 1677-84, was the most significant non-Hebrew source of Kabbalistic knowledge up to the end of the 19th century, and the source of much Golden Dawn Kabbalah. It contained a number of Kabbalistic classics by various authors, like Luria, Vital, Gikatilla, and Cordovero's *Pardes Rimmonim*, and was not just a partial translation of the *Zohar*, as many people seem to think. It even contained works like *Aesch Mezareph* (or *Esh ha-Mezareph)*, which was translated into English by Westcott, and for which the Hebrew text was subsequently lost.

### Helena Petrovna Blavatsky (1831-1891)

Blavatsky co-founded the Theosophical Society in 1875. As a result of this plus her monumental works, *The Secret Doctrine* and *Isis Unveiled,* she introduced a lot of Eastern esoteric and philosophical thought into the West, and was probably responsible for the concept of secret Masters that so fascinated Mathers, and for Crowley's enthusiasm for all things Eastern. Indirectly she is responsible for the Vedic and Buddhist Columns in this book.

---

[1] In a letter to Sir Thomas Savile edited by J O Halliwell and published in 1841.

*S L MacGregor Mathers (1854 - 1918)*

Mathers was the primary scholar-magician behind the creation of the Hermetic Order of the Golden Dawn. He translated parts of the second volume of von Rosenroth's *Kabbalah Denudata* and published it as the *Kabbalah Unveiled*. This, along with the *Sepher Yetzirah*, formed the basis of most Golden Dawn speculations upon the Kabbalah.

His work also included the transcription and translation of various key grimoires, such as the *Key of Solomon, Goetia* (part I of the *Lemegeton*)[1], *Almadel*, and the *Sacred Magic of Abramelin the Mage*. Many of the angels and demons in this volume are drawn from these books.

Mathers also wrote and brought together the knowledge lectures of the Golden Dawn, which were later embellished and published by Aleister Crowley as *Liber 777*.

*Aleister Crowley (1875-1947)*

A poet, mountain climber and major figure in 20th century occultism. His most important work was probably *Magick in Theory and Practice*. He was responsible for editing and putting into print a lot of MacGregor Mathers' work including the rituals of the Golden Dawn (in Volume I of the *Equinox*), the *Goetia* and the Golden Dawn 'Book of Correspondences' as *Liber 777*.

*Israel Regardie (1907-1985)*

Like Crowley, Israel Regardie also broke his vows and published the Golden Dawn (or Stella Matutina in his case) rituals and knowledge lectures. He had a precedent for this as he was Crowley's secretary for a while in Paris and London. Regardie published the four volume set of Golden Dawn rituals and Knowledge lectures in 1937-1940, and his edition of MacGregor Mathers' work forms the basis for many columns in the present Volume.

Amongst modern researchers in this field, the names that stand out for original magical scholarship are Adam McLean (for his Hermetic Sourceworks series), Donald Tyson (for his edition of Agrippa's *Three Books of Occult Philosophy*), and Joseph Peterson (for his editions of John Dee's works and the *Lemegeton*, not to mention the *Twilight Grotto* CD collection of classical magical texts).

David Godwin (for his *Cabalistic Encyclopedia*), David Hulse (for his two massive volumes on the *Western Mysteries* and the *Eastern Mysteries*) and Bill Whitcomb, need to be acknowledged for the encyclopaedic work they have done in bringing together much of the above in a more easily accessible form.

---

[1] The standard edition of the *Lemegeton* is that edited by Joseph Peterson. Dr Rudd's version of the *Goetia* is published as Volume 3 of Sourceworks of Ceremonial Magic, Golden Hoard Press, London & Singapore, 2007.

# Bibliography

Agrippa, H. C. *Three Books of Occult Philosophy*. Translated by James Freake [John French]. Edited by Donald Tyson. Llewellyn, St Paul, 1993.

Agrippa, H. C. *Fourth Book of Occult Philosophy*. First facsimile edition Askin Publishers, London, 1978. It includes:

> *Of Occult Magical Ceremonies* by Agrippa;
> *Heptameron or Magical Elements* by Peter de Abano;
> *Of the Nature of Spirits* by Georg Villinganus;
> *Arbatel of Magick*;
> *Of Geomancy* by Agrippa;
> *Of Astronomical Geomancy* by Gerard Cremonensis.

> Modern edition edited and annotated by Stephen Skinner, Nicolas-Hays, Berwick, 2005.

Bardon, Franz. *Initiation into Hermetics*. Osiris-Verlag, Koblenz, 1962.

Bardon, Franz. *The Practice of Magical Evocation*. Pravica, Graz-Puntigam, 1967.

Barry, Kieren. *The Greek Qabalah: Alphabetic Mysticism and Numerology in the Ancient World*. Samuel Weiser, York Beach, 1999.

Ch'ien, Kineta [Trans.] *The Great Grimoire of Pope Honorius.*, Trident, Seattle, 1999.

Charlesworth, James [Editor]. *The Old Testament Pseudepigraphia: Apocalyptic Literature and Testaments*. Doubleday, New York, 1983.

Collins, Andrew. *From the Ashes of Angels*. Signet, London, 1997.

Conway, D. J. *Magick of the Gods and Goddesses*. Crossing Press, Berkeley, 2003.

Crowley, Aleister (edited by Gerald Yorke). *777 Revised*. Neptune Press, London, 1955. Limited to 1,100 copies. [First published anonymously in 1909.]

Crowley, Aleister. *Magick in Theory and Practice*. Lecram Press, Paris, 1929.

Cumont, Franz. *Astrology and Religion among the Greeks and Romans*. Dover, NY, 1960

Davidson, Gustav. *A Dictionary of Angels*. Free Press, New York, 1967.

Driscoll, Daniel J. *The Sworn Book of Honorius the Magician.*, Heptangle, New Jersey, 1977.

Dumas, Francois Ribadeau. *Grimoires et Rituels Magiques*. Pierre Belfond, Paris, 1972.

Fanger, Claire. *Conjuring Spirits: Texts and Traditions of Medieval Ritual Magic*. Pennsylvania State University Press, Pennsylvania, 1998.

Gilly, Carlos, 'The rediscovery of the original of Großschedel's Calendarium Naturale Magicum Perpetuum,' in Carlos Gilly, Cis van Heertum (ed.) *Magia, Alchimia, Scienza Dal '400 al '700*. L'influsso di Ermete Trismegisto Centro, Florence, 2002, vol. 1 pp. 310-317.

Godwin, David. *Godwin's Cabalistic Encyclopedia*. Llewellyn, St Paul, 2004.

Gollancz, Hermann. [Foreword by Stephen Skinner.] *Sepher Maphteah Shelomoh (Book of the Key of Solomon)*. Teitan, York Beach, 2008.

Hand, Robert. *Chronology of the Astrology of the Middle East and the West by Period*, Arhat, Reston, 1998.

Hedegard, Gosta. *Liber Iuratus Honorii.* Almqvist & Wiksell, Stockholm, 2002.

Hepburn, James. *Virga Aurea,* Rome, 1616.

Hulse, David Allen. *The Eastern Mysteries: an Encyclopedic Guide to the Sacred Languages & Magical Systems of the World.* Book I, Llewellyn, St. Paul, 2004.

Hulse, David Allen. *The Western Mysteries: an Encyclopedic Guide to the Sacred Languages & Magical Systems of the World.* Book II, Llewellyn, St. Paul, 2004.

James, Geoffrey. *The Enochian Evocation of Dr John Dee.* Heptangle, New Jersey, 1984.

Kieckhefer, Richard. *Forbidden Rites: a Necromancer's Manual of the Fifteenth Century.* Sutton, Stroud, 1997.

Kiesel, William [Editor]. *Picatrix: the Ghayat al-Hakim.* Books I-IV. Ouroboros Press, Seattle, 2002 [Volume I] and 2008 [Volume II].

Kaplan, Aryeh. *Sepher Yetzirah: The Book of Creation.* Weiser, Boston, 1997.

Karr, Don and Stephen Skinner [Editors]. *Sepher Raziel,* SWCM Volume 6, Golden Hoard Press, Singapore, 2010.

Kuntz, Darcy [Editor]. *The Grand Grimoire.* Holmes, Sequim, 2005.

Laycock, Dr Donald. *The Complete Enochian Dictionary.* Askin, London, 1978.

Luck, Georg. *Arcana Mundi.* Crucible Aquarian, London, 1987.

Mathers, S.L. MacGregor. *The Kabbalah Unveiled.* Weiser, New York, 1974.

Mathers, S L MacGregor. *The Sacred Magic of Abramelin the Mage.* Watkins, London, 1900.

Mathers, S L MacGregor. *The Key of Solomon the King (Clavicula Salomonis).* Kegan Paul, London, 1909.

Matt, Daniel C. *The Zohar.* Pritzker Edition. Stanford University Press, Stanford, 2004.

McLean, Adam. *The Magical Calendar.* Magnum Opus Hermetic Sourceworks Volume 1. Edinburgh, 1979. Limited edition of 100 copies.

McLean, Adam. *A Treatise on Angel Magic: being a Complete Transcription of MS Harley 6482.* Magnum Opus Hermetic Sourceworks Volume 15, Edinburgh, 1982. Reprinted Phanes Press, 1990.

Naveh, Joseph. *Origins of the Alphabet.* Jerusalem Publishing, Jerusalem, 1994.

Parkhurst, John. *An Hebrew and English Lexicon without Points.* Faden, London, 1762.

Peterson, Joseph [Editor] *John Dee's Five Books of Mystery* [Sloane MS 3188]. Weiser, Boston, 2003.

Peterson, Joseph [Editor] *The Lesser Key of Solomon: Lemegeton Clavicula Salomonis.* Weiser Books, York Beach, 2001.

Peterson, Joseph. *Grimorium Verum.* CreateSpace, Scotts Valley, 2007.

Rankine, David. *Heka: The Practices of Ancient Egyptian Ritual & Magic.* Avalonia, London, 2006.

Rankine, David. *Climbing the Tree of Life.* Avalonia, London, 2005.

Rankine, David & Sorita D'Este. *The Isles of the Many Gods.* Avalonia, London, 2007.

Regardie, Israel. *The Golden Dawn. 4 Vols.* Llewellyn, St. Paul, 2005.

Regardie, Israel. *A Garden of Pomegranates.* Llewellyn, St. Paul, 1970.

Regardie, Israel. *The Tree of Life: a Study in Magic.* Rider, London, 1932.

Robinson, James. *The Nag Hammadi Library in English.* Harper, San Francisco, 1990.

Rosenroth, Knorr Baron von. *Kabbalah Denudata.* Frankfort, 1677-1684.

Rudy, Gretchen [Trans.] *The Grand Grimoire,* edited by Antonio Venitiana del Rabina, Trident & Ars Obscura, Seattle, 1996.

Scarborough, John. 'The Pharmacology of Sacred Plants, Herbs, and Roots' in *Magika Hiera: Ancient Greek Magic and Religion* ed. Faraone and Obbink. New York: OUP, 1991, pp. 138-174.

Shah, Idries. *The Secret Lore of Magic: the Books of the Sorcerers.* Muller, London, 1957.

Skinner, Stephen. *Geomancy in Theory and Practice* (previously entitled *Terrestrial Astrology).* RKP, London, 1980, revised Golden Hoard, Singapore, 2011.

Skinner, Stephen. *Sacred Geometry,* Gaia Books (Hamlyn), London, 2006.

Skinner, Stephen (ed.) and Meric Casaubon (ed). *Dr John Dee's Spiritual Diaries,* being revised *True & Faithful Relation…* Golden Hoard Press, London, 2011.

Skinner, Stephen & Rankine, David. *The Practical Angel Magic of John Dee's Enochian Tables,* SWCM Volume 1, Golden Hoard Press, London & Singapore, 2004.

Skinner, Stephen & Rankine, David. *The Keys to the Gateway of Magic: Summoning the Solomonic Archangels and Demon Princes.* SWCM Volume 2, Golden Hoard Press, London & Singapore, 2005.

Skinner, Stephen & Rankine, David. *Dr Rudd's Goetia: Angels & Demons,* SWCM Volume 3, Golden Hoard Press, London & Singapore, 2007.

Skinner, Stephen & Rankine, David. *The Veritable Key of Solomon,* SWCM Volume 4, Golden Hoard Press, London & Singapore, 2008.

Skinner, Stephen & Rankine, David. *The Grimoire of St Cyprian: Clavis Inferni,* SWCM Volume 5, Golden Hoard Press, London & Singapore, 2009.

Skinner, Stephen. *Techniques of Graeco-Egyptian Magic.* Golden Hoard Press, Singapore, 2014.

Thorndike, Lynn, *A History of Magic and Experimental Science,* Columbia University Press, New York, 1958.

Tishby, Isaiah. *The Wisdom of the Zohar.* 3 Volumes, Littman Library, Oxford, 1989.

Trithemius, Abbot Johannes. *Steganographia.* Frankfurt, 1606.

Trithemius, Abbot Johannes. *Polygraphia.* 1518.

Wang, Robert. *The Rape of Jewish Mysticism by Christian Theologians.* Marcus Aurelius, Columbia, 2001.

Waite, Arthur. *The Holy Kabbalah.* Williams & Norgate, London, 1926.

Warnock, Christopher. *The Mansions of the Moon.* Renaissance Astrology, 2006.

Whitcombe, Bill. *The Magician's Companion.* Llewellyn, St Paul, 2004.

# Full Index of Individual Columns

D2. Planet – Agrippa.

D3. Zodiacal Sign – Agrippa.

D4. Names of the Parts of the Earth.

D5. Names of the parts of the Earth drawn from Dee's reformed Angelic table.

D6. 30 Spheric Aethers of the good Princes of the Air.

D7. Tripartite number of good servants of each Order.

D8. Total Number of tripartite good servants in each Order.

D9. 12 Angel Kings ruling their 30 Orders, who rule also over 12 Tribes.

D10. 12 Tribes of Israel at their dispersal.

D11. Zodiac Mapped on to the Geography of the Ancient World.

D12. John Dee's 49 *Bonorum Angelorum*.

D13. Day of Week.

D14. The Heptarchical Kings (without their initial 'B').

D15. The Heptarchical Princes (without their initial 'B').

D16. John Dee's *Sigillum Dei Aemeth*.

D17 *Clavicula Tabularum Enochi*.

D18. The Tablet of Union.

D19. Watchtowers – Direction and Quadrant.

D20. Watchtower Colour (Dee).

D21. Watchtower Colour (Golden Dawn).

D22. The Kings and Seniors of the *Tabularum Enochi*.

D23. Angels of the *Tabularum Enochi*.

E1. Alchemical Elements on the Tree of Life – 1.

E2. Alchemical Elements on the Tree of Life – 2.

E3. Chemical Elements (Golden Dawn).

E4. Chemical Symbol and Latin Names of Planetary Metals.

E4a. Periodic Table for Planetary Metals: Number, Row & Column.

E5. Alchemical Processes – Lapidus.

E6. Ripley's *Twelve Gates*.

E7. *Splendor Solis* Emblems.

E8. *Splendor Solis* – Images in the Surrounding Frame.

E9. *Book of Lambspring* Emblems.

E10. *The Twelve Keys* of Basil Valentinus Emblems.

E11. *Atlanta Fugiens* Emblems.

F1. Taoism and Trigrams of the Former Heaven Sequence.

F2. Taoism and Trigrams of the Former Heaven Sequence – English.

F3. The *kua*.

F4. The Five Chinese Planets – Chinese.

F5. The Five Chinese Planets – English.

F6. Five Chinese Elements.

F7. Five Colours.

F8. Seasons.

F9. Five Directions.

F10. Five Traditional Emperors.

F11. Five Sacrifices and Five Key Feng Shui points.

F12. Five Spirits or *shen*.

F13. Later Heaven Sequence Numbers.

F14. Former Heaven Sequence Numbers.

F15. Five Tastes.

F16. Five Odours.

F17. Five Organs.

F18. Five Musical Notes.

F19. Five types of Creature.

F20. Heavenly Stems – Chinese.

F21. Heavenly Stems – English.

F22. Heavenly Stems – Yin or Yang.

F23. Heavenly Stems – Element.

F24. Heavenly Stems – Associated Spirit – Chinese.

F25. Heavenly Stems – Associated Spirit – English.

F26. Chinese Astrology – 12 'Zodiacal' Animals.

F27. Chinese Astrology – 12 'Zodiacal' Animals.

F28. The Twelve Branches – Chinese.

F29. The Twelve Branches – English.

F30. The Twelve Branches – Yin and Yang.

F31. The Twelve Branches – Elements.

F32. Triplicity of Harmonious Branches.

F33. Triplicity of Punishment Branches.

F34. Post Horse Branches.

F35. Nine Flying Stars – Chinese.

F36. Nine Flying Stars – Transliterated.

F37. Nine Flying Stars – English.

F38. Nine Flying Stars – usual Chinese order.

F39. Talismans of the Nine Stars.

F40. The Nine Stars – Chinese.

F41. The Nine Stars – Secret Star Name.

F42. The Nine Stars – Compass Direction.

F43. The Nine Stars – Trigram.

F44. The Nine Stars – Position on the *lo shu*.

F45. The Nine Stars – Element.

F46. Eight Taoist Immortals *pa hsien* – Chinese.

F47. Eight Taoist Immortals *pa hsien* – English.

F48. Eight Taoist Immortals – Qualities and Symbols.

F49. 12 of the *shen* of the 60 *Chia-Tzu* Cyclical characters – Chinese.

F50. 12 of the *shen* of the 60 *Chia-Tzu* Cyclical characters – Transliterated.

F51. The 12 *Ting-Chia* Spirits – Chinese.

F52. The 12 *Ting-Chia* Spirits – Transliterated.

F53. Chinese Animal and Element Year 60-Year Cycle.

F54. Start of the Chinese Lunar New Year.

F55. Chinese Animal and Element Year – Luck, Vitality and Destiny Cycles.

F56. The 24 Mountains of the *lo p'an* or Chinese compass.

G1. Geomantic Binary Figures.

G2. Traditional Meaning.

G3. Geomantic Elements.

G4. Geomantic Attributions to the Zodiac.

G5. Latin Names from Hugh of Santalla.

G6. Other Latin from *Geomantie Nova*.

G6a. Latin from Gerard of Cremona (1114-1187)

G7. Traditional Arabic Names.

G8. Traditional Arabic Meanings.

G9. Arabic Names in Kordofan (Sudan).

G10. Divinatory Meaning in Kordofan (Sudan).

G11. Greek Geomantic Names – Pierre de Montdore,

G12. Greek Geomantic Names – Georges Midiates.

G13. French Provençale Names.

G14. Hebrew Names.

G15. Hebrew Names – Meaning.

G16. Hebrew Names – in Hebrew Characters.

G17. Malagasy Hova Interior Dialect Name.

G18. Malagasy Antanosy & Sakalava West Coast Name.

G19. Malagasy Name from Fort Dauphin Region.

G20. Central African Tribal Name from Sara Madjingaye

G21. Central African Tribal Name from Sara Deme Figure

G22. Central African Name from Dakhel (NE Chad).

G23. West African Tribal name from Dahomey.

G24. Islamic Patriarchs – Bambara (Mali).

G25. Dr. Rudd's Geomantic Intelligence – Hebrew.

# Commentary

# Commentary

M18. Demons of the *Goetia* by Rank, Planet and Zodiacal Sign.

M19. Demons of the *Goetia* by Title, Planet and Legions.

M20. Good and Evil Aerial Spirits (of the Compass) from *Theurgia Goetia* (*Lemegeton* Book II*).

M20a. Good and Evil Aerial Spirits (Wandering Princes) from *Theurgia Goetia* (*Lemegeton* Book II*).

M21. Emperors of the Good and Evil Aerial Spirits from *Theurgia Goetia* (*Lemegeton* Book II*).

M22. Spirits of the Hours from *Ars Paulina* Part 1 – *Lemegeton* (Book III – 1).

M23. Angels of the Degrees of the Zodiac from *Ars Paulina* (Part 2) *Lemegeton* (Book III – 2).

M24. Angels of the Altitudes (*Choras*) from *Ars Almadel* – *Lemegeton* (Book IV).

M25. Hours of the Day and Night from *The Key Of Solomon*, and the Angels that rule them.

M26. The Servient Spirits from *Abramelin*.

M27. Hierarchy of the Abramelin Demons.

M27a. Grimoire Magical Equipment.

M28. Abramelin Magical Operations.

M29. Magical Objectives and Abilities.

M30. Franz Bardon's Spirit Hierarchy from *Practice of Magical Evocation*.

M31. Magical Squares of the Planets – Key Numbers.

M32. Intelligences of the Planets – Hebrew.

M33. Intelligences of the Planets – Transliteration.

M34. Intelligences of the Planets – English.

M35. Intelligences of the Planets – Numeration.

M36. Spirits of the Planets – Hebrew.

M37. Spirits of the Planets – Transliteration.

M38. Spirits of the Planets – English.

M39. Spirits of the Planets – Numeration.

M40. The Familiar Shapes of the Planetary Spirits.

M41. The Visible Appearance of the Planetary Spirits.

M42. Olympic Spirits.

M43. Olympic Spirits – Greek Orthography.

M44. Olympic Spirits – Numeration.

M45. Olympic Spirits – Ministers.

M46. Olympic Spirits – Legions Commanded.

M47. Olympic Spirits – Provinces.

M48. Olympic Spirits – Powers & Attributes.

M49. Olympic Planetary Spirits – Days.

M50. Olympic Planetary Spirits – Years Ruled.

M51. Hebrew Name of Element.

M52. Bodily Humour & Elemental Qualities.

M53. Kings of the Elemental Spirits.

M54. The Rulers of the Elements.

M55. The Rulers of the Elements – English.

M56. The Rulers of the Elements – Numeration.

M57. Angels of the Elements.

M58. Angels of the Elements, English.

M59. Angels of the Elements – Numeration.

M60. Traditional Names of the Elementals.

M61. Enochian Elemental Kings.

M62. Demon Kings of the Quarters.

M63. Traditional Demon Kings.

M64. Hebrew Demon Princes.

M65. Cardinal Directions.

M66. Winds of the 4 Quarters.

M67. Rivers of Hell.

M68. The 4 Kerubs.

M69. Demons of the *Grimorium Verum*.

M70. Demons of the *Grand Grimoire*.

M71. Demons of Faust's *Dreifacher Höllenzwang*.

M72. Planetary Angels and Spirits of the *Steganographia* Book III.

M73. Graeco-Egyptian Magic – headwords and types

M74. Graeco-Egyptian *nomina magica*

N1. Animals – Real.

N2. Animals – Imaginary and Legendary Orders of Being.

N3. Birds.

N4. Extended Plant Planetary Correspondences.

N5. Plants.

N6. Vegetable and Synthetic Drugs.

N7. The 16 Traditional Magical Plants of Albertus Magnus.

N8. Precious and Semi-Precious Stones.

N9. Metals and Minerals.

N9a. Rocks, Metals and Semi-Precious Stones according to the *Picatrix*.

N10. Stones of the High Priest's Breastplate.

N11. Perfumes and Incenses.

N12. Zodiacal Perfumes (Ascendant Decans).

N13. Zodiacal Perfumes (Succedent Decans).

N14. Zodiacal Perfumes (Cadent Decans).

N15. Planetary Perfume Compounds.

N16. Complete Perfumes from *Liber Juratus*.

N17. Perfumes of the Sub-Elements.

N18. Fumigations from the *Mystical Hymns of Orpheus*.

N19. Incense from the *Greek Magical Papyri*.

N20. Perfumes and their Plant Source.

N21. Incenses in the *Book of Jubilees* and the *PGM*.

N22: Magical Ingredient Codenames from the *PGM*.

O1. Mithraic Initiation Grades.

O2. Mithraic Initiation Grades – Translation.

O3. Mithraic Initiation Grades – Greek Numeration.

O4. Mithraic Grade Symbols.

O5. Mithraic Planetary Symbols.

O5a. Mithraic Zodiacal and Elemental Animals & Symbols.

O5b. Mithraic Constellation.

O6. Grades of the Hermetic Order of the Golden Dawn.

O7. Cipher Manuscript Grades.

O8. Cipher Manuscript Grades – Hebrew.

O9. Golden Dawn Passwords of the Grades – Hebrew.

O10. Golden Dawn Passwords – English.

O11. Golden Dawn Passwords – Numeration.

O12. Golden Dawn Passwords – Meaning.

O13. Pre-Golden Dawn Grades.

O14. Numbers Associated with Grade.

O15. Symbols by which a Lodge Superior knows his Inferior.

O16. Grade Name (used also in the Golden Dawn).

O17. Grade 'Consulates'.

O18. Golden Dawn Temple Officers: Neophyte Grade.

O19. Female form of Officers' Title.

O20. Corresponding Egyptian God/Goddess.

O21. Officers in a Masonic Lodge.

O22. Masonic Grades – Relaxed Observance.

O23. Masonic Grades – Rite of Philalethes.

O24. Masonic Grades – Philosophic Scottish Rite.

O25. Masonic Grades – 33 degrees of the Scottish or Ancient and Accepted Rite.

O26. Masonic Grades – 33 degrees of the Antient and Primitive Rite.

O27. Masonic Grades – Rite of Mizraim.

O27a.. Masonic Grades – Oriental Rite of Memphis.

# Commentary

O28. Grades and Magical Mottos adopted by Crowley.
O29. Grades of the OTO – Crowley 1917.
O30. Grades of the OTO – Modern.
O31. The Grades of the A∴ A∴.
O32. The Order Divisions and Portal Grades of the A∴ A∴.
O33. A∴ A∴. Practices and Attainments for each Grade.
O34. Magical 'Weapons' and Temple Equipment.
O35. Magical Formulae.

P1. Sumerian Gods.
P2. Akkadian, Assyrian, Mesopotamian Gods.
P3. Babylonian Planetary Gods.
P4. Planetary Gods  Numeration.
P5. Persian Gods.
P6. Phoenician and Canaanite Gods.
P7. Pre-Islamic Arabian Peninsular & Nabatean Gods.
P8. Syrian Gods.
P9. Egyptian Gods.
P10. Egyptian Gods as used ritually by the GD.
P11. Egyptian Gods and the Bodily Attributes of the
        Perfected Man.
P12. Egyptian Gods and their Attributes.
P12a. Egyptian Gods of the Hours of the Day from  *PGM*
P12b. Egyptian Gods of the Zodiac from the *PGM*
P13. Ophitic Gnostic Gods & Archons.
P14. Gnostic Gods – Corresponding Meaning or Name.
P14a. Alternative Ophite Archon names.
P15. Gnostic Archons – Numeration.
P16. Greek Gods.
P17. Main Greek Gods – Greek.
P18. Main Greek Gods – Numeration.
P19. The Orphic Theology.
P20. Greek Muse Governing.
P21. Greek Muses – Type of Lyric.
P22. Roman Gods.
P23. Etruscan Gods.
P24. Celtic Gods.
P25. Celtic Gods – Ireland.
P26. Celtic Gods – Wales.
P27. Slavic Gods.
P28. Baltic Gods.
P29. Norse & Scandinavian Gods with Days of the Week.
P30. Hindu Gods.
P31. Japanese Shinto Gods.
P32. Chinese Taoist Gods.
P33. Meditation Buddhas & Dakinis.
P34. Dahomean Gods.
P35. Yoruba Orishas.
P36. Santeria Gods.
P37. Voodoo Rada & Petra Loa Gods.
P38. Other African Gods.
P39. Aztec Gods.
P40. Inca Gods.
P41. Mayan Gods.

Q1. Knights on the Round Table at Winchester Castle.
Q2. Knights of the Round Table – Mallory c. 1470.
Q3. Knights of the Round Table – Relationships.
Q4. The Tinctures of Chivalry.

R1. The King Scale of Colour (World of Atziluth) – *Yod*.
R2. The Queen Scale of Colour (World of Briah) – *Heh*.
R3. The Emperor Scale of Colour (World of Yetzirah) – *Vav*.

R4. The Empress Scale of Colour (World of Assiah) – *Heh*
    · final.
R5. Mathers' Combined King & Queen Colour Scale.
R6. Rainbow Colours of the Zodiac.
R7. Rainbow Colours of the Zodiac – Wavelength .
R8. Rainbow Colours of the Zodiac – Frequency .
R9. Traditional Kabbalistic Colours.
R10. Rabbi Azriel's Colours.
R11. Dr Jellinek's Colours.
R12. Tattwa Flashing Colours.

S1. Planetary Equatorial Radius.
S2. Planetary Mass.
S3. Planetary Distance from the Sun.
S4. Planetary Sidereal Period of Rotation.
S5. Planetary Rotation on own axis.
S6. The Platonic Solids.
S7. Number of Edges.
S8. Number of Planes.
S9. Number of Faces.
S10. Number of Vertices (Corners).
S11. Shape of Face.
S12. Surface Area.
S13. Volume.
S14. Figures, Numbers, Platonic Solids and Perfect
        Geometric Shapes.
S15. Points of the Pentagram (Elements).
S15a. Points of the Hexagram (Planets).
S16. Sacred Geometry Conversion Factors.

T1. Names and Numbers of the Tarot Trumps (G. D.).
T2. Court Cards and Suits of the Tarot Minor Arcana.
T3. Titles of the Tarot Trumps (Golden Dawn).
T3a. Titles of the Tarot Trumps (Crowley).
T4. Design of the Tarot Trumps.
T5. The Titles of the Wands Court Cards.
T6. The Titles of the Cups Court Cards.
T7. The Titles of the Swords Court Cards.
T8. The Titles of the Coins Court Cards.
T9. Titles of the Wands Suit.
T10. Titles of the Cups Suit.
T11. Titles of the Swords Suit.
T12. Titles of the Coins Suit.
T13. The Wands Court Cards of the Tarot, with their
        Golden Dawn Zodiacal Dominion.
T14. The Cups Court Cards of the Tarot, with their Golden
        Dawn Zodiacal Dominion.
T15. The Swords Court Cards of the Tarot, with their
        Golden Dawn Zodiacal Dominion.
T16. The Coins Court Cards of the Tarot, with their Golden
        Dawn Zodiacal Dominion.
T17. Zodiacal Attributions of the Wands Suit.
T18. Zodiacal Attributions of the Cups Suit.
T19. Zodiacal Attributions of the Swords Suit.
T20. Zodiacal Attributions of the Coins Suit.
T21. Pairs of Angels Ruling Wands.
T22. Pairs of Angels Ruling Wands – Transliteration.
T23. Pairs of Angels Ruling Cups.
T24. Pairs of Angels Ruling Cups – Transliteration.
T25. Pairs of Angels Ruling Swords.
T26. Pairs of Angels Ruling Swords – Transliteration.
T27. Pairs of Angels Ruling Coins.
T28. Pairs of Angels Ruling Coins – Transliteration.
T29. Tarot of Mantegna – A. Astrology series.

T30. Tarot of Mantegna – B. Virtues series.
T31. Tarot of Mantegna – C. Liberal Arts series.
T32. Tarot of Mantegna – D. Nine Greek Muses series.
T33. Tarot of Mantegna – E. Estates of Man
T34. Tarot Emblems: Set 1 – The Estates of Man.
T35. Tarot Emblems: Set 2 – the 7 Planets & the Zodiac.
T36. Tarot Emblems: Set 3 – the 7 Virtues.
T37. Tarot Emblems: Set 4 – Christian Theology.
T38. Planetary Attributions – *Sepher Yetzirah* Planetary
    Order.
T39. Tarot Trumps based on the usual *Sepher Yetzirah*
    Planetary Order.
T40. Planetary Attributions modified by Mathers for G.D.
T41. Tarot Trumps based on the Planetary Order as
    modified by Mathers for the G.D.

U1. Magicians Timeline.
U2. Kabbalists Timeline.
U3. Astrologers Timeline.
U4. Alchemists Timeline.
U5. Masters of the Knights Templar.
U6. Masters of the Knights Templar – years of rule.
U7. Alleged Masters of the *Prieure de Sion*.
U8. Alleged Masters of the *Prieure de Sion* – years of rule.
U9. Gnostic Movements and their Founders.

V1. Five Hindu Tattwas (Elements).
V2. Hindu Tattwas – Colour and Shape.
V3. Hindu Tattwas – Flashing Colour.
V4. Hindu Tattwas – Associated Sense.
V5. Nadas – Associated Internal Sounds.
V6. Observances – *Niyama*.
V7. Hindu Chakras.
V8. Hindu Chakras – Location in Body.
V9. Hindu Chakras – Interpretation.
V10. Hindu Chakras – Number of Petals.
V11. Hindu Chakras – Number of Rays.
V12. Tattwa Ruling this Chakra.
V13. Hindu Chakras – Shape of Mandala.
V14. Hindu Chakras – *Bija* syllable and its Vahana.
V15. Hindu Chakras – Devata.
V16. Hindu Chakras – Sakti of the Dhatu.
V17. Other Tattwas and organ of sense.
V18. Hindu Meditations & Yoga Results.
V19. The Ten Traditional Yamas.
V20. The Ten Traditional Yamas – Meaning.
V21. The Ten Vayus.

W1. Seasonal Quarters of the Year – Pagan.
W2. Seasonal Quarters of the Year – Christian.
W3. Seasonal Quarters of the Year – Astronomic.
W4. Genii of the Twelve Hours from the *Nuctameron*.
W5. Table of Planetary Hours.
W6. Months of the Jewish Calendar – Hebrew.
W7. Months of the Jewish Calendar – Translation.
W8. Months of the Jewish Calendar – Commencement
    Dates 2006.
W9. Months of the Egyptian Calendar.
W10. Egyptian Mystery Celebrations.
W11. Months of the Egyptian Calendar – Theoretical
    Commencement Dates.
W12. Months of the Ancient Greek Lunar Civil Calendar.
W13. Months of the Ancient Babylonian Calendar.
W14. The 24 mini-Seasons of the Chinese Solar Calendar.

X1. Greek Isopsephy.

Y1. The 64 Hexagrams in the Order of their Position on
    the *lo p'an.*
Y2. King Wen's Sequence of the Hexagrams.
Y3. Eight Trigrams or *pa kua.*

Z1. The Human Body.
Z2. The Members of the Body of Terrestrial Man.
Z3. *Sepher Yetzirah* (Long Version) Body Attributions.
Z4. Typical Diseases.
Z5. Chinese Acupuncture Meridians.
Z6. Chinese Acupuncture Meridians – Element.
Z7. Chinese Acupuncture Meridians – origin *hsueh.*
Z8. Chinese Acupuncture Meridians – which run via
Z9. Chinese Acupuncture Meridians – terminus *hsueh.*
Z10. The Kabbalistic Parts of the Soul.
Z11. The Kabbalistic Parts of the Soul – English.
Z12. Kabbalistic Parts of the Soul – Meaning.
Z12a. The Esoteric Makeup of Man.
Z13. Egyptian Parts of the Soul (Crowley).
Z14. Egyptian Parts of the Soul (Crowley - Whitcombe).
Z15. Egyptian Parts of the Soul (Wallis Budge & Farr).
Z16. Egyptian Parts of the Soul.
Z17. Hindu Parts of the Soul (Theosophy).
Z18. Raja Yoga divisions of the Soul.
Z19. Lower Worlds of Theosophy.
Z20. The Planes – Golden Dawn and Case derived from
    Theosophy.
Z21. The Five Hindu Khandas/Skandhas making up Self.
Z22. The Five Hindu Khandas/Skandhas making up Self -
    English.
Z23. The Senses.
Z24. The Body.
Z25. Bodily Functions.